ANNUAL REVIEW OF IRISH LAW 1990

Annual Review
of Irish Law 1990

Raymond Byrne
B.C.L., LL.M., Barrister-at-Law
Lecturer in Law, Dublin City University

William Binchy
B.A., B.C.L., LL.M., Barrister-at-Law
Research Counsellor, The Law Reform Commission

THE ROUND HALL PRESS
DUBLIN

The typesetting for this book was produced by
Gilbert Gough Typesetting, Dublin for
The Round Hall Press, Dublin

BRITISH LIBRARY CATALOGUING IN PUBLICATION DATA
A catalogue record for this book
is available from the British Library.

ISBN 0-947686-69-X

ISSN 0791-1084

Printed by
Colour Books Ltd, Dublin

Contents

Preface

In this fourth volume in the Annual Review series, our purpose continues to be to provide a review of legal developments, judicial and statutory, that occurred in 1990. In terms of case law, this includes those judgments which were delivered in 1990, regardless of whether they have been (or will be) reported and which were circulated up to the date of this preface.

It is a pleasure to thank those who made the task of completing this volume less onerous than might otherwise have been the case. Mr Justice Brian Walsh (the originator of the concept of an Annual Review of Irish Law) continues to be most supportive and we are very grateful for this. Ms Peggy McQuinn, of the Office of the Supreme Court, was especially helpful in dealing with a number of queries. Ms Margaret Byrne and Ms Mary Gaynor, of the Library of the Incorporated Law Society of Ireland, once again gave us considerable help and access to material. Mr John Armstrong, of the King's Inns Library, was as always extremely kind in assisting with any difficulties. And the facilities provided by Ms Jennifer Aston, Librarian in the Law Library, Four Courts, were also availed of by us, and once again were of great benefit. We are also extremely grateful for the assistance provided us by Mr Ben Ó Floinn in connection with this Review.

We are also grateful on this occasion to the trustees of the Arthur Cox Foundation for their generous financial research assistance in connection with the preparation of this volume.

Finally, the production of the Annual Review series would not be possible without the considerable expertise of the Round Hall Press, and in particular the professionalism of Michael Adams, Gilbert Gough and Martin Healy. Our best thanks are due to them.

Raymond Byrne and William Binchy,
Dublin,
October 1991.

Table of Cases

Annual Review of Irish Law 1990

Other Tables

IRISH STATUTES

STATUTORY INSTRUMENTS

EUROPEAN COMMUNITY LAWS

COUNCIL OF EUROPE LAWS

INTERNATIONAL AGREEMENTS

ANNUAL REVIEW OF IRISH LAW 1990

Administrative Law

GOVERNMENT FUNCTIONS

Appropriation The Appropriation Act 1990 provided as follows. For the year ended 31 December 1987, the Act provided £1,000 to make good the supply granted and also provided £30,749 for appropriations-in-aid. For the year ended 31 December 1990, the amount for supply grants was £6,620,549,000 and for appropriations-in-aid was £713,857,000.

Civil service *Whelan v Minister for Justice*, High Court, 29 June 1990 concerned the purported dismissal of a probationary prison officer.

On 14 February 1987 the applicant had been appointed a prison officer. The conditions of appointment included a provision stating that he must serve a probationary period which would normally be of two years duration. However, by virtue of an agreement between the Prison Officers' Association and the respondent Minister, the applicant's probationary period would have terminated on 14 March 1989. In April 1989, the applicant was informed that the Minister had terminated his services under s.7 of the Civil Service Regulation Act 1956, as amended by s.3 of the Civil Service Regulation (Amendment) Act 1958. S.7 provides for termination where the Minister is satisfied that a probationer has failed to fulfil the conditions of probation. In the instant case, the Minister based his determination on the applicant's unsatisfactory sick absence record. The applicant sought judicial review of the Minister's decision. Pursuant to an order for discovery, it emerged that the termination of the applicant's services was recommended to the Minister by a memorandum dated 10 March 1989, and that this was endorsed by the Minister on 21 March 1989.

In light of the timing of the Minister's endorsement, Blayney J found that, during the period of the applicant's probationary period, there was no evidence that the Minister was satisfied that the applicant had failed to fulfil his conditions of probation. Blayney J therefore held that the Minister had acted ultra vires s.7 of the 1956 Act (as amended by s.3 of the 1958 Act) in purporting to dismiss the applicant. The consequences of this finding was that the termination was void and the applicant was entitled to a declaration that he remained an established civil servant, and was in the same position as any other probationer who had completed his probation period and had not been found to be unsatisfactory.

Blayney J added two important comments. He opined that s.7 of the 1956 Act, as amended, does not in terms require that the termination occur during the probationary period, provided the Minister reached his decision within the period of probation. However he noted that the actual conditions under which the applicant had been appointed as a probationary officer appeared to require that the termination occur within the period. That, of course, is a matter of contractual form, unrelated to the terms of s.7.

International Development Association   The International Development Association (Amendment) Act 1990 was passed to approve Ireland's latest replenishment to the fund of this affiliate of the World Bank: see the 1988 Review, 3. Ireland's latest contribution was fixed at IR£12,740,000, i.e. 0.10% of the total figure.

Marine   The Dún Laoghaire Harbour Act 1990 transferred the control of Dún Laoghaire Harbour from the Commissioners of Public Works to the Minister for the Marine. This is part of an overall strategy to place all major harbours under the Minister's control.

National Parks   An Blascaod Mór National Historic Park Act 1989 (Forms) Regulations 1990 (SI No. 340) concern CPOs and Vesting Orders under the 1989 Act (1989 Review, 4).

Semi-State bodies
1 B & I Line   The B & I Line Act 1990 increased from £100 million to £106 million the amount of additional share capital which the Minister for Finance may invest in the B & I Line.

2 Bord Glas   The Bord Glas Act 1990 established An Bord Glas, the Horticultural Development Board. The Board is empowered, under s.4 of the Act to develop, promote, facilitate, encourage, co-ordinate and assist the production, marketing and consumption of horticultural produce in the State. Increased exports and job creation are to be particular areas of attention for the Board. The Act came into effect on 28 February 1990 and An Bord Glas was established on 22 March 1990: Bord Glas Act 1990 (Establishment Day) Order 1990 (SI No. 66).

3 Bord na Móna   The Turf Development Act 1990 allows Bord na Móna to establish subsidiary companies, create specialist sub-boards and to engage in activities outside the State. The Act also increases Bord na Móna's ability to engage in commercial activities generally.

4 Foir Teoranta   The Foir Teoranta (Dissolution) Act 1990 provides for the dissolution of the State rescue company, Foir Teo. Its assets and liabilities were transferred to the Industrial Credit Corporation plc.

5 *Industrial Credit Corporation plc* The Industrial Credit (Amendment) Act 1990 increased the amount of borrowing which the ICC may undertake from £800 million to £1,000 million. The Act also empowers the Minister for Finance to guarantee the borrowings of the company up to the same sum.

6 *National Treasury Management Agency* The National Treasury Management Agency Act 1990 established the Agency of its title. The purpose of the Act is to delegate the borrowing and debt management functions hitherto under the direct control of the Department of Finance to the Agency, which will have the advantage of being able to attract personnel form the private sector with expertise in debt management. It was also pointed out that Department of Finance personnel involved in debt management had, in the past, been drawn to the better salaries in the private sector and that the Act was an attempt to prevent this in the future. The primary aim of the Act, moreover, is to reduce the cost of servicing the national debt. Interest payments of over £2 billion on the overall debt of £25 billion were made in 1989. The Act provides that, while the Agency will have day-to-day responsibility for management of the national debt, overall control remains within the Department of Finance. The Minister for Finance argued that this ensured that the Act did not breach Article 28.2 of the Constitution as to the exercise of executive power. The Act came into effect on 17 July 1990 and the Agency was established on 3 December 1990: National Treasury Management Agency Act 1990 (Establishment Day) Order 1990 (SI No. 276). The National Treasury Management Agency Act 1990 (Delegation of and Declaration as to Functions) Order 1990 (SI No. 277) sets out the detail of the functions to be peformed by the Agency.

JUDICIAL REVIEW

Availability: effect of decision In *McDonough v Minister for Defence* [1991] ILRM 115 and *Ahern v Minister for Industry and Commerce (No. 3)*, High Court, 6 July 1990 the common issue for decision was whether the applicants had been adversely affected by decisions to the extent that judicial review was available.

In the first case, *McDonough v Minister for Defence* [1991] ILRM 115, the applicant, a member of the Naval Service, had been involved in the transport section at Haulbowline Naval Base for approximately three years. He was advised by a Captain Holmes that there were a number of complaints about his driving, that disciplinary action would be taken against him and that he was 'grounded'. The applicant was taken off transport duties, with a consequent loss, in the form of subsistence allowances, of approximately £200 per month. His Naval permit to drive was also revoked. The applicant sought a hearing before the commanding officer of the Base but this was refused. After a further request, he was seen by Captain Holmes and the applicant regarded this as an attempt to frustrate him. He then applied to see the Legal Officer, who advised him as to what steps to take. The applicant stated that, subsequent to the meeting with the Legal Officer he was informed that this meeting could result in his being charged in respect of the driving complaints. Charges were laid against the applicant but were not in fact proceeded with. After the charges were not proceeded with, the applicant sought a return to driving duties but this was refused. The applicant sought judicial review of his suspension from driving duties. The respondents argued that, as the suspension was an internal administrative Naval Service matter, it was not subject to judicial review. Lavan J did not accept the respondents' argument and he granted the relief sought by the applicant.

He stated that he had formed the view that the charges had not been proceeded with because they were trivial in nature and did not warrant a military court investigation. He also held that it had been unreasonable for the commanding officer to refuse to see the applicant as was his decision to delegate to Captain Holmes the conduct of the interview with the applicant, having regard to the fact that Captain Holmes had initially informed the applicant about the disciplinary procedures. Third, he was satisfied that the reason that disciplinary proceedings were pursued to any extent was that the applicant had consulted the Legal Officer.

Crucially, Lavan J held that the suspension from driving duties was amenable to judicial review since it affected the applicant's ability to earn additional monies as a member of the Naval Service. He also held that the revocation of the applicant's Naval driving permit constituted the imposition of a penalty, and that he was entitled to an opportunity to hear the complaints against him and of answering these before the revocation would take place. In this respect, Lavan J quoted with approval the approach taken by Barron J in *Flanagan v University College Dublin* [1989] ILRM 469 (1988 Review, 14-5). In the circumstances, the revocation had occurred in breach of the rules of natural justice and the applicant was entitled to have the decision quashed. Finally, Lavan J added that any such revocation should be stated to be for a reasonable period, and an open-ended revocation such as occurred in the instant case was not acceptable.

In the second case in this area, *Ahern v Minister for Industry and Commerce (No. 3)*, High Court, 6 July 1990 a discovery issue in the case was discussed in the 1988 Review, 334-5 and another preliminary issue is discussed, below, 10-11.

The applicant, a civil servant in the Patents Office, had been placed on compulsory sick leave with pay in the light of an incident which formed part of a pattern of events involving an unhappy professional relationship between the applicant and other staff in the Office. Prior to the applicant being placed on compulsory sick leave, he was asked to attend a psychiatrist. The applicant initially agreed to this, but subsequently did not attend. He was placed on compulsory sick leave by the Personnel Officer after medical reports had been received on the applicant. The applicant sought to quash this decision. Blayney J declined the relief sought, but also held that the matter was susceptible to judicial review.

He concluded that the issue raised by the applicant was justiciable since, although he had not lost pay, the suspension affected his right to work and carried an innuendo that he was unfit for work. In this context, he quoted with approval the well-known dicta of Palles CB in *R. (Wexford County Council) v Local Government Board for Ireland* [1902] 2 IR 349 to the effect that a decision is liable to judicial review where it imposes liabilities or affects rights.

Blayney J went on to hold that since the applicant had not been made aware of the medical reports which formed the basis for his suspension and since the medical opinions formed had been made without an examination of the applicant, the applicant had established grounds on which to challenge the decision to place him on compulsory sick leave. However, applying the decision of the Supreme Court in *The State (Abenglen Properties Ltd) v Dublin Corporation* [1982] ILRM 590; [1984] IR 381 he concluded that, in the exercise of his discretion he would decline to grant judicial review. This was based on a number of factors: the applicant's refusal to see a psychiatrist, his allegation that the Personnel Officer had acted out of mala fides and also the fact that his being on compulsory sick leave would not affect his promotion prospects so that an order of certiorari would confer no benefit on him.

Deference to decision-making body The reluctance of the courts to interfere with the decision-making power of a body whose decision is being reviewed was expressly adverted to by the Supreme Court in *Stroker v Doherty*, Supreme Court, 26 July 1990 (14-16, below) and *O'Keeffe v An Bord Pleanála*, High Court, 31 July 1990; Supreme Court, 15 February 1991 (16, below).

Fair Procedures/Natural Justice
1 Audi alteram partem: hearing In *Goode v Veterinary Council*, High Court, 14 December 1989 Hamilton P quashed the plaintiff's suspension from the Register of Veterinary Surgeons on the basis that he had not been

given an opportunity to make representations before the Council itself.

Similarly, in *Cooney v An Post*, High Court, 6 April 1990 Lavan J quashed the applicant's dismissal by An Post. The applicant had been charged with certain offences concerning used stamps, but a nolle prosequi was entered in respect of these matters. The applicant had been interviewed in respect of these matters, and in his affidavit in the High Court he stated that the investigators had indicated to him that the matters were relatively minor and that his job was not in question. During this interview, the applicant appeared to confirm that he had re-used certain stamps in the course of various transactions and that the sums involved amounted to £40. Subsequently, the Personnel Officer of An Post informed him that dismissal was being considered. The applicant sought, at a meeting with the Personnel Officer, to question the investigators who had interviewed him, but this was refused. This turned out to be a crucial point in the case.

Subsequent to this meeting with the applicant, the Personnel Officer talked to the investigators and later informed the applicant that he had been dismissed. Lavan J held that the procedures adopted by An Post were defective. The real issue in the case, he concluded, was that the applicant had been refused an opportunity to question the investigators. Lavan J also regarded as significant that the investigators had not filed any affidavits which contradicted the applicant's version of the interview during which he had made his statement. While he accepted that the courts should be reluctant to interfere with the internal disciplinary procedures of a company such as An Post (citing dicta of Griffin J in *The State (Keegan) v Stardust Victims Compensation Tribunal* [1987] ILRM 202; [1986] IR 642), he nonetheless held that the applicant's dismissal could not stand in the light of what amounted to an uncontroverted guarantee to him of continued employment.

For a similar case see also Lavan J's decision in *McDonough v Minister for Defence* [1991] ILRM 115 (5, above).

2 *Audi alteram partem: non-participation in hearing process*   In *Corcoran v Electricity Supply Board*, High Court, 10 May 1990 (364-5, below, in the Labour Law chapter) Barron J held that the plaintiffs were precluded from complaining about alleged deficiencies in a process which resulted in their dismissal where they had refused to participate in that process.

3 *Audi alteram partem: no right to appeal*   In *Carroll v Minister for Agriculture and Food*, High Court, 28 February 1990 (21, below, in the Agriculture chapter) Blayney J held that in certain circumstances there was no breach of the audi alteram partem rule where a decision was not amenable to appeal within the decision-making process established.

4 *Audi alteram partem: prior hearing*   In *Hickey v Eastern Health Board*

[1990] ELR 177, the Court held that there was no general right to a hearing prior to the dismissal of an employee: see 356-7, below, in the Labour Law chapter. In *McDonough v Minister for Defence* [1991] ILRM 115, however, Lavan J held that a hearing prior to a decision taking effect was required: 5, above. These two decisions are not incompatible.

5 Bias   In *Bord na Móna v J. Sisk & Son Ltd (No. 2)*, High Court 31 May 1990 (see 25-7, below, in the Commercial Law chapter), Blayney J applied the 'objective likelihood' approach to the question whether bias was established in the context of an arbitration hearing. He quoted with approval comments to the same effect made by Murphy J in what appears to be his uncirculated judgment in *Dublin and County Broadcasting Ltd v Independent Radio and Television Commission and Ors*, High Court, 12 May 1989. It is unfortunate that Blayney J would not have had available to him the *ex tempore* decision of the Supreme Court in *O'Neill v Beaumont Hospital Board* [1990] ILRM 419 (1989 Review, 7-9), in which the Supreme Court had taken a slightly different view on bias to that expressed by Murphy J in that case. Although *O'Neill* was decided in July 1989, it was not reported until after the judgment in the *Bord na Móna* case was delivered. It is unlikely, however, that the Beaumont Hospital decision would have had a dramatic impact on the decision in the instant case.

It is, indeed, of interest to note that Murphy J himself applied the Supreme Court decision in the Beaumont Hospital case in his judgment in *O'Neill v Irish Hereford Breed Society Ltd* [1991] ILRM 612 without adverting to the fact that the Supreme Court had differed to some extent from his views in that case. In the instant case, Murphy J held that the defendant Society, in circumstances remarkably similar to those in the Beaumont Hospital case, had not breached the bias rule. Murphy J cited in particular the necessity rule described by the Chief Justice in the Beaumont Hospital case (1989 Review, 8-9). It might also be noted that this was a plenary summons case and not a judicial review, but Murphy J referred to the case law on the bias rule. See also, 26-7, below.

6 Constitutional case: Attorney General   The requirement to give notice to the Attorney General under O.60 of the Rules of the Superior Courts 1986 was held by the Supreme Court to extend to a High Court judge in *The People v Ellis* [1991] ILRM 225 (sub nom. *Application of Ellis* [1990] 2 IR 291): see 162, below, in the Constitutional Law chapter.

7 Reasons to be given   The move towards requiring decision-making bodies to furnish the reasons for their decisions (see the 1988 Review, 17-18) continued with the decision of the Supreme Court in *Breen v Minister for Defence*, Supreme Court, 20 July 1990 (see 265-6, below, in the Defence

Forces chapter) and of Johnson J in *Sherlock v Governor of Mountjoy Prison*, High Court, 21 December 1990 (see 456-7, below, in the Prisons chapter). However the Supreme Court's decision in *O'Keeffe v An Bord Pleanála*, High Court, 31 July 1990; Supreme Court, 15 February 1991 would appear to have placed some limits on this area: see 16, below.

Legitimate expectation   In *Cosgrove v Legal Aid Board*, High Court, 17 October 1990 (see 144, below, in the Constitutional Law chapter), Gannon J made brief reference to the decision of the Supreme Court in *Webb v Ireland* [1988] ILRM 565; [1988] IR 353. The applicant in *Cosgrove* had applied for civil legal aid from the respondent Board and she sought a number of declarations and other relief on judicial review. In the course of his judgment, Gannon J rejected the argument that she had a legitimate expectation of financial legal aid from the Board or from any institution of the State, there being no evidence of any representation to her on which she relied to her detriment. This emphasis on the procedural and estoppel nature of legitimate expectation is in line with the recent trend to limit the extent of this concept in Irish law: see the 1988 Review, 20-30 and 1989 Review, 9-12.

Cannon v Minister for the Marine [1991] ILRM 261 also indicates that legitimate expectation may hold less attractions as a head of relief than it at first had appeared: see 328-9, below, in the Fisheries chapter.

However, the doctrine was successfully invoked in two cases in 1990. In *Philips v Medical Council*, High Court, 11 December 1990 Costello J held that the Council was estopped from relying on changes in its rules for registration of medical practitioners in relation to the plaintiff. This was because the plaintiff had already made an application to the Council under previous rules which both parties had treated as being applicable. In those circumstances, the Council was not entitled to rely on new rules which would effectively prevent the plaintiff from being entitled to obtain registration. And in *Sherlock v Governor of Mountjoy Prison*, High Court, 21 December 1990, the doctrine was successfully invoked in the context of procedural fairness in connection with the withdrawal of temporary release (parole): see 456-7, below, in the Prisons chapter.

For further discussion of the case law, see Delany (1990) 12 DULJ 1.

Practice and Procedure

1 Additional grounds   In *Ahern v Minister for Industry and Commerce (No. 2)* [1990] 1 IR 55, Blayney J held that O.84, r.23(2) of the Rules of the Superior Courts 1986 did not allow an applicant for judicial review to seek, at an interlocutory stage, to have additional grounds for relief added to those allowed at the 'leave to apply' stage. Thus the applicant in the instant case was held confined to those grounds on which he had originally based the application for leave to apply. Blayney J also held that the general power of the Court under O.125, r.1 of the 1986 Rules to amend pleadings at any time did not extend to judicial review, since a statement grounding an application for leave to apply did not constitute pleadings under O.125. However, Blayney J noted that the applicant could apply to have additional grounds added at the hearing of the application for judicial review itself. The applicant's appeal to the Supreme Court was struck out: see [1990] 1 IR 58n. For the substantive proceedings in the case, see 6-7, above.

2 Alternative remedies   The decision of the House of Lords in *O'Reilly v Mackman* [1983] 2 AC 237 was not followed by Costello J in *O'Donnell v Dun Laoghaire Corporation* [1991] ILRM 301. The effect is that declaratory relief will not be refused merely because a plaintiff has not established an inability to obtain *certiorari*. Thus, O.84 of the Rules of the Superior Courts 1986 should not be regarded as a self-contained code. See the comments by Hogan, (1990) 12 DULJ 114. The *O'Donnell* case is discussed below, 407-10, in the Local Government chapter.

3 Costs   In *Kelly v O'Sullivan*, High Court, 11 July 1990 (discussed in the Criminal Law chapter, 197-8, below) the applicant had succeeded on one point only, the Court holding that the order made by the respondent had been made *per incuriam* through following a long-established practice. A number of other points had been put forward unsuccessfully by the applicant. In the circumstances, Gannon J made no order as to costs.

4 Damages   In *O'Donnell v Dun Laoghaire Corporation* [1991] ILRM 301, Costello J applied the Supreme Court decision in *Pine Valley Developments Ltd v Minister for the Environment* [1987] ILRM 747; [1987] IR 23 in holding that no damages were awardable for *ultra vires vires* actions by a statutory body, in the absence of mala fides or the commission of a tort: see 410, below, in the Local Government chapter.

5 Delay   In *Director of Public Prosecutions v McDonnell (Dumbrell, Notice Party)*, High Court, 1 October 1990 the respondent Justice had refused to adjudicate in a prosecution brought by the Director against the Notice Party after a previous order made by the respondent had been quashed on certiorari. The respondent's decision was made on 1 December 1989. On 1 March 1990, the Director applied for judicial review of the respondent's decision. Gannon J accepted that, having regard to the method of computing time in O.122, r.1 of the Rules of the Superior Courts 1986, the application was within the three month time limit specified in O.84, r.21(1). However, he declined to entertain the application for judicial review. He stated that, while O.84, r.21 sets a limitation period for judicial review applications, it also creates a specific obligation on an applicant to seek such relief promptly; and since there was no explanation for the failure to bring the application until the last day permitted by the 1986 Rules, he held that the Court would decline to entertain the application for judicial review.

6 Discretion to refuse   In *Ahern v Minister for Industry and Commerce (No. 3)*, High Court, 6 July 1990 Blayney J exercised his discretion to refuse judicial review: see 6-7, above. The exercise of discretion also arose in *Grimes v Smithwick*, High Court, 15 May 1990, 237 below, *O'Donnell v Dun Laoghaire Corporation* [1991] ILRM 301: see 407-10, below, in the Local Government chapter, and in *Banerjee v Medical Council*, High Court, 23 November 1990, 338-9, below, in the Health Services chapter.

In *Osborne v Hickey*, High Court, 2 May 1990 Hamilton P decided to grant judicial review to the applicant even though it had been suggested he had available to him an alternative remedy. He had challenged the validity of a refusal to grant him travelling expenses as an environmental health officer attached to a health board, of which the respondent was chief executive officer. The President granted mandamus, since this achieved a just resolution of the dispute with minimal inconvenience. He applied *dicta* of Gannon J to that effect in *The State (Glover) v McCarthy* [1981] ILRM 47.

7 Notice parties   The Supreme Court in *O'Keeffe v An Bord Pleanála and Anor*, High Court, 31 July 1990; Supreme Court, 15 February 1991 (see 16, below) issued what amounted to a Practice Direction on aspects of appeals in planning cases. Delivering the Court's leading judgment, the Chief Justice made two important points at the end of that judgment. First, an applicant for judicial review must seek to join, and the court should normally join, any party who is likely to be affected by the avoidance of the decision impugned. The second point, concerning an oral hearing, is discussed below.

8 No useful purpose   In *Ahern v Minister for Industry and Commerce (No. 3)*, High Court, 6 July 1990 Blayney J declined judicial review on the basis that no benefit would accrue to the applicant: 6-7, above. On the differing views in this area, see the 1988 Review, 35-6.

9 Oral hearing   The second point made by the Chief Justice in *O'Keeffe*, above, was that where judicial review is by way of a plenary summons, the action should be presented by way of oral evidence, unless the court by express order directs a hearing on affidavit or accepts from the parties an expressly agreed statement of facts.

10 Public law/Private law   In *O'Neill v Iarnród Éireann* [1991] ILRM 129 the Supreme Court declined to give an authoritative ruling as to the precise scope of the judicial review procedure in O.84 of the Rules of the Superior Courts 1986.

The applicant had sought judicial review of his dismissal by the respondent company. The respondent was a statutory body limited by shareholders, and had been created by the Transport (Re-Organisation of Coras Iompair Éireann) Act 1986. The applicant claimed that judicial review lay on the ground that in dismissing him, the respondent was acting under statutory authority. In the High Court, Barr J declined to allow the applicant leave to apply for judicial review but on appeal the Supreme Court, by a majority, (Finlay CJ and McCarthy J; Hederman J dissenting) allowed him to proceed, though without indicating whether in fact he came within the terms of O.84 of the 1986 Rules. Finlay CJ and McCarthy J referred to the conflicting High Court decisions on the scope of O.84 of the 1986 Rules, including *Murphy v Turf Club* [1989] IR 171 (see the 1989 Review, 14) and *Ryan v VIP Taxi Co-Op Ltd*, Irish Times Law Reports, 10 April 1989. Finlay CJ also referred to the decision of the Court itself in *O'Neill v Beaumont Hospital Board* [1990] ILRM 419, in which leave to proceed under O.84 had been granted with considerable reluctance. And McCarthy J noted that he had expressed grave reservations, *ex tempore*, in *Gupta v Trinity College Dublin*, Supreme Court, 14 April 1990, as to the applicability of O.84 to the decision of the relevant body of the College in that case.

In view of the conflicting views which had been expressed by different High Court judges as to the scope of O.84 of the 1986 Rules and of the ambivalence of the Supreme Court itself, the majority felt that the Court should await a case in which a substantive argument as to the scope of the judicial review procedure could be argued. Therefore the applicant was allowed to proceed to apply for judicial review, although both the Chief Justice and McCarthy J noted that he ran the risk of finding that the High Court had no jurisdiction to hear his application. And both Finlay CJ and McCarthy J stated that they would refuse the applicant any interim relief by way of a stay on his dismissal under O.84, r.20 of the 1986 Rules, relief which the applicant's counsel made clear was one of the few practical advantages of applying under O.84 in the first place. In dissent, Hederman J concluded quite simply that O.84 was not applicable and he would have struck out the application and required the applicant to institute plenary proceedings.

One would have thought that, given the general rule that a court does not act in vain, the Chief Justice and McCarthy J were engaging in what might be described as a sin of commission in this regard. Since the applicant had conceded that interim relief under O.84 was, perhaps, the only reason for applying under O.84 the majority were certainly doing him no favours, and they seemed to be remitting the case to the High Court in a manner that might be regarded as more at home in *Bleak House* than in the Supreme Court in 1990. The approach taken by Hederman J in dissent seems more appropriate in a case of this kind where a net legal issue arises. It is difficult to see why the majority should want to postpone giving a definitive judgment on what is a very important practical issue. The argument used by Finlay CJ and McCarthy J is that they would prefer to wait until the issue arose in a substantive way so that they could hear full submissions on the point. While that might well be a reasonable point in the normal course, it is difficult to imagine how this particular point will be teased out to any greater degree than has already occurred in the leading textbooks or indeed by Barr J in *Murphy v Turf Club* [1989] IR 171. The issue is as uncomplicated as could be envisaged, and it is unfortunate that its definitive determination should have been postponed. It may be noted that in his informative note on the case Hogan concludes that, in effect, the majority decision has restricted the scope of O.84: see (1990) 12 DULJ 119-27.

11 Public law/private law: non-statutory scheme   In *Cosgrove v Legal Aid Board*, High Court, 17 October 1990, (144, below) Gannon J held that judicial review was available in respect of decisions of the respondent Board, established under the non-statutory *Scheme of Civil Legal Aid and Advice* (1979). This confirms the views taken in cases such as *The State (Hayes) v Criminal Injuries Compensation Trubunal* [1982] ILRM 210. This approach is not affected by the doubts expressed in the *O'Neill* case, above.

Reasonableness   In *Breen v Minister for Defence*, Supreme Court, 20 July 1990 (265-6, below, in the Defence Forces chapter), *Stroker v Doherty*, Supreme Court, 26 July 1990 (below) and *O'Keeffe v An Bord Pleanála and Anor*, High Court, 31 July 1990; Supreme Court, 15 February 1991 (16, below), the Supreme Court applied the test of reasonableness it had pro-pounded in *The State (Keegan) v Stardust Victims Compensation Tribunal* [1987] ILRM 202; [1986] IR 642.

In *Stroker v Doherty and Ors*, Supreme Court, 26 July 1990, the question at issue was whether certain allegedly lewd conduct of the applicant Garda was sufficiently grave to warrant dismissal from the Force.

The applicant had been a member of the Garda Síochána for 14 years when he was involved in an incident in a public house in the rural locality in which he was stationed. It was alleged, inter alia, that he made lewd remarks to an acquaintance in relation to his (the applicant's) wife; and that when the licensee of the premises called for the applicant's wife to leave the premises at closing time the applicant failed to assist his wife to leave the premises. The applicant was charged with a number of disciplinary offences under Reg.6 of the Garda Síochána (Discipline) Regulations 1971 (which have since been replaced by 1989 Regulations of the same title), being alleged to be conduct prejudicial to the Force. After a disciplinary inquiry under the Regulations and an appeal to an Appeal Board, he was ultimately only convicted in relation to the lewd comments and the failure to assist his wife to leave the licensed premises. The Appeal Board recommended dismissal from the Force and this was implemented by the Garda Commissioner. The applicant sought judicial review, seeking to have the convictions and dismissal set aside, inter alia, for unreasonableness. In the High Court, Barron J granted the relief sought: [1989] ILRM 428; [1989] IR 440 (1989 Review, 276-8). On appeal by the Commissioner, this decision was reversed by the Supreme Court (Finlay CJ, Griffin and McCarthy JJ).

Ultimately, the courts differed over the application of the reasonableness test laid down by the Supreme Court in *The State (Keegan) v Stardust Victims Compensation Tribunal* [1987] ILRM 202; [1986] IR 642. All judges agreed that, since there was no claim that there had been a procedural defect in the decision-making process, the decisions made could only be quashed if they flew in the face of fundamental reason and common sense, as Henchy J had described it in the *Keegan* case. In the High Court, Barron J felt the decisions had been unreasonable, the Supreme Court held they were not. Delivering the main judgment, McCarthy J (with whom Finlay CJ agreed, while Griffin J delivered a short concurring judgment) indicated the 'hands off' approach which the courts should adopt in cases of this kind:

> The consideration of such matters as to whether or not a particular incident amounts to conduct prejudicial to discipline or likely to bring discredit to the Force is peculiarly appropriate for determination by the Gardaí themselves; so also is the assessment of the penalty appropriate to any such breach or breaches. In the regulation and enforcement of discipline where a decision depends upon the assessment made by the Commissioner or by an Appeals Board, in my view, the courts should be reluctant to interfere.

Applying this general approach to the incidents in question, the Court was not prepared to quash the decision of the Appeal Board as unreasonable, and like considerations applied to the penalty chosen by the Appeal Board under the 1971 Regulations. McCarthy J expressed clearly the limits of the Court's willingness to interfere when he accepted that views could differ on the conduct engaged in by the applicant:

> There are, no doubt, many who would consider the incident in question as tasteless and offensive but irrelevant to An Garda Síochána as such, whatever about its relevance to the individual Garda. There are some who would consider that what a Garda says off duty and in plain clothes as strictly his own business. There are others who would consider that, in a small country community, members of the Gardaí should be setting an example of decent conduct. *Quot homines tot sententiae.*

Although this passage appears to indicate that the 'setting an example' group might appear to represent a minority ('others' as opposed to 'many'), nonetheless the Court considered that the Commissioner and Appeals Board were entitled to act on the basis of protecting that particular view of Garda conduct in a rural community. However, McCarthy J can hardly have meant that his reference to Terence, *Phormio* ('as many men, so many minds or opinions') could be taken literally. Otherwise, of course, the opinion of a particularly unrepresentative section of a community might be taken into account, and a decision based on such narrow constraints might easily fall into the category of flying in the face of reason and common sense. It may be that the dicta quoted from *Doherty* express too broadly the extent to which the courts will allow a domestic tribunal to regulate its own procedures.

To some extent the same may be said of the decision in *O'Keeffe v An Bord Pleanála and Anor*, High Court, 31 July 1990; Supreme Court, 15 February 1991, the case concerning the 'Radio Tara' transmission mast.

The applicant sought judicial review of the decision of the respondent Planning Board to grant planning permission to a company, Radio Tara Ltd, for the erection of a long wave radio transmitting station, including a 300 metre mast, in County Meath. The application for planning permission to Meath County Council had been rejected by the elected members pursuant to a motion under s.4 of the City and County Management (Amendment) Act 1955 directing the County Manager to refuse planning permission. The County Manager declined to follow the direction, and he granted planning permission subject to certain conditions. The applicant appealed to the respondent Board, which upheld the planning permission, subject to certain conditions.

The judicial review focused on the decision-making procedures adopted by the Board and, what appeared to Costello J in the High Court, its apparent disregard for the views of experts. The Board had appointed an Inspector and an expert from Eolas, the Science and Technology Agency, to prepare a Report on the effect of the transmission station. The Eolas Report indicated that there would be 'widespread and sustained' electro-magnetic interference within a 7 km radius of the mast; electric fencing would require temporary earthing when not in use; telephones would be subject to consistent nuisance or impairment of enjoyment; radios and hearing aids would be difficult to operate free of interference and burglar alarms would be affected. The Inspector's report indicated the possible effect of the mast on the value of houses in the area surrounding the mast. S. 26(5) of the Local Government (Planning and Development) Act 1963 requires the Board, on appeal from a 'decision' of the planning authority, to determine the matter as if made to it in the first place; and the Board is thus required in its decision to consider the proper planning of the area in question. The Board's formal decision was notified by means of a statement that the permission was granted as being consistent with the proper planning of the area. A Schedule of the conditions was attached to this statement.

In the High Court, Costello J quashed the Board's decision, but this was unanimously overturned on appeal to the Supreme Court (Finlay CJ, Griffin, Hederman, McCarthy and Lynch JJ). While there was agreement in the courts on the relevant principles of judicial review, clear differences emerged in their application to the particular circumstances of the case. In particular, the courts took quite different approaches to the application of the well-established reasonableness rule as well as the more recently-established rule requiring reasons for decisions.

There was one preliminary point which Costello J dealt with and on which there was, apparently, no appeal. This was as to whether, if the County Manager's grant of planning permission was *ultra vires*, the Board had jurisdiction to hear an appeal under the 1963 Act. Assuming, without deciding the point, that the Manager's decision was indeed *ultra vires*, Costello J held it nonetheless constituted a 'decision' within s.26(5) of the 1963 Act and the Board therefore had jurisdiction to hear the appeal. In this respect, he expressly adopted the approach taken by the Privy Council in *Calvin v Carr* [1980] AC 574 and the general principles expressed by the Supreme Court in *The State (Abenglen Properties Ltd) v Dublin Corporation* [1982] ILRM 590; [1984] IR 381.

However, as already indicated, Costello J's views on the reasonableness of the Board's decision and the adequacy of its reasons were overturned by the Supreme Court. As to reasonableness, Costello J accepted the principles laid down in the leading decision *Associated Provincial Picture Houses Ltd v Wednesbury Corporation* [1948] 1 KB 223 as applied by the Supreme Court in *The State (Keegan) v Stardust Victims Compensation Tribunal* [1987] ILRM 202; [1986] IR 642. On the question of giving reasons, he referred to the decision of the Supreme Court in *The State (Creedon) v Criminal Injuries Compensation Tribunal* [1989] ILRM 104; [1988] IR 51 (1988 Review, 17-18).

Applying these decisions, Costello J concluded that while the Board might reasonably have granted permission on the basis of taking a different view to that of the inspector on the likely impact on the value of houses in the area of the mast, it had acted unreasonably in disregarding the Report prepared by the expert from Eolas as to the widespread and sustained nuisance which would be caused in the surrounding area. On this basis he held that the applicant was therefore entitled to have the decision quashed for unreasonableness. He also held that the applicant was entitled to have the Board's decision quashed on the ground that it had failed to conduct its decision-making process in a manner which would enable the courts to ascertain the reasons why it made its determination, applying what he considered to be the holding in the *Creedon* case.

On appeal to the Supreme Court, Radio Tara Ltd was joined as a party by order of the Court. On both the substantive issues in the case, the Supreme Court (Finlay CJ, Griffin, Hederman, McCarthy and Lynch JJ) allowed the Board's appeal.

Delivering the leading judgment of the Court, the Chief Justice adopted a quite conservative approach to the courts' role on judicial review. He referred to a number of authorities which had warned on the dangers of the judges themselves usurping another body's decision-making power, and reiterated the views of Lord Brightman in *Chief Constable of North Wales Police v Evans* [1982] 1 WLR 1155 on that topic (noting that Griffin J had quoted the same passage in the *Keegan* case). He also noted that the courts cannot interfere merely because they might have reached a different decision or because the case against the decision made by the body under review was much stronger than the case for it.

The Chief Justice felt that these considerations were particularly important in the planning context. He continued:

> Under the provisions of the Planning Acts the legislature has un-equivocally and firmly placed questions of planning, questions of the balance between development and the environment and the proper convenience and amenities of an area within the jurisdiction of the planning authorities and the Board which are expected to have special skill, competence and experience in planning questions. The Court is not vested with that jurisdiction, nor is it expected to, nor can it exercise discretion with regard to planning matters.
>
> I am satisfied that in order for an applicant for judicial review to satisfy a court that the decision-making authority had acted irrationally . . . so that the court can intervene and quash its decision, it is necessary that the applicant should establish to the satisfaction of the court that the decision-making authority had before it no relevant material which would support its decision.

The Court held that, in the instant case, the applicant had not discharged the onus placed on him in this regard. But even aside from the issue of onus of proof, the Supreme Court held that the Board had been entitled to reach the conclusion it did on a perusal of the entire of the Reports before it, notwithstanding the strength and clarity of the actual recommendations against granting permission made in them. On this basis, the decision of the High Court was reversed on this ground also.

On the issue of the Board giving reasons for its decisions, the Supreme

Court looked at a combination of the decision itself and the conditions attached to the decision; and having regard to the clarity of the conditions in the instant case, the Board had complied with its obligation to give reasons under reg.48 of the Local Government (Planning and Development) Regulations 1977.

The Court also rejected a point on the Board's procedure for keeping minutes. It held that there was no obligation on the Board to keep contemporaneous minutes of its proceedings; and that, in any event, having regard to the failure of the applicant to seek a minute of its proceedings its procedure was not infirm for judicial review purposes. This would appear to limit to some extent the range of the decision of the Supreme Court itself in *P. & F. Sharpe Ltd v Dublin City and County Manager* [1989] ILRM 565; [1989] IR 701 (1988 Review, 296-301).

It is clear that the Supreme Court in the *O'Keeffe* case intended to place limits on the circumstances in which judicial review may be successfully claimed in certain cases. In this, the five member Court affirmed the approach adopted by the three judges in *Stroker v Doherty*, Supreme Court, 26 July 1990, 14-6, above. It also reflects the approach in recent years in, for example, appeals from arbitrations: see *Keenan v Shield Insurance Co. Ltd* [1988] IR 89 (1988 Review, 43-6) and *McStay v Assicurazioni Generali Spa* [1991] ILRM 237 (27-8, below, in the Commercial Law chapter). No doubt, as with the *Keenan* and *McStay* decisions, there may be good reasons for restricting the availability of judicial review to those circumstances in which clear errors of principle have occurred in decision-making bodies under review.

However, the points raised by the Chief Justice in *O'Keeffe* could equally be countered by countervailing quotations on the importance of the 'great remedy' of certiorari and also of the emerging trends in other jurisdictions in which the distinction between judicial review and appeals on points of law has been eroded. Indeed, that erosion has been adverted to in this jurisdiction: see Hogan and Morgan, *Administrative Law in Ireland* (Sweet & Maxwell, 1991) pp.353-4. The reference by the Chief Justice to the competence and expertise of the planning authorities (echoing the views in the *Stroker* case concerning Garda disciplinary procedures) also reflects a 'hands off' doctrine which has traditionally been used as a mechanism for judicial restraint. That approach was used, for example, by the Chief Justice as President of the High Court in cases such as *The State (Smullen) v Duffy* [1980] ILRM 46 (school discipline), *Cahill v Governor of the Curragh Military Detention Barracks* [1980] ILRM 191 (prison discipline) and *Savage v Director of Public Prosecutions* [1982] ILRM 385 (State security). Of course, the Chief Justice reiterated the point that decisions can be quashed for unreasonableness and other errors, but the real message seems to be that the courts should be cautious to interfere with a statutory 'code' in which original jurisdiction has been given to bodies other than the courts.

Although the *O'Keeffe* decision appears to indicate a reversion to an approach in which 'jurisdictional error' might again become a major issue for discussion, the Supreme Court did not really tease out the implications of this. Such implications will require another decision and a full review of recent Irish authorities which seemed to indicate a departure from the approach indicated in *O'Keeffe*. Perhaps in a desire to put a policy-based cap on certain types of judicial review, the Supreme Court may have tramped over recent expansions in judicial review jurisprudence. Assuming that this was not the Court's intention, the more open but relatively modest approach of the Court itself in *Breen v Minister for Defence*, Supreme Court, 20 July 1990 (265-6, below, in the Defence Forces chapter), of Lavan J in *Cooney v An Post*, High Court, 6 April 1990 (8, above) and of Costello J in *O'Donnell v Dun Laoghaire Corporation* [1991] ILRM 301 (see below, 407-10, in the Local Government chapter) may reflect more accurately the true position of the courts in judicial review.

Agriculture

ANIMAL DISEASE ERADICATION

BSE The Diseases of Animals (Bovine Spongiform Encephalopothy) (Amendment) Order 1990 (SI No. 98) amends the 1989 Order (1989 Review, 17) by increasing the compensation payable for slaughtered animals with BSE. The Diseases of Animals (Bovine Spongiform Encephalopothy) (Amendment) (No. 2) Order 1990 (SI No. 195) concerns control on movement and compensation under the 1989 Order. The Diseases of Animals (Bovine Spongiform Encephalopothy) (Amendment) (No. 3) Order 1990 (SI No. 196) prohibits the feeding to ruminants (cattle) of food from ruminants.

Bovine TB The Bovine Tuberculosis (Attestation of the State and General Provisions) (Amendment) Order 1990 (SI No. 182), which reduced to 45 days the validity of the pre-movement test, was revoked by the Bovine Tuberculosis (Attestation of the State and General Provisions) (Amendment) (No. 2) Order 1990 (SI No. 230), which increased the validity of the test to 2 months.

Movement permits The operation of movement permits arose for discussion again in *Carroll v Minister for Agriculture and Food*, High Court, 28 February 1990. The applicant was a farmer in Roscommon, an area which had been designated in January 1989 by the Eradication of Animal Disease Board (ERAD) as a 'black spot' area for bovine TB. The result of this designation was that, where a TB test resulted in an inconclusive reading for TB the animal would be treated as a reactor animal for the purposes of the Bovine Tuberculosis (Attestation of the State and General Provisions) Order 1978 and that a restriction order would be placed on the associated herd. One of the applicant's cattle was tested for TB by a veterinary surgeon in October 1989 pursuant to the 1978 Order and the test resulted in an 'inconclusive' reading. The District Veterinary Office served a restricted holding order on the applicant under Art.12 of the 1978 Order. A new restricted holding order was served on the applicant pursuant to Art.12 of the Bovine Tuberculosis (Attestation of the State and General Provisions) Order 1989 after the 1978 Order had been held *ultra vires*: see *Howard v Minister for Agriculture and Food*, High Court, 3 October 1989 (discussed in the 1989 Review, 17). The applicant sought to have the restricted movement order declared invalid and also argued that the 1989 Order was defective in failing to provide for an appeal against a veterinary test. Blayney J refused the relief sought.

He pointed out that a restricted movement order was mandatory under Art.12 of the 1989 Order where there were reasonable grounds for believing that the animal in question had TB, and in the instant case there was evidence to support such reasonable belief so that the District Veterinary Office was obliged to make the restricted movement order. On the second argument put forward, Blayney J adopted a pragmatic stand. He felt that having regard to the importance of controlling bovine TB in the interest of the economy and its possible impact on inter-Community trade, strict measures were necessary to control TB. On this analysis, he concluded that Art. 12 did not therefore lack fair procedures in not permitting an appeal against the test findings of a veterinary surgeon since any delays might jeopardise the entire TB eradication scheme. Nor did he consider that there an obligation on the respondent to provide another test for the animal in question.

It is unfortunate that Blayney J's judgment does not contain any references to the case law in this area, since this might have required him to examine the interesting line of authority concerning the absence of a right of appeal within a decision- making code: see for example the decisions of Doyle J in *Moran v Attorney General* [1976] IR 400 and of Carroll J in *Gammell v Dublin County Council* [1983] ILRM 413. Looking at these decisions, there is at least an arguable case that the applicant in the instant case should be given some opportunity to displace the profound effect of the initial veterinary finding. However, the emphasis by Blayney J on the overriding public policy factors, namely the impact of TB on the Irish economy and on EC trade, finds an echo in the similar view taken by the Supreme Court in *The State (Lynch) v Cooney* [1983] ILRM 89; [1982] IR 337. In that case it will be recalled that the failure to provide a hearing prior to the making of a ministerial order under s.31 of the Broadcasting Authority Act 1960 (as amended) was excused on the basis of the exigencies of the particular security circumstances arising in that case. To that extent, therefore, Blayney J's approach may not be entirely inconsistent with the existing jurisprudence in the area. Nonetheless, it is a pity that these issues were not teased out to any great extent.

EUROPEAN COMMUNITIES

Milk quota schemes   In *O'Brien v Ireland* [1990] ILRM 466, *Dowling v Ireland*, High Court, 18 January 1990 and *Condon v Minister for Agriculture and Food*, High Court, 12 October 1990, the validity of aspects of the milk quota system were upheld: see 281-4, below, in the European Communities chapter.

Regulations   A number of important EC-based statutory regulations concerning Agriculture are referred to in in the European Communities chapter, 284-6, below.

HORSES

The Horse Breeding Act 1990, which repeals the Horse Breeding Act 1934, abolishes the requirement that stallions be licensed.

IMPORTATION OF LIVESTOCK

The Importation of Livestock (Amendment) Order 1990 (SI No. 43) requires that a licence be obtained to import from Northern Ireland bovine animals less than six months old.

Commercial Law

AGENCY

Essfood Eksportlagtiernes Sallgsforening v Crown Shipping (Irl) Ltd [1991] ILRM 97 concerned the application of well-accepted principles. The plaintiff, a Danish company in the pig meat business, had bought a consignment of meat from a company, Ballybay Meat Exports Ltd. The defendant company was the shipping agent for the meat, which was due to be delivered to Japan. When arrangements had been made for the shipment of the meat, the plaintiff paid Ballybay. Ballybay went into receivership while the meat was in transit. The defendant, which was owed substantial sums by Ballybay, purported to exercise a lien over the meat consignment and wished to sell it to offset the money owed by Ballybay.

The plaintiff successfully prevented the defendant from seling the meat and Costello J ordered that the defendant deliver its bills of lading over the consignment to the plaintiff and take such steps as were necessary to enable the plaintiff obtain possession of the goods.

Costello J rejected the argument that the defendant had any common law lien over the goods, since when they came into the defendant's possession they were already the property of the plaintiff. In addition, once the defendant parted with physical possession it had lost any lien that might otherwise have existed, applying the decision in *Hathesing v Laing* (1873) LR 17 Eq 92 in this context.

As to the bills of lading, they gave no possessory title to the goods to the defendant. But the defendant also argued that the contract entered into with Ballybay entitled it to claim a lien over the goods. Costello J stated that this could not bind the plaintiff since there was no relationship of agency between the plaintiff and defendant when the defendant entered into its contract with Ballybay. It might have been of some interest had Costello J been referred to the Privy Council decision in *New Zealand Shipping Co. Ltd v Satterthwaite & Co. Ltd* [1975] AC 154, though the particular circumstances in that case were somewhat unusual.

Finally, Costello J also rejected the argument that the doctrine of ostensible authority should apply. He quoted with approval the decision of the Court of Appeal in *Freeman and Lockyer v Buckhurst Park Properties Ltd* [1964] 2 QB 480 in this context to emphasise that the doctrine is dependent on representations being made by the principal, and no such representations had been made in the instant case. It is disappointing that Costello J was not referred to the Supreme Court decision in *Kett v Shannon* [1987] ILRM 364 or to his own judgment in *T. Williamson Ltd v Bailieborough Co-Op Ltd*, High Court, 31 July 1986, in both of which the doctrine was discussed. No doubt, reference to these cases would not have led to a different result, and the fact that they were not cited might be explained by the fact that in the instant case the application for interlocutory relief was treated by consent as the hearing of the full action.

ARBITRATION

1 Extension of time to set aside   In *Bord na Mona v J Sisk & Son Ltd (No. 2)*, High Court, 31 May 1990 Blayney J declined to extend the period of time for setting aside an arbitration award. For a preliminary point as to discovery which arose in the case see *Bord na Mona v J. Sisk & Son Ltd* [1990] 1 IR 85 (1989 Review, 350).

The plaintiff had been involved in arbitration proceedings against the defendants. Part of the plaintiff's claim had been dismissed by the arbitrator in awards made in January and March 1988. In the course of seeking to enforce another part of the claim, in which it had been successful, the plaintiff became aware in December 1989 that the arbitrator was, at the time of the arbitration hearing, being retained as an architect by a company associated with the first defendant in connection with the Swan Centre in Rathmines in Dublin. The plaintiff sought to have the arbitration set aside on the ground that the arbitrator had failed to disclose that he was being retained by the company associated with the first defendant. By the time the plaintiff became aware of this fact, the six week time limit specified in O.56, r.4 of the Rules of the Superior Courts 1986 had long since passed and so the plaintiff sought an extension of time under the Rules, but as indicated Blayney J refused the extension.

Blayney J discussed each of the factors as to whether an extension should be granted as outlined in the leading textbook Mustill and Boyd, *Commercial Arbitration*, 2nd ed (Butterworths, 1989) p.568. Blayney J also accepted the dicta of the co-author of that text, Mustill J, when speaking in his judicial capacity in *Citiland Ltd v Kanchan Oil Industries PVT Ltd* [1980] 2 Lloyd's Rep 274, that the weight to be given to each of the relevant factors would vary according to the circumstances of the case. In the instant case, the factor which weighed most with Blayney J was whether the plaintiff had a good arguable case on the merits. He also took account of the possible prejudice to the defendants in having to defend their position again at this stage.

Looking at whether the plaintiff had an arguable case, Blayney J noted that the main challenge to the arbitration related to the question as to whether the arbitrator was in breach of the rule on bias. He referred with approval to the test of bias put forward by Griffin J in *Corrigan v Irish Land Commission* [1977] IR 317 and approved by Murphy J in *Dublin and County Broadcasting Ltd v Independent Radio and Television Commission*, High Court, 12 May 1989. From these authorities Blayney J considered that the test was whether a right minded person with full knowledge of the facts would have been led to conclude that there was a real likelihood of bias, as opposed to a mere suspicion of bias, in the arbitrator acting in the instant arbitration. From this highly objective point of view, Blayney J concluded that it could not be said that the arbitrator could be thought to be biased, taking account of the large amount of publicity which attended his continued involvement in the Swan Centre development, much of which was current immediately prior to his appointment as arbitrator in the instant case. On this basis, therefore, Blayney J held that the plaintiff had failed to establish an arguable case on the merits and would have refused the extension sought on this ground. However, he also indicated that a further factor of importance was the prejudice which the defendants might suffer from having to defend their position in connection with a contract which had, from their point of view, been completed in 1978 and been dealt with in the arbitration hearings in 1988.

The decision of Blayney J deserves comment in particular by virtue of the manner in which he dealt with the bias issue. The authorities on the subject have, on occasion, held that the mere appearance of bias is sufficient to invalidate a decision. This is the approach which gave rise to the oft-quoted dictum of Lord Hewart CJ in *R. v Sussex Justices, ex p. McCarthy* [1924] 1 KB 256 that 'justice should not only be done but should manifestly and undoubtedly be seen to be done.' And that was certainly the view taken by Kenny J in *O'Donoghue v Veterinary Council* [1975] IR 398, to which Blayney J referred in the instant case. The competing view in the case law is, in fact, the view taken by Blayney J, following the approach of Griffin J in the *Corrigan* case (in which Kenny J dissented on this point) and of Murphy J in the *Dublin and County Broadcasting* case. This approach requires proof of something approaching actual bias, as opposed to the appearance of, or suspicion of bias as Blayney J described it. While Blayney J did not have the benefit of being referred to the then unreported ex tempore decision of the Supreme Court in *O'Neill v Beaumont Hospital Board* [1990] ILRM 419 (see the 1989 Review, 7-9), it is of interest that the Supreme Court also took the objective approach to bias in that case.

It thus seems that this view is now firmly in the ascendancy and that a mere appearance of bias is not sufficient to ground a claim in such cases. While there are, no doubt, good practical reasons for taking this approach, it may be that confidence in such decision-making processes from the point of view of the 'consumer' will be adversely affected. While the appearance of justice is not sufficient to cloak a manifestly unfair decision, a 'mere suspicion' of bias may be enough for disappointed persons to feel that the hearing they received was less than what they expected. See Hogan and Morgan, *Administrative Law in Ireland*, 2nd ed. (Sweet & Maxwell, 1991), 420ff.

2 *Interest on award In McStay v Assicurazioni Generali Spa and Anor* [1991] ILRM 237 the recent 'hands off' trend in arbitration matters was confirmed. Some of the difficulties associated with this approach were also expressly referred to. The plaintiff was the receiver of a company which had agreed to refer a dispute to arbitration. The arbitrator, in making his award, stated that he had no jurisdiction to award interest on the sum which he declared was due by the first defendant to the plaintiff. The plaintiff applied for an order remitting to the arbitrator the portion of the arbitration award which related to interest. In the High Court, Carroll J refused the relief sought: [1989] IR 248 (1989 Review, 20) and this was upheld by the Supreme Court (Finlay CJ, Hederman and O'Flaherty JJ), though with a dissenting view expressed by O'Flaherty J as to remitting the case to the arbitrator.

The Court was unanimous, however, in the view that where a precise issue of law has been referred to an arbitrator, the courts should not interfere with the decision arrived at by the arbitrator on that issue of law and should refrain even from investigating whether the arbitrator has made an erroneous decision. In this respect the Court adopted the views of Lord Russell of Killowen in *Absalom Ltd v Great Western Garden Village Society Ltd* [1933] AC 592.

As to the particular issue raised, the award of interest, Finlay CJ (with whose judgment Hederman J agreed) considered that the terms of reference of the arbitrator in the instant case included the precise issue of awarding interest, so that Carroll J had, in his view, rightly refrained from investigating the correctness of the decision arrived at by the arbitrator. This was even though he accepted that in a future appropriate special case stated under s.35 of the Arbitration Act 1954 the courts might decide that an arbitrator had such jurisdiction. The Chief Justice appeared to acknowledge this approach posed a problem, because he felt moved to say that it might be said that the plaintiff appeared to suffer an injustice if the courts were to decide in the future that an arbitrator has jurisdiction to award interest on an award. His answer to this was that the effect in the instant case that the arbitration made a final determination on the point was just and adequate, having regard to the right which the parties had at any time to seek a special case stated in order to have the point of law determined by the High Court.

It was on this aspect of the *Keenan* approach that O'Flaherty J differed from the majority. He accepted the essential point that the courts should be reluctant to become involved in an excessive way in arbitrations, but he felt that in the special circumstances of the case it was appropriate to remit the matter to the arbitrator. This view did not, however, prevail.

3 Stay of proceedings: Supreme Court   *Mitchell v Budget Travel Ltd* [1990] ILRM 739 is an important case as to the power to stay proceedings pursuant to s.12 of the Arbitration Act 1954, as amended by s.5 of the Arbitration Act 1980. The plaintiffs had booked a holiday with the defendant, and subsequently instituted proceedings in the District Court for breach of contract. The defendants applied in the District Court to stay these proceedings pursuant to the arbitration agreement common to such holiday contracts. The District Justice declined to grant the application, but adjourned the case to allow an application to be made to the High Court. In the High Court, Gannon J granted the stay.

The plaintiffs appealed to the Supreme Court (Finlay CJ, Griffin and Hederman JJ). In a unanimous decision delivered ex tempore by the Chief Justice, the Court held that the District Court was empowered under s.5 of the 1980 Act to determine the application for a stay. The Court therefore set aside the order made by Gannon J and remitted the case to the District Court.

The Chief Justice referred to the slight change in wording between s.12 of the 1954 Act and s.5 of the 1980 Act. S.12 had stated that a party which commences proceedings in 'any court . . . may . . . apply to that court to stay the proceedings' whereas s.5 of the 1980 Act provides that any party which commences proceedings in 'any court . . . may . . . apply to the court to stay the proceedings.' Finlay CJ did not consider that the change from 'that court' to 'the court' was sufficient to indicate that exclusive jurisdiction to stay was being conferred on the High Court. He pointed out that much clearer language would be required to take away the inherent jurisdiction of any court to stay proceedings pending an arbitration. He also noted that an exclusive High Court jurisdiction would cause a great number of costly inconveniences, though obviously this could not determine the interpretation issue. The decision will thus be welcome to parties seeking to enforce arbitration agreements, particularly where proceedings are instituted in the District Court and Circuit Court.

BAILMENT

Sheehy v Faughnan, High Court, 14 December 1990 concerned the onus of proof on a bailee to disprove negligence by the bailor. The case is discussed in full in the Torts chapter, 528-9, below.

BANKRUPTCY

In re Casey, a Bankrupt [1991] ILRM 385 is an important decision on the effect of an adjudication in bankruptcy on prior contracts with the bankrupt.

The bankrupt was a beet farmer who supplied the beet to Comhlucht Siúicre Éireann Teo (the company). The terms of the contracts entered into from time to time between the bankrupt and the company allowed the bankrupt to obtain various goods on credit, and these were set off against the beet to be supplied. In April 1981, a contract was entered into which provided that previous credits would be payable out of sums due from the company, and were a charge against his account with the company. The adjudication in bankruptcy took place in July 1981. The company was informed of the adjudication by letter from the Official Assignee of 12 November 1981. The letter indicated that sums due to the bankrupt should be forwarded to the Official Assignee. The company applied to claim in bankruptcy for the sums owed by the bankrupt. Hamilton P (High Court, 21 July 1986) held that the letter from the Official Assignee had terminated the contract between the company and the bankrupt and that the company was not entitled to what would amount to a preference in the bankruptcy. On appeal the Supreme Court (Finlay CJ, Griffin and O'Flaherty JJ) unanimously reversed this decision.

Delivering the only reasoned judgment, the Chief Justice held that the adjudication in bankruptcy could not have the effect of terminating the contract between the company and the bankrupt, but instead it amounted to a novation of the contract so that the Official Assignee became entitled to the bankrupt's rights and obligations under it, unless these were disclaimed. He went on to conclude that the Official Assignee's letter did not amount to a disclaimer of the contract under s.97 of the Bankruptcy (Ireland) (Amendment) Act 1872 (see now s.56 of the Bankruptcy Act 1988) and was precisely to the contrary effect. Therefore, he concluded, by virtue of the terms of the contract, the company had no liability in the bankruptcy and was entitled to prove in the bankruptcy as a creditor against the estate for the balance between the value of the beet supplied by the bankrupt and the goods supplied on credit.

CONSUMER PROTECTION

1 Consumer Credit: APR The ambit of the Consumer Information (Consumer Credit) Order 1987 was discussed in *Director of Consumer Affairs and Fair Trade v Irish Permanent Building Society* [1990] ILRM 743.

The 1987 Order requires that all institutions involved in providing consumer credit include the total annual percentage rate of charge (APR) in all advertisements in connection with such credit. The APR is defined by the 1987 Order to include: (i) the total amount of interest on the credit payable under the agreement and (ii) all other charges at any time payable under the transaction or as a direct consequence of the agreement. The APR is further defined by the Order as excluding any ancillary costs, and it refers specifically in this context to maintenance charges under a hire-purchase contract not imposed by the creditor. The Director of Consumer Affairs and Fair Trade sought a declaration that, in mortgage agreements entered into by the defendant building society, two items in particular should be included in calculating the APR: (a) the cost of house insurance, and (b) the cost of mortgage protection insurance, the latter type of insurance being required by the terms of the Building Society Regulations 1987. Murphy J dismissed the Director's claim.

While he acknowledged that there were some difficulties in interpreting some provisions of the 1987 Order, Murphy J was clear as to the overall purpose of the Order. Thus, he was quite happy with the concept of excluding 'ancillary costs' from the ambit of APR, but found some difficulty in the particular example given in the 1987 Order, namely maintenance charges under a hire-purchase contract. However, by looking at the 1987 Order in the context of its overall purpose, he was able to come to a firm conclusion on the issue posed by the Director.

He held that, in mortgage agreements, the primary beneficiary of both types of insurance was the insured person or the dependents of the insured. Since neither form of insurance involved initial or periodic payments from which the lender could derive a financial benefit of any description, Murphy J concluded that it would be improper to infer that the legislature intended in the 1987 Order to incorporate payments made in respect thereof as forming part of the charge made by the building society.

2 *Legal aid service*   A Consumer Personal Service was established in 1990 by the Consumers' Association of Ireland in conjunction with a grant aid from the European Commission. The intention was to provide consumers with a legal aid service for a fixed fee: see *Irish Times*, 6 June 1990.

3 *Report of Director*   The Annual Report of the Director of Consumer Affairs and Fair Trade for 1989 (Pl. 7571) was published in December 1990. This was the final Report of the first Director, Jim Murray. A point worthy of interest in the Report was the Director's criticism of existing funding for the Office of Consumer Affairs and Fair Trade, particularly in the light of recent increased legislative responsibilities, through the integration of the functions of the Examiner of Restrictive Practices with those of the Office.

CURRENCY

The Decimal Currency Act 1990 provided for the following matters: to amend the Decimal Currency Act 1969 to allow for the introduction of the £1 coin; to allow the Central Bank alter the composition of 1p and 2p coins; and to allow for the minting of coins to commemorate the Irish presidency of the EC Council of Ministers in 1990. The dimensions of the £1 coin are detailed in the Coinage (Dimension and Design) (One Pound Coin) Regulations 1990 (SI No. 83), while the Coinage (Weight and Composition of and Remedy for Certain Copper Coins) Regulations 1990 (SI No. 100) gave effect to the new provisions on the 1p and 2p coins.

EXCHANGE CONTROL

Continuance The Exchange Control (Continuance) Act 1990 continued in force s.2 of the Exchange Control Act 1954 until 31 December 1992. While the Exchange Control (Continuance) Act 1986 was predicted to be the last such Act in view of EC currency liberalisation (see Hogan's annotation, Irish Current Law Statutes Annotated), the 1990 Act may very well attain that title.

Gulf crisis The Exchange Control Regulations 1990 (SI No. 213) required Central Bank approval for dealings with Iraq and Kuwait, in the light of the invasion of Kuwait.

FINANCIAL SERVICES

Building Societies The Building Societies Act 1989 (Commencement) Order 1990 (SI No. 107) brought Part IX of the 1989 Act (on savings protection) into force from 1 May 1990. The Building Societies (Savings Protection) Regulations 1990 (SI No. 108) give detailed effect to Part IX of the 1989 Act by providing that Part II, Chapter V of the Central Bank Act 1989 applies to building society savings.

International Financial Services Centre In 1990, the firm McCann Fitzgerald published a helpful *Guide to the Legal, Regulatory and Taxation Issues Affecting Companies Establishing in Dublin's International Financial Services Centre*.

TSBs The Trustee Savings Banks Act 1989 (Commencement) Order 1990 (SI No. 21) was referred to in the 1989 Review, 40.

Unit Trusts   The Unit Trusts Act 1990 is a comprehensive measure concerning the regulation of unit trusts. It updates and replaces the Unit Trusts Act 1972. Control of unit trust schemes was transferred by the Act from the Minister for Industry and Commerce to the Central Bank. This conforms with the 1989 legislation giving overall supervision to the bank in most areas of financial services: see the 1989 Review, 22-42. The Bank's approval is now required for any scheme covered by the Act, including the advertisement of any such scheme. The Act does not apply to UCITS, which continue to be governed by EC Directives as implemented in Irish law.

GUARANTEE

In *International Commercial Bank plc v Insurance Corporation of Ireland (Meadows Indemnity Co. Ltd, Third Party)*, High Court, 19 October 1990, Blayney J considered the distinction between a contract of guarantee and one of insurance.

The case arose in the following way. A Greek businessman, operating through a Swiss company Amaxa SA (Amaxa), wished to buy out his father's interest in the family hotel and needed to arrange a loan, amounting to over IR£6 million, for this purpose. He was turned down for the loan by a number of banks on the basis that there was inadequate security for the loan sought. Ultimately, he was told that a bank might be willing to make such a loan on the security of a Credit Guarantee Insurance Agreement (CGI Agreement). The general manager of the defendant company's (ICI) London office was approached with a view to entering into such a CGI Agreement. He brought the proposal to the third party, Meadows, to which he acted as consultant, with a view to re-insuring the CGI Agreement. Meadows agreed to this, on condition that the loan to Amaxa itself be properly secured. The plaintiff bank (the bank) was then approached to effect the loan to Amaxa, the bank requiring ICI to 'front' the CGI Agreement, that is act as principal since it was not satisfied that Meadows had sufficient capital to take on the Agreement. The loan agreement between the bank and Amaxa was executed, and the following day the CGI Agreement was executed.

Amaxa defaulted on the loan agreement, and the bank then sought payment from ICI under the CGI Agreement. ICI repudiated liability under the CGI Agreement on the basis that it was a contract of insurance and that there had been non-disclosure of material information by the bank. As to non-disclosure, it was alleged that the bank was aware that it would not be lawful, in Greek law, to apply the loan fully for the purpose of buying out the Greek businessman's family hotel. ICI claimed that this should have been disclosed to it by the bank. ICI also argued that, if it was liable under the contract, it was entitled to a full indemnity from Meadows. Meadows argued, however, that it had entered into the contract on condition that the loan be properly secured through transfer of ownership of the hotel in the event of default on the loan by Amaxa, but that this was never effected by ICI.

Blayney J held that the CGI Agreement was one of guarantee, not of insurance, so that ICI was not entitled to default to the bank. In addititon he held that ICI was not entitled to an indemnity from Meadows, since ICI had failed to secure the Amaxa loan properly. Thus, ICI was left with sole liability in the transaction.

On the question of the CGI Agreement between the bank and ICI, Blayney J was required to interpret the effect of an agreement that had in its title the two words 'guarantee' and 'insurance'. In finding that the agreement was one of guarantee, he referred to a number of important factors. First, he quoted with approval the judgment of Romer LJ in *Seaton v Heath* [1899] 1 QB 782, where the substantial character of the agreement and how it came to be effected were stated to be important factors. As to how the agreement in the instant case came to be effected, he noted that ICI had been approached initially, long before the bank became involved in the transaction. This distinguished the agreement from the situation normally occurring in insurance, where the bank might wish to cover itself in the event of default. As to the character of the agreement, Blayney J noted that the wording corresponded very closely to the precedent for a guarantee in *Butterworth's Encyclopaedia of Forms and Precedents*, 4th ed., Vol. 9, p. 785. This also led him to conclude that the CGI Agreement was one of guarantee and not of insurance. The agreement itself also made no reference to a premium, and the only reference to Amaxa paying a premium to ICI was to be found in a separate cover note sent by ICI to the bank. Finally, he noted the words of Romer LJ in the *Seaton* case to the effect that a contract of insurance was one of speculation, where the insured has knowledge of the risk while the insurer does not. Blayney J felt that, in the instant case, the bank did not have greater knowledge than ICI of the risk posed by the loan to Amaxa; if anything, ICI was in a better position to judge the risk, having been involved in considering the loan for a longer period of time than the bank.

In any event, Blayney J was also doubtful about whether ICI could have succeeded even if it had established that the contract was one of insurance. He pointed out that ICI was arguing that the bank knew about the possible illegality of applying the full loan to the purchase of the hotel by way of information in the hands of the brokers acting for Amaxa. Blayney J noted that this knowledge, if it was relevant, came to the broker's attention *before* it had approached the bank with the loan proposal. It could only be deemed to be acting as agent for the bank (if at all) *after* it approached the bank. Applying a passage from *McGillivray and Parkington on Insurance Law*,

7th ed., para. 811, Blayney J concluded that such information could not be imputed to the bank. This point was not, of course, necessary in view of his conclusion on the CGI Agreement itself, but it was important in terms of indicating whether ICI might have considered an appeal to the Supreme Court.

Turning then to the claim by ICI for a complete indemnity from Meadows under what he referred to (presumably for convenience) as the 're-insurance' agreement, the single issue was whether Meadows entered into this agreement conditional on proper security for the loan. On that point, Blayney J reviewed the precise circumstanecs under which Meadows entered into the agreement, and concluded that Meadows did expressly stipulate that such security be obtained. He found that, although some efforts were made by ICI to effect such security after the agreement had been entered into, these ultimately came to nothing, partly it appeared because of difficulties associated with Greek law. Blayney J thus held that ICI were not entitled to obtain an indemnity from Meadows. He did not consider, in this context, that the fact that ICI had 'fronted' the arrangement with the bank was in any way relevant, as the evidence indicated that this was mere jargon. Perhaps inadvertently, Blayney J summed up the position as follows: 'ICI was the insurer, with all the responsibilities that that involved, and Meadows was the re-insurer.' Of course, he had already found that ICI was not, in fact, an insurer, but this sentence may be translated to indicate that ICI was the principal in the transaction, and that Meadows relied on ICI to effect a proper security for the loan to Amaxa. Having defaulted on ensuring compliance with this condition, he concluded that ICI was not entitled to rely on the indemnity given by Meadows.

INDUSTRIAL AND PROVIDENT SOCIETIES

Kerry Co-Op Creameries Ltd and Ors v An Bord Bainne Co-Op Ltd [1990] ILRM 664 (HC); Supreme Court, 21 March and 14 May 1991 concerned a number of important issues as to the operation of the Irish dairy co-operative movement. As the judgments in the case point out, while the Irish co-ops have grown into large commercial undertakings, they remain by and large in the same legal form as in their humble beginnings, industrial and provident societies. The proceedings arose from changes which the defendant Board proposed to make in its rules.

The Board, also an industrial and provident society, was formed in 1972 to market Irish dairy produce abroad. The Board membership consisted exclusively of dairy co-operatives. The members of the Board agreed that no dividends would be paid on the members' shares, but that instead profits would be distributed to those members who traded with it. Rules were adopted by the Board in 1975 which had the effect of guaranteeing members a fixed price regardless of the market price at the time, provided that the produce was sold to the Board. Membership could be terminated if a member failed to sell produce to the Board, but in fact no membership had ever been terminated. In 1981, the Board agreed a waiver to the 1975 Rules, without explicitly amending them, by which members were gievn a freer choice as to whether to sell produce to the Board or to export produce directly.

The plaintiffs had traded exclusively with the Board up to 1987 when they decided to export some produce directly. In 1987 also the Board decided formally to alter its 1975 Rules. The plaintiffs, as members of the Board, sought unsuccessfully to oppose the changes in the Rules. The effect of the changes was that members who traded exclusively through the Board would be treated more favourably than those who exported some produce directly. The changes also involved changes in the composition of the Board itself as well as the issue of bonus shares. The plaintiffs challenged the validity of the rule changes on the grounds, *inter alia*, that the changes constituted an expropriation of property and a breach of property rights; that the rules constituted an unreasonable restraint of trade; that they were *ultra vires* the Industrial and Provident Societies Act 1893; and were in breach of Articles 85 and 86 of the Treaty of Rome.

All of these claims were rejected by Costello J in the High Court and the Supreme Court upheld all of the domestic law conclusions reached, but decided to refer the EC law issues to the European Court of Justice. Since this reference has yet to be resolved, it is convenient to deal with the domestic law issues in this Review.

In his lengthy judgment, Costello J began by outlining the essential provisions of the Industrial and Provident Societies Act 1893, and he drew attention in particular to the differences between such a society and a limited liability company governed by the Companies Act 1963. Of importance in the instant case was that the 1893 Act contained no provisions regulating in any way the manner in which a society may increase or decrease its capital. In general, he concluded that a society was virtually free to manage its own affairs under the 1893 Act, particularly where that society was registered, as Bord Bainne was, under the terms of the Act.

He went on to consider the constitutional dimension to the plaintiffs' claims, in particular the extent to which it could be argued that they had property rights arising from membership of Bord Bainne. He accepted that, in accordance with the decision in *Private Motorists' Provident Society Ltd v Moore* [1984] ILRM 88; [1983] IR 339, the plaintiffs as shareholders had certain rights which could be described as property rights, but he added that the nature of these rights could only be ascertained by reference to the contract which had been entered into with Bord Bainne in accordance with Bord Bainne's own rules, quoting with approval the judgment of Kenny J in *Attorney General v Jameson* [1904] 2 IR 644.

Approving the decision of Goulding J in *Mutual Life Insurance Co of New York v Rank Organisation Ltd* [1985] BCLC 11, Costello J held that there was no implied contractual obligation that the fractional interest which the member of a society obtained in its shareholding would not be reduced during the period of its membership. Indeed, Costello J referred to the increases and decreases in share capital in which both plaintiffs had engaged internally, noting that there were no restrictions on doing so, in contrast to the situation which obtained for registered companies under the Companies (Amendment) Act 1983. He therefore concluded that there had been no infringement of any property rights the plaintiffs had under Article 40.3 of the Constitution, nor did he consider that there had been an infringement of the equality guarantee of Article 40.1.

Turning to the common law issues in the case, Costello J applied the test of reasonableness concerning restraint of trade clauses, as set out in the House of Lords decision in *McEllistrim v Ballymacelligot Co-Op Society Ltd* [1919] AC 548. Costello J also contrasted Bord Bainne's rules with those condemned in *Tipperary Creamery Society v Hanley* [1912] 2 IR 586, where a member of the society was required to deliver to the society's creamery all the milk produced from the member's cows and where there was no provision for voluntary withdrawal except on transfer of shares. Costello J upheld Bord Bainne's rules because each member was free to trade outside the society. It is of interest that, in dealing with the restraint of trade issue, Costello J applied the traditional 'reasonableness' test. Towards the end of this part of his judgment, however, he also noted that the 'fairness' test suggested by Lord Diplock in *Schroeder Music Publishing Co Ltd v Macauley* [1974] 3 All ER 616 had been relied on. Without expressing a view as to whether this test should be preferred to the reasonableness test, he concluded that, in the instant case, the arrangements made between the plaintiffs and Bord Bainne could not be attacked as unfair.

Then Costello J considered whether the 1988 amended rules were *ultra vires* Bord Bainne. While repeating that the 1893 Act left the society virtually at large, he stated that this was subject to the rule that a majority cannot abuse its position by adopting changes which were outside the scope of the original venture contemplated by the members, citing the views of Lord Atkin in the House of Lords decision *Hole v Garnsey* [1930] AC 472. Looking at the matter in an objective manner by reference to the venture when the plaintiffs joined, Costello J did not consider that the 1988 rules were *ultra vires* Bord Bainne. He felt that the new rules were consistent with the maintenance of the central marketing organisation which it had established, bearing in mind the changed circumstances which had arisen in the intervening period.

Costello J was also required to deal with the role of the Registrar of Friendly Societies, who was required to register the amended rules under the 1893 Act. Applying the Supreme Court decision in *Irish Civil Service Building Society v Registrar of Friendly Societies* [1985] IR 167, he pointed out that the Registrar was confined to considering whether submitted rules conflicted with the terms of the 1893 Act; but was not required to determine whether such rules were otherwise contrary to law. In that light, the Registrar does not commit an actionable wrong in registering rules that might be invalid for some reason other than a breach of the 1893 Act.

Finally, Costello J decided that, in the absence of an application by the plaintiffs to the EC Commission in respect of Articles 85 or 86 of the Treaty of Rome, he would be prepared to assume that Bord Bainne was entitled to claim an exemption under Council Regulation 26/62/EEC. In the Supreme Court, it was felt that the EC dimension required a reference under Article 177 to the Court of Justice. On all the domestic law issues arising, the Court, as already indicated, upheld the decision of Costello J.

INSURANCE

European Communities   Insurance-related Regulations made pursuant to EC obligations are referred to in the European Communities chapter, 285, below.

Fees   The Insurance (Fees) Order 1990 (SI No. 149) prescribes the fees for a solvency certificate and for the depositing of accounts with the Minister for Industry and Commerce under s.7 of the Insurance Act 1989.

Guarantee or insurance   The distinction between a contract of guarantee and one of insurance was considered by Blayney J in *International Commercial Bank plc v Insurance Corporation of Ireland plc*, High Court, 19 October 1990: see 32-4, above.

Intermediaries   The Insurance Act 1989 (Part IV) Commencement Order 1990 (SI No. 136) brought Part IV of the 1989 Act (on the regulation of insurance intermediaries) into effect on 1 October 1990. The Insurance (Bonding of Intermediaries) Regulations 1990 (SI No. 191), which also came into effect on 1 October 1990 were made under s.47 of the 1989 Act.

Irish Life   The Insurance Act 1990 provided for the restructuring, public flotation, and sale of a large segment of the State's shareholding in the Irish

Life Assurance plc. It has been suggested that the attempt by the government to maintain the company's 'Irish ethos' (by retaining a 34% shareholding and prohibiting any one person from holding more than 15% for up to 5 years after the flotation) may be in breach of Article 90 of the Treaty of Rome: see Hogan, Annotation, *Irish Current Law Statutes Annotated*. The Act came into effect on 1 August 1990: Insurance Act 1990 (Commencement) Order 1990 (SI No. 197). The scheme for the transfer of the shares was approved by Costello J in the High Court: *Irish Times*, 7 November 1990. The public flotation took place in 1991.

INTELLECTUAL PROPERTY

1 Copyright:compilations In *Allied Discount Card Ltd v Bord Fáilte Éireann* [1990] ILRM 811, Lynch J considered whether the defendant had used the fruits of the plaintiff company's original work in compiling certain booklets.

The plaintiff had been engaged by the defendant to prepare booklets of discount vouchers for tourists in order to attract visitors to Ireland in the off-peak tourist season. The defendant placed a firm order for 1,000 such booklets, to be delivered by October 1985 in order to allow the defendant to gauge the market for such booklets for Spring 1986. The defendant intended that these booklets would be sold to travel agents and others. The plaintiff successfully approached a number of businesses in Ireland with a view to their inclusion in the discount promotion booklets. However, the plaintiff was unable to deliver to the defendant the 1,000 printed booklets by October 1985. The plaintiff sought instead to obtain an order for 5,000 booklets, which the defendant ultimately agreed to. The booklets were delivered in January 1986, and in view of the lateness of delivery, the defendant felt that it was required to distribute the booklets free rather than to sell them to tourist outlets abroad.

Because of these difficulties, the defendant indicated that it would not require the plaintiff's services in the future. However, in advance of the 1987 Spring season the defendant wrote to the 97 outlets in Ireland which had been included in the plaintiff's 1986 booklet, and 57 such outlets agreed to be included in the 1987 booklet which was prepared solely by the defendant. For the 1988 booklets, 56 outlets agreed to be included. Many of the entries were identical to those for the 1986 booklet, but in some instances alterations were made. The plaintiff claimed damages for breach of copyright and unjust enrichment in respect of the 1987 and 1988 booklets. Lynch J awarded damages primarily on the basis of the breach of copyright.

As to whether copyright existed in the booklets, Lynch J followed the decision of Lardner J in *Radio Telefís Éireann v Magill TV Guide Ltd (No. 2)* [1990] ILRM 534; [1989] IR 554 (see the 1989 Review, 200-1). Lynch J was of the view that, having regard to the definition of literary work in ss.2 and 8 of the Copyright Act 1963 and to the decision in the *Magill TV Guide* case, there was no doubt that copyright can exist in compilations and that in the instant case the plaintiff was entitled to claim copyright in respect of the 1986 booklet.

He went on that while the defendant would not necessarily be in breach of copyright simply by canvassing the traders who had been included in the 1986 booklet, there would be such breach where there was minimal input by the defendant into settling the wording of the vouchers to be included in the 1987 and 1988 booklet. Having regard to the evidence it appeared to him that for 1987 there were 40 repeats of the plaintiff's wording in the 1986 booklets and that for 1988 there were 30 entries based substantially or wholly on the plaintiff's work. On this basis Lynch J concluded that breach of copyright had been established.

As to the measure of damages, he pointed out that since the defendant had indicated to the plaintiff that for 1987 and 1988 there might be orders for something in the region of 50,000 booklets, the plaintiff had incurred expenses in preparing the 1986 booklet on the reasonable expectation that that would be the level of future orders; and the plaintiff was thus entitled to damages based on that level of potential orders. He assessed damages as amounting to £19,250 in total in respect of the 1987 and 1988 booklets. As to any further claims, he concluded that the plaintiff was not entitled to damages for any further years since its original work would be too remote beyond 1988.

2 Copyright: designs In *Costelloe v Johnston and Ors*, High Court, 16 May 1990 the plaintiff claimed that the defendants had infringed his copyright in the registered design of a door. The defendants successfully claimed that the plaintiff's registration of the design under the Industrial and Commercial Property (Protection) Act 1927 was invalid because the design had already been published. Having reveiwed the evidence, Blayney J accepted that the defendants had imported and sold a door of a design virtually identical to the door in respect of which the plaintiff had obtained the design registration.

In the circumstances, Blayney J granted a declaration to the defendants that the registration was invalid and that they were entitled to have the registration expunged for the Register of Designs. However, he did not feel he could actually expunge the registration from the Register under s.129 of the 1927 Act, since the Controller of Patents, Designs and Trade Marks had not been served with any proceedings under O.94, r.50 of the Rules of the Superior Courts 1986.

3 Trade Marks V' Soske Shops Inc v V' Soske Joyce Ltd, High Court, 25 May 1990 concerned the interpretation of a contract involving trade marks: see 186, below, in the Contract Law chapter.

MERGERS AND TAKE-OVERS

Anglo-Irish Beef   The Proposed Merger or Take-Over Conditional Order 1990 (SI No. 93) prohibited the deal between Anglo-Irish Beef Processors Ltd and Master Meat Packers (Bandon) Ltd except on certain conditions. The Proposed Merger or Take-Over Conditional (No. 2) Order 1990 (SI No. 94) No. 93) prohibited the deal between Anglo-Irish Beef Processors Ltd and DJS Meats Ltd except on certain conditions.

British Steel   The Proposed Merger or Take-Over Prohibition Order 1990 (SI No. 42) prohibited for a time the deal involving British Steel plc and C. Walker & Sons (Holdings) Ltd on the ground that it was an enterprise controlled in this State. The Order was revoked by the Proposed Merger or Take-Over Prohibition Order 1990 (Revocation) Order 1990 (SI No. 115) on the basis that the EC Commission had approved the merger.

RESTRICTIVE PRACTICES

Commission's Report   The Report of the Fair Trade Commission for 1988 and 1989 (for which no government publication number was given) was published in November 1990.

Legal profession   The Fair Trade Commission Report Into Restrictive Practices in the Legal Profession was published in June 1990: see 437-9, below, in the Practice and Procedure chapter.

National Lottery   The Restrictive Practices (National Lottery) Order 1990 (SI No. 13) provides that the National Lottery may not prohibit its retail agents from selling other lottery tickets.

Company Law

THE COMPANIES (AMENDMENT) ACT 1990

This Act introduces a new procedure into Irish law, providing a breathing space for businesses in financial difficulties but with the prospect of continued survival, in part or whole. It enables the court to appoint an examiner for a limited period during which the examiner forms an assessment of the chances of viability. The effect of a petition to appoint an examiner is to place the company under the protection of the court, so that no proceedings for its winding up may be commenced, nor other enforcement remedies pursued. If the examiner's assessment is positive, then, with the court's blessing, he sets about formulating proposals for a compromise or scheme of arrangement. He organises meetings of interested parties (including creditors of the company) and seeks their approval for his proposals. In due course, the examiner returns to court with his proposals, which the court may confirm (with or without modification) or reject. Thereafter the business reemerges from the protection of the court into the open market. The hope, of course, is that the combination of the examiner's proposals, the give-and-take of mutual concessions, and the exercise by the examiner of wide-ranging ancillary powers will have gradually improved its overall financial standing.

The Act began its life as Part IX of the Companies (No 2) Bill 1987: see the 1987 Review, 53. International developments in 1990 altered its progress. Iraq's invasion of Kuwait, followed by the UN trade embargo, had serious consequences for the substantial Irish beef export trade with Iraq. This led to the Act's being rushed through the Oireachtas in 48 hours and signed by the President into law on 29 August 1990. That day Hamilton P appointed an examiner to Goodman International and 25 related companies. See McCormack, *The New Companies Legislation* (1991), 185-6, Lynch, 'Goodman International and the 1990 Companies (Amendment) Act', *Dlí*, Spring 1991, p. 21.

A few minor amendments to the Act were effected by Part IX of the Companies Act 1990, which became law four months later. In our consideration of the Companies (Amendment) Act 1990, we take account of these subsequent changes.

For detailed consideration of the Act, see McCormack, *op. cit.,* chapter 11, Keane, *Company Law in the Republic of Ireland* (2nd ed., 1991) chapter

39, Lynch, *op. cit.* The legislation was followed by a number of seminars, including *Companies under Court protection and Appointment/Role of Examiner*, organised by Grant Sugrue & Co. on 10 October 1990. Barry O'Neill's paper at that seminar, 'Review of Companies (Amendment) Act 1990', contains several points of theoretical and practical interest. We refer to a number of them below.

The petition A petition for the appointment of an examiner may be presented by the company, its directors, a creditor, or contingent or prospective creditor (including an employee) of the company or, finally, members of the company holding at least a tenth of such of the paid up capital as carries the right of voting at general meetings: s. 3(1).

Where it appears to the court that the company is unable to pay its debts, that no resolution subsists for its winding up and that no order for its winding up has been made, the court *may*, on the presentation of the petition, appoint an examiner 'for the purpose of examining the state of the company's affairs and performing such duties in relation to [it] as may be imposed by or under th[e] Act': s. 2(1). The court may, in particular, make such an order if it considers that it would be likely to facilitate the survival of the company, and the whole or any part of the undertaking, as a going concern: s. 2(2). In deciding whether to make an order, moreover, the court may also have regard to whether the company has sought from its creditors significant extensions of time for the payment of its debts, from which it could reasonably be inferred that it was likely to be unable to pay its debts: s. 2(4).

The broad discretion given to the court under s. 2 may be contrasted with the specificity of s. 8 of Britain's Insolvency Act 1986: see McCormack, *op. cit.*, 188-90.

Under s. 2(3), a company is *unable to pay its debts* if:

(a) it is unable to pay its debts as they fall due;
(b) the value of its assets is less than the amount of its liabilities taking into account its contingent and prospective liabilities, or
(c) it has failed to pay a creditor a debt of at least £1,000 for more than three weeks after being demanded in writing to pay it or a judgment is unsatisfied (cf Keane, *op. cit.*, paras. 38.09, 39.03).

The petition must nominate a person to be appointed as examiner, and be supported by such evidence as the court may require to show that the petitioner has good reason for requiring the appointment of an examiner: s. 3(3)(a) and (b). Where it is presented by the company or its directors, the petition must include a statement of the assets and liabilities of the company (in so far as these are known to the petitioners) as they stand on a date not earlier than seven days before the presentation of the petition: s. 3(3)(c).

The petition must be accompanied by a consent signed by the person nominated to be examiner and by a copy of any proposals for a compromise or scheme of arrangement in relation to the company's affairs which have been prepared for submission to interested parties for their approval: s. 3(4).

The court is not to give a hearing to a petition presented by a *contingent or prospective creditor* until such security for costs has been given as it thinks reasonable and until a *prima facie* case for the protection of the court has been established to its satisfaction: s. 3(5) (as amended by the Companies Act 1990, s. 180(1)(a)).

If a receiver has stood appointed to the company for at least three days before to the presentation of the petition, the court is not to give a hearing to the petition: s. 3(b) (as amended by the Companies Act 1990, s. 180(1)(a)). The Companies (Amendment) Act 1990 provided for a period of 14 days, but this was reduced to three days in the Companies Act 1990. Mr Leyden was of the view that this would give 'considerable comfort' to receivers who would be much more certain of their position as well as requiring company managements, and their creditors, to make up their minds within a shorter period whether to apply to the court for the appointment of an examiner: 403 Dáil Debs, col. 1128 (1990).

The court has wide powers on hearing a petition: it may dismiss it, adjourn the hearing conditionally or unconditionally, or may make any interim order or any other order it thinks fit: s. 3(7). An interim order may restrict the exercise of any powers of the directors of the company (whether by reference to the consent of the court or otherwise): s. 3(8).

Where it appears to the court that the total liabilities of the company (taking into account its contingent and prospective liabilities) do not exceed £25,000, the court may, after making such interim or other orders as it thinks fit, order that the matter be remitted to the judge of the Circuit Court in whose circuit the company has its registered office or principal place of business: s. 3(9)(a). When this is done, the Circuit Court has full jurisdiction to exercise all the powers of the court conferred by the Act in relation to the company: s. 3(9)(b). If it appears to the Circuit Court that in fact the total liabilities *exceed* £25,000, it must transfer the case back to the High Court, having made such interim orders as it thinks fit: s. 3(9)(c).

Related companies S. 4 (as amended by the Companies Act 1990, s. 180(1)(b)) deals with *related companies*. Where the court appoints an examiner to a company, it may, then or at any later time, appoint the examiner to be examiner to a related company or confer on the examiner, in relation to that company, all or any of the powers or duties conferred on him in relation to the company to which the court appoints him examiner: s. 4(1). In deciding whether to take this course, the court is to have regard to whether it would be likely to facilitate the survival of the company, or of the related company, or both, and the whole or any part of it or their undertaking, as a joint concern: s. 4(2). The idea behind this power is to avoid unnecessary duplication.

S. 4(5) provides that a company is *related to another company* if:

(a) that other company is its holding company or subsidiary,

(b) more than half in nominal value of its equity share capital (as defined in s. 155(5) of the 1963 Act) is held by the other company and companies related to that other company (whether directly or indirectly, but other than in a fiduciary capacity),

(c) more than half in nominal value of the equity share capital (as defined by s. 155(5) of the 1963 Act) of each of them is held by members of the other (whether directly or indirectly, but other than in a fiduciary capacity),

(d) that other company or a company or companies related to the other company or that other company together with a company or companies related to it are entitled to exercise or control the exercise of more than half of the voting power at any general meeting of the company,

(e) the business of the companies has been so carried on that the separate business of each company, or a substantial part of it, is not readily identifiable, or

(f) there is another body corporate to which both companies are related.

For the purposes of s. 4, 'company' includes any body which is liable to be wound up under the Companies Acts: s. 4(6).

Effect of petition to appoint examiner on creditors and others   S. 5 deals with this matter. During the period beginning with the presentation of a petition for the appointment of an examiner to a company and (subject to the periods for extension of time permitted by s. 18(3) or (4)) ending on the expiry of three months from the date of presentation or on the withdrawal or refusal of the petition, whichever first happens, the company is deemed to be under the protection of the court: s. 5(1).

S. 5(2) (as amended by the Companies Act 1990, ss. 180(1)(b) and 181(1)(c)) provides that, for as long as a company is thus under the protection of the court, the following provisions have effect:

(a) no proceedings for its winding-up may be commenced or resolution for winding-up passed;

(b) no receiver over any part of the property or undertaking of the company may be appointed, or, if so appointed before the presentation of a petition, may (subject of s. 6) be able to act;

(c) no attachment, sequestration, distress or execution may be put into force against the property or effects of the company, except with the consent of the examiner;

(d) where any claim against the company is secured by a charge on the whole or any part of the property, effects or income of the company, no action may be taken to release the whole or any part of the security, except with the consent of the examiner;

(e) no steps may be taken to repossess goods in the company's possession under any hire-purchase agreement (defined by s. 11(8) as including a conditional sales agreement, a retention of title agreement and an agreement for the bailment of goods which is capable of subsisting for more than three months), except with the consent of the examiner;

(f) where, under any enactment, rule of law or otherwise, any person other than the company is liable to pay all or any part of the debts of the company —

(i) no attachment, sequestration, distress or execution is to be put into force against the property or effects of that person in respect of the debts of the company, and
(ii) no proceedings of any sort may be commenced against that person in respect of the debts of the company

(g) no order for relief is to be made under s205 of the 1963 Act against the company in respect of complaints as to the conduct of its affairs or the exercise of its directors' powers before the presentation of the petition.

(h) no set-off between separate bank accounts of the company is to be effected, save with the consent of the examiner.

Subject to s. 5(2), no other proceedings in relation to the company may be *commenced* except by leave of the court and subject to such terms as the court may impose and the court may on the application of the examiner make such order as it thinks proper in relation to any *existing* proceedings including an order to stay them: s. 5(3).

Complaints concerning the conduct of the affairs of the company while it is under the protection of the court are not to constitute a basis for the making of an order for relief under s. 205 of the 1963 Act: s. 5(4).

Effect on receiver or provisional liquidator of order appointing examiner Where the court appoints an examiner to a company and a *receiver* stands appointed to the whole or any part of the property or undertaking of that company the court may make such order as it thinks fit including the following:

(a) an order that the receiver is to cease to act as such from a date specified by the court;
(b) an order that the receiver is to act as such only in respect of certain specified assets;
(c) an order directing the receiver to deliver to the examiner all books, papers and other records relating to the property or undertaking of the company that are in his possession or control;
(d) an order directing the receiver to give the examiner full particulars of all his dealings with the property or undertaking of the company: s. 6(1).

Where a *provisional liquidator* stands appointed to a company to which the court appoints an examiner, the court may against make such order as it thinks fit, including:

(a) an order that the provisional liquidator be appointed as examiner of the company;
(b) an order appointing some other person as examiner of the company;
(c) an order that the provisional liquidator is to cease to act as such from a specified date;
(d) an order directing him to deliver all records in his possession or control to the examiner;
(e) an order directing the provisional liquidator to give the examiner full particulars of all his dealings with the property or undertaking of the company: s. 6(2).

In deciding whether to make an order that a receiver is to cease to act as such or to act as such only in respect of certain specified assets or that a provisional liquidator is to cease to act as such, the court is to have regard to whether the making of the order would be likely to facilitate the survival of the company, and the whole or any part of its undertaking, as a going concern: s. 6(3). Likelihood has been interpreted in England as encompassing 'a real prospect of survival' rather than the balance of probabilities: *Re Primlaks (UK) Ltd* [1989] BCLC 734. Commenting on this power of the court to 'freeze' the receiver, Barry O'Neill (*op. cit.*, para 9.2) observes that it:

is a radical statutory provision. It remains to be seen how the power is exercised by the Court. In many instances, receivers are not welcomed by the directors of the company. Now, the directors have a statutory right to seek the appointment of an examiner and, thereby, the possibility of retrieving their powers of management (which will have ceased on the appointment of the receiver). The court will be obliged to distinguish between the petitioner who genuinely believes that rescue is possible and the petitioner who is really trying to frustrate the 'unwelcome receiver'.

Powers of an Examiner   S. 7 sets out in detail the powers of an examiner. It first provides that any provision of the Companies Acts relating to the powers of an auditor of a company and the supplying of information to and co-operation with an auditor are, with the necessary modifications, to apply to an examiner: s. 7(1). The examiner has power to convene, set the agenda for, and preside at meetings of the board of directors and general meetings of the company to which he is appointed and to propose motions or resolutions and give reports to these meetings: s. 7(2).

The examiner is, moreover, entitled to reasonable notice of, to attend and be heard at, all meetings of the board of directors and all general meetings of the company to which he is appointed: s. 7(3).

Where the examiner becomes aware of any actual or proposed act, omission, course of conduct, decision or contract by or on behalf of the company to which he has been appointed, its officers, employers, members or creditors or any other person in relation to the income, assets or liabilities of that company which, in his opinion, is or is likely to be to the detriment of the company or any innocent party, he has full power, subject to *bona fide* third party rights for value, to take whatever steps are necessary to halt, prevent or rectify the effects of that venture: s. 7(5). As to the power of the examiner to rectify the effects of a creditor's act, Barry O'Neill (*op. cit.*, para 11.7) comments that:

> [t]here are many situations arising in typical insolvencies which could fall within the scope of this provision for instance, where, say, Telecom Éireann cut off telephone service, there will have been 'an act' by a 'creditor' relating to 'the assets [or] liabilities' of the company which is to the 'detriment' of the company. Can the examiner 'rectify' this situation by forcing Telecom Éireann to restore the service? It remains to be seen.

The examiner may apply to the court to determine any question arising in the course of his office, or for the exercise in relation to the company of any of the powers the court may exercise under the Act, on the application to it of any member, contributory, creditor or director of a company: s. 7(6). If so directed by the court, the examiner has power to ascertain and agree claims against the company to which he has been appointed: s. 7(6).

Production of documents and evidence S. 8 (as amended by the Companies Act 1990, s180(1)(e)) gives the examiner wide-ranging powers in relation to the production of documents and evidence. All officers and agents of the company or a related company must produce to him all books and documents of or relating to any such company which are in their custody or power, attend before him when required to do so and 'otherwise . . . give him all assistance in connection with his functions which they are reasonably able to give': s. 8(1). If the examiner considers that some *other* person is or may be in possession of any information concerning the company's affairs, he may require that person to give him similar assistance: s. 8(2).

The examiner has power to insist that a director, past director, shadow director or connected person of the company give him all documents in his possession or under his control relating to a bank account into which has been paid any money which has resulted from or been used in the framing of any transaction, arrangement or agreement particulars of which have not been disclosed in the company's accounts as required by law or any money which has been 'in any way connected' with misconduct on his part (fraudulent or otherwise) towards the company or its members: s. 8(3) (as amended by the Companies Act 1990, s. 180(1)(d) and (e)).

The examiner may examine an oath, either orally or by written interrogatories the officers or agents of the company or others who may be in possession of any information concerning the company's affairs, in relation to the company's affairs: s. 8(4). If the person thus called to account refuses to produce a book or document which it is his duty to produce, refuses to attend when required to do or refuses to answer any question put to him by the examiner with respect to the affairs of the company, the examiner may certify the refusal under his hand to the court, and the court may thereupon inquire into the case and, after hearing any witnesses who may be produced against or on behalf of the alleged offender and any statement which may be offered in defence, punish the offender in like manner as if he had been guilty of contempt of court: s. 8(5).

After a hearing under s. 8(5), the court may make any order it thinks fit, including an order to attend or re-attend before the examiner or produce particular books or documents or answer particular questions put by the examiner: s. 8(5a) (inserted by the Companies Act 1990, s. 180(1)(e)). Subs. (5a) was introduced in order to offer more wide-ranging, sensitive options to the court than merely the crude mallet of contempt. Legally protected information is protected under s8 in the same way as it is in relation to the investigation procedure under Part II of the Companies Act 1990: s. 8(5b) (inserted by the Companies Act 1990, s. 180(1)(e)).

Further powers of the Court S. 9 gives the court power, on application by the examiner, to make an order that all or any of the functions or powers of the directors are to be performable or exercisable by the examiner: s. 9(1). In deciding whether to make such an order the court is to have regard to the following matters:

> (a) that the affairs of the company are being conducted, or are likely to be conducted, in a manner calculated or likely to prejudice the interests of the company or of its employees or of its creditors as a whole, or
> (b) that is expedient, to preserve the company's assets or safeguard the interests of the company, its employees or its creditors as a whole, that the carrying on of the company's business by, or the exercise of the powers of, the directors or management should be curtailed or regulated in any particular respect, or
> (c) that the company, or its directors have resolved that such an order should be sought, or
> (d) any other matter in relation to the company which the court thinks relevant: s. 9(2).

In any event, an order under s. 9 may give the examiner all or any of the powers that he would have if he were a liquidator appointed by the court in respect of the company: s. 9(4). Where the order so provides, the court has all the powers that it would have if it had made a winding-up order and appointed a liquidator in respect of the company concerned: *id.*

Incurring of certain liabilities by examiner S. 10 (as amended by the Companies Act 1990, s180(1)(f)) treats certain liabilities incurred by the company during the protection period as expenses properly incurred by the examiner (or the purposes of s. 29 of the Act: these are liabilities which the examiner certified at the time as, in his opinion, incurred in circumstances *where the survival of the company as a going concern would otherwise be seriously prejudiced.*

Disposal of charged property The examiner, with the consent of the court, may dispose of property subject to a floating charge or other security or goods in the possession of the company under a hire purchase agreement if the court is satisfied that this would be likely to facilitate the survival of the whole or part of the company as a going concern: s. 11(1) and (2). The holder of the floating charge is given the same priority in relation to the proceeds as he would have had in respect of the property disposed of: s. 11(3). On the disposition of property subject to other security or of goods in the possession of the company under a hire purchase agreement, the net proceeds of the disposal or if they are less than the amount that would be realised on their sale in the open market to a willing vendor, the amount required to make good the deficiency, must be applied towards discharging the sums secured by the security or payable under the hire purchase agreement: s. 11(4).

Mr Brennan explained that it had been put to him that a company 'could be effectively hamstrung' during the protection period if some of its assets, such as buildings incurring heavy overheads, were the subject of a fixed security. This could clearly be a drain on the company's resources during the protection period: 121 Seanad Debs, col. 87 (21 September 1988).

Examination of the affairs of the company   When the examiner has been appointed, it is his duty to conduct an examination into the affairs of the company and report to the court, within 21 days (or longer if the court allows this) the results of his examination: s. 15(1).

The report must comprise the names and addresses of the officers and (so far as he can establish) any one in accordance with whose directions the directors are accustomed to act (s. 16, clause (a)), the names of other companies of which the directors are also directors (*id.*, clause (b)), a statement as to the affairs of the company, including particulars of assets, debts, liabilities and securities (*id.*, clause (c)), the examiner's opinion as to whether any deficiency between assets and liabilities has been satisfactorily accounted for or, if not, whether there is evidence of a substantial disappearance of property that is not adequately accounted for (*id.*, clause (d)), a statement of his opinion as to whether the company, and the whole or any part of its undertaking, would be capable of survival as a going concern and a statement of the conditions which he feels are essential to ensure that survival, whether as regards the internal management and controls of the company or otherwise (*id.*, clause (e)), his opinion as to whether the formulation, acceptance and confirmation of proposals for a compromise or scheme of arrangement would facilitate that survival (*id.*, clause (f)), his opinion as to whether an attempt to continue the whole or any part of the undertaking of the company would be likely to be more advantageous to the members as a whole and the creditors as a whole than a winding up (*id.*, clause (g)), recommendations as to the course he thinks should be taken in relation to the company (including, if warranted, draft proposals for a compromise or scheme of arrangement) (*id.*, clause (h)), his opinion as to whether the facts disclosed would warrant further inquiries with a view to proceeding for imposing personal liability for fraudulent or reckless trading (*id.*, clause (i)), such other matters as he thinks relevant or the court directs (*id*, clause (j)), and his opinion as to whether his work would be assisted by a direction of the court extending the role or membership of a creditors' committee under s. 21 (*id.*, clause (k)).

To assist the examiner in preparing his report, the company's directors must, within a week of his appointment, submit a statement as to the affairs of the company, giving particulars of its assets, debts and liabilities, the names and addresses of creditors, securities held by them and such further information as may be prescribed or as the court may direct: s. 14(1) and (2). This obligation is backed by a criminal sanction: s. 14(3).

When the examiner has completed the report, he must deliver a copy to the company on the same day as he delivers it to the court (s. 15(3)) as well as to any interested party on written application, with such omissions as the court thinks fit (s. 15(4)).

The court must hold a hearing to consider matters arising out of the examiner's report where the examiner has expressed a *negative* opinion as to the company's future viability or as to what appears to be past misdeeds (in terms of evidence of a substantial disappearance of property that has not been adequately accounted for or other serious irregularities): s. 17(1). At this hearing, there is an automatic right to appear and be heard for the examiner, the company, any interested party and anyone who is referred to in the context of suspected misdeeds: s. 17(2).

The court has a very broad discretion as to what orders it may make (s. 17(3)); these may, for example, include an order for winding up, an order for the sale of all or part of its undertaking and the formulation of the examiner of proposals for a compromise or scheme of arrangement (s. 17(4)). The examiner (or such other person as the court may direct) must deliver an office copy of an order made under s. 17 to the registrar of companies for registration (subs. (5)).

S. 18 deals with the situation where the examiner's opinion is *positive*, that is:

(a) that the whole or part of the undertaking of the company would be capable of survival as a going concern, *and*

(b) that an attempt to continue the whole or part of the undertaking would be more likely to be more advantageous to the members as a whole, and to the creditors as a whole, than a winding up, *and*

(c) that the foundation, acceptance and confirmation of proposals for a compromise or scheme of arrangement would facilitate this survival (subs. (1)).

In these circumstances, the examiner must formulate proposals for a compromise or scheme of arrangement (*id.*).

The normal requirements as to notice of general meetings do not apply: the examiner can convene and preside at such meetings of members and creditors as he thinks proper, to consider his proposals, subject to three days' notice: subs. (2). He must report on the outcome to the court within 42 days of his appointment (or longer, if the court allows this): *id.*

The examiner's report must include:

(a) the proposals placed before the required meetings;
(b) any modification adopted at them;
(c) the outcome of each required meeting;
(d) the recommendation of the committee of creditors;
(e) a statement of the company's assets and liabilities as at the date of his report;
(f) a list of creditors, the amounts they are owed, the security they hold and their respective priority status;
(g) a list of officers of the company;
(h) the examiner's recommendations, and
(i) such other matters as the examiner deems appropriate or the court directs (s. 19).

The rules as to circulation of the examiner's report (s. 18(5) and (6)) are the same as for a report made under s. 16, which we have already outlined.

The examiner's proposals for a compromise or scheme of arrangement, which he will present to a meeting of members or creditors under s. 23, must:

(a) specify each class of members and creditors of the company;
(b) specify any such class whose interests or claims will *not* be impaired by the proposals;
(c) specify any such class whose interests or claims *will* be thus impaired;
(d) provide equal treatment for each claim or interest of a particular class unless the holder of a particular claim or interest agrees to less favourable treatment;
(e) provide for the implementation of the proposals;
(f) if the examiner considers it necessary or desirable to do so to facilitate the survival of the company and all or part of its undertaking as a going concern, specify whatever changes should be made in relation to the management or direction of the company;
(g) if he considers it thus necessary or desirable, specify any changes he considers should be made in the memorandum or articles of the company, whether as regards the management or direction of the company or otherwise;
(h) include such other matters as he deems appropriate (s. 22(1)).

In this context, the interest of a member of a company in a company is *impaired* if:

(a) the nominal value of his shareholding is reduced,

(b) where he is entitled to a fixed dividend in respect of his shareholding, its amount is reduced,

(c) he is deprived of rights accruing to him by virtue of his shareholding,

(d) his percentage interest in the total issued share capital is reduced, or

(e) he is deprived of his shareholding (s. 22(6)).

S. 22 does not define *class*, which is, of course, crucial to the operation and effect of the section as a whole. Experience in relation to the operation of s. 201 of the 1963 Act is to the effect that, '[n]ormally the classes that will have to be considered in the case of a proposal affecting members are the ordinary and preference shareholders; and in the case of a proposal affecting creditors, the preferential, secured and unsecured creditors. But there may be further categories to be considered. . . .': Keane, *op. cit.*, para 34.05. Bowen LJ's statement in *Sovereign Life Assurance Co. v Dodd* [1892] 2 QB 573, at 583 is widely quoted by the commentators in this context:

It seems plain that we must give such a meaning to the term 'class' as will prevent the section being so worked as to result in confiscation and injustice, and that it must be confined to those persons whose rights are not so dissimilar as to make it impossible for them to consult together with a view to their common interest.

The extent to which this approach permits standard 'obvious' classifications to be 'trumped' by classifications based on a contingent confluence of circumstances in particular cases in a matter of debate: see the discussion of *In re Pye (Ireland) Ltd*, Supreme Court, 17 April 1985, reversing High Court, Costello J, 11 March 1985, in Keane, *op cit,* para 34.05, McCormack *op. cit.*, 202-3. Barry O'Neill (*op. cit.*, para 26.3) thinks that it 'would seem logical that secured creditors should be in separate classes if their debts are secured on different properties or, if secured on the same property, they are to rank in different orders of priority'.

With every notice summoning a meeting which is sent to a creditor or member, there must also be sent a statement explaining the effect of the compromise or scheme of arrangement; in particular it must state any material interests of the directors of the company, whether as directors or members or creditors or otherwise, and the effect on them of the compromise or arrangement, insofar as it is different from the effect of the like interest of the persons: s. 23(8).

At a meeting of members, or a class of them, summoned by the examiner to consider his proposals for a compromise or scheme of arrangement, these proposals are deemed to have been accepted by the members, or the class, if a majority of votes cast, whether in person or by proxy, are in favour: s. 23(3). At a meeting of creditors, or a class of them, similarly summoned, proposals are deemed to have been accepted when a majority in number representing a majority in value of the claims represented at the meeting have voted, whether in person or by proxy, in favour: s. 23(4). This preference for a simple majority, in contrast to the 75% of requirement under s. 201 of the 1963 Act, has been identified by Irene Lynch (*op. cit.*, at 21) as 'run[ning] contrary to the principle of increased creditor protection'.

The report of the examiner is in due course set down for consideration by the court (s. 24(1)). At the hearing, the company, the examiner and any creditor or member whose claim or interest would be impaired if the proposals were implemented may appear and be heard (s24(2)). That creditor or member may object in particular to confirmation of the proposals on any of following grounds: (a) that there was some material irregularity in relation to a meeting summoned by the examiner to consider his proposals, (b) that acceptance of the proposals was obtained by improper means, (c) that proposals were put forward for an improper purpose, or (d) that they unfairly prejudice the interests of the objector (s. 25(1)). An objector who voted to accept the proposals may object to them only on the grounds that they were obtained by improper means or that, after so voting, he became aware that they had been put forward for an improper purpose (s. 25(2)).

At the hearing (and subject to s. 25, which we consider presently), the court may, as it thinks proper, confirm, with or without modifications, or refuse to confirm the proposals (s. 24(3)). It is *not* to confirm the proposals:

> (a) unless at least one class of members of creditors whose interests or claims would be impaired by implementation of the proposals has accepted them, or
> (b) if the sole or primary purpose of the proposals is the avoidance of payment of tax due, or
> (c) unless the court is satisfied that:

>> (i) the proposals are fair and equitable in relation to any class of members that has not accepted them and whose interests or claims would be impaired by implementation, and
>> (ii) they are not unfairly prejudicial to the interests of any interested party (s. 24(4)).

Where the court confirms proposals (with or without modifications), they are binding on all the members or class affected by them and also on the company (s. 24(5)). Moreover, they are binding on all or a class of the creditors affected by them in respect of claims against the company and others who are liable for its debts (s.24(6)). The court has power to confirm proposed alterations in the memorandum and articles of the company regardless of whether these comply with the requirements of the Companies Act (s.24(7)). A compromise or scheme of arrangement which is confirmed by the court comes into effect on the date fixed by the court, not later than 21 days after this confirmation (s. 24(9)).

Where the court refuses to confirm the examiner's proposals, it may, if it considers it just and equitable to do so, make an order for the winding up of the company, or any other order as it deems fit (s. 24(11)). If the court confirms the examiner's proposals, a copy of the order must be delivered (by the examiner or such other person as the court directs) to the registrar of companies for registration. The company or any interested party may, within 180 days of the confirmation of the proposals of the court, apply to it for revocation of the confirmation on the ground that it was procured by fraud; if so satisfied, the court may revoke the confirmation on such terms and conditions as it deems fit, particularly with regard to the protection of the rights of parties acquiring interests or property in good faith and for value in reliance on the confirmation (s. 27). This short time limit may be contrasted with the generally open-ended policy of limitation periods towards fraud.

Commercial realities dictate a short limitation period in the present context. This will not, of course, prevent injured parties (including corporate entities) from suing in tort for fraud or conspiracy in appropriate cases.

Repudiation of company's contracts Where proposals for a compromise or scheme of arrangement are to be formulated in relation to a company, the company, subject to the court's approval, may affirm or repudiate any contract under which some element of performance other than payment remains to be rendered both by the company and the other party (s. 20(1)). Anyone suffering loss as a result of repudiation stands as an unsecured creditor for the amount of the loss (s. 20(2)). The examiner is not a necessary party to an application but he must be served notice of it and may appear and be heard (s. 20(4)). 'Hiving down' provisions such as s. 20 are a useful means of 'salvaging the viable parts of a business and disposing of them without the encumbrance of crippling liabilities': McCormack *op. cit.*, 206.

Publicity The examiner (or such other person as the court directs) must within 14 days after the delivery to the registrar of companies of every order made under s. 17 (on the hearing of matters arising from the examiner's report) or s. 24 (on confirmation (or otherwise) of the examiner;s proposals), have published in *Irish Oifigúil* notice of that delivery: s. 30(1). This obligation is backed by the criminal sanction of a £1,000 maximum fine: s. 30(2).

S. 31 permits the whole or part of any proceedings under the Act to be heard otherwise than in public if the court, in the interests of justice, considers that the interests of the company concerned or of its creditors as a whole so require. This provision was used in the *Goodman* case on 29 August 1990, where Hamilton, in *in camera* sittings in his home, appointed the examiner to Goodman international and 25 related companies: see McCormack, *op. cit.*, 206, fn. 50. As to constitutional considerations, cf. *In re R. Ltd* [1989] ILRM 747; [1989] IR 126, analysed in the 1989 Review, 55-8, 351-2.

COMPANIES ACT 1990

The Companies Act 1990 began its life as the Companies (No. 2) Bill 1987: see the 1987 Review, 51-3. Work at departmental level went back as far as 1982. The legislation introduces radical changes in company law on such matters as insider dealing, restrictions on directors, the duties of receivers, company accounts and audits, investigations of companies and the disclosure of interests in shares. Most of these reforms sprang from the growing unease at the relative indulgence towards malpractice apparent in the earlier state of the law. The legislation also implements a number of European Community directives on company law.

In our analysis of the Act, we will examine each of its Parts in sequence, concentrating on their more significant provisions.

As will become immediately clear, we have leant heavily on Gerard McCormack's text for our understanding of many aspects of the legislation. Our frequent debts of acknowledgement show how much is to be gained from his book. We have also derived great benefit from Keane J's second edition of his textbook on company law, published in 1991. This contains a succinct and insightful analysis of the Act, which clarifies even the most impenetrable of its provisions.

Part I: Preliminary

This part contains the normal preliminary provisions for legislation of this type. Of greatest practical significance in s. 2, which enables the Minister by order to prescribe differing commencement dates with reference to particular purposes or provisions.

Part II: Investigation

Part II introduces important changes in the process of inspection of companies. Under the 1963 Act, the Minister had the exclusive function of appointing inspectors, a power rarely invoked. See McCormack, *op. cit.*, 13. P. Ussher, *Company Law in Ireland* (1986), chapter 13.

The strategy of the 1990 Act is to give to the *court* the power of ordering an investigation of a company's affairs. The Minister's power in this context is reduced to that of an applicant to the court.

Appointment of inspectors

(i) On application by shareholders, creditors etc. S. 7 authorises (but does not oblige) the court in any of five cases to appoint one or more competent inspectors to investigate the affairs of a company in order to enquire into matters specified by the court and to report on them in such a manner as the court directs. These are:

> (a) where a company has a share capital, on the application of at least 100 members or a member or members holding at least one-tenth of the paid up share capital of the company;
>
> (b) where a company has not a share capital, on the application of at least one-fifth of the persons on the company's registered members;
>
> (c) on the application of the company;
>
> (d) on the application of a director; and
>
> (e) on the application of a creditor (sub. (1)).

The application must be supported by such evidence as the court may require, including such evidence as may be prescribed (subs. (2)).

The court may require an applicant to give security for the costs of the investigation, of between £500 and £100,000 (subs. (3)). The provision specifies no criteria by which the ordering of security and of its quantum are to be determined.

(ii) On application of the Minister S. 8(1) authorises the court, *on the application of the Minister,* to appoint inspectors to investigate and report on the affairs of a company, as under s. 7, in *three* cases. These occur where the court is satisfied that there are circumstances suggesting:

> (a) that the company's affairs are being or have been *conducted with intent to defraud its creditors* or the creditors of any other person or otherwise for a *fraudulent or unlawful purpose* or in an *unlawful manner* which is unfairly prejudicial to some part of its members or that any *actual or proposed act or omission* of the company is or *would be so prejudicial,* or that it was *formed for any fraudulent or unlawful purpose;*
>
> (b) that persons concerned with its formation or the management of its affairs have, in connection with this function, been *guilty of fraud, misfeasance or other misconduct towards it or its members;* or

(c) that its *members have not been given all the information relating to its affairs which they might reasonably expect.*

The court may order an investigation under s. 7 or 8 even where the company is in the course of being wound up: s. 8(2).

Investigation into related companies The inspectors appointed under ss. 7 and 8 have power, with the court's approval, to investigate and report on the affairs of companies *related* to the company whose affairs they were appointed to investigate where they think it necessary for the purposes of the investigation to do so: s. 9. (We examine the notion of related companies presently, in our discussion of s. 140(5), in Part IV of the Act.)

Production of documents and evidence on inspection S. 10 lays down stringent rules as to compliance with the requirements of the inspectors in the course of their investigation. It is the duty of all officers and agents of the company (or related company in a case to which s. 9 applies) to produce to the inspectors all books and documents of or relating to the company which are in their custody or power: subs. (1). They must attend before the inspectors when required to do so and otherwise give them all assistance in connection with the investigation which they are reasonably able to give: *id.*

If the inspectors consider that some other person may be in possession of any information concerning the company's affairs, a similar duty of assistance falls on him: subs. (2).

S. 10(3) contains special provisions applying to directors (present or past), shadow directors (present or past) or persons 'connected with' a director (a term defined in s. 26) of a company whose affairs are under investigation. These provisions deal with the situation where the investigator has reasonable grounds for believing that any of these people has, or had, a bank account, here or elsewhere, into or out of which has been paid:

(a) any money resulting from or used for a transaction, arrangement or agreement —

(i) particulars of which have not been disclosed in the notes of the accounts of any company for the financial year as required by s. 41;
(ii) in respect of which any amount outstanding was not included in the aggregate amounts outstanding in respect of certain transactions, arrangements or agreements, as required by s. 43, or
(iii) particulars of which were not included in any register of transactions, arrangements and agreements, as required by s. 44, or

(b) any money connected with any act or omission (or series of acts or omissions) which on the part of the director or other such person constituted misconduct (whether fraudulent or not) towards the company or its members.

In such circumstances, the inspector may require the director to produce all documents in his possession or under his control relating to the bank account. 'Bank account' is defined as including accounts with persons exempt by virtue of s. 7(4) of the Central Bank Act 1971 from the requirement of holding a licence under s. 9; these include accounts with the following: the ACC, the ICC, the Post Office Savings Bank, the Trustee Savings Banks, Building Societies, credit unions, industrial and provident societies, friendly societies, investment trust companies and unit trusts: 385 Dáil Debs, col. 1530 (14 December 1988). But, as Mr Willie O'Dea, TD, pointed out (*id.*), the definition contained 'a large loophole', in omitting pension funds and funds managed by life assurance companies. (The Pensions Act 1990, which we consider in the Labour Law Chapter below, pp. 357-63, contains important new controls in relation to pension funds.)

Inspectors may examine on oath, either orally or on written interrogatories, the officers and agents of the company or other persons whom they consider may be able to help them; they may administer the oath and reduce the replies to writing and require that they be signed: subs. (4). If a person fails to produce the relevant documents, to attend before the inspectors when required to do so or to answer any question put to him by the inspectors with respect to the company, the inspectors may certify this refusal under their hand to the court: subs. (5); the court may thereupon enquire into the case and, after hearing witnesses for or on behalf of the alleged offender and any statement offered in defence, the court may punish the offender 'in like manner as if he had been guilty of contempt of court'. *id.* The Law Reform Commission in its *Consultation Paper on Contempt of Court* (1991), p. 224 deprecates this strategy and hints at doubts about its constitutionality in the light of *In re Haughey* [1971] IR 217.

After a hearing of this kind, the court is empowered to make any order or direction it thinks fit. This can include a direction to the person concerned to attend or re-attend before the inspector or produce particular books or documents or answer particular questions put to him by the inspector, or a direction that he need not do such things: subs. (6).

It should be noted that 'officers' and 'agents' in s. 10 include *past* officers and agents; moreover 'agents' include the bankers and solicitors of a company and those employed as the company's auditors: subs. (7).

Inspectors' reports Inspectors may make *interim reports* to the court and must do so if the court so directs. They must make a *final report* to the court at the conclusion of their investigation: s. 11(1). The court must furnish the Minister a copy of every report it receives. It has a discretion, if it thinks fit, to forward a copy to the company's registered office and, on payment of the prescribed fee to a range of others:

> (i) any member of the company which is the subject of the report;
> (ii) anyone whose conduct is referred to in the report;
> (iii) the company's auditors;
> (iv) the applicants for the investigation;
> (v) any one else, including an employee whose financial interests appear to be affected by the matters dealt with in the report (whether a creditor or otherwise) and
> (vi) the Central Bank, where the report relates, even partly, to the holder of a licence (s. 11(3) (b)).

The court may also, if it thinks fit, cause the report to be printed and published (s. 11(3) (c)). In any case, the court may direct that a part of the report be omitted from copies furnished to those whom the court holds entitled to receive it or from the report as printed and published (s. 11(3) (4)).

Proceeding on inspectors' report Having considered the inspectors' report, the court has a broad discretion to make such order as it deems fit in relation to matters arising from it (s. 12(1)). This includes an order, on its own motion, for the winding-up of the company or an order 'for the purpose of remedying any disability suffered by any person whose interests were adversely affected by the conduct of the affairs of the company' (s. 12(1)(b)); in making the latter order the court must have regard to the interests of any other person who may be adversely affected by it (*id.*). Even with this limitation the breadth of the court's powers here are worthy of note.

Where it appears to the Minister, on the basis of the inspectors' report (or any other information or document obtained by him under Part II) that a petition for the company's winding up should be presented, he may do so, seeking the winding up if the court thinks this just and equitable (s. 12(2)).

Expenses of investigation Finding a fair solution to the problem of who should pay the expenses of an investigation under Part II is not easy. Suspicions may have been properly aroused but turn out to be unfounded. The applicant for a petition is not in quite the same position as a plaintiff, even though the court has power to make an order for 'remedying any disability suffered by a person whose interests were adversely affected by the conduct of the affairs of the company' (s. 12(1)(b)). There is, moreover, a clear public interest in policing companies through the investigation system.

The Act adopts a compromise approach. The expenses are to be defrayed in the first instance by the *Minister for Justice* (s 13(1)). The court may, however, direct that a *company dealt with in the report* or the *applicants for the investigation* are to be liable to repay the Minister for Justice, to such extent as it may direct, up to an aggregate amount in the case of the applicants of £100,000. (The company can avail itself no such limit.) Moreover, the court may seek a retrospective contribution to expenses from the following three categories of person:

(a) those *convicted on indictment* of an offence on a prosecution instituted as a result of an investigation;

(b) those *ordered to pay damages or restore any property* in proceedings brought as a result of an investigation;

(c) those *awarded damages or to whom property is restored* in proceedings brought as a result of an investigation (s. 13(2)).

The court may order a partial or a full contribution save in the case of those awarded damages or to whom property is restored: here the amount cannot exceed *one-tenth of the amount of the damages or the value of the property* (*id.*).

Ministerial investigation into share ownership   Ss. 14 and 15 confer on the Minister a new power to investigate into the ownership of a company, s. 14 involves the assistance of inspectors; s. 15 deals with situations where their assistance seems unnecessary and the Minister relies on the replies of these who are required by him to give the relevant information.

Under s. 14, the Minister may appoint inspectors to investigate and report on the membership of a company to determine the true persons who are or have been financially interested in its success or failure (real or apparent) or able to control or materially influence its policy (subs. (1)). The Minister may take this course if of opinion that there are circumstances suggesting that it is necessary —

(a) for the effective administration of the law relating to companies;

(b) for the effective discharge by the Minister of his functions under any enactment; or

(c) in the public interest (s. 14(2)).

In carrying out their investigation, the inspectors have all the powers that they possess in carrying out inspections into a company's affairs under ss. 7 and 9, save those in respect of directors' private bank accounts. Refusal to comply with their demands can thus be referred by them to the court, which may punish the offender 'as if he had been guilty of contempt of court' (s. 10(5); cf s. 14(5)(c)). McCormack, *op. cit.*, 32 considers that the constitutional difficulties relating to s 10(5) are accentuated in respect of s. 14(5)(c): 'The added dimension derives from the fact that the inspector has been appointed not by a court but by the Minister'.

S. 15 enables a Minister, on the same grounds as for s. 14, to investigate the ownership of any shares in or debentures of a company, where he considers it unnecessary to appoint an inspector for this purpose. He may require anyone whom he has reasonable cause to believe to possess to be able to obtain any information as to the present or past interests in the shares or debentures (and related matters) to give him the information (subs. (1)). This power is backed by a criminal sanction (subs. (3)).

Freezing of shares and debentures   S. 16 gives the Minister power, where, during an investigation on enquiry, it appears to him that there is difficulty in finding out the relevant facts about any shares (whether issued or to be issued), to direct that transactions involving the shares are, in effect, to be frozen until further notice: subs. (1). While this direction is in force,

(a) any transfer of the shares (or, in the case of unissued shares, any transfer of the right to be issued with them and any issue of them) will be void;
(b) no voting rights are exercisable in respect of the shares;
(c) no further shares are to be issued in right of those shares or in pursuance of an offer made to their holder, and
(d) except in a liquidation, no payment is to be made of any sums due from the company or the shares, whether in respect of capital or otherwise (subs. (12)).

These restrictions apply to debentures as they do to shares: subs. (17). The freezing process is backed by criminal sanctions: subs. (14).

A right of appeal to the court against a Ministerial direction under subs. (1) freezing transactions relating to shares is provided for: subs. (5). The court may lift the restriction only if it or the Minister is satisfied that the relevant facts about the shares have been disclosed to the company and no unfair advantage has accrued to any person as a result of the earlier failure to make that disclosure *or* if the shares are to be sold and the court or Minister approves the sale: subs. (6). The *denial* to the court of power to lift the Ministerial restriction where an unfair advantage to *any* person has accrued seems so arbitrary as to cast a shadow of unconstitutionality over the section. The person thus advantaged might be an enemy of the company whose investigation he maliciously instigated. Perhaps a teleological interpretation will salvage the provision's validity.

Ministerial power to require production of documents   S. 19 gives the Minister power to require a company to produce specified books or documents in certain circumstances (subs. (1)). (He may depute one of his officers to do so as well (*id.*)). Eight circumstances warrant the exercise of this power, based on the Minister's opinion that there are circumstances suggesting that

(a) it is necessary to examine the company's books and documents with a view to determine whether an inspector should be appointed;

(b) the company's affairs are being or have been conducted with intent to defraud creditors of any person or the members of the company;

(c) the affairs of the company are being or have been conducted for some other fraudulent purpose;

(d) the affairs of the company are being or have been conducted in a manner unfairly prejudicial to some part of its members;

(e) an actual or purported act or omission of, or on behalf of, the company is or would be unfairly prejudicial to some part of its members;

(f) an actual or proposed act or omission of, or on behalf of, the company is or is likely to be unlawful;

(g) the company was formed for a fraudulent purpose, or

(h) the company was formed for an unlawful purpose (subs. (2)).

Where the Minister (or authorised officer) has power to require the production of books or documents from a company, he has a like power to require their production from anyone who appears to be in possession of them (subs. (3)).

Failure to comply with a requirement is an offence (subs. (5)). Moreover, a statement made by a person in compliance with a requirement may be used in evidence against him (subs. (b)).

The Ministerial power is backed by the power to request a search warrant from a District Justice (s. 20). No information, book or document relating to a body obtained under s. 19 or 20 may be published or disclosed without the previous consent in writing of that body, save where this is required (i) with a view to instituting proceedings under the Companies Acts or for offences entailing misconduct in relation to the body's affairs, (ii) with a view to criminal proceedings relating to exchange control or regulations on insurance under the European Communities Act 1972, (iii) so as to comply with the statutory functions relating to reports by inspectors under Part III, (iv) with a view to instituting winding-up proceedings, or (v) for the purposes of s. 20, relating to search warrants (s. 21)(1)). Where one of these five cases exists, the matter may be published or disclosed only to a 'competent authority', a term which includes the Minister for Industry and Commerce, a person authorised by him, an inspector, the Minister for Finance, an officer authorised by him, a court of competent jurisdiction, the Central Bank and a supervisory authority in respect of regulations relating to insurance made under the 1972 Act (s. 21(3)). Moreover legal professional privilege applies (s. 23(1)). A further protection, in relation to banking, restricts the power of the Minister to require a banker to produce a document relating to the affairs of a customer save where it appears to the Minister that it is necessary to do so for the purpose of investigating the affairs of that bank or the customer is person on whom a requirement has been imposed under s. 19 (s. 23(2)).

Ministerial power to make supplementary regulations   S. 24 gives the Minister power to make supplementary regulations modifying any provision of Part 1, where it appears necessary to or expedient to do so in order to remove any difficulty in relation to its operation. This strategy is also used elsewhere in the Act (cf ss. 121, 201, 261) and has a well established statutory pedigree: cf McCormack, *op. cit.*, 36. It appears to present no danger of offending against the test for legislative delegation which the Supreme Court laid down in *Cityview Press Ltd v An Chomhairle Oiliúna* [1980] IR 381.

Part III: Transactions involving directors

Part III introduces wide ranging controls on transactions involving directors and 'shadow directors'. The latter concept embraces persons in accordance with whose directions or instructions the directors of a company are accustomed to act save in cases where this is 'by reason only that they do so on advice given by [these persons] in a professional capacity': s. 27(1). Thus professional advisers, such as lawyers and accountants, will not normally be 'shadow directors': see McCormack, *op. cit.*, 71, fn. 1. The general rule is that shadow directors are treated as directors of the company for the purposes of Part III and thus subject to the liability it prescribes in several sections (save in relation to licensed banks under s. 44(8)): see s. 27(1) and (2).

(a) Directors' contracts of employment   S. 28 of the Act seeks to mitigate the problems for companies resulting from the removal of a director. Whereas, under s. 182 of the 1963 Act, it is quite easy to remove a director, the effect of s. 182(7), which preserves the director's right to compensation, coupled with the practice of directors' of 'entrench[ing] themselves by contracts of service' (McCormack, *op. cit.*, 72), was to make it very expensive to fire them. S. 28 requires prior approval by resolution at a general meeting of the company employment contracts between a company and a

director for a period of more than five years, where the contract is one that cannot be terminated by the company by notice or can be so terminated only in specified circumstances.

Subs. (3) frustrates the device of entering into new agreements more than six months before the execution of a contract within the prescribed period; if this is done, the original period must be added to the new period and if their combined term exceeds five years, they are caught by the section. It is also futile to structure the contract as one of services rather than service since these are captured by the definition of 'employment': s. 28(7).

(b) Substantial property transactions S. 29 seeks to control substantial property transactions involving directors (and persons connected with directors) whereby a director (or connected person) acquires non-cash assets of the requisite value from the company or *vice versa*. Prior approval by a resolution of the company in general meeting must have been obtained: s. 29(1). If the director or connected person is a director of the company's holding company or a person connected with such a director, a resolution in general meeting of the holding company is also required: *id.*

The *value* of a transaction or arrangement in the case of a loan is the *principal* of the loan: s. 25(4)(a). The value of a transaction or arrangement other than a loan, quasi-loan, guarantee or security is determined by the test of reasonableness: s. 25(4)(e). The value of a transaction or arrangement which is not capable of being expressed as a specific sum of money (because the amount of any liability arising under it is unascertainable or for some other reason) is deemed to exceed £50,000, even if liability under it has been reduced: s. 25(5).

An asset is of the *requisite* value if at the time the arrangement is entered into its value is not less than £1,000 and either exceeds £50,000 or 10% of the amount of the company's relevant assets: s. 29(2). This amount is the value of the company's net assets, determined by reference to accounts prepared and laid in accordance with s. 148 of the 1963 Act in relation to the last preceding financial year in respect of which such accounts were so laid; where no accounts have been prepared and laid before that time, the amount of the company's relevant assets is that of its called-up share capital. Since most private companies are not obliged to prepare accounts, and have a nominal share capital of small amount (cf. McCormack, *op. cit.*, 78), the effect of this definition is that s. 29 will apply to the large majority of property transactions between private companies and their directors (and connected persons), subject to the £1,000 threshold. It should be noted that s. 29 is not limited to cases where the transaction involves sharp practice or sale at an under-value: Keane, *op. cit.*, para 29.19.

Where a breach of s. 29 occurs, the transaction is *voidable* at the instance of the company unless (a) restitution is no longer possible or the company has been indemnified for the loss or damage; (b) rights acquired *bona fide* for value and without actual notice of the contravention would be affected; or (c) the arrangement is, within a reasonable period, affirmed by the company in general meeting: s. 29(3).

S. 29(4) gives a non-exhaustive list of sanctions on directors and connected persons who enter into transactions in contravention of the section, as well as directors who authorised it: they are liable to account for any gain they made and to indemnify the company for any loss. Where an arrangement is entered into by a company and a person connected with a director of the company or a holding company, in contravention of the section, that director will not be subject to these sanctions if he shows that he took all reasonable steps to secure the company's compliance with the section: s. 29(5). Neither a person connected with a director nor a director who authorised a transaction will be subject to such sanctions if he shows that, at the time, he did not know the relevant circumstances constituting the contravention: *id.*

(c) Options dealing by directors   In conjunction with the prohibition on insider trading contained in Part V of the Act, s. 30 prohibits, under criminal sanction, the dealing by directors of a company in options to buy or sell certain shares in, or debentures of, the company or associated companies. The justification for this total prohibition is that 'options are inherently speculative instruments and directors and their close family relations should not be allowed to profit from what is *informed* speculation by the very nature of their office': McCormack, *op. cit.*, 75.

Let us look at the terms of s. 30 in more detail. Subs. (1) makes it an offence for a director of a company to buy a right to call for, or to make, delivery at a specified price (including a specified price range: s. 30(4)) and within a specified time of a specified number of relevant shares or a specified amount of relevant debentures or a right (as he may elect) to call for, or make, such delivery. 'Relevant shares' here are those in the company, or its subsidiary or holding company, for which dealing facilities are provided by a stock exchange (whether within the State or elsewhere): s. 30(2). No penalty attaches to a person who buys a right to subscribe for shares in, or debentures of, a body corporate that confer on the holder a right to subscribe for, or to convert the debentures into, shares of the body: s. 30(3).

S. 30(5) extends criminal liability to persons who are not directors but who buy one of the rights to which the section applies, on behalf of or at the instigation of a director. Those who buy *on behalf of* directors are clearly their agents; those who buy at the *instigation of* directors may be so, but it does not seem essential that there be an undertaking or even likelihood that the instigating director should personally benefit from the transaction.

(d) Loans to directors Before the 1990 Act, there were no restrictions on the making of loans by a company to its directors: see Keane, *op. cit.*, para 27.12 (1st ed., 1985). Although statutory prohibitions had existed in England since 1948, the Cox Committee in its 1958 Report recommended against their development here on the basis that it would be impractical.

That judgment no longer holds sway. S. 31(1) of the 1990 Act sets out the general rule prohibiting a company from engaging in the following three types of transaction with its director, a director of its holding company or a person connected with such a director:

(a) loans or quasi-loans;
(b) credit transactions where the company is creditor for the director or person so connected;
(c) guarantees or the provision of security in connection with a loan, quasi-loan or credit transaction made by another person for such a director or person so connected.

Subs. (2) prevents a company from defeating the prohibition contained in subs(1) by arranging for the *assignment to it or assumption by it* of rights, obligations or liabilities under a transaction which, if the company had entered into it, would have been a prohibited transaction under subs. (1). Subs. (3) kills the possibility of evasion by using a third party to enter into what would have been a prohibited transaction to a director or connected person and who is paid back by the company. As McCormack, *op. cit.*, 78, notes, '[t]his catches, in particular, back to back arrangements where a company agrees to make loans to the directors of another company in return for a loan to its own directors. It would also apply where, in return for the company's business, a director obtains a loan from a bank on favourable terms'.

Some important definitions should be noted. Under s. 26, a person is *connected with a director* if he or she is:

(a) the director's spouse, parent, brother, sister or child (including stepchild and adopted child (s. 3(1));
(b)a person acting in his or her capacity as the trustee of any trust, the principal beneficiaries of which are the director, his spouse or any of his children or any body corporate which he controls; or
(c) a partner of the director; or
(d) a body corporate controlled by the director.

A director *controls* a body corporate where he (either alone or together with any connected person) is interested in more than a half of its equity share capital or entitled to exercise or control the exercise of more than a half of the voting power at any general meeting of the body corporate: s. 26(3). A spouse or other relation, trustee or partner will not be treated as a connected person where he or she is also a director of the company: s. 26(1).

S. 25(2) defines a *quasi-loan* as a transaction where one person (the creditor agrees to pay (or pays otherwise than in pursuance of an agreement) a sum for another (the borrower) or agrees to reimburse (or reimburses otherwise than in pursuance of an agreement) expenditure incurred by another party for another (the borrower), either on terms that the borrower will reimburse the creditor or in circumstances giving rise to his liability to do so. S. 25(3) defines *a credit transaction* as one under which the creditor:

(a) supplies goods or sells land under a hire-purchase agreement or conditional sale agreement;
(b) leases or licenses the use of land or hires goods in return for periodical payments;
(c) otherwise disposes of land or supplies goods or services on the understanding that payment is to be deferred.

Exceptions to s. 31 prohibitions   To the general rule in s. 31 prohibiting loans, quasi-loans and credit transactions to directors and connected persons there are some important exceptions.

Arrangements which in total involve less than 10% of company's assets   The first exception, under s. 32, permits such arrangements where the value of the particular arrangement and the total amount outstanding under any other such arrangements entered into by the company amount when com- bined to less than 10% of the company's relevant assets. We have already met the notion of relevant assets when discussing the control on substantial property transactions under s. 29.

The situation can arise where, by reason of a fall in a company's assets, the amount outstanding on these arrangements comes to exceed the 10% limit. When the directors become aware, or ought reasonably to become aware, that there exists such a situation, it becomes the duty of the company, its directors and persons for whom the arrangements were made to amend the terms of the arrangements within two months, so as to comply with the 10% limit: s. 33. The section lays down no rules of priority or proportionality, for example, as to how this is to be done.

Inter-company loans and transactions with a holding company   The second and third exceptions to the prohibition under s. 31 are inter-company loans in the same group of companies (s. 34) and transactions with a holding company (s. 35).

Directors' expenses The fourth exception, under s. 36, permits a company to provide its directors with funds to meet vouched expenditure properly incurred or to be incurred by them for the purposes of the company or for the purpose of enabling them properly to perform their duties as officers of the company or doing anything to enable them to avoid incurring this expenditure: subs. (1). Any such liability must be discharged within six months (subs. (2)) under criminal sanction (subs. (3)) for which the maximum penalty, on summary conviction, is a fine of £1,000 and 12 months' imprisonment or, on conviction on indictment, a fine of £10,000 and three years' imprisonment (s. 240(1)).

Whether these payments may each be characterised as loans has been doubted: see McCormack, *op. cit.*, 79. This difficulty certainly arises in regard to payments for expenditure which has *already* been incurred; it is easy, however, to envisage cases where what are in fact loans could plausibly be described as an imprest for *future* expenditure.

Loans and other transactions in the ordinary course of business The fifth and final exception to the prohibition under s. 31 concerns loans, quasi-loans and credit transactions in the ordinary course of the company's business. These are permissible provided their value is not greater and their terms no more favourable, in respect of the persons for whom they are made, than those which the company ordinarily offers (or it is reasonable to expect the company to have offered) to or in respect of a person of the same financial standing but unconnected with the company: s. 37. Thus a bank or finance house may still lend to its directors, provided it does not give them special terms.

Civil remedies S. 38 prescribes civil remedies for breach of s. 31. These are substantially similar to those we have already described in relation to substantial property transactions involving directors and connected persons under s. 29: see subs. (3) to (5) of that section. Briefly, the offending transaction or arrangement is voidable at the instance of the company, save where restitution is no longer possible, the company has been indemnified or a third party has acquired *bona fide* rights for value without notice: s. 38(1). (There is no equivalent to s. 29(3)(c), allowing for subsequent affirmations by the company at a general meeting). The obligation of those who benefitted from or were involved in the authorisation of the transaction to account for and indemnity the loss is drafted in the same terms as s. 29(4) and (5): see s. 38(2) and (3).

Criminal penalties S. 40 deals with *criminal* penalties. An officer of a company who authorises or permits, or a person who procures, the company to enter into a transaction or arrangement knowing or having reasonable cause to believe that the company is thereby contravening s. 31 is guilty of an offence. Commentators have been struck that the remit of the criminal sanction is thus, unusually, wider than its civil counterpart, since s. 38 catches (*inter alia*) directors who *authorised* the transaction or arrangement whereas s. 40 penalizes officers of a company who *authorise or permit* it to enter into a prohibited transaction. See McCormack, *op. cit.*, 81. At all events, it seems that passive acquiescence by a director at a board meeting, rather than positive opposition to the proposal to make a loan prohibited by s. 31, should render him liable, in the Minister's intent, provided of course that he knew or had reasonable cause to believe that it was so prohibited. See McCormack, *op. cit.*, 81, fn. 35.

Personal liability for company debts   Arrangements that fall within s. 32, as we have seen, are those which do not push the combined amount outstanding beyond the 10% barrier of the company's relevant assets. While therefore these arrangements do not offend against s. 31, they may have unpalatable effects for those who engage in them. Under s. 39, if a company is being wound up and is unable to pay its debts, and the court considers that such an arrangement has contributed materially to the company's inability to pay its debts or has substantially impeded its orderly winding up, the court, on the application of the liquidator or any creditor or contributory of the company, may, if it thinks it proper to do so, declare that any person for whose benefit the arrangement was made is to be personally liable, without any limitation of liability for part or all of the company's liabilities: subs. (1).

In deciding whether to make this declaration, the court is to have particular regard to whether, and to what extent, any outstanding liabilities arising under such an arrangement were discharged before the commencement of the winding-up: subs. (2). (This offers an incentive to discharge liabilities before winding-up, since the personal liability which the court can impose under subs. (1) is not limited to the amount of the liability arising under the particular arrangement from which the person in question benefited). In deciding the extent of any personal liability, moreover, the court is to have particular regard to the extent to which the arrangement in question contributed materially to the company's inability to pay its debts or substantially impeded the orderly winding up of the company: subs. (3).

Disclosure of loans and other arrangements in accounts   The rigorous controls on loans, quasi-loans and other transactions which we have already examined are supplemented by stringent requirements of disclosure in companies' annual accounts. These requirements are more wide-ranging than the controls: companies are obliged to give a very full picture as regards transactions even where they are perfectly lawful.

S. 41(2) requires that, as a general principle, the accounts should contain the following particulars:

(a) any transaction or arrangement of a kind described in s. 31;

(b) any agreement by the company or its subsidiary to enter into such a transaction or arrangement;

(c)any other transaction or arrangement with the company in which a person who at any time during the relevant period was a director of the company or its holding company had, directly or indirectly, a material interest.

A transaction or arrangement between a company and a director of the company or its holding company or a person connected with him is treated as one in which the director is *interested*: s. 41(5)(a). An interest is not material if, in the opinion of the majority of the directors (other than the director in respect of whom the transaction or arrangement was done), it is not material: s. 41(5)(b). Whether judicial review is available where arguably there was no basis on which such an opinion could reasonably have been formed is in the view of Keane J (expressed extra-judicially) 'uncertain': *op. cit.*, para 32.19. As Keane J points out (*id.*):

There are recent decisions by the High Court to the effect that the judicial review procedure established by the Rules of the Superior Courts in 1986 is not confined to public law matters, but the Supreme Court, while expressly reserving the question [in *O'Neill v Iarnród Éireann*, [1991] ILRM 129 have expressed doubts *obiter* as to whether they were correctly decided.

See further the Administrative Law Chapter, above, 12-4.

Particulars which are required to be contained in accounts must be given to way of *notes*: s. 41(3). S. 42 spells out what particulars must be included. They include such matters as the names of the relevant parties, the amount of liability, in respect of principal and interest, at the beginning and end of the relevant period, the maximum amount of that liability during this period and the amount of unpaid interest. The accounts must also disclose loans and other transactions relating to *officers* of the company who are *not* directors (s. 43(2)), save where in respect of that officer the aggregate amount outstanding is no more than £2,500 (s. 43(3)).

A similar exception from the obligation of disclosure in the accounts applies to transactions relating to directors and connected persons (s. 45(1)). Transactions (other than loans, quasi-loans and credit transactions) in which a director has a material interest need not be disclosed if their value did not at any time exceed £1,000 or, if more, did not exceed £5,000 or 1% of the net assets of the company as at the end of the relevant period for the accounts, whichever is the less (s. 45(2)). (The Minister may, by order alter this limit or, indeed, any other financial limit in Part III: s. 48.)

We need here only note, without elaboration, the fact that licensed banks are given some privileges as regards disclosure requirements. They must disclose only the *aggregate* amounts outstanding at the end of the relevant period in respect of transactions and arrangements involving directors, and connected persons, as well as the *number of persons* for whom they were made: s. 43(5) and (6). They need make no reference to transactions entered into in the course of business where their value is not greater and on terms no more favourable for the persons for whom they are made than those which the bank ordinarily offers to person of the same financial standing but unconnected with the company: s. 43(6)(b).

Balancing these privileges, s. 44(1) obliges licensed banks to maintain a register containing a copy of all these transactions. (If they were not in writing, written memoranda must set out their terms.) The register must cover transactions extending back over the previous ten years. Transactions involving connected persons need not thus be recorded if they fall within the ordinary course of the bank's business and are not on preferential terms: s. 44(2).

For a period of 15 days before a licensed bank's annual general meeting, it must make available at its registered office, for inspection by its members, a statement containing particulars of those transactions which, if it were not a licensed bank, it would be obliged to disclose in its accounts: s. 44(3). In contrast with the ten year rule applicable to the register, here the members are entitled only to a statement covering transactions taking place within the *past financial year*. Moreover, the bank need not include particulars of transactions entered into in the ordinary course of its business on non-preferential terms: s. 44(4).

The bank's auditors are required to examine the statement published to members under s. 44(3) and to make a report to them stating whether in their opinion it contains the necessary particulars: s. 44(5) and (6). If, in their opinion, it does not, they must include in the report, so far as they are reasonably able to do so, a statement giving the required particulars: s44(6). Backing this control are criminal sanctions on the company and its directors: s. 44(8) and (9).

Disclosure by directors of interests in transactions   Returning to the general field from our brief consideration of the special provisions relating to banks, we must now consider the changes the legislation effects in relation to contracts between a company and its directors. These were controlled by s. 194 of the 1963 Act, which requires a director to disclose the nature of his interest in any proposed contract when its conclusion is first considered: see Keane, *op. cit.*, para 29.31. S. 47 of the 1990 Act extends this obligation of disclosure to proposed loans, quasi-loans, credit transactions and the provision of guarantees or securities for directors, shadow directors or connected persons: subs. (1) and (2). A general notice given by a director to the other directors to the effect that:

(a) he is a member of a specified company or firm and is to be regarded as interested in any contract which may, at the date of the notice, be made with that company or firm, or
(b) that he is to be regarded as interested in any contract which may be made with a specified person who is connected within him (within the meaning of s. 26 of the 1990 Act),

is deemed a sufficient declaration of interest for the purposes of s. 194: subs. (3).

Inspection of directors' service contracts   S. 50 contains disclosure provisions designed to enable shareholders to be informed about service contracts between the company and its directors. Every company is required to keep at an appropriate place copies of written contracts of service of each director with the company or its subsidiary as well as memoranda sitting out the terms of oral contracts of service. Variations in the terms of these contracts must similarly be recorded: s. 50(1). An 'appropriate place' is the company's registered office (or the place where its register of members is kept if this is elsewhere) or its principal place of business: s. 50(3). This obligation does not apply to contracts requiring the director to work wholly or mainly outside the State: s. 50(5).

Companies are bound, under criminal sanction (s. 50(7)), to keep these particulars open to the inspection of any member of the company without charge for at least two hours every day: s. 50(6). In cases of a refusal of an inspection, the court may by order compel its immediate inspection: s. 50(8).

The obligation under s. 50 does not require a company to keep particulars of a contract where its unexpired portion is less than three years or at a time when the contract can, when the next three years, be terminated by the company without payment of compensation: s. 50(9).

Register of directors and secretaries   S. 51 amends s. 195 of the 1963 Act so as to 'enable members of the company who are allowed by s. 195(5) to inspect the register during business hours, to examine the track record, as it were, of directors of the company': McCormack, *op. cit.*, 76. It requires that the register contain the date of birth of directors (to avoid confusion as between family members), as well as particulars of any other directorships of bodies corporate, whether incorporated in the State or elsewhere, held by directors currently or within the previous ten years. Within 14 days of a change among its directors or in its secretary or in any of the particulars contained in the register, a company must notify the registrar of companies.

Directors' duty to have regard to the employees' interests　S. 52 introduces a new principle, of uncertain scope. It provides that the matters to which the directors of a company are to have regard in the performance of their functions are to include the interests of the company's employees in general, as well as the interests of its members (subs. (1)). It goes on to provide that, '[a]ccordingly', the duty imposed by the section on the directors is to be owed by them to the company (and the company alone) and is to be enforceable in the same way as any other fuduciary duty owed to a company by its directors (subs. (2)).

The provision is of English provenance, deriving from a recommendation of the Bullock Committee of Inquiry on Industrial Democracy in 1977. It first appeared there as s. 46 of the Companies Act 1980, and now contained in s. 309 of the Companies Act 1985.

The precise import of the section has puzzled commentators. Thus Keane J (*op. cit.*, para 29.24) observes that,

> while the motives which prompted it are understandable, it suffers from the same probably inescapable defect as its English counterpart. There is no guidance as to how the board are to resolve the conflict which may arise between those interests and the interests of the shareholders which they must also protect. In practice, a management which regularly disregards the interests of its employees will find itself in difficulties anyway and the occasions on which it is in the shareholders' interests to antagonise the workforce must be rare.

Of course, the issue of conflicting claims for attention may arise at the *end* of a company's life, where the goodwill or hostility of the employees will no longer be capable of having any claim to attention for pragmatic considerations. In this instance clearly the questions of principle must be squarely freed.

Judicial authority under former law was ill-disposed to recognising the moral claims of employees. As Bowen LJ observed in *Hutton v West Cork*

Railway Co. (1883) 23 Ch D 654, at 673, 'there are to be no cakes and ale except such as are required for the benefit of the company'. See *Roper v Ward* [1981] ILRM 408, *Parke v Daily News* [1962] Ch 927, Keane, *op. cit.*, para 28.06, McCormack, *op cit,* 75. Later in this chapter below, 120-1 we examined O'Hanlon J's decision in *In re Clubman Shirts Ltd* [1991] ILRM 43, which evinces a sensitive concern for employee interests.

At all events, s. 51 describes the duty as one owed to *the company* by the directors. McCormack, *op. cit.*, 76, is pessimistic as to its impact:

> [O]ne might conclude that directors' duties to employees are effectively unenforceable.

Part IV: Disclosure of interests in shares

Part IV strengthens and extends the obligation of disclosure of interests in shares in three respects: Chapter 1 deals with share dealings by directors, secretaries and their families; chapter 2 deals with individual and group acquisitions; and chapter 3 deals with disclosure orders in respect of companies other than public limited companies.

Chapter 1: Share dealings by directors, secretaries and their families

(a) Obligation of notification   S. 190 of the 1963 Act required companies to maintain a register of directors' shareholdings: see Keane, *op. cit.* (1st ed., 1985), para 27.37. Chapter 1 of Part IV greatly extends the scope of this requirement. See Keane, *op. cit.* (2nd ed, 1991), paras 29.44-29.51, McCormack, *op. cit.*, 86-90.

S. 53 requires a director or secretary to notify the company in writing of his or her interest in its shares and of any dealings by him in the company or its subsidiary or holding company: subs. (1) and (2). (This obligation applies also to shadow directors: subs. (9).) An 'interest' here is widely defined, so as to include, *inter alia*, a beneficial interest in property held on trust, interests involving options and the entitlement to exercise or control the exercise of at least one-third of the voting power at general meeting: s. 54. (For exceptions, see s. 55.)

A director or secretary is also obliged to notify the company of any similar interest of his or her spouse or a minor child: s. 64.

(b) Sanctions for failure to notify   Failure to comply with these notification requirements within the prescribed time (of five days from the time the director or secretary becomes aware of the event giving rise to the obligation (s. 56)), as well as being an offence (where the failure is without reasonable

excuse (s. 58(7)), has dire civil consequences. The party in breach of this obligation can enforce 'no right or interest of any kind whatsoever' in respect of the shares: s. 58(3). This bleak position may be ameliorated on application to the court for relief, under s. 58(4), if the court is satisfied that the default was accidental, or due to inadvertence, or 'some other sufficient cause', or that on other grounds it is just and equitable to grant relief. The court may *not* grant relief, however, if it appears that the default arose as a result of any deliberate act or omission on the part of the applicant: s. 58(5).

One may question whether this limitation on the power of the court to grant relief is defined with sufficient sensitivity: it is quite easy to envisage cases where the default arose from deliberate conduct on the part of the applicant which was entirely lacking in moral default and, indeed, which might have sprung from an entirely laudable motivation, as where he acted in good faith on the basis of another's fraud. (In the constitutional context, we later criticise a similar process of identifying the deliberate quality of conduct as generating negative legal consequences, regardless of the *bona fides* and reasonableness of the person engaging in that conduct: see below).

(c) Maintenance of register   The company is obliged to keep a register of all these interests (s. 59(1)) and to record all pieces of information received from a director or secretary (s. 59(2)). The register is to be kept open for at least two hours a day during business hours and open to the inspection of any person (non-members being subject to a charge of no more than 30p) (s. 59(5)). Moreover, the register is to be open and accessible to anyone attending the company's annual general meeting at least 15 minutes before it is scheduled to begin, and during its continuance (s59(9)). These requirements are backed by criminal sanction (s59(10)), and refusal to permit inspection can be met by a court order to do so (s. 59(11)).

Chapter 2: Individual and group acquisitions   Chapter 2 of Part IV introduces detailed provisions requiring disclosure of individual or group interests amounting to at least 5% in voting share capital of public limited companies.

(a) Obligation of disclosure   S. 67(1) imposes an obligation of disclosure on a person who:

> (a) to his knowledge acquires an interest in shares comprised in a public limited company's relevant share capital, or ceases to be interested in these shares, or
> (b) becomes aware that he has acquired, or lost, an interest in shares in which he was previously interested.

The concept of 'interest' here is very wide (s. 77), similar to that in respect of directors and secretaries (s. 54) which we have already mentioned. 'Relevant share capital' here means the company's issued share capital of a class carrying rights to vote in all circumstances at general meetings of the company: s. 67(2). A temporary suspension of voting rights does not take the shares out of this category: *id.*

An obligation of disclosure also arises where a person acquires a notifiable interest in circumstances other than by acquisition or disposal of shares such as where the company's share capital is reduced so that the party's interest breaches the 5% barrier. While 5% is the notifiable percentage, s. 70 gives the Minister power to prescribe a different percentage, either universally or in relation to companies of different classes or descriptions. In Britain the figure was reduced from 5% to 3% in 1989.

A person's obligation to make a notification must be performed within 5 days of the time it arises; the notification must be in writing: s. 71(1). As to details which are required in the notification, see s. 71(2)-(6), McCormack, *op. cit.*, 93-94.

A person is taken to be interested in any shares in which his or her spouse or minor child is interested: s. 72. (This approach echoes that applicable to directors and secretaries in Chapter 1). Moreover, a person is taken to be interested in shares if a company is interested in them and either that company or its directors is or are accustomed to act in accordance with his directions or he is entitled to exercise (or control the exercise) of one third or more of the voting power at general meetings of that company: s. 72(2). Where a person is entitled to exercise (or control the exercise) of one third or more the voting power at general meetings of a company which in turn has an entitlement of these proportions in respect of another company, then that person is deemed to have an interest in shares held by the second company: s. 72(3).

(b) Concert parties   Chapter 2 also deals with 'concert parties', imposing on them similar obligations of disclosure. These are groups of people acting in concert with the design of sidestepping the notification obligation. Each of their individual interests would be less than the disclosure threshold but together they might represent a formidable interest. The definition in s. 73(1) of such groups follows the lead of s. 204 of Britain's Companies Act 1985. It embraces an agreement between two or more persons which includes provision for the acquisition by any one or more of them of interests in shares comprised in relevant share capital or a particular public limited company ('the target company') *if* (i) this agreement also includes provisions imposing obligations or restrictions on any one or more of them with respect to their use, retention or disposal of interests in the shares thus acquired, *and* (ii) an

interest in the company's shares has in fact been acquired. 'Agreement' is widely defined so as to include undertakings, expectations or understandings operative under any arrangement and any provision, express or implied, absolute or otherwise: s. 73(4). However, s. 73 does not apply to an agreement which is not legally binding unless it involves mutuality in the undertakings, expectations or undertakings of the parties to it: subs. (5).

Once an interest has been thus acquired, the agreement remains a concert party agreement, in spite of changes in its parties or variation of its terms, so long as the agreement continues to include provisions imposing obligations and restrictions in respect of the parties' use, retention or disposal of interests in the target company's shares: s. 72(3).

S. 74 treats all the parties to a concert party agreement as being interested in all the shares of the target company in which any other party is interested apart from the agreement whether or not the interest of the other party was acquired, in part of whole, in pursuance of the agreement. The notification requirement obliges a party to a concert party agreement to disclose its existence, and give the details he has as to the names, addresses and respective shares of its parties. This is backed by an obligation on parties to such agreements to keep each other informed on relevant particulars: s. 75.

(c) Sanction for failure to disclose   Failure to comply with the notification requirement under Chapter 2 is not only visited with a criminal sanction (s. 79(7) and (8)) but also results in rendering unenforceable the person's rights or interests in respect of any shares in the company concerned (s. 79(3)), subject to the court's power to grant relief where the default was accidental or due to inadvertence or some other sufficient case (s. 79(4)). This power is not available where the default arose from a deliberate act or omission on the part of the person in default (s. 79(5)). (We criticise this approach in respect of an equivalent provision (s. 58(5)) in Chapter 1).

(d) Obligation to keep register   Every public limited company is obliged to keep a register to record information supplied to it under ss. 67-71. See McCormack, *op. cit.*, 100.

(e) Company investigations   A public limited company may require a person whom it knows or has reasonable cause to believe to be or, within the previous three years, to have been interested in shares comprised in the company's relevant share capital to confirm this fact and to give particulars of his own past or present interest in such shares, particulars of such other interests as may be required by the notice, and (in relation to past interests) particulars of the identity of his successor: s. 81. See McCormack, 101-3. The definition of 'interest' in this context is wider than that for notification purposes: subs. (7).

S. 83 enables members of the company holding at least 10% of the paid up capital carrying a right of voting at general meetings to *require* the company to exercise its powers of investigation under s. 81. The company is under a duty to prepare a report of the information received in pursuance of that investigation and to make it available at its registered office within a reasonable period (s. 84(1)) not exceeding 15 days after the conclusion of the investigation (s. 84(3)). If the investigation takes longer than three months, the company must produce interim reports (s. 84(2)). Both the company's register of interests in shares and its reports under s. 84 are available for inspection by members and non-members: s. 88.

Where a person fails to comply with a s. 81 notice, he is guilty of an offence (s. 85(3)) unless the requirement to give the information was frivolous or vexatious: s. 85(4)). Under s. 85(1), failure to comply also entitles the company to apply to the court for an order directing that the shares in question be subject to restrictions under s. 16 (which we have already discussed in relation to Part II of the Act). For detailed consideration of English caselaw in relation to s. 216 of Britain's Companies Act 1985, equivalent to our s. 85(1), see McCormack, *op. cit.*, 104-6.

(f) The 1988 Directive   Chapter 2 of Part IV also gives effect to the Council Directive 88/627/EEC of 12 December 1988 (OJ No. L348, 17 December 1988, p. 62) on the information to be published when a major holding in a listed company is acquired or disposed of: see s89. The Directive is on the same general lines as Part IV but somewhat less strict: see McCormack, *op. cit.*, 106. It requires disclosure of an interest when that interest passes certain thresholds: 10%, 25%, 50% and 75%: s. 91(3). More narrowly than the provisions which we have already discussed, the Directive applies only to interests in shares in public limited companies that are *officially listed on the Stock Exchange*: s. 91(1). In addition to notifying the company of the acquisition or disposal of an interest, the party must also report this to the relevant authority of the Stock Exchange (that is, its committee of management, or manager: s. 90(2)), which, within three days of receipt of this notification, must publish this information. The Stock Exchange may decide not to publish the information if satisfied that disclosure would be contrary to the public interest or seriously detrimental to the company concerned, provided, in the latter case, that a decision not to publish would be unlikely to mislead the public with regard to the facts and circumstances knowledge of which is necessary for the assessment of the interest in question: s. 91(6).

The relevant authority of the Stock Exchange is obliged to report any suspected breach of s. 91 to the Director of Public Prosecutions: s. 92. See further McCormack, *op. cit.*, 107-108.

Chapter 3: Disclosure orders   Chapter 3 makes provision for disclosure
of share ownership in companies other than public limited companies. This
is not a general entitlement, but rather one to be granted in only fairly limited
circumstances.

(a) Application for order   S. 98 enables any person with a financial interest
in a company to apply to the court for a disclosure order in respect of all or
any of the shares of or debentures in that company (subs. (1)); the application
must be supported by such evidence as the court may require (subs. (2)). A
disclosure order is one obliging any person whom the court believes to have
or be able to obtain information as to persons interested in the shares and
debentures of a company, to give that information to the court; it embraces,
moreover, the power to order a person to disclose whether he is or has been
interested in such shares or debentures and to give any further information
the court may require (subs. (1)). A financial interest justifying an application
includes any interest as member, contributory, creditor, employee,
co-adventurer, examiner, lessor, lessee, licensor, licensee, liquidator or
receiver, in relation to the company in question or a related company (subs.
(6)).
    The court may make a disclosure order only if

    (a) it deems it just and equitable to do so and
    (b) it is of opinion that the financial interest of the applicant is or will be
    prejudiced by non-disclosure (subs. (5)).

(b) Scope of order   S. 100 spells out in detail the scope of the disclosure
order which the court may make. It may require the person to whom it is
addressed to give particulars of his own past or present interest in shares or
debentures and, where his interest is a past interest, to give so far as lies within
his knowledge particulars of the identity of his successor: subs (1). Moreover,
family and corporate interests and interests held by others in a concert
agreement are similarly subject to the obligation of disclosure: subs. (3). The
court has wide-ranging powers as to rescission or variation of a disclosure
order (s. 101(1)) or exemption from its requirements (s. 101(3)).

(c) Sanction for non-compliance   Where a person fails to comply with a
disclosure order or makes a false statement knowingly or recklessly, he loses
the right to enforce any interest in respect of the shares or debentures he holds,
subject to the power of the court to grant relief where satisfied that the default
was accidental or due to inadvertence or some other sufficient cause: ss.
104(1) and (2). The court may not grant this relief if it appears that the default
has arisen as a result of any deliberate act or omission on the part of the

applicant: s. 104(3). (We have already criticised a similarly drafted provision in s. 58(5) above).

Part V: Insider dealing

At common law, the sanctions against insider dealing were poor enough. The decision in *Percival v Wright* [1902] 2 Ch 421 appeared to give directors a fairly free hand; the duty to account to the company for the profit made, which looked a promising remedy (cf. MacCann, 'Liability for Insider Trading', Part I, (1991) 9 *ILT* (ns) 130, at 130-1), did not turn out to be so in practice. As McCormack, *op. cit.*, 118 explains:

> The problem with the ... principle [of the duty to account] as an effective sanction against insider dealing lies in the fact that only rarely will a company be prompted into action against profiteering insiders. Such actions are as rare as the midnight sun, save perhaps for a situation ... where control of the company has changed hands. Moreover, it appears that abuses originating from misuse of corporate information may be ratifiable or indeed sanctioned in advance by the company.

Part V imposes wide-ranging civil and criminal sanctions on insider dealing, and backs them by the establishment of a formidable investigative machinery involving the Stock Exchange. Whether these provisions will yield a rich crop of 'insiders' has been debated. Some have argued that the pool of information in this country is so small that insider dealing is an inevitable part of business life here. Others, including the Minister, have replied that the creation of a sound legal system of controls, with sharp teeth, is likely to improve, if not transform, the position.

(a) Definition of 'securities' S. 107 defines 'securities' in such a way as to extend only to those for which dealing facilities are (or are to be) provided by a recognised stock exchange. Thus, the controls in Part V do not apply to private companies or unquoted public companies. In such circumstances, as MacCann, *op. cit.*, at 131, points out, 'the only applicable restriction would appear to be [the] equitable duty imposed on fiduciaries of the company such as directors, not to misuse confidential information coming into their possession by reason of the fiduciary position'. In the Bill as initiated, the definition of 'securities' embraced shares or debentures of public companies, whether listed on the Stock Exchange or not. In proposing an amendment narrowing the scope of the term, the Minister, Mr Brennan, argued that it would not be realistic to have the Stock Exchange investigating suspected insider dealing cases involving companies outside its direct sphere of

operation and control. There was 'no particular evidence' suggesting that insider dealing was a significant problem in the case of unquoted companies though he added that this was a matter of knowledge and information which he did not have: 119 Seanad Debates, col. 730 (4 May 1988). Of course the establishment of a significant monitoring function for the Stock Exchange with regard to listed companies did not logically require the extension of that function to unlisted public companies as a precondition of bringing unlisted public companies within the *rules* of Part V. How these companies might appropriately be monitored was surely a separate question.

(b) Unlawful dealings by insiders   S. 108 is a core provision. It provides that it is not lawful for a person who is or, within the preceding 6 months, has been connected with a company to deal in any securities of that company if, by reason of his so being or having been connected with the company, he is in possession of information that is not generally available, but, if it were, would be likely materially to affect the price of those securities: subs. (1).

Secondly, it is not lawful for such a person to deal in securities of *another* company if in possession of such price-sensitive information relating to any transaction (actual or contemplated) involving both companies or involving one of them and securities of the other, or the fact that any such transaction is no longer contemplated: sub. (2). So, if an employee of company A is aware of the fact that his company's published intention to take over company B will not go ahead, and he then deals in company B's shares, exploiting this secret knowledge, he will be acting unlawfully.

A third basis of liability is where a person ('a tippee') deals in securities having received such price-sensitive information directly or indirectly from another, knowing or having reason to be aware of facts or circumstances by which that other person is precluded from dealing in the securities: subs. (3). The use of 'received' in subs. (3) instead of 'obtained' obviated a debate about whether active solicitation was integral to the unlawfulness, a matter which caused difficulty in England in *R. v Fisher,* (1988) 138 NLJ 294 (Crown Court), rev'd [1989] 1 All ER 321 (CA) and by HL, *sub nom AG's reference (No. 1 of 1988)* [1989] AC 71. See McCormack, *op. cit.,* 124.

A fourth basis of liability under s. 108 occurs where a person, precluded from dealing on any of the first three grounds, causes or procures anyone else to deal in the securities: subs. (4). A fifth, and related, basis occurs where a person is precluded from dealing under any of the first three grounds by reason of his being in possession of any information, and he communicates that information to another, knowing, or having reason to know, that the other will make use of it to deal or cause or procure another to deal in the securities: subs. (5).

A sixth basis of liability rests on companies as opposed to individuals. Subs. (6) makes it unlawful for a company to deal in securities at a time when any of its officers is precluded on any of the first three grounds from dealing in those securities. (An 'officer' here includes an employee: s. 107). This potentially vast liability is cut down by the 'Chinese Wall' contained in subs. (7) whereby a company is not precluded from entering into a transaction by reason only of information in the possession of its officers if:

(a) the decision to do so was taken on its behalf by a person other than the officer,
(b) it had in operation at the time written arrangements to ensure that the information was not communicated to that person and that no advice relating to the transaction was given to him by a person in possession of the information, and
(c) the information was not so communicated and such advice was not so given.

For detailed consideration of the Chinese Wall strategy see McCormack, *op. cit.*, 125-7. Mr McCormack (*id.*, 127) finds it difficult to see a Chinese Wall operating effectively in the Irish context:

Employees of a firm are likely to be transferred from one department to another during the course of their career and to see former colleagues socially. When they do meet, it is only natural that they should talk shop.

Among the other cases where a company or person is not precluded from dealing in securities under s. 108 is that covered by subs. (10). This permits a person to deal in securities if, while not otherwise taking advantage of his possession of information that is not generally available which would be likely to materially affect the price of the securities if it were so available,

(a) he gives at least 21 days' notice to a relevant stock exchange of his intention to deal in the securities of the company concerned,
(b) the dealing taken place within a period beginning 7 days after the publication of the company's interim or final results and ending 14 days after this publication, and
(c) the notice is published by the exchange immediately on its receipt.

This provision enables a director within price-sensitive information to trade for a limited period each year in shares if he does not take advantage of this information. Lyndon MacCann (*op. cit.*, at 132) expresses concern as to the difficulty of applying this distinction in practice. Of course, the post-publication period is one in which the potential for insider trading may generally be expected to be at its nadir but this will not be so in every case.

(c) Definitions of 'dealing' and 'persons connected with a company'
Finally, it is worth noting the definitions of *dealing* and *persons connected with a company*. Dealing means first (whether as principal or agent), acquiring, disposing of, subscribing for or underwriting the securities. It also includes making or offering to make, or inducing or attempting to induce a person to make or to offer to make, an agreement which either (a) is for or relating to acquiring (or otherwise acting as already mentioned in relation to) these securities or (b) is one whose purpose or purported purpose is to secure a profit or gain to a person who acquires (or otherwise acts as already mentioned in relation to) these securities or to any of the parties to the agreement in relation to the securities: s. 107.

A person is connected with a company if:

(a) he is the officer of that company or of a related company,
(b) he is a shareholder of it or a related company,
(c) he occupies a position (including a public office) that may reasonably be expected to give him access to price-sensitive information of the kind specified in s. 108(1) and (2), because of

(i) any professional, business or other relationship existing between himself (or his employer or a company of which he is an officer) and that company or a related company, or
(ii) his being an officer or a substantial shareholder in that company or in a related company: s. 108(II).

A substantial shareholder is one holding shares in a company in excess of the notifiable percentage for the time being in force under s. 70: s. 108(12). (This, as we have seen, is 5%, or such other percentage as the Minister may at any time specify.)

(d) Exempt Transactions S. 110 exempts certain transactions from the general prohibition on insider dealing. These include:

(i) acquiring securities under a will or an intestacy;
(ii) acquiring securities pursuant to an employee profit sharing scheme;
(iii) the obtaining in good faith by a director of a share qualification;
(iv) the entering of a transaction in good faith by a person in accordance with his obligations under an underwriting agreement;
(v) the entering of a transaction in good faith by a personal repre-

sentative, trustee, liquidator, receiver or examiner in the performance
of the functions of his office;
(vi) the entering of a transaction in good faith by way of, or arising out
of, a mortgage of or charge on securities or a mortgage, charge, pledge
or lien on documents of title to securities;
(vii) the entering of transactions by Ministers of the Government or the
Central Bank (or persons on their behalf) in pursuit of monetary,
exchange rate, national debt management or foreign exchange reserve
policies.

For comparison with the English approach, see McCormack, *op. cit.*, 127.

(e) Civil Sanction   The question whether insider dealing warrants a *civil*
sanction is controversial. Against imposing one, it has been argued that the
person with whom the guilty party deals is happy to buy or sell at the stated
price. He has been improperly 'induced' to do so only by a most procrustean
extension of the concept of inducement. If the action were one of fraudulent
misrepresentation, the insider dealer would be free of liability. Why, therefore, should a person who happens to have participated in a transaction which
had an outcome for him in harmony with his expectation be entitled to
compensation merely because it benefited the insider dealer in a way which
the person did not appreciate at the time?

The argument in favour of imposing civil liability is essentially based on
general deterrence. Moreover, the principle of unjust enrichment extends to
cases where the party from whom the unjust enrichment was made did not
rely on the wrongdoer and suffered no loss. The making of an illegitimate
gain by dishonest treatment of another person may be considered to justify
the requirement to compensate that other for damaging the foundation of trust
on which the transaction proceeded.

It has further been argued that 'the person who sells his shares [to an insider
dealer] is getting less than he would if he knew the facts of which the insider
is aware and, to that extent, can properly be regarded as being at a loss':
Keane, *op. cit.*, para 36.08. As against this, if *this* seller has suffered a loss,
why should not other sellers who sold to other purchasers at the same price
also not be regarded as selling at a loss? To say that they did sell at a loss but
that the insider did not *cause* it might be regarded as somewhat artificial. The
advantage that the insider dealer derives is (normally) obtained at the expense
of all who participate in the market, not just the person with whom he directly
does business.

At all events, s. 109 of the 1990 Act (in contrast to its British counterpart)
imposes civil liability on an insider dealer to compensate any other party to
the transaction who was not in possession of the relevant information for any

loss he sustained by reason of any difference between the price at which the securities were dealt in in that transaction and the price at which they would have been likely to have been dealt with at that time if that information had been generally available: subs. (1)(a). If the defendant has already been found liable to compensate the plaintiff by reason of the same act or transaction, the amount he had to pay will be deducted: subs. (2).

As well as having to compensate the other party, the insider dealer must account to the company that issued or made available the securities for any profit accruing to him: subs. (1)(b). This is in line with the pre-existing common law approach: see Keane, *op. cit.*, para 29.30, *Regal (Hastings) Ltd v Gulliver* [1967] 2 AC 134n, [1942] 1 All ER 378 (HL).

A two-year limitation period applies to actions for compensation or account, running from the date of the transaction in which the loss or profit occurred: s. 109(4).

(f) Criminal Sanctions   Part V imposes wide-ranging criminal sanctions for insider dealing: see MacCann, 'Liability for Insider Dealing', Part II, (1991) 9 *ILT* (ns) 151, at 151-2. S. 111 provides that a person who deals in securities in a manner declared unlawful by s108 is to be guilty of an offence. Moreover, s. 113 makes it an offence for a person to deal on behalf of another person if he has reasonable cause to believe or ought to conclude that the deal would be contrary to s. 108. The maximum penalty for these offences, on summary conviction, is imprisonment for 12 months and a fine of £1,000 or, on conviction on indictment, imprisonment for 10 years and a fine of £200,000: s. 114.

A person convicted of unlawful dealing may not deal for a period of 12 months thereafter: s. 112(1). Breach of this prohibition is a criminal offence (S. 112(3)), with the same maximum penalty as for dealing (s. 114).

McCormack, *op. cit.*, 129, raises the important question of whether the offence prescribed by s. 111 should be subject to some qualification of *mens rea* or *scienter*. He raises the spectre of a person being convicted where he was unaware of his connection to a company, on account of a complicated group structure, or unaware that the information he possessed was not generally available. The general presumption of *mens rea* in statutory offences suggests that it should be implied. McCormack comments that '[a]gainst such implication might be argued the deliberate contrast with the UK position' (where *mens rea* is integral to the offence). Our borrowings from British legislation have been so widespread that a decision *not* to copy a specific provision may indeed give pause for thought. It is a depressing commentary on the jadedness of our legislators and the caution of their advisers that the failure to copy British legislation can have such an effect.

(g) Enforcement   Part V gives the Stock Exchange the roles of informer and policeman in relation to suspected insider dealing. The Stock Exchange is required to report to the Director of Public Prosecutions and co-operate with him thereafter, if it appears to its 'relevant authority' that anyone has committed an offence relating to insider dealing: s. 115 (1). A relevant authority is the management body or the manager: s. 107. Moreover, where it appears to a member of the Stock Exchange that anyone has committed an offence of this type, he must report the matter forthwith to the relevant authority: s. 115(2).

Supplementing these provisions, s. 115(5) enables the Minister to *direct* the relevant authority to use its powers under Part V where it appears to the Minister, arising from a complaint to a relevant authority of the Stock Exchange concerning an alleged offence under Part V, that there are circumstances suggesting that it ought to use its powers but has not done so.

The Stock Exchange's role as policeman is conferred by s. 117, which gives wide ranging investigative powers to the 'authorised persons' to enable them obtain any information necessary for the exercise of the Stock Exchange's functions under s. 115. An authorised person is the manager of the Stock Exchange or a person nominated by a relevant authority of the Stock Exchange, who has been approved by the Minister: s. 117(1). The powers of investigation include those of requiring persons whom the authorised person has reasonable cause to believe to have dealt in securities (or to have any information about dealings) to give particulars regarding these transactions and to give him facilities for inspecting and taking copies of any documents relating to the matter as he reasonably requires: s. 117(3). In contrast to the position in Britain, these powers do not include that of requiring persons to attend and to examine them on oath, though conferring this function would seem to be within the Minister's remit in the exercise of his wide-ranging powers to make supplementary regulations in relation to the powers of authorised persons under s. 121 (2)(a). See McCormack, *op. cit.*, 132-3. (Whether this would contravene Articles 15, 34 or 38 of the Constitution may be debated.)

An important judicial control on the powers of authorised persons should be noted. Under s. 117(5)-(9), the court, on the application of either an authorised person or a person on whom he has made a requirement, may at its discretion declare that the exigencies of the common good *do* or, as the case may be, *do not* warrant the exercise by the authorised person of the powers conferred on him by s. 117. If they do so require, then the person on whom the requirement is made must comply with it under sanction of contempt of court. If they do not, then the requirement must be withdrawn. McCormack, *op. cit.*, 133-6 raises interesting questions as to the extent to which the exigencies of the common good may require disclosure of off-shore and nominee holdings or of information imparted in confidence or may interfere with the privilege against self-incrimination.

(h) International Co-Operation   Part V contains a number of provisions derived from the EC Insider Trading Directive (OJL 334, 13 November 1989) designed to encourage co-operation between Stock Exchanges in Member States of the European Communities in detecting and penalising insider trading. See McCormack, *op. cit.*, 136-7. Where a relevant authority of the Stock Exchange receives a request from a similar authority in another Member State in relation to the exercise by the foreign authority of its functions under any enactment of the European Communities relating to unlawful dealing, whether here or elsewhere, it is obliged, so far as it is reasonably practicably able to do so, to obtain and provide the requested information: s. 116(1) and (2). It must first, however, advise the Minister, who may direct it not to provide all or part of the requested information on being satisfied that:

>   (a) communication of the information might adversely affect the sovereignty, security or public policy of the State;
>   (b) civil or criminal proceedings in the State have already commenced in the State against a person in respect of any acts in relation to which the request for information has been received; or
>   (c) any person has been convicted in the State of a criminal offence in respect of any such acts (s. 116(3) and (4)).

Also of note is s.118, which, as we have seen, prohibits the disclosure by the Stock Exchange authorities of information obtained by virtue of the exercise of its functions under Part V save in accordance with law. This prohibition does not prevent a relevant authority of the Exchange from disclosing any information to the Minister or to a similar authority in another Member State.

Part VI: Winding up and related matters

Part VI contains important reforms, building on earlier provisions which extended the range of assets accessible for distribution on insolvency. See McCormack, *op. cit.*, chapter 12.

Civil liability for fraudulent or reckless trading   S. 138 of the 1990 Act supplements s. 297 of the 1963 Act (which imposed civil liability on those party to the carrying on of the business of a company in a fraudulent manner). If, in the course of winding up in cases where the company is deemed unable to pay its debts, it appears that an officer of the company was knowingly a party to the carrying on of any business of the company in a reckless manner or any person who was knowingly a party to the carrying on of any business of the company with intent to defraud creditors of the company, or creditors of any other person or for any fraudulent purpose, the court, on the application of the receiver, examiner, liquidator or any creditor or contributory of the company, may, if it thinks it proper to do so, declare that that person is to be personally responsible, without any limitation of liability, for all or any part of the debt or other liabilities of the company as the court may direct: s. 297A(1) and (3) of the 1963 Act, inserted by s. 138 of the 1990 Act.

An 'officer' here includes an auditor, liquidator, receiver or shadow director: s. 297A(10).

The section goes on to specify that an officer of a company is deemed to have been knowingly a party to the carrying on of any business of the company in a reckless manner if either:

(a) he was party to the carrying on of that business and, having regard to the general knowledge, skill and experience that may reasonably be expected of a person in his position, he ought to have known that his actions or those of the company would cause loss to the creditors of the company, or

(b) he was a party to the contracting of a debt by the company and did not honestly believe on reasonable grounds that the company would be able to pay the debt when it fell due for payment as well as all its other debts (taking into account the contingent and prospective liabilities) (S. 297A(2)).

Where it appears to it that the officer has acted honestly and responsibly the court may relieve from personal liability (wholly or in part) on such terms as it may think fit: S. 297A(6).

Court's power to summon persons for examination S. 126 reenacts, with embellishments, s. 245 of the 1963 Act, dealing with the power of the court to summon before it and examine on oath any officer of the company or person suspected of having in his possession any property of the company or supposed to be indebted to it or any other persons whom the court deems capable of giving information relating to the company's affairs. Now, before the examination takes place, the court may require the person to place before it a statement of any transactions between him and the company of a type or class which the court may specify: subs. (4) of s. 245, as substituted by s. 126 of the 1990 Act. These powers are backed by stringent controls, by way of contempt (subs. (7)) and arrest on *quia timet* grounds (subs. (8)).

S. 127 backs up s. 126 by inserting a new section — s. 245A — in the 1963 Act. Under s. 245A, if, in the course of an examination under s. 245, it appears to the court that a person being examined either is indebted to the company or has in his possession or control property or books or papers of the company, the court may order him to pay to the liquidator part or all of the debt or to convey or transfer to the liquidator part or all of the money, property, books and papers in his possession or control. It is not necessary that the liquidator have applied for this order. See McCormack, *op. cit.*, 218.

Fraudulent preference   S. 135 of the 1990 Act substitutes a new s. 286 for the original in the 1963 Act. It introduces a new rule relating to fraudulent preference whereby a transaction is deemed to be a fraudulent preference if made in favour of a 'connected person' within two years before the commencement of the winding up of the company, unless the contrary is shown. See further McCormack, *op. cit.*, 219-22.

Circumstances in which floating charge is invalid   S. 136 of the 1990 Act re-enacts s. 288 of the 1963 Act with some amendments. The general rule is that, where a company is being wound up, a floating charge on the undertaking or property of that company created within 12 months before the commencement of the winding up is invalid, except as to money actually advanced or paid, or the actual price or value of goods or services sold or supplied to the company at the time of or subsequently to the creation of, and in consideration for, the charge, together with 5% p.a. interest. This rule does not apply if it is proved that the company immediately after the charge was solvent. The original model of s. 288 had limited itself to 'cash paid' (see Keane, *op. cit.* (1st ed., 1985), paras 21.29-21.31) and had not embraced the actual price or value of goods or services sold or supplied: see McCormack, *op. cit.*, 222.

   S. 136 goes on to provide (in subs. (3) and (4) of the new s. 288) that, where a floating charge on the undertaking or property of a company is created in favour of a 'connected person', the relevant period is 2 years rather than 12 months; a 'connected person' is one who, when the transaction was made, was a director or shadow director of the company, a person connected with a director (within the meaning of s. 26(1) of the 1990 Act), a related company (within the meaning of s. 140 of the 1990 Act) or a trustee of, or surety or guarantor for, the debt due to a director, shadow director or person connected with a director.

Requirement to contribute to debts of related companies   Part VI also contains important provisions, inspired by developments in New Zealand (cf McCormack, *op. cit.*, 226-7) but having no parallel in Britain, whereby a company may be required to contribute to the payment of debts of its related companies. S. 140(1) provides that, on the application of the liquidator or any creditor or contributory of a company that is being wound up, the court may, if satisfied that it is just and equitable to do so, order that any company that is or has been related to it is to pay the liquidator an amount equivalent to the whole or part of all or any of the debts provable in that winding-up.

A company is related to another company if:

(a) the other company is its holding or subsidiary company,

(b) more than half in nominal value of its equity share capital is held by the other company and companies related to the other company (other than in a fiduciary capacity),

(c) more than half in nominal value of the equity share capital of each of them is held by members of the other (again other than in a fiduciary capacity),

(d) the other company (or a company related to the other company or the other company together with a company or companies related to it) is (or are) entitled to exercise or control the exercise of more than a half of the voting power at any general meeting of the company,

(e) the businesses of the companies have been so carried on that the separate business of each of them, or a substantial part of it, is not readily identifiable, or

(e) there is another company to which both companies are related (s. 140(5)).

There are important limitations on the exercise of this new power. In deciding whether it is just and equitable to make an order under subs. (1) the court must have regard to:

(a) the extent to which the related company took part in the management of the company being wound up,

(b) the conduct of the related company towards the creditors of the company being wound up, and

(c) the effect which the order would be likely to have on the creditors of the related company (s. 140(2)).

The court is not to make an order unless satisfied that the circumstances giving rise to the winding up of the company are attributable to the actions or omissions of the related company (s. 140(3)). Moreover, it is not just and equitable to make an order if the only ground for doing so is the fact that one company is related to another, or that creditors of the company being wound up have relied on the fact that another company is or has been related to the first mentioned company (s. 140(4)). It should also be noted that 'creditor' is defined in s. 14(6) as one or more creditors to whom the company being wound up is indebted, *by more, in aggregate, than £10,000.*

Pooling of assets of related companies   S. 141 provides for the *pooling of assets of related companies*. Where two or more companies are being wound up and the court, on the application of the liquidator of any of them, is satisfied that it is just and equivalent to make an order under the section, it may order that the companies be wound up together as if they were one company: subs. (1).

It should be noted that an order under s141(1) does not affect the rights of secured creditors of any of the companies (subs. (3)(c)). Moreover, debts of a company that have priority in payment by virtue of s. 285 of the 1963 Act (cf. Keane, *op. cit.*, para 38.72) are, to the extent that they are not paid out of the assets of that company, subject to the claims of holders of debentures under a floating charge created by any of the other companies (subs. 3(d)).

Compensation by promoter, officer, reciver, etc.   S. 142 of the 1990 Act re-enacts s. 298 of the 1963 Act with amendment. It concerns a case where, in the course of winding up a company it appears that any person who has taken part in its formation or promotion, or any past or present officer, liquidator, receiver or examiner of the company, has misapplied or retained or become liable or accountable for any money or property of the company, or has been guilty of any misfeasance or other breach of duty or trust in relation to the company. In such circumstances, the court may, on the application of the liquidator or any creditor or contributory, examine into the conduct of the person in default and compel him either to repay or restore the money or property (with interest) or to contribute a sum to the assets of the company by way of compensation. The section applies regardless of whether the wrongdoer is also criminally liable.

This re-draft of s. 298 extends the range of persons to whose wrongdoing liability attaches, by bringing *receivers* within its scheme: see McCormack, *op. cit.*, 230; cf *In re B Johnson & Co Builders Ltd* [1955] Ch 634. Moreover, the re-draft extends the range of wrongdoing it covers from 'misfeasance or breach of trust' to cover 'misfeasance or other breach of duty or trust in relation to the company'. The intention is to bring negligence within the scope of the section: see McCormack, *op. cit.*, 230.

Part VII: Director disqualification and restriction

Under the 1963 Act, apart from bodies corporate, undischarged bankrupts and auditors of the company, the only people who could not be directors of a company were those expressly prohibited from being so by a court order after they had been found guilty of fraud or dishonesty: Keane, *op. cit.*, para 29.52. Part VII of the 1990 Act radically improves the controls on the 'Phoenix syndrome', by introducing *restrictions* on the ability of directors of insolvent companies to resurrect a new company from the ashes, and by enabling the court to *disqualify* a person from acting as director in a number of circumstances: see Whelan, 'When the Board has to walk the plank', *Sunday Tribune*, 27 January 1991. Part VII has not met with universal acclaim. Mr Justice Keane is reported as having observed that it 'almost equates insolvency with dishonesty', and it is 'unduly harsh' and that the minimum share capital requirements may be very onerous for many small traders to meet: *Sunday Business Post*, 7 April, 1991, p. 13.

Restrictions on directors of insolvent companies   Chapter 1 of Part VII deals with restrictions on directors of insolvent companies. The general principle is that, where a company is wound up and unable to pay its debts, the court is to declare that any director, former director holding office within the previous 12 months and shadow director (s. 149(5)) is not, for a period of five years, to act as a director or secretary of a company unless it meets the following requirements:

(a) the nominal value of its allotted share capital must be at least £100,000 in the case of a public limited company or £20,000 in the case of any other company;
(b) each allotted share up to the minimum prescribed capital must be fully paid up including the whole of any premium; and
(c) such allotted share and premium must have been paid for in cash: s. 150(3).

The Minister has power to vary these amounts by order: s. 158. See further McCormack, *op. cit.*, 141-2.

The court is not to make a restriction order if satisfied:

(a) that the person concerned acted honestly and responsibly in relation to the conduct of the affairs of the company and that there is no other reason why it should be just and equitable that he should be subject to a restriction order; or
(b) that the person concerned was a director of the company solely by reason of his nomination as such by a financial institution in connection with the giving to credit facilities to the company by the institution and the institution has not obtained from any director of the company a guarantee of repayment to it of the loans or other forms of credit advanced to the company; or
(c) that the person concerned was a director of the company solely by reason of his nomination as such by a venture capital company in connection with the purchase of, or subscription for, shares in it by the venture capital company: s. 150(2).

A person to whom a restriction order applies may, within a year of its making, apply to the court for relief, either in whole or in part, from its restrictions: s. 152(1). The court may, as it deems it just and equitable to do so, grant that relief on whatever terms and conditions it sees fit: *id.* See McCormack, *op. cit.*, 142.

Chapter 1 applies not only to cases where the company has been wound up but also to those where 'a receiver of the property' is appointed: s. 154. Whether this expression is restricted to cases where the receiver is appointed over *all* the company's property is a matter of some uncertainty: see McCormack, *op. cit.*, 143.

A person who acts in relation to a company in a manner which he is prohibited from doing by virtue of s. 150 is guilty of an offence: s. 161. Where a declaration has been made under s. 150 against a person, he must notify any company of this fact within 14 days before acting as a director of it or otherwise taking part in its promotion or formation: s. 155(5).

Several important restrictions attach to companies in relation to which a person subject to a s. 150 declaration is appointed or acts in any way as a director or in respect of their promotion or formation. First they are not permitted to avail themselves of the exception to the general prohibition on the giving of financial assistance by companies for the purchase of their shares where this is done under the authority of a special resolution of the company: s. 155(2). Secondly, an expert valuation is required for the acquisition of non-cash assets from directors and persons involved in their promotion or formation as well as subscribers to the memorandum: s. 155(3); this contrasts with the normal rule which limits the need for such valuation to the acquisition of non-cash assets from a subscriber to the memorandum within the period of two years of the issuing of a certificate of entitlement to the company to do business: see McCormack, *op. cit.*, 146. Thirdly, a company in relation to which a person subject to s.150 order acts is prohibited from making loans or quasi-loans to its directors, or from engaging in credit transactions on their behalf, even where these are for less than 10% of the company's assets or are on normal commercial terms: s. 155(4).

The court may, if it deems it just and equitable to do so, grant relief to a company to which these restrictions under s. 155 apply, in respect of an act or omission which amounted to a contravention or provision of the Companies Acts by virtue of s. 155. The court may similarly grant relief to a person adversely affected thereby. In either case, the court may grant the relief on whatever terms and conditions it sees fit, including exemption from the provision in question: s. 157(1). No relief can be granted, however, where the company was notified (as required by s. 155(5)) by the director, within the 14 days preceding his appointment or acting as a director, that he was a person to whom s. 150 applied: s. 157(2).

Disqualification of directors   Chapter 2 of Part VII contains provision for the disqualification of persons from acting as directors, echoing and strengthening former legislative provisions on the subject.

S. 160(1) prescribes *mandatory* disqualification for a period of five years unless the court, on application of the prosecutor, orders otherwise (whether longer or shorter). This rule applies where a person is convicted on indictment of any indictable offence in relation to a company, or involving fraud or dishonesty. The disqualification is from acting as an auditor, director or other officer, receiver, liquidator or examiner or in any other way, directly or indirectly, being concerned or taking part in the promotion, formation or management of any company. See McCormack, *op. cit.*, 148-9. (Undischarged bankrupts who act as officers of a company or are otherwise involved in its management, save with leave of the court, are guilty of an offence: (s. 169) and on conviction deemed subject to a disqualification order (*id.*)).

S. 160(2) provides for *discretionary* disqualification for such period as the court thinks fit, in six circumstances:

(a) where a person has been guilty, while a promoter, officer, auditor, receiver, liquidator or examiner of a company, of any fraud in relation to it or its members;

(b) where a person in that position in a company has been guilty of a breach of his duty in respect of that position;

(c) where a declaration of personal responsibility for the debts of a company has been made under s. 297A of the 1963 Act (inserted in s. 138 of the 1990 Act);

(d) where the conduct of a person in that position makes him unfit to be concerned in the management of a company;

(e) where, in consequence of a report of inspectors appointed by the court or the Minister under the Companies Acts, a person's conduct makes him unfit to be concerned in the management of a company; or

(f) where a person has been persistently in default in relation to the relevant requirements (cf. s. 159) relating to the filing, delivery or notice of any returns, accounts or other documents. (Persistent default may be conclusively proved by showing that within the past five years the person has been adjudged guilty of at least three such defaults (s. 160(3)(a)). (This 'conclusive' proof would not seem to offend against the rule that legislation must not foreclose a judicial resolution of factual evidential issues: cf. *Maher v Attorney General* [1973] IR 140. What is here envisaged is a *definitional* clarification of what constitutes persistence in default.)

In making a discretionary order of this discretionary kind, the court may act on its own motion or as a result of an application to it: s. 160(2). Application in respect of the first four of the six grounds may be made by the Director of Public Prosecutions or by any member, contributory, officer, employee, receiver, liquidator, examiner or creditor of a company in relation to which the person sought to be disqualified has been acting or is proposing to act or has been or is proposing to be concerned with its promotion, formation or management: s. 160(4). The Director of Public Prosecutions may apply under ground (e): (s. 160(5)). Either the Director of Public Prosecutions or the registrar of companies may apply under ground (f): (s. 160(b)).

A person who is subject to a mandatory or discretionary disqualification order may apply to the court for relief, and the court may grant this, if it deems it just and equitable to do so, on whatever terms and conditions it sees fit (s. 160(8)).

Enforcement   Chapter 3 of Part VII deals with enforcement of orders of restriction and disqualification. If a person subject to a restriction or dis-qualification order acts contrary to its provisions he is guilty of an offence (s161(1)), and the period of disqualification is extended for a further period of ten years from the date of conviction or such other further period as the court (on application of the prosecutor) may order (s. 161(3)).

Breach of the terms of a restriction order or of a disqualification order can also have important civil effects. Where any consideration is given by the company for an act done or service performed by the person in breach, while he was acting in this prohibited capacity, the company may recover from him, as a simple contract debt, the consideration or an amount representing its value: s. 163(2). Moreover, if the company begins to be wound up while he is so acting or within 12 months thereafter and the company is insolvent, the court may declare him personally liable for all or part of the company's debts or other liabilities incurred when he was so acting: s. 163(3). Where a company which has received notification under s. 155(5) that a person has been restricted by an order made under s. 150 and that company carries on business afterwards without the requirements of s. 150(3) (as to minimum capitalisation, *inter alia*) being fulfilled within a reasonable period and the company is later wound up in a state of insolvency, the court may, declare that officers of the company who knew or ought to have known that it had been so notified are to be personally liable for part or all of its debts or other liabilities: s. 163(4).

In respect of each of these three instances of personal liability, the court has a power to grant relief when it considers it just and equitable to do so: s. 163(5). Directors and other officers or members of committees of management or trustees of companies who act in accordance with the directions or instructions of another person knowing that, in giving these directions or instructions, he is acting in contravention of any provision in Part VII are guilty of an offence: s. 164(1). Those who are convicted under s 164 are personally liable for the company's debts incurred when they were so acting; the court has a discretionary power to grant relief from this liability: s. 165.

Part VIII: Receivers

Part VIII of the Act, introduces a number of changes in the law relating to *receivers* of companies. See McCormack, *op. cit.*, chapter 10; while some of these changes are clearly welcome, others may be criticised for their failure to resolve important issues of policy and principle as fully as might have been expected.

(a) Disqualification   S. 170(1) extends the range of disqualification of persons for appointment as receiver. Five categories are now excluded: undischarged bankrupts, person who are, or within the previous year have been, officers or servants (including auditors) of the company, the parents, spouse, brothers, sisters and children of officers of the company, persons who are partners of or in the employment of officers or servants of the company, and finally persons not qualified for appointment as receiver of the property of any other body corporate which is that company's subsidiary or holding company or a subsidiary of the holding company. The Minister has power by regulations to add to his list: s. 237(2). Receivers who become disqualified must thereupon vacate their office and give notice within 14 days to the company, the registrar of companies or, as the case may be, the debenture-holder or the court: s. 170(2). It is an offence (involving a daily default fine) to act when disqualified or to fail to give the relevant notice: s. 170(3).

(b) Application to Court for directions   S. 171 extends the eligibility to apply to the Court for directions in relation to a receivership. Formerly only the receiver could apply. Now, as well as the receiver, so also may an officer, member or creditor of the company, a liquidator or a contributory, and employees of the company comprising at least half of those employed in a full-time capacity. The application may be for directions 'in relation to any matter in connection with the performance or otherwise by the receiver of his functions'. The court has an equally broad remit on hearing the application: it 'may give such directions or make such order declaring the rights of persons before the court or otherwise, as [it] thinks just'.

All applications save those by the receiver are to be supported by such evidence that the *applicant is being unfairly prejudiced* by any actual or proposed action or omission of the receiver as the court may require. This narrows the scope of entitlement. It is not sufficient for the applicant to show that a course of action is damaging to others; he must show that it is unfairly prejudicing *himself.* How an applicant could succeed in establishing *actual* prejudice from *proposed* action is difficult to see (in at least most cases); one suspects that the court will not construe the words of the provision too narrowly, since it is designed to prevent meddlesome interventions rather than to obstruct genuine applications. While the provision requires the applicant to support the application by 'such evidence [of unfair prejudice] as the court may require', it seems clear that the court's discretion is restricted, not only by the general rule that it be exercised judicially in a non-arbitrary fashion, but also by constitutional considerations: cf *Bula Ltd v Tara Mines Ltd* [1988] ILRM 149 (High Court, Murphy J, 1987), discussed in the 1987 Review, pp. 282-3.

(c) Duty of receiver to sell property at best price reasonably obtainable   S. 172 modifies the position in relation to the duty of receivers when selling property of a company. Formerly the courts accepted that the receiver is under a duty, when selling, to take reasonable care to obtain the best price for the company: cf *Holohan v Friends Provident and Century Life Office* [1966] IR 1 (duty of mortgagee); *Lambert Jones Estates Ltd v Donnelly,* High Court, O'Hanlon J, 5 November 1982, *McGowan v Gannon* [1983] ILRM 516. The willingness of the courts to impose a duty of care on the receiver, notwithstanding his potentially conflicting duties, may be contrasted with their reluctance to do so in other, related, contexts: cf. McMahon & Binchy, *op. cit.,* chapter 6, *McMahon v Ireland, the Attorney General and the Registrar of Friendly Societies* [1988] ILRM 610, discussed in the 1987 Review, 312-4, *Yuen Kun-yeu v Attorney General for Hong Kong* [1988] 2 AC 175, *Rondel v Worsley* [1969] 1 AC 191. The difference in approach is probably attributable to the *public* dimension to the conflict of duties in these latter cases.

At all events, Irish courts had not resolved the question whether the duty to take reasonable care to obtain the best price imported a *temporal* element: if the market is down today but likely to be up tomorrow, may the receiver sell today oblivious of probable future trends? In England, the judges were divided on this issue: Salmon LJ in *Cuckmere Brick Co. v Mutual Finance Ltd* [1971] Ch 949 (CA) thought that delay was not required: Lord Denning MR, however, in *Standard Chartered Bank Ltd v Walker* [1982] 3 All ER 938 (CA), thought that the issue of how long the receiver should wait was part of the wider requirement of taking reasonable care. The court in *Bank of Cyprus (London) Ltd v Gill* [1980] 2 Lloyd's Rep 51, favoured Salmon LJ's approach. In Ireland, Carroll J in *McGowan v Gannon, supra,* raised, but preferred not to resolve, the question.

S. 172 of the 1990 Act deals with the situation in a somewhat tentative and unsatisfactory manner. It inserts a new s. 316A in the 1963 Act, subs (1) of which provides that:

> [a] receiver, in selling property of a company, shall exercise all reasonable care to obtain the best price reasonably obtainable for the property as at the time of sale.

This provision 'no more than reflects developments in the case law' (McCormack, *op. cit.*, 179) but can be criticised in two respects. First, it imposes an obligation on the receiver to exercise *all reasonable care* when selling, but does not attempt to prescribe the persons (if any) who may sue for compensation if the receiver breaches this obligation. The law of negligence proceeds on the basis that a person 'is entitled to be as negligent as he pleases towards the whole world if he owes no duty to them': *Le Lievre v Gould* [1893] 1 QB 491, at 497 (CA, *per* Esher MR). Thus, assuming that the defendant owes a duty of care *at all*, the crucial question concerns the persons to whom he owes that duty. The fact that the subsection makes no attempt to determine this issue *could* mean that it should be persons foreseeably suffering loss from the receiver's failure to exercise all reasonable care, *who would have a right of action in common law negligence*; on this interpretation, the courts would continue to deny a remedy to plaintiffs who, although foreseeable victims of the receiver's negligence, fell outside the range of persons to whom he owed a *duty* to care: cf the recent English decisions of *Caparo Industries plc v Dickman* [1990] 2 AC 605, *Morgan Crucible Co. plc v Hill Samuel Bank Ltd* [1991] 1 All ER 148, *James McNaughton Papers Group Ltd v Hicks Anderson & Co. (afirm)* [1991] 1 All ER 134. (Whether the Irish courts would necessarily endorse the retrenchment which these decisions involve is far from clear.) Is there not, however, a case for interpreting the subsection, not as clarifying the common law rules, but rather as establishing a new statutory duty, in relation to the breach of which civil liability should be imposed in accordance with the well established principles relating to actions for breach of statutory duty? If this approach were adopted, the ghosts of foreseeability and duty would not be entirely exorcised but would fall to be determined under the rubrics of *persons whom the statutory provision is designed to protect* and the *type of damage against which it affords protection*: see McMahon & Binchy, *op. cit.*, 385-8.

The point is of more than academic interest, since it links up with the second criticism that may be made of the subsection. This is that it appears to limit the obligation of the receiver to one of obtaining the best price reasonably obtainable *as at the time of sale*, thereby impliedly relieving him of the obligation to exercise due care in the selection of what time to sell. Against this interpretation, it can be argued that the subsection professes to deal only with the narrow issue of the obligation to take reasonable care to obtain the best price *on the day*, and that it does not address the separate issue of whether there is a duty of care in respect of *when to sell*. If the subsection is to be understood as an attempt to clarify of common law rules, then it is, perhaps, easier to construe it as impliedly excluding a duty of care as to when to sell. If, however, it is to be interpreted as creating a specific statutory duty, without prejudice to the common law rules — as is the case with statutory duties in general — then the question left unanswered by Carroll J still awaits resolution.

S. 316A(2) gives some support to the view that what subs. (1) envisages is a distinct new statutory duty, rather than a modification of common law principles of negligence. It provides that it is not to be a defence to any action or proceeding brought against a receiver in respect of his duty under subs. (1) that he was acting as agent of the company or under a power of attorney given by the company; nor is he to be entitled to be compensated or indemnified by the company 'for any liability he may incur as a result of a breach of his duty under this section'. The language here suggests that the duty envisaged by subs. (1) is exclusively of statutory character, fully articulated in the subsection.

McCormack, *op. cit.*, 181, points out that the section leaves untouched other possible devices for excluding or limiting the liability of a receiver in this context. A question of public policy may arise as to whether these devices, in particular those of a flagrantly evasive nature, should defeat or substantially restrict civil liability for breach of the obligation which subs (1) places on receivers. An unthinking application of the *inclusio unius* rule would lead a court to hold that, outside the specific contexts specified by the legislation, a contractual free-for-all should prevail. A more sensitive judicial approach would have regard to the inequalities of bargaining power which can arise between a financially-battered company and a lending bank. Any devices whereby the bank could easily shake off the liability of a receiver for neglect of the company's interests when selling its property at an under-value should be closely scrutinised.

S. 316A(b) prevents a receiver from selling by private contract a 'non-cash asset' of the 'requisite value' to a person who is or, within the three years prior to the receiver's appointment, has been an officer of the company (including a person connected with a director (cf s. 26 of the 1990 Act), and a shadow director) without having given at least 14 days' notice of his intention to do so to all creditors of the company who are known to him or who have been intimated to him. (We have seen that, under s. 29 of the Act, a non-cash asset of the requisite value is (normally) property other than cash whose value is not less than £1,000 and which exceeds £50,000 or 10% of the amount of the company's relevant assets). As McCormack, *op. cit.*, 182, explains, the intention 'clearly is to prevent directors of the company, who are in a better position as regards knowledge than other prospective purchasers, from buying company assets "on the cheap" from a receiver'.

(d) Submission to receiver of statement of affairs Under ss. 319 and 320 of the 1963 Act, a receiver on his appointment must give notice of it immediately to the company. Within 14 days thereafter, or such longer period as the court or receiver may permit, the directors and secretary of the company must submit to the receiver a statement of affairs. This statement of affairs involves a fairly full confession as to the company's present financial situation, as well as details as to its personnel.

Prior to the 1990 legislation, this requirement, though backed by a criminal sanction, was inefficacious, since directors rarely complied with it: *Keane, op. cit.* (1st ed, 1985), para 23.14. S. 173 of the 1990 Act increases the criminal sanction to a maximum of three years' imprisonment and £5,000. Moreover, where a statement of affairs has not been submitted, s. 174 enables the court, on the application of a receiver or creditor, to make 'whatever order it thinks fit, including an order compelling compliance with ss. 319 and 320'. Breach of such an order would be contempt of court. An interesting question arises as to whether that contempt should be characterised as criminal or civil. Cf. the Law Reform Commission's *Consultation Paper on Contempt of Court* (1991), chapter 6.

(e) Removal of receiver S. 175 enables the court, on cause shown, to remove a receiver and appoint another receiver. Notice of removal proceedings must be given to the receiver and the debenture holder, both of whom may appear and be heard. The section is largely confirmatory of the previous legal position, at all events as regards receivers appointed by the court though, as McCormack, *op. cit.*, 174, points out, the courts have 'not [been] so vocal' as to receivers appointed out of court.

(f) Determination or limitation of receivership S. 176 provides that, on the application of the liquidator of a company that is being wound up (other than by means of a members' voluntary winding up), the court may order a receiver to cease to act, and prohibit the appointment of any other receiver, or order the receiver to act only in respect of certain specified assets. The receiver and debenture-holder must have been given 7 days' notice of the hearing and are entitled to be heard by the court in respect of the application. An order made under the section is not to affect any security or charge over the undertaking or property of the company.

S. 176 reflects the previous practice so far as court-appointed receivers are concerned, but 'appears to represent a radical transformation' of the existing position so far as concerns privately appointed receivers: McCormack, *op. cit.*, 176.

(g) Resignation of receiver S. 177 permits a receiver appointed *out of court* to *resign*, on one month's notice to the holders of floating and fixed charges and the company or its liquidator. It permits a receiver *appointed by the court* to resign only with the authority of the court and on such terms and conditions as the court lays down. Previously a receiver appointed out of court could resign *with the consent of the debenture holder* (whether given in the debenture or subsequently); if he did not have this consent, he could be sued for damages for breach of contract: see McCormack, *op. cit.*, 173.

(h) Power to order return of improperly transferred assets S. 178 adapts to the context of receiverships the provisions of s. 139, which applies to companies in liquidation. S. 139, as we have seen, gives the court power to order the return of assets which have been improperly transferred.

(i) Notification of suspected criminal offence S. 179 requires receivers who become aware of circumstances tending to show that a criminal offence has been committed in relation to a company to report this to the Director of Public Prosecutions, and requires receivers, as well as officers and agents (including bankers, solicitors and auditors) of the company, to give all reasonable assistance to the Director: see McCormack, *op. cit.*, 183-4.

Part IX: Companies under protection

This Part contains two sections (ss. 180 and 181) which amend aspects of the Companies (Amendment) Act 1990. In our discussion of that Act above, 41-56, we have already taken account of these amendments.

Part X: Accounts and audit

Part X of the Act implements the Eighth EEC Company Law Harmonisation Directive on the qualification of auditors (84/253/EEC, OJ No. L126.20, 10 April 1984), introduces more stringent duties for the keeping of accounts and strengthens the hand of auditors in their dealings with companies. See McCormack, *op. cit.*, chapter 9.

Qualifications for appointment as auditor First let us consider the question of *disqualification.* S. 187(2), replacing s. 6 of the Companies (Amendment) Act 1982, provides that the following persons are not qualified for this position:

(a) an officer or servant of the company,

(b) a person who has been an officer or servant of the company within a period in respect of which accounts would fall to be audited by him if he were appointed auditor of the company,

(c) a parent, spouse, brother, sister or child of an officer of the company,

(d) a person who is a partner of or in the employment of an officer of the company,

(e) a person who is disqualified for appointment as auditor of a subsidiary or holding company of the company or a subsidiary of the company's holding company,

(f) a person disqualified for appointment as a public auditor of a society that is a subsidiary or holding company of the company or a subsidiary of the company's holding company.

The former indulgence to private companies so far as concerned auditors who were partners of, or in the employment of, an officer of the company no longer prevails: 'the laxity of yore has been swept away by the Eighth . . . Directive' (McCormack, *op. cit.*, 157).

Giving further effect to the Directive, Part X contains detailed provisions for the minimum educational and professional requirements for auditors, which we need not examine in any detail. For a thorough discussion, see McCormack, *op. cit.*, 158-61. Membership of a recognised body of accountants suffices (s. 187(1)(a)(i)). Also sufficient is an accountancy qualification which is, in the Minister's opinion, not less than that required for membership of such a body and which would entitle the person in question to a practising certificate if he were a member of that body, if the Minister gives his authorisation (s. 187(1)(a)(ii)). Those who on 31 December 1990 were members of a body of accountants recognised under s162(1)(a) of the 1963 Act also qualify (s. 187(1)(a)(iii)). Moreover those holding a direct authorisation from the Minister before February 1983 are qualified (s. 187(1)(a)(iv)), as are persons undergoing appropriate training on 1 January 1990 (s. 187(1)(a)(v)) and persons with appropriate qualifications obtained outside the State (s. 187(1)(a)(vi)).

Acting as an auditor while disqualified is an offence: s. 187(6)(7) and (9). See further McCormack, *op. cit.*, 162.

Register of auditors In compliance with the requirements of Article 28 of the Directive, s. 198 obliges the registrar of companies to maintain a register of the names and addresses of persons who have been notified to him as qualified for appointment as auditor of a company or as a public auditor. S. 199 obliges recognised bodies of accountants to deliver to the registrar the names and addresses of members thus qualified to act and also requires others

---

104   *Annual Review of Irish Law 1990*

who are authorised by the Minister so to act similarly to notify the registrar. A body of accountants which fails to comply with this obligation is guilty of an offence: subs. (4). Cf. the Special Committee Debate 31, No. 20, 12 June 1990, cols. 1145-51.

Ministerial power to make supplementary regulations S. 201 gives the Minister power to make supplementary regulations which he may consider necessary for the proper and effective implementation of the Directive, within three years of the commencement of Part X. Mr Leyden explained that the question of allowing auditors to form companies and of allowing these companies to act as auditors of companies or as public auditors had to be examined. S. 201 would enable the Minister to make appropriate regulations if he considered it 'desirable to go down that road at a later stage': *id.*, col. 1154.

Removal of an auditor Prior to the 1990 Act, a company might remove a first-appointed auditor at a general meeting and substitute one nominated for appointment by any member of the company where notice of the nomination had been given to the other members at least 14 days beforehand: s. 160 of the 1963 Act. The shareholders had no similar power with respect to the removal of other auditors though they could decline to reappoint a retiring auditor: Keane, *op. cit.*, para 32.35. S. 183 of the 1990 Act greatly extends their powers, subject to certain due process protections. *Any* auditor may now be removed (and replaced by another qualified auditor) by ordinary resolution at a general meeting, provided extended notice (of at least 28 days) has been given to the company and proper notice has been given to the auditor.

An auditor whose removal is proposed may make representations in writing to the company which must not exceed a reasonable length. The company must send them out to the members of the company; if it does not do so because they were received too late or on account of the company's default, the auditor may insist that the representations be read out at the meeting. He may, moreover, make an oral presentation at the meeting.

The auditor's right to have his representations circulated (or read out at the meeting) is qualified by the rule that, on the application of either the company or of any one who claims to be aggrieved, the court may dispense with the company's obligation to circulate or read out these representations if satisfied that the auditor's right is being abused to secure needless publicity for defamatory matter.

An auditor who has been removed is nonetheless entitled to attend, and be heard at, the annual general meeting of the company at which, but for his removal, his term of office as auditor would have expired and the general meeting of the company at which it is proposed to fill the vacancy occasioned by his removal: s. 161(2A) of the 1963 Act, as amended by s. 184(1) of the 1990 Act.

Resignation of auditor   S. 185 of the 1990 Act introduces a means for an auditor to resign before his term has expired. This is by way of notice in writing served on the company: subs. (1). The notice must contain a statement of the circumstances connected with the resignation that the auditor considers should be brought to the notice of the members or creditors of the company, if such circumstances exist: subs. (2).

S. 186 enables a resigning auditor to requisition the convening of a general meeting of the company for the purpose of receiving and considering such account and explanation of the circumstances connected with his resignation as he may wish to give to the meeting: subs. (1). Where the auditor takes this course, he can also have a further statement in writing, prepared by him, of circumstances connected with the resignation brought to the notice of the members (subs. (3)), subject to the power of the court to prevent this if satisfied that the auditor is abusing this entitlement in order to secure needless publicity for defamatory matter (subs. (4)).

An auditor who resigns has the right to attend and be heard at the subsequent annual general meeting and the general meeting at which it is proposed to appoint his successor: subs. (5).

Auditors' functions   S. 193 of the 1990 Act (replacing substantially similar provisions in the 1963 Act) sets out the auditor's functions: these now include the general duty to carry out the audit 'with professional integrity' (subs. (6), echoing the Directive). S. 196(1) imposes on a subsidiary company incorporated in the State and its auditors the duty (backed by criminal sanction (subs. (2)) to give to the auditors of the holding company such information and explanations as the auditors may reasonably require. Where the subsidiary is incorporated elsewhere, the holding company has the duty, if its auditors require, to take all such steps as are reasonably open to it to obtain from the subsidiary such information and explanations as may reasonably be required: (subs. (3)), again subject to criminal sanction (subs. (2)).

S. 197 supplements these obligations of assistance by a wide-ranging series of offences. An officer (including an employee (subs. (5)) of a company who makes a statement to the auditors (whether orally or in writing) which conveys or purports to convey any information which they require under the Companies Acts, or are entitled so to require, as auditors, is guilty of an offence where the statement is misleading, false or deceptive in a material particular and he makes the statement knowingly or recklessly: subs.

(1) and (2). Moreover, an officer commits an offence where he fails to provide the auditors of the company or of its holding company, within two days of being required to do so, any information or explanations that they require as auditors of the company or of its holding company, when it is within his knowledge or can be procured by him: subs. (4). As to the overlap between ss. 197 and 242, see McCormack, *op. cit.*, 167.

Keeping of books of account   Ss. 202 and 203 of the Act strengthen the requirements of the 1963 Act in relation to the keeping of financial records. S. 202 expands the scope of s. 147 of the 1963 Act, and gives more specific guidelines on the matters to be dealt with in company books: see McCormack, *op. cit.*, 168. Every company must keep proper books of account, 'whether in the form of documents or otherwise' (so computerised systems are quite permissible: see Keane, *op. cit.*, para 32.04). These must be such as:

(a) correctly record and explain the transactions of the company;
(b) enable at any time the financial position of the company to be determined with reasonable accuracy;
(c) enable the directors to ensure that any balance sheet, profit and loss account or income and expenditure account of the company complies with the requirements of the Companies Acts, and
(d) enable the accounts of the company to be readily and properly audited. (Subs. (1)).

The books of account must be kept on a continuous and consistent basis: this means that the entries must be made in a timely manner and be consistent from one year to the next (subs. (2)).

A company that contravenes s. 202 or a director who fails to take all reasonable steps to secure the company's compliance or who has by his own wilful act been the cause of any default by the company in this regard, is guilty of an offence (subs. (10)). Where, however, a person is charged with failure to take such reasonable steps, it is a defence to prove that he had reasonable grounds for believing and did believe that a competent and reliable person was charged with the duty of ensuring that those requirements were complied with and was in a position to discharge that duty (*id.*). Moreover, a person is not to be sentenced to *imprisonment* (though he may be fined up to £10,000 on indictment or £1,000 on summary conviction (s. 240(1)) unless, in the opinion of the court, the offence was committed *wilfully* (s. 202(10)).

S. 203 imposes criminal liability on every *officer* of the company who is in default in cases where a company that is being wound up and that is unable to pay all of its debts has contravened s. 202 and the court considers that this contravention has contributed to the company's inability to pay all of its debts or has resulted in substantial uncertainty as to the assets and liabilities of the company or has substantially impeded its orderly winding up (subs. (1)). The officer has the defence that he took all reasonable steps to secure compliance by the company with s. 202 or he had reasonable grounds for believing and did believe that a competent and reliable person was charged with this task (akin to the director's defence under s. 202(10): subs. (2)).

McCormack, *op. cit.*, 169, notes that the term 'officers' is not further defined in s. 203. This may be contrasted with s. 197(5), which, as we have seen, extends the term so as to incorporate any employee of the company, for the purposes of the offence of making false statements to auditors. It may thus be assumed that the remit of the term in s. 203 falls short of embracing all employees.

S. 204, which links in with s. 203, has been described as containing '[p]erhaps the most potent remedy to ensure the keeping of proper books of account': McCormack, *op. cit.*, 169. It imposes *civil* liability on the officers and former officers of a company where proper books have not been kept as required under s. 202. The 'trigger' for doing so is the same as in s. 203: the company must be being wound up and unable to pay its debts and the court must consider that the s. 202 contravention has contributed to the company's inability to pay its debts or resulted in substantial uncertainty as to assets and liability or substantially impeded its orderly winding up (subs. (1)).

The term 'officer' is given a broad meaning (subs. (6)). It includes a person who has been convicted of an offence under s. 194, 197 or 242 in relation to a statement concerning the keeping of proper books of account by a company. See further McCormack, *op. cit.*, 169-70.

Part XI: Acquisition by a company of its own shares

Part XI reverses the old common law rule (as reinforced with modifications by statute) that a company may not acquire its own shares. The reasons for the change are multifold: it enables a company to buy out a dissident shareholder; it facilitates the retention of family control where one member of the family wants to cash in his shares and the other members have not the present ability to buy his interest; it assists the operation of employee share schemes; and enables companies vulnerable to takeover after a Stock Exchange crash to take defensive action. See McCormack, *op. cit.*, 40-1, 47. Whether Part XI represents the best solution to the issue has been debated. Mr Justice Keane is reported as having expressed the view that its provisions allowing a company to buy its own shares and permitting the redemption of shares appear to be 'unnecessarily complicated' and that they 'will make life difficult for everyone': *Sunday Business Post*, 7 April 1991, p. 13.

Power to issue redeemable shares Under former law, a company, if authorised by its articles, was entitled to issue redeemable preference shares and shares redeemable at the option of the company. Under s. 207(1) of the 1990 Act, a company limited by shares or limited by guarantee and having a share capital may, if authorised by its articles, issue redeemable shares (whether preference or equity) and redeem them accordingly.

This entitlement is subject to a number of conditions (s. 207(2)). No redeemable shares may be issued or redeemed at any time when the nominal value of the issued share capital which is not redeemable is less than one tenth of the nominal value of the total issued share capital of the company. The shares may not be redeemed unless they are fully paid, and the terms of redemption must provide for payment on redemption. As a general rule these shares are to be redeemed out of profits available for distribution. Where, however, the company proposes to cancel shares on redemption, they may also be redeemed out of the proceeds of a fresh issue of shares made for the purpose of redemption. As a further general rule, the premium payable on redemption must have been provided for out of the profits available for distribution. Where, however, the shares were issued at a premium, the premium payable on their redemption may be paid out of the proceeds of a fresh issue of shares made for the purpose of redemption up to an amount equal to either the aggregate of the premiums received by the company on the issue of the shares that are redeemed or the current amount of the company's share premium account (including sums transferred to it in respect of premiums on the new shares), whichever in the less. The amount of the company's share premium account is to be reduced by a sum corresponding to the amount of any payment made out of the proceeds of the issue of new shares.

Cancellation of shares on redemption S. 208 provides that shares may be cancelled on redemption. In such circumstances, the amount of the company's issued share capital is reduced by the nominal value of the shares that are redeemed, but this is not to be taken as reducing the amount of the company's authorised share capital. Where the shares are redeemed wholly out of the profits available for distribution then a sum equal to the nominal amount of the shares redeemed is to be transferred to the capital redemption reserve fund. Where the shares are redeemed wholly or partly out of the proceeds of a fresh issue and the aggregate amount of the proceeds is less than the aggregate nominal value of the shares redeemed, then a sum equal to the aggregable difference is to be transferred to the capital redemption reserve fund. The provisions of the 1963 Act relating to the reduction of the share capital of a company apply as if the capital redemption reserve fund were paid-up share capital. Another provision applicable to the cancellation of shares is that a company has power to issue shares up to the nominal amount of the shares redeemed as if those shares had never been issued; no chargeable transaction occurs for the purpose of stamp duty.

Power to convert shares into redeemable shares S. 210 gives companies power (subs(l)) to convert any of their shares into redeemable shares, subject to fairly stringent conditions. No conversion is possible if the holder of the shares has notified the company of his unwillingness to have them converted (subs. (2)). No shares may be converted into redeemable shares if, as a result, the nominal value of the non-redeemable issued share capital would be less than a tenth of the nominal value of the total issued share capital (subs. (4)). Moreover the power to convert is subject to the provisions of the Companies Acts governing the variation of rights attached to classes of shares and the alteration of a company's memorandum or articles (subs. (1)). For consideration of the complex variation of rights procedure in the companies legislation, see McCormack, *op. cit.*, 46-7.

Power of company to purchase its own shares S. 211(1) establishes the general principle that a company, if authorised by its articles, may purchase its own shares (including any redeemable shares). This is not permitted, however, where, as a result of the purchase, the nominal value of the issued share capital which is not redeemable would be less than one tenth of the nominal value of the total issue of the shared capital: s. 211(3). The aim is 'clearly to prevent a company from purchasing itself out of existence': McCormack, *op. cit.*, 48. The provisions of the legislation relating to the redemption of shares apply in the same way to the purchase by a company of its shares, without this necessarily being effected on the terms and in the manner provided by the articles (cf. s. 207(3)): s. 211(2).

Off-market and market purchases The Act draws a distinction between *off-market* and *market* purchases. With an off-market purchase, the shares are purchased either otherwise than on a recognised stock exchange or, if purchased on such an exchange, they are not subject to a 'marketing arrangement': s. 212(1)(a). Shares are subject to a marketing arrangement on a recognised stock exchange where either they are listed on that stock exchange or the company has been afforded facilities for dealing in those shares to take place there without prior permission for individual transactions and without limit on to the time during which those facilities are to be available: s. 212(2). A market purchase is one where the shares are purchased on a recognised stock exchange and are subject to a marketing arrangement: s. 212(1)(b). As McCormack, *op. cit.*, 48, puts out, '[i]t follows therefore that purchase by

private and non-listed public companies and over-the-counter purchases by
listed companies are within the regime for off-market purchase. . . .'

Authority to make off-market purchase   A company may make an off-
market purchase of its own shares only in pursuance of a contract whose
terms have been authorised by special resolution before it is entered into (s.
213)(1) and (2)). This authority may be varied, revoked or from time to time
renewed by special resolution (s. 213(2)). Where public limited companies
are concerned, any authority thus granted must specify the date on which it
is to expire, which can not be later than 18 months thereafter: s. 216(1). (A
narrow exception to this time limit enables a public limited company to make
a purchase after the expiry of the time limit where the *contract of purchase*
was concluded *before* the authority expired and the terms of the authority
permit the company to make a contract of purchase which might be executed
after the authority expired: s. 216(2)).

S. 213 contains detailed procedural requirements as to notice of proposed
contracts of purchase; for consideration of them, see McCormack, *op. cit.*,
49-50.

S. 215 deals with *market purchases*. These create the danger of market
rigging (which of course is no problem in relation to off-market purchases);
moreover, of the nature of things, prior approval cannot be obtained for each
individual contract of purchase: McCormack, *op. cit.*, 50. The approach
favoured in s. 215 enables a company to make a market purchase of its own
shares if this has been authorised by the company in general meeting: subs.
(1). This authority may be varied, revoked or from time to time renewed by
the company in general meeting: *id.* It is not necessary that a particular
contract for the market purchase of shares be authorised: *id.*

In the case of a public limited company, any authority for a market
purchase must:

> (a) specify the maximum number of shares authorised to be acquired,
> and
> (b) determine both the maximum and minimum prices which may be
> paid for the shares: s. 215(3).

The resolution granting authority as to the maximum and minimum prices
to be paid for the shares may determine either of these prices by specifying
a particular sum or by providing a basis or formula for calculating the amount
of the price in question without reference to any person's discretion or
opinion: s. 215(4).

The problem of insider dealing may arise in this context. S. 223 introduces
a Chinese Wall protection, akin to s. 108(7) but without the requirement of

there being written arrangements in operation to ensure that the information is not communicated to the person who made the decision to enter into the transaction in question and that no advice was given to him by a person in possession of the information. See further McCormack *op. cit.*, 51-2.

Contingent purchase contracts S. 214 requires that a company's purchase of its own shares in pursuance of a contingent purchase contract have been authorised beforehand by a special resolution of the company. The section subjects such transaction to the same procedural requirements as for off-market purchases of shares. A contingent purchase contract is one relating to any of the company's shares which does not amount to one of purchase but under which the company may become entitled or obliged to purchase those shares. 'Put' or 'call' options on shares fall within this definition: McCormack, *op. cit.*, 50. Payment for the option must be made out of the distributable profits of the company: s. 218.

Assignment and release of contractual rights A company may not *assign* its rights under a contract to purchase its own shares: s. 217(1). The intention here 'clearly is to prevent a company from speculating against its own share price by buying and selling purchase rights': McCormack, *op. cit.*, 52. A company may, however, *release* such rights, provided, in the case of contracts for off-market or contingent purchase, this has been previously authorised by special resolution of the company: s. 217(2).

Treasury shares An innovation in the 1990 Act is the establishment of treasury shares. The inspiration is North American: British company law still shows no interest in introducing them. Neither is Mr Justice Keane (*op. cit.*, para 15.07) an euthusiast:

> The[ir] object would seem to be to enable the company to keep in reserve unissued share capital which can be re-issued if, for example, an employees sharing scheme were envisaged. They would seem to be of little practical utility: under the present law, there is nothing to prevent a company from making a new issue, even where its authorised share capital will be exceeded, by passing the necessary special resolutions.

S. 209(1) provides that a company, instead of cancelling shares upon their redemption, may hold them (as treasury shares). These may be dealt with in one of two ways: they may either be cancelled or re-issued as shares of any class or classes: s. 209(4).

The nominal value of treasury shares held by a company may not at any time exceed 10% of the nominal value of the issued share capital of the company: s. 209(2)(a). (In determining this percentage, account must be taken of shares held in the company by any subsidiary or by any person acting in his own name but on the company's behalf: s. 209(2)(b).) A company must not exercise any voting rights in respect of treasury shares; any purported exercise of those rights is void: s. 209(3)(a). Moreover, no dividend or payment, including one in a winding-up, is to be payable to the company in respect of those shares: s. 209(3)(b).

Shares reissued on the market are not subject to legislative controls. This contrasts with off-market re-issues. The maximum and minimum prices at which treasury shares may thus be re-issued must be determined in advance by the company in general meeting: s. 209(6)(a). Where the treasury shares to be re-issued are derived from shares purchased by the company, the re-issue price range must have been previously determined by special resolution of the company: s. 209(6)(b). This determination remains effective for a maximum period of 18 months, the resolution being capable to specifying a lesser period: s. 209(6)(e)(ii).

Failure of company to redeem or purchase   Where a company fails to redeem or purchase redeemable shares, shares that have been converted into redeemable shares or shares which it has agreed to purchase, it is not liable in damages to the holder of the shares: s. 219(2); nor may the court grant an order for specific performance of the terms of redemption or purchase of these shares if the company shows that it is unable to meet the cost involved out of profits available for distribution: s. 219(3).

When it comes to winding up, the general rule is that the terms of redemption or purchase may be enforced against a company with respect to shares that have not been redeemed or purchased: where this happens, the shares are treated as *cancelled:* s. 219(4). This general rule is set aside in two cases: *first,* if the terms of redemption or purchase provided for the redemption or purchase to take place at a date *later than that of the commencement of the winding up,* and *second,* if, *during the period from the date when redemption or purchase was to have taken place to the commencement of the winding up, the company could not at any time have lawfully made a distribution equal in value to the price at which the shares were to have been redeemed or purchased:* s. 219(5). The amount due to a shareholder in this context is payable only after the creditors and preferential shareholders have been paid: s. 219(6).

Facilities for inspection of documents   Companies are obliged under criminal sanction to keep available for public inspection at their registered office copies of contracts for the purchase of their own shares, for ten years after their full performance: s. 222(1)-(3). The refusal of an inspection may prompt a court order to allow it: s. 222(4).

Validation of invalid issue, redemption or purchase of shares   S. 227 of the 1990 Act substitutes a new s89 in the 1963 Act, designed to permit retrospective validation in certain circumstances. If a company has created or issued shares in its capital or acquired any of its shares by redemption or purchase in purported compliance with Part XI of the 1990 Act, and if there is reason to apprehend that the shares were invalidly created, issued or acquired, the following persons may apply to the court:

(i) the company,
(ii) a holder or former holder of the shares,
(iii) a member or former member,
(iv) a creditor, or
(v) a liquidator of the company.

The court may declare that the creation, issue or acquisition is to be valid for all purposes if satisfied that it would be just and equitable to do so. Thereupon the shares are retrospectively deemed to have been validly created, issued or acquired. The court may not make this declaration in four cases, however just and equitable it might appear to do so. These are where the shares have been redeemed or purchased in contravention of para. (d) (e) or (f) of s. 207(2) or s. 207(3) of the 1990 Act, which we have already discussed. For discussion of the parameters of s. 227, see McCormack, *op. cit,* 56-7.

The discretion afforded by s. 227 is very broad and the section makes no attempt to guide the court in the exercise of its powers.

Shares held by subsidiary in its holding company   S. 224 enables a subsidiary company to acquire and hold shares in its holding company (subs. (1)), subject to a number of conditions. *First,* the consideration for the acquisition must be provided out of the profits of the subsidiary available for distribution (subs. (2)(a)). *Secondly,* for as long as the shares are held by the subsidiary, the profits of the subsidiary available for distribution are for all purposes to be restricted by the total cost of the shares acquired (subs. (2)(b)(i)). *Thirdly*, the shares must be treated in the consolidated accounts in the same manner as treasury shares (subs. (2)(b)(iii)). *Finally,* the subsidiary is not to exercise any voting rights in respect of the shares (subs. (2)(b)(iii)).

A contract for the acquisition by a subsidiary of shares in its holding company requires the prior authorisation of both the subsidiary and the holding company on the model of the requirements in ss. 214 to 217, relating to the purchase of a company of its own shares: s. 224(3). Where a subsidiary has acquired shares in its holding company within six months before it is wound up in an insolvent state, the court, on the application of a liquidator, creditor, employee or contributory of the company, may declare that the directors of the holding company are jointly and severally liable to repay to the company the total amount paid by the company for the shares: s. 225(1). By way of mitigation, where it appears to the court that a director believed on reasonable grounds that the purchase of the shares was in the best interests of the company, it may relieve him, wholly or in part, from personal liability on such terms as it thinks fit: s. 225(2). McCormack, *op. cit.*, 58 observes that the personal liability under subs. (1) 'is completely discretionary so it is not clear what purpose is served by s. 225(2) save to structure that discretion'. A narrow reading of the section as a whole would construe subs. (2) as representing the only basis on which personal liability may be avoided.

Registration obligations   Companies which have purchased shares under Part XI must when 28 days after delivery to them of the shares, make a return to the registrar, giving details of the shares of each class purchased, their number and nominal value and their date of delivery to the company: s. 226(1). Public limited companies, in their returns, must also state the aggregate amount paid for the shares and the maximum and minimum prices paid for each class: s. 226(2). These obligations are backed by a summary criminal sanction at the suit of the registrar: s. 226(4) and (5).

Ministerial regulatory power   S. 228(1) gives the Minister a wide-ranging power to make regulations governing the purchase by companies of their own shares or shares in their holding companies, and the sale by companies of their own shares held as treasury shares. There regulations may provide in particular for:

> (a) the *class* or description of shares which may (or may not be purchased or sold,
> (b) their *price*,
> (c) the *timing* of the purchase or sales,
> (d) the *method* of purchase or sale, and
> (e) the *volume of trading* which may be carried out by companies (s. 228(2)).

This regulatory power is backed by a criminal sanction (s. 228(3)).

Stock Exchange participation   Whenever shares for which dealing facilities are provided on a recognised stock exchange have been purchased either by the company which issued the shares or its subsidiary, the company must (under criminal sanction) notify that stock exchange of the matter, before the end of the following day: s. 229. The stock exchange may publish, in such a manner as it may determine, any of this information: s. 229(1).

This obligation is backed by a parallel reporting obligation placed on the Stock Exchange by s. 230. If it appears to a relevant authority of a recognised stock exchange that there has been a breach of s. 229 (or of s. 228, relating to Ministerial regulations), it must forthwith report the matter to the DPP, and support this with available information and opportunity for inspecting and copying relevant documents: s. 230(1). A similar duty rests on members of the stock exchange to inform the relevant authority of the stock exchange of suspected breaches of s. 228 or 229: s. 230(2).

Part XII: General

(a) Qualification of secretary Among the miscellany of provisions contained in Part XII, s. 236 imposes a duty on directors of *public* limited companies to take all reasonable steps to secure that the secretary of the company is a person who appears to them to have the requisite knowledge and experience to discharge his functions *and* complies with one of the following further requirements:

(a) he was secretary of the company on the commencement of the section;
(b) he was secretary of a company (not necessarily a public limited company) for at least three of the five years immediately preceeding his appointment as secretary;
(c) he is a member of a body for the time being recognised for the purposes of the section by the Minister; or
(d) he is a person who, 'by virtue of his holding or having held any other position or his being a member of any other body, appears to the directors to be capable of discharging those functions'.

As Mr Leyden noted during the Parlimentary Debates, ground (d) 'would essentially give the directors considerable freedom to appoint a person who may not be professionally qualified but whom they consider to be appropriately equipped to do the job': Dáil Debs, Special Committee, D31, No. 21, col. 1251 (26 June 1990). Mr Bruton welcomed this ground, since it ensured that there would be 'no closed shop': *id*.

We have already noted that s. 237 empowers the Minister, by regulation, to add to the list of persons in s. 315 of the 1963 Act (inserted by s. 170 of the 1990 Act) who are not to be qualified for appointment as *receiver*. S. 237 confers a similar power on the Minister in respect of *liquidators*.

(b) Minister's power to make regulations for transfer of securities   S. 239
empowers the Minister by regulations to make provision for enabling title to
securities to be evidenced and transferred without a written instrument,
subject to safeguards protecting investors and ensuring that competition is
not restricted, distorted or prevented. See further McCormack, *op. cit.*, 13-14.

(c) Penalties for offences   Ss. 247-9 contain provisions designed to ensure
that the information given to the registrar of companies pursuant to legal
obligation is appropriately classified and in legible form. See further
McCormack, *op. cit.*, 12-13.

Finally, we may note that s. 240(1) provides that a person guilty of an
offence under the Companies Acts for which no punishment is specifically
provided is liable, on summary conviction, to a maximum fine of £1,000 and
one year's imprisonment or, on conviction on indictment, to a maximum fine
of £10,000 and three years' imprisonment.

Part XIII: Investment companies

Part XIII provides for a particular kind of investment company known as an
investment company with variable capital. In the financial world this type of
investment vehicle is usually known by its French abbreviation SICAV: see
127 Dáil Debs, col. 301 (13 December 1990). Prior to the 1990 Act, this type
of company could operate here but only in the context of the European
Communities Undertakings for Collective Investment in Transferable
Securities Regulations 1989 (the 'UCITS Regulations'): *id.*

There is a demand internationally for types of investment vehicle which
fall outside the scope of the investment constraints of the UCIT regulations.
This demand has been catered for elsewhere, notably in Luxembourg. The
reason for facilitating their development here was to enable them to operate
in the International Financial Services Centre. Mr O'Malley observed that
'the IFSC competes for investment business with several other centres
throughout the world and it is important that companies operating in the
centre are able to market a full range of products': *id.*

Accordingly Part XIII dispenses with certain general principles of
company law, mainly in relation to the maintenance of capital, where
companies of this type are concerned. The Central Bank is given a crucial
role, with power to attach conditions to the authorisation of these companies
and to require a minimum paid up capital below which an investment
company with variable capital will not be allowed to operate: *id.*, cols. 301-2.
For a comprehensive analysis, see McCormack, *op. cit.*, chapter 4.

Consolidation of actions   In the 1989 Review, 54-5, we discussed the case of *O'Neill v Ryan, Ryan Air Ltd, Aer Lingus plc, et. al.* [1990] ILRM 140 (High Court, 1989), in which the plaintiff sought relief under s. 205 of the Companies Act 1963 as well as damages on foot of misrepresentation, breach of contract, inducing breach of contract, conspiracy and breach of Articles 85 and 86 of the European Community Treaty. Lynch J dismissed the action against four defendants, and the plaintiff appealed to the Supreme Court against that order.

One of the remaining defendants, Dr Thomas Anthony Ryan, sought to have the proceedings for relief and the plenary action for damages heard simultaneously. Blayney J, in a judgment delivered on 21 May 1990, made an order for simultaneous trial. Applying the test expressed by Fitzgibbon J in *Malone v Great Northern Ry Co.* [1931] IR 2, at 13, he was satisfied that to do so would result in a substantial saving of expenses and inconvenience since the two proceedings had their origin in the same circumstances and each proceedings on its own could take six to eight weeks. Moreover, the issue of assessment of damages had been raised in both proceedings; this could best be addressed in a simultaneous trial.

The argument against taking this course was that the number of defendants was still in issue pending the resolution of the Supreme Court appeal, and the Supreme Court had refused an application for an early hearing. Blayney J considered that this did not tilt the balance against a simultaneous hearing. If the plaintiff succeeded against the defendants who were still parties it was unlikely that he would need to pursue his appeal to the Supreme Court. If he failed, it would still be open to him to pursue his appeal and, if successful, to reactivate the plenary proceedings against the four defendants, though Blayney J considered that in practice this was hardly a real possibility, since if he failed against the defendants still parties to the action, there would be little chance of his succeeding against the other four.

DIRECTORS' MEETINGS

In *Holland v McGill*, High Court, 16 March 1990, Murphy J, in an *ex tempore* judgment, addressed issues relating to the requirements of proper notice and an agenda for a directors' meeting of a private company. The plaintiff, one of three shareholders of the company, sought to enforce the terms of a draft agreement, which dealt with the subject of sale of shares. This draft agreement had been circulated to the other two shareholders, who were defendants. A crucial question was whether, in the circumstances of the case, it was binding on them. The plaintiff's solicitor had made it clear to the defendants that the plaintiff would not seek to rely on it. Nevertheless, in the proceedings the plaintiff sought to go back on his assurance because, he argued, the defendants had not relied on it. He contended that, at a directors' meeting, the defendants had dealt with the disposal of shares on terms inconsistent with those of the draft agreement and that he had been misled as to what would be on the agenda at that meeting.

Murphy J dismissed the action, holding, on the evidence, that the defendants had indeed relied on the assurance made by the plaintiff's solicitor. The plaintiff was accordingly estopped from relying on its terms. As to the plaintiff's complaint about the meeting, Murphy J held that it had validity but did not assist the plaintiff in the outcome. There could be no complaint about the amount of notice given for the meeting (which is not clear from the judgment). It was common case that the law did not stipulate any defined period as being required for notice to be given:

> Due notice is what was required and this is usually established among the parties.

Here the plaintiff had been told when the meeting would be held, agreed to the date and stipulated the time.

The plaintiff had sought an agenda for the meeting, but this had not been provided, and he had not known the topics to be considered. Murphy J considered that this was not a ground for complaint:

> [T]he law is clear in that regard. There is no requirement to provide an agenda for directors' meetings, though in practice it may be desirable that it be done occasionally if not frequently.

The plaintiff had good grounds of complaint, however, that he had been *misled* as to what the agenda would be. Whilst the defendant with whom the plaintiff had discussed the forthcoming meeting had been under no obligation to disclose what would be on the agenda, he owed the plaintiff a duty not to mislead him as to what the parties intended to discuss. Nevertheless, in the circumstances of the case, had the plaintiff been properly apprised of what would be on the agenda, the ultimate outcome would not have been different since, if he had sought an injunction to retain the implementation of the proposed transaction on the basis of the draft agreement, he would have been defeated by the defence of estoppel.

TORTIOUS CONSPIRACY

In *Taylor v Smith, Kape Investments et. al.*, Supreme Court, 5 July 1990, which we also discuss in the Torts Chapter, below, pp. 542-5, the question arose as to whether there is any legal reason why a company and a person who controls that company should not be capable of being held liable in tort for having conspired with each other to the plaintiff's detriment. The Supreme Court held that there was not, and that accordingly liability might be imposed on both.

McCarthy J (Finlay CJ and Hederman J concurring) analysed the issue as follows. In principle, it would seem invidious that the assets of a limited company should not be liable to answer for the conspiracy where its assets had been augmented as a result of the action alleged to constitute the conspiracy. To fail to render a company liable in such circumstances would permit it 'to lift its corporate veil as and when it suits'.

McCarthy J could see no reason why the mere fact that one individual controlled a company of limited liability should give immunity from suit to both in the case of an established arrangement for their benefit to the detriment of others. If this was so, it would follow that a like arrangement to the advantage of two companies of limited liability, both controlled by the same individual, 'would give an equal immunity from suit to both companies, and so on'.

One may perhaps wonder whether this would *necessarily* follow. A decision not to impose liability for conspiracy on a company and the person who controls it would be based on the fact that in reality there is here only one entity, *and conspiracy needs a combination of two entities.* If two companies, both controlled by the same person, combine to cause another person harm, there is a difference since there are now *two separate entities — the two companies —* which have acted in combination. Now it would, of course, be possible for a court to hold that, in spite of this fact, the phenomenon of their being controlled by one person renders their apparently separate identities illusory; but a court is not *obliged* so to hold as a result of holding that a single company and its controller should be treated as one. The separate identity of two companies is a different question from the separate identity of a company and its controller. On the basis that a company and its controller should be treated as a single person for the purpose of the tort of conspiracy, a court might well conclude that two or more companies, controlled by that person, should be similarly treated; but it is difficult convincingly to argue in the reverse order.

VALUATION OF SHAREHOLDING

In *In re Clubman Shirts Ltd* [1991] ILRM 43 (High Court 1990), O'Hanlon J returned to the issue of how a shareholding should be valued where O'Hanlon J had ordered that the majority shareholders who had resisted a petition for relief under s. 205 of the Companies Act 1963 to buy out the petitioner's shareholding at a valuation based on the true value of the shares when the company had been transferred to new owners in 1980: [1983] ILRM 323. In a judgment on 8 June 1988, O'Hanlon J addressed procedural aspects of this valuation.

Briefly, the background to the case was that the company had fallen into serious financial difficulties, to the extent that, in spite of Foir Teoranta's assistance, the company's bankers were intending to appoint a receiver. After extended negotiations, a rescue package was put together whereby the company would transfer to new owners all its disclosed liabilities and assets, its liabilities would be discharged and the jobs of its three hundred employees secured. The shareholders under this arrangement would waive their claims to any payment for their shares. The petitioner was the sole objector to this solution. Under the new regime one of the directors of the old company became an executive director and apparently acquired a franchise formerly held by the old company.

Having granted the petitioner relief in the basis of the value of his shares at the time of the new owners, O'Hanlon J was later requested to assess their value. Adopting a *dictum* of Oliver LJ in *In re Bird Precision Bellows Ltd* [1985] 3 All ER 523, at 529 he proceeded on the basis that the court had a wide discretion to have regard to all the circumstances of the particular case when arriving at what it considers to be a fair value.

The evidence indicated that at the time of the transfer the company was very near collapse. The hope for its survival was to do as had been done. The alternative was the appointment of a receiver and 'the scenario was one pointing to liquidation thereafter'. In the circumstances the petitioner's shares should not be valued on the basis that the company was a going concern; they were unsaleable in the open market and had no value if assessed on a dividend yield or earnings yield basis. The petitioner therefore had to fall back on a net asset valuation basis to support a claim for payment.

The expert adviser appointed by the Court had assessed the shares value at £1.96 per share on the basis that, after the rescue package the threatened appointment of the receiver had receded. O'Hanlon J thought it better to proceed on a different basis. While the business had survived,in that the manufacturing process continued to operate and the employees' jobs were saved, the original company had '[gone] to the wall just as significantly as if it had been put into liquidation'. The price it had to pay for release from its disclosed liabilities had been to divest itself of all its assets so that all that remained at the end of the day was a 'shell' company. It had ceased to be a viable company in its own right. The valuation criterion was thus that of its 'break up' value.

O'Hanlon J had some difficulty in assessing the value of the shares, having regard to deficiencies in the evidence as the valuation of stock and the subsequent history of the business after the 1980 deal had been carried into effect. He regarded evidence of these matters as relevant when attempting to assess whether the directors had been justified in the decision to give away the entire business of the company, with no financial gain whatever coming back to the shareholders.

O'Hanlon J commented:

> On the one hand it seems unfair that all the other shareholders should be left with worthless pieces of paper in their hands while the petitioner should receive a substantial sum of money for his shares. On the other hand, none of the other shareholders who have lost out in the process have told the court of their motivation for accepting the arrangement which was made on their behalf.

O'Hanlon J assessed the value of the petitioner's shares at 60p per share (without interest, as he considered that this figure might 'err on the side of generosity').

WINDING UP

1 Grounds for application for winding up Two of the grounds on which a company may be wound up by the court are, first, that the court is of opinion that it would be just and equitable that this should be done (Companies Act 1963, s. 213(f)) and, second, that the court is satisfied that the company's affairs are being conducted in a manner oppressive to any member or in disregard of his interests as a member and that winding up would be justified by the general circumstances of the case (*id.*, s. 213(g)). In *In re Dublin and Eastern Regional Tourism Organisation Ltd* [1990] 1 IR 579, Costello J had to consider the application of these grounds to an environment where commercial issues merged with broader issues of national socio-economic policy.

Bord Fáilte Éireann, the petitioner, was established by the Oireachtas to put forward and promote a proper policy for tourism in Ireland and to encourage and promote its development. To assist it in carrying out these statutory duties, Dublin and Eastern Regional Tourism Organisation Ltd was established. Bord Fáilte Éireann was a principal shareholder in this company, whose memorandum and articles of association stated that its object was to promote the development of tourism in accordance with the policies and directions of Bord Fáilte Éireann and to co-ordinate with it.

Disagreement arose between the chairman and some other members of the company, on the one hand, and Bord Fáilte Éireann on the other, as to how best to carry out the policies for the development of tourism in the Dublin area.

Bord Fáilte Éireann successfully petitioned for a winding up of the company on grounds (f) and (g). Costello J stressed that this was 'a unique type of company . . . established in the public interest by Parliament to carry out certain public functions'. The company's memorandum and articles of association, in clearly stating the object of the company in terms of promoting the development of tourism and in spelling out the requirement of compliance with the policies and direction of the petitioner, and of co-ordination with it, placed the responsibility of members of the company in 'a completely different position' to that of members or directors of a company engaged in commerce.

The petitioner had a statutory function; it was not the court's function to consider whether the policies which the petitioner conceived as necessary to carry out its functions were correct.

The disagreement had led to the proceedings because the company could not carry out its statutory duties. In these circumstances, Costello J concluded that the company was no longer able to continue to pursue the purposes for which it had been incorporated and that it would be just and equitable to wind it up.

In taking this approach, Costello J echoed earlier caselaw to the effect that it may be 'just and equitable' to wind a company up on the basis of crippling disharmony at board level, without having to investigate and adjudicate upon the source and rights and wrongs of this state of affairs. The mere fact, however, that the there was an element of public policy in the rationale for a company's existence should not *require* a court, inevitably, to make an order for winding up. As Costello J pointed out, it is not the function of the court to adjudicate on the merits of policy options; But this does not mean that the context of a disagreement involving companies of this type will inevitably be outside the range of justiciability.

Costello J went on to hold that a case for winding up had also been made out on ground (g). While that ground was frequently used when there was an allegation of oppression of a minority, the facts of the instant case were very exceptional in that the directors of the company were carrying out a quasi-public function under the overall direction of the petitioner, its principal shareholder, whose role in the company was a predominant one. The evidence established that the affairs of the company were being conducted by the chairman and a small group of members who were 'sufficient to stop resolutions being passed in the interests of the proper development of tourism' and that they were doing this in disregard of the interests of the petitioner.

Perhaps it could be argued that, whereas a 'no-fault', non- intrusive judicial approach may be appropriate to *ground (f)* in cases of serious disharmony among members of the board of a company with public rather than strictly commercial functions to discharge, there is reason to hesitate before adopting the same approach in respect of *ground (g)*. If, without seeking to enter into the actual merits of the instant case, we assume for the purposes of argument that the chairman and members of similar viewpoint favoured an approach which was capable of being shown empirically to be preferable to that of the petitioner, and sought to effectuate that approach as energetically as they could, this could hardly amount to disregard of the interests of the petitioner. It is one thing to fail to have regard to another's interests; it is another to have a genuine disagreement with another as to what is the best approach to take towards matters of common concern. Costello J rightly emphasised the fact that the role of the petitioner in the company was designed to be, and was accepted as, a predominant one. Having regard to this factor, there comes a point when adherence to a point of view (however strongly believed in and, indeed, however preferable it may be) must give way to the point of view of a predominant party, in order to effectuate the object of the company. But the point remains worth noting (though not crucial on the facts of this case) that, even in relation to companies with a public policy dimension, a winding up on ground (f) does not *necessarily* entail a winding up on ground (g) as well.

2 Fraudulent Preference In *Parkes (John C.) & Sons Ltd (In Liquidation) v Hong Kong and Shanghai Banking Corporation* [1990] ILRM 341, the owner of one company had control over a second company, the claimant in the proceedings. After a fire in the claimant's premises, the owner transferred its business to the first company's premises. The first company owed the respondent bank £200,000. The owner guaranteed its indebtedness up to this sum with the respondent. It ceased trading shortly afterwards and its entire stock was purchased by the claimant. The respondent continued to press for repayment of the debt. The owner promised that the first company would deposit the title deeds of his premises with the respondent as soon as a prior charge had been released and that the claimant would guarantee the amount due. The proceeds of the sale of the claimant's former premises were to be used to repay the amount owed to the respondent. The charge was in due course paid, but the sale of the site of the claimant's former premises was delayed by a difficulty over title. The respondent informed the owner that it was not prepared to continue to support the first company unless it obtained a guarantee from the claimant supported by a mortgage over the claimant's site. Three days later, the guarantee and mortgage were executed. Both the claimant and the first company were insolvent on this date. In consideration of this security the respondent agreed not to call in the loan for a further four and half months, provided interest was paid. Six weeks after this period had expired, a petition for the winding up of the claimant on the grounds of insolvency was successfully presented. Questions arose as to whether the claimant's guarantee of the first company was a fraudulent preference under s. 286 of the Companies Act 1963, whether the mortgage was similarly a fraudulent preference, and whether the creation of both was *ultra vires* the claimant.

Blayney J answered all of these three questions in the negative. As to the first, where (as here) a third party paid a creditor of an insolvent company in circumstances where this would have constituted a fraudulent preference if made by the company itself, the payment could not be a fraudulent preference because it was not made by the company but by a third party.

Blayney J considered that the guarantee and mortgage constituted a single security, which could have been created by a single deed. The fact that it was not was irrelevant, since the course of drawing up two deeds had been adopted merely for convenience.

Blayney J went on to hold that, even if the creation of the mortgage could have been a fraudulent preference, the owner's dominant motive had been to save the claimant company rather than to prefer the respondent.

As to the third question, Blayney J was of the view that the guarantee and mortgage had not been *ultra vires* the company. These were based on consideration, which consisted of the giving of time for a period of months. The fact that the company was insolvent at the time they were made did not mean that any disposition of its assets by the company was *ultra vires*: if it were, it would mean that s. 286 of the Companies Act 1963 and its statutory predecessors would have been unnecessary as the dispositions could and would have been void on the basis that the company was insolvent at the time they were made. While a disposition in such circumstances might constitute a breach of duty on the part of the directors, it did not follow that it would be *ultra vires* the company. In the present case there was no evidence that the owner knew that the company was insolvent when he engaged in these transactions.

In *In re Frederick Inns Ltd (in liquidation)* [1991] ILRM 582, Lardner J was requested by the liquidator of a holding company and a number of subsidiaries, all of them insolvent, to determine whether it had been proper from them to make payments to the Revenue Commissioners in partial discharge of each other's tax liabilities. The companies had been trading for several years under the shadow of the threat of being wound up on the application of the Revenue Commissioners, to whom they owed substantial amounts. An agreement was worked out whereby a number of public houses belonging to separate subsidiaries would be sold and the money realised would be apportioned between the companies in the group in accordance with their respective shares of the group's total tax liabilities.

Lardner J held that this solution broke a number of basic rules of company law. First, insofar as the payments by any of these companies exceeded their liabilities for tax and were intended to be applied in reduction of the tax liabilities of other companies in the group, they could only be regarded as voluntary payments without consideration for the benefit of third parties and, in the absence of any evidence that these excess payments were for the benefit of the paying companies they were 'clearly *ultra vires*'. It was not possible to treat the tax liabilities of the separate companies as though it were a group liability.

Secondly, these gratuitous payments had been made when the companies were insolvent. It had not been contended that they amounted to fraudulent preferences, the necessary proof of dominant purpose to prefer the Revenue being difficult to establish, in Lardner J's view. (This seems clearly correct: the pressures under which the companies made the arrangement were surely such as to deny them the freedom of choice that is essential to the making of a fraudulent preference). Nevertheless, Lardner J considered that the payments had been made in breach of the duty which the company and the directors owed to the general creditors of the insolvent companies.

S. 8 of the Companies Act 1963 did not assist the Revenue Commissioners since, even if the companies had been empowered by their Memoranda and Articles to make gratuitous payments for the benefit of third parties out of their assets (which clearly was not the case), no such power extended to the situation where the companies were insolvent.

In the circumstances, Lardner J held that the Revenue Commissioners had received and held the payments as trustees on a constructive trust for the payer companies and that their purported appropriation in reduction of the tax liabilities of other companies in the group was a breach of trust. He considered that the action for money had and received lay against the Revenue Commissioners at the suit of the holding company with regard to the sum that exceeded its tax liabilities. Evidence had not been directed to what the Revenue Commissioners had done with the payments they received and Larder J adjourned consideration of this aspect to enable this to be done and for further argument, if this should be necessary.

As far as the subsidiaries were concerned, since the amounts they owed the Revenue exceeded the amounts of the payments they had diverted to either members of the group, the solution was to credit these amounts in reduction of their tax debts.

Conflict of Laws

FOREIGN ADOPTIONS

The question of the recognition of foreign adoptions has not generated much litigation over the years in Ireland: see Binchy, *Irish Conflicts of Law* (1988) 372-6. For this reason, MacKenzie J's decision in *M.F. v An Bord Uchtála* [1991] ILRM 399 (High Court, 1987) (*ex tempore*), is of considerable interest. The facts are unusual. A young unmarried Irish woman had given birth to a child in August 1973 when she was seventeen. She had gone to England during her pregnancy in March of that year, to avoid the 'strident social stigma' then attracting to unmarried motherhood. She had given the child the surname of the natural father, whom she hoped she might marry. After the birth this relationship had come to an end. She had returned to live in Ireland with her child in February 1974. On the advice of a social worker she adopted the child in England primarily to avoid the effect of the legal states of illegitimacy. She had applied for this adoption order while still in England. It was made in October 1974. Three years later she married a man who was not the child's father. She and her husband applied to An Bord Uchtála to adopt the child.

An Bord Uchtála was faced with a private international question on which there was no clear Irish authority. It could make an adoption order only if the child was illegitimate or an orphan. Clearly the child had been born illegitimate but did Irish private international law recognise the change of status brought about by the English adoption order? MacKenzie J was content to adopt the English rules for the recognition of foreign adoptions, as set out in Dicey & Morris's *Conflict of Laws*, 10th ed., rule 69(3), at pp 495-496, to the effect that recognition should be afforded to an adoption obtained in the foreign country where, at the time of the adoption, the adoptive parent was domiciled.

Applying this test, MacKenzie J concluded that the English adoption should not be recognised. The mother had returned to Ireland as soon as she felt the stigma had passed. She had had no intention of making England her home. She had at all times retained her domicile of origin. Accordingly An Bord Uchtála was free to make an adoption order in relation to the child.

MacKenzie J also made it plain that, in the exercise of its statutory functions, An Bord Uchtála was entitled to come to legal conclusions on facts it decided. These legal conclusions could extend to the question whether a foreign adoption would be recognised under Irish private international law. Like any other statutory body, such decisions might be 'subject to review in the courts'.

The case raises interesting issues as to the *purpose* of recognition rules in relation to foreign adoptions. Lawyers unfamiliar with private international law can tend to be bemused by the formidable technical complexities of the concept of domicile and lose sight of the fact that domicile is no more than a connecting factor considered best suited to link a person with the most appropriate legal system to deal with his or her *long-term* interests, such as relate to personal status, marriage and divorce, for example. Far from being an unthinking dictator, domicile should be the servant of the law; if its application yields unjust or otherwise inappropriate results in particular contexts, then it is time to look again at the strategy of automatically referring to it for the answer rather wring one's hands. MacKenzie J's consideration of the English Court of Appeal decision of *In re Valentine's Settlement: Valentine v Valentine* [1965] Ch 831 evinces some degree of unhappiness with the effects of a domicile-based test in this context. Perhaps the best solution is to review any recognition rules of a mechanical nature which carry with them the likelihood of inappropriate results in a significant range of instances.

The matter may be considered moot in view of the enactment of the Adoption Act 1991, which sets out a long list of grounds for recognition of foreign adoptions. Nevertheless, in the context of the particular issue raised in *M.F. v An Bord Uchtála* it is worth giving some attention. (The 1991 Act has its own difficulties, of a constitutional nature: we will discuss them in the 1991 Review.)

Recognition rules in relation to adoption are difficult to determine because of the wide range of factual permutations that can occur and the complex and potentially conflicting social policy issues that must be confronted. For our private international law to *fail* to recognise a foreign adoption may result in hardship to a child (or, as the years pass, an adult) whose long-term connections are clearly Irish. Yet too broad a range of recognition rules would be unjust to natural parents and in some instances their children, as well as raising issues of justice as between the peoples of rich and poor nations. This latter concern is a real one, as the sad state of the trafficking in Romanian children has shown.

Three quite different types of situations may arise. In the first, the adopters and the child share a common attachment to a particular country, whether on account of domicile, habitual residence or nationality. Here, assuming that that attachment is considered sufficiently strong to warrant the application of the law of that country to the adoption, it is relatively easy to be generous with rules of recognition (subject, of course, to constitutional and public policy limitations). In the second situation, the adopters and the child do *not* share a common attachment to a particular country. This is the classic 'inter-country adoption'. Here, recognition rules are hard to devise, as the potential for injustice is high. There are less than fully convincing arguments in favour of (i) applying the adopters' *lex domicilii*, (ii) applying the child's *lex domicilii* or (iii) applying a cumulative test: see the 1989 Review, 81-2. In the third situation, which arose in *M.F. v An Bord Uchtála*, the adoption takes place abroad in a country with which neither the adopters nor the child have any close connection (such as domicile) but they have a close connection with Ireland. In *M.F. v An Bord Uchtála*, the mother was (it seems safe to assume) an Irish national; she was domiciled at all times in Ireland; whether her soujourn in England constituted habitual residence may perhaps be debated but, at all events, she was not habitually resident there when the adoption order was made. The child was of Irish domicile.

The 1974 adoption was unusual in that it involved no third party. In no sense, therefore did it raise the difficult policy issues that affect adoption where the adopters do not share a common attachment to a particular country. Adoption by the child's mother is also permitted under Irish domestic law. The real question in this case had nothing to do with the mechanical application of domicile-based recognition rules. The situation was clear and simple. Under Irish domestic adoption law, if a mother adopts her child and then marries a man who is not the father, it is not possible for her and her husband thereafter to adopt the child. Whether the policy underlying this rule is correct may be debated but there is at least no argument that this rules applies to all such adoptions. If, when the mother in *M.F. v An Bord Uchtála* had adopted her child in England, she had intended to stay there but had later changed her mind and returned to Ireland, what policy could justify her being *prevented* from later joining her husband in adopting her child while an equally lawful adoption made in England by her when still domiciled *in Ireland* should be *ineffective* in preventing her from doing what she could not have done had she adopted the child in Ireland or in England when domiciled there? The answer is surely that there is no policy justifying this anomalous and arbitrary result.

When private international law rules yield an outcome so indefensible as this, it is surely time to contemplate their reform. One need not be a slavish follower of Cavers to express concern about the inadequacy of 'jurisdiction-selecting' rules in this context. Adoption law contains a significant element of public policy: in Currie's lexicon, the governmental interests on some aspects of the subject are tangible and should not be ignored in the formulation of conflicts strategies. Perhaps the court should seek to identify the policies underlying the domestic prohibition on the re-adoption of a child who has been adopted by its mother. Having done this, it should attempt to determine whether those policies would be served or frustrated by the mechanical application of a domicile-based conflicts rule. It is frankly difficult to see how they could be served in any way by a rule which lets an Irish mother's *tenuous* connection with the country where the adoption occurs result in the *non*-application of the domestic prohibition while a *strong* connection on her part with the foreign country will result in the *application* to her case of the domestic prohibition.

INTERNATIONAL ROAD TRANSPORT

The International Carriage of Goods by Road Act 1990 enables Ireland to accede to the *Convention on the Contract for the International Carriage of Goods by Road*, generally known as CMR, from its French title: *Convention Relative au Contrat de Transport International de Marchadises par Route*. See para 1 of the helpful Explanatory and Financial Memorandum published by the Department of Tourism and Transport with the Bill as initiated, and D.M. Day, *The Law of International Trade* (1981), 89-92.

The Convention is the subject of a very useful and detailed text: D.J. Hill & A.D. Messent, *CMR: Contracts for the International Carriage of Goods by Road* (Lloyd's of London Press, 1984).

The Convention was opened for signature in 1956 under the aegis of the United Nations Economic Commission for Europe; it came into force in 1961. There are now twenty four Contracting Parties to the Convention; Ireland is the last Member State of the European Communities to join. The thirteen non-EC States are Austria, Bulgaria, Czechoslavakia, Finland, the German Democratic Republic (prior to its incorporation into a United Germany), Hungary, Norway, Poland, Romania, Sweden, Switzerland, the USSR and Yugoslavia.

Of these twenty four States all but six (Bulgaria, Czechoslovakia, Hungary, Poland, the USSR and Yugoslavia) are also Contracting Parties to a 1978 Protocol substituting units of account (for example Special Drawing Rights of the International Monetary Fund) for francs in the limit on the account of damages under the Convention: see the International Carriage of Goods by Road Act 1990 (CMR Contracting Parties) Order 1991 (SI No. 160 of 1991). The Convention, as amended by the Protocol, entered into force for the State on 1 May 1991, the same date as the Act came into operation: International Carriage of Goods by Road Act 1990 (Commencement) Order 1991 (SI No. 22 of 1991).

The Convention sets out standard conditions of contract for international carriage of goods by road, it prescribes the respective rights and obligations of the consignor, carrier and consignee, spelling out in detail the circumstances and quantum of liability of the carrier. The Convention applies to carriage into or from a CMR State, regardless of where the carriage originates or ends. It does not, however, apply to carriage solely between the State and Britain or Northern Ireland. Uniquely the 1956 Protocol of Signature to the Convention agreed by the State and Britain, but not signed by these parties, provided for this exclusion, apparently to avoid any additional burden for hauliers concerned: 399 Dáil Debs, col. 1263 (1 June 1990). With the forthcoming completion of the EC Internal Market according to uniform rules, this exception had a limited future. It seems that before the 1990 legislation, the practice was to apply the Convention on a voluntary basis to carriage between the State and Britain or Northern Ireland, especially in relation to the carriage of perishables: *id.* The 1990 Act does not abolish the exception since a change in the British legislation is also necessary. S. 9(2)(b) of the Act enables this change to be effected by order of the Minister for Tourism and Transport. Support for this course of action (and for the legislation generally) was received from representative organisations of Irish hauliers and the British authorities raised no objection: *id.*

Scope of application   The Convention's scope of application can be sketched briefly. It applies to contracts for the carriage of goods by road in vehicles for reward when the place of taking over the goods and the place designated for delivery are situated in two different countries, of which (as we have seen) one must be a contracting country, irrespective of the place of residence and nationality of the parties: Article 1, para 1. It also applies where the vehicle containing the goods is carried over part of the journey by sea, rail, inland waterways or air, provided the goods are not unloaded from the vehicle (except where circumstances make it impossible to complete carriage in accordance with the conditions laid down in the consignment note): Article 2, para 1. The Convention applies where carriage coming within its scope is carried out by States or by Governmental institutions or organisations: Article 1, para 3.

The Convention does not apply to (a) carriage performed under the terms of any international postal convention; (b) financial consignments; or (c) furniture removal: Article 1, para 4.

The consignment note   The consignment note plays a crucial part in the operation of the Convention. The contract of carriage must be confirmed by the making out of a consignment note (Article 4) in three original copies signed by sender or carrier (Article 5, para 1). (These signatures may be printed or replaced by the stamps of the sender and carrier if the law of the country in which the consignment note has been made out so permits (Article 5, para 1)). The first copy is handed to the sender, the second accompanies the goods and the third is retained by the carrier (*id.*). Article 6 sets out the particulars which the consignment note must contain: these relate to identifying the parties, describing the goods, specifying relevant charges, and prescribing requisite instructions for Customs and insurance.

On taking over the goods, the carrier must, so far as is reasonably possible, check the accuracy of the statements in the consignment note as to the number of packages and their marks and numbers and the apparent condition of the goods and their packaging; if he has no reasonable means of checking the accuracy of these statements, or the apparent condition of the goods and packaging he is to enter his reservations in the consignment note. These reservations do not bind the sender unless he has expressly agreed to be bound by them in the consignment note: Article 8, para 2.

The consignment note is *prima facie* evidence of the making of the contract, the conditions of the contract and the receipt of the goods by the carrier: Article 9, para 1. If it contains no specific reservation by the carrier, it is presumed, unless the contrary is proved, that the goods and packaging appeared to be in good condition when the carrier took them over and that the number of packages, their marks and numbers corresponded with the statements in the consignment note: Article 9, para 2.

Defective packing   Article 10 provides that the sender is liable to the carrier for damage to persons, equipment or other goods, and for any expenses due to defective packing of the goods, unless the defect was apparent or known to the carrier at the time when he took over the goods and he made no reservation concerning it. It should be noted that this article imposes no liability on the sender relative to *third parties*.

Customs and other formalities   Article 11 deals with cases where documents are required for the purposes of Customs or other formalities. The sender must attach the necessary documents to the consignment note or place them at the disposal of the carrier and furnish him with all the information he requires. The carrier is not under any duty to enquire into either the accuracy or the adequacy of the documents or the information. The sender is liable to the carrier for any damages caused by the absence, inadequacy or irregularity of the documents and information, save in the case of some wrongful act or neglect on the part of the carrier. Since the carrier is not under any obligation to provide or check the relevant documentation, and this position cannot be overridden by any contractual stipulation to the contrary (cf. Article 41), the only circumstance in which the carrier could be guilty of a wrongful act of default in this context would appear to be where the carrier either misused or mislaid the documentation or information with which he was provided: see Hill & Messent, *op. cit.*, 49-50.

It appears that liability as agent here embraces liability to the sender or (after he acquires the right of disposal of the goods) the consignee for any negligence: Hill & Messent, *op. cit.*, 50.

The right of disposal   Article 12 deals with the right to dispose of the goods, in particular by asking the carrier to stop the goods in transit, to change the place at which delivery is to take place or to deliver the goods to a consignee other than is indicated in the consignment note. The key moment is *when the second consignment note is handed to the consignee:* before then the consignor has the right of disposal, afterwards the consignee: Article 12, para 2.

Disposal of goods on delivery   Article 13(1) provides that, after arrival of the goods at the place designated for delivery (cf. Article 6(d)), the consignee may require the carrier to deliver to him, against a receipt, the second copy of the consignment note and the goods. If the goods are lost or have not arrived which the period specified by Article 19, the consignee may enforce in his own name against the carrier any rights arising from the contract of carriage.

Article 13(2) requires the consignee who avails himself of the rights granted under Article 13(1) to pay the charges shown to be due on the consignment note; in the event of dispute on this matter the carrier is not required to deliver the goods unless the consignee has furnished security. (Hill & Messent, *op. cit.*, 57, criticise the absoluteness of this requirement).

Impossibility in relation to the carriage   Article 14(1) deals with the situation arising where for any reason it is (or becomes) impossible to carry out the contract in accordance with the terms laid down in the consignment note before the goods reach the place designated for delivery. In these circumstances the carrier must ask for instructions from the person entitled to dispose of the goods in accordance with Article 12. If the carrier fails to do this and acts on his own initiative, 'he will be liable for any loss, whether or not he acted reasonably: the provisions of CMR operate to deprive him of any degree of implied agency or the like': Hill & Messent, *op. cit.*, 59.

If, however, the circumstances allow the carriage to be carried out under conditions differing from those laid down in the consignment note and if the carrier has been unable to obtain instructions in reasonable time from the person entitled to dispose of the goods in accordance with Article 12, he must take such steps as seem to him to be in the best interests of the person entitled to the goods: Article 14(2).

Impossibility in relation to delivery of the goods Article 15 deals with the situation where circumstances prevent delivery of the goods after their arrival at the place designated for delivery. The carrier must ask the sender for his instructions. If the consignee refuses the goods, the sender is entitled to dispose of them without being obliged to produce the first copy of the consignment note: subs. (1). Even if he has refused the goods, the consignee may nevertheless require delivery so long as the carrier has not received contrary instructions from the sender: subs. (2). When circumstances preventing delivery of the goods arise after the consignee, in exercise of his right of disposal under Article 12(3), has given an order for the goods to be delivered to another person, Article 16(1) and (2) apply as if the consignee were the sender and the third party were the consignee: subs. (3).

Expenses The carrier is entitled to recover the cost of his request for instructions and any expenses entailed in carrying out these instructions, unless the expenses were caused by his own wilful act or neglect: Article 16(1).

Unloading and storing the goods Article 16(2) deals with the situation where the carrier is prevented from performing the contract of carriage in accordance with the consignment note under Article 14(1) or from delivering the goods under Article 15: see Hill & Messent, *op cit.*, 62-3. The carrier may immediately unload the goods for account of the person entitled to dispose of them; thereupon the carriage is deemed to be at an end. The carrier then holds the goods on behalf of the person so entitled. He may, however, entrust them to a third party; if he does so, he is not under any liability save for the exercise of reasonable care in the choice of that third party. The charges due under the consignment note and all other expenses remain chargeable against the goods.

Sale of goods by the carrier Article 16(3) permits the carrier to sell the goods, without awaiting instructions from the person entitled to dispose of them, if they are perishable or their condition warrants this course, or when the storage expenses would be out of proportion to the value of the goods. He may also proceed to the sale of the goods in other cases if, after the expiry of a reasonable period, he has not received from the person entitled to dispose of the goods instructions to the contrary which he may reasonably be required to carry out.

If the goods have been sold pursuant to Article 16, the proceeds of sale (after deduction of the expenses chargeable against the goods) are to be placed at the disposal of the person entitled to dispose of the goods: Article 16(4). If these charges exceed the proceeds of sale, the carrier is entitled to the difference: *id*. The procedure in the case of sale is determined by the law or custom of the place where the goods are situated: Article 16(5).

Liability of the carrier   The general rule is that the carrier is strictly liable for the total or partial loss of the goods and for damages thereto occurring between the time he takes over the goods and the time of delivery, as well as for any delay in delivery: Article 17, para 1. (As to delay, see Articles 19 and 20, Hill & Messent, *op. cit.*, chapter 7). The carrier is, however, relieved of liability if he proves (Article 18) that the loss, damage or delay was caused:

(i) by the wrongful act or neglect of the claimant,
(ii) by the instructions of the claimant given otherwise than as the result of a wrongful act or neglect on the part of the carrier,
(iii) by inherent vice of the goods, or
(iv) through circumstances which the carrier could not avoid and the consequences of which he was unable to prevent. (Article 17, para 2).

As a general rule the maximum liability limit for carriers under the Convention is 25 francs per kilogram of gross weight short — approximately £7,000 per metric tonne: see Article 23, para 3 and 399 Dáil Debs, col. 1261. Higher compensation may be claimed only where the value of the goods or a special interest in delivery has been declared by the sender, against payment of an agreed surcharge, in accordance with Articles 24 and 26: see Article 23, para 6, Hill & Messent, *op. cit.*, 143ff.

A claimant is entitled to claim interest at 5% per annum on compensation payable, from the date when the claim was sent in writing to the carrier (or the date on which legal proceedings were issued if no such claim was made): Article 27.

Goods of a dangerous nature   Article 22 deals with goods of a dangerous nature. See Hill & Messent, *op cit.*, chapter 8. Para 1 requires the sender, when handing goods of this type to the carrier, to inform him of the exact nature of the danger and to indicate, if necessary, the precautions to be taken. If this information has not been entered in the consignment note, the burden of proving, by some other means, that the carrier knew the exact nature of the danger rests on the sender or consignee. Para 2 provides that goods of a dangerous nature which the carrier did not know were dangerous may, at any time or place, be unloaded, destroyed or rendered harmless by the carrier without compensation; further, the sender is liable for all expenses loss or damage arising out of their handing over for carriage or of their carriage. S. 3(5) of the 1990 Act requires a carrier who proposes to unload, destroy or render harmless goods pursuant to Article 22, para 2 first to notify the National Authority for Occupational Safety and Health, the local fire authority, the local Gardai and, in the case of any substance known or suspected to be radioactive, the Nuclear Energy Board. The carrier should wait 24 hours after the notification before embarking on his proposed course of action, unless it is not reasonably possible to do this. This statutory requirement is backed by a criminal sanction.

Successive carriers A carrier who has paid compensation in compliance with the provisions of the Convention may recover that compensation from the other carriers who have taken part in the carriage, subject to the rule that the carrier or carriers responsible for the loss or damage are solely liable for the damage; if it cannot be ascertained to which carriers liability is thus attributable, they all share it in proportion to the shares of the payment for the carriage which are due to them: Article 37. In the event of the insolvency of any of them, the share of the compensation due from him and unpaid by him is divided proportionately among the others on the same principle: Article 38. Carriers are free to agree among themselves on provisions other than those laid down in these two articles: Article 40. See below, 139.

Prohibition on contracting-out Apart from Article 40, any stipulation which would directly or indirectly derogate from the provision of the Convention is null and void: Article 41, para 1. An arbitration clause is permissible if the clause conferring competence on the tribunal provides that the tribunal is to apply the Convention: Article 33.

Integration of Convention with Irish domestic legislation S. 3 of the 1990 Act 'marries' the Convention to certain provisions of Irish law. S. 3(1) applies the provision of the Statute of Limitations 1957 regarding extension of limitation periods in cases of fraud, mistake and disability. This is required by Article 32, para 3 of the Convention. S. 3(2) applies Part I and II of the Arbitration Act 1954 to arbitrations in respect of or arising out of carriage to which the Convention applies as if the arbitrations were pursuant to arbitration agreements and as if the Convention were an arbitration agreement, except in so far as Part II of the 1954 Act is inconsistent with the Convention or its authorised rules or procedure. S. 3(3) makes clear that contracts for the carriage of goods falling within the scope of the Convention are not to be affected by the Carriers Act 1830, s. 7 of the Railway and Canal Traffic Act 1854 (limiting the liability of railway companies for loss of or damage to goods or animals), the Sale of Goods Act 1893 and the Sale of Goods and Supply of Services Act 1980. S. 3(4) requires Coras Iompair Éireann (and its subsidiary Iarnrod Éireann) when attaching terms and conditions to a contract of carriage governed by the Convention to conform to the terms and conditions of the Convention for the time being.

Private international law aspects   How does the Convention fit into the rules of Irish private international law? The answer is that its practical effect is to exclude other choice of law options. While the Convention does not expressly rule them out, an Irish court must apply the terms of the Convention as the *lex fori*, regardless of the proper law of the contract of carriage. As Dicey & Morris, *The Conflict of Laws* (11th ed, 1987) p. 1274 observe in relation to equivalent English legislation implementing the Convention, 'since the Convention is, to all intents and purposes, a comprehensive codification of the mutual rights and duties of carrier, sender, and consignee, there is little scope in practice for the application of any other law'. In view of the harmonisation brought about by the Rome Contracts Convention of 1980 and the Contractual Obligations (Applicable Law) Act 1991, the potential for dissonant conflicts rules throughout the Communities is further reduced.

The Convention does not seek to prescribe general private international law rules for delictual liability arising in respect of contracts of carriage to which the Convention applies. It does, however, lay down important limitations on the freedom of States to let this matter be governed by their choice of law rules for tort. Article 28 provides as follows:

> 1. In cases where, under the law applicable, loss, damage or delay arising out of carriage under this Convention gives rise to an extra-contractual claim, the carrier may avail himself of the provisions of this Convention which exclude his liability on which fix or limit the compensation due.

> 2. In cases where the extra-contractual liability for loss, damage or delay of one of the persons for whom the carrier is responsible under the terms of article 3 is in issue, such person may also avail himself of the provisions of this Convention which exclude the liability of the carrier or which fix or limit the compensation due.

Under Article 3, a carrier is vicariously liable for the acts and omissions of his servants, agents and others of whose services he makes use for the performance of the carriage, acting within the scope of their employment.

The effect of para 1 of Article 28 in that even if, under the applicable law of tort, the defendant carrier is fully liable, the defendant will nonetheless be permitted to invoke the provisions of the Convention which exclude or limit his liability. The Convention is concerned only with a carrier's liability 'for the total or partial loss of . . . goods and for damage thereto . . . [and] delay in delivery' Article 17, para 1. Thus a carrier guilty of a tort committed in the course of a carriage to which the Convention applies, causing personal injury or death, such as where a lorry loaded with goods runs over a cyclist, would not be permitted to invoke any limitation of liability contained in the Convention.

As regards para 2 of Article 28, there is much uncertainty in common law jurisdictions as to how to identify the applicable law for vicarious liability. Some commentators have argued that vicarious liability should be based on the proper law of the contract (if any) from which the vicarious liability is derived. Para 2 seems to involve a more radical intermingling of contract and tort. It protects a person who is sued in tort where the carrier is vicariously liable for that person's misconduct under Article 3: the provisions of the Convention excluding or limiting the carrier's liability may be invoked by that person also in defence against that delictual claim. Otherwise the claimant, by suing that person rather than the carrier, could effectively side-step the limitations of liability envisaged by the Convention or exclusion in those cases where Article 3 applies. To allow that would shatter the unity of the principles of vicarious liability and limitation (or exclusion) of liability envisaged by the Convention as a whole.

Article 31 of the Convention deals with jurisdiction. Para 1 provides that, in legal proceedings arising out of carriage under the Convention, the plaintiff may bring an action in any court or tribunal of a contracting country designated by agreement between the parties and, in addition, the courts or tribunals of a country within whose territory:

(a) the defendant is ordinarily resident, or has his principal place of business, or the branch or agency through which the contract was made, or

(b) the place where the goods were taken over by the carrier or the place designated for delivery is situated.

No other courts or tribunals have jurisdiction.

As regards the first of these jurisdictional grounds it should be noted that the agreement need not have been at the time of the making of the contract of carriage. Dicey & Morris, *op cit.*, p. 515 consider that if the designation is in the original contract it would seem to be binding on the consignee of the goods the subject of the contract as the consignee's rights are those 'arising from the contract'. The expression 'arising from the contract' occurs in Article 13, para 1 which, as we have seen, entitles the consignee, in the event of loss of the goods or failure of due delivery, to enforce in his own name against the carrier any rights arising from the contract of carriage. It seems that *Dicey & Morris* are mistaken in suggesting that a choice of jurisdiction between consignor and carrier in the original contracts *binds* the consignee. Even if Article 13 is relevant in the context of choice of jurisdiction it merely *entitles* rather than obliges the consignee to enforce in his own name any rights arising from the contract of carriage. The idea that he should be obliged to submit to a choice of jurisdiction made by the consignor and the carrier, apart from the impracticality and injustice that it could involve, seems unwarranted by the terms of Article 13, para 1.

A further, and crucial difficulty with Dicey & Morris's suggested interpretation in that the reference to 'the parties' in Article 31, para 1 seems capable of referring only to the *plaintiff* and the *defendant* (or defendants); it does not seem capable of also including of also including an agreement made between the defendant and a non)party (the consignor).

It seems that the effect of Article 31 is to enable a plaintiff to ignore, at his option, an *exclusive* jurisdiction agreement properly entered into between him and the defendant and to sue in the courts or tribunals of another country provided this fulfils the jurisdictional requirements of paragraph (a) or (b) of Article 31.

The Act contains no provisions relating to the procedure for asserting jurisdiction under Article 31. On principle it should not be necessary to seek the prior approval of the High Court or the Master before suing out of the jurisdiction. The procedure now available under the amendment to the Rules of the Superior Courts in 1989 to take account of the Jurisdiction of Courts and Enforcement of Judgments (European Communities) Act 1988 would seem appropriate. In England a change was made in the Rules of the Supreme Court to take account of cases such as this: cf. O. 11, r. 1(2)(b) and Dicey & Morris, *op cit.*, Rule 27. It may be desirable for the Rules to be amended on these lines to clarify the position.

Article 31, para 2 gives effect to an approach similar to that of Articles 19 and 20 of the Brussels Judgments Convention. Where in respect of a claim under the 1956 Convention, an action is pending before a court or tribunal with jurisdictional competence or where, in respect of such a claim, a judgment has been entered by that court or tribunal, no new action is to be started between the same parties on the same grounds unless the judgment of the court or tribunal before which the first action was brought is not enforceable in the country where the fresh proceedings are brought.

The provisions relating to recognition and enforcement of judgments are broadly similar to those of the 1988 Act: see Article 31, paras 3-4 and s. 4 of the 1990 Act. Under s. 4, an application for recognition or enforcement must be made to the High Court. Where the law of the Contracting Party in which the award was made or judgment given provides that interest is recoverable at a particular rate, the Irish order may incorporate this aspect into it. (The possibility of divergence as between States on this matter raises the prospect of forum shopping to the limited extent that this is permissible under Article 31, para 1). S. 4(3) requires that an application for recognition or enforcement by the High Court must be accompanied by the following documentation: the original or a certified copy of the award or judgment; the original or a certified copy of a document signed by the arbitrator, judge or an officer of the court stating that the award or judgment is enforceable in the state where it was made or given; in the case of a default award or judgment, the original or a certified copy of a document establishing that due notice of the proceedings was given to the defendant; and, finally, the original or a certified copy of a document establishing that the defendant has received due notice of the award or judgment. S. 5 enables interested parties to a similar set of documents in respect of proceedings taken here.

Chapter VI of the Convention (Articles 34-40) deals with carriage performed by *successive* carriers. See Hill & Messent, *op. cit.*, chapter 11. Article 34 spells out the basic rule: if carriage governed by a single contract is performed by successive road carriers, each is responsible for the performance of the whole operation, the second and each succeeding carrier becoming a party to the contract of carriage, under the terms of the consignment note, by reason of his acceptance of the goods and the consignment note. See further above, 135.

JURISDICTION

The decision of *Taher Meats (Ireland) Ltd v State Company for Foodstuff Trading and Rafidain Bank*, High Court, 18 December 1990 raised interesting and difficult issues relating to jurisdiction. The case involved a dispute between an Irish company, an Iraqi company and an Iraqi bank. The plaintiffs had entered into a contract to supply meat to the Iraqi company, for a price of over 16 million dollars. The contract was made in Iraq and the meat was to be supplied there. The Iraqi company had entered into a guarantee bond with the Iraqi bank whereby the bank was required to pay over 1 million dollars in the event of the plaintiffs' default under the terms of the main contract. Before entering into this guarantee, the bank had obtained a counter-indemnity from an Irish bank in Dublin.

The plaintiffs instituted proceedings against the Iraqi company and the Iraqi bank in Ireland. As against the company they claimed they were not bound by the terms of the contract; as against the bank they sought an injunction preventing it from demanding payment from the Irish bank on foot of the counter-indemnity. Their reason for seeking this injunction was that, if the Irish bank paid the Iraqi bank, the latter would, in turn, seek reimbursement from the plaintiffs.

The plaintiffs had no difficulty with the jurisdictional issue so far as the Iraqi *company* was concerned since the company had accepted the jurisdiction of the Irish courts to determine the dispute relating to the contract. The Iraqi *bank* proved a more formidable adversary in this regard. While the plaintiffs obtained an order from Barrington J for service out of the jurisdiction under O. 11, r. 1(e) and (g), the bank applied to Costello J under O. 12, r. 26 to have Barrington J's order set aside.

Costello J rejected this application and upheld Barrington J's order. He first dealt with Order 11, rule 1(e) which permits service out of the jurisdiction whenever 'the action is one brought to enforce, rescind, dissolve, annul, or otherwise affect a contract, or to recover damages or other relief for or in respect of the breach of a contract . . . or is one brought in respect of a breach committed within the jurisdiction of a contract wherever made ...'. See Binchy, *op. cit.*, 144-7. Costello J was satisfied that the plaintiffs could invoke this ground because there had been a breach of the contract committed within the State. The Iraqi company had been required to make available certain letters to credit under the contract. Whilst it was true that the contract had not specifically provided that the letters of credit were to be opened in Ireland, in at least one instance they had been so opened. Therefore, if the plaintiffs were correct in their contention, they would have established that the Iraqi company's breach of contract had occurred within the jurisdiction. There had admittedly been no breach within the jurisdiction by the Iraqi bank of the contract into which *it* had entered. But, said Costello J,

> the contract between the plaintiffs and the [Iraqi bank] is ancillary to the main contract, namely, the supply contract. No claim on foot of this ancillary contract could be made if the principal contract is unenforceable by the [Iraqi company]. So it seems to me that the link between the two contracts is very close and is such as to give the Irish Court jurisdiction to determine the issues under the ancillary contract when a breach in this jurisdiction of the main contract has been raised as an issue in the proceedings.

This analysis raises two questions, one more important than the other. The first, and less important, question is whether the *main* contract had been *broken* in Ireland. The basis on which Costello J appeared to find a breach was that of non-performance of an obligation which ought to have been performed here: see Binchy, *op. cit.*, 144-7. In order for this ground to be established, it is not sufficient to show that a particular obligation had, as a matter of fact, been performed here on occasions prior to its non-performance here: it is essential to show that the contract *required* its performance here. Now it is true that most contracts do not specify in express terms where particular obligations are to be performed; it is quite sufficient for this intention to be gleaned from the circumstances of the case, including a course of dealing between the parties: see *O'Mara Ltd v Dodd* [1912] 2 IR 55 (KB Div, Kenny J, 1911). In assessing the proper inferences to be drawn from a course of dealing, it would be wrong to infer too easily from the fact that an obligation happens to have been performed within the jurisdiction that there was an obligation that it be performed here and *nowhere* else. Applying these principles to *Taher Meats*, they would justify the finding of a breach within the jurisdiction if the finding of the court was that there was an *obligation* to open letters of credit here. This appears to be at least consistent with Costello J's holding.

The more important question is whether, if parties, together or with others, make several contracts, where these are closely interconnected so far as the economic relationship and expectations of the parties are concerned, the breach of the most important contract in Ireland entitles the court to make an order for service out of the jurisdiction under O. 11, r. (1)(e) with regard to a dispute between the injured party to that contract and a party to another, related, contract. There may be excellent sense and justice in doing so, but the language of the rule does not appear to warrant it. Rightly or wrongly, O. 11 must be treated as being 'obviously exhaustive — *expressio unius est exclusio alterius*; it plainly deals with the only subjects of suit in which leave can be given to serve personally out of the jurisdiction': *O'Connor v The Star Newspaper Co. (Ltd)*, 30 LR Ir 1, at 4 (QB Div, *per* O'Brien CJ, 1891). This view represents the dominant one among the judiciary (see Binchy, *op. cit.*, 133) though there is the odd statement supporting a broader approach to extend the net to catch cases 'clearly within the spirit of the rules where there is a question of substance to be determined, which really ought to be, on analogy at least to the rest of the rules, submitted to the Irish Courts, and where no reason to the contrary, founded on convenience, [is] alleged': *Russell v Le Bert* [1896] 1 IR 334, at 339 (Porter MR, 1895). *Taher* may be considered just such a case.

Costello J was of the view that the court had jurisdiction also under O. 11, r. 1(g), which empowers the court to make an order for service out of the jurisdiction where 'any injunction is sought as to anything to be done within the jurisdiction. . . . whether damages are or are not also sought in respect thereof'. It seemed to him that the claim against the Iraqi bank fell squarely within the terms of this rule. The claim was not of an ancillary nature in respect of a substantive claim which the defendant could not be required to meet within the jurisdiction (as in *Caudron v Air Zaire* [1986] ILRM 6; [1985] IR 716, Binchy, *op. cit.*, 153-145). Here the claim was of a substantive nature. Moreover, the injunction sought against the Iraqi bank related to 'something to be done within the jurisdiction', namely, the payment in this jurisdiction by the Irish bank of a sum of money to the Iraqi bank. Perhaps a more convincing identification of what had to be done here would be the Iraqi bank's demand for payment from the Irish bank on foot of the indemnity. The injunction which the plaintiffs sought was to prevent that act; it was not against the Irish bank at all.

Two problems arise in this context. First there is the metaphysical debate as to whether the making of a demand by the Iraqi bank on the Irish bank should be located in Iraq (where it is transmitted) or in Dublin (where it is received). Secondly, and more substantially, it might be argued that O. 11, r. 1(g) should not be invoked where, in reality, the remedy sought is ancillary to another grievance with another party. There is a slight dissonance in the identification of the Iraqi bank's contract as ancillary for the purposes of O. 11, r. 1(e) and the rejection of its ancillary status for the purposes of O. 11, r. 1(g). It is clear that relief in respect of an ancillary contract is not necessarily to be characterised as ancillary for the purposes of O. 11, r. 1(g); but the truth of the matter is that the plaintiffs' claim against the Iraqi bank was very much ancillary to their claim against the Iraqi company.

The final issue in the case was one involving judicial discretion. The plaintiffs and the Iraqi bank had agreed in their contract that the Iraqi courts should have jurisdiction. (Costello J's reference to 'the parties' here embraces at least these two parties but the context suggests that the agreement as to jurisdiction may also have included the resolution of disputes arising under the contractual relationship between the plaintiffs and the Iraqi company.) Costello J was quite satisfied that the case was a proper one in which the Irish court should assume jurisdiction. The Iraqi bank accepted that no claim against it by the Iraqi company on foot of the performance guarantee could arise if the plaintiffs' claim succeeded. The Iraqi company had accepted the jurisdiction of the Irish courts to determine the dispute relating to the main contract. It seemed to Costello J, therefore, that it would be contrary to the proper administration of justice that the Irish courts should relinquish jurisdiction to a foreign court to determine the same issue which was going to be determined, properly, in the Irish courts.

Whilst the particular circumstances of this case may be considered to support the assertion of Irish jurisdiction in the face of a specific choice by the parties of the courts of another jurisdiction, there is perhaps reason to hesitate before endorsing any over-zealous assertion of jurisdiction by our courts in the face of party autonomy. It is one thing to ensure that our courts do not too easily disavow a jurisdiction selected by the parties (cf. *Kutchera v Buckingham International Holdings Ltd* [1988] ILRM 501, [1988] IR 61 (Supreme Court), analysed in the 1988 Review, 84-9); it is quite another that our courts, on the grounds of practical convenience, should override the free choice of the parties.

ORDINARY RESIDENCE

In *Quinn v Waterford Corporation* [1991] ILRM 433; [1990] 2 IR 507, which we discuss in detail in the Constitutional Law Chapter, below, pp. 175-6, the Supreme Court endorsed the views of the judges of the former Supreme Court in *The State (Goertz) v Minister for Justice* [1948] IR 45 that the expression 'ordinarily resident' was to be construed in its ordinary meaning, with the aid of such light as is thrown on it by the general intention of the legislation, and that it involved no more than that the residence was not casual or uncertain, the addition of the word 'ordinarily' to 'resident' making little difference. Counsel had conceded that this approach was correct. McCarthy J (Finlay CJ and Hederman J concurring) was of the view that this concession had properly been made.

The effect of this definition was that a person might be ordinarily resident in more than one location at the same time. This contrasts, of course, with the concept of domicile, which, in Irish and English law, is a connecting factor of exclusive referential import. See *Shannon Deceased*, 76 ILTR 53, at 54 (NI KB Div, Andrews LCJ, 1942), Binchy, *op. cit.*, 50-1. While Cook argued that domicile is a relative concept, varying in meaning according to the particular contexts in which it is applied (*Logical and Legal Bases of the Conflict of Laws* (1942) 194ff), it would be difficult to find such a clear tendency in the Irish cases over the years, even in such sensitive areas as foreign divorces and annulments.

Constitutional Law

ACCESS TO COURTS

Costs: family law   In *F. v L.* [1990] ILRM 886, Barron J considered the question of the award of costs in a nullity petition: see 322-5, below, in the Family Law chapter.

Legal aid   In *Cosgrove v Legal Aid Board and Ors*, High Court, 17 October 1990 Gannon J rejected the argument that the Constitution recognised a right to civil legal aid. The circumstances of the case were, briefly, that the applicant, who was the respondent in a nullity petition, applied to the respondent Board for civil legal aid in accordance with the non-statutory *Scheme of Civil Legal Aid and Advice* (Prl.8543), laid before the Oireachtas by the Minister for Justice in 1979 and operated by the Board. She applied to the Board for legal aid in November 1989 but no decision was made as to whether her application should be granted. The applicant claimed, inter alia, that her constitutional right of access to the courts was infringed by the failure of the State to provide her with legal aid. Gannon J granted certain declaratory relief to the applicant but rejected in full the constitutional argument.

He stated that the fact that the applicant was the respondent in a nullity petition did not create any duty to her personally by any of the respondents, and that the validity or invalidity of her marriage did not involve the State or any agency of the State. He went on, in an important passage, to comment:

> The State does provide the forum for resolution of such disputes, namely the courts, but without any obligation on her or on the petitioner to have recourse thereto. By contrast criminal matters may be resolved only in the courts as the investigation of crime is a matter of public duty. . . .
>
> The duty of administering justice and adjudicating by due process does not create any obligation on the State to intervene in any private civil litigation so as to ensure that one party is as well equipped for their dispute as is the other. The fact that the existence of fundamental personal rights is expressly recognized by the Constitution does not impose on the State any duty to intervene in aid of a party involved in any private civil dispute in relation to any such personal rights. The temporary exigencies of circumstances special to a particular individual

cannot afford a ground for drawing the State into a civil dispute of a private nature.

By adopting the Scheme for funding Legal Aid and Advice to impecunious litigants the State provides resources to enable such persons to obtain the services of skills adequate to that of an adversary in civil litigation. In my opinion, the adoption of that Scheme does not impose any duty on the State or on the Legal Aid Board to any litigant involved in civil litigation other than to ensure that the Scheme is implemented fairly to all persons and in a manner which fulfils its declared purpose. I am not convinced that there is any provision in the Constitution which imposes a duty on the State to provide any form of support for civil litigation among citizens. In the absence of such duty I can find no express or implied right in any citizen to require the State to provide financial support for, or to afford free facilities for, civil litigation of a dispute with another citizen.

These views invite comment on the nature of the right of access to the courts in Irish constitutional law. First, it can be said that this is the clearest indication that the right of access to the courts does not include a State-backed 'level playing pitch.' Clearly, for Gannon J to have conceded a blanket right to State-funded civil legal aid would have financial implications which might have proved difficult to accept. Such considerations were also to the fore in the judgment of O'Keeffe P in *O'Shaughnessy v Attorney General*, High Court, 16 February 1971, in which a general constitutional right to civil legal aid was rejected.

However, such financial considerations did not prevent the Supreme Court from 'constitutionalising' the Criminal Justice (Legal Aid) Act 1962 in *The State (Healy) v Donoghue* [1976] IR 325. Indeed that decision provides a useful analogy for *Cosgrove*, since Gannon J sought, in the passage quoted, to draw a distinction between civil and criminal disputes. And although he did not do so explicitly, it must be assumed that he was rejecting the analogy (referred to earlier in his judgment) which counsel for the applicant had sought to make between her position and that of the defendants in *Healy*.

Healy is particularly apt because Gannon J was the High Court judge in that case and had, in effect, rejected the constitutional dimension to legal aid in criminal cases for impecunious defendants. In many ways, the approach he took in *Healy* is remarkably reminiscent of the views reflected in the passages quoted above from *Cosgrove*. In *Healy*, Gannon J emphasised the importance of ensuring procedural fairness ('due process') at the trial, but that this could not be taken to include a constitutionally guaranteed right to State-funded legal aid. He was prepared to leave the paramaters of such matters to the Oireachtas. The Supreme Court took a different view, of course.

Nonetheless, the subsequent history of *Healy* is also of interest because an attempt was made shortly after the Supreme Court decision to extend the constitutional reach of access to legal advice into the Garda station. This attempt, in *The People v Farrell* [1978] IR 13, was flatly rejected by the Court of Criminal Appeal. In *Farrell*, O'Higgins CJ (delivering the Court's judgment) took the view that, as far as access to a lawyer was concerned, the courts' constitutional remit did not extend 'back' to the Garda station. He held that the courts should be concerned to ensure that proper procedures were observed, but this did not extend to what might be described as a pro-active right to a lawyer. That also seems to reflect the thinking in *Cosgrove*. It is notable, however, that in *The People v Healy (P.)* [1990] ILRM 313; [1990] 2 IR 73 (1989 Review, 137-9) the Supreme Court was prepared to acknowledge the constitutional origin of the right of access to a lawyer in Garda custody. Significantly, the present Chief Justice in *The People v Healy* linked access to a lawyer with the concept of a 'fundamental standard of fairness in the administration of justice', a phrase which is not, of course, confined to criminal trials but extends to the whole range of functions performed by the judges under the Constitution. It thus seems that the Supreme Court has acknowledged that fair procedures can only be achieved through pro-active rights such as access to a lawyer. To that extent, at least, the judgment of Gannon J in *Cosgrove* seems unduly conservative from the point of view of constitutional jurisprudence.

Whether the courts are prepared to extend the fairness notion to a State-funded right of access to legal advice is, however, another matter. A reticence to become involved in financial/policy issues can be traced back to the judgment of Kenny J in *Ryan v Attorney General* [1965] IR 294. But that general reticence has not deterred the courts from making decisions such as those in *The State (Healy) v Donoghue* (above), *Murphy v Attorney General* [1982] IR 241 or *Blake v Attorney General* [1982] IR 117; [1981] ILRM 34. Financial implications, it seems, cannot always take priority over constitutional requirements.

It might be relevant in this context to refer to another aspect of the *Cosgrove* judgment which Gannon J alluded to earlier in his judgment without comment. This is the decision of the European Court of Human Rights in *Airey v Ireland* (1979) 2 EHRR 305, which was the spur to the introduction of the 1979 Scheme itself. Counsel for Mrs Cosgrove sought to use the *Airey* case in support of the constitutional argument. The decision in *Airey* is not, of course, binding in an Irish court (see *Norris v Attorney General* [1984] IR 36), but it is, perhaps, disappointing that it did not receive some discussion. This is particularly so because the Court of Human Rights expressly addressed the economic aspects of civil legal aid in its judgment. It accepted that free civil legal aid was not the sole mechanism to give effect to the right of access to courts under Article 6 of the European Convention. Other means included simplication of procedure. The crucial test, as far as the Court was concerned, was effective access. This requirement, the Court stated:

> may sometimes compel the State to provide for the assistance of a lawyer when such assistance proves indispensable for an effective access to court either because legal representation is rendered compulsory, as is done by the domestic law of certain contracting states for various types of litigation, or by reason of the complexity of the procedure or of the case.

This approach by the Court might have served as a starting point for discussion of the 'due process' element referred to by Gannon J in his judgment in *Cosgrove*. It is unfortunate that his outright rejection of the concept of even a limited State duty in this respect, in the passage from his judgment already quoted, did not include a discussion of what might appear to be a persuasive precedent on the subject.

Mental treatment: leave to commence proceedings   In *Murphy v Greene* [1991] ILRM 404; [1990] 2 IR 566, the Supreme Court considered the requirement in s.260 of the Mental Treatment Act 1945 that leave to commence proceedings be obtained from the High Court before a claim for damages can be made in respect of committal to a psychiatric hospital. S.260 requires that the Court is 'satisfied' that the applicant has established 'substantial grounds' for contending that there was bad faith or want of reasonable care before leave will be granted. The case arose against the following background.

The plaintiff had been brought to a Garda station after his wife had made complaints to the Gardaí that the plaintiff had beaten his daughter. The wife had previously obtained a protection order against the plaintiff in the District Court. The wife then contacted the defendant doctor who was on call for another doctor. The defendant had never attended the plaintiff. The wife explained the circumstances in which the plaintiff had been taken to the Garda station and she requested the defendant to certify that the plaintiff be committed to a psychiatric hospital under the 1945 Act. The defendant attended the plaintiff in the Garda station, concluded that the plaintiff was intoxicated and certified that he should be committed as an addict under the 1945 Act and that he required 6 months treatment. The plaintiff was escorted by the Gardaí in an ambulance to a psychiatric hospital. He was released from the hospital approximately 12 hours later. In seeking leave under s.260 to bring proceedings against the defendant, the plaintiff averred that he was not an alcoholic, that the defendant did not conduct a proper examination of him in the Garda station and that a second opinion should have been obtained by him. In the High Court, MacKenzie J granted leave under s.260, but the Supreme Court (Finlay CJ, Griffin, Hederman, McCarthy and O'Flaherty JJ) unanimously reversed this and allowed the defendant's appeal.

Finlay CJ delivered the main judgment, with which Hederman J agreed. Griffin, McCarthy and O'Flaherty JJ delivered separate concurring judgments. The Chief Justice acknowledged that the requirement in s.260 of the 1945 Act that the Court must be satisfied that there are substantial grounds for contending that there was bad faith or want of reasonable care is a restriction on the constitutional right of access to the courts under Article 40.3. As such, he stated that it must be strictly construed in the sense that the restriction must not be availed of except where it is essential to do so, citing *In re R. Ltd* [1989] ILRM 757; [1989] IR 126 (1989 Review, 55-8) in support.

However, he went on to hold that the restriction on the right of access to the courts in s.260 was reasonable. A crucial issue in this context was the standard of proof required under s.260, and this involved an examination of the Court's decision in *O'Dowd v North Western Health Board* [1983] ILRM 186. Griffin J in that case had suggested that the word 'satisfied' in s.260 suggested a standard higher than the civil standard of the balance of probabilities. O'Higgins CJ had stated that the civil standard was sufficient. In *Murphy*, Griffin J reconsidered his *O'Dowd* judgment in the light of *In re R Ltd*, above, and agreed with the other members of the Court that it was not necessary for the plaintiff to establish the grounds for proceeding on any standard greater than that in ordinary civil proceedings.

But the picture is somewhat more complicated than this, because the judges in *Murphy* also held that it was not sufficient that the plaintiff merely bring forward a *prima facie* case of bad faith or want of reasonable care since this would not be consistent with the requirement to serve notice under s.260 on any intended defendant. Thus, the Court appeared to suggest some other 'intermediate' standard of proof, lying somewhere between *prima facie* proof and establishing the case on the balance of probabilities. The Griffin intermediate test in *O'Dowd* has therefore been replaced by another form of intermediate test. This appears inconsistent with the Court's own approach to standards of proof. For example in *Banco Ambrosiano Spa v Ansbacher & Co. Ltd* [1987] ILRM 669 (1987 Review, 165) the Court rejected the idea that civil fraud claims should be based on a higher standard of proof than any other civil claims. Henchy J noted that any intermediate standard of proof would 'introduce a vague and uncertain element' into fraud cases. It is unfortunate that the Court in *Murphy* did not address this point; in the absence of such consideration, one is left with the impression that the Court regarded s.260 proceedings as a situation in which it should take a paternalistic approach, as indeed the 1945 Act was itself characterised in *In re Clarke* [1950] IR 235. In *Murphy*, O'Flaherty J alluded to this in his concurring judgment when he stated:

> Because of the nature of the legislation [the 1945 Act] the court will of necessity look at the individual seeking to sue. Is he a crank? Is he paranoid? Has he a case of any description? These are the first questions that must be asked and, it may be very often, the only questions that need to be answered.

With respect, these questions are nowhere to be found in the 1945 Act, so that it is unclear how they might be in any respect relevant to the issue which a Court might be required to decide under s.260. An applicant might be both a 'crank' and paranoid but be perfectly entitled within the terms of the Act to bring proceedings. It must also be assumed that by referring to paranoia O'Flaherty J did not intend to exclude other forms of illness. But the passage does indicate that the courts seem to treat the s.260 application for damages by a person who has been committed to a psychiatric hospital as quite different from any other form of proceedings. Thus, the Court failed to deal with the issue on the basis that s.260 might be repealed in its entirety. Although McCarthy J alluded to the inherent jurisdiction of the Court to dismiss proceedings for abuse of the process of the courts 'in what may be termed ordinary litigation', that principle is quite different since the courts will examine a case on its individual merits. The impression given in s.260 applications is that the courts act on the basis of a presumption arising from the committal of a person, the very act which is under question where leave to commence proceedings is sought.

Another issue not addressed by the Court was the relevance of Article 40.4.1 of the Constitution. The Court did, of course, refer to the right of access to the courts under Article 40.3 and McCarthy J made a tantalising reference to Article 40.4.2, though only in the context of indicating that this appeared to be the only provision which conferred an express right of access to the courts. But where a person is deprived of liberty through committal to a psychiatric hospital under the 1945 Act, it is clear that such deprivation occurs without the judicial procedures normally associated with such deprivation. The judicial acceptance of the paternalistic approach, as in the *Clarke* case, seems to continue in the *Murphy* case but this marks out committal cases as almost unique in terms of the short-cuts which appear acceptable in this area of deprivation of liberty. The Article 40.4.1 dimension of such cases did not even receive short shrift from the judges in *Murphy*. We will return to this point presently.

To revert to the *Murphy* case itself, however, the Court concluded that the plaintiff had failed to bring forward evidence which satisfied the Court of substantial grounds of want of reasonable care, since a mis-diagnosis did not necessarily signify want of reasonable care. Nor did the Court consider that a second opinion was required, and in the circumstances leave under s.260 of the 1945 Act was refused. In many respects, the Court comes very close to determining the substantive case by approaching the s.260 application in this way.

It is of interest to contrast the approach of the Supreme Court in *Murphy* with that of MacKenzie J (who, it will be recalled, had been the High Court judge in *Murphy*) in the earlier decision, *Brady v St John of God's Hospital*, *Irish Times*, 16 February 1990. In that case, the applicant obtained an order for her release from hospital pursuant to an enquiry under Article 40.4 of the Constitution. As noted already, McCarthy J made a passing reference to this 'direct' right of access to the High Court in his judgment in *Murphy v Greene*, above. The application under Article 40.4 required, in the *Brady* case, a full examination of the basis for the applicant's detention under the 1945 Act. MacKenzie J was satisfied that there was no basis for the applicant's detention and he ordered her release. It may be that applications under Article 40.4, where these are possible, could be used to circumvent the limitations imposed by s.260 of the 1945 Act.

It is also of interest that, in the immediate aftermath of the *Brady* case, the Minister for Health informed the Dáil that legislation amending the 1945 Act would be brought before the Oireachtas before the end of 1990: *Irish Times*, 17 February 1990. While such legislation has yet to appear, the Minister of State at the Department of Health indicated later in 1990 that a review of the 1945 Act was ongoing: *Irish Times*, 12 April 1990.

Summary proceedings   The *ex tempore* decision of the Supreme Court in *Calor Teo v Colgan*, Supreme Court, 22 June 1990 is referred to 452, below, in the Practice and Procedure chapter.

ACCESS TO LAWYER

Walsh v Ó Buachalla and Anor, High Court, 26 November 1990 might have produced an extensive discussion of the extent of the right of access to a solicitor in Garda custody. Instead, Blayney J applied an approach which relegated the right of access to what appears to be a result-based level. He may have been influenced in this by what he appeared to believe to be a lack of 'merit' in the case.

The applicant had been arrested under the Road Traffic Act 1961 on suspicion of driving a vehicle while in breach of the blood-alcohol provisons of the Act. He was brought to a Garda station. On his arrival, he was given a document entitled 'Information for Persons in Custody', a document issued under the Criminal Justice Act 1984 (Treatment of Persons in Custody in Garda Síochána Stations) Regulations 1987 (the Custody Regulations). This document included a statement that he was entitled to communicate privately with a solicitor. This is in compliance with the limited right of access recognised in s.5 of the Criminal Justice Act 1984. The applicant was told to read the document and he did so. He did not request to see a solicitor. Some 40 minutes later, he was brought to the Garda doctor for a blood sample to be taken in accordance with s.13(1) of the Road Traffic (Amendment) Act 1978. The applicant then requested, for the first time, to see a solicitor. This request was refused by the Garda in question on the ground that it was not a genuine request and that it would be some time before a solicitor would arrive, it being approximately 1 a.m. at that time. The blood sample was taken, and when analysed it showed the applicant to be in excess of the permitted levels. The applicant was convicted in the District Court under the 1961 Act. On judicial review, the applicant argued that the blood sample had been taken in breach of his constitutional right of access to a solicitor. Blayney J declined the relief sought.

For the purposes of argument, Blayney J first assumed that the applicant's right of access to a solicitor had been breached. However, he cited a passage from the judgment of Finlay CJ in *The People v Healy (P.)* [1990] ILRM 313; [1990] 2 IR 73 (1989 Review, 137-9, and discussed above, 146, with the *Cosgrove* case) to argue that this was not sufficient, and that the applicant was also required to establish a causative link between the infringement of the right and the evidence in question. Blayney J found that the applicant failed to establish the link. He stated:

In my opinion the evidence here was not obtained as a result of the violation of the applicant's constitutional rights. It is a case of *post hoc sed non propter hoc* — the evidence was obtained after the violation but not as a result of the violation. The applicant was obliged by statute [s.13 of the 1978 Act] to give a specimen of his blood or urine. No advice from a solicitor could have altered that. So his being refused access to a solicitor did not in any way lead to the specimen of blood being obtained. . . .

It was submitted on behalf of the applicant that if he had had access to a solicitor he could have been advised by him. But what advice could a solicitor have given him? He would certainly not have advised him to commit an offence by refusing to give one or other of the specimens.

All he could have done was to confirm that the applicant was required by law to provide a specimen of blood or urine.

On this basis, he found the conviction should stand. Blayney J also added some comments at the end of his judgment, indicating that he doubted there had in fact been a breach of any right. He stated that, while it might have been better for the Gardaí to have allowed the applicant to telephone a solicitor when he requested to do so, it was doubtful if the applicant's constitutional right of access had been infringed having regard to the length of time during which the applicant had had an opportunity to telephone a solicitor but chose not to do so.

There is a common thread running through Blayney J's judgment which invites comment. He took the view, in the passage quoted, that access to a solicitor would have brought no benefit to the applicant since he was obliged to provide a blood or urine sample under the terms of the Road Traffic Acts. This seems a dubious point of constitutional law. Blayney J had already referred to the *Healy* case in which the Supreme Court had recognised for the first time the constitutional origin of the right of access to a lawyer. It is regrettable that this constitutional dimension was not emphasised by Blayney J. Instead, he focused on the admissibility of evidence point, when in fact there was no admissibility issue involved in the case. By presenting the case as one on admissibility of evidence, the status of the right of access to a lawyer is diminished and made to appear like another 'technicality' to avoid a conviction under the Road Traffic Acts.

In some ways, of course, all arguments about admissibility of evidence constitute technical points. But in *The People v Madden* [1977] IR 336, the Court of Criminal Appeal declared inadmissible a confession which was completed after, but begun before, the time limits under s.30 of the Offences against the State Act 1939 had elapsed. The constitutional right to liberty excised the entire confession, because the interference with the constitutional right 'poisoned the fruit'. And in *The People v Healy (P.)* [1990] ILRM 313; [1990] 2 IR 73, above, the Supreme Court excluded a confession where access to a lawyer had been refused. The point in the present context is that in neither case did the courts ask whether the violations of the different constitutional rights 'made a difference'. They were concerned solely with whether the violations had actually taken place. Similarly, in *The People v Kenny (M.)* [1990] ILRM 569 (SC); [1990] 2 IR 90 (CCA & SC) (202-5, below, in the Criminal Law chapter) the unintended violation of the constitutional inviolability of the dwelling through the use of an invalid search warrant resulted in the exclusion of physical evidence found on the premises of the accused. Could it be argued, as Blayney J did in the instant case, that such evidence was obtained after the constitutional violation but not as a result of the violation?

The courts have rejected a result-based approach in the evidence cases because otherwise they would be involved in 'punishing' bad police behaviour. Instead they have preferred to rely on the approach that rights should be protected in a positive way. It is, perhaps, instructive to refer to the leading Irish case on access to a lawyer, *The State (Healy) v Donoghue* [1976] IR 325 (also discussed with the *Cosgrove* case, above). In that case, the Supreme Court did not decide that access to a lawyer is for the innocent only; the right extends to people who may be unable to prepare themselves, as Henchy J indicated, for the 'alien complexity of courtroom procedures'. The decision in *The People v Healy (P.)*, above, reaffirms that access to a lawyer is about fair procedures and a 'level playing pitch' in the equally alien environment of a Garda station.

It may very well be, as Blayney J indicated, that a solicitor's advice would not have produced a different result for the applicant in the instant case. On the other hand it might: the solicitor might have advised one type of sample as opposed to another, on the ground that one might be more accurate than another; or there might have been defects in the procedure adopted to that stage of the arrest and detention which may have gone unnoticed by the applicant, but which would be apparent to a solicitor. However, as already indicated, it seems that the approach adopted by Blayney J requires a person to establish that some legal benefit will accrue before access to constitutional rights will be granted. The existing case law seemed to indicate, to the contrary, that access to constitutional rights have their own inherent value.

Blayney J's closing comments in his judgment are also worthy of comment. He indicated, to some extent, that he was unhappy as to the merits of the applicant's request for a solicitor, coming as it did 40 minutes after receiving the document given to him. The Gardaí certainly took the view that the applicant's silence in some way amounted to an indication that he did not wish to see a solicitor. Is such an inference always to be drawn from silence? For instance, the person may not have the name of a solicitor immediately to hand. We have already noted that Blayney J addressed in a peripheral manner the constitutional dimension to the instant case; it is equally to be regretted that he did not examine the statutory basis for the document given to the applicant. The document was presented to the applicant in pursuance of the duty to inform the detained person under s.5 of the Criminal Justice Act 1984. If Blayney J had approached the case on the basis that the statutory duty must be deemed (in the light of the *Healy* case) to be premised on a constitutional foundation, the right of access might have been afforded greater weight, and the difficulties associated with effective implementation of the right of access might have been addressed.

Although the judgment was delivered over 8 months after the *Martin Committee on Criminal Procedure* reported on the need for changes in this precise part of the 1987 Custody Regulations (see 240-2, below, in the Criminal Law chapter), no amending Regulations had reached even draft stage. Any such amending Regulations could not have influenced directly the outcome in the instant case, though it might have influenced a different approach to the issue of access. Indeed, it is noteworthy that the UK equivalent of our Custody Regulations 1987, the Code of Practice under the Police and Criminal Evidence Act 1984 (PACE), was amended in 1990 precisely because there were difficulties in giving full effect to the right of access to a solicitor: see [1991] *Crim LR* 232, at 235. The *Walsh* decision appears to indicate that such difficulties exist on this side of the Irish Sea also, and that action on the Martin Committee recommendations should be regarded as a matter of urgency.

ADMINISTRATION OF JUSTICE

Definition of administration of justice   The difficulty of describing the boundaries of the administration of justice arose again in 1990 in a number of cases. In *Deighan v Hearne* [1990] 1 IR 499 (see 459-60, below, in the Revenue Law chapter) the Supreme Court held that the raising of a Revenue assessment did not constitute the administration of justice. On the other hand, in *Murphy v Wallace and Ors*, High Court, 17 July 1990 (465-6, below, also in the Revenue Law chapter) Barron J held that the use by the Revenue of penal warrants under the Excise Management Act 1827 was an unconstitutional exercise of the judicial power. In *The People v Neilan* [1991] ILRM 184 (sub nom. *Application of Neilan* [1990] 2 IR 267), Keane J held that the detention of a person pursuant to the Trial of Lunatics Act 1883 formed part of the administration of justice, but the effect of this decision was reversed in early 1991 by the Supreme Court decision in *The People v Gallagher* [1991] ILRM 339 (see 157-68, below). In *Glavin v Governor of Training Unit Mountjoy Prison* [1991] ILRM 478, below, suggestions were made that sending forward on a preliminary examination may be part of the administration of justice.

Discovery of documents   The well-established principle that it is a matter for the courts to determine points of privilege in connection with discovery was reiterated in *Smurfit Paribas Bank Ltd v AAB Export Finance Ltd* [1990] ILRM 588; [1990] 1 IR 469: see 435-6, below, in the Practice and Procedure chapter.

Interference with judicial process   In the 1989 Review, 94-5, we discussed the March 1990 decision of the Supreme Court in *Shelly v Mahon*
[1990] 1 IR 36. It will be recalled that, in that case, the applicant had been
convicted by the first respondent of an offence under the Road Traffic Acts.
At the time of the conviction, the respondent had reached the retirement age
for District Justices but this was unknown to the authorities. The Courts (No.
2) Act 1988 (see also the 1988 Review, 337-8) was enacted with the express
purpose of validating any orders made by the first respondent during the time
in issue in the *Shelly* case, but the 1988 Act also included an express saver
that it would not operate where it would conflict with any constitutional
rights. In *Shelly*, the Supreme Court held that the 1988 Act could not operate
so as to validate a trial which had not been conducted in due course of law
by a judge validly appointed as required by Articles 34.1 and 38.1 of the
Constitution. The Court concluded that neither of these constitutional
conditions were met by the circumstances which existed in the case.

In the 1989 Review, 95, we suggested that this approach seemed to be
different from that taken by the Supreme Court in cases such as *The State
(Byrne) v Frawley* [1978] IR 326 and *Murphy v Attorney General* [1982] IR
241. It is of interest to note that it has since emerged from the report of
counsel's arguments that the Court's attention was drawn to the *Murphy* case
(see [1990] 1 IR, at p.41). To that extent, it would appear that established
limits on retrospection in constitutional cases, particularly those identified in
the *Byrne* case, are being given some form of quietus.

This would appear to be confirmed by the second case arising from the
Courts (No. 2) Act 1988, *Glavin v Governor of Training Unit Mountjoy
Prison* [1991] ILRM 478.

The applicant had been charged in 1986 with offences under the Larceny
Act 1916, as amended. He appeared before District Justice Mahon, who
conducted a preliminary examination under Part II of the Criminal Procedure
Act 1967 and sent him forward for trial in the Circuit Court. There, the
applicant pleaded guilty and was sentenced to 10 years imprisonment. In
1987, the Court of Criminal Appeal reduced this to 6 years. As in the *Shelly*
case, at the time that District Justice Mahon conducted the preliminary
examination in the applicant's case, he had in fact reached retirement age,
but due to a misunderstanding as to his correct age no warrant continuing
him in office had been issued under the Courts of Justice (District Court) Act
1949. As already noted, the Courts (No. 2) Act 1988 purported to validate
retrospectively orders made by District Justice Mahon, but without prejudice
to any constitutional rights which might have been affected by his orders.
The applicant sought an inquiry and release under Article 40.4.2 of the
Constitution. Hamilton P and, on appeal, the Supreme Court ordered his
release.

In the High Court, Hamilton P first examined the case as a matter of jurisdiction to try. Applying the decision of the Supreme Court in *The People v Boggan* [1958] IR 67, he held that since the preliminary examination conducted by District Justice Mahon was null and void, the Circuit Criminal Court thus had no jurisdiction to try him.

Then he examined the effect of the *Shelly* decision. He opined that, while the applicant did not have a constitutional right to a preliminary examination, the applicant's trial was not conducted in due course of law within Article 38.1 of the Constitution. Thus, the 1988 Act had not validated the applicant's trial since it was enacted on the express basis that the Oireachtas did not intend to infringe any person's constitutional rights.

Finally, the President considered whether he should return the matter to the District Court. He held that, in the particular circumstances, as the applicant had served over 3 years in prison, it would be unjust and inequitable to return the matter to the District Court. He therefore ordered that the applicant be released immediately.

On appeal by the respondents the Supreme Court (Griffin, Hederman, McCarthy, O'Flaherty and Keane JJ) upheld the conclusions of Hamilton P. However some interesting comments were added on the constitutional dimension to the case and the Court was also of the view that it was no part of the Court's function to even consider returning the case to the District Court.

Three reasoned judgments were delivered, by Griffin, O'Flaherty and Keane JJ. All three judgments were in agreement that a trial in due course of law within Article 38.1 of the Constitution required compliance with steps provided for in legislation, including those which are required as preliminary to a trial on indictment. They concluded that the applicant thus had a constitutional right to have a preliminary examination conducted by a District Justice duly appointed in accordance with the Constitution. In this context, Keane J (with whose judgment McCarthy J concurred in full) in particular doubted certain *dicta* of Lardner J in *O'Shea v Director of Public Prosecutions* [1989] ILRM 309; [1988] IR 655, in which the act of sending a person forward for trial was regarded as falling outside the administration of justice for the purposes of Article 38.1. In fact counsel for the State (now Denham J) expressly declined to rely on the *O'Shea* case. It is also of interest to note that O'Flaherty J (with whom Hederman J concurred) questioned whether it would be constitutionally permissible for legislation to be enacted which would remove the right to have a preliminary examination prior to trial on indictment. Of course that point did not arise for decision, but a majority in the Court clearly expressed a preference for regarding the preliminary examination as part of the constitutional aspect of trial on indictment. While this is not necessarily in complete conflict with the *O'Shea* decision, it does cast some doubt on the analysis in the Supreme Court judgment in that case: see also the comments in the 1988 Review, 166-8.

To revert to the *Glavin* case itself, the Supreme Court went on to hold, applying its *Shelly* decision, that since the 1988 Act by its terms did not purport to validate any orders made in conflict with constitutional rights, it did not alter the invalidity of the preliminary examination conducted in the applicant's case. Thus, as the return for trial was null and void the applicant was entitled to the relief sought. And, taking a different line to that of Hamilton P, it held that once the applicant's conviction had been found invalid, the High Court must immediately order his release and that it was not within its competence to consider whether the case should be returned to the District Court, this being a matter for the Director of Public Prosecutions.

To sum up, the *Shelly* and *Glavin* cases adopted an approach which is quite at variance (unintentionally?) with the views expressed in *The State (Byrne) v Frawley* [1978] IR 326 (also an Article 40.4 inquiry) and, to a lesser extent, in cases such as *Murphy v Attorney General* [1982] IR 241. It is, to say the least, greatly to be regretted that the Court did not, in either *Shelly* or *Glavin*, advert to these decisions, even though in *Shelly* the *Murphy* case was specifically referred to in argument. No doubt, the judges are entitled to defend this by stating that they are not in the business of writing academic articles. However, question marks must now be placed beside the *Byrne* and *Murphy* cases.

One might also pose this question: what would have been the judicial view if, after the discovery of the difficulty associated with District Justice Mahon, it had been decided by the government not to bring to the Oireachtas any 'mending' legislation such as the Courts (No. 2) Act 1988? It will be recalled that, after the decision of the Supreme Court in *deBurca v Attorney General* [1976] IR 38, no legislation was brought forward to 'mend' prior unconstitutional jury decisions. In the *Byrne* case, the Supreme Court decided that such unconstitutional verdicts were, in effect, immune from attack. Is this bad law after *Glavin*? Perhaps the relevance of *Byrne* would have been clearer if there had never been a Courts (No. 2) Act 1988. However, it may be said that the existence of the Act should surely not have distracted attention to such an extent.

Separation of the powers and insanity verdicts   A mentally incompetent person in a civilised society should not be held criminally responsible for his acts; but what should be the fate of that person where he is adjudicated free of legal guilt on that account? In the days of the British system of the nineteenth century, the solution seemed simple enough. On a finding by the jury that the accused was 'guilty of the act .. charged . . . but insane . . . at the time he did the act. . . .' (Trial of Lunatics Act 1883, s. 2(1)), the trial judge was obliged to order him to 'to be kept in custody as a criminal lunatic, in such place and in such manner as the court shall direct till the pleasure of the Lord Lieutenant shall be known' (s. 3). The question of subsequent release was thus characterised as one for executive rather than judicial resolution.

This approach caused no great difficulty in 1883. The doctrine of a rigid separation of the powers was repellant to British constitutional theory. Moreover, the *M'Naghten Rules* were so circumscribed and narrow in their application that, as O'Hanlon J rightly pointed out in *The People v Ellis* [1991] ILRM 225; [1990] 2 IR 291, '[i]t was hardly to be expected that a person labouring under a type of insanity so severe and so deep-rooted, in the ordinary course of events would recover his sanity at a later stage'.

With the replacement of British constitutional norms by an indigenous constitutional framework, in which the three organs of state are more rigidly separated, together with the extension of the scope of the defence of insanity (*Doyle v Wicklow County Council* [1974] IR 55), the issue has come into central focus, since many defendants acquitted of serious crimes on the ground of insanity may regain their full mental faculties shortly after the crime, indeed in some cases even by the time of the trial. The question whether their release is a matter for the judiciary or the executive is thus one of pressing relevance.

Three cases addressed the issue in 1990, with their sequelae extending into 1991. Before discussing them it may be useful to refer briefly to the constitutional backdrop.

In *The State (O.) v O'Brien* [1973] IR 50, the Supreme Court had considered the constitutional dimensions of a related, but not identical, provision: s. 103 of the Children Act 1908. This provided that a sentence of death should not be pronounced against a young person but that instead the court should sentence him to be detained 'during His Majesty's pleasure'. (By s. 133 the powers exercised by 'His Majesty' were exercisable in Ireland by the Lord Lieutenant.) The prosecutor, then aged sixteen, had been convicted of murder by a jury in the Central Criminal Court and had been sentenced by the trial judge to be detained 'until the pleasure of the Government be made known concerning him'. The following year he was certified to be insane and transferred to the Central Mental Hospital. Twelve year later he applied for an order of *habeas corpus*. O'Keeffe P directed his release and the Supreme Court (McLoughlin J dissenting) affirmed.

A difference in analysis was apparent between Ó Dálaigh CJ and Walsh J. It was agreed that the trial judge had been wrong in prescribing a period of detention 'till' the pleasure of the Government be known, rather than 'during' its pleasure. The 'till' formula was from the 1883 rather than the 1908 Act. But on the constitutional dimensions there was no unanimity. In the Chief Justice's view, the determination of the length of sentence for a criminal offence, which s. 103 envisaged, was '. . . essentially a judicial function'. By British constitutional norms this had remained part of the executive authority. Article 51 of the 1922 Constitution had transferred that executive authority to the Saorstat; and Article 49.1 of the 1937 Constitution had declared that this power belonged to the People. S. 2 of Article 49, in conjunction with Article 34, had made the courts the repository of this judicial power previously vested in the Lord Lieutenant by ss. 103 and 133 of the 1908 Act. S. 103 withstood constitutional challenge, surviving as an operable provision authorising the court to determine the length of a young person's sentence.

In contrast, Walsh J was of opinion that the crucial date was not 1937 but 1922. The fact that the executive was charged with the function of determining the fate of a person found guilty but insane did not mean that the function should be characterised as executive rather than judicial: the quality of the act was 'to be determined by the act itself, not by the person who is doing the act'. The King, in British constitutional law, exercised a plurality of functions, including powers of a judicial character. Walsh J noted that '[w]hat was called the prerogative of mercy or the Sovereign right to commute sentences or grant reprieves was the exercise of part of this power; the fact that, by convention, it came to be exercised on the advice of the Executive did not change its character'.

Walsh J went on to note that Article 2 of the 1922 Constitution 'quite clearly did not accept the Crown as the fountain of justice'; it expressly stated that all powers of government, including judicial, in Ireland were derived from the people of Ireland and to be exercised in the Irish Free State through the organisations established by or under, or in accord with, the Constitution. Article 64 had provided that the judicial power should be exercised by the judges. Article 51, which declared that the executive authority of Saorstat Éireann should be vested in the King and exercisable by his representative in accordance with Canadian constitutional usage, referred only to the exercise of executive authority and was not to be taken as conferring any other powers which were enjoyed by the King in Canada. After the enactment of the 1922 Constitution, neither the King nor his representative here had any function whatsoever in the selection of punishment in the administration of justice or in any other exercise of the judicial power save that expressly mentioned (in Article 66) with reference to an appeal to the Privy Council, and the appointment of judges.

Walsh J concluded that the words 'during His Majesty's pleasure' in s. 103 were inconsistent with the provisions of the 1922 Constitution and were not carried over by virtue of Article 73 of that Constitution. Stripped of this inconsistency, s. 103 should be interpreted as giving the court power to order detention for an indeterminate period which, during its currency, might be remitted by virtue of the provisions of Article 13, s. 6 of the Constitution and the consequent statutory provisions enacted by the Constitution.

We should here mention the passage of Walsh J's judgment which has assumed importance in subsequent decisions: it involves his contrasting the language of s. 103 of the 1908 Act ('during His Majesty's pleasure') with that of s. 2(2) of the 1883 Act ('till Her Majesty's pleasure be known'). Walsh J noted the differences as follows:

> In the first place, in the case of an insanity verdict, no sentence is being passed. . . . Under s. 103 . . . there is the important distinction that the person there being dealt with is a person who has been convicted of an offence and who has to be sentenced by the terms of the statute. Therefore, the question of punishment is what is contemplated. . . . . [F]rom the very moment of sentence the convicted person is undergoing punishment for a term which the judge was not to determine but which was to be determined by 'His Majesty' or by the Lord Lieutenant.

Budd J concurred with Walsh J's judgment. Fitzgerald J agreed that the appeal should be dismissed but gave no indication as to which of the competing analyses be preferred.

The chronological sequence of the cases dealing with s. 2(2) of the 1883 Act proved important. The first was *The People v Ellis* [1991] ILRM 225; [1990] 2 IR 291. There the applicant had been found guilty but insane at a trial in 1987. O'Hanlon J had ordered that he be detained in the Central Mental Hospital until further order of the court. This formula was clearly inconsistent with the express requirements of s. 2(2). It was, however, in accord with what had become the practice of the courts in recent years. Why that practice should have developed is not certain but probably reflected a view that it was required in view of what had been said in *The State (O.) v O'Brien*.

In July 1989, on the basis of a psychiatric report, O'Hanlon J had ordered the release of the applicant for a probationary period of six months, after which a further psychiatric report was to be made available. After that period had elapsed the matter came before O'Hanlon J again; the psychiatric report was again to the effect that the applicant should be regarded as sane in all respects.

In his judgment, delivered in February 1990, O'Hanlon J observed that the verdict under the 1883 Act was one of acquittal concurrent with a finding of insanity at the time the deed was committed. There was no question of the court's imposing a sentence in such circumstances. Its only function in the ordinary case of an acquittal was to discharge the accused and, in the case of a special verdict under s. 2(2), to order the accused to be kept in custody as a criminal lunatic. The duration of that detention was to be determined by the

Lord Lieutenant. O'Hanlon J considered that this was an executive function of the Crown, which did not come under the umbrella of 'law and justice' so as to be transferred to the Minister for Justice by s. 11 of the Adaptation of Enactments Act 1922; it had been transferred to the Government of Ireland under the Constitution and was not merely an administrative function. (O'Hanlon J made no reference to the location of the power between 1922 and 1937).

O'Hanlon J considered that:

> when the court makes the appropriate order under the Trial of Lunatics Act 1883, it is *functus officio*, and . . . there is no inconsistency with the provisions of the Constitution in the further provisions of the Act of 1883 which vested in the executive the power to make the decision when the detention of the person concerned in a mental institution should be brought to an end. Like any other power vested in the executive, however, an allegation of abuse of such power could be made the subject of investigation by the High Court in proceedings brought for that purpose.

O'Hanlon J noted that s. 165 of the Mental Treatment Act 1945 afforded another example of the intervention of the executive power of the State for the purpose of having a person believed to be insane taken into custody and subjected to examination as to his mental condition. On proper certification, that person could then be detained as a person of unsound mind. All these steps could be taken without resort to the courts and without the necessity of a court order to validate what had been done.

O'Hanlon J accordingly concluded that it had been 'unnecessary' to depart from the formerly prevailing practice whereby the order directed that the accused, found guilty but insane, should be kept in custody as a criminal lunatic in the Central Mental Hospital till the pleasure of the Government of Ireland should be known. He thereupon made an order in these terms, expressing the view that he had no jurisdiction to make any order in relation to the application before the court for the applicant's release from detention. That application should be made in the first instance to the proper executive authority.

The Supreme Court allowed the applicant's appeal. Finlay CJ (with whose judgment Griffin, Hederman, McCarthy and O'Flaherty JJ concurred) identified three objections going to the root of the validity of the order made in the High Court. First, it was an order with important effect on the liberty of the defendant in a case which had originated as a criminal charge against him and it had been made without affording the defendant or his counsel any opportunity to be heard on the legal issues on which it was founded. This omission amounted to a major breach of the constitutional guarantee of fair procedures to which the defendant was entitled. Secondly, whilst a judge had in certain circumstances an inherent right to correct his own order which he believed to have been made in error, the lapse of time which had occurred in the instant case between the making of the order in 1987 and the making of the order in February 1990 and the assumption of jurisdiction by the court in the intervening period with the acquiescence of all the parties concerned, made a rescission of the order of 1987 unjust. Thirdly, the failure to direct in the High Court service of a notice under O. 60 of the Rules of the Superior Courts 1986 on the Attorney General so as to permit him to intervene in the raising of what was a new constitutional issue had to raise significant doubts and queries as to the validity of the procedures leading to the making of the order.

In the view of Finlay CJ, justice required that the original order of 1987 should stand and O'Hanlon J should decide, on the evidence before him, as to the further detention, if any, or other control or supervision which he would apply to the defendant. Although 'to some extent' arguments had been submitted to the Supreme Court on the interpretation and constitutional consistency of the provisions of the 1883 Act, the Chief Justice was satisfied that it was inappropriate that these issues should be decided in the instant case and that a decision on them had to await their presentation to the Supreme Court in a case which had been fully argued in the High Court.

In *The People v Neilan* [1991] ILRM 184; [1990] 2 IR 267, Keane J addressed the issue, during the period between O'Hanlon J's judgment in *Ellis* and the Supreme Court appeal. In *Neilan* the defendant had been found guilty but insane in 1983 and, in accordance with the practice that had by then grown up, Keane J had ordered that he be detained in the Central Mental Hospital until further order of the Court. Over the years Keane J had made a number of orders for the defendant's temporary release into the care of his family. In 1989 he had made an order transferring the defendant to another psychiatric hospital. When it was later proposed that the defendant be discharged to the out-patient care of that hospital, Keane J, in the light of O'Hanlon's judgment in *Ellis*, required the submission of argument on behalf of the defendant and the DPP.

After a detailed analysis of the distinction between the exercise of the judicial power and of executive functions, Keane J concluded that the order of the Court made after a finding of guilty but insane fell within the former category. Although there was at that time no justiciable controversy to be resolved, it by no means followed that the order made involved a purely executive function:

A criminal trial — and, indeed, the same could be said of a civil trial — is not a disjointed sequence of unrelated events: it is a continuum which begins with the arraignment of the accused and does not conclude until he has been either sentenced by the court or unconditionally discharged. In the former case, the correctness in law of the conviction or the sentence may be reviewed on appeal or there may be no appeal in which case the detention of the accused and his subsequent release becomes solely a matter for the executive. Whether or not there is an appeal, the criminal trial itself has come to a definitive and unmistakable end. Where the accused has been neither convicted nor unconditionally discharged, the court retains its seisin of the case.

That the criminal trial itself involves a controversy — and the most important which it falls to the judicial power of the State to resolve — cannot be gainsaid. The fact that the order made by the court of trial allows of the exercise of no discretion by the court is immaterial: the life sentence which the court would have been obliged to impose in the present case had the accused been found guilty of murder would have been as much a part of the administration of justice as the verdict of the jury itself. It is undoubtedly not material, in my view, that the order now sought does not, in that sense, seek to resolve any justiciable issue between the parties.

Keane J noted some features of the procedures that would have to be employed by the executive in dealing with applications by persons found guilty but insane. The psychiatrists might not necessarily be in total agreement as regards what was the most desirable course. In such a case, the executive (whether the government in the collective sense or the Minister for Justice) would 'have to adjudicate — I use the word advisedly — between these conflicting views'.

Keane J identified the order following such applications as one that was normally part of the administration of justice, for four reasons: it was in no sense an order of an arbitrary nature, since it emanated unequivocally from the State; it derived its legal efficacy from the jury resolving disputed issues of fact which had as its necessary consequence an order affecting the constitutional liberty of the defendant; it was undoubtedly an order which, as a matter of history, was one characteristic of the courts in this country; and it ultimately derived its efficacy from the order made by a judge presiding at a criminal trial. The power of a member of the Garda Síochána to take into custody a person believed to be of unsound mind where he is of opinion that this is necessary for the safety of the public or the person concerned was plainly an executive function which could legitimately be entrusted to the executive since it did not purport to interfere with or override the jurisdiction of any court established under the Constitution. The same could be said of the involuntary reception orders which could be made in respect of persons appearing to require institutional treatment for mental illness under the provisions of the 1945 Act.

Keane J noted the distinction between the power purportedly assigned to the executive under the 1883 Act and the right of pardon and power to commute or remit punishment imposed by a court which Article 13.6 of the Constitution vested in the President (subject to conferment by legislation on other authorities). In cases where the right of pardon and powers of commutation and remission applied, a guilty person was relieved of some of the consequences following from his act. In contrast a person to whom the 1883 Act applied was a citizen innocent of any crime. If his continued detention was no longer required by considerations of the public welfare or of his own safety, he was entitled to be set free, not as a matter of privilege or concession, but because his being at liberty was necessary to protect and vindicate his right to liberty under the Constitution. No useful comparison could be drawn between the two procedures in determining whether the function of determining the fate of a person ordered to be detained as a result of a verdict of guilty but insane was appropriately part of the administration of justice.

Keane J accordingly concluded that the order which he had been asked to make constituted part of the administration of justice and that to assign the determination of any of the matters in issue to the executive was inconsistent with the separation of the powers enjoined by the Constitution.

The question remained as to whether it was a necessary consequence of this finding that the words beginning 'till Her Majesty's pleasure shall be known' had not survived the enactment of the 1937 Constitution. Keane J expressed a preference for what he identified as 'the view taken by Walsh J when a somewhat similar issue arose' in *The State (O.) v O'Brien*. Like Walsh J, Keane J was of the view that the power of the King in the judicial sphere did not exist at all in Saorstát Éireann, save in respect of the right to appeal to the Privy Council under Article 65. It followed that the words beginning 'till her Majesty's pleasure shall be known' had been inconsistent with the 1922 Constitution.

Keane J went on to deal with the application before him relating to the continued detention of the defendant, and made an order whereby he might be released subject to an overnight stay of at least one night a week in hospital, for a projected initial minimum period of six months.

In *The People v Gallagher* [1991] ILRM 339, the appellant had been found guilty but insane in July 1989. The trial judge, Johnson J, had ordered that he be detained in the Central Mental Hospital until further order. In January 1990, the appellant applied to Johnson J for an order granting his release. Johnson J amended his original order so as to direct, on 14 December 1990, that the appellant be detained in the Central Mental Hospital until the pleasure of the Government of Ireland be known. In coming to this position Johnson J had the benefit of the competing analysis of his judicial colleagues in *Ellis* and *Neilan*; he preferred O'Hanlon J s approach. The appellant appealed to the Supreme Court, which affirmed Johnson J's order.

McCarthy J delivered the only judgment, with which Finlay CJ, Hederman, O'Flaherty and Barr JJ concurred. He quoted the crucial passage of Keane J's judgment in *Neilan* and expressed the view that there was a link missing in the 'chain of logical conclusion'. The overriding circumstance was that the verdict of guilty but insane was a verdict of acquittal.

> [T]he trial is concluded; the court does not pronounce a sentence; the role of the court is to order the detention of the person, the former accused, until the executive, armed with both the knowledge and resources to deal with the problem, decides on the future disposition of the person. At that stage also the Director of Public Prosecutions ceases to have his ordinary statutory role. The result of the prosecution has been an acquittal but the statute which permits the special verdict requires that the former accused be detained at least for some minimum time.

McCarthy J rejected the argument for the Attorney General that the relevant words in s. 2(2) of the 1883 Act constituted the administration of justice in a criminal matter:

> If it is the administration of justice, then clearly the statute consigns it to the executive, which is constitutionally not permissible. But it is not the administration of justice. It is the carrying out of the executive's role in caring for society and the protection of the common good.

In McCarthy J's view, the role of the executive on the making of an order by the court under s. 2(2) was similar to that of the executive in s. 165 of the Mental Treatment Act 1945. No criticism had been levelled against *In re Clarke* [1950] IR 235, in which the former Supreme Court had upheld the constitutional validity of s. 165.

McCarthy J went on to state that where, as in the instant case, a person detained pursuant to s. 2(2) sought to secure his release, he might apply to the executive on the grounds that he was not suffering from any mental disorder warranting his continued detention in the public and private interests:

> [T]hen the executive, in the person of the Government or the Minister for Justice, as may be, must inquire into all of the relevant circum-

stances. In doing so, it must use fair and constitutional procedures. Such an inquiry and its consequence may be the subject of judicial review so as to ensure compliance with such procedures.

The aftershocks of the Supreme Court's decision in *Gallagher* continue to reverberate.

On 19 July 1991, O'Hanlon J in the light of *Gallagher* decided that Mr Ellis should return to the Central Mental Hospital until the pleasure of the Government was known. It appeared to him that earlier orders he had made releasing Mr Ellis on a temporary basis had to be regarded as a usurpation of a function clearly vested in the executive and not in the judiciary: see *Irish Times*, 20 July 1991, p. 3. Mr Ellis appealed unsuccessfully to the Supreme Court on 25 July 1991. His counsel did not seek to disturb the general approach favoured in *Gallagher* but argued that, in the light of Mr Ellis's experience of having been treated like a 'human shuttlecock' between detention and liberty, as well as by virtue of the terms of the Supreme Court's judgment in *Ellis*, the matter of Mr Ellis's liberty had to be determined by the court rather than the executive. The Supreme Court rejected this contention. It applied *Gallagher* without qualification, which had been a 'full decision on the fundamental question of the separation of the powers'. The Court in *Ellis* had expressly declined to resolve the constitutional question which it ultimately determined in *Ellis (No. 2)*. There was an obligation on the executive, 'without any possible delay' to inquire into all relevant circumstances relating to Mr Ellis. In doing so, it had to use fair and constitutional procedures, having an obligation to determine, in the light of both public and private considerations, whether it was safe to release him. See *Irish Times*, 26 July 1991, p. 4.

Immediately after the Supreme Court judgment in *Ellis (No. 2)*, it was reported that the Minister for Justice was to set up an advisory panel to advise the Minister on what action the Government should take in relation to Mr Ellis and Mr Gallagher. The panel was likely to consist of a barrister, a psychiatrist and a general medical practitioner. It would hear submissions from interested parties and was likely to hold its inquiry before October. In the light of this development, Mr Gallagher did not proceed with his application before Johnson J seeking his release, on 26 July 1991: see *Irish Times*, 27 July 1991, p. 3.

This trilogy of cases raises interesting and troublesome issues. The first relates to the nature and scope of the administration of justice. Some may consider that Keane J's understanding was more attractive, and less formalistic, than that favoured by the Supreme Court. It is difficult to see how the mandatory order for the incarceration (for life) of a person found guilty of murder *is* within the scope of the administration of justice and an order for the incarceration of a person found guilty but insane is *not*. In neither instance has the court any discretion as to the type of order it can make; in both instances the question of when the person is to be released is a matter for determination by the executive.

This brings us to the second question. *Why* should a person who has been acquitted on account of lack of mental capacity at the time of the act be subjected to automatic compulsory detention by virtue of that acquittal? The easy answer is that such an acquittal justifies at least a *prima facie* inference that the person's mental condition is such as to warrant that step. The problem of course is that the finding relates, not to his mental condition at the time of the acquittal but at the time of the act, which may perhaps have been a year on more prior to the trial. The psychiatric evidence may have been to the effect that the mental incapacity was completely transitory and that it is almost certain never to recur. Is it a sufficient justification of detention in all cases that *most* cases will involve a mental incapacity of temporal dimensions extending beyond the trial and acquittal? The Supreme Court's answer seems to be that it is. The fact that the executive is obliged to act without delay in cases where the evidence indicates that the acquitted person is now in sound mental condition would probably be invoked in support of the legitimacy of the universal requirement of an order for detention.

In this context it is interesting to contrast the approach favoured by the Supreme Court in *Gallagher* with that of the Court in *The People v Ryan* [1989] ILRM 333; [1989] IR 399, on the question of bail: see the 1988 Review, 144-7. In *Ryan* the Court identified as (unconstitutional) *punishment* the detention of a person charged with an offence who was likely to commit an offence if granted bail. The fact that a judge thus proposing to incarcerate a defendant in no way intended to punish him did not remove the punitive quality of that incarceration, in the view of the Supreme Court. It is difficult to see, therefore, how the compulsory order of detention of a person found guilty but insane lacks this punitive quality. The evil effects of incarceration, not only of the direct loss of liberty but also in relation to family life and business management, are no less real for this person.

This brings us to the third issue: that of characterisation of the court's order under s. 2(2). It is true that it is not a 'sentence', but this is so only because courts do not sentence persons found not guilty of offences. If it is not part of the administration of justice, could it be argued that s. 2(2) is unconstitutional by amounting to an improper interference with the administration of justice? Rather than characterising the trial as having concluded at the moment of acquittal (as the Court does in *Gallagher*) could not the process more plausibly be described as continuing to the point where the defendant's fate consequential on that acquittal is determined by the court? There is surely something artificial about an analysis which regards the making of an order

for detention consequent on that acquittal as separate from the trial which
generated that acquittal. If this is so, and if (for the sake of argument) it is
accepted that the order for detention is part of the trial, could it not be regarded
as involving an improper interference in the administration of justice because
it prevents the court from making the order (or merely announcing the fact)
that the defendant, by virtue of the acquittal, is free to go?

At all events, if it is conceded that, as a result of *Gallagher* and *Ellis*, the
executive is to be charged with the task of determining the fate of a person
acquitted by reason of insanity, the question arises as to the factors which it
must, or may, take into account in exercising this jurisdiction. It is easy to
disguise the answer with comforting labels such as reasonableness and
professional judgment. Of course these come into play, but other less
comfortable matters must also be addressed. The most crucial question is
whether the lawfulness of the act — a sexual violation of a child, for example
— may play any part in the executive's determination of when to release the
detained person. Logically it seems that it should not, since the defendant's
conduct lacked legal and moral responsibility. One suspects, however, that
many people would object to this exclusion of all consideration for the
objective dimensions of the act. In many instances, this objection could be
reduced to unthinking, unsophisticated prejudice, but is it possible for the
executive to dismiss the problem out of hand? We suggest that it is not. In a
perfect world, with perfect laws and perfect understanding of the relationship
between moral responsibility and psychiatric disability in every specific case,
it would seem safe to dismiss all consideration of the objective elements of
the act. But this is not our world. The law relating to insanity has many rough
edges. The philosophic debate as to the scope of moral responsibility for
conduct continues unabated. (Internationally, one has the curious situation
replicated in court after court of psychiatrists addressing the issue of insanity
in a philosophic framework, premised on free will, when many of them
adhere to a determinist philosophy, in which free will for *anyone* is regarded
as a troublesome illusion). A further element of potential deviation from a
perfect outcome is the uncertainty of how a trial will run and the
unpredictability of juries. All of these factors in combination can on occasion
result in popular perception having some element of rationality, which cannot
invariably be dismissed as total prejudice.

ASSOCIATIONS AND UNIONS

The extent of the limits on associations and unions permitted by Article
40.6.1.ii of the Constitution was alluded to in *National Union of Journalists*

and Ors v Sisk and Ors, High Court, 31 July 1990; Supreme Court, 20 June 1991. We will discuss this case in the 1991 Review.

AVOIDANCE OF CONSTITUTIONAL ISSUES

In *McDaid v Sheehy* [1989] ILRM 342 (HC); [1991] ILRM 250 (SC) (464-5, below, in the Revenue Law chapter) the Supreme Court applied the well-established rule that constitutional issues should be avoided where a case may be decided on a different point. See also the 1987 Review, 83-5.

BODILY INTEGRITY

In both *Finucane v McMahon* [1990] ILRM 505 (SC); [1990] 1 IR 348 (HC & SC) and *Clarke v McMahon* [1990] ILRM 648; [1990] 1 IR 228, the Supreme Court emphasised the obligation on the courts to protect the bodily integrity of citizens pursuant to Article 40.3: see 220-2, below, in the Criminal Law chapter.

EQUALITY

In *McGimpsey v Ireland and Ors* [1990] ILRM 440; [1990] 1 IR 110, the Supreme Court briefly dealt with an argument arising under Article 40.1: see 172, below. The point was also discussed by Barron J in *K. v W. (No. 2)* [1990] ILRM 791 (317, below, in the Family Law chapter).

FAIR PROCEDURES

Much of the case law on fair procedures in 1990 is discussed in the Administrative Law chapter, 7-10, above. The issue is also discussed in the context of summary trial in *Kelly v O'Sullivan*, High Court, 11 July 1990 (see 197-8, below, in the Criminal Law chapter).

FAMILY

The State (F.) v Superintendent B. Station [1990] ILRM 243 (HC); Supreme Court, 3 May 1990 is discussed in the 1989 Review, 267-9. See also the cases discussed in the Family Law chapter, below.

INTERNATIONAL RELATIONS

In *McGimpsey v Ireland and Ors* [1990] ILRM 440; [1990] 1 IR 110, the Supreme Court held that the Anglo-Irish Agreement of 1985 was not in breach of the Constitution. While the Court thus upheld the order made by Barrington J in the High Court ([1989] ILRM 209; [1988] IR 567), the basis for reaching the same conclusion differed markedly. The general background to the case was described in the 1988 Review, 118-20. The status of the Anglo-Irish Agreement of 1985 is, it will be recalled, that of a treaty signed between the Irish and United Kingdom governments and deposited with the United Nations in accordance with the provisions of the U.N. Charter. The Agreement states, in Article 1, that the two governments affirmed that any change in the status of Northern Ireland would only come about with the consent of the majority of the people of Northern Ireland, and that the present position of a majority of the population of Northern Ireland was for no change in its status; and that if the position changed in the future both governments would support legislation to give effect to a wish for a United Ireland.

In the High Court, Barrington J, in dismissing the plaintiffs' claim, had attempted to eschew any definitive interpretation of Articles 2 and 3 of the Constitution. However, it appeared that he preferred the view expressed in *In re the Criminal Law (Jurisdiction) Bill 1975* [1977] IR 129, namely that the description of the National Territory as comprising the entire island of Ireland represented a political aspiration rather than a legal claim: see the 1988 Review, 121-3. The Supreme Court (Finlay CJ, Walsh, Griffin, Hederman and McCarthy JJ) unanimously rejected the 'aspiration' view and unequivocally stamped Article 2 as expressing a legal claim. In doing so, the Chief Justice borrowed the words 'constitutional imperative' from the judgment of Hederman J in *Russell v Fanning* [1988] ILRM 333; [1988] IR 505, and these have now entered the lexicon of Irish politics.

The judgment of Finlay CJ contains a passage worth quoting in full in this context. He stated:

> With Articles 2 and 3 of the Constitution should be read the Preamble, and I am satisfied that the true interpretation of these constitutional provisions is as follows:
>
> 1. The re-integration of the national territory is a constitutional imperative (cf. Hederman J in *Russell v Fanning* [1988] IR 505).
>
> 2. Article 2 of the Constitution consists of a declaration of the extent of the National Territory as a claim of legal right.

3. Article 3 of the Constitution prohibits, pending the re-integration of the National Territory, the enactment of laws with any greater area or extent of application or extra-territorial effect than the laws of Saorstat Eireann, and this prohibits the enactment of laws applicable in the counties of Northern Ireland.

4. The restriction imposed by Article 3 pending the re-integration of the National Territory in no way derogates from the claim as a legal right to the entire National Territory.

The Chief Justice went on to state that Article 3 must be regarded as an express denial that the frontier between what he described as 'the State and Northern Ireland' is or can be accepted as conclusive of the matter, or that any prescriptive title is created by that frontier or that any estoppel is created as to the applicability of the laws of the State in Northern Ireland.

Some difficulties present themselves as to the reference by the Chief Justice to Hederman J's judgment in *Russell v Fanning*. Barrington J had also referred to the passage in that judgment in the High Court in *McGimpsey*. *Russell* was, of course, a case concerning the political offence exception under the Extradition Act 1965. The relevant paragraph of Hederman J's judgment in *Russell* begins with the description, without reference to any previous judicial authority, of the re-integration of the National Territory as a 'constitutional imperative', and in the context of that case he immediately went on to state that the only question of policy which arises is as to the manner in which that aim of re-integration is to be achieved. On this, Hederman J stated: 'It is undoubtedly within the competence of the government of Ireland and the Oireachtas to decide from time to time whether or not this aim should be pursued by peaceful means or by warlike means'.

Hederman J's judgment in *Russell* was a dissenting one, and this may explain why, in *McGimpsey*, Barrington J did not place a great deal of emphasis on Hederman J's view. But in *Finucane v McMahon* [1990] ILRM 505; [1990] 1 IR 165 (212-6, below, in the Criminal Law chapter), 'the analysis and the conclusions' of Hederman J's minority judgment (though not specifically the passage quoted above) were approved in the leading judgment delivered by Walsh J: [1990] ILRM at 522; [1990] 1 IR at 217. And while the *Finucane* decision was delivered two weeks after the decision of the Supreme Court in *McGimpsey*, it is interesting to note that legal submissions in *Finucane* had taken place before those in *McGimpsey*. The legal arguments in *Finucane* may thus have been fresh in the mind of the Chief Justice in *McGimpsey*.

Although Hederman J's judgment now has a greater standing in the light of *Finucane*, it would seem wrong to conclude that the Chief Justice's allusion in *McGimpsey* to the phrase 'constitutional imperative' in any way amounted to an incorporation by reference of the statement by Hederman J as to the means by which that aim could be achieved by the government or Oireachtas. That issue of means did not arise for decision in *McGimpsey*, and if only for that reason it is perhaps unfortunate that Finlay CJ's judgment happened to contain a reference to a passage from what was at the time a dissenting judgment in which that topic had been discussed in trenchant language.

Moving on from its approach to Articles 2 and 3 of the Constitution, the Chief Justice proceeded to explain why the Anglo-Irish Agreement did not breach any constitutional provision. He held that Article 1 of the 1985 Agreement did not violate Articles 2 or 3 of the Constitution since the Agreement merely recognised the de facto status of Northern Ireland, but does so expressly in Article 2(b) of the Agreement without abandoning the claim to the re-integration of the National Territory. He did not consider that this was affected by Articles 4(c) or 5(c) of the Agreement, which referred to a change of status in Northern Ireland requiring the consent of a majority of the people of Northern Ireland, since such provisions were compatible with Article 29.1 and 29.2 under which Ireland affirms its devotion to friendly co-operation between states and pacific settlement of international disputes. This view is particularly intriguing in light of the reference earlier to the judgment of Hederman J in *Russell*, in which he had of course stated that the government would be perfectly entitled to engage in warfare to achieve the 'constitutional imperative' of the re-integration of the National Territory. Finlay CJ does not attempt to reconcile these views.

As to the Court's decision in *Crotty v An Taoiseach* [1987] ILRM 400; [1987] IR 713 (1987 Review, 91-4) he stated that the 1985 Agreement did not fetter the conduct of the government's foreign policy. He noted that the manner of implementation of the provisions of the 1985 Agreement were a matter exclusively for the government, and not subservient to other considerations, such as those which in *Crotty* had doomed Title III of the Single European Act.

The Court also rejected arguments based on Article 40 of the Constitution. Finlay CJ stated that the provisions of Articles 4(c) and 5(c) of the Agreement, by which the interests of the 'minority' community in Northern Ireland as to devolution would be put forward by the Irish government were not in breach of the equality guarantee in Article 40.1 of the Constitution, since the 1985 Agreement was not a 'law' within the meaning of Article 40.1. Nor did he consider that these provisions of the Agreement were in conflict with Article 40.3 of the Constitution since they in no way amounted to an abandonment of concern by the government for the majority community in Northern Ireland.

For discussion of the case, see Morgan: *Irish Times*, 5 March 1990. The decision also resulted in further discussion of possible changes to Articles 2 and 3 of the Constitution, for example at a meeting of the Irish Association: *Irish Times*, 7 May 1990. Alternative texts for Articles 2 and 3 were suggested by Mary Robinson SC (as she then was) in an article on the subject: *Irish Times*, 21 April 1990. It was reported that the *McGimpsey* case may proceed to the European Commission of Human Rights: *Irish Times*, 11 September 1990.

IRISH LANGUAGE

In *Delap v Minister for Justice and Ors*, High Court, 13 June 1990 (see 440-1, below, in the Practice and Procedure chapter), O'Hanlon J held that it was not necessary, for the Rules of the Superior Courts 1986 to have legal efficacy, that the State publish an Irish language version of the Rules. However, he did hold that, to facilitate the right of a person to conduct legal proceedings through the first offical language, Article 8 of the Constitution did require that an Irish language version be available to litigants. See also Editorial (1991) 9 *ILT* 173.

LIBERTY

The exclusive jurisdiction given to the High Court under Article 40.4 to enquire into the legality of a person's detention was adverted to in *Keating v Governor of Mountjoy Prison* [1990] ILRM 850: see 262-4, below, in the Criminal Law chapter.

LIVELIHOOD

Cox v Ireland and Ors, High Court, 2 October 1990; Supreme Court, 11 July 1991 was a successful challenge to the constitutional validity of s.34 of the Offences against the State Act 1939. Doubts had been expressed judicially and extra-judicially about the validity of s.34: see Walsh J in *The People v Quilligan* [1987] ILRM 606; [1986] IR 495 and Hogan and Walker, *Political Violence and the Law in Ireland* (1989), 265-6.

The plaintiff, a qualified vocational teacher, had pleaded guilty in the Special Criminal Court to certain firearms offences and was sentenced to two years' imprisonment. While serving his term of imprisonment, his teaching position was filled on a temporary basis. On his release, he was informed that by virtue of s.34 of the 1939 Act, his teaching position had been forfeited and that he was disqualified from holding the position for a period of seven years. The plaintiff instituted proceedings claiming that s.34 of the 1939 Act was in breach of the Constitution. In the High Court Barr J granted the declaration sought, and this decision was subsequently upheld by the Supreme Court.

Barr J stated that the State was entitled, in the interest of the common good, to impose conditions of employment by statute, even outside the public sector, but that such intervention in the relationship of master and servant must be even-handed. He concluded that s.34 failed this test. Since it applied to employees of a wide range of statutory bodies such as those of the ESB and of local authorities, but not to comparable employees in the private sector, it appeared to lack any logical justification and its operation in practice seemed to him to be capricious and was therefore in breach of Article 40.1 of the Constitution.

He also considered that s.34 constituted an unreasonable and unjustifed interference with personal rights under Article 40.3 of the Constitution, such as the right to practice a particular profession or vocation. In particular, he held that it constituted a penalty which arose from conviction only for scheduled offences under the 1939 Act and only for conviction in the Special Criminal Court. Echoing his conclusions in connection with Article 40.1, he pointed out that s.34 thus operated in a capricious manner.

Finally, he held that the plaintiff was also entitled to damages for having been deprived of his teaching post.

As already noted, the decision of Barr J was upheld by the Supreme Court in a decision of 11 July 1991. The *Cox* case will be discussed more fully in the 1991 Review.

LOCUS STANDI

Declaratory proceedings   In *O'Leary v Attorney General* [1991] ILRM 454 (discussed, 178-82, below) Costello J questioned whether the High Court should have entertained declaratory constitutional proceedings where the plaintiff, who was challenging his conviction, had not moved to seek judicial review. Despite these misgivings, however, he proceeded to deal with the substantive issues raised.

Exception to normal rule   In *McGimpsey v Ireland and Ors* [1990] ILRM 440; [1990] 1 IR 110, the Supreme cast severe doubt on the standing of the plaintiffs to maintain their constitutional challenge to the Anglo-Irish Agreement 1985: see 170, above. It will be recalled that the plaintiffs resided in Northern Ireland and were members of the Unionist Party of Northern

Ireland. That political party was, of course, implacably opposed to the Anglo-Irish Agreement. In the High Court, Barrington J had liberally applied the Supreme Court decision in *Crotty v An Taoiseach* [1987] ILRM 400; [1987] IR 713 in deciding that the plaintiffs had standing: see the 1988 Review, 120-1.

In the Supreme Court in *McGimpsey*, the Chief Justice, delivering the leading judgment, stated that in view of the findings of fact made by the trial judge concerning the plaintiffs' standing, and the absence of any cross-appeal by the defendants as to *locus standi* (for example, as to whether it was correct to describe the plaintiffs as Irish citizens as Barrington J had done) the Court decided to entertain the case on its merits. However, he added that there must be considerable doubts as to whether a person may challenge an act of the executive or legislature for the sole purpose of achieving an objective directly contrary to the purpose of the constitutional provision invoked in such challenge. McCarthy J, usually expansive on the standing question, concurred in expressing doubts about the plaintiffs' *locus standi*.

Normal rule In *McDaid v Sheehy* [1991] ILRM 250, the Supreme Court declined to deal with a constitutional issue where the applicant's interests were not shown to have been affected by the impugned provisions: see 464-5, below, in the Revenue chapter.

NOTICE TO ATTORNEY GENERAL

High Court judge The requirement to serve a notice on the Attorney General pursuant to O.60 of the Rules of the Superior Courts 1986 was held by the Supreme Court to extend to a High Court judge in *The People v Ellis* [1991] ILRM 225 (sub nom. *Application of Ellis* [1990] 2 IR 291): see 162 above.

OIREACHTAS

Double electoral registration In *Quinn and Ors v Waterford Corporation* [1991] ILRM 433; [1990] 2 IR 507, the appellants established what may turn out to be a short-lived right to registration in two constituencies. The right will be removed if s.11(1) of the Electoral Bill 1991 is enacted.

The appellants were students at the Waterford Regional Technical College. None of the students' homes were in Waterford, but for the academic year they resided within the County Borough of Waterford. They were all on the Register of Electors for their 'home' constituency. They applied for registration on the Register of Electors for Waterford County Borough for 1988/1989. The County Registrar refused their application. This decision was upheld on appeal to the Circuit Court on the grounds that the students were not 'ordinarily resident' in the Borough within the meaning of s.5 of the Electoral Act 1963 and also that the Registrar was entitled to take account of the risk of double voting having regard to the fact that the appellants were also registered to vote in their home constituency. This approach was overturned on case stated to the Supreme Court (Finlay CJ, Hederman and McCarthy JJ).

The appellants relied on *Fox v Stirk and Bristol Electoral Registration Officer* [1970] 2 QB 463, in which the English Court of Appeal had held that students were capable of being 'resident' in the constituencies at which they attended college. The Circuit Court judge had noted that the 1963 Act referred to 'ordinarily resident', and had distinguished the *Fox* case on that basis. However, the respondents conceded in the Supreme Court that the appellants were 'ordinarily resident' in the Waterford County Borough for at least the period of the academic year, within the meaning of s.5 of the 1963 Act. McCarthy J, delivering the only judgment for the Court, accepted that this concession had been properly made.

But McCarthy J went further and suggested that the appellants might also be ordinarily resident in Waterford for the full calendar year, on the basis that the wording of s.5(4) of the 1963 Act appeared to envisage ordinary residence in more than one constituency. It was this point which appears to have resulted in s.11(1) of the Electoral Bill 1991.

Finally, McCarthy J stated that, while the Registrar was entitled under Article 12 of the Registration of Electoral and Juries Acts (Specification of Dates) Regulations 1963 to require information in carrying out his duties, he was restricted to matters that lie within his constituency. It was, thus, irrelevant to the exercise of his statutory functions that registration might result in double registration within a larger European Parliament constituency since Article 16.1.4 of the Constitution prohibited double voting and not double registration. This distinction between double registration and double voting will, of course, become somewhat redundant if s.11(1) of the Electoral Bill 1991 is enacted.

Electoral boundaries   The Electoral (Amendment) Act 1990 gave effect to the boundary changes recommended by the *Dáil Eireann Commission Report 1990* (Pl.7520). The number of Dáil seats remains unaltered at 166. It may be noted that the 1990 Commission Report followed the unimplemented 1988 Report which had been compiled by a differently constituted Committee: see the discussion of *O'Malley v An Taoiseach* [1990] ILRM 461 in the 1989 Review, 107-10.

Regulation of discipline The suspension of Senator David Norris from the Seanad and a subsequent challenge to that suspension gave rise to some debate on the extent to which the courts could exercise judicial review of internal Oireachtas disciplinary matters. As the case was subsequently settled, the point was not decided in any definitive manner. See, however, Morgan's article: *Irish Times*, 20 March 1990.

PRESIDENT

The limits to the powers of the Presidency under the Constitution were discussed in a series of articles written in the context of the 1990 Presidential election. Three articles were written by Jim Duffy: *Irish Times*, 24, 25 and 26 September 1990. These became the subject of some controversy during the election itself, giving rise to disagreement as to whether certain Dáil deputies had attempted to contact the then President Patrick Hillery on the night of the dissolution of the Dáil in November 1982.

The election also produced proposals from the candidates as to the possible expansion of the functions of the President. For discussion of these, see Morgan, *Irish Times*, 3 October 1990.

PRESUMPTION OF CONSTITUTIONALITY

Post-Constitution Act In *Hegarty v O'Loughran* [1990] ILRM 403; [1990] 1 IR 148, the Supreme Court appied the presumption to the Statute of Limitations 1957: see 389, below, in the Limitation of Actions chapter.

Pre-Constitution statute In *The State (F.) v Superintendent B. Station* [1990] ILRM 243 (HC); Supreme Court, 3 May 1990 (discussed in the 1989 Review, 267-9) the Supreme Court held that, while the Children Act 1908 did not enjoy the presumption of constitutionality, it remained part of the legislative framework until it was found to be inconsistent with the Constitution. While remaining part of that framework, it did so subject to the provisions of the Constitution itself. This 'quasi' presumption, first outlined by O'Higgins CJ in *Norris v Attorney General* [1984] IR 36, has, as Casey has noted, tended to 'blur the distinction between pre- and post- Constitution Acts': Casey, *Constitutional Law in Ireland* (1987), p. 287.

PRIVACY

The issue of privacy arose in the context of the presence of a doctor in a Garda station under the Road Traffic (Amendment) Act 1978 in *Director of Public Prosecutions v Kenny*, High Court, 8 March 1990: see 244-5, below, in the Criminal Law chapter.

SEVERABILITY OF UNCONSTITUTIONAL PROVISIONS

In *Murphy v Wallace*, High Court, 17 July 1990 Barron J declined to sever an unconstituional provision from the remainder of s.90 of the Excise Management Act 1826, as amended by s.76 of the Courts of Justice Act 1936: see 465-6, below, in the Revenue chapter.

TRIAL OF OFFENCES

Burden of proof *O'Leary v Attorney General* [1991] ILRM 454 involved an important analysis by Costello J of the connection between the Constitution, the presumption of innocence and the burden of proof in criminal trials. The judgment would appear to approve, from a constitutional standpoint, many statutory provisions which shift the evidential burden to the accused. To that extent, it may be that the decision indicates that the Irish criminal justice system is not really accusatorial in nature. The proper conclusion might be that the system is, in practice, inquisitorial with an option on accusatorial rhetoric.

The *O'Leary* case involved a constitutional challenge to sections in the Offences against the State Act 1939 and in the Offences against the State (Amendment) Act 1972. The plaintiff had been convicted by the Special Criminal Court of membership of an unlawful organisation, the IRA, and possession of incriminating documents relating to the IRA, the latter contrary to s.24 of the Offences against the State Act 1939. His conviction was upheld in the Court of Criminal Appeal: *The People v O'Leary* (1988) 3 Frewen 163 (see the 1988 Review, 162-4 and 190-1).

On the membership charge, a Chief Superintendent gave evidence of his belief that the plaintiff was a member of the IRA on the date specified in the indictment. Under s.3(2) of the 1972 Act, such evidence of belief 'shall be evidence that [the accused] was then such a member.' The prosecution also produced evidence of finding in the plaintiff's possession 37 copies of a poster showing a man holding a rifle with the words 'IRA calls the shots' displayed on it. The prosecution claimed that these were 'incriminating documents' within s.24 of the 1939 Act, which provides that proof to the satisfaction of the trial court that such documents were found in the accused's possession 'shall, without more, be evidence until the contrary is proved that such person was a member of the [unlawful] organisation at the time alleged in the . . . charge.'

The plaintiff sought declarations that s.3 of the 1972 Act and s.24 of the 1939 Act were in breach of the Constitution by infringing the presumption of innocence. Costello J dismissed the claim, and his judgment provides a great deal of food for thought on the issues raised.

Costello J accepted the plaintiff's basic argument that the Constitution conferred on an accused a right to the presumption of innocence. Costello J referred to the explicit recognition of that right in Article 11 of the United Nations Universal Declaration of Human Rights and in Article 6 of the European Convention on Human Rights, as well as other international Conventions and Charters. In order to 'domesticate' such international recognition of the presumption, he noted that, in accordance with the Supreme Court decision in *The State (Healy) v Donoghue* [1976] IR 325, he should interpret the Constitution in the light of contemporary concepts of fundamental rights. In any event, he was satisfied that in 1937 the presumption of innocence had been an integral part of the common law system which had been carried over by the Constitution, citing in support McCarthy J in *The People v Ryan* [1989] ILRM 333, sub nom. *Ryan v Director of Public Prosecutions* [1989] IR 399 (see the 1988 Review, 144-7). Costello J was thus able to conclude:

> The Constitution of course contains no express reference to the presumption [of innocence] but it does provide in Article 38[.1] that 'no person shall be tried on any criminal charge save in due course of law'. It seems to me that it has been for so long a fundamental postulate of every criminal trial in this country that the accused was presumed to be innocent of the offence with which he was charged that a criminal trial held otherwise than in accordance with this presumption would, *prima facie*, be one which was not held in due course of law. It would follow that *prima facie* any statute which permitted such a trial so to be held would be unconstitutional.

This is an important description of the basic elements required by the Constitution for a valid criminal trial, but it was to prove of little comfort to the plaintiff. Having accepted this basic premise, Costello J went on to pose the crucial question, namely, whether the relevant provisions of the 1939 and 1972 Acts infringed the presumption of innocence. In answering this question in the negative, Costello J set out what he described as four general observations. In effect, these observations had the effect of undermining the benefit of the 'presumption of innocence' which he had described in the passage quoted.

First, he noted that many statutory provisions (mentioning, inter alia, the Explosive Substances Act 1883, the Larceny Act 1916 and the Misuse of Drugs Acts 1977 and 1984) shifted the onus of proof in certain circumstances from the prosecution to the accused. It was the nature and effect of such provisions which he said needed to be considered. Second, Costello J noted the two different meanings of the phrase 'burden of proof'. He noted that most statutory 'shifting' of the burden affected the 'evidential burden of proof' in establishing a particular issue against the accused by casting some burden on the accused after the prosecution has met certain stated criteria. Such provisions, he pointed out, were without prejudice to the 'legal burden of proof' on the prosecution to prove its case beyond reasonable doubt, and in each case the Court must examine the particular effects of the shift in the evidential burden to the accused. Based on these first two observations, Costello J drew a significant conclusion:

> [I]t is clear that if the effect of the statute is that the court *must* convict an accused should he or she fail to adduce exculpatory evidence then its effect is to shift the legal burden of proof (thus involving a possible breach of the accused's constitutional rights) whereas if its effect is that notwithstanding its terms the accused *may* be acquitted even though he calls no evidence — because the statute has not discharged the prosecution from establishing the accused's guilt beyond a reasonable doubt — then no constitutional invalidity could arise.

This passage anticipates the outcome of the case, since the provisions of the 1939 and 1972 Acts fall neatly within the category where a court *may* acquit even where the accused decides not to give evidence. In many instances, an accused is given the 'benefit of the doubt': see the 1988 Review, 163, and Hogan and Walker, *Political Violence and the Law in Ireland* (1989), 249. That, of course, was of little consolation to the plaintiff in the instant case, since his court of trial signally failed to give him the 'benefit of the doubt.'

Costello J went on to make two more observations which further limit the potential for constitutional challenges to such statutory provisions. He stated that even where the statutory provision *requires* a conviction if the accused fails to adduce exculpatory evidence, it is possible that such a provision may be constitutionally permissible if it merely gives legal effect to an inference which it is reasonable to draw from facts which the prosecution establish. He cited s.27A of the Firearms Act 1964, inserted by s.8 of the Criminal Law (Jurisdiction) Act 1976 as an instance here. Finally, he stated that a limitation on the presumption of innocence could be constitutionally permissible under the 'due course of law' of Article 38.1 where a rational basis could be demonstrated between facts established by the prosecution and the inference to be drawn from them. He referred with approval in this context to the 'rational connection' test established by the United States Supreme Court in cases such as *Leary v United States*, 395 US 6 (1969) and *County Court of Ulster County, New York v Allen*, 442 US 140 (1979). It is of interest to note that his approval of these decisions is consistent with the views expressed by the Law Reform Commission in its Report on Receiving Stolen Property (Report No. 23), in which the Commission indicated that existing law in the area of receiving stolen property unduly favoured the accused. The changes recommended by the Commission on this point (though not on others) were implemented in the Larceny Act 1990 (see 231-2, below, in the Criminal law chapter).

After these observations, it was not surprising that Costello J dismissed the plaintiff's constitutional action. He concluded that s.3(2) of the 1972 Act did not affect the accused's right to enjoy the presumption of innocence, since it did *not* provide that a court of trial is *required* to convict an accused on the basis of the evidence of belief of the Chief Superintendent. And while he noted that s.24 of the 1939 Act was differently worded to s.3(2) of the 1972 Act and its object was different, it did not infringe the plaintiff's rights, since it did not impose any obligation on the accused to give evidence to avoid conviction. Distinguishing the 1939 Act from the statutory provisions invalidated by the Supreme Court of Canada in *R. v Oakes* (1986) 26 DLR (4th) 200 he noted that a court of trial would still be required to evaluate the extent of the 'incriminating' nature of the document and the extent to which the accused person was in 'possession' of the document, so that the court would in some circumstances be required to acquit an accused even in the absence of exculpatory evidence.

The outcome of the *O'Leary* case was, perhaps, predictable. The original failure of the court of trial and of the Court of Criminal Appeal to give the plaintiff the 'benefit of the doubt' constituted the real problem: see the comments in the 1988 Review, 162-4. This failure in an individual case was unlikely to affect the outcome of a constitutional case given the presence of that other important presumption — of constitutionality. However, the comments of Costello J in the case appear to give a green light to most statutory 'shifts' of proof. His judgment even allows for constitutionally valid limits on the presumption of innocence.

Such a view probably reflects accurately the actual situation in the Irish criminal justice system, though it is difficult to square with the rhetoric of judicial pronouncements (including Costello J's own in the instant case) on the importance of the presumption of innocence. What is disturbing is that the courts have accepted the legislative inroads on the presumption as reference points for their interpretation of the Constitution itself. This must surely be bad constitutional law. Even those judges who might be considered as in the vanguard of constitutional development in the criminal justice system have, for example, implicitly accepted that provisions such as s.30 of the Offences against the State Act 1939 do not infringe the Constitution: see for example the judgment of Walsh J in *The People v Shaw* [1982] IR 1. Such 'statutory inroads' are to be seen as 'exceptions' to the normal constitutional rule. This may be a comfortable explanation of 'awkward' exceptions but it may be criticised for lack of intellectual rigour.

Indeed, it may be said that the judgment of Costello J, aside from his opening flourish on the importance of the presumption of innocence, represents a judicial acknowledgment of reality. It poses the ultimate question as to whether the courts may be required to revise the rhetoric of what purports to be an accusatorial system of justice. If it is now accepted that statutory inroads may be made on the presumption of innocence, then it may be more accurate to describe the system of criminal justice in this State as inquisitorial in reality, with an option on accusatorial rhetoric. That may be an unpleasant prospect for some judges, but it may reflect more accurately the extent of the *laissez faire* approach to this area in which the courts have engaged. See also the view of the DPP, 239-40, below.

Preliminary examination In *Glavin v Governor of Training Unit Mountjoy Prison* [1991] ILRM 478, suggestions were made that the preliminary examination might be constitutionally required: see 155-7, above.

Contract Law

AGENCY

In *Essfood Eksportlagtiernes Sallgsforening v Crown Shipping (Ireland) Ltd* [1991] ILRM 97, which we consider in detail in the Chapter on Commercial Law, above, pp. 24-5, Costello J held that the purchaser of meat bought from an Irish company and shipped through Irish forwarding agents was not bound by the terms of the contract between the seller of the meat and the forwarding agents in which the seller warranted that it was the authorised agent of the purchaser, to whom title to the goods had passed, and that it accepted the entitlement of the forwarding agents to a lien, not just on their own behalf but as agents on behalf of the owner of the meat. Costello J was satisfied on the evidence that the purchaser had given the seller no authorisation, express or implied, to make such a warranty. Nor was this a case of ostensible authority: no representation by an agent as to the extent of his authority could amount to a 'holding out' by the principal. Even if the forwarding agents were aware of the identity of the purchaser, this did not entitle them to conclude that the purchaser had authorised the seller to make such a warranty on their behalf.

The decision of *Allied Pharmaceutical Distributors Ltd and All-Phar Services Ltd v Walsh, et al*, High Court, 14 December 1990, which involved the issue of ostensible authority, is analysed in the Torts Chapter, in the section on Vicarious Liability, below, at 561-2.

BREACH OF WARRANTY

In *O'Callaghan v Meath Vocational Education Committee, McCormack and the Minister for Education*, High Court, 20 November 1990, Costello J dismissed an action for breach of warranty on the basis of lack of privity of contract. We analyse the case in the Labour Law Chapter below, 365-7.

CONSTRUCTION OF TERMS

The law of contract, in enforcing bargains, does not operate in a social vacuum. It cannot ignore the fact that contracts may have been made with the sole purpose of avoiding the application of a particular social policy, in relation to taxation, for example. Courts sometimes have to decide whether a contract which has no rational justification for having been made other than to sidestep the unpalatable policy should be recognised as valid rather than contrary to public policy. On other occasions the question is not one of contractual validity but rather of *characterisation*: if the contract professes to be of one type, should the court read between the lines and characterise it as being of another, when it is clear from the context that this other characterisation more accurately reflects the substance as opposed to the form?

Of course, legislation is well able to deal with this type of problem if the Oireachtas sees it coming. Thus, for example, the provisions of the Sale of Goods and Supply of Services Act 1980 relating to consumer protection override attempts at contractual avoidance.

At the heart of the matter is the question whether the law of contract should be viewed formalistically or in substantive terms. A formalistic approach would result in an unarticulated policy preference in favour of facilitating the sidestepping of social policies. It would treat the law's deference to contractual autonomy as an unarguable datum rather than as involving a (controversial) conclusion that this best serves the goals which law is designed to achieve, of justice in accordance with norms of practical social and economic nationality. No doubt formalistic strategies are attractive to courts which do not feel comfortable about openly addressing the full and complex issues of principle and policy.

In *O'Grady v Laragan Quarries Ltd*, High Court, 27 June 1990, Murphy J, on a case stated from the Circuit Court, had to determine an issue of characterisation of a contract, whose purpose appeared to be to avoid the application of s. 17 of the Finance Act 1970 (as amended). S. 17 imposes an obligation on contractors to deduct tax of 35% at source from payments made to those engaged in the haulage for hire of materials. The respondents had entered into contractual arrangements with lorry drivers whereby the drivers agreed to bring quarry materials from a company of which the respondents had part control and to sell the materials to the respondents, delivering them to customers nominated by the respondents; further contractual arrangements between the seller, the drivers and the respondents provided that the amounts owing by the drivers to the seller were to be deducted from the amounts owed to the driver by the respondents. No deduction of 35% tax was made in these agreements.

The case stated required Murphy J to determine whether, in spite of the language of buying and selling, the lorry drivers were in fact engaged in 'the haulage for hire of materials'. The Circuit Court Judge had held that they were not. On behalf of the Inspector of Taxes it was argued that the majority decision in *Irish Shell & BP Ltd v Costello* [1981] ILRM 66 supported an approach whereby the agreements should be read as a whole and in the light of the surrounding circumstances so as to ascertain the purpose and substance of the matter.

Murphy J noted the dissonance between expressed and actual intention that can arise in contractual arrangements designed to minimise liability to taxation, as well as in relation to retention of title clauses, debentures and landlord and tenant and rent restriction legislation. In the *Irish Shell* case, the majority of the Supreme Court had interpreted an agreement relating to the use of a petrol station as creating the relationship of landlord and tenant rather than of licensor and licensee. While Griffin J had said that it was 'right and indeed necessary to look at the substance of the matter', his remarks should not be interpreted as deciding that one could ascertain the substance of a contract by ignoring the actual bargain between the parties and substituting for it an agreement which would be in closer harmony with the commercial realities of the situation. As Griffin J himself had made clear elsewhere in his judgment as well as in *Gatien Motor Co. v Continental Oil* [1979] IR 406, one had to look at the transaction itself and see what in fact had been effected by the agreement, rather than let labels put on the transaction determine the outcome.

It seemed to Murphy J that neither the terms of the agreements in the instant case nor the terminology used in them created any ambiguity. He saw no reason why an agreement expressed to be for the sale of quarry materials should not take effect as such. The parties were free to conduct their affairs in such manner as they thought fit and to take advantage of whatever consequences followed from the arrangements they chose.

Murphy J pointed out that not all the consequences of this arrangement were beneficial: for example, if goods were lost or damaged in transit the loss would have to be borne by the lorry drivers rather than the respondents. The arrangement did not prevent the accrual of the lorry drivers' liability for tax; it merely affected the means of collecting it. Murphy J made it clear. however, that neither consideration would affect the proper interpretation of the agreements or their legal effect.

The parties had deliberately and effectively arranged that the relationship between them should not constitute a hiring of the services or vehicles of the lorry owners; thus s. 17 had no application. It was not open to a court of law to hold that, merely because the arrangement was commercially unusual or practically unnecessary, its terms and effect should be ignored and that the actual bargain should be replaced by a more conventional agreement which would have substantially the same effect but would fall within the provisions of s. 17.

Murphy J's approach is in general harmony with that favoured by the

Supreme Court in *McGrath v McDermott (Inspector of Taxes)* [1988] ILRM
647; [1988] IR 258, which we analysed in the 1988 Review, pp. 356-8. The
long term result is likely to be an extended game of legislative cat and mouse.

In *V'Soske Shops Incorporated v V'Soske Joyce Ltd*, High Court, 25 May
1990, Blayney J was called on to construe the terms of an agreement between
the owners of a trade mark and an Irish company which acquired the right to
use it. The key clause provided that the use of the name by the Irish company
with its products was 'subject to an annual payment of £100 a term of five
years, which term is to be renewable at the request of [the Irish company]
with the consent of [the owners of the trade mark] not to be withheld
unreasonably'.

Blayney J construed the phrase 'to be renewable' as meaning renewable
every five years rather than once only. He invoked the *contra proferentem*
rule against the owners of the trade mark, who had drawn up the agreement.
He then was required to consider whether the owners of the trade mark were
reasonable in refusing consent to a renewal save on new terms, involving the
payment of a royalty of 2% of the Irish company's total turnover per annum,
and the requirement to channel exports to the United States through them in
New York. He concluded that the clause did not permit the imposition of any
conditions, whether reasonable or unreasonable. Its requirement that the
owners give their consent unless they had reasonable grounds for withholding it envisaged situations such as where the Irish company might
produce goods of an inferior quality or might refuse to elect a director from
the owners of its board, as the contract required. It did not permit the
imposition of additional conditions, no matter how reasonable they appeared,
followed by the withholding of consent because these conditions had not
been accepted.

The broader economic background to the agreement supported this construction. When it was made the owners had decided to withdraw from the
Irish operation which had become too costly for them to run at a distance
from their main business in Puerto Rico. Their concern was to ensure that
their name would be used only on products of high quality standard. The
prospect of royalties in the future was not on their minds. The fact that the
Irish company had done well, as a result of the efforts of its shareholders,
might have encouraged the owners to take a commercial view and seek what
would be a normal royalty for the use of their name but this was not justified
by the terms of the contract which they themselves had drawn up.

EVIDENTIAL ASPECTS

In *Duggan et al v Donegal Co-Operative Creameries Ltd*, High Court, 26 November 1990, Gannon J dismissed a claim for breach of implied warranty and negligence with regard to the sale of barbed wire to be used on a mountain area in Co. Donegal. Gannon J's comments as to the quality of some of the evidence adduced on behalf of the plaintiffs were as barbed as the subject matter of the litigation. He concluded that all the wire was suitable for its purpose, and that the plaintiffs had not in any respect material to the nature and quality of the barbed wire relied on the skill or judgment of the defendants. In dismissing the claim he observed:

> [I]f the plaintiffs' evidence does no more than present a mystery for which they cannot provide a solution they have failed to discharge the onus of proof, as I have no function of solving mysteries. In respect of some aspects of the matters in issue I feel the whole truth was not reached, and my conclusions are founded on the credibility, and lack of it, as it appeared to me of the witnesses and the circumstantial evidence presented.

GUARANTEES

In *International Commercial Bank plc v Insurance Corporation of Ireland plc and Meadows Indemnity Co. Ltd*, High Court, 19 October 1990, Blayney J held that a particular credit guarantee insurance agreement should be characterised as a contract of guarantee rather than of insurance. We examine the case in detail in the Commercial Law Chapter, pp. 32-4. In the 1989 Review, 66-8, 353-4, we examined the jurisdictional issue which first needed resolution.

IMPLIED TERMS

We discussed the important Supreme Court decision of *Burke v Dublin Corporation*, 26 July 1990 in the 1989 Review, 117-25.

QUANTUM MERUIT

In *Travers Construction Ltd v Lismore Homes Ltd*, High Court, 9 March 1990, Gannon J analysed the circumstances in which a *quantum meruit* remedy is available. The plaintiff's action was for this remedy (among others) in respect of work done pursuant to a building contract. That contract had professedly been terminated by the parties before its intended completion. The plaintiff claimed that he had been wrongfully misled and pressurised into terminating the contract and sought *quantum meruit* in respect of the work he had done under the contract.

On the evidence, Gannon J rejected the plaintiff's claim that the termination had been wrongfully induced. As to the law, Gannon J noted that a *quantum meruit* claim was available only in circumstances from which an unexpressed agreement would be implied by law. If parties intending to enter into an agreement mistakenly proceeded as if *ad idem* and found they were not, any performance in the mistaken belief of agreement would be rewarded on a *quantum meruit* basis. But if parties who were *ad idem* on the terms of their agreement discharged the agreement before completion, the premature discharge, being itself a new agreement, left the past performance to be rewarded only on the terms originally agreed if not varied by the new agreement for discharge. The difficulty for the plaintiff in complaining that his entering into an agreement had been wrongfully procured or entered into in vitiating circumstances was that he could not enforce that agreement to the extent that it favoured him and repudiate his own obligations under it. He might find himself, when trying to set the agreement aside, with no alternative other than to be restored to the position in which he would have been had he not entered the agreement. This presented grave difficulties if the purported agreement in respect of of which complaint was made was itself an agreement for the discharge of earlier obligations under a previous agreement.

UNJUST ENRICHMENT

In *Allied Discount Card Ltd v Bord Fáilte Éireann* [1990] ILRM 811, Lynch J held that the plaintiff should be awarded damages for infringement of copyright or receive restitution for unjust enrichment where the defendant obtained an unfair benefit for work done by the plaintiff in canvassing traders and in preparing and printing booklets for a discount voucher scheme for retail outlets. The plaintiff had done this work for one year pursuant to a contract with the defendant. Thereafter the defendant continued the scheme, with some modifications. Lynch J held that it was permissible for the defendant to canvass the same traders as had proved receptive for the plaintiff but that it had been wrong merely to repeat the wording that had been included in the plaintiff's booklets, even if the traders were happy with this being done. We examine the case in the chapter on Commercial Law, above, 38-9.

Coroners

FEES

The Coroners Act 1962 (Fees and Expenses) Regulations 1990 (SI No. 19) set out the level of fees and expenses payable to a coroner under the 1962 Act.

INQUEST VERDICT

The effective ban on returning a suicide verdict at an inquest, deriving from the decision of O'Hanlon J in *The State (McKeown) v Scully* [1986] ILRM 133; [1986] IR 524, was confirmed in *Green v McLoughlin*, High Court, 1 December 1989. The applicant's son had died as the result of a gunshot wound which appeared to have been self-inflicted. The respondent Coroner presided over an inquest into the death. Over objections from the solicitor for the applicant, the Coroner allowed evidence to be adduced from a doctor as to the mental condition of the deceased prior to the death. The Coroner left to the jury a number of possible verdicts. The verdict reached was that death was due to discharge from a rifle in accordance with the medical evidence while the balance of the mind was disturbed. The applicant sought judicial review on the ground that it was in excess of the jurisdiction conferred by s.30 of the Coroners Act 1962. Johnson J agreed and granted the applicant an order of certiorari quashing the verdict.

He noted that s.40 of the 1962 Act allowed an inquest jury to reach a verdict of murder, manslaughter or infanticide, but that this was confined to third party involvement in a death, and in all other instances the jury was prohibited from reaching a verdict which involved attaching criminal liability.

He went on to hold that the Coroner should not have allowed the medical evidence as to the deceased's state of mind, since this brought up for the jury the whole question of criminal liability in respect of possible suicide. Referring to the decision in the *McKeown* case, Johnson J concluded that the verdict was in excess of the jurisdiction conferred by s.30 since it asked the jury why the death had occurred and not just how, when and where.

Criminal Law

ARREST

1 Access to solicitor The issue of access was raised in *Walsh v Ó Buachalla*, High Court, 26 November 1990: see 150-4, above, in the Constitutional Law chapter.

2 Criminal Justice Act 1984: detention powers and arrest *The People v O'Toole and Hickey*, Court of Criminal Appeal, 20 July 1990 provided the Court with one of the first opportunities to examine the substance of the detention powers in s.4 of the Criminal Justice Act 1984. While the Court purported to require strict compliance with the terms of s.4 of the 1984 Act, the conclusions reached in the case might lead one to believe that in fact there was very little analysis of the nature of the new detention powers enacted in the 1984 Act.

The applicants had been convicted of murder in the Central Criminal Court. They had been arrested at common law on suspicion of murder and brought to a Garda station. On arrival, they were detained pursuant to the provisions of s.4 of the 1984 Act. S.4 of the Act requires that a Garda described as the 'member in charge of the station' must have 'reasonable grounds for believing' that the detention is 'necessary for the proper investigation of the offence.' In the instant case, the member in charge of the station had been informed earlier that morning by the arresting Gardaí that they intended to proceed with search warrants to the houses which they knew to be occupied by the applicants. It was this piece of police intelligence which was the basis for the detention of the applicants for the initial six hour period authorised by s.4 of the 1984 Act. Before the expiration of that initial six hour period of detention, the applicants made statements indicating their participation in the robbery of the deceased person. The Gardaí consulted the Director of Public Prosecutions who indicated that they should not be charged with murder at that stage. A further six hour period of detention of the applicants was ordered under s.4 of the 1984 Act. The investigating Gardaí then arranged for an identification parade at which the applicants were identified. A further statement was made by one of the applicants during the second period of detention. Evidence was also given at their trial of statements from the applicants as to whether there had been a common design between them to murder the deceased or to rob him only.

The Court of Criminal Appeal (Hederman, Egan and Johnson JJ) dismissed the applications for leave to appeal and upheld the convictions in the case. Delivering the Court's lengthy judgment, Hederman J repeated the well-established judicial approach that s.4 'must be interpreted strictly and the Court must be vigilant to ensure that the Gardaí fully comply with all the provisions of s.4.' Notwithstanding this dictum, however, the Court seemed to adopt a wide interpretation of s.4 in some respects.

The first issue dealt with was as to the basis on which the member in charge authorised the original detention of the applicants. The Court stated that:

> the member in charge of the Garda Síochána station must have an independent *bona fide* belief that the person who has arrived in custody without warrant is a person who should be detained by the [member in charge] for a period not exceeding six hours from the time of the arrest as a necessary part of the proper investigation of the offence for which the person has been brought in to the Station. That independent opinion . . . can be formed as a result of information given to the [member in charge], either prior to the arrest or even when the arrested person is brought to the Station. What is necessary under the section is that the [member in charge] makes an independent decision on the information supplied . . . and comes to his or her own personal decision that the detention of the person brought to the Station is then necessary for the proper investigation of the offence for which he has been charged.

It could be said that this passage identifies in a clear manner the independent nature of the decision-making process of the member in charge of the Station under s.4 of the 1984 Act. Indeed, there appear to be parallels with the recent case law of the courts requiring that search warrants issued under legislative powers be based on an independent decision made by a District Justice, rather than the mere say-so of a Garda swearing an information: see for example *Byrne v Grey* [1988] IR 31 (discussed in the 1988 Review, 192-4) and *The People v Kenny (M.)* [1990] ILRM 569; [1990] 2 IR 110 (below, 202). A closer examination of the conclusion arrived at by the Court of Criminal Appeal in *O'Toole* and *Hickey*, however, reveals that the 'independent' decision of the officer in charge is less that what it appears. In concluding that the evidence in the instant case indicated that the member in charge had reasonable grounds for believing that the applicants' detention was necessary for the proper investigation of the offence of murder and was thus entitled to exercise the powers conferred on him by s.4 of the 1984 Act, the Court quoted with apparent approval the following pasage from the ruling of Barr J, the trial judge in the case:

It is not necessary for the member in charge to make inquiries and weigh up the evidence. He must have a particular belief at a particular time. It is sufficient as in the present case for the member in charge to be aware that there is a bona fide Garda investigation into a particular offence and that the person to be detained has been arrested on suspicion [*sic*] of having committed that offence.

Two difficulties arise from this passage, neither of which were addressed by the Court of Criminal Appeal. First, Barr J clearly does not seem to require that the member in charge make a truly independent decision — he expressly does not require the member in charge to make inquiries or weigh up any evidence. This is a far cry from what would ordinarily be required in an independent decision-making process, and it stands in stark contrast to the approach taken by the judges in the search warrant cases referred to above. Second, Barr J, perhaps inadvertently, transmuted the statutory basis for the arrest of a person who is brought to a Garda station under s.4. He refers to a person being 'arrested on suspicion' of having committed an offence. 'Suspicion' implies a purely subjective basis for arrest, whereas s.4 of the 1984 Act requires that the arrest can only be made by a Garda who 'with reasonable cause, suspects' that the arrested person has committed an offence. The 'reasonable cause' requirement implies that the arrest must be, at least in part, based on objectively verifiable criteria.

It may be imposing a counsel of perfection to require that, in giving his presumably ex tempore ruling in the Central Criminal Court, Barr J should be expected to advert to this distinction, but it seems at least arguable that his failure to do so 'infected' the previous sentence in the passage quoted, leading him to the view that the member in charge was not required to 'make inquiries and weigh up the evidence.' Had he adverted to the objective nature of the arrest power in s.4, he might have reached a different conclusion on this point. What is less understandable is that the Court of Criminal Appeal apparently fell into the same elementary error in the course of a reserved judgment in which the relevant provisions of s.4 were quoted in full less than two pages after the relevant passage from Barr J's ruling had been quoted. In doing so, the Court has left the impression that the dictum as to requiring strict compliance with s.4 should not be taken as strictly as might have been hoped.

A number of other related issues were also addressed by the Court. It held that the Gardaí had acted properly in contacting the Director of Public Prosecutions to seek advice as to whether they should charge the applicants with murder after they had made their initial statements admitting involvement in the robbery of the deceased. The Court also concluded that the Gardaí had acted correctly in deciding to hold an identification parade rather

than charging the applicants immediately after they had made their statements, since the obtaining of statements was only part of an investigation of
an offence, and the Gardaí had been entitled to extend the period of detention
of the applicants under s.4 of the 1984 Act for a further period of six hours
for the purposes of facilitating the identification parade.

Other issues are dealt with separately below (201 and 236).

3 *Opinion grounding arrest Director of Public Prosecutions v Lynch*, High
Court, 7 November 1990 is an important decision on the explicit evidence
required to establish that a Garda had formed the necessary opinion on which
to ground an arrest under s.49 of the Road Traffic Act 1961: see 243, below.

COURT OF CRIMINAL APPEAL

Limit of appellate jurisdiction   In *The People v Egan (L.)* [1990] ILRM
780, the Supreme Court affirmed the well- established limits on the Court of
Criminal Appeal's appellate function. In so doing, the Court rejected the
attempted importation of the 'lurking doubt' concept. For previous discussion of the Court of Criminal Appeal's own approach see the 1989
Review, 178-9.

In *Egan*, the appellant had been convicted of rape in the Circuit Criminal
Court and sentenced to 10 years penal servitude. He applied for leave to
appeal to the Court of Criminal Appeal, which dismissed the application on
the ground that to allow the appeal would be to substitute the verdict of the
Court of Criminal Appeal for that of the jury. The Court certified, however,
that the case raised a point of law of exceptional public importance under
s.29 of the 1924 Act. The Supreme Court (Finlay CJ, Hamilton P, Griffin,
McCarthy and O'Flaherty JJ) dismissed the appeal. Judgments were
delivered by McCarthy and O'Flaherty JJ, and the other three members of
the Court agreed with both.

The judgments were in agreement that the Court of Criminal Appeal had
no jurisdiction under s.34 of the Courts of Justice Act 1924, as applied by
s.12 of the Courts (Supplemental Provisions) Act 1961, to overturn the
verdict of a jury on subjective criteria such as a 'lurking doubt' as to the
correctness of the verdict reached in the trial court. Once again, therefore,
the Irish courts rejected the suggested test posited by the Court of Appeal
(Criminal Division) in *R. v Cooper* [1969] 1 QB 267. It preferred the
established Irish approach as indicated by the Court of Criminal Appeal in
The People v Mulligan (1980) 2 Frewen 16 and indeed the decision of the
Supreme Court itself in *The People v Kelly (No. 2)* [1983] IR 1.

Applying that approach to the instant case, the Supreme Court concluded that that since the trial judge had correctly directed the jury as to the legal issues arising and that as the verdict was peculiarly one for the jury in the light of the conflicting evidence which had been presented in the trial court, the Court of Criminal Appeal had been correct in refusing to interfere with the verdict reached.

It must be assumed that this decision represents the authoritative view by the Irish courts on the limits to their appellate functions in criminal matters. While this no doubt reinforces well-established case law, the reference to the English decision in *R. v Cooper* [1969] 1 QB 267 is of wider interest than the Supreme Court seems to have indicated. The 'lurking doubt' concept was floated by the English Court of Appeal (Criminal Division) in the context of the then newly- created reference procedure created by the U.K. Criminal Appeal Act 1968. This is, of course, the procedure by which the British Home Secretary may refer a matter to the Court of Appeal in what might be described colloquially as 'miscarriages of justice' cases, such as the Guilford Four and Birmingham Six cases. The 'lurking doubt' concept might be regarded as an attempt by the English judges to recognise the novel nature of the reference procedure under the 1968 Act. However, as was pointed out by O'Higgins CJ in *The People v Kelly (No. 2)* [1983] IR 1, later decisions of the Court of Appeal (Criminal Division) had sought to retreat to traditional principles in outlining the limited appellate function of the Court of Appeal (Criminal Division) under the 1968 Act.

What is of interest, therefore, is that that the Supreme Court in the *Egan* case, following the lead in the *Kelly* case, would appear to be signalling in advance what its attitude would be in the event that the Court of Criminal Appeal is given an appellate jurisdiction along lines similar to those in the English Criminal Appeal Act 1968. The Court's indications in *Egan* might lead one to conclude that the Oireachtas should not anticipate any revolutionary change in the operation of the Court of Criminal Appeal's traditional approach to criminal appeals. In other words, the Irish judiciary is unlikely to deal with any Irish 'miscarriages of justice' by reference to a 'feel' for the case or a 'lurking doubt' about the safety of convictions. In so far as the *Egan* decision is a pointer on this, the Irish courts have indicated that they would be just as uncomfortable as their English counterparts in pushing out the well-established boundaries of the appellate court's function in this regard.

The *Egan* decision was referred to approvingly in *The People v McDonagh and Cawley*, Court of Criminal Appeal, 24 July 1990: see 238-9, below.

DEATH PENALTY ABOLITION

S. 1 of the Criminal Justice Act 1990 provided for the formal abolition of the death penalty in Irish law. No execution had in fact taken place in the State since 1954. The Criminal Justice Act 1964 had abolished the death penalty for murder, except for certain categories of murder such as of members of the Garda Síochána acting in the course of their duty. The decision of the Supreme Court in *The People v Murray* [1977] IR 360 established the need for specific knowledge or recklessness before the capital offence would be deemed to be committed. While the courts had, since *Murray*, handed down a number of death sentences in respect of murders of members of the Garda Síochána, these sentences had invariably been commuted by the President acting on the advice of the government to ones of 40 years penal servitude.

Despite this practice, the death penalty remained on the statute books but the 1990 Act has finally removed it entirely, following a number of previous failed legislative attempts to do so. The 1990 Act has, in a sense, made the practice a legislative rule by providing, in s.3, that the categories of murder which attracted the death penalty under the 1964 Act will now carry a minimum mandatory sentence of 40 years imprisonment. S.5 of the 1990 Act provides that, while 40 years will be the normal actual sentence to be served, the constitutional power to pardon, commute and remit under Article 13.6 of the Constitution is not affected. This appears to leave some element of flexibility in the actual term which might be served.

The 1990 Act was passed over the objections of Garda representatives in particular who argued that the residual continuation of capital punishment was a necessary defence against armed violence in the State. Nonetheless, the Act was broadly accepted and the Minister for Justice argued that the 40 year prison sentence constituted a continuing deterrent in this respect. There remains some doubt, however, as to whether a mandatory sentence of this nature is compatible with the rehabilitative goals of sentencing expressed by the courts. See, for example, the discussion of the principle stated by Walsh J in *The People v O'Driscoll* (1972) 1 Frewen 351 in the 1988 Review, 179-84.

DELAY IN ISSUING AND PROSECUTING CHARGES

C. v Director of Public Prosecutions, High Court, 2 October 1990 is another decision on the effects of delay in bringing a criminal prosecution. The applicant's niece, aged 9 years, made a statement to the Gardaí, in the course of an interview concerning another person, that the applicant had engaged in buggery and indecent assault with her. This statement had been made in the presence of the niece's mother, the applicant's sister. The applicant's sister then also made a statement to the effect that the applicant had frequently had full sexual intercourse with her while she had been living at home.

The Director of Public Prosecutions decided not to prosecute the applicant in respect of the statement made by his niece, but a prosecution was brought in respect of the statement made by his sister. The book of evidence contained a statement by the sister in which she stated that she had not previously made a complaint to the Gardaí about the applicant because she was afraid of him. She had, however, complained to their father who, she stated, had protected her from the applicant to some extent. The book of evidence contained no statement from the father of the applicant and his sister, the complainant. The offences were alleged to have taken place nine years before the charges were brought.

The applicant sought an order of prohibition preventing his trial from going ahead, on the ground that the delay had prejudiced his right to a fair trial, arising from his difficulty in recalling the events of nine years ago. Barr J granted the order sought. He accepted that the applicant's sister might have had good grounds for not informing the Gardaí about the applicant, having regard to a general reluctance by a young person to discuss such matters outside the family setting. However, he was also prepared to accept that she had complained to her father about the matter, and that there had been no explanation from him as to why he had not brought the matter to the attention of the Gardaí. Barr J concluded that the delay of nine years was an unreasonable one and that, in the circumstances, the applicant had been prejudiced in his ability to prepare his defence and that he had been deprived of his constitutional right to fair procedures and a fair trial.

It is disappointing that Barr J did not refer to any Irish authority on this area, particularly the decision of the Supreme Court, affirming Gannon J, in *O'Flynn and Hannigan v Clifford* [1990] ILRM 65; [1989] IR 524 (1988 Review, 147-50 and 1989 Review, 141). In that case, the Court had affirmed the point that delays between the commission of an offence and the bringing of charges were to be treated quite differently from delays after the charges have been brought. The only case that Barr J did refer to was the decision of the House of Lords in *R. v Lawrence* [1982] AC 510, a case concerning delays *after* charges were brought. Had Barr J referred to the *O'Flynn* case, his approach might have been quite different. No doubt, the delay in the instant case was quite long, but as Walsh J pointed out in the *O'Flynn* case no person has the *right* to be charged with an offence of which they were suspected. This might be applied a fortiori to the instant case, where the Gardaí had no inkling whatever that an offence had been committed. This is not to say that in all such cases the prosecution should be allowed to go ahead; but it indicates that the approach adopted by Barr J may not be reliable. It is one thing to prohibit a prosecution based on the inactivity of State institutions; it seems quite difficult to transplant the same reasoning to the private reasons for inactivity which arose in the instant case.

DISTRICT COURT

Advance notice of evidence In *Kelly v O'Sullivan*, High Court, 11 July 1990 Gannon J appeared to rule out any situation in which the prosecution in a summary trial might be required to give advance notice of its case to the defence. The applicant had been tried summarily in the District Court on charges of using threatening language and of conduct likely to lead to a breach of the peace. The offences were alleged to have taken place on a lake in the course of a protest against the rod licence legislation, the Fisheries (Amendment) (No. 2) Act 1987 (1987 Review, xiii and 214). The applicant was one of 18 people involved in the protest all of whom were charged with similar offences.

The applicant was represented in the District Court by a solicitor who also represented all the other defendants. In advance of the District Court hearing, the solicitor sought by letter from the Director of Public Prosecutions some precise information as to, *inter alia*, the time of the alleged incidents on which the charges were based as well as agreement to have separate hearings of the charges against the defendants. The solicitor acting for the DPP replied that such requests were not appropriate in a summary prosecution. In the District Court all cases were heard together and a number of the defendants were found guilty. The respondent Justice indicated to the applicant that he was prepared to apply the Probation of Offenders Act 1907 if the applicant apologised for his actions. The applicant, having been advised by his solicitor as to the implications involved, declined to apologise. The applicant was convicted and bound over to keep the peace for 12 months. The applicant sought judicial review of the conviction. Gannon J remitted the case to the District Court, though in substance he affirmed the major elements of the respondent's approach.

Gannon J first of all held that the respondent Justice had been correct in treating the applicant's case as any other case of summary jurisdiction, and that the trial had been conducted in a regular and proper manner. He also held that there was no basis for the contention that the respondent should have had from the prosecution information as to how it intended to conduct the trial. While informality is, no doubt, the distinguishing feature of the summary procedure, it may be questioned whether a blanket refusal to provide advance information is constitutionally sound. Article 38.1 requires that all criminal trials be conducted in due course of law, while Article 40.3 constitutes a guarantee of fair procedures in decision-making processes. In many instances the courts have recognised that fair procedures may require advance notice as well as simply the opportunity to challenge evidence. For example, in *Nolan v Irish Land Commission* [1981] IR 23 the Supreme Court ordered the Land Commission to permit the plaintiff advance access to papers in its possession prior to a compulsory acquisition hearing. And in *The State (Williams) v Army Pensions Board* [1983] IR 308, the Court rejected the respondent Board's refusal to allow access to certain papers in its possession, which the Board had attempted to defend on the basis of 'settled practice.' These cases indicate that, in certain instances, the requirements of fair procedures must outweigh established practice. It also may be relevant to note that in Britain, specific information prior to a Magistrates' Court summary trial may be required in certain instances.

To revert to the *Kelly* case, the applicant had also argued that he had been put under undue pressure to plead guilty, but Gannon J concluded that the suggestion by the respondent Justice that he might apply the Probation of Offenders Act 1907 in the event of an apology by the applicant did not constitute an interference with the applicant's right to fair procedures. He took particular account of the fact that the applicant had been given the opportunity of considering the effect of this suggestion by consulting his solicitor.

As for binding the applicant over, he held that there was evidence before the District Court to indicate the possibility that the behaviour complained of might be repeated. To that extent, the indicia required to bind a person over, as described by Palles CB in *R. (Boylan) v Londonderry Justices* [1912] 2 IR 374 and approved by Gannon J in the instant case, appeared to be present. However, he noted that a finding by the respondent of such apprehension was not actually recorded in the order made, so that the jurisdiction to make the order had not been established. In the circumstances Gannon J concluded that it was appropriate to remit the matter to the District Court to enable the respondent to make the order he intended.

Finally, Gannon J made no order as to costs, because of the fact that the respondent's order had been made *per incuriam* by following a long-established practice and also because the applicant had failed to establish the other grounds put forward.

Note of proceedings The year saw a number of cases that virtually resurrected a point of procedure arising from the Petty Sessions (Ireland) Act 1851. In *Friel v McMenamin* [1990] ILRM 761; [1990] 2 IR 210 and *Hegarty v Fitzpatrick* [1990] 2 IR 377, Barron and Murphy JJ, respectively, held that the failure by a District Justice to keep a note of criminal proceedings did not invalidate those proceedings.

The circumstances in the *Hegarty* case were as follows. The applicant had been convicted by the respondent Justice of an offence under s.49 of the Road Traffic Act 1961, as amended. The applicant sought judicial review of the conviction on the following grounds: (i) that the District Court (Courts Act 1971) Rules 1972, which inserted new rr.84 and 85 of the District Court Rules 1948, were *ultra vires* in purporting to revoke the right to obtain copies of a note of evidence taken by a Justice. It was claimed that such a note was required under s.20 of the Petty Sessions (Ireland) Act 1851; (ii) the respondent acted contrary to s.20 of the 1851 Act in failing to keep a note of the evidence in the case, thus denying the applicant his right to natural and constitutional justice; (iii) there was no adequate proof before the respondent of the complaint on which the charge was made. Murphy J dismissed the application for judicial review.

Following the decision of Barron J in the *Friel* case, above, Murphy J held that the 1972 Rules were not *ultra vires*, on the ground that the right to obtain copies of a note kept in accordance with s.20 of the 1851 Act had been conferred by the 1948 Rules, and therefore it was permissible for the District Court Rules Committee to revoke such right in the 1972 Rules.

Murphy J also held that, although the respondent had failed to keep a note of the evidence as required by s.20 of the 1851 Act, this did not invalidate his order convicting the applicant, there being no dispute between the parties as to the evidence adduced before the respondent. The fact that the parties agreed on the evidence adduced may be significant in future cases, where the legislative intention of s.20 of the 1851 Act may be examined in more detail. It might be argued, for example, that the purpose of s.20 was to ensure that an independent record of proceedings be kept in the event of a disagreement between the legal representatives of prosecution and defence as to the precise course of events. While such disagreements may be few, it can hardly be argued that s.20 has no legislative substance. It may prove extremely inconvenient in the context of the enormous workload of the District Court, but unless and until it is repealed it can hardly be ignored, unless it can be regarded as having fallen 'into a limbo of disuetude', in the words of Henchy J in *Waterford Harbour Commissioners v British Railways Board* [1979] ILRM 296, 353 (quoted in *The State (Feeley) v O'Dea* [1986] IR 687)

Finally, in *Hegarty*, although the evidence before the respondent indicated that a complaint had been made on a date which was different from that stated on the summons, the respondent was entitled pursuant to r.88 of the 1948 Rules to deal with the matter once satisfied that a valid complaint had been made.

On a separate note, Murphy J drew attention to what he thought was a serious error of punctuation in s.14 of the Courts Act 1971 and that this error might preclude any reference to any record of a decision of a Justice of the District Court. The error concerns the position of a bracket in s.14, which if taken at face value would have the effect, as Murphy J indicated, of precluding any reference to any record of a District Justice's decision. Of course, it is unfortunate when an error of this kind occurs but it may be that, if this particular issue arose, the courts would ignore the defect in order to avoid an unintelligible provision. Not all 'obvious errors' will be 'corrected' by the courts, of course, and in the absence of an amended s.14 a fine distinction might be required between such cases as *The State (Murphy) v Johnson* [1983] IR 235 (error not corrected) and *The State (Rollinson) v Kelly* [1984] ILRM 625; [1984] IR 248 (error corrected).

Preliminary examination   In *Glavin v Governor of Training Unit Mountjoy Prison* [1991] ILRM 478, the suggestion was made that the preliminary examination was a constitutionally required procedure: see 155-7, above, in the Constitutional Law chapter.

Striking out   In *Carpenter v Kirby* [1990] ILRM 764 the applicant had been charged with firearms offences for which he was remanded by the first respondent for serving of the book of evidence under the Criminal Procedure Act 1967. After his remand, it came to the attention of the Director of Public Prosecutions (the second respondent) that the charge sheet on which he had been charged omitted to state that the offence had occurred within the Dublin Metropolitan District area. The Director applied to have the charge struck out and the respondent acceded to the request. The applicant sought judicial review on the grounds that the respondent acted in excess of s.8 of the 1967 Act and that the decision had involved fundamentally unfair procedures but Barr J dismissed the application.

He held that the striking out was the appropriate order for the respondent to make where he considered that he might not have jurisdiction to deal with the charge. Barr J did add, however, that the Director and the respondent may have been unduly cautious on the jurisdiction question having regard to Article 2(a) of the District Court Districts (Dublin) (Amendment) Order 1982.

As to delay, Barr J concluded that although there had been some delay in recharging the applicant, this did not taint the second charging. In fact the point was, in effect, conceded by counsel for the applicant and it must be assumed that Barr J saw no prejudice arising from the recharging of the applicant.

The report of the case also notes that the Supreme Court (Griffin, McCarthy and O'Flaherty JJ) affirmed Barr J's decision *ex tempore* on 25 May 1990.

ENTRY ON PREMISES

The decision in *Minister for Justice (Clarke) v Wang Zhu Jie*, High Court, 5 October 1990 involved a net but important point as to the use of entry powers by the Gardaí. In this instance the Gardaí had entered a restaurant in a routine entry as part of their supervision of the Aliens Act 1935. The Gardaí had no evidence to indicate that any breach of the Aliens Act 1935 was occurring in the restaurant at the time, and it appeared that such entries were very common. The evidence indicated that the Gardaí did not seek search warrants under the 1935 Act, that they were well known and that invariably entry was not refused.

The defendant had approached the Gardaí, who were in plain clothes and asked them 'How many?', indicating that he would bring them to a table. After a brief conversation, the defendant was arrested under the Aliens Act. The manager of the restaurant continued talking to the Gardaí after the arrest had been effected. Costello J held that, in the circumstances the Gardaí could not be considered trespassers on the premises so that the arrest of the defendant had been lawful. Costello J held that the circumstances in the instant case were quite different from those in *Director of Public Prosecutions v McMahon* [1987] ILRM 87; [1986] IR 393. In *McMahon*, the Supreme Court held that, in the absence of the agreement or the invitation of the owner of premises, the Gardaí must be treated as trespassers on such property where they enter without a warrant authorising entry. The background to the entry in the instant case was quite different from that in *McMahon*; another point of distinction being that in *McMahon* the entry was with a view to law enforcement against the occupier of the premises rather than against any person found on the premises.

Costello J also declined to grant leave to appeal to the Supreme Court, and the Supreme Court, in judgments delivered on 7 May 1991, held that it had no jurisdiction to hear an appeal against such refusal. That decision will be considered in the 1991 Review.

EVIDENCE

1 Confessions: Custody Regulations In *The People v O'Toole and Hickey*, Court of Criminal Appeal, 20 July 1990 (the circumstances of which are outlined above, 190) the Court dealt, briefly, with one aspect of the Criminal Justice Act 1984 (Treatment of Persons in Custody in Garda Síochána Stations) Regulations 1987 (SI No. 119). As was pointed out in the 1987 Review, 119, failure to observe the terms of the 1987 Regulations does not in itself affect the admissibility of confessions obtained as a result: see s.7(3) of the Criminal Justice Act 1984. The procedures to be followed in the 1987 Regulations constitute, therefore, a statutory form of the Judges' Rules, though the Judges' Rules also appear to continue to operate. It is a matter for the trial judge to decide, as a matter of discretion, whether confessions obtained in breach of the Regulations should be admitted in evidence. In *O'Toole and Hickey* one of the applicants complained that he had been questioned for in excess of 4 hours. Reg.12(4) of the 1987 Regulations provides that '[i]f an interview has lasted for four hours, it shall be either terminated or adjourned for a reasonable time.' The Court of Criminal Appeal, upholding the view taken by Barr J, the trial judge, concluded that since the statement made by the applicant had not been made after four hours continuous questioning, the question of the judge's discretion did not in fact arise. And although the applicant now argued that he had been confused, oppressed, disorientated and fatigued at the time the statement was made, this line of argument was also rejected by the Court on the basis that these points had not been put at his trial.

2 Constitutional rights: deliberate and conscious violation In the 1989 Review, 146, we described the judgment of the Supreme Court in *The People v Kenny (M.)* [1990] ILRM 569 (SC); [1990] 2 IR 110 (CCA & SC) as a landmark decision. In its July 1990 judgment, the Supreme Court held that evidence obtained by means of an action by a member of the Garda Síochána, which violated a constitutional right of an accused person, was inadmissible regardless of whether the Garda who obtained the evidence was aware that a right had been violated. As mentioned in the 1989 Review, the decision clarifies, therefore, the meaning of the phrase 'deliberate and conscious violation' which first appeared in the Supreme Court decision in *The People v O'Brien* [1965] IR 142.

The background to the case was as follows. The appellant had been charged in the Circuit Criminal Court with offences under the Misuse of Drugs Acts 1977 and 1984. The principal evidence against him consisted of quantities of controlled drugs which had been found in his flat pursuant to a search warrant obtained by the Garda Síochána under s.26 of the 1977 Act, as amended by the 1984 Act. The Garda applying for the search warrant had sworn an information stating that he suspected that controlled drugs were in the flat in contravention of the 1977 Act, as amended. The Peace Commissioner who granted the warrant acted on the sworn information without further evidence. At the appellant's trial, the trial judge ruled admissible the evidence obtained on foot of the search warrant, and the appellant was subsequently found guilty of the offences charged. The appellant unsuccessfully appealed to the Court of Criminal Appeal, but on further appeal pursuant to s.29 of the Courts of Justice Act 1924 his conviction was set aside by the Supreme Court.

As to the invalidity of the search warrant, there was no disagreement between the courts. The Court of Criminal Appeal (McCarthy, O'Hanlon and Lardner JJ) approved the decision of Hamilton P in *Byrne v Grey* [1988] IR 31 (see the discussion in the 1987 Review, 85-6 and the 1988 Review, 192-4), and in line with that decision, the Court concluded that the search warrant was invalid since the Peace Commissioner had acted purely on the say-so of the Garda who applied for the warrant and had failed to exercise any independent judicial discretion as required by s.26 of the 1977 Act, as amended by the 1984 Act. But the Court of Criminal Appeal concluded that this did not affect the admissibility of evidence obtained in the course of the search since any breach of the appellant's constitutional rights had not been 'deliberate and conscious': see the 1989 Review, 146-8. The Supreme Court disagreed and, by a 3-2 majority (Finlay CJ, Walsh and Hederman JJ; Griffin and Lynch JJ dissenting), ruled inadmissible the evidence obtained in the search.

The *Kenny* case thus involves a clear connection between breach of constitutional rights and the exclusion of evidence so obtained, and so required yet another re-appraisal of the exclusionary rule first referred to in *The People v O'Brien* [1965] IR 142. There have been a number of decisions since then, both of the Court of Criminal Appeal and of the Supreme Court, which have demonstrated a clear division of opinion among the judges as to how that exclusionary rule works: see the informative discussion by O'Connor, (1982) 17 *Ir Jur (ns)* 257. Much of the disagreement centres on the meaning of the phrase 'deliberate and conscious violation of con- stitutional rights', the litmus test of admissibility in *O'Brien*. Is evidence inadmissible under this test only where a member of the Garda Síochána engages in an intentional violation of a constitutional right? Yes said the Court of Criminal Appeal in *Kenny*; no said the Supreme Court.

The answer to this question is not simply a matter of a dictionary definition of the words 'deliberate and conscious'; it involves important policy issues concerning the purpose of the exclusionary rule. This has been a major discussion point in the United States Supreme Court where a strict ex- clusionary rule had been introduced many years prior to the *O'Brien* decision. Through a number of decisions in the 1960s, the US Supreme Court had explained that the rule was intended to deter unlawful activity by the police. The 'penalty' was to exclude unconstitutionally obtained evidence. By the 1980s, with a differently constituted Supreme Court, there was a degree of drawing back from the exclusionary rule. The decision in *United States v Leon*, 468 US 897 (1984) is representative of this change of heart by the United States Supreme Court. The question thus posed in the *Kenny* case was whether the Irish exclusionary rule was intended as a deterrance against unlawful police conduct. The Supreme Court decision has made it plain that its primary purpose is quite different: the vindication of constitutional rights. We do not take issue with the basic premise, but we will argue here that the phrase 'deliberate and conscious' may have outlived its usefulness.

Delivering the leading judgment for the majority of the Court, Finlay CJ held that the exclusionary rule should be based on an approach which would be likely to provide a stronger and more effective defence and vindication of constitutional rights. He pointed out that to exclude evidence only where a person knows or ought reasonably to know that he is invading a constitutional right would be to impose a negative deterrent. However, to exclude evidence on the basis of what the Chief Justice described as the absolute protection rule of exclusion (that is in circumstances where there is a conscious and deliberate violation of rights without regard to the state of knowledge of the policeman) incorporates, he said, an additional positive encouragement to those involved in crime prevention and detection to consider in detail the effects of their powers on the personal rights of the citizen.

He acknowledged that although the absolute protection rule of exclusion might lead to anomalies in its application, and might hinder the capacity of the courts to arrive at the truth and thus to administer justice effectively, this could not outweigh the obligation to protect personal rights pursuant to Article 40.3. Accordingly the courts must rule inadmissible evidence obtained in violation of constitutional rights unless the act constituting the breach was committed unintentionally or accidently, or there are extraordinary excusing circumstances justifying its admissibility. To the extent that the majority decision in *The People v Shaw* [1982] IR 1 appeared to be in conflict with this approach, the Chief Justice stated that he would not be prepared to follow it. And the rationale for the exclusionary rule put forward in *United States v Leon*, 468 US 897 (1984) was expressly disapproved. The Court's decision in *The People v Healy (P.)* [1990] ILRM 313 (see the 1989 Review, 137) was followed.

In conclusion, the majority held that since the acts of the Gardaí in the instant case were neither unintentional or accidental and there were no extraordinary excusing circumstances present, the evidence obtained was inadmissible even though the Gardaí had no knowledge that they were invading the constitutional rights of the appellant. Accordingly the appellant's conviction was quashed. In dissent, Griffin and Lynch JJ considered that the acts of the Gardaí could not be regarded as amounting to conscious and deliberate violations of the appellant's constitutional rights, within the meaning of the case law to date.

The view of Lynch J in dissent is worthy of some discussion. In essence, his view points up the unreality of the continued use of the phrase 'conscious and deliberate'. It is difficult to describe the activities of the Gardaí in the instant case as a conscious decision to breach the defendant's rights except in the very limited sense of 'not unconscious.' It is accepted that the Gardaí intended to obtain the search warrants in issue in the instant case: in that sense the action was conscious. But it is more difficult to read into their actions a deliberate attempt to violate a constitutional right. Indeed, at the time of the application for a warrant, an informed observer might readily have said that the procedure adopted appeared to conform with all constitutional requirements. It was only when the case came before the Court of Criminal Appeal that it was 'discovered' — in the light of *Byrne v Grey* [1988] IR 31 — that the action was in fact in breach of constitutional requirements. Judicial decisions at the time of the application for the search warrant had failed to signal to the Gardaí that the warrant was fatally flawed. Looked at in this light, the 'conscious and deliberate' test does not assist an analysis of why the evidence obtained was declared inadmissible. The judgment of Lynch J indicates this weakness. Indeed, it might even be said that the 'conscious and deliberate' test merely masks the fact that the *Byrne v Grey* decision operated retrospectively, because the search warrant in *Byrne* was obtained on 3 August 1986 (the High Court decision in the case being given on 9 October 1987), while the search warrant in *Kenny* had been obtained on 29 September 1984 (over 3 years before any Irish judge had suggested that the procedure adopted was defective).

In reality, the courts held in *Kenny* that a constitutional right was violated and that this fact in itself was sufficient to render the evidence inadmissible. But the terminology of 'conscious and deliberate violation' seems redundant set against the background of what occurred. There was no intentional violation of rights in the ordinary sense of the word, as where inhuman and degrading treatment is used or where an interrogation is knowingly continued beyond permitted statutory time limits. Nor was it a case of a 'clerical error' as in the *O'Brien* case. The *Kenny* case was simply one where the state of mind of the Gardaí was irrelevant, but the use of the 'conscious and deliberate' test made it seem relevant. This allowed for the criticism of the decision in Lynch J's judgment. Perhaps, in a future case the Supreme Court may return to this and acknowledge that a better approach is to state simply that the judicial process cannot be tainted by evidence obtained in violation of constitutional rights, regardless of the state of mind of the Gardaí who obtained that evidence. That approach was endorsed by O'Higgins CJ in *The People v Lynch* [1981] ILRM 389; [1982] IR 64, quoting Warren CJ in *Terry v Ohio*, 392 US 1 (1968). If this approach can be used — without the somewhat dubious rationale employed in the US that it is intended to punish police misconduct — then the less useful 'conscious and deliberate' test may be discarded. The essential exclusionery rule would still remain.

3 Forensic evidence The Criminal Justice (Forensic Evidence) Act 1990 provides the Gardaí with the power to take various bodily samples from persons detained under either s.30 of the Offences against the State Act 1939 or under s.4 of the Criminal Justice Act 1984. In effect, the Act is designed to facilitate DNA or genetic fingerprinting techniques.

S.2(1) of the Act contains the list of bodily samples which may be taken from a person in custody. These include samples of blood, hair, urine, saliva, nail, swabs from body parts, a dental impression or a footprint. S.2(8) provides that samples of blood, urine or of swabs from a body orifice or a genital region may only be taken by a registered medical practitioner and a dental impression may only be taken by a registered dentist or registered medical practitioner.

S.2(4) requires that authorisation for the taking of a sample can only be given by a Garda not below the rank of superintendent. S.2(5) requires that such authorisation shall not be given unless: (a) the Garda in question has reasonable grounds for suspecting the involvement of the person from whom the sample is to be taken in the offence in respect of which he is in custody; and (b) the Garda has reasonable grounds for believing that the sample 'will tend to confirm or disprove the involvement of the person from whom the sample is to be taken' in the offence in respect of which he is in custody. The second precondition, at first sight, may appear difficult to comply with in some instances. Thus, a Garda may be hard pressed to explain why a sample is being taken from a person already in custody in order to 'disprove' involvement in the offence for which the person has been detained. Does 'confirm or disprove' indicate conjunctive or disjunctive belief in the mind of the authorising Garda? Is it sufficient, in other words, if the Garda believes that the sample may tend to confirm involvement of the detained person? Or does it indicate that the Garda should have an 'open mind' on the possible result of the DNA fingerprint that arises from the sample?

The Act contains important provisions on consent. S.2(4) requires the consent of the detained person where any of the following is being sought: (i) blood; (ii) pubic hair; (iii) urine; (iv) saliva; (v) a swab from a body orifice or a genital region; or (vi) a dental impression. However, s.3 goes on to provide that where a person refuses 'without good cause' to consent to the samples in question, a court of trial 'may draw such inferences, if any, from the refusal as appear proper.' The section also provides that the refusal may be treated as 'corroboration of any evidence in relation to which the refusal is material', though a person may not be convicted solely on the basis of a refusal. In addition, s.3 requires that the full implications of refusal must be made known to the person detained. S.3 of the 1990 Act is modelled on the 'inference' sections in the Criminal Justice Act 1984 (ss.18 and 19). The constitutional validity of such inferences has never been tested in this State and it remains to be seen whether they could withstand a challenge. Two points at least might arise in any such challenge. The first is whether what amounts to compulsive bodily invasion constitutes an unjust attack on the right to bodily integrity under Article 40.3 of the Constitution. The second then relates to the effect of inferences on the evidential burden and the burden of proof in criminal trials. No doubt the relatively sanguine approach of Costello J in *O'Leary v Attorney General* [1991] ILRM 454 may be relevant in this context (see the discussion, 178-82, above in the Constitutional Law chapter).

For a critical analysis of the reliability of DNA testing as well as of the implications of the 1990 Act for the criminal justice system see Fennell's article in the inaugural edition of the *Irish Criminal Law Journal* (1991) *ICLJ* 34. See also the Family Law chapter, 315-16, below.

4 Identification parade: when required In *The People v O'Reilly* [1991] ILRM 10, the Court of Criminal Appeal provided some guidance as to the circumstances in which formal identification parades should take place.

The applicant had been convicted of larceny in the Circuit Criminal Court and sentenced to four years penal servitude. The principal prosecution witness was an 85 year old woman from whom a sum of money had been stolen by a gang of people. Her description referred to one of the gang as having 'a most notorious face, an awful face.' She was brought by the Gardaí from her home in Athlone to Edgeworthstown, Co Longford in a Garda car from which she was asked whether she recognised any of the people on the street. Having made a partial identification of one person among a group of three, she made a positive identification of the applicant, the person alleged to have the singular face she had earlier described. At the trial of the applicant, she again identified him as the person involved in the robbery of her money. The trial judge gave a warning to the jury on the danger of convicting on the identification evidence of the prosecution witness. The Court of Criminal Appeal (O'Flaherty, Barr and Lavan JJ) allowed the applicant's appeal and quashed his conviction.

Delivering the Court's judgment, O'Flaherty J held that in the circumstances which arose, a formal identification parade should have been held. While he was prepared to accept the Garda contention that they had acted out of a mistaken belief that the method of identification used might be for the benefit of the applicant, O'Flaherty J concluded that this explanation was 'less than satisfactory', the phrase which had been used by the Court in *The People v Fagan* (1974) 1 Frewen 375. O'Flaherty J's judgment stated that while it was important that the Gardaí should be scrupulous in looking to the rights of the accused, he suggested that the decision as to what is best for the accused:

must be primarily a matter for the decision of the accused and his legal
adviser (if he has a legal adviser at the time).

It would, of course, be unfortunate were members of the Garda Síochána
to misinterpret this comment. It clearly should not be taken to dilute in any
manner the constitutional and other legal obligations placed on Gardaí to
observe the law of the State. It should also be borne in mind that, as the law
stands at present, an accused person does not have a clear right to have a
lawyer present during interrogation. The provisions of the Criminal Justice
Act 1984 do represent some element of such a right, and the courts have
indicated that access to a solicitor in Garda custody has a constittuional
dimension: *The People v Healy (P.)* [1990] ILRM 313; [1990] 2 IR 73 (1989
Review, 137-9). Nonetheless, in many instances the Garda in charge of a
prosecution will be the only person in a position to influence what is 'best
for the accused.' In this context it is of interest to note also that the Criminal
Justice Act 1984 (Treatment of Persons in Custody in Garda Síochána
Stations) Regulations 1987 envisage that the rights of the accused person
should be taken into account by the Gardaí at all times.

To return to the *O'Reilly* case, the Court of Criminal Appeal, without
laying down that a formal identification was required in all cases, emphatically denied that they had not outgrown their usefulness. O'Flaherty J
pointed out that the parade was a procedure in which the accused person (or
his legal adviser) has an input to ensure its fairness, as opposed to the informal
mechanism used in the instant case; and the court of trial would also have
the benefit of a detailed account of the parade. And without attempting to
describe in an exhaustive manner the elements involved in a formal parade
(noting that some criticism was made of the particular parade in *The People
v O'Driscoll* (1972) 1 Frewen 351), the Court provided a useful outline of
agreed elements, which is worth quoting:

> It involves that there are assembled eight or nine people of similar age,
> height, appearance, dress and walk of life as the suspect; that the parade
> will be supervised by an independent Garda (that is, one not concerned
> with the actual investigation); that full details will be kept of the
> description of the various people making up the parade; and that the
> witness should not have any opportunity of seeing the suspect in
> advance of the holding of the parade.

Without indicating whether the absence of a formal parade would, in itself,
have been fatal to the conviction, the Court also noted that in the instant case
the identification witness had in fact been given a photograph of the applicant
prior to the informal identification which had taken place. The Court felt that

this added to its concern as to the safeness of the conviction. It pointed out that defence counsel had been 'left with Hobson's Choice' since, to mention this fact during the trial would have suggested that the accused was possibly a person of bad character. This potential for prejudice to the accused by such disclosure seems indeed to be significant: see *Doob and Kirschenbaum* (1972) 15 *Crim LQ* 88 and *Sealy and Cornish* (1973) 36 *MLR* 496.

In *O'Reilly*, the Court held that the trial judge's ruling was required on the admissibility of the identification evidence obtained in what the Court described as 'such frail circumstances.' While the phtograph given to the witness in the instant case may have been pivotal, it is useful to bear in mind that, in a future case, the question as to whether to hold an identification parade might turn on the other factor which faded into the background in the instant case, namely the singular appearance of the accused. The *Fagan* case is strong authority for the proposition that an identification parade in wuch circumstances would be invidious to such a person, for obvious reasons. This brings us back to the question of concern for the rights of the accused.

Ultimately, the Court in *O'Reilly* concluded that the trial judge had fallen into the trap identified in the seminal decision of the Supreme Court in *The People v Casey (No. 2)* [1963] IR 33. The judgment of Kingsmill Moore J in that case was quoted extensively by O'Flaherty J to reiterate the dangers of convicting on identification evidence; and that a trial judge must be extremely cautious not to fall into a stereotyped direction to a jury on this point. Although the trial judge had given a warning on this, the Court of Criminal Appeal felt that there was a need in the instant case for more than a general warning, particularly having regard to the absence of a formal identification parade. In the result, the Court held that since the defects in the original trial could not be put right, it would not order a re-trial, and therefore the conviction was quashed outright.

It may be noted here that in *The People v O'Toole and Hickey*, Court of Criminal Appeal, 20 July 1990 (the circumstances in which are discussed above, 190) the Court held that, even where confessions have been obtained by the Gardaí from a person detained under s.4 of the Criminal Justice Act 1984, the Gardaí acted correctly in extending the period of detention for a further period in order to facilitate the holding of an identification parade.

5 Visual identification: security officer The status of visual identification evidence given by a security officer arose in *The People v O'Callaghan*, Court of Criminal Appeal, 30 July 1990. The case also concerned the majority verdict provisions of the Criminal Justice Act 1984.

The applicant had been convicted of robbery arising from an armed hold-up of a bank. The robbers had worn face disguises in the course of the robbery, but the security officer on duty at the bank identified the applicant as one of the robbers. The officer stated that he had been face to face with the applicant before being told to get down on the ground. He stated that he had also remembered seeing the applicant and another person in the bank two days before the robbery and that they had been acting suspiciously. He had also studied the bank's video recording of both occasions, and this was available to the trial court also. The trial judge delivered a warning to the jury on the dangers of convicting on the basis of identification evidence. The jury deliberated for one hour and 43 minutes and returned to court stating that they could not agree on a verdict. The judge told them to attempt to arrive at a unanimous verdict but that he would accept a majority verdict of 10 of them once they had deliberated for over two hours. The Court of Criminal Appeal (Griffin, O'Hanlon and Egan JJ) dismissed an application for leave to appeal.

The Court held that the trial judge had acted correctly in leaving the security officer's evidence to the jury. Delivering the Court's decision, O'Hanlon J noted:

> The witness was not a mere casual passer-by, but a security officer who had worked in that capacity in the bank for over a year prior to the robbery. His duties required him to stand near the entrance to the bank and observe carefully the people who entered and left the bank. The video film shows that he was watchful on the [date two days before the robbery] when the two men entered and that he kept them under constant observation. It also shows that on the occasion of the armed robbery he was face to face with the armed robber and looked directly into his face from a distance of only a few feet for an appreciable time before complying with the order to lie on the ground.

This passage confirms that the combination of the security officer's role and the presence of 'corroborating' technology is likely to have an important influence on the application of rules of evidence.

This may also have affected the judges in their approach to the warning on the visual identification rule, the Court holding that the trial judge had correctly issued a warning to the jury (in accordance with the Supreme Court decision in *The People v Casey (No. 2)* [1963] IR 33) on the dangers of convicting on visual identification, and that it was then a matter for the jury to determine and should not be interfered with.

On the question of the majority verdict, the Court held that since s.25 of the Criminal Justice Act 1984 only prohibits the trial judge from *accepting* a majority verdict after the expiration of two hours, he had not been in breach of s.25 by *informing* the jury that he would accept a majority verdict after two hours deliberation. The Court also opined that the trial judge was free to tell the jury that he would accept a majority verdict at any time before the expiration of the two hour period. It is difficult to detect a precise trend from this particular decision, but it does appear to indicate a somewhat laxer approach by the Court to the majority verdict section. It certainly seems out of kilter with the strict construction approach favoured in *The People v Kelly (J.)* [1989] ILRM 370 (1988 Review, 174). Perhaps like with many such provisions, what is at first seen as a 'signal departure' from traditional protections can eventually become a matter of less importance. It would be highly regrettable if this was to occur in connection with the verdicts of juries in serious criminal trials.

6 Visual identification: warning In *The People v McDermott*, Court of Criminal Appeal, 17 December 1990 the Court (Finlay CJ, Egan and Johnson JJ) in an *ex tempore* judgment overturned a conviction based on identification evidence. While the Court accepted that a *Casey* warning (see above) had been given by the trial judge, the Court noted that it had failed to take account of the particular circumstances of the identification and had not drawn attention to the greater reliability of a formal identification parade. The Court referred with approval to the decision of the Court in *The People v O'Reilly* [1991] ILRM 10, above, 207. In the circumstances, the Court discharged the appellant and did not order a re-trial.

EXTRADITION

1 Correspondence of offences In *Ellis v O'Dea (No. 2)* [1991] ILRM 346, the High Court and Supreme Court dealt with correspondence issues in connection with conspiracy to cause explosions: see 218-9, below.

2 Investigation of conviction In *Clarke v McMahon* [1990] ILRM 648; [1990] 1 IR 228 the Supreme Court held that, exceptionally, there might be a case for investigating the circumstances leading to a conviction on foot of which extradition is sought: see 222, below.

3 Political offence: 1965 Act In 1990, the Supreme Court delivered two important judgments, in the *Finucane* and *Carron* cases, on the political offence exception in s.50 of the Extradition Act 1965. In both, the Supreme Court reversed Divisional High Court decisions of 1989 (1989 Review, 156-9). In essence, the Supreme Court decisions opened up the exception after it had been severely limited in *Quinn v Wren* [1985] ILRM 410; [1984] IR 322 and *Russell v Fanning* [1988] ILRM 333; [1988] IR 505. By declining to extradite the two people involved in the applications the decisions created more tensions in Anglo-Irish relations: see *Irish Times*, 14 and 15 March 1990. A third case, *Clarke v McMahon* [1990] ILRM 648; [1990] 1 IR 228 also resulted in a refusal to extradite: 221-2, below. By the end of the year, however, in *Ellis v O'Dea (No. 2)* [1991] ILRM 346, the Court indicated that extradition was still possible. Perhaps significantly, however, in this case the political offence point was not pressed. The *Ellis* case is of some additional interest, however, because in the High Court the effects of the Extradition (European Convention on the Suppression of Terrorism) Act 1987 were discussed. Because of the relevance of the 1987 Act, we will discuss *Ellis* under a separate heading, below, 217.

In *Finucane v McMahon* [1990] ILRM 505 (SC); [1990] 1 IR 165 (HC & SC), the applicant had been convicted in Northern Ireland in 1982 of possession of firearms with intent to endanger life and was sentenced to 18 years imprisonment. In 1983, he escaped from prison custody in a mass escape. In the course of the escape, a prison officer died after being stabbed. In a subsequent investigation of the escape, the applicant appeared to be identified as the prisoner who stabbed the prison officer. Many prisoners were immediately recaptured and the same investigation concluded that a number of the prisoners had been beaten by prison officers and were refused access to medical attention. Some prisoners were charged with the man-slaughter of the prison officer, but were acquitted on the ground that it had not been proved that the stabbing caused the prison officer's death, it being established that he had had a heart condition. A number of the prisoners involved in the escape also brought claims for damages for assault, and in 1988, in *Pettigrew v Northern Ireland Office* [1989] 3 BNIL 83, Hutton LCJ awarded damages and concluded that there had been a conspiracy to pervert the course of justice on the part of prison officers in the prison. No disciplinary proceedings were brought against any prison officer arising from the escape.

The applicant's extradition to Northern Ireland was ordered in the District Court. He applied to the High Court under s.50 of the 1965 Act and Article 40.4 of the Constitution seeking his release on the grounds, inter alia, that, as he had been identified as being involved in the stabbing of the prison officer, if extradited to Northern Ireland he would be subjected to ill-treatment in the prison and that, in any event, his offence was a political offence or an offence connected with a political offence. In the High Court, his application was refused by a Divisional High Court (Hamilton P, Gannon and Costello JJ) primarily on the grounds that the offence did not fall within the political offence exception and that he had not established that there was a likelihood of his being ill-treated if returned to Northern Ireland: see the 1989 Review, 157-9. On appeal by the applicant, the Supreme Court (Finlay CJ, Walsh, Griffin, Hederman and McCarthy JJ) Court reversed on both these points and released the applicant pursuant to s.50 of the 1965 Act, altering the legal landscape in this area to a considerable degree. The ill-treatment point is dealt with below, 220-1, and the present discussion focuses on the political offence issue.

It will be remembered that in *Quinn v Wren* [1985] ILRM 410; [1985] IR 322, the Supreme Court decided unanimously that the activities of the plaintiff on behalf of the INLA could not attract the political offence exception under s.50 of the 1965 Act. While all the judges stated that each case should be decided on its individual merits, they also unanimously decided that the plaintiff's activities were treasonable under Article 15.6 of the Constitution. The Court in that case comprised Finlay CJ, Henchy, Griffin, Hederman and McCarthy JJ. In *Russell v Fanning* [1988] ILRM 333; [1988] IR 505, a change in the voting pattern became apparent. Finlay CJ, Henchy and Hederman JJ affirmed the *Quinn* decision, and categorised the plaintiff's escape from prison (the same escape as was to be in issue in *Finucane*) in pursuit of the aims of the IRA as treasonable (1988 Review, 154). Hederman and McCarthy JJ, however, took a strong line in dissent, arguing that, if each case is to be considered individually and a 'blanket' approach avoided, some IRA or INLA cases could constitute 'political' activity for extradition purposes. They considered that the escape constituted a 'political' offence under s.50.

The approaches of both (at that stage dissenting) judges are of interest. Thus, McCarthy J had stated in *Quinn* as follows:

> The appellant [Quinn]... committed the offence in order to obtain money to fund the campaign of the INLA which campaign is described in a manner which necessarily includes the overthrow by force of arms of the organs of the State, including the courts. The proposition . . . that the courts should grant protection to a person charged with an offence stamped with such a purpose is ludicrous.

Hederman J also delivered a reasoned judgment in *Quinn* in which he agreed that the activities of the INLA involved treason as contemplated by Article 39 of the Constitution, and as such could not be described as 'political' within the terms of the Extradition Act 1965.

In *Russell*, the plaintiff stated on affidavit that, in carrying out the activities of the IRA (including the prison escape) he did not seek to overthrow the 1937 Constitution but rather sought to reintegrate the National Territory and that if these objectives were achieved the democratic principles of the Constitution would govern the 32 county State thereby established. The majority in effect upheld the view taken by O'Hanlon J in *Russell* that this was merely an attempt to circumvent the *Quinn* decision. However, this 'subjective' factor was crucial to the change in the approach of Hederman and McCarthy JJ between *Quinn* and *Russell*.

They also argued that to apply *Quinn* in the way indicated by the majority in *Russell* would render s.50 virtually meaningless. McCarthy J took judicial notice of what he perceived to be the case that extradition applications from the United Kingdom involved IRA or INLA cases exclusively, so that the *Quinn* approach would deprive all such applicants of any redress under the 1965 Act. Neither he nor Hederman J were prepared to accept that consequence.

This view became orthodoxy in *Finucane*. Between the decision in *Russell* and that in *Finucane*, there was only one change of personnel: Henchy J had resigned to become Chairman of the Independent Radio and Television Commission, and Walsh J became the fifth member of the Court for the *Finucane* case. His judgment in *Finucane* proved to be pivotal.

Essentially, in *Finucane*, the minority *Russell* view simply became the majority view with the presence of Walsh J on the Court. Walsh, Hederman and McCarthy JJ reiterated the test that whether any particular offence falls within the political offence exemption in s.50 of the Extradition Act 1965 must be decided in the light of its own particular facts and circumstances. Thus, the mere fact that the applicant committed his offences on behalf of the IRA did not, in itself, lead to the conclusion that such activity was treasonable under Article 15.6 of the Constitution, and thus incapable of attracting the exemption in s.50.

Of the other two judges on the Court in *Finucane*, Finlay CJ in particular appeared to be swayed by what he described as 'the most comprehensive and detailed consideration of all the relevant factors' in Walsh J's judgment. The Chief Justice changed his own view, as expressed in *Quinn* and *Russell*, to fall in with the majority in *Finucane*. Though Griffin J was less enthusiastic, he also felt that the Court should now accept the Walsh view. What had been a minority view in *Russell* now became the unanimous view by virtue of the views of Walsh J.

Because Walsh J's judgment had such a dramatic effect on the voting pattern, it might be thought that his analysis contained new insights into the political offence issue. Rather, it may be said that the judgment contains much the same views as expressed by Hederman and McCarthy JJ in *Russell*. Indeed, the analysis and conclusions of both judgments were expressly approved by Walsh J. The analysis deployed by Walsh J in *Finucane* was, perhaps, more detailed than in some previous cases. He referred, for example, to the distinction between terrorism and political activity as in the European Convention on the Suppression of Terrorism. This reflects very much the analysis in *McGlinchey v Wren* [1983] ILRM 169; [1982] IR 154. In *McGlinchey*, the Court accepted that the use of violence did not necessarily take the activity in question outside the realm of political activity. Significantly, Walsh J expressly approved the approach taken in *McGlinchey*.

Again, Walsh J made the point that the use of the word 'terrorism' in British legislation such as the Prevention of Terrorism Act should not be given great weight, since authorities in power are apt to describe insurgents of any type as 'terrorists.' The fact that an act may be described in different ways depending on the context is, in fact, implicit in all extradition cases. The 'political' label in an extradition context does not estop the courts from treating as an 'ordinary' criminal act the very activities in respect of which they might refuse extradition. Thus the applicant in *Finucane* might have been charged in this State's courts, under the Criminal Law (Jurisdiction) Act 1976, with the offence of prison breach in respect of the prison escape. It would be *nihil ad rem* in that context for him to argue that the offence was 'political' in character. But, interesting as this may be (and perhaps confusing to the non-lawyer), it hardly amounts to a new point.

To the extent that the decision in *Quinn v Wren* [1985] ILRM 410; [1985] IR 322 could be explained as consistent with his judgment in *Finucane*, Walsh J (with the concurrence of Hederman and McCarthy JJ) was prepared to accept that it stands as a correct statement of the law. In other words, the Court in *Finucane* held that the actual conclusion in *Quinn* was correct. But *Russell v Fanning* [1988] ILRM 333; [1988] IR 505 was declared bad law in so far as it expanded the treason approach in *Quinn* to all IRA and INLA activity. The reality of the situation is, however, that the treason approach has been emasculated and *Quinn v Wren* will now be accorded the dubious status of 'a decision on its own particular facts.'

Finlay CJ in effect accepted as much in *Finucane*, while Griffin J still argued that the *Quinn* approach was correct. However, both the Chief Justice and Griffin J stated that in view of the importance of certainty in the jurisprudence of the Supreme Court, the views of the majority in *Finucane* (Walsh, Hederman and McCarthy JJ) are those which should be applied in all future cases. This was an extraordinary concession. In view of the fact that two definitive Supreme Court decisions, *Quinn* and *Russell*, had already taken a particular approach it was, to say the least, remarkable that these decisions were not treated with the respect normally reserved for them having regard to *stare decisis*.

Instead, Walsh, Hederman and McCarthy JJ approached the matter virtually as if the question was *res integra*. Walsh J appeared to regard *Quinn* and *Russell* as the Supreme Court might regard High Court decisions. His lengthy judgment contains no reference to the respect to be accorded previous Supreme Court decisions. McCarthy J makes reference to *stare decisis* for the purpose of arguing that O'Hanlon J had ignored the doctrine in *Russell*! McCarthy J himself then immediately goes on to state that since *Russell* had been challenged in *Finucane*: 'I am free to differ from its conclusion'.

On the contrary, he might perhaps have said that, since his view had not been accepted in *Russell*, he was *bound* by that decision. Equally, Hederman J might have followed this course also. Indeed, the judges who formed part of the majority in *Russell*, Finlay CJ and Griffin J, also acquiesced in the rejection of that decision by accepting that, since the views which were accepted in *Russell* had now been turned into a minority they also felt obliged to depart from *Russell* and apply *Finucane* in all future cases.

The other remarkable feature of *Finucane* is that it concerned the same prison escape as was in issue in *Russell*. The different results in the two cases might give rise for concern even in the absence of the important Supreme Court decision in *McMahon v Leahy* [1985] ILRM 423; [1984] IR 525. In that case it will be remembered that the plaintiff successfully resisted extradition on the basis that co-escapees from the Newry Courthouse escape of 1975 had successfully resisted extradition in late 1975 and early 1976. The plaintiff's extradition was requested in 1983, in the wake of the *McGlinchey* case. Despite the change in the judicial approach to the political offence exemption, the Supreme Court unanimously decided that the applicant in *McMahon* should be treated in the same way as his co-escapees. However, the prison escape in *Finucane* was destined to be regarded as different from the same prison escape in *Russell*. For whatever reason, the *McMahon* case was not discussed by the judges in *Finucane*. No doubt, in *Finucane* it could be argued that the 'like case' of *Russell* is irrelevant where the liberty of the individual and the protection of constitutional rights is concerned. What remains, however, is the sense that once again the judges have altered their view on the political offence exception without a clean analysis of existing precedent.

It might be said that the *Finucane* case at least establishes a unanimous position on the political offence exception. Should all new appointees to the Supreme Court follow the concession made by two judges, Finlay CJ and Griffin J, in *Finucane*? A mischevious user of the doctrine of precedent might argue, perhaps with a sense of irony, that since the majority in *Finucane* — Walsh, Hederman and McCarthy JJ — felt free to depart from a decision of the Supreme Court once it was challenged, then *Finucane* stands for the proposition that *Finucane* itself is open to review once it is challenged. For a trenchant defence of the decision in *Finucane* see Humphreys' note, (1990) 12 *DULJ* 127.

A second decision was delivered by the Supreme Court less than a month after *Finucane*, namely *Carron v McMahon* [1990] ILRM 802 (SC); [1990] 1 IR 239 (HC & SC). As indicated already, the Court also reversed the High Court decision in this case and declined to order the applicant's extradition. The case arose from quite different circumstances to those in *Finucane*. On foot of warrants for his arrest issued in Northern Ireland, the applicant was arrested and the District Court ordered his extradition. The warrants alleged that the applicant had, on a particular date, in his possession in a car specified arms and ammunition with intent to endanger life. The other occupant of the car in which the applicant had been found was convicted of the offences charged. In an affidavit, the other occupant stated that the firearms offences of which he was convicted were offences committed as part of his political aim of forcing British troops to leave Northern Ireland so that the country of Ireland may be reintegrated. The applicant denied that he knew that weapons were being carried in the car and also stated that he did not support the use of violent means to achieve political change in Northern Ireland.

The applicant appealed against the decision of the District Court under s.50 of the Extradition Act 1965 and also sought his release pursuant to Article 40.4 of the Constitution on the grounds, inter alia, that the offences with which he was charged were political offences or offences connected with political offences, and that if returned to Northern Ireland he would be subjected to ill-treatment. A Divisional High Court (Hamilton P, Gannon and Costello J) refused the relief sought on all grounds: see the 1989 Review, 157-8. The Supreme Court (Finlay CJ, Griffin, Hederman, McCarthy and Blayney JJ) allowed the appeal and ordered the applicant's release on the political offence point only.

Delivering the leading judgment, the Chief Justice stated that in view of the applicant's disavowal of any knowledge of the contents of the car in which he was found and that he did not support violence to achieve political aims, he could not claim that the offences alleged were political offences. However, applying the *Finucane* decision, the Court held that the offences were connected with political offences, in view of the affidavit of the other occupant of the car and in the absence of any evidence that the weapons would be used in any atrocity which would take the offence outside the concept of a political offence. On this basis, extradition was refused.

The Court rejected the other grounds raised. As to risk of ill-treatment, it was held that there were no grounds for interfering with the finding of the High Court that, on the evidence, the applicant would not be ill-treated if returned to Northern Ireland. Finally, the Supreme Court held that the High Court had not erred in its assessment of the limits of the role of the Minister for Justice and of the District Court under s.44 of the 1965 Act (see the 1989 Review, 157).

4 Political offence: 1987 Act   The political offence point emerged again in *Ellis v O'Dea (No. 2)* [1991] ILRM 346. But what was in the High Court a case on the political offence issue — with the added interest of the impact of the Extradition (European Convention on the Suppression of Terrorism) Act 1987 — became, in the Supreme Court, a quite different case. Its status, therefore, is somewhat confusing.

The applicant's extradition to England had been ordered by the District Court on foot of warrants issued in England alleging that he had conspired with other named persons between 1981 and 1983 to cause explosions likely to endanger life, contrary to the Explosives Substances Act 1883 and the Criminal Jurisdiction Act 1975 (the latter an Act of the British Parliament). The applicant sought his release under s.50 of the Extradition Act 1965 and also instituted an enquiry under Article 40.4.2 of the Constitution in connection with the order of the District Court. Hamilton P dismissed the applicant's claims, and this order was ultimately upheld by the Supreme Court but on quite different grounds.

Hamilton P followed the decision of the Supreme Court in *Finucane v McMahon* [1990] ILRM 505; [1990] IR 165, above, but at the same time he distinguished the circumstances in the instant case from those in *Finucane*. Having regard to the seriousness of the offences alleged against the applicant, the use of violence involved and that they created a collective danger for persons, he concluded that they could not be regarded as political offences within the meaning of s.4 of the Extradition (European Convention on the Suppression of Terrorism) Act 1987.

Even aside from the 1987 Act, the President felt that the offences alleged against the applicant could not be regarded as political offences or offences connected with political offences within the meaning of s.50 of the 1965 Act. On this part of the case, he relied on the test laid down by O'Higgins CJ in *McGlinchey v Wren* [1983] ILRM 169; [1982] IR 154, which he considered, rightly, did not appear to have been overruled by the *Finucane* case.

An intriguing aspect of Hamilton P's decision was his reference to s.3 of the 1987 Act. This is the section which excludes certain categories of offences from being designated as political offences, and the President held that this section had no application to the instant case since it specified offences involving explosives where their use endangers 'persons', whereas the explosives offences with which the applicant was charged involved dangers to only one person or property. The Supreme Court judges went out of their way to raise a doubt over this interpretation of s.3 of the 1987 Act, stating that this point would require consideration of s.11 of the Interpretation Act 1937. The Supreme Court did not, however, make a final determination on the point.

As to the delay in proceeding against the applicant, Hamilton P noted that since any delay between 1983 and the present in proceeding with the case was due to the applicant's own actions, including absconding from the State and serving a prison sentence, it would not now be unjust or oppressive within the meaning of s.47 of the 1965 Act to order his extradition.

The judgment then dealt with correspondence, and the decision in *Wyatt v McLoughlin* [1974] IR 379 was relied on to support the conclusion that the offences alleged against the applicant corresponded to offences in Irish law under the Explosives Substances Act 1883 and the Criminal Law (Jurisdiction) Act 1976. This point was upheld by the Supreme Court.

The applicant had argued that, if extradited, there was a risk to his constitutional rights which required the intervention of the courts. Applying the decision in *Finucane* again, Hamilton P pointed out that the applicant was required to discharge the burden of proof on him in connection with establishing this point. Applying this rule, he held that there was sufficient evidence to ground the request for extradition, having regard to the evidence sworn; that there was no evidence that the applicant would not receive a fair trial arising from the rules and procedures which apply in conspiracy cases in the United Kingdom; that while the applicant might be subjected to a certain amount of publicity prior to his trial, it was a matter for the trial judge to ensure that the jury would not be prejudiced thereby; and that while some forensic evidence proferred in previous trials might have been unreliable, this was not a ground for proceeding on the basis that all forensic evidence in future cases would be unreliable and this was a matter for challenge in the court of trial. On this basis, therefore, he concluded that the applicant had not discharged the onus on him, and the extradition order was confirmed.

On appeal by the applicant to the Supreme Court (Finlay CJ, Griffin, Hederman, McCarthy and O'Flaherty JJ) an important tactical change was made in the sense that no challenge was made to the High Court's findings on the political offence issue. No comment is made in the judgments delivered on this about face. It is thus difficult to judge the status of Hamilton P's decision on the effect of the 1987 Act on this area. The Court firstly held that the offences contained in the extradition warrants corresponded to offences within this State. Of particular significance in this context was that the Court accepted that in Irish law a person could be charged with conspiracy to commit an offence even though at the time of the conspiracy that person was not physically within the State. It seemed to be accepted that the applicant was not in Britain at least for part of the time during which the alleged conspiracy is said to have occurred. This point also gave rise to further difficulties after the applicant was in fact extradited to England, as the magistrate before whom the applicant appeared felt that physical presence in the jurisdiction was required for a conspiracy charge. She therefore substituted different charges. This procedure appeared, however, to undermine the rule of specialty and ultimately (after a successful judicial review of the magistrate's decision) the original charges were proceded with and the applicant was acquitted. It may also be noted that the conspiracy issue had been adverted to in a previous application by the applicant: *Ellis v O'Dea* [1990] ILRM 87; [1989] IR 530 (1989 Review, 161).

To revert to the Supreme Court's decision, it was held that there was no evidence of any prejudice to the applicant arising from the failure to inform him, between 1983 and the initiation of the extradition proceedings, of an intention to prosecute him for the offences involved in these proceedings. Nor did the Court consider that the evidence given on the applicant's behalf established a risk of prejudice to his constitutional rights if extradited.

5 *Risk of ill-treatment*   In *Finucane v McMahon* [1990] ILRM 505 (SC); [1990] 1 IR 165 (HC & SC), (212, above) the Supreme Court held that the applicant should not be extradited to Northern Ireland since he had been singled out as a possible target for ill-treatment arising from his participation in the 1983 mass prison escape is which he had participated.

The five Supreme Court judges were in full agreement on this point. As the Chief Justice pointed out, it was clear from the *Pettigrew* decision (referred to above, 212) that ill-treatment of prisoners in Northern Ireland would be condemned and remedied in the courts of Northern Ireland. However, Finlay CJ was equally of the view that the courts of this State had, under Article 40.3 of the Constitution, the primary obligation of preventing such invasions of the applicant's rights and an award of compensation after they had been invaded would not be sufficient. Thus, having regard to the total absence of repercussions on the staff of the prison arising from the escape and that the applicant had been identified, rightly or wrongly, with the death of the prison officer, the applicant was a probable target for ill-treatment if returned to Northern Ireland and his extradition would be refused for that reason. The Court thus showed no sympathy for the suggestion that a conspiracy of silence prevented the Northern authorities from taking disciplinary action.

This view represents as much a departure from previous case law as the political offence point, though the five judges did not see it this way. In the previous cases, the risk of ill-treatment had been given relatively short shrift. It is true that the judges had placed some emphasis in those previous cases on the ongoing disciplinary investigations against prison officers to indicate the *bona fides* of the Northern Ireland prison authorities. Of course, the minority in the Supreme Court in *Russell v Fanning* [1988] ILRM 333; [1988] IR 505 had not been convinced that such investigations were fully acceptable. It seems that this minority view has been accepted along with the (former) minority view on the political offence test.

On the risk of ill-treatment point, however, the test applied by the five judges seems rather a difficult test to apply in practice. It is, of course, laudable that the judges have sought to emphasise the preventive nature of the constitutional duty to protect personal rights, but this hardly seems a realistic prospect in practical terms. If the judges must defend rights by preventing breaches of such rights, will they be required to apply that approach to the protection of rights 'internally' in this State? It is a daunting task, which on past experience the courts have been reluctant to involve themselves in.

Take, for example, the whole area of conditions in prisons in this State, which seems to be the nearest case to the point raised in *Finucane*. In *The State (Richardson) v Governor of Mountjoy Prison* [1980] ILRM 82, Barrington J declined to release the prosecutrix from prison even though he accepted that her conditions of confinement were in breach of the Constitution. Instead, he allowed the prison authorities an opportunity to remedy these conditions. And in *Cahill v Governor of the Curragh Military Detention Barracks* [1980] ILRM 191, the present Chief Justice (then Finlay P) declined to release the applicant even though he accepted that he was being detained in breach of a number of the relevant statutory provisions concerning detention. These cases indicate that, at most, post-violation remedies may be granted, however less satisfactory they may actually be. The case law indicates that pre-violation applications for relief are unlikely to receive a favourable response from the courts. However, in the light of *Finucane*, perhaps the courts will re-examine the precise status of their 'preventive' duty under the Constitution.

In *Clarke v McMahon* [1990] ILRM 648; [1990] 1 IR 228, in which judgment was delivered on the same date as *Finucane*, the Court delivered a second decision on the ill-treatment point. The case concerned the same mass prison escape as in *Finucane*. Judged in isolation, it might have been thought that the 'singling out' of the applicant in *Finucane* had been a significant factor for the Court, but this turned out not to be the case, and the Court emphasised instead the lack of repercussions for the prison officers.

The applicant in *Clarke* had been convicted in 1979 in Northern Ireland of attempted murder and other offences. The evidence against the applicant was contained in statements made by him while in police custody. The applicant did not contest the admissibility of the statements at his trial and the trial judge ruled them admissible. As already indicated, in 1983 the applicant escaped from custody in the same escape as discussed in *Finucane*. The applicant's extradition to Northern Ireland was ordered by the District Court. The applicant claimed that he should not be extradited to Northern Ireland on the grounds, inter alia, that his conviction was obtained by means of inhuman and degrading treatment in that his confession had been compelled and that, if extradited to Northern Ireland, he would be ill-treated by prison officers in the prison because of his involvement in the 1983 escape. In the High Court, Costello J refused his application, but the Supreme Court (Finlay CJ, Walsh, Griffin, Hederman and McCarthy JJ) allowed the applicant's appeal and ordered his release under s.50 of the 1965 Act.

The Court accepted that the applicant in this case was not identified as having been involved in the death of the prison officer in the prison escape, so that he was in a different position to his fellow escapee in *Finucane*. Despite this, the Court concluded unanimously that, having regard to the absence of any repercussions for prison staff involved in the ill-treatment of those prisoners who had been recaptured immediately after the escape, it was necessary for the Court to protect the applicant's constitutional rights under Article 40.3 by declining to permit his delivery to Northern Ireland. Concurring, McCarthy J pointed out that his conclusions in the *Finucane* case had not been premised on the fact that there had been a 'singling out' of one person over another. It was the lack of repercussions for prison officers which was crucial. As indicated already, this seems to take the approach in *Finucane* even further, and it must be reiterated whether the Court considered whether application of this test to the State's own institutions would be practical.

On the other point raised in *Clarke*, the circumstances in which the applicant made his confession, the Court held that while there might be circumstances in which the inherent jurisdiction of the High Court to protect his constitutional rights would require an investigation of an applicant's original trial, this was not such a case. Thus, while the Court would have declined to order his release under this heading, the approach leaves open the possibility of going behind a conviction, at least in some circumstances. To that limited extent, therefore, the decision of Finlay P in *Archer v Fleming*, High Court, 21 January 1980, in which he stated that there could be no such investigation in any circumstances under the 1965 Act, no longer represents a complete statement of the law. It is still true to say that the 1965 Act does not authorise such an investigation, but such an inquiry may, it seems, now be conducted in appropriate cases under the High Court's inherent constututional jurisdiction to protect constitutional rights.

Finally, in *Carron v McMahon* [1990] ILRM 802 (SC); [1990] 1 IR 239 (HC & SC), the Supreme Court upheld a finding of the High Court that there was no evidence that the applicant would be liable to be subjected to ill-treatment if extradited to Northern Ireland. This case did not involve the prison escape discussed in *Finucane* and *Clarke*. In any event, the applicant's extradition was refused on the political exemption ground (216, above).

6 Treaties   The Extradition (European Convention on the Suppression of Terrorism) Act 1987 (Designation of Convention Countries) (Amendment) Order 1990 (SI No. 131) amended the 1989 Order (1989 Review, 164) by adding Finland to the list of States who are party to the Convention.

FIREARMS

Garda use   The circumstances under which the Gardaí may use firearms gave rise to discussion in 1990 in the light of two armed robberies on banks. The first occurred in Athy, Co. Kildare in January and the second in Enniscorthy, Co. Wexford in May. The second instance was unusual in that uniformed Gardaí were involved in the use of firarms. The instructions for the Gardaí in the use of firearms are discussed in *Irish Times*, 19 January 1990. The decision of Hanna J in *Lynch v Fitzgerald (No. 2)* [1938] IR 382 remains the definitive decision on the 'necessity' test in the use of firearms.

Statutory control   The Firearms and Offensive Weapons Act 1990, introduced as a Bill in 1989, tightens the criminal law in this area.

1 Amendments to Firearms Acts   The Act deals first with weapons which have recently come into vogue among criminals. These are crossbows, stun guns and other weapons 'for causing any shock or other disablement to a person by means of electricity or any other kind of energy emission': s. 4(1)(d). S. 4 of the Act amends the Firearms Act 1925 (and its progeny) so as to incorporate these weapons into the definition of 'firearms', and thus subject them to all the controls applicable to firearms, the most important being the offence under s. 2 of the 1925 Act of possession of a firearm without having been authorised or with a firearms certificate. Who is likely to obtain a certificate for a stun gun? The Minister for Justice, Mr Collins, did not envisage that *any* such certificate would be granted. He thought that no justifiable case could be made, in view of 'the very practical concern that if these weapons are available at all they will find their way into criminal hands': 122 Seanad Debates, col. 246 (22 February 1989). Crossbows were, of course, different: they were used in the sport of archery, by members of archery clubs, the sport being particularly suitable for disabled people with an interest in it. The certificate system would ensure that they could be used for legitimate sporting and recreational purposes.

An amendment by Mr McCartan TD, at Committee stage in the Dáil, that the *longbow* be brought within the remit of the legislation was resisted by Mr Burke (who was now Minister) on the basis that it was so cumbersome as to be ineffective for use in committing crime, in contrast to crossbows, which could be fitted with a telescopic sight and pressed to fire by the simple squeeze of a trigger. The amendment was withdrawn: see 396 Dáil Debates, cols. 1736-43 (7 March 1990). At Report Stage, Deputies Flanagan and O'Keeffe put the same amendment, which was defeated: see 398 Dáil Debates, cols. 1144-8 (9 May 1990).

The definition of 'firearms' is extended to bring within the definition of *component parts* certain telescope sights and silencers: s. 4(g). This, in conjunction with s. 5, enables Ireland to ratify the Council of Europe Convention on the control and acquisition and possession of firearms by individuals. The Convention enables states who are party to it either to adopt a notification system or the more radical 'double authorisation' system, whereby they undertake not to allow a resident of their state to transfer or sell a firearm to a resident of another contracting state until they have first satisfied themselves that the receiving state has authorised the transaction. S. 5 amends the 1925 Act to bring this about.

S. 7 introduces new strict controls on silencers. Under the former law they were treated as accessories rather than components. Now it is necessary for specific permission to be given by a Superintendent for the possession, sale or transfer of a silencer, when satisfied that the person seeking it is the holder of a certificate for a firearm to which the silencer can be fitted, that this will not endanger the public safety or the peace and that the person has a special need, sufficient, in the superintendent's opinion to justify granting the authorisation (which may be made subject to conditions). Those likely to be granted an authorisation are vets and others concerned with the destruction of animals: 393 Dáil Debates, col. 1943 (28 November 1989).

The reckless discharge of a firearm is an offence with a maximum penalty on indictment of a fine or five years' imprisonment or both: s. 8. This fills a gap in the existing law; it covers such situations as where a person fires a gun at another's house to intimidate the occupant, with the serious risk of injury but no provable intent to injure or endanger life: 393 Dáil Debates, col. 1943.

Part II of the Act came into operation on 1 January 1991: Firearms and Offensive Weapons Act 1990 (Part II) (Commencement) Order 1990 (SI No. 313).

3 Offensive Weapons   S. 9 makes it an offence for a person to have with him in any public place a knife or any other article which has a blade or which is sharply pointed (subs. (i)), without good reason or lawful authority (subs. (2)); proof by the accused that he had the article for use at work or for a recreational purpose will be a defence (subs. (3)). (One may expect that the court would not be receptive to the argument from a bouncer that his work involves the use of such weapons: the defence contains no restriction that the use at work be a justified or lawful one. The reference to 'a recreational purpose' presumably will be understood as excluding socially damaging recreations, such as teenage gang warfare).

A 'public place' includes highways or other premises or places at which at the material time the public have or are permitted to have access, whether on payment or otherwise. The expression includes club premises and trains, vessels or vehicles used for the carriage of persons for reward: subs. (8).

When the Bill was initiated, criminal liability for this offence was restricted to cases where the possession was in specified public premises (which included dance halls, discotheques, cinemas, amusement halls and premises in which food or drink was served to the public). A series of serious stabbing incidents on the streets, in one of which a British visitor was fatally injured, led the Minister to extend the scope of 'public place' so radically: 398 Dáil Debates, col. 1151 (9 May 1990).

S. 9(4) makes it an offence for a person, without lawful authority or reasonable excuse (the onus of proving which lies on him), to have with him a flick-knife (defined in subs. (9)) or any other article whatsoever made or adapted for use for causing injury to or incapacitating a person.

Trespassing with a knife, weapon of offence or other article to which s. 9(1) applies is an offence: s. 10. Where a person, while committing or appearing to be about to commit an offence or, in the course of a dispute or fight, produces in a manner likely unlawfully to intimidate another any article capable of inflicting serious injury, he is guilty of an offence: s. 11. There are also criminal prohibitions on the manufacture, importation, sale, hire or loan of offensive weapons (s. 12) as well as a power of forfeiture given to the court on convicting a person of an offence under ss. 9 to 12. S. 14 confers the power of arrest without warrant on the Gardaí with respect to a reasonable suspicion that a person is in the act of committing an offence under ss. 9, 10 or 11. A search warrant may be obtained in respect of suspected offences under s. 12. The Firearms and Offensive Weapons Act 1990 (Offensive Weapons) Order 1991 (SI No. 66) specifies descriptions of weapons falling within the scope of s. 12. Apart from old reliables, such as the flick-knife and knuckleduster, it mentions an impressively international array, including the blow pipe, shuriken, shaken or death star, balisong or butterfly knife, kusari gama, and footclaw.

S. 16 confers on the Gardaí a wide-ranging power of search without warrant. It applies to a situation where a number of people are congregated in a public place and a breach of the peace is occurring, or a member of the Garda Síochána has reasonable grounds for believing that it has occurred or may occur there when the people were or are congregated there: subs. (1). In such circumstances, if the Garda suspects with reasonable cause that a person has with him an article in contravention of s. 9, he may search him in order to ascertain whether this is the case: subs. (2). If the Garda suspects that some one or more of the people present has or have such an article, then, even if he has no reason to suspect that any particular one of the people present has with him any such article, he may search any of those people if he considers that a search is necessary in order to ascertain whether any of them has with him any such article or articles: subs. (3). This power to search persons in respect of whom, *as individuals rather than as members of a group*, there is no reason to believe that they are in possession of an offensive weapon, may seem too broadly cast. It would arguably have been defensible in respect of the more narrowly defined 'public place' which the Bill as initiated contained. As Mr Burke observed in respect of this narrower definition, 'experience would show that it is in such places that the greatest danger of abuse of offensive weapons arises': 398 Dáil Debates. col. 1152. With the expansion of the definition of 'public place', any citizen walking down the road is at risk of being searched if he has the misfortune to congregate at a place where a breach of the peace has occurred or may reasonably be suspected as having done so or of occurring in the future. The entitlement of the Garda to search him is based on his consideration that this is necessary in order to ascertain whether *any* members of the public thus congregated has such an article with him. That consideration apparently need not even be a reasonable one. The section makes no provision for what are the evidential implications for material found in these trawls which relate to possible wrongdoing entirely unconnected with offensive weapons.

S. 17 inserts a new paragraph into s. 8 of the Criminal Law Act 1976, which empowers the Garda to search vehicles and persons in vehicles for evidence for certain offences. The effect of s. 17 is to add the offences under s. 12(1) of the Firearms and Offensive Weapons Act 1990 to the list.

Finally s. 18 subtracts from s. 4 of the Vagrancy Act 1824 elements of an offence of being armed with offensive weapons on the basis that these are adequately covered by the 1990 Act.

LEGAL AID

The Criminal Justice (Legal Aid) (Amendment) Regulations 1990 (SI No.20) prescribe revised fees for work done under the Criminal Justice (Legal Aid) Act 1962.

OFFENCES

Criminal Libel   In *Hilliard v Penfield Enterprises Ltd* [1990] 1 IR 138, helpfully analysed by Marie McGonagle, (1990) 12 *DULJ* 138 and by Adrian Hardiman SC, (1991) 1 *ICLJ* 52, Gannon J exercised the jurisdiction under s. 8 of the Defamation Act 1961 which amounts to a judicial filter of criminal prosecutions for libel against newspaper defendants. The applicant was the widow of a Church of Ireland rector who had died during the course of an intrusion in his home. The respondent had published an article in its magazine shortly afterwards which, under the guise of a commentary on his funeral, had alleged that the deceased had twenty years previously been an intelligence officer in the IRA, had provided contacts to lead to massive bank robberies and had set fire to houses and cars on behalf of the IRA. S. 8 provides that no criminal prosecution may be commenced against the proprietor, publisher or editor of a newspaper for libel published in it without the order of a judge of the High Court sitting *in camera* being first obtained. The section requires notice to be given to the accused, who has an opportunity of being heard against the application.

The case was clearly a legally troublesome one, since the crime of defamatory libel is somewhat antiquated with too small a volume of litigation over the years to have resulted in a fully successful modernisation by the courts. Central to Gannon J's consideration was the fact that the defamation had been made of a deceased person. At civil law, no claim for defamation would be sustainable in such circumstances: M. McDonald, *Irish Law of Defamation* (1987), 281. So far as criminal libel is concerned, the courts evinced much reluctance to permit proceedings to go on where the defamed person was deceased at the time of the defamation; they would permit it where the defendant had sought to cause injury to the surviving members of the deceased's family or to provoke a breach of the peace: see *R. v Ensor* (1887) 3 TLR 366 but not, it seems, otherwise. (As we shall see, this statement of law can be made only tentatively.)

In *Hilliard*, Gannon J held that the case should not proceed further. Having quoted extensively from *Ensor*, and other cases expressing principles of more general relevance, he expressed the conclusion that the application had to be refused because it seemed to him that the defamation of the widow and daughter of the deceased, even assuming it to be proved to have been intentional and malicious, did 'not have the gravity in law to require prosecution for a criminal offence'. Gannon J did not enlarge on the precise nature of this lack of 'gravity'. Several possible interpretations thus call for consideration. The first is that the mere fact that the object of the libel is dead should not, of itself, defeat a prosecution for criminal libel. On this view, all that the prosecutor should have to do to pass the hurdle prescribed by s. 8 of the 1961 Act is to satisfy the Court that the particular circumstances are sufficiently serious to warrant prosecution. Such questions as the intention of the defendant to defame living persons or to provoke a breach of the peace would be but factors to be taken into account in a global assessment of the seriousness (or otherwise) of the particular case. Against this interpretation, it may be argued that it is quite inconsistent with the decisions cited by Gannon J. It could nonetheless be replied that the lack of a clear rule emerging from these decisions encourages an independent, non-categorical, approach.

The second interpretation is that a prosecution for criminal libel may be brought only where there appears to have been a defamation of *living* persons. This interpretation gains some support from parts of Lord Coleridge CJ's judgment in *R. v Labouchere* (1884) 12 QBD 320, at 323 and Stephen J's judgment in *R. v Ensor, supra*, at 366. As against this, Gannon J expressed no preference for it; nor do other passages from the earlier judgments support it.

The third interpretation permits a prosecution for criminal libel only where the defendant intended to breach the peace and there was objectively such a likelihood. This approach has the support of Stephen J elsewhere in his judgment in *R. v Ensor*, at 367, as well as the approval of Lord Kenyon in *R. v Topham*, 4 Term Rep 126 (1791). The difficulty with this interpretation of Gannon J's laconic remarks is again that he expressed no such clear preference. It is, moreover, difficult to harmonise with Gannon J's rejection of the general principle, expressed in the older cases, that a likelihood of a breach of the peace was a necessary requirement for prosecution. Gannon J was of the view that a prosecution might be brought where the libel had so serious an impact on the public conscience as to generate 'a substantial volume of protest in the form of public assembly or correspondence to newspapers or protest by other means of mass communication'. Perhaps libelling the dead could be treated as an exception to this general rule, in re-quiring the intent and likelihood of a breach of the peace (cf. the English Law Commission's Working Paper No. 84, *Criminal Libel*, para 3.10 (1982)).

Gannon J adverted to the fact that s. 8's judicial filter applies only to *newspaper* defendants. He commented that it might well be that in modern times the protection thus afforded to newspapers should be withdrawn if found to be frequently abused. On the other hand, he noted, it might appear to be an omission that the same protection had not been afforded to other modern means of mass communication. These, however, were matters for consideration by the legislature and could 'form no part of the consideration by the court', which had to accept and apply the law as it was.

Gannon J's deference to the Oireachtas bears a strong similarity to Henchy J's approach, in relation to civil defamation, in *Hynes-O'Sullivan v O'Driscoll*, [1989] ILRM 349, at 361; [1988] IR 436, at 450, which we discussed in the 1988 Review, 442-3.

Fraud The adequacy of arrangements for dealing with alleged major frauds in the State arose in the wake of a decision by the Director of Public Prosecutions not to proceed with a particular prosecution arising from the collapse of a merchant bank: *Irish Times*, 25 September 1990. Further disquiet over these arrangements in September 1991 may give rise to the creation of a Serious Fraud Agency along the lines of the UK Serious Fraud Office: *Irish Times*, 23 and 24 September 1991.

Larceny: non-presence In *Director of Public Prosecutions v O'Reilly*, High Court, 31 October 1990 Egan J confirmed that physical presence at a robbery was not required in a prosecution under the Larceny Act 1916.

The defendant had been charged with aggravated burglary contrary to s. 23B of the 1916 Act, as inserted by s. 7 of the Criminal Law (Jurisdiction) Act 1976. The only incriminating evidence against the accused was a statement made by him under caution. The statement indicated that he had been asked to drive his van behind another person 'to do a stroke', that he brought the van to a particular place, that after a long wait other persons wearing balaclavas and carrying guns and a box arrived at the place where he was parked, that he then drove these people out of Dublin and left them at that place. In the District Court, the Justice found that the persons who had been driven in the accused's van had participated in an armed robbery of a Post Office. He concluded that the prosecution was required to establish in an aggravated burglary charge that the accused was present physically on or about the premises at which the burglary occurred. He stated a case for the High Court as to whether such was required. Egan J held it was not.

He referred to of s. 35 of the Larceny 1916, which provides that any person who aids, abets, counsels, procures or commands an offence under the Act can be prosecuted as a principal. From this section, he was of the clear view that physical presence of the accused was not required in order for him to be treated as a principal offender. In the circumstances, he ordered that the case should be remitted to the District Court to consider whether, on the evidence, it had been established that the accused had knowingly and wilfully aided and abetted the commission of the crime within s. 35 of the Larceny Act. Egan J ended his judgment by suggesting that the Justice might receive some assistance from the decision of the Court of Criminal Appeal in *The People v Egan (M.)* [1989] IR 681 (1989 Review, 174-5).

Larceny: lack of care in purchasing In *The People v Smith*, Court of Criminal Appeal, 5 November 1990 the Court (Finlay CJ, Costello and Lardner JJ) in an *ex tempore* decision noted that mere want of due care in purchasing jewellery was not sufficient to ground a conviction for receiving stolen property. The applicant, an antiques dealer, had been convicted of receiving certain stolen jewellery. Since the impression might have been given by the trial judge's charge to the jury that such mere want of care was sufficient, the Court ordered a re-trial on this issue. It is, perhaps, significant that a requisition had been made on the point to the trial judge but that he had refused to redirect the jury. It should also be noted that the mens rea issue is discussed in the Larceny Act 1990, below.

Larceny: receiving The Larceny Act 1990 introduces important changes in the law relating to receiving (now 'handling') stolen goods and other aspects of the law of larceny. For helpful analysis of the legislation as it proceeded through the Oireachtas, see John Larkin (1989) *ILT* 314 and Willie O'Dea, 83 *Gazette ILSI* 421 (1989). Paul McCutcheon's Annotation to the Act, *ICLSA* and his article (1991) *ICLJ* 23, provide a wide-ranging and perceptive commentary.

It will be recalled that in their report No. 23-1987, Receiving Stolen Property, analysed in the 1987 Review, 147-54, the Law Reform Commission made wide-ranging proposals for the reform of the law of receiving stolen property. The problem with the position prior to the 1990 Act was that it was very hard to prove beyond reasonable doubt that a defendant *knew* the goods were stolen or otherwise illegally obtained. An odd one presented no great difficulty: why were there five thousand cigarettes hidden in the defendant's attic? In most cases, however, if the defendant was prudent enough to keep his mouth shut, the facts would not speak for themselves to the point of removing reasonable doubt. The second deficiency in the previous law concerned the *actus reus*. Certain forms of dealing with stolen goods might involve high culpability but not constitute *receiving* as the guilty person might never actually have the goods in his possession.

The Commission's proposed solution was, broadly speaking, to endorse the extension of the *actus reus* made in England by the Theft Act 1968, and to endorse a *mens rea* approach centring on *recklessness*, which was favoured by the American Law Institute in the Model Penal Code.

The Act favours a somewhat different approach. To assist our discussion, it may be helpful to set out section 3 in full. It substitutes in the 1916 Act the following new section 33 in replacement of the former section:

> (1) A person who handles stolen property knowing or believing it to be stolen property shall be guilty of felony and shall be liable on conviction on indictment to imprisonment for a term not exceeding 14 years or to a fine or to both.

> (2) For the purpose of this Act —

> (a) a person handles stolen property if (otherwise than in the course of the stealing), knowing or believing it to be stolen property, he dishonestly:
> (i) receives the property or
> (ii) undertakes or assists its retention, removal, disposal or realisation by or for the benefit of another person, or
> (iii) arranges to do any of the things specified in subparagraph (i) or (ii) of this paragraph

(b) where a person:—

(i) receives stolen property, or

(ii) undertakes or assists in its retention, removal, disposal or realisation by or for the benefit of another person, or

(iii) arranges to do any of the things specified in subparagraph (i) or (ii) of this paragraph, in such circumstances that it is reasonable to conclude that he knew or believed the property to be stolen property, he shall be taken to have so known or believed unless the court or the jury, as the case may be, is satisfied having regard to all the evidence that there is a reasonable doubt as to whether he so knew or believed and

(c) believing property to be stolen property includes thinking that such property was probably stolen property;

(3) A person to whom this section applies may be indicted and convicted whether the principal offender has or has not be previously convicted or is not amenable to justice.

A number of features of this section may be noted. First, the *actus reus* of the offence is broadly similar to that proposed by the Commission. Secondly, the *mens rea* is quite different from what the Commission envisaged. Instead of a recklessness-based test, it must be shown that the handler *knows* or *believes* the property to be stolen property. Knowledge is not defined in the section. As has been mentioned, it was the sole *mens rea* ingredient of s. 33 in its former incarnation. The scope of the concept was considered by the Supreme Court in *Hanlon v Fleming* [1982] ILRM 69; [1981] IR 489, where it was stressed that knowledge embraces a 'substantial degree of certainty', in contrast to belief, which need not necessarily do so. As to belief, it is to be noted that, by virtue of subs. (2)(c), believing property to be stolen property includes thinking that it was *probably* stolen property. 'Thinking' here presumably connotes a settled rather than a tentative belief; thus a person who asked himself whether the property was, or was probably, stolen, would not be held to have 'thought' this until he came to a settled decision on the matter. A difficulty with the concept is that many persons who receive or otherwise dispose of stolen property may ask themselves a question as to its provenance but leave its resolution in abeyance. It requires a degree of self-honesty to clarify one's thoughts on a matter where leaving issues unresolved is more psychologically comfortable. See further Paul McCutcheon's interesting discussion of the issue in his Annotation to the Act, General Note to s. 3.

Subs. (2)(b) is worthy of particular attention. Where the defendant has received or otherwise disposed of the property in such circumstances that it is reasonable to conclude that he knew or believed it was stolen, then he is to be 'taken to have so known or believed' unless the court or jury is satisfied having regard to all the evidence that there is a reasonable doubt as to whether he so believed. The Minister for Justice explained that 'once the accused is shown to have handled stolen property in these circumstances then, unless the defence can raise a reasonable doubt as to the guilty mind of the accused by, for instance, offering an explanation for the handling which points to the accused's innocence, he or she should be convicted'. 124 *Seanad Debs.*, col. 347 (1 March 1990). This would appear to place an evidential, as opposed to legal, burden on the accused: cf. A Keane, *The Law of Evidence* (2nd ed, 1989), 49-50, 59-61.

A difficulty with this interpretation is that the provision makes no reference to the prosecution or the accused. Instead it lays down a rule to apply to the jury's deliberations regardless of which side adduced the evidence before them. It may be argued that, in a case where the prosecution makes its case and the defendant elects *not* to adduce evidence and the prosecution's evidence as to the *actus reus* is such that in the circumstances it is reasonable to conclude that the defendant knew or believed the property to be stolen, the jury must take him to have so known or believed, *unless they are satisfied having regard for all the evidence that there is a reasonable doubt as to whether he so knew or believed.* What is this if not the conventional test of proof beyond reasonable doubt expressed in a most curious manner? If the jury in the case are of the view that on the evidence there is a reasonable doubt, they have to acquit. This is the test they always apply.

The justification for adopting the test of knowledge or belief, rather than recklessness, proved controversial. This was that it was 'based with modification on [a test] which has actually proven to be effective in a neighbouring jurisdiction as a means for bringing to justice those who handle stolen property'. (124 *Seanad Debs.*, col. 347), rather than the 'as yet, untried formula . . . [which] could result in a considerable amount of litigation by way of appeal as defence lawyers endeavoured to test the new law to its limits. The ensuing uncertainty could encourage rather than inhibit criminal activity'. *Id*, cols. 347-348.

This rationale perhaps reveals more about the propensity in some key places to favour British legislation (which will almost always represent a 'trusted and tried' model) than it does about the reality of the danger of a flood of litigation. It is, moreover, untenable for three reasons. First, the test of knowledge or belief, adopted in s. 22 of England's Theft Act 1968 proved a good deal less than successful: so confused were the courts there and so unable were they to confront the philosophical ramifications of these concepts that a commentator observed that 'sometimes you would think that the courts were trying to make a dog's breakfast of the law of handling stolen goods': Spencer, 'The Mishandling of Handling', [1981] *Crim L Rev* 682, at 682.

Secondly, the formula for recklessness, far from being untried, is integral to Irish criminal law: cf. *The People v Murray* [1977] IR 360. It is true that there is some judicial disagreement as to its precise scope, but the Irish courts have been considerably more circumspect in this regard than their British counterparts. The specificity of definition of the concept proposed by the Law Reform Commission would, moreover, have removed the risk of a major split in judicial opinion. The failure of the legislation to adopt the recklessness test makes it harder for the Commission to produce consistent proposals for the codification of criminal law. As they note in their *Eleventh Report* (Pl 7448, 1989) para 23, recklessness 'has already a familiar and well tried 'pedigree' in our criminal law, is a concept basic to offences such as capital murder, rape and malicious damage and would be a cornerstone concept of any codification'.

As to the definition of 'stolen property', the receipt or other disposal of which might render a person guilty of an offence, s. 33(1) of the 1916 Act required that the property should have been 'stolen or obtained in any way whatsoever under circumstances which amount to felony or misdemeanour'. An accused, charged with receiving property obtained under circumstances amounting to a misdemeanour, would have to know that the property 'fell into the general category of property which has been obtained under circumstances which amount to misdemeanours': *R. v Nieser*, 93 Cr App Rep 35, at 93 (1958), and similarly in respect of property obtained by felony. See Gooderson, [1959] *Camb L J* 14, Smith, (1960) 79 *L Q Rev* 78, at 94-96. The Law Reform Commission were anxious to prevent a defendant charged with receiving (or 'handling') stolen property from escaping liability on the basis that he thought it was smuggled when in fact it was stolen (and *vice versa*). They proposed a definition of 'unlawfully obtained' to cover smuggling, and that it should not be necessary to specify how the goods were unlawfully obtained. The strategy adopted in the Act of giving an extended definition of 'stolen property' does not go so far as to include smuggled property, thus (as the Commission pointedly notes in its *Eleventh Report*, para 23) 'leaving receivers with a tried and trusted defence and the law with a loophole through which, for example, many a stolen car will be driven'.

The Act removes the lacuna created by s. 3 of the Adaptation of Enactments Act 1922 whereby receiving within the jurisdiction property stolen in England, Scotland or Wales (as opposed to Northern Ireland) no longer fell within the scope of the offence of receiving: *The People (AG) v Ruttledge* [1978] IR 376, *The State (Gilsenan) v McMorrow* [1978] IR 360. See Binchy, *Irish Conflicts of Law* (1988). S. 7 of the 1990 Act provides that the offence of handling applies whether the property was stolen within the State or elsewhere, provided that the stealing amounted to an offence where and at the time when the property was stolen.

S. 8 of the Act permits alternative verdicts in the sense that a person charged with stealing, embezzlement, fraudulent conversion or extortion may be convicted of handling, and *vice versa*. This does not solve the problem, highlighted in the Commission's Report, which arises where a defendant is wrongfully convicted of stealing and acquitted on larceny (or *vice versa*) and the appellate court is unable to rectify the situation because of the acquittal: *O'Leary v Cunningham* [1980] IR 367. The Commission's proposed solution was that all thieves should automatically be guilty of handling as well. In any case where there was a doubt as to whether the suspect stole or handled goods, he could thus safely be charged with handling. The Commission's recommendation that larceny and handling should both attract the same maximum penalty of ten years fitted in with this proposal. The Act does not implement this recommendation either, the Minister preferring to retain the fourteen-year maximum for receiving. However, s. 9 introduces a uniform maximum sentence of 10 years for all the larceny offences covered by the 1916 Act, as well as embezzlement, fraudulent conversion, false pretences and blackmail. Moreover it introduces the option of a fine as an adjunct or an alternative.

The Bill as initiated had proposed to restate, with modifications, the thrust of s. 43 of the 1916 Act, which enabled the prosecution to adduce evidence of the accused's previous convictions for offences of dishonesty, or his having been found previously in possession of stolen property, in order to show his *mens rea* in a trial for receiving stolen property. The Commission had expressed serious doubt as to the constitutional propriety of s. 43, in view of *King v Attorney General* [1981] IR 233, and, fortified by the fact that it was seldom if ever relied on by the prosecution, had recommended its repeal. During the Dail debates, the Minister resisted arguments against the retention of any echo of s. 43, but by the time the Bill reached the Seanad he had accepted that the better approach would be a straightforward repeal of the section. S. 5 accomplishes this.

S. 2 of the Act modernises and extends the old offence of being in possession of housebreaking implements. It creates two types of offence. First it is an offence for a person, when not at his place of abode, to be in possession of any article with the intention that it be used in the course of or in connection with larceny, burglary, fraud, embezzlement, blackmail or taking a vehicle without consent of the owner. Secondly it is an offence for a person, without lawful authority or reasonable excuse, to be in possession of any article made or adapted for use in the course of or in connection with any of these six offences. The difference between the two offences may be explained by examples. The first offence would be committed by a person who is in possession of an ordinary item, outside his house, with the intention that it be used in the course of or in connection with larceny, burglary etc. The task of the prosecution in proving *mens rea* may perhaps be discharged by a confession, or by circumstances pointing to the preliminary stages of a theft or burglary. It is to be noted that the offence would not be committed where a person had such an article with the requisite intent *in his own place of abode*. This is scarcely a lacuna, however: the phenomenon of hosts stealing from their private guests is rare enough.

An example of a case falling within the scope of the second offence is where the defendant is in possession, anywhere, of a device for abstracting coins from a telephone box: here the article is 'made or adapted' for use for this purpose, rather than one of general use. The maximum penalty for these two offences is five years' imprisonment or a fine or both. Moreover forfeiture of the article for the possession of which the accused was convicted is permissible. There is still a cloud of uncertainty as to the precise constitutional status of forfeiture provisions. The decisions are not easy to reconcile. One rationale, suggested by Professor Casey (*Constitutional Law in Ireland*, (1987), p. 252) is based on whether the forfeited article is designed for the criminal purpose. Such a rationale would justify the forfeiture of an article under the second, but not necessarily the first, of the two offences. Perhaps the permissive, rather than mandatory, format of the forfeiture provision ensures its constitutional validity since the court in the exercise of its power may be presumed to act in harmony with the Constitution. See further Paul McCutcheon's Annotation to the Act, General Note to s. 2.

Finally, it may be noted that s. 10 of the Act amends the penalties for certain offences under the Post Office Act 1908 relating to larceny and fraudulent conduct in respect of the mails.

Murder   The reluctance of juries to bring in verdicts of murder was pointed up by Paul Carney SC (now Carney J) in his article on the subject: *Irish Times*, 2 June 1990.

Sexual offences   Because of the large amount of material concerning sexual offences, these are dealt with under a separate heading of Sexual Offences, 246, below.

PARTIES

Accessory: forgery   Whether it was established that an accused person had knowledge that certain bank notes were forgeries was in issue in *The People v Harrington*, Court of Criminal Appeal, 31 July 1990.

The applicant had been charged, along with two others, with possession of forged bank notes contrary to s. 8 of the Forgery Act 1913. It was established in evidence that the applicant had been present with the two co-accused on the occasion when undercover police officers had arranged to exchange money for the forged bank notes. The applicant admitted that he had been asked whether he would like to make a few pounds for moving a few bags, that he knew that what was involved was 'not straight' but that he did not know that it would involve thousands of bank notes. It was accepted that the applicant had played a minor part in the transaction. It was also accepted that it was necessary under s. 11 of the 1913 Act to establish knowledge on his part that the notes were forged. The trial court convicted the applicant on the basis that he had been involved in a common design and that he had been aware in broad terms of what he was doing. On appeal by the applicant the Court of Criminal Appeal (Hederman, Lardner and Johnson JJ) allowed the application and quashed the conviction.

The Court concluded that while the applicant may have been aware that the transaction involved illegality, the prosecution had failed to establish beyond reasonable doubt that he had been aware that the bank notes were forgeries as required by s. 11 of the Forgery Act 1913, and so the conviction could not stand.

Common design: murder   In *The People v O'Toole and Hickey*, Court of Criminal Appeal, 20 July 1990 (the circumstances in which have been outlined above, 190), the Court dealt with the issue as to whether there had been sufficient evidence of a common design between the applicants in connection with the murder of which both had been convicted. One of the applicants had given evidence that it had been his intention to 'just jump on him [the murdered person] and empty his pockets'. He also stated that he did not have any weapon with him and that he was unaware that the other applicant had had a knife at the time. He stated that he had no intention of injuring the murdered person. The Court of Criminal Appeal approved the direction of the trial judge, Barr J. In his direction, he had dealt with what the Court of Criminal Appeal described as the physical and mental elements. On the physical side, Barr J had stated that common design could arise from encouragement by one of the parties to the other. As to the *mens rea*, Barr J noted that the intention to rob had been established as well as the violence used in the robbery, and that it was then a matter for the jury to infer from that what the intentions of the applicants had been. If the jury was satisfied that the person who actually stabbed had been encouraged to do so, then that was sufficient to convict of murder the person encouraging that stabbing. As indicated, this direction was approved by the Court of Criminal Appeal, and this appears to be in line with the decisions of the Court in *The People v Ryan* (1966) 1 Frewen 304, *The People v Madden* [1977] IR 336 and *The People v Eccles* (1986) 3 Frewen 36. The Court concluded that there was sufficient evidence from other witnesses to justify the jury's conclusion that the accused in question had intended to cause serious injury to the murdered person and that this was sufficient to satisfy the requirements of s. 5 of the Accesories and Abettors Act 1861 (though the Court inadvertently referred to s. 5 of the Criminal Justice Act 1984 in its judgment in this context).

PROCEDURE

Advance notice: summary proceedings   The limits on advance notice of evidence in summary proceedings is discussed above, 197.

Bail   Calls for changes in the law to restrict availability of bail emerged again in 1990. Fine Gael published a private member's Bill on the subject. For a defence of the present system see Michael McDowell's article: *Irish Times*, 14 July 1990. See also the discussion of *The People v Ryan* [1989] ILRM 333, sub nom. *Ryan v Director of Public Prosecutions* [1989] IR 399 in the 1988 Review, 144-7.

Consent to trial of linked charges   In *Grimes v Smithwick and Ors*, High Court, 15 May 1990 the Court considered aspects of circumstances in which the Director of Public Prosecutions had consented to certain linked charges being tried together.

The applicant had been charged on nine counts of offences under the Transport (Tour Operators and Travel Agents) Act 1982. He objected to a number of these charges being tried summarily. The Director of Public Prosecutions' instructions to the State Solicitor who appeared before the respondent Justice was that he would not consent to summary trial of linked charges against the applicant. The applicant withdrew his objection to a summary trial on one of the 'linked' charges and accordingly the State Solicitor consented to summary trial of these charges. The applicant then changed his attitude to these charges being tried summarily. He sought an order of prohibition to prevent the first respondent from proceeding with depositions on the charges which were due to heard on indictment. Blayney J refused judicial review.

He did not accept the applicant's argument that the Director of Public Prosecutions had, in fact, changed his attitude. He held that the State Solicitor had not altered any consent by the Director to summary trial, since the only consent had been to have linked charges tried together. It was, Blayney J held, the change of attitude of the applicant to summary trial that had nullified the Director's original consent.

The applicant also argued that there was a risk of double jeopardy where 'split' trials might arise. Blayney J held, however, that it was a matter for the first respondent to determine whether there was a risk of double jeopardy as between the charges to be heard on indictment and those to be dealt with summarily, and that this could be determined after a preliminary examination had taken place.

Finally, Blayney J noted that the applicant should not be refused relief merely because he had had three previous unsuccessful applications for judicial review in 1989, since those applications were unconnected with the instant proceedings: see 12, above.

Court of Criminal Appeal's appellate jurisdiction   In *The People v Egan (L.)* [1990] ILRM 780, the Supreme Court rejected the attempted importation of the 'lurking doubt' concept: see 193, above. The *Egan* decision was referred to approvingly by the Court of Criminal Appeal in *The People v McDonagh and Cawley*, Court of Criminal Appeal, 24 July 1990, below, 239.

Cross-examination: rape   *The People v McDonagh and Cawley*, Court of Criminal Appeal, 24 July 1990 appears to be the first reserved judgment of the Court to deal with the cross-examination procedures in s. 3 of the Criminal Law (Rape) Act 1981. The changes to s. 3 made by the Criminal Law (Rape) (Amendment) Act 1990 (discussed below, 258) do not affect the particular points raised in the *McDonagh* and *Cawley* decision.

The applicants were tried on charges of rape. In the course of the trial, the applicants applied for leave to cross-examine the complainant pursuant to s. 3 of the 1981 Act. The applicants sought to adduce evidence that the complainant had accepted money for sexual intercourse from the applicants and from others, and that she was known by some people as a prostitute. The trial judge initially refused to allow such questioning, but on a further application he allowed questioning along these lines. It also emerged towards the end of the trial that the complainant had apparently perjured herself in that she had denied having been convicted of receiving stolen property and also denied that she had previously been known by the name of a man she had once lived with. The trial judge drew the attention of the jury to the apparent perjury in the complainant's testimony. The jury convicted the applicants. The Court of Criminal Appeal (Finlay CJ, Carroll and Murphy JJ) upheld the convictions.

In delivering the judgment of the Court, the Chief Justice commented on the procedure to be followed where an application under s. 3 is made:

> It is obviously desirable where it is practicable for a ruling to be made at an early stage in the trial on any such application. It may not, however, always be possible to rule it on one occasion only, and there is nothing inconsistent with the provisions of [s. 3 of the 1981 Act] in a further or different application at a later stage in the trial or with the renewal of an application or the postponement of a decision on it. The grounds on which the learned trial judge shall exercise his discretion are very clearly set out at section 3(2)(b), and solely consist of the question as to whether he is satisfied that if the evidence or question was not allowed the jury might reasonably be satisfied beyond a reasonable doubt that the accused person is guilty, whereas the effect of allowing the evidence or question might reasonably be that they would not be so satisfied.

Applying these general criteria to the instant case, the Court held that the delayed or deferred decision of the trial judge in the instant case did not give rise to any disadvantage to the applicants, so that the application for leave to appeal on this ground failed.

On the other ground raised, the Court concluded that since the trial judge had clearly drawn attention to the apparent perjury in the complainant's testimony, it should not interfere with what was an issue of credibility for determination by the jury, and the decision could not be overturned as perverse. The Chief Justice referred in this context to the decision of the Supreme Court in *The People v Egan (L.)* [1990] ILRM 780 (193, above).

Double jeopardy: summary and indictable trials The possibility of double jeopardy arising where a summary trial and a trial on indictment might arise from connected charges was discussed in *Grimes v Smithwick and Ors*, High Court, 15 May 1990: see 237, above.

Jury majority verdicts In *The People v O'Callaghan*, Court of Criminal Appeal, 30 July 1990 the Court appeared to adopt a somewhat lax approach to the question of the majority verdict provision in s. 25 of the Criminal Justice Act 1984: see 210-1, above.

Law reform: inquisitorial system The Director of Public Prosecutions, speaking to the annual conference of the Incorporated Law Society, has suggested that a move away from the accusatorial system to one involving an inquisitorial examination of cases might be justified: *Irish Times*, 5 May 1990. This would appear to reflect the views he expressed to the UCG Law Graduates Association in 1989: see *Dli* (Gazette of the UCG Law Graduates Association), Summer 1989, p.5. As to whether the Irish criminal justice system can accurately be described as an accusatorial system, see the discussion of *O'Leary v Attorney General* [1991] ILRM 454 (178-82, above, in the Constitutional Law chapter).

Law reform: Martin Committee   The Report of the *Committee to Enquire into Certain Aspects of Criminal Procedure*, chaired by Judge Frank Martin, was published in March 1990 (no government publication number was assigned to the Report). The Committee had been established in November 1989 in the wake of the release of the Guildford Four and in the light of disquiet expressed as to whether Irish criminal procedure was adequate in terms of protections against potential miscarriages of justice.

The Committee was given two terms of reference: whether there was a need for a procedure for the further review of cases after normal appeals have been exhausted; and, given that uncorroborated confessions are sufficient to ground a conviction, whether additional safeguards are required to ensure that such confessions are properly obtained.

On its first term of reference, the Committee recommended the establishment of an independent inquiry body with powers broadly similar to a tribunal established under the Tribunals of Enquiry (Evidence) Acts 1921 and 1979. The purpose of this Body would be to investigate the circumstances of a conviction, but it would not have the power to make recommendations (unlike a tribunal established under the 1921 and 1979 Acts). The question of the status of any convictions would be a matter for the government to consider, the Martin Committee recommended. The Committee referred to the government's power to pardon under the Constitution.

This recommendation clearly envisages a procedure quite different from that currently existing under the UK Criminal Appeal Act 1968, under which cases may be referred by the Home Secretary to the Court of Appeal (Criminal Division). No doubt there are good reasons for the Committee's recommendation that a case not be referred back to, for example, the Court of Criminal Appeal, but it is unfortunate that the procedure envisaged does not involve the possible quashing of a conviction where this would seem justified in the light, for instance, of new evidence. For other criticisms of the use of the pardon power, see Michael McDowell's article, (1991) 1 *ICLJ* 9.

The Committee rejected the idea of involving the Supreme Court in this process in a curious passage in its Report. The Committee noted that Article 34.4.6 of the Constitution provides that all decisions of the Supreme Court are 'final and conclusive' and that the decision in *The People v Conmey* [1975] IR 341 envisaged a direct appeal from the Central Criminal Court to the Supreme Court. The Committee then concluded (p.11) that where a person had intially made an unsuccessful appeal to the Supreme Court under the *Conmey* rule, a referendum would be required to facilitate a further appeal. This conclusion cannot be sustained. The *Conmey* decision is premised on the basis that no legislation has been enacted under Article 34.4.3 restricting the Supreme Court's appellate jurisdiction in this area. Indeed the Criminal Justice Act 1984 was to have included such a restriction, but this was never enacted: see Kelly, *The Irish Constitution, 2nd ed.* (1987 Supp.), p.92. Thus, no referendum is required to remove this difficulty. In any event, the Committee would seem to have taken an excessively literal view of Article 34.4.6. In *Ryan v Attorney General* [1965] IR 294, the Supreme Court had long ago pointed out that its decisions should not be taken as 'once and for all' judgments. And, the courts have also made clear that the doctrine of *res judicata* is limited in many respects. Thus, there would appear to be no real constitutional barrier to a statutory reference procedure to the Supreme Court, contrary to the view of the Martin Committee.

The Committee's Report contains a brief (pp.18-19) but welcome reference to compensation for persons wrongly imprisoned. The Committee considered that a right to have compensation determined by a court should be established, rather than having an ex gratia system.

On the second aspect of the Committee's terms of reference, it must be noted that the Committee was restricted in its approach. Thus, it was precluded from recommending that uncorroborated confessions should no longer be sufficient to found a conviction, a point which was raised in the immediate wake of the Guildford Four release (see the 1989 Review, 145). It is also of interest to note that this point will be the subject of discussion by the Royal Commission on Criminal Procedure which was established after the release of the Birmingham Six in 1990. It may therefore return as an issue for discussion in the future.

Given this limit on the Committee's terms of reference, the Report contains vitally important recommendations on current Garda practice in the taking of confessions. The Committee pointed up the unsatisfactory nature of the present procedure from the point of view of the Gardaí in that there was no independent mechanism for determining the procedure by which a confession, or 'statement', is compiled. In effect, such 'statements' amount to a condensed version of many hours questioning. The Committee recommended that the only satisfactory method of precluding allegations of improper techniques was to have such questioning sessions taped. The Committee recommended that video taping be investigated in the light of advances in that area of technology. Significantly, the Committee went so far as to suggest that videoing should take place not only in Garda stations but also in Garda vehicles where necessary. Special warnings to juries as to the dangers of convicting on confessions alone were also recommended by the Committee. Finally, the Committee recommended that changes be made to the Criminal Justice Act 1984 (Treatment of Persons in Custody in Garda Síochána Stations) Regulations 1987, particularly in the context of ensuring effective access to a solicitor. The Committee was influenced in this context by the decision of the Supreme Court in *The People v Healy (P.)* [1990] ILRM 313; [1990] 2 IR 73 (1989 Review, 137-9).

The Minister for Justice indicated that the government accepted the recommendations of the Martin Committee in principle: *Irish Times*, 31 March 1990. However, the necessary administrative or statutory changes required have not been implemented at the time of writing. The issue of potential miscarriages of justice in Irish courts arose again later in the year in the light of a television documentary on what has become known as the 'Tallaght Two' case. In the light of the documentary, the Minister for Justice requested a report on the case from the Director of Public Prosecutions: *Irish Times*, 11 October 1990.

Note of proceedings   The requirement imposed on a District Justice to take a note of proceedings under the Petty Sessions (Ireland) Act 1851 is discussed, above, 198-200.

Preliminary examination   In *Glavin v Governor of Training Unit Mountjoy Prison* [1991] ILRM 478, the suggestion was made that the preliminary examination might be constitutionally required: see 156, above, in the Constitutional Law chapter.

Remand in custody: alleged illegality   The effects of an allegedly unlawful arrest on the subsequent remand in the District Court was considered in *Keating v Governor of Mountjoy Prison* [1989] IR 286 (HC); [1990] ILRM 850 (SC): see 262-4, below.

ROAD TRAFFIC

Access to solicitor   In *Walsh v Ó Buachalla and Anor*, High Court, 26 November 1990, access to a solicitor in Garda custody was discussed: see 150-4, above in the Constitutional Law chapter.

Arrest: opinion In *Director of Public Prosecutions v Lynch*, High Court, 7 November 1990 O'Hanlon J took a strict view of s. 49(6) of the Road Traffic Act 1961, as inserted by s. 10 of the Road Traffic (Amendment) Act 1978, which sets out the basis for an arrest for the blood-alcohol offence.

The respondent had been acquitted in the District Court on a charge under s. 13 of the 1978 Act of failure to permit a designated medical practitioner to take a specimen of his blood or urine. The respondent had been arrested by a Garda when the respondent approached a Garda checkpoint. The Garda stated in evidence in the District Court that he had formed the opinion that the respondent was incapable of driving a mechanically propelled vehicle and that he then arrested him under s. 49(6) of the 1961 Act as inserted by s. 10 of the 1978 Act. The Garda did not state that he informed the respondent at any time that he had so formed the opinion. The respondent later declined to provide a sample of his blood or urine to a registered medical practitioner. The District Justice accepted that there was no evidence to validate the arrest under s. 49 since the Garda had not informed the respondent that he (the Garda) had formed the relevant opinion. On a case stated O'Hanlon J upheld the decision of the District Justice.

He held that it was not sufficient for a Garda to state to the person under arrest merely that he was being arrested under s. 49 of the 1961 Act, and the Court should not always infer that the Garda had concurrently formed the opinion that the person placed under arrest is committing or has committed an offence under s. 49. Distinguishing the instant case from the decision of the Supreme Court in *Director of Public Prosecutions v O'Connor* [1985] ILRM 333, O'Hanlon J stated that it was only where the surrounding circumstances clearly indicated that such opinion must have been formed that the Court could draw such an inference in the absence of positive evidence to that effect. In the instant case he concluded that the Justice had been correct in dismissing the charge against the respondent.

It remains open to question whether O'Hanlon J's approach in the instant case is fully compatible with such decisions as that of the Court of Criminal Appeal in *The People v McCaffrey* [1986] ILRM 687. In that case, the Court, in effect, showed that it was prepared to make some concessions to the exigencies of an arrest situation. The Court dismissed the suggestion that communication of the opinion on which an arrest is founded need be made to the arrested person.

Compliance with Act: presumption In *D.P.P. (Crowley) v Connors*, High Court, 10 May 1990 the issue of compliance by the Medical Bureau of Road Safety with the terms of the Road Traffic (Amendment) Act 1978 arose again.

The defendant had been charged with driving a mechanically propelled vehicle when the level of alcohol in his system was in excess of the permitted levels, contrary to s. 49 of the Road Traffic Act 1961, as amended by the 1978 Act. At his trial in the District Court, he gave evidence that he resided at a campsite on which a number of persons with his first and last name also resided. He also stated that he did not receive a copy of the certificate of the Medical Bureau of Road Safety as to the results of the blood test carried out by the Bureau under the terms of the 1978 Act. Evidence was given by a postman that he had delivered the certificate to one of the houses on the site, and that he was aware that there were a number of persons living there with the defendant's name. The District Justice dismissed the charge against the defendant on the ground that it had not been shown that the Bureau had complied with its statutory duty to forward the test results to the defendant as required by s. 22 of the 1978 Act. On a case stated Lavan J remitted the matter to the District Court.

Applying in particular the decision of Gannon J in *Director of Public Prosecutions v Walsh* [1985] ILRM 243, Lavan J held that, having regard to the presumption of compliance with statutory duties contained in s. 23 of the 1978 Act, it was not sufficient for the defendant to indicate that the Bureau's certificate had not been delivered to him. The *Walsh* case had confirmed the judicial view that s. 22 of the 1978 Act did not place an absolute duty on the Bureau to ensure actual delivery; the obligation is to take all practicable steps to send the results by post to the relevant address. Lavan J therefore concluded that the case should be re-entered in the District Court to enable the Justice to hear any submissions which might be made by the defendant as to whether the Bureau was in breach of such duties, the onus of establishing non-compliance being on the defendant.

On a procedural point, Lavan J echoed the words of Gannon J in the *Walsh* case when he commented that there was a difficulty identifying the precise question of law posed in a case stated where the legal submissions made in the lower court are not identified in the case stated itself and where a general question is posed. See also the comments of Murphy J in *The Racing Board v Ó Culachain*, High Court, 27 April 1988 (1988 Review, 320-1) and the advice of Blayney J in *Mitchelstown Co-Op Society Ltd v Commissioner of Valuation* [1989] IR 210 (1989 Review, 345).

Medical practitioner in station   In *Director of Public Prosecutions v Kenny*, High Court, 8 March 1990 the defendant raised a novel point concerning the taking of a sample by a medical practitioner under s. 13 of the Road Traffic (Amendment) Act 1978.

The defendant had been charged with driving a mechanically propelled vehicle when he was under the influence of an intoxicant to such an extent as to be incapable of having proper control of his vehicle, contrary to s. 49

of the Road Traffic Act 1961, as amended. The defendant had been arrested under s. 49 and brought to a Garda station where he consented to having a registered medical practitioner take a blood sample. No analysis was made of this sample. At his trial in the District Court, the defendant objected to evidence being given by the medical practitioner as to his opinion of the defendant's level of intoxication. The objection was on the ground that such evidence was obtained in breach of the defendant's right to privacy. On a case stated Barron J rejected the defendant's argument.

Citing the decision of Hamilton P in *Kennedy v Ireland* [1988] ILRM 472; [1987] IR 587, he agreed that the defendant had a right to privacy while in police custody. However, since the defendant had not argued that there had been an abuse of s. 13 of the 1978 Act, under which the medical practitioner was in the Garda station, he felt that the full nature of that right did not arise in the present case. The case thus turns on the point that, in a sense, the doctor could not be regarded as an intruder or trespasser, and the case thus bears comparison with *Minister for Justice (Clarke) v Wang Zhu Jie*, High Court, 5 October 1990 (see 201, above).

However, the status of the right of privacy may fall to be determined in a future case, and no doubt the limits to the right may be dealt with in that context. In addition to the limits indicated in the *Kennedy* case, the comments of Barrington J in *The State (Richardson) v Governor of Mountjoy Prison* [1980] ILRM 82 may also prove instructive in such a case.

To return to the *Kenny* case, counsel also relied on a passage from the judgment of Davitt P in *Sullivan v Robinson* [1954] IR 161 in which he had raised the need for a caution where a person was undergoing a test of some description in a Garda station to ascertain sobriety. Barron J distinguished the *Sullivan* case on the basis that where the doctor was lawfully in the Garda station under the 1978 act and where the defendant had consented to the sample being taken by the medical practitioner it was perfectly permissible for the doctor to give evidence of his observation of the defendant.

SENTENCING

Alternatives to prison Two interesting articles on alternatives to imprisonment by Tom O'Malley of UCG appeared in *Irish Times*, 29 and 30 January 1990. See also his more detailed article on the European Convention for the Prevention of Torture and Inhuman and Degrading Treatment or Punishment (1990) 8 *ILT* 216.

Consecutive In *The People v Farrell*, Court of Criminal Appeal, 23 July 1990 the Court (O'Flaherty, Egan and Barr JJ), in an ex tempore decision suspended part of a consecutive sentence which had been imposed under s. 11 of the Criminal Justice Act 1984, which relates to offences committed on bail. The applicant had been sentenced to seven and a half years imprisonment in respect of an attack on a 70 year old man. The consecutive sentence, of eight years, was in respect of an aggravated burglary on a shop. It was accepted that both sentences were, in themselves, right in principle. However, the Court took note of the dicta of McCarthy J in *The People v Healy* [1990] 1 IR 388 (1989 Review, 183-4) in adjusting the totality of the sentence downwards by suspending the last four years of the consecutive sentence. The main purpose of this was to give the applicant some hope of taking his place in society at a relatively early date.

While the approach of the Court indictes an important place for the concept of rehabilitation, one might query whether the Court considered in full the legislative policy behind s. 11 of the 1984 Act. Might it be argued that the mandatory language of s. 11 indicated an intention by the Oireachtas that, in respect of offences committed on bail, the sentencing approach should be: prison term A plus prison term B minus zero. In *Farrell*, of course, the Court took the view that it retained the discretion to adjust the totality of the sentence. It may be that, implicitly, the Court accepted that if s. 11 was interpreted as not allowing such discretion, its constitutional validity would be open to doubt in view of the comments of Walsh J in *The State (O.) v O'Brien* [1973] IR 50 as to the propriety of mandatory sentencing provisions.

Death penalty abolition The Criminal Justice Act 1990 is discussed above, 195.

Lenient sentences Perceived difficulties concerning the inability to appeal against lenient sentences were raised in 1990 in the light of a suspended sentence given to a person who had pleaded guilty to unlawful carnal knowledge of an 11 year old girl: see *Irish Times*, 13 January 1990.

SEXUAL OFFENCES

Child sexual abuse The Law Reform Commission, in August 1989, published a Consultation Paper on Child Sexual Abuse. In September 1990 they published their Report on the subject (LRC 32-1990), containing their final recommendations. Our analysis concentrates almost exclusively on the Commission's Report.

On the civil side, the Commission recommend imposing a duty on doctors, psychiatrists, psychologists, health workers, social workers, probation officers and teachers to report cases of suspected child sexual abuse to the relevant health board. To speak here of 'suspected' child sexual abuse is misleading, since the Commission propose that a person could be convicted of the offence, not merely where in fact he or she suspected child sexual abuse but also where he or she *might reasonably to be aware that sexual abuse had occurred*. Failure 'without good reason' to report would be an offence carrying a maximum penalty of six months' imprisonment or a fine of £1,000 or both. A person who *bona fide* and *with due care* reported a suspicion of child sexual abuse to the appropriate authority should be immune from legal proceedings, such as defamation or malicious prosecution, for example. Due care is thus essential whether the decision is to report or not to report. Lack of due care in respect of the former generates civil liability; in respect of the latter, criminal liability.

The Commission go on to make several recommendations relating to child care proceedings. They propose that the District Justice should be able to appoint an independent, legally qualified, representative for the child where in his or her opinion this appears to be necessary in the interests of child. As to barring orders, the Commission recommend a substantial widening of their present scope. They should be available in respect of any person who is or has been a member of the abused child's household or who comes into regular contract with the child. A health board should be given power to seek a barring order as an alternative to a care order, and the District Court should be given power to grant a barring order as an alternative to a care order when satisfied that this is the most appropriate method of securing the child's protection. The right to seek the barring order should be extended to the child.

In formulating their proposals in relation to substantive offences, the Commission state their philosophy frankly in terms which give the criminal law no role in enforcing standards of morality save to the extent of preventing coercive or injurious acts or conduct exploiting immaturity. This approach may be contrasted with the majority decision in *Norris v Attorney General* [1984] IR 36, at 64-65, where O'Higgins CJ, for the majority, made it plain that, on the grounds of (*inter alia*) the Christian nature of the State and of the fact that homosexual conduct 'is morally wrong', criminal sanctions on buggery and gross indecency among males could not be regarded as inconsistent with the Constitution.

The Commission propose that, while it should in general continue to be an offence to have sexual intercourse with a girl under seventeen, it should no longer be an offence where the girl is aged between fifteen and seventeen save where the defendant is a 'person is authority' or is at least five years older than the girl. A 'person in authority' would be a parent, stepparent, grand parent, uncle or aunt, guardian or person *in loco parentis* or any person responsible, even temporarily, for the education, supervision or welfare of a person under seventeen. The maximum penalty would be seven years' imprisonment where the girl was between the ages of thirteen and seventeen, and penal servitude for life where she was younger.

In place of 'indecent assault with consent' (which arises only where the person on whom the assault is alleged to have been committed is under fifteen years of age), the Commission propose a new offence of 'child sexual abuse' or 'sexual exploitation', which involves sexual activity engaged in for the sexual gratification of the accused or another, or as an expression of aggression, threat or intimidation. It would be possible to commit this offence where the boy or girl was under fifteen, or, if he or she was between fifteen and seventeen where the perpetrator was a person in authority. Reasonable mistake as to age would constitute a defence for any consensual offence.

In relation to homosexual offences, the Commission's proposals are based, not on a detailed assessment of the constitutional implications of the Supreme Court decision in *Norris v Attorney General*, but on the premise that our legislation will be changed in the light of the European Court of Human Rights' decision in *Norris v Ireland* (1988) 14 EHRR 149. The Commission explain their reluctance to engage in such an analysis of O'Higgins CJ's judgment on the basis that '[a]ny remarks on [it] which might suggest that he viewed legislation which decriminalised homosexual actions between consenting adults as constitutionally suspect — and it is by no means clear that this is what he intended to convey — were accordingly not necessary for the purpose of that decision and *obiter*'. It is perhaps odd that in formulating recommendations on the subject the Commission should consciously determine not to address the question of their constitutional validity on the basis that a Supreme Court judgment, so far that it addressed the subject, was *obiter*. The Minister for Justice could scarcely introduce a Bill without assessing its constitutional validity in the light of the existing body of jurisprudence and its likely future development.

It is worth noting in this context that, in their *Report on Sexual Offences aginst the Mentally Handicapped*, para 12 (LRC 33-1990) , the Commission state that '[t]here is no specific reference to a right to sexual relations in the Constitution . . . As judicially interpreted, however, the Constitution guar-antees the right of all citizens to be protected against intrusions on their privacy not warranted by the requirements of the common good'. This contention finds some support in existing case law, such as *McGee v Attorney General* [1974] IR 284, but it is somewhat difficult to reconcile with *Norris v Attorney General*. O'Higgins CJ, for the majority, gave no express recog-nition to a constitutional right of sexual privacy outside the context of marriage. Indeed what he had to say seems directly opposed to it:

> [T]he plaintiff says that the continued operation of such laws was inconsistent with a right of privacy which he enjoys. Here, in so far as

the law and the State are concerned, he asserts a 'no go area' in the field of private morality. I do not accept this view either as a general philosophical proposition concerning the purpose of law or has having particular reference to a right of privacy under the Constitution. I regard the State as having an interest in the general moral wellbeing of the community and as being entitled, where it is practicable to do so, to discourage conduct which is morally wrong and harmful to a way of life and to values which the State wishes to protect.

The specific holding in *Norris v Attorney General*, central to its *ratio*, makes it clear that the right of privacy asserted by the plaintiff, if it has any constitutional status, is defeated by factors more wide-ranging than that of the common good.

Returning to the Commission's Report on Child Sexual Abuse: the Commission recommend that the present legislation prohibiting buggery and gross indecency between males should be repealed. In its place, the Commission propose that buggery of boys and girls under the age of seventeen should be an offence, on the basis of its associated medical risks.

In regard to consensual offences involving underage girls, the Commission recommend that the present rule should continue whereby the girl is not subject to any criminal liability. They go on to recommend that '[t]he same should apply to any offence of anal penetration where committed by a person in authority five years older than the boy in question or other sexual activity with boys under a specified age'.

A matter not brought out in the Report is the effect of the Commission's recommendations on lesbian conduct. At present lesbian conduct is not criminal where the parties are over the age of fifteen. Under the Commission's proposals lesbian conduct would be criminal where the defendant was a person in authority, such as a teacher, for example, and the conduct took place with a girl under the age of *seventeen*.

The Commission in their Discussion Paper (para 4.22) had made tentative noises in relation to the abolition of the offence of incest:

If an offence based on abuse of authority were introduced, it would render incest to that extent less necessary and relevant an offence. We welcome views as to its retention as a specific offence, independent of the ordinary criminal law, e.g., for brothers and sisters.

Of course, it is not true that the creation of an offence for abuse of authority would make the offence of incest in any way 'less necessary and relevant an offence' *so far as incest between consenting adults is concerned*. On the basis of the Commission's philosophy that the criminal law must not enforce standards of morality further than is necessary to effect a limited number of specific purposes, it would seem that the Commission should logically be in favour of abolishing the crime of incest between consenting adults so far as its underlying rationale relates to the wrongfulness of the conduct. Indeed abolition would harmonise with the principle of the right to sexual fulfilment, which forms the basis of the Commission's Report on Sexual Offences with the Mentally Handicapped: see below, 253. Yet this philosophy does not emerge in the Commission's treatment of the issue in their Report. They state:

> There was some strongly voiced opposition to any change in the present law and it is in any event the fact that the considerations involved are to a large extent outside our present terms of reference. We accordingly recommend no change in the present law of incest and content ourselves with pointing out the need for prosecutorial and judicial discretion in unusual cases of long parted siblings who embark on an emotional relationship in later life, such as have occurred in other jurisdictions.

Those who would wish to see the present criminal prohibition on incest retained may perhaps breathe a sigh of relief; but it is of interest that nowhere in the passage quoted does the Commission give an indication that they have any principled objections to removing the criminal sanction in respect of consensual incest between adults.

It is worth recalling that in *Norris v Attorney General*, O'Higgins CJ regarded the State as being entitled to condemn incest on the basis that it is morally wrong. Moreover, he considered that the State had an interest in the general moral well-being of the community. This philosophy, endorsed by the majority in *Norris*, seems incompatible with the philosophy that, save for limited purposes, of which the wrongfulness of the conduct in question is not one, the criminal law has no function to enforce standards of morality.

Turning to the law of evidence, the Commission make wide-ranging proposals. The competency of children to give evidence has provoked much interest in recent years: see Myers, 'The Testimonial Competence of Children' (1986) 25 *J of Family L* 1 and the Ontario Law Reform Commission's *Report on Child Witnesses* (1991), chapter 1. The Commission recommend that the test should be that of capacity to give an intelligible account of events which the child observed. The corroboration requirement for the unsworn evidence of a child should be abolished, as also the requirement to warn the jury before they can convict on the sworn evidence of a child. The Court should be able to hear the evidence of children under the age of fourteen without requiring them to give evidence on oath or affirm when satisfied that the children are competent to give evidence.

The Commission recommend that, in general, expert evidence should be admissible as to competence and as to children's typical behaviourial and emotional reactions to sexual abuse. The Commission are not in favour of the introduction of the various exceptions to the rule against hearsay which have been adopted in many jurisdictions in the United States.

As to procedure, the Commission recommend that the use of closed circuit television (or, if unavailable, a screen) should be the rule where a witness in a case of child sexual abuse is under seventeen, unless the Court, for special reason, decides otherwise.

The Commission recommend that the Criminal Procedure Act 1967 should be amended to provide for the video recording of the District Court deposition taken from a witness under seventeen years in these cases, unless the court, for special reasons, rules that the deposition be taken in the ordinary way. The video recording would be presented as the child's evidence at all trials on indictment, as the normal procedure, unless the Court decides, on an application by the accused, that, in the interests of justice and fair procedures, the child should give evidence at the trial. In that event, the evidence would be given on closed circuit television or from behind a screen.

The Commission go on to propose the admissibility in evidence of a video-recorded interview with a child recorded out of court and conducted by an 'appropriate person', such as an appropriately qualified child examiner, a doctor, a psychologist, a woman Garda, or a social worker, provided the child is made available for cross-examination. In cases going forward for trial on indictment, the video-recorded testimony would be first shown in the District Court on notice to the defence. The child could then be cross-examined and the cross-examination recorded so that it could be played at the trial. The child would not have to give evidence at the trial itself unless the Court deemed it necessary in the interests of justice for the child to do so.

The Court of trial would decide whether any such video-recorded evidence would be admissible. This procedure could be followed in addition to or in substitution for the recording of the child's deposition in the District Court. The Commission recommend that provision be made in addition for the admission of a preliminary video in evidence for the first time at the trial itself, with or without additional cross-examination as the Court may direct. In any case where the Court requires the child to be cross-examined at the trial, the child could give evidence on closed circuit television.

The Commission propose that, in a prosecution for child sexual abuse, the court should have power to appoint an examiner, for special reason, on the application of the DPP. The accused, however, should continue to be entitled to cross-examine the alleged victim himself or through his counsel or solicitor at the deposition stage and (when the presence of the child is required) at the trial, except where the court is satisfied that, having regard to the age or mental condition of the alleged victim, the interests of justice require that the cross-examination be conducted through a child examiner, in which event the examiner should be required to put to the alleged victim any question permissible under the rules of evidence requested by the defence. Child examiners would be experienced at interviewing children and specially trained in child language, psychology and the relevant law with particular emphasis on the law of evidence.

Where an offence of child sexual abuse is to be tried by a jury, the Commission recommend that the preliminary examination should be dispensed with and the District Justice should return the accused for trial as if the preliminary examination had been waived under s. 12 of the Criminal Procedure Act 1967, having first taken and recorded any depositions sought from the complainant or any cross-examination of the complainant in respect of any preliminary video-recording of an interview, then shown in court and having taken any other deposition sought by the prosecution or the accused. The accused should be entitled in every such case to apply to the court of trial before he is arraigned for an order directing that he be discharged on the ground that there is no *prima facie* case against him.

The Commission are not in favour of the appointment of a *guardian ad litem* for the complainant. Any such additional representation 'would be perceived as tilting the constitutional balance in favour of the prosecution. It is the function of the judges to ensure that cross-examination is conducted properly'.

Among other recommendations, it is to be noted that the Commission recommend that at no stage in the investigation process in relation to child sexual abuse prosecutions should the child be subjected to leading questions in relation to any matters of significance. Moreover, this exclusion of leading questions should apply also in civil cases where an issue of child sexual abuse arises.

The Commission also recommend that the use of anatomical dolls and other demonstrative aids in the investigation of child sexual abuse cases should not be outlawed. The validity and reliability of the use of anatomical dolls have yet to be established. Writing in 1989 (23 *Family L Q* 383, at 400), the American family law scholar, Robert Levy, observed that:

> [t]he literature inspires little confidence regarding the validity of any proposition concerning the meaning of children's play with anatomically correct dolls. . . . The three empirical studies reported in the literature (and regularly cited in workshops and by experts testifying in courts) should not relieve any sensible person's doubts about the propriety of using the dolls. In fact, they are shallow as well as narrow, extravagant only in the conclusions their authors draw as to the

implications of their research for the validity of doll-assisted expert testimony.

The Commission in their earlier Discussion Paper on the subject, published in 1989, cited only one of these studies. In relation to it, after a detailed critique, Professor Levy observes (*id.*, at 401, fn 82): 'To be charitable, it suffices only that this is not the kind of "rigorous, scientific study" child sexual abuse experts have called for on other occasions'.

Mentally handicapped The law relating to sexual offences against mentally disabled persons raises distinctive difficulties. At a practical level, there is of course the problem of the capacity of the victim to give evidence. At the conceptual level there is the question of what constitutes a valid consent to sexual activity. At the social and philosophical level, there is the issue of what is the appropriate basis for the criminal law in this area.

The Law Reform Commission addressed the subject in 1990, first by active consultation with judges, legal practitioners, psychiatrists, psychologists and social workers with particular skills in the area and then by publishing their *Report on Sexual Offences Against the Mentally Handicapped* (LRC 33-1990).

The Commission express the central philosophical premise on which they base their recommendations in these terms:

It is, in the view of the Commission, fundamentally wrong to approach and study the mentally handicapped or mentally ill as children. They should be approached as persons, adults and children, who suffer from disabilities in varying degrees of severity. The emphasis should be on approaching them as people who enjoy the same rights as other more fortunate members of the community but who may also require the protection of the law in the area of sexual activity.

It follows, in our view, that the law must respect the rights of the mentally handicapped and mentally ill to sexual fulfilment and should not pose unnecessary obstacles to intimate relationships which find sexual expression where one of the partners is mentally disabled.

(The Commission note that most of those consulted were 'in wholehearted agreement' with this general approach.)

The Commission's notion of a right to *sexual fulfilment* is of course crucial. It presents no difficulties in relation to sexual fulfilment in marriage but it is controversial in relation to sexual activity outside marriage. Although the Commission refer to a constitutional right to privacy (citing *McGee v*

Attorney General [1974] IR 284, which was concerned exclusively with *marital* sexual activity), it is clear that our courts have not recognised any constitutional right to non-marital sexual fulfilment if by that term is envisaged some positive right, enforceable against the State and other citizens, to achieve sexual satisfaction by engaging in consensual non-marital sexual activity. Indeed, having regard to the express terms of the Constitution and in particular to Article 41, it would seem that such an asserted right of non-marital sexual fulfilment can receive no constitutional benediction. Whether the Constitution requires a barrier against legislation trenching on an asserted right of sexual, non-marital privacy is, it should be noted, a quite separate issue. It is one thing to argue that certain sexual activities, regardless of their morality, should be beyond the restraint of criminal sanction. It is quite another to argue that engaging in these activities is a moral desideratum worthy of characterisation as a right, to be upheld by the law.

To speak in terms of the right to sexual fulfilment may seduce casual readers into endorsing a radical shift in moral principle without fully appreciating its significance. The concept of fulfilment may suggest a counterpoint of frustration and inadequacy. Such a theory is well developed by Francis Bennion in *The Sex Code: Morals for Moderns* (1991). The aim of the work is to provide a guide to secular sexual ethics. Mr Bennion posits 'sex-acceptance' and 'sex-negativism' as counterpoints. The following passage (p. 103) encapsulates part of his thesis:

> Sexuality is indeed the key to human joy. But that joy is the birthright of every human being. If a man or woman has not linked with a soulmate because the right person has not come along, or diffidence or shyness has conquered, or life with another has seemed a huge step, or the responsibility to serve has prevailed, that joy is still not to be denied. It is to be taken as best it may — freely, openly and in good heart.

Applying these principles to the sexual fulfilment of mentally disabled persons (p. 121) Mr Bennion is unhappy about the effects on mentally disabled patients of the criminal prohibition on sexual activity with them:

> Society seeks to condemn such women, unnecessarily and for no fault of their own, to a life-long sexual deprivation. Because a medical expert will testify that theirs is not a 'true' consent, their factual agreement to a harmless act that gives simple pleasure is overruled.

Of course the Commission do not follow so far down this philosophic avenue. They are resolute that all exploitative conduct should be fully criminalised. (Indeed, by and large, their recommendations on the subject are likely to be widely and deservedly welcomed as they represent a humane and prudent delimitation of boundaries on this most difficult and sensitive subject.) It is, however, unfortunate that the Commission sought to base their analysis on a radically different philosophy from what finds support in our constitutional jurisprudence, and one so vulnerable to the argument that non-exploitative sexual conduct with persons whose mental disability is so significant as to deprive them of the capacity to consent might, after all, be entirely laudable.

The notion of sexual fulfilment is one that merits serious analysis and reflection. It raises profound ethical issues going to the heart of morality, social relations and the law. If we repudiate 'sex-negativism', in the sense of some rooted objection to the expression of sexuality, and if we accept the obvious fact that sexuality is an integral part of human flourishing, the important questions really only begin at that point. Should seeking and attaining sexual satisfaction be regarded in isolation or is this interconnected with other aspects of human flourishing, such as developing and maintaining secure family relationships? Is the risk of exploitation so characteristically associated with sexual desire that the law should seek to anticipate this? (See our discussion of sexual harassment, in the Labour Law chapter below, pp. 344-6). In short, no ethical or legal system could adequately cater for the sexual dimension of human beings by seeking to address it exclusively in terms of accommodating physical and psychological stimuli. To do so would misunderstand the complexity of human life and the need to integrate sexuality into the fulfilment of the whole person.

The present law relating to sexual offences against the mentally handicapped is unsatisfactory in a number of respects. First, it is confined to acts of sexual intercourse: Criminal Law Amendment Act 1935. In harmony with the approach favoured in relation to child sexual abuse, the Commission recommend an extension of the offence to other acts of sexual exploitation.

A second difficulty with the present law is its terminology for mentally handicapped persons. The terms have become words of insult and contempt in common parlance. The Commission consider that the best solution is for the legislation to describe those whose protection is at issue as 'persons suffering from mental handicap to such a degree as to render them susceptible to exploitation'. The Commission prefer this approach to one which would expressly incorporate the World Health Organisation classification of persons by reference to IQ ranges. That classification is as follows:

Mild mental handicap:	IQ range 50 to 70
Moderate mental handicap:	IQ range 35 to 49
Severe mental handicap:	IQ range 20 to 34
Profound mental handicap:	IQ range less than 20

The Commission take the view that, while their proposed definition would probably include persons suffering from profound and severe mental handicap, a workable statutory definition based on this categorisation 'would be extremely difficult and would inevitably result in cases which might properly be within the section creating the offence being excluded because of an over rigid scheme of statutory classification'.

A third difficulty with the present law, though one on which an argument against change can be made, concerns the question of *mens rea*. Under s. 4 of the 1935 Act the prosecution must prove that the accused *knew* of the woman's mental incapacity. The Commission's analysis of the issue is summary. It notes that '[t]he fact that the offence created by s. 7 of the English Sexual Offences Act 1956 is one of strict liability does not appear to have given rise to any unease among commentators in that jurisdiction'. S. 7 does not actually involve strict liability: subs (2) gives the defendant a complete defence if he 'does not know and has no reason to suspect' that the person involved is a 'defective': see Rook & Ward, *Sexual Offences* (1990), para 7.09). Consultations 'fully confirmed' the Commission's provisional view that the requirement of proof of knowledge is an unnecessary obstacle to the prosecution of such offences and is not reasonably required in the interests of justice to the accused. The Commission propose therefore that it should be presumed until the contrary is shown that the accused was aware of the fact that the complainant was suffering from the relevant degree of mental handicap at the time of the alleged offence. They also propose that the legislation should provide that a person is not guilty of the offence if, at the time the offence is alleged to have been committed, he did not know, and had no reason to suspect, that the complainant was suffering from mental handicap as defined. The cumulative effect of these proposals is a stringent *mens rea* test. If the prosecution proves that the complainant was suffering from the relevant degree of mental handicap at the time of the alleged offence, and that the accused had sexual intercourse (or engaged in other exploitative sexual activity) with the complainant, then the accused will be convicted unless he can show *both* (i) that he did not know of the fact that the complainant suffered from that handicap *and* (ii) that he had no reason to suspect this.

A fourth difficulty with the existing law, which has already been mentioned, relates to the capacity of the victim to give evidence. The Commission propose that the requirements as to giving evidence on oath or affirmation for persons with mental handicap 'should be the same as for other witnesses'. Where appropriate, however, the court should satisfy itself that a person with mental handicap is capable of giving an intelligible account of events which he has observed. The Commission recommend that there should be no requirement of corroboration. They propose that any special legislative arrangements facilitating the giving of evidence by children by the use of closed circuit television, video recordings and skilled examiners should apply also in cases of sexual offences against persons with mental handicap or suffering from mental illness.

The Commission recommend that, since this area of the law is peculiarly one in which the exercise of prosecutorial discretion is of the greatest importance, the consent of the Director of Public Prosecutions should be required before prosecutions are initiated. They recommend that there should continue to be higher penalties where the relevant offences are committed by persons in charge of, or employed in, mental institutions or where the accused person had the care or charge of the other participant. The definition of 'mental institution' in the Mental Treatment Act 1945, they propose, should be expanded so as to include residential centres and community-based residences. The maximum sentence for the offences of unlawful sexual intercourse and exploitative sexual activity should be seven years, or ten years where the offence is committed by a person having care or charge of the complainant in a mental institution or otherwise.

Consistent with its approach to the matter of child sexual abuse, the Commission recommend the repeal of s. 4(2) of the 1935 Act, which requires that prosecutions be brought within twelve months of when the offence is alleged to have been committed. In view of the fact that disclosure is often delayed through fear or ignorance, they see no reason for this limitation being satisfied that the Director of Public Prosecutions will 'presumably exercise normal prosecutorial criteria' in respect of delay. See the discussion of *C. v Director of Public Prosecutions*, High Court, 2 October 1990, 195-7, above.

The Commission adopt the same attitude towards homosexual activity involving mentally handicapped persons as in relation to homosexual activity with young persons. They proceed on the basis that the present criminal prohibitions on all homosexual activity will be restricted in the wake of the judgment of the European Court of Human Rights in *Norris v Ireland* (1988) 14 EHRR 149. On this basis anal penetration and other exploitative sexual activity with males suffering from the relevant degree of handicap will, on the Commission's proposed approach, be treated identically with heterosexual activity.

Up to this point we have described the Commission's proposals so far as they relate to persons with *mental handicap*. In fact the Commission propose to extend the net of criminal liability to sexual intercourse, anal penetration or other acts of sexual exploitation with persons *suffering from mental illness* of such a nature or degree that they are incapable of guarding themselves against exploitation. This proposal might have been considered to merit detailed analysis. Whilst incapacity to protect oneself against exploitation is a legitimate common theme, it is not clear that the range of criminal liability should be the same for sexual activity with mentally handicapped as it is for sexual activity with mentally ill persons. The Report contains no discussion of this possible divergence.

In England, a distinction is drawn between the offence of unlawful sexual intercourse with a 'defective' (that is one who suffers from severe impairment of intelligence and social functioning) and the offence of unlawful sexual intercourse with a mental patient. The former offence is very close to the one proposed by the Commission, but clearly does not penalise sexual intercourse with mentally *ill* persons; the latter offence does penalise sexual intercourse with mentally ill persons but only where the defendant is employed in the hospital or mental nursing home where the victim is receiving treatment; if the victim is an in-patient, it is irrelevant where the offence takes place; if the victim is an out-patient, the offence is committed only if the sexual intercourse takes place on the premises. The defence of lack of knowledge or reason to suspect that the victim was a mentally disordered patient is available but manifestly is of little practical utility for defendants: see Rook & Ward, *op. cit.*, para 7.63.

Rape The Criminal Law (Rape) (Amendment) Act 1990 gives substantial effect to the recommendations of the Law Reform Commission in their Report on *Rape and Allied Offences* (LRC24 – 1988) which we discussed in the 1988 Review, pp. 176-8. On a couple of important issues, it departs from the Commission's proposals.

The Act introduces new categories of offences. It retains rape as a substantive offence. It relabels indecent assault on a male or female as 'sexual assault' (s. 2(1)) but does not attempt to change the ingredients of the former offence, save to render it a felony, thus enabling the Gardaí to arrest a suspected offender without warrant: see the remarks of the Minister for Justice, Mr Burke, 127 Seanad Debates col. 35 (12 December 1990). Following the Commission's approach it introduces a new offence, as a species of the genus of sexual assault, which is designated 'aggravated sexual assault'. This connotes an assault that involves serious violence or the threat of serious violence or is such as to cause injury, humiliation or degradation of a grave nature to the person assaulted (s. 3(1)). The maximum penalty is imprisonment for life (s. 3(2)).

Part of the *raison d' être* of the offence of aggravated sexual assault was to provide an effective penalty for degrading penetrative assaults, which under the existing legislation were categorised as indecent assault, carrying a maximum penalty of only ten years' imprisonment (Criminal Law (Rape) Act 1981, s. 10). The Commission favoured this approach in their Consultation Paper on Rape, published in October 1987. By the time they published their Report in 1988, three members of the Commission had come to the view that the offence of rape should be extended to include these penetrative assaults. The President, Keane J, and Commissioner Simon O'Leary had opposed this extension. See the 1988 Review, 177.

When the Bill on the subject was introduced, it adopted the approach favoured by Keane J and Commissioner O'Leary. At the Report Stage in the Seanad, where the Bill had been returned after having been amended in the Dáil, the Minister moved an amendment introducing a new offence, to be known as 'rape under section 4'. This is defined as a sexual assault that includes (a) penetration (however slight) of the anus or mouth by the penis, or (b) penetration (however slight) of the vagina by any object held or manipulated by another person: s. 4(1). The maximum penalty for this offence, which is a felony (s. 4(3)), is life imprisonment (s. 4(2)).

The Minister Mr Burke, explained that, from his discussion with individuals and various women's interest groups, he was aware that this was an issue over which many women felt strongly. It had been represented to him that serious sexual assaults of this nature needed to be termed rape 'to provide the psychological re-assurance and sense of vindication necessary for the well-being of the victims of those horrendous offences': 127 Seanad Debates, col. 32 (12 December 1990). By virtue of s. 4, it would be possible to provide the psychological reassurance sought by victims of these crimes without attracting any of the disadvantages of interfering with the existing definition of rape.

The provision dealing with alternative verdicts (s. 8) enables a person indicted for rape to be convicted of rape under s. 4, but does not enable a person charged with rape under s. 4 to be convicted of rape. Perhaps the thinking here is that rape, in spite of carrying the same maximum penalty as rape under s. 4, is still to be regarded as a more serious offence.

The Government's approach to the question of definition of the offence may be contrasted with what it favoured in the earlier stages of the Oireachtas debates. Then, it took the view that victims' trauma would be reduced if degrading penetrative acts were re-categorised as serious sexual assault carrying the same penalty as the offence of rape. Rape should continue to be regarded as a distinct offence. Echoing what Keane J and Commissioner O'Leary had said in the Law Reform Commission's Report on *Rape and Allied Offences*, para. 61, Dr Woods, the Minister for Social Welfare (deputising for Mr Collins the then Minister for Justice) had observed that the essential ingredient of rape is the absence of consent to an act which in proper circumstances constitutes an expression of human love. A further distinguishing feature, he noted, was that 'unlike any of the other offences in question, only the act of rape can give rise to pregnancy': 393 Dáil Debates, col. 929 (16 November 1989).

S. 5(1) of the Act abolishes the common law immunity whereby, in at least some circumstances, a husband could not be guilty of the rape of his wife. Following the lead of the Oireachtas Joint Committee in its Fourth Report on Sexual Violence, s. 5(2) requires the consent of the Director of Public Prosecutions for such a charge. Fear of 'spiteful or mischievous complaints against a husband . . . by a wife or even a third party' (393 Dáil Debates, col. 927) appears to underlie this restriction.

S. 6 removes the irrebuttable presumption that a boy under 14 is incapable of rape in the first degree. This change is in line with the recommendations of the Joint Oireachtas Committee, and the Law Reform Commission, and in harmony with legislative changes or proposals in many common law jurisdictions: cf. the Law Reform Commission's *Consultation Paper on Rape*, para. 44. In removing this immunity, s. 6 makes no change in the *doli incapax* principle (cf. Osborough, (1975) 10 *Ir Jur* 48). From one standpoint, it might be considered curious that at a time when some voices are heard arguing for a raising of the age of criminal responsibility, the law should here be reducing the age in respect of one of the most serious offences on the statute book. The explanation must surely be that this change is made without prejudice to the wider question of the minimum age for criminal responsibility. This was the basis on which the Law Reform Commission made their recommendation: cf the *Consultation Paper*, para. 44.

S. 7 abolishes the universal obligation on the trial judge in prosecutions for offences of a sexual nature to give a warning to the jury about the dangers of convicting on the uncorroborated evidence of the complainant. (See O'Connor (1985) 20 *Ir Jur* (ns) 43, Clarke, [1980] *Crim L Rev* 362). In its place, the section provides that it is for the judge to decide *in his or her discretion*, having regard to all the evidence given, whether the jury should be given the warning. This is in line with the recommendations of the Law Reform Commission in their *Report*, para. 32. The Commission in their *Consultation Paper*, para 103, had been divided on the issue. While all had been of the view that *prohibiting* the giving of any such warning would be an unjustifiable interference with the exercise of the judicial function — an assessment surely vindicated by the subsequent decision of the Court of Criminal Appeal in *The People v T.* (1988) 3 Frewen 141 (discussed in the 1988 Review, 151-3) — the (unidentified) majority had felt that, on balance, no useful purpose would be served by changing the existing law. The minority had thought that the requirement of a warning should be abolished or that, at a minimum, some restrictions should be placed on the manner in which the warning might be given, so as to prohibit, for example, any reference by the judge to the supposed mendacity of rape complainants.

S. 9 seeks to clarify the law by declaring that, in relation to an offence which consists of or includes the doing of an act to a person without the consent of that person, any failure or omission by that person to offer resistance to the act does not of itself constitute consent to the act. This again reflects part of the thinking of the Law Reform Commission, in line with legislation in Western Australia, New Zealand and Canada: cf the Commission's *Report*, para 17. In their *Consultation Paper*, the Commission had been opposed altering the law in this way. They were not aware of any problems having arisen as a result of the failure of the existing law to define consent and were 'loath to suggest changes in an area where no problems has arisen' (para. 64). By the time the Commission prepared their *Report*, no such cases had emerged but the Commission deferred to the strong opinion of the Irish Association for Victim Support that the absence of a definition had influenced verdicts. They recommended that the legislation should provide, not merely that failure to offer resistence to a sexual assault does not of itself constitute consent to a sexual assault but also that consent means a consent freely and voluntarily given and, without in any way affecting or limiting the meanings otherwise attributable to these words, that a consent is not freely and voluntarily given if obtained by force, threat, intimidations, deception or fraudulent means.

S. 9 does not change the law, since it was clear already that the failure of the victim to offer resistance does not of itself constitute consent to the act, but this does not mean that the section will have no *practical* effect. It would be an interesting area for empirical research to determine whether juries can fully understand trial judges' legal directions on fairly complex and nuanced distinctions. They will be told that failure to offer resistance 'does not of itself constitute consent to the act', but, to come to a proper verdict, they will have to appreciate also that failure to offer resistance may in some circumstances, taken in conjunction with all the facts of the case, afford sufficient evidence to justify, or warrant, the finding of consent. The key words are 'of itself'. To ensure that this is adequately absorbed by a jury the trial judge may have some hard work to do. Even if the jury fully grasp this point, they have to assess it in conjunction with the definition of *mens rea*, which, in the case of the offence of rape, requires that, at the time of the act, the defendant 'knows that [the victim] does not consent to the intercourse or he is reckless as to whether she does or does not consent to it': Criminal Law (Rape) Act 1981, s. 2(1). Thus, the jury have to understand that, even where failure to resist did *not* amount in the circumstances to consent, the accused must be acquitted if, however unreasonably, he thought that it did. In determining that question, the jury must have regard to the presence or absence of reasonable grounds for a belief that the victim consented, in conjunction with any other relevant matters, in considering whether he so believed: *id.*, s. 2(1). The reasonableness of the alleged belief impinges only on the issue of the credibility of the accused in asserting that belief. It may be that jurors can absorb all of this but there is also the danger that some do not. Inclusion in the trial judge's charge to the jury of references to non-resistance and to the reasonableness of belief may have the effect in some cases of leading some jurors mistakenly to believe that the State's burden of proof is lighter than it is, according to the rather complex rules which the legislation has ordained.

S. 10 provides that the Central Criminal Court is to try all prosecutions for a wide range of serious sexual offences, including rape, rape under s. 4 and aggravated sexual assault. This change was intended to be seen as an expression of the seriousness with which these crimes should be regarded. The change will have the greatest impact in Dublin: on average only about six rape trials were held outside Dublin in a year: 393 Dáil Debates, col. 931.

TRIAL OF OFFENCES

1 Remand in custody: alleged illegality in arrest In *Keating v Governor of Mountjoy Prison* [1989] IR 286 (HC); [1990] ILRM 850 (SC), the question arose as to whether an unlawful remand could affect the jurisdiction of the trial court dealing with the issue.

The applicant had been arrested in relation to larceny charges and was then detained in custody under s. 4 of the Criminal Justice 1984, during which time he was alleged to have made certain statements to the Gardaí relating to the offences. At the remand hearing in the District Court, his solicitor had raised the legality of the applicant's detention in Garda custody under s. 4 of the 1984 Act as a ground for refusing to remand the applicant in custody. The District Justice declined to enter into the question of the validity of the applicant's detention under the 1984 Act, and proceeded to remand him in custody. On an inquiry under Article 40.4.2 of the Constitution it was argued that once the issue of the applicant's detention under the 1984 Act had been raised the District Justice was obliged to consider the matter. In the High Court ([1989] IR 286), Barrington J did not accept this point: see the 1989 Review, 185-6. This view was upheld by the Supreme Court (Finlay CJ, McCarthy and O'Flaherty JJ) in dismissing the applicant's appeal.

Delivering the leading judgment, McCarthy J (with whom Finlay CJ agreed) stated:

> In the present case, no hindrance has been offered to the [applicant] in seeking an enquiry under Article 40. The holding of such an enquiry is constitutionally the role of the High Court. . . . The District Court has no such function. It is . . . wholly inconsistent with the constitutional role of the High Court that, in a case of this kind, a District Justice should embark upon the constitutional enquiry as to the validity of detention.

He concluded that the District Justice in the instant case had taken the correct course of remanding the applicant in custody and thus facilitating any application under Article 40.4 which he might be advised to take. In a concurring judgment, O'Flaherty J stated that issues of the kind raised in the instant case were more properly raised in the context of the admissibility of evidence in the course of a trial.

No doubt the decison of the Court in this case reflects a traditional approach to such matters, and that there has been a tendency to leave matters which might affect the admissibility of evidence to a court of trial. However, as noted in the 1989 Review, 186, the courts have not always displayed a consistency of approach in this area. And it would appear that, after s. 4 of the Criminal Justice Act 1984 came into effect in 1987, it was the practice of some District Justices to scrutinise the validity of a s. 4 detention before completing the preliminary examination. In *Keating*, the Court held that this trampled on the Article 40.4 function.

Trimbole v Governor of Mountjoy Prison [1985] ILRM 465; [1985] IR 550 was cited in support of the applicant's argument that such issues may be dealt with in an Article 40.4 inquiry, but the Supreme Court distinguished it on the ground that the arrest in *Trimbole* was mala fide. McCarthy J held out some prospect that a person would not be remanded in custody where some 'outrage' was committed against a person brought before the Court. However, where the issue touched on the 'validity of detention' the proper course was to remand the person in custody to enable that person to make an application under Article 40.4. While this seems to meet the requirement that a remedy be available to deal with an injustice, the decision in *Keating* appears to indicate that, even where an Article 40.4 inquiry is launched the High Court and Supreme Court are likely to say, as in this case, that such matters are for the trial court. This would appear to involve a delay of the hearing of the issues concerned. As *O'Mahony v Melia* [1990] ILRM 14; [1989] IR 335 indicates (1989 Review, 186) such issues have certainly been considered in the past as preliminary matters, with criminal trials being postponed pending determinations of such issues. Perhaps the prospect of a glut of preliminary applications in criminal trials disturbed the Supreme Court, and the preference for the unitary criminal trial won out. The reality of such a prospect must be doubted, on the ground that defence lawyers will rarely be tempted to reveal their defence prior to trial; and the result of *Keating* is that some cases which might be disposed of at a preliminary stage will be required to continue to full hearing.

YOUNG OFFENDERS

The non-availability of secure residential accommodation for young offenders — otherwise than in the prison regime — arose during the year. In the case of one 15 year old girl, *Director of Public Prosecutions v X.*, District Justice Hubert Wine declined on a number of occasions to accept a direction from the Director of Public Prosecutions that assault charges against her be struck out. He took the view that secure accommodation should be provided for her under the direction of a health board. He also rejected the suggestion that the girl be remanded to the Women's Unit in Mountjoy Prison, stating that this would be unsuitable for a person of her age: see *Irish Times*, 19, 24 and 27 February 1990. Ultimately, the District Justice dismissed the charges when the Eastern Health Board and Dun Laoghaire Corporation undertook to provide secure accommodation for the girl in question: *Irish Times*, 2 March 1990.

Later in the year, the detention of a 15 year old boy in Mountjoy Prison was upheld by the Court of Criminal Appeal: *The People v Y.*, *Irish Times*, 26 July 1990. The Court pointed out that s. 102 of the Children Act 1908 provided for such detention of a 15 year old of 'unruly character.' While it noted that detention in Mountjoy Prison was 'unusual' and that, on his 16th birthday, the boy in question would be eligible for transfer to the, arguably, more suitable St Patrick's Institution, the Court declined to interfere with the detention ordered by the Circuit Court judge in this instance.

Finally, the case of two other 15 year old girls also attracted considerable publicity: *Director of Public Prosecutions v G. and McD.*, *Irish Times*, 13 and 19 October 1990. In this instance, the two girls had been remanded to the Women's Unit in Mountjoy Prison pursuant to s. 102 of the 1908 Act, there being no other secure accommodation available for them. An application seeking their release under Article 40.4.2 on the ground that s. 102 was inconsistent with the Constitution was also later rejected: *G. and McD. v Governor of Mountjoy Prison*, High Court, 7 March 1991. This decision will be discussed in the 1991 Review.

While there were continuing delays and some criticism of the failure to provide secure accommodation for the type of offenders discussed in the above cases (see, for example, *Irish Times*, 5 September 1990), it would appear that such accommodation will become available in late 1991. See also O'Malley's article on the European Convention against Torture (1990) 8 *ILT* 216.

Defence Forces

DISCIPLINE

The decision in *McDonough v Minister for Defence* [1991] ILRM 115, on the application of the rules of natural justice and reasonableness to disciplinary procedures in the Defence Forces, is discussed in the Administrative Law chapter, 5-6, above.

PENSIONS

Breen v Minister for Defence, Supreme Court, 20 July 1990 is an important decision on the extent of the Minister for Defence's discretion in terminating a defence forces pension.

The applicant had been a member of the Defence Forces. By virtue of a road traffic accident in an Army vehicle, the applicant suffered severe personal injuries, and in a subsequent claim recovered £60,000 damages, though a large portion of this award went to meet debts of the applicant and to meet solicitor and client costs. In the meantime, the applicant had been awarded a disability wound pension under the Army Pensions Acts 1923 and 1927. The Minister, after lengthy correspondence with the applicant's solicitors, purported to terminate the applicant's wound pension, pursuant to his powers under s.13(2) of the Army Pensions Act 1923, as amended by s.3(1) of the Army Pensions Act 1927. In the High Court, O'Hanlon J declined to grant judicial review of the Minister's decision: [1988] IR 242 (see the 1988 Review, 196). On appeal by the applicant, the Supreme Court (Finlay CJ, Hederman and O'Flaherty JJ) unanimously reversed the decision of O'Hanlon J as to whether the Minister had acted reasonably.

Delivering a judgment with which the other members of the Court agreed, O'Flaherty J firstly, however, agreed with O'Hanlon J that a wound pension could be abated under the 1923 and 1927 Acts even where such wound was not sustained on active service. That no doubt will continue to be an important factor in future such cases.

But the Supreme Court took a different view on the actual procedures adopted by the Minister. O'Flaherty J noted that the fair procedures requirement spelt out by the Court in *The State (Thornhill) v Minister for Defence* [1986] IR 1 may not have been fully appreciated at first by the authorities in the instant case, though correspondence between the parties indicated that its relevance was acknowledged. He then quoted with approval the reasonableness test laid down by the Court in *The State (Keegan) v Stardust Victims Compensation Tribunal* [1987] ILRM 202; [1986] IR 642. Applying that test, he held that, while the courts would not interfere with an administrative discretion merely because the courts might have reached a different conclusion, the Minister in the instant case did not appear to have responded to the representations made on the applicant's behalf as to why the pension in the instant case should not have been abated. And although he accepted that a decision of this kind did not in all cases require a reasoned judgment, the Minister's decision was *ultra vires* for unreasonableness since it appeared not to have taken into account the individual circumstances of the applicant. Accordingly the Minister's abatement of the pension was quashed.

Emphasising that decisions of this type dispose of procedural rather than substantive issues, O'Flaherty opined that the Minister would have been clearly right if he had taken into account half of what had been awarded in the applicant's damages claim.

REMUNERATION AND CONDITIONS

The Report of the Commission on Remuneration and Conditions of Service in the Defence Forces was published in July 1990. The Commission, chaired by Dermot Gleeson SC, constituted the first independent assessment of the general conditions of work and of pay scales for the permanent defence forces since the foundation of the State. The Commission was established in the wake of widespread dissatisfaction concerning conditions in the defence forces. This also led to the enactment of the Defence (Amendment) Act 1990, discussed below. The government accepted the recommendations of the Gleeson Commission.

REPRESENTATIVE ASSOCIATIONS

The Defence (Amendment) Act 1990 provides for the establishment of representative associations within the Defence Forces. This is one of the most significant innovations in the Defence Forces and, in subtle ways, will no doubt lead to a fundamental change in the command structure of the Forces. The 1990 Act resulted from considerable pressure exerted, first, by a loosely-based Defence Forces Spouses' Association and the establishment of the Permanent Defence Forces Other Ranks Association (PDFORRA). The establishment of PDFORRA was in direct conflict with the Defence Act 1954 and when its spokesperson began giving media interviews disciplinary action was initiated within the Army. The reaction to this, coupled with the impact of the Spouses' Association in the 1989 General Election campaign, led the incoming government to proceed with the 1990 Act as well as establish a review of army conditions under the Glesson Commission: see above.

S. 2 of the 1990 Act provides that the representative associations may not be involved in operational matters, but are entitled to discuss pay and connected issues. It also provides that the associations must not constitute trade unions.

The Defence (Amendment) Act 1990 (Commencement) Order 1991 (SI No. 119) brought the 1990 Act into effect from 16 May 1991.

Education

SUPERANNUATION SCHEMES

The Teachers' Superannuation (Amendment) Act 1990 amends ss.5 and 6 of the 1928 Act by providing that superannuation schemes for primary and secondary level teachers will take effect when laid before the Houses of the Oireachtas, subject to negative resolution. Under the 1928 Act, such schemes required a positive resolution by both Houses. For a similar move from positive to negative resolutions see the Restrictive Practices (Amendment) Act 1987 (1987 Review, 34).

STATUTORY FRAMEWORK

In *O'Callaghan v Meath Vocational Education Committee*, High Court, 20 November 1990 (discussed in the Labour Law chapter, 365-7, below) Costello J pointed out that many decisions in the education area were effected by administrative circulars which lacked any statutory basis. These comments are of interest in the context of the commitment given by the Minister for Education to introduce a comprehensive Green Paper on Education which it is intended will lead to the enactment of an Education Act. See also *Irish Times*, 27 November 1990.

Electricity and Energy

PETROLEUM

Whiddy   The Fuels (Control of Supplies) (Strategic Storage of Petroleum Oils) Order 1990 (SI No. 227) provided for extra storage of oil supplies at Whiddy Island arising from the invasion of Kuwait by Iraq.

Whitegate offtake   The Petroleum Oils (Regulation or Control of Acquisition, Supply, Distribution or Marketing) (Continuance) Order 1990 (SI No. 298) continued for a further year the regime outlined in the 1988 Order of the same title: see the 1988 Review, 198.

Equitable Remedies

CHAMPERTOUS AGREEMENTS

In *McElroy t/a Irish Genealogical Services) v Flynn and O'Flynn* [1991] ILRM 294, Blayney J applied well-established legal principles relating to champertous agreements, in holding void contracts whereby the plaintiff, a specialist in tracing next-of-kin, had undertaken to identify a deceased person to two beneficiaries and actively to assist in the recovery of the shares to which they were entitled in that deceased person's estate. The beneficiaries, in consideration of that undertaking, had agreed to the plaintiff's entitlement to a cut of 25% of their respective shares. Although the deeds between the parties incorporated merely an undertaking by the plaintiff to disclose to the next-of-kin the identity of the deceased, Blayney J was satisfied that the deeds were part of a wider agreement by which the plaintiff undertook active assistance in the recovery of their shares.

The law on the subject seemed clear: an agreement to communicate information on terms of obtaining a share of any property that may thereby be recovered by the recipient of that information is not champertous: *Spyre v Porter* (1856) 7 E & B 58; but if the agreement involves not merely the giving of that information but also an undertaking to recover the property or actively to assist in its recovery by procuring evidence or by similar means, it is champertous and void: *id*; *Stanley v Jones* (1831) 7 Bing 369, *Hutley v Hutley* (1872) LR 8QB 112.

In view of his holding, Blayney J did not have to consider the further evidence in the case, which involved deliberate misrepresentations of fact of which the specialist was guilty during his interview with one of the beneficiaries. When asked by her who the deceased was, he said he did not know, and when asked specifically whether it was the deceased, he said it was not. (The defendants had not sought to resist the claim on the grounds of fraud, though they had alleged undue influence.) The specialist was, however, seeking equitable relief in the form of a declaration of his entitlement to a 25% share and a mandatory injunction directing the defendants to give effect to the assignment of this share. Blayney J observed that the plaintiff's claim would fall to be determined in the light of equitable principles, and a court in applying those principles would take into account the elements of deceit in the plaintiff's conduct. In the absence of argument, he was not prepared to express an opinion as to what conclusion would be reached; but he had little doubt that, if the defendants had sought to invoke equitable principles, apart from undue influence, this aspect of the facts would have been 'highly relevant'.

One may perhaps debate the merits of the distinction between the giving of information and the taking of more active steps in aid of litigation. In the present case, it seems clear that, on receipt of the relevant information, the next-of-kin would have been perfectly able, and surely equally willing, to assert their legal entitlements to shares in the estate. That the law should strike down the agreements as void on account of the mere processing of their claims is not an immediately attractive approach. Far from fomenting litigation, the plaintiff was doing little more than a mechanical exercise, in aid of the administration of the estate. The theoretical possibility that the claims might be contested is surely not one which should render void an agreement, otherwise valid. The real issue, we suggest, is whether the trading in disclosures of legal entitlements should be discouraged to the extent of rendering it illegal. There may seem to many people to be something unpleasant about this trade, but it does, after all, serve a useful social function. Perhaps the better solution would be to leave the matter to be governed by legislation prescribing, *inter alia*, maxima for the proportions or the share that may lawfully be assigned.

The law on the subject of champerty is based on principles which have a long history: see Winfield (1919), 35 *LQ Rev* 50, 143, Tan, (1990), 106 *LQ Rev* 656 (1990). Perhaps the area of its greatest potential contemporary significance is in relation to agreements between a client and solicitor that the solicitor is to have a share in the award if the contemplated litigation has a successful result. This raises the whole question of the 'contingent fee', on which there is no clear consensus in the legal profession.

ESTOPPEL BY REPRESENTATION

In *Phillips v The Medical Council*, High Court, 11 December 1990, which we analyse in the chapter on Torts, below, pp. 533-4, Costello J applied the doctrine of estoppel by representation where an applicant for full registration on the General Register of Medical Practitioners had been sent a set of rules purporting to be those governing the determination of eligibility. There was another set of rules, of which the plaintiff had no knowledge, which were later alleged to be the correct ones to govern his application. Costello J held that, even of this were so, the plaintiff's application should be governed by the set that had been sent to him.

Costello J considered this to be an instance of estoppel by conduct:

An estoppel by conduct may arise from a representation of fact made either mistakenly or innocently. So if there is an unambiguous representation of fact, and an intention (or conduct raising a reasonable presumption thereof) that the injured party was meant to act upon the representation and the party relying on the representation has in fact acted on it to his own detriment and the representation was the proximate cause of the detriment, then the rule will be applied.

Costello J cited *Phipson on Evidence* (13th ed., 1982), pp. 1063-7 in support.

All the ingredients were fulfilled in the instant case. There had been a clear representation, intended to be, and actually, acted upon. Detriment was established since, if the plaintiff had been aware that the other set of rules was to apply, he would have realised that he was ineligible by them to practice in Ireland on a permanent basis; he would have contemplated other career options; he would, moreover, have had the opportunity of taking legal advice as to the constitutional and statutory validity of this other set of rules and the option of instituting immediate proceedings against the Medical Council.

The case also involved the issue of *legitimate expectation*, in respect of subsequent aspects of the plaintiff's attempt to practice here on a permanent basis. We discuss this issue below.

INJUNCTIONS

1 Interlocutory injunctions In *HB Ice-cream Ltd v Masterfoods Ltd, t/a as Mars Ireland* [1990] 2 IR 463, Lynch J evinced little hesitation in granting an interlocutory injunction against the defendant's wrongful interference with the plaintiff's contractual rights with retailers to whom it had supplied freezer cabinets, and the wrongful interference with its property rights in these freezer cabinets. HB had invested £7 million in the purchase of these cabinets; it supplied them on free hire to retailers in return for the exclusive storage of HB ice cream products. HB spent about £1 million per year in servicing and replacing these cabinets free of charge to the retailers. The agreement with the retailers enabled either party to terminate the arrangement on two months' notice. The retailer was not restricted from selling the products of HB's competitors; the only limitation was that HB's cabinets could not be used for this purpose. It appeared that, when Mars entered the Irish market in 1989, a number of retailers stored their products in HB's freezer cabinets.

Lynch J was satisfied that HB had established that there was a serious case to be tried on the issue of wrongful interference with the plaintiff's property rights in its freezer cabinets. Mars had argued that the interference was not unlawful because HB's arrangements with the retailers were contrary to Articles 85 and 86 of the Treaty of Rome and Article 9 of the Restrictive Practices (Groceries) Order 1987. As to the Treaty of Rome, the defendant had contended that the contracts were subject to acceptance by the retailers of 'supplementary obligations which, by their nature or according to commercial usage ha[d] no connection with the subject of such contracts' (Articles 85(1)(c), 86(d)). Lynch J was satisfied that a breach of this category did 'not arise at all'. The terms with which Mars took issue related to the very basis of the contract of bailment, namely the purpose for which the freezing cabinets were bailed to the retailers. Those terms were not supplementary obligations, nor by their nature or according to commercial usage did they lack an essential connection which the contracts of bailment.

Mars could still argue that the contracts, though not breaching any of the grounds specified in Articles 85 and 86, nonetheless contravened the general intention of these Articles; however, Lynch J was satisfied that Mars had not made out a sufficient case that this had occurred. While Mars had established a serious case to be tried that HB enjoyed a dominant position within the Irish ice-cream market, it had not established such a case of *abuse* of dominant position so as to affect trade between Member States or at all.

Turning to Article 9 of the 1987 Order, which prohibits suppliers, wholesalers and retailers from being parties to any agreement, arrangement or undertaking having or likely to have the effect of limiting or restricting entry to trade in any grocery goods, Lynch J was not satisfied that Mars had established a sufficiently serious case to be tried. There was nothing to prevent a rival of HB from canvassing retailers to take its products and to offer rival storage facilities. In effect, Mars was seeking terms of entry to the Irish ice-cream trade more favourable to it than those available to other suppliers, by 'seeking to have available to it the £7 million capital investment and £1 million annual maintenance and replacement of freezers free, gratis and for nothing'.

The balance of convenience lay in HB's favour. Mars had achieved it sales' target in 1989 and had not suffered any real loss to date. On the other hand, HB's property and contractual rights had been 'set at nought'. If an injunction were refused, there was a danger that other suppliers might seek to poach HB's freezer space on the basis that an injunction would be unlikely to be given against them if it had not been given against Mars. The damage suffered by HB was incapable of calculation and bad will would be created between HB and the retailers.

In *Paramount Pictures Corporation v Cablelink Ltd*, High Court, 31 July 1989 and 8 March 1990, Murphy J applied the equitable principles relating to injunctions in a commercial context with a commendable consciousness of commercial realities. His observations on the proper scope of these principles are of general interest.

The plaintiffs, on behalf of themselves and an association of film producers (AGICOA), sought an injunction to restrain the defendants from infringing, by the use of their cablelink system, the plaintiffs' copyright in films. On 31 July 1989, Murphy J declined to grant the injunction but refused to do so only on the terms that the defendants should lodge into a joint bank account a monthly sum totalling 8% of the annual net subscription income received by the defendants — an amount representing the plaintiffs' alleged loss. Later the plaintiffs sought a new injunction to restrain the defendants from infringing their copyright by the use of a multi-point microwave distribution system (MMDS). The defendants raised defences under Articles 85 to 86 of the Treaty of Rome, involving a challenge to the constitutionality of Irish domestic legislation.

The plaintiffs contended that the defendants' introduction of the MMDS system was an intensification of the defendants' user, technically severable from the Cablelink system so that an injunction could be granted separately in respect of it. The defendants replied that, while the introduction of the MMDS system involved a technical change in the electronic or engineering sense, the true *status quo* consisted of their continuous provision for about twenty years of a diffusion service.

Murphy J conceded that both arguments obviously had substance. The *Campus Oil* test [1983] IR 88) should be applied. Murphy J summarised the first element of that test in terms of whether the plaintiffs had established 'a statable case' in support of an injunction. He added:

> The question whether the plaintiffs have established a statable case does not and never did cause any problem. The difficulty in this regard was whether or not the defendants showed a statable defence because it must be clear that an injunction will issue immediately and as a matter of right on an interlocutory application if the plaintiffs' right is not open to challenge. That is so stated as a proposition but it is sometimes over-looked. Because of the fact that other matters are ordinarily considered at the interlocutory state, including the balance of convenience and the adequacy of damages as a remedy, it does not mean that those considerations would be considered . . . [if] the defendants have no defence. There is no reason why the plaintiffs' rights or the remedies to vindicate their rights should be postponed if the defendants have no defence.

Murphy J's reminder to courts and practitioners that the questions of balance of convenience and adequacy of damages arise only where the defendant has offered some element of a legal contest to the plaintiff's case is a useful one.

In the instant case, since the plaintiffs had shown they had a statable case 'and the defendants a statable defence', Murphy J thought it right to proceed to the second and third elements of the *Campus Oil* test. What he had to say here was again of general interest: it seemed to him that it was perhaps mistaken to view as separate or watertight compartments the questions of balance of convenience and the adequacy of damages as a remedy since one would necessarily impinge on the other. In the instant case, he thought it best to approach the matter solely by a consideration of the latter. Murphy J is surely correct to perceive an overlap between these two elements. The balance of convenience seems a sufficiently broad and generic concept to embrace the question of adequacy or damages as a specific element. This is not to suggest that Murphy J was wrong to have concentrated on the question of the adequacy of damages to the apparent exclusion of other aspects of the balance of convenience; in truth, the *only* issue arising under the genus of balance of convenience was the specific matter of the adequacy of damages.

Applying the adequacy of damages test, Murphy J re-adopted the novel solution he had favoured on 31 July 1989, which was to secure through a bank account the amount that the plaintiffs claimed to be losing by the continuation of the *status quo*. Murphy J observed:

> The plaintiffs' interests will be safeguarded and they will be fully compensated for their continuing loss if it turns out that they have that right. In that regard one recognises that if, in fact, an injunction were granted, there would be no comparable benefit accruing to the plaintiffs because by definition the defendants would not have been utilising the plaintiffs' property. It may be . . . that [the plaintiffs] would benefit in other respects, but the obvious benefit would be lost if an injunction is granted. Of course, I am not saying that the plaintiffs would not be entitled to an injunction at the end of the day if they succeed in the case. If their right is established notwithstanding the defences, they would, of course, be at liberty and entitled at that stage to claim a permanent injunction and I would assume that such an order would be made so as to vindicate their property right in that event.

> By preserving the *status quo* I will do justice to the plaintiffs without unfairly prejudicing the defendants. It seems to me that the provision of a sufficient sum of money to meet the amount of the plaintiffs' claim as it is at present accruing meets the full justice of the case.

Accordingly Murphy J refused the application for an interlocutory injunction and let his earlier orders continue. He expressed strong support for a restructuring of the arrangement, preferably with an agreement of the parties, whereby the very substantial sum of money involved would be invested in Government securities or some other procedure adopted which would secure the interests of both parties.

The effect of Murphy J's approach is to force the plaintiffs to engage in compulsory economic relations with the defendants at the defendants' behest. Murphy J was probably correct in assuming that the plaintiffs would not seriously object to thus doing business with the defendants, but it would be far from every case, even in a strongly commercial context, where it would be proper to refuse to grant an interlocutory injunction on this ground. At the end of the day, it normally is for the plaintiff, and not the court or defendant, to decide as to those with whom he has commercial relations.

2 Damages in lieu of injunction   In *Falcon Travel Ltd v Owners Abroad Group plc t/a Falcon Leisure Group*, High Court, 28 June 1990, perceptively analysed by Paul Coughlan (1991) 9 ILT (ns) 138, the plaintiff travel agency operating a retail business in Dublin and Wicklow sought an injunction against the defendants, very substantial tour operators on the wholesale side, who had carried on business in Britain for about ten years and had recently launched a brochure directed to the Irish public, backed up by the opening of an office here. There was no question of any attempt by the defendants to expropriate the plaintiff's business or reputation. It seems that the plaintiff may have gained rather than lost customers as a result of the confusion that followed from the extension into Ireland of the defendants' business.

The defendants, resisting the injunction, argued that an essential ingredient in the tort of passing off was proof of existence or the real likelihood of damage to the plaintiff and that this was lacking on the facts. Murphy J accepted the defendants' proposition as to the requirement of proof of actual or likely damage but he considered that the plaintiff had indeed suffered damage — in that its reputation had become 'submerged in that of the defendants'.

In the circumstances of the case Murphy J considered damages rather than an injunction the appropriate remedy. The confusion resulting from the defendants' arrival in Ireland had lessened in recent months. An injunction would cause the defendants enormous expense. The damages which the plaintiff should be awarded would primarily enable it to mount an advertising campaign explaining to the public and those in the travel agency business the very real differences between it and the defendants.

LEGITIMATE EXPECTATION

Since its broad articulation by the Supreme Court in *Webb v Ireland* [1988] ILRM 565, [1988] IR 353 (discussed in the 1987 Review, 162-4), the doctrine of legitimate expectation has not yet blossomed into a fully-fledged private law equitable remedy of significance: see the 1988 Review, 20-30, the 1989 Review, 9-12, 194-6 and above, 10. Hamilton P's decision in *Duggan v An Taoiseach and Ors* [1989] ILRM 710 (discussed in the 1988 Review, pp 21-4) is one exception. In *Philips v The Medical Council*, High Court, 11 December 1990, to which we have already referred earlier in this Chapter, Costello J applied the doctrine as part of his holding, with repercussions in both the private and public law contexts.

Very briefly, the plaintiff, of Sudanese background but now an Irish citizen married to an Irish woman, had applied to the Medical Council for full registration on the General Register of Medical Practitioners. The Council had had sent him a set of rules by which his application would purportedly be determined. These rules had since been rescinded and new ones adopted, which would have rendered his application certain to fail.

Costello J invoked *Webb* and *Duggan* in holding that the Council was required to consider the plaintiff's application under the rules sent to him as well as using these rules as the yardstick to determine the plaintiff's action for breach of statutory duty. In Costello J's view, it would be 'grossly unfair to allow the Council to rescind the rules when an application was pending under these and adopt new ones which effectively make it impossible for the plaintiff to be registered'.

In *Philips*, the Medical Council had delayed unreasonably in making its determination: Costello J thought that three months would suffice but, after three years, it still had not come to a conclusion. If this element is removed from the formula, the question arises whether the legitimate expectation doctrine should always require a decisionmaker to freeze the criteria for determination to those prevailing when the application is made. Courts might understandably hesitate before committing themselves to an affirmative answer. It is far from every case where an applicant could truly be considered to have had such an expectation.

SECRET TRUSTS

In *In re the Estate of Prendiville, Deceased*, High Court, 5 December 1990, Barron J expounded on the principles relating to secret and half secret trusts. The testator had left all his property to his wife 'to be used by her accordingly to my wishes — as she had been advised'. During his lifetime he had informed one of his sons that he had written out his wishes as to the passing of his estate after his wife's death. He had then showed him a document in his handwriting which included a clause to the effect that another son was 'to get preference of Cluincorrig house — on a reasonable valuation . . .'. After the death of the testator, his widow gave this document to the son to whom it had been shown. She made a statutory declaration acknowledging her acceptance of the terms of her late husband's written instructions. In this, she declared that, after her death, the residence and lands of Cluincorrig should, in the first instance, be offered to the son named by the testator in the document for £6000. Other aspects of this declaration did not fully coincide with the document. By her will, some years later, she gave an option to purchase to the son for £6000. Ten years after this, she revoked the will; in a further statutory declaration, she again acknowledged that her later husband's instructions had been communicated to and accepted by her, but now she declared that the sum of £6000 had never been mentioned as the option price.

The issue in the proceedings before Barron J was whether there was an enforceable secret or half secret trust whereby the named son should have an option to purchase the residence and lands of Cluincorrig house at a reasonable valuation. After a review of the case law, Barron J held that there was an enforceable half secret trust which had been communicated to the testator's wife and accepted by her during his lifetime. He held, further, on the evidence, that the expression 'Cluincorrig house' was intended to connote the *entire* holding, including the residence and surrounding lands and that it had been so understood by the wife.

Counsel seeking to dislodge the trust had argued, on the basis of *In re Keen's Estate; Evershed v Griffiths* [1937] 1 All ER 452, that a half secret trust cannot be established unless its terms are *communicated prior to the execution of the will*. Barron J rejected this interpretation of that decision; it had turned on the construction of a particular clause in a will where the terms had never been communicated to the persons named in it subsequent to the execution of the will; there was no suggestion in it that acceptance of the terms of a trust could not be effected if made after the execution of the will.

Barron J endorsed the seven rules set out in Monroe J's judgment in *in re King's Estate*, 21 LR Ir 273, at 277-8 (1888):

> 1. A testator cannot reserve to himself the right of declaring trusts by an instrument informally executed subsequent to the execution of his will. This would be to repeal the Statute of Wills.

> 2. If a testator at or before the execution of his will communicate to a person to whom he proposes to give a legacy that the legacy is given

upon trust to be applied in a particular way, and if the legatee expressly or tacitly consents to take the legacy on these terms, the Court of Chancery will not permit him to be guilty of a fraud, but will compel the execution of the trust so communicated.

3. This rule applies whether the existence of a trust be indicated on the face of the will, or the legacy by the terms of the instrument be given absolutely.

4. The rule applies when the communication is made subsequently to the execution of the will. . . .

5. It is essential to the creation of a valid trust that the communication should be made to the legatee in the testator's lifetime, and that the legatee should not object to execute the trust.

6. If the bequest be to two or more legatees, a valid trust is created if the communication be made to any of them, before or at the time of the execution of the will. If the communication be made after the execution of the will, it must be made to all the legatees on whom the trust is sought to be imposed.

7. The terms on which the trust is expressed must not be vague or uncertain.

In Barron J's view, the principles of law applicable to half secret and secret trusts were identical. The only difference was that the person named in the will was 'an express trustee in the first case and a beneficiary in the latter'. A person who had on his own behalf agreed to hold an apparently beneficial gift on trust could not in conscience refuse to carry out the trust. The same rule should apply in the case of a half secret trust where the recipient had not made any such promise to the testator.

SPECIFIC PERFORMANCE

In *Noonan Construction Co. Ltd v Tinne*, High Court, 30 July 1990, Barr J ordered specific performance of the sale of a house to a builder. Some difficulties with the title had led to the inclusion of conditions in the contract permitting either party to rescind if the vendor (the defendant) should be unable to acquire the superior interests, and permitting either party to terminate the contract, on seven days' notice in writing, if within three months, the vendor was unable to comply with certain conditions relating to title including the acquisition of the superior interests. The vendor's solicitor purported to terminate the contract on behalf of his client. He later made damaging allegations about an accountant, a mutual acquaintance of the parties, which, he claimed, had been conveyed to him by his client.

Barr J rejected the solicitor's allegations, and rejected his evidence on crucial issues. In any event, Barr J interpreted the seven-day notice as not entitling unilateral termination without giving the other party the opportunity to do in the meantime what was necessary to uphold the contract.

Barr J declined to award the builder damages. He accepted evidence that the cost of building had increased by 5% over the period of delay, but weighed against this the increase in the value of the property in the meantime, which was 'obviously inconsistent with a decline in the new house prices in that area'. He thus implicitly rejected evidence of a decline of 5% in house prices in the area. Barr J also had regard to the probability that at least six months would pass before the new houses would be built on the property. He considered himself:

> entitled to take cognisance of the fact that interest rates are presently in decline. This trend may continue and, if so, there is likely to be a corresponding reduction in mortgage interest rates which in turn will tend to stimulate the price of new housing by increasing demand for such property.

European Communities

ABUSE OF DOMINANT POSITION

The issue of abuse of a dominant position was raised in *Paramount Pictures Corp v Cablelink Ltd*, High Court, 8 March 1990 (see 275-6, above, in the Equitable Remedies chapter), *HB Ice-cream Ltd v Masterfoods Ltd* [1990] 2 IR 463 (see 272-5, above, in the Equitable Remedies chapter), *Dunlea v Nissan (Irl) Ltd*, High Court, 24 May 1990 and *Kerry Co-Op Creameries Ltd v An Bord Báinne Co-Op Ltd* [1990] ILRM 664; Supreme Court, 21 March and 14 May 1991 (see 34-7, above, in the Commercial Law chapter).

COMMUNITY REGULATIONS IN IRISH LAW

Three cases in 1990 dealt with important aspects of the 'quota' system in Ireland.

In *O'Brien v Ireland* [1990] ILRM 466, Murphy J upheld the application of the 'Mulder' Council Regulation in relation to the plaintiff. The background was, briefly, as follows. Council Regulation 1078/77/EEC introduced the system under which milk producers were encouraged to cease production by being paid a premium based on their level of production in the year preceding the application for the premium. The farmers involved were required to give an undertaking that they would cease milk production for 5 years. Council Regulation 857/84/EEC was intended to further discourage milk production by introducing milk production quotas for the first time, with penalties for excess production. This Regulation was successfully challenged before the Court of Justice in *Mulder v Minister van Landbouw en Visserij* [1989] 2 CMLR 1 on the basis that it excluded from quota allocation those farmers who had availed of the premium system introduced in 1977. Council Regulation 764/89/EEC, referred to as the 'Mulder' Regulation, extended the category of farmers entitled to obtain quotas.

In *O'Brien*, the plaintiff, who had availed of the premium system, was allocated a quota of 30,000 gallons under the Mulder Regulation. For various reasons, he was unable to produce this quota from the land in respect of which he had obtained the premium under the 1977 Council Regulation. He therefore proposed to lease 40 cows as well as take on licence 60 acres of land from his brother. The authorities agreed that the plaintiff was entitled to lease the 40 cows to come within the Mulder Regulation, but they considered that the plaintiff was not entitled to take on licence the 60 acres as proposed. The question, therefore, was whether the Mulder Regulation required a farmer to operate a quota from the same land as that from which a premium had been claimed under the 1977 Council Regulation.

Murphy J held, in finding against the plaintiff, that the authorities were correct in their interpretation of the Mulder Regulation. Murphy J pointed out that in both the 1977 (Premium) Regulation and in the 1984 (Quota) Regulation, the word 'holding' was defined by reference to land 'managed' and 'operated' respectively by the milk producer. He also referred to his own judgment in *Lawlor v Minister for Agriculture* [1988] ILRM 400 (1987 Review, 92-4) in which he had held that quotas must relate to the holdings on which the milk is produced. He then noted that the 1989 (Mulder) Regulation was in fact an amendment to the 1977 and 1984 Regulations and was to be construed as such. Noting that the plaintiff had accepted that the Mulder Regulation was not designed to give Mulder farmers a windfall profit, Murphy J concluded that in the overall context of all the Council Regulations, the 1989 Regulation should properly be construed as requiring that production be from the land in respect of which the premium under the 1977 Regulation had been obtained originally.

Accepting this interpretation of the Mulder Regulation then required Murphy J to consider whether this breached either the principles of proportionality or certainty. He held that, as to proportionality, the Mulder Regulation would inevitably involve some difference of treatment as between Mulder and non-Mulder producers but he did not consider that the particular scheme chosen by the Council in the 1989 Regulation breached the principle. Neither did he consider that the certainty principle had been breached in the context of the word 'holding' in the 1989 Regulation.

It may be noted, finally, that in the *O'Brien* case the Supreme Court has referred to the Court of Justice the question whether the 1989 Regulation requires that the Mulder quota be produced from the land in respect of which the non-production premium had originally been obtained: see [1990] ILRM at 484.

The second case on the quota system was *Dowling v Ireland*, High Court, 18 January 1990. In a judgment delivered on the same date as *O'Brien*, Murphy J dealt with a case involving a farmer who had ceased milk production and taken advantage of the 1977 Premium Regulation. In 1980 he had then unfortunately developed a heart condition which precluded him from resuming milk production. He was thus unable to obtain the benefit of the 1984 Quota Regulation, which based the quota on 1983 production, even though the period during which he was precluded from resuming milk production had expired in 1982. A Commission Regulation of 1988 amended the 1984 Regulation to allow a producer who had suffered occupational incapacity to obtain a quota by reference to another calendar reference year 'within the 1981 to 1983 period.' This amendment was of no benefit to the plaintiff on a literal interpretation since there was no milk production in any of these years.

The plaintiff in *Dowling* argued that, since the 1988 Regulation had failed to anticipate the gap which was involved in the instant case, the court should dispense with the literal rule and adopt the teleological approach, an approach discussed by Murphy J in the *Lawlor* case, above (see the 1987 Review, 312-3). However, in *Dowling*, although Murphy J accepted that, on the authorities opened to him, the teleological approach of interpretation allowed the courts to depart from the literal interpretation of legislation, he felt compelled by the clear language of the 1988 Regulation to find against the plaintiff. Of particular interest was that he stated that the presumption of constitutionality applied by the Supreme Court in *East Donegal Co-Op Ltd v Attorney General* [1970] IR 317 was consistent with the teleological approach. Indeed, Murphy J had noted the limits to the schematic or teleological approach in a domestic context in *Rafferty v Crowley* [1984] ILRM 350.

The third case on the quota system was *Condon v Minister for Agriculture and Food*, High Court, 12 October 1990. Here, Lynch J upheld the procedure by which the detailed implementation of EC Regulations in agriculture matters is done by way of non-statutory schemes. In this instance the scheme in question was one implementing the milk quota and clawback system under Council Regulation 857/84/EEC. Lynch J accepted that the Regulation had immediate effect in Irish law and was, to that extent, immune from constitutional challenge under Article 29.4.3. The Minister, he concluded, therefore had an option to implement the Council Regulation by means of statutory order under s.3 of the European Communities Act 1972 or, as had been done here, by means of communicating his scheme to interested parties in the agricultural sector.

However, Lynch J added that once it was decided to implement a scheme it might be open to challenge for unreasonableness or unfairness. In this respect, he stated that an unreasonable or unfair scheme could not be said to be 'necessitated' by Article 29.4.3. As to the interpretation of 'necessitated', see the 1987 Review, 93-4. Having considered the operation of the scheme in question on this basis, Lynch J held that it did not operate in an unreasonable or unfair manner.

It is notable that the list of cases cited which Lynch J helpfully provided at the end of his judgment includes the Supreme Court decision in *Cityview Press Ltd v An Chomhairle Oiliúna* [1980] IR 381. While he did not rely on this decision expressly in his judgment, his approach is similar to the 'detail filling' approach of the Court in that case.

COURT OF FIRST INSTANCE

An informative discussion of the operation of the Court of First Instance of the European Communities, delivered by Judge Donal Barrington to members of the Irish Bar, was published in (1990) 12 DULJ 92.

IRISH REGULATIONS

The following regulations and orders were made in 1990 pursuant to the provisions of s.3 of the European Communities Act 1972 (or other statutory powers) involving implementation of Community law obligations.

European Communities (Agricultural or Forestry Tractors Type Approval) Regulations 1990 (SI No. 338): amend the 1979 Regulations, as already amended.

European Communities (Asbestos Waste) Regulations 1990 (SI No. 30): require procedures connected with the transport and disposal of asbestos waste, and provide penalties for failure to comply.

European Communities (Cereal Seed) (Amendment) Regulations 1990 (SI No. 341): amend the 1981 Regulations and provide for certification procedures to conform with international schemes of certification.

European Communities (Construction Plant and Equipment) (Permissible Noise Levels) (Amendment) Regulations 1990 (SI No. 297): amend the 1988 Regulations (see the 1988 Review, 208).

European Communities (Control of Veterinary Medicinal Products and Their Residues) Regulations 1990 (SI No. 171) extend the impact of the European Communities (Control of Oestrogenic, Androgenic, Gestragenic and Thyrostatic Substances) Regulations 1988.

European Communities (Control of Water Pollution by Asbestos) Regulations 1990 (SI No. 31).

European Communities (Co-responsibility Levy on Milk and Milk Products) (Amendment) Regulations 1990 (SI No. 37): amend the 1977 Regulations and provide for penalties for breach.

European Communities (Co-responsibility Levy on Cereals) (Amendment) Regulations 1990 (SI No. 38): amend the 1988 Regulations and provide for penalties for breach.

European Communities (Cosmetic Products) Regulations 1990 (SI No. 265): prohibit the marketing of cosmetic products likely to cause harm to health.

European Communities (Counterfeit Goods) Regulations 1990 (SI No. 118): allow for applications to the Revenue Commissioners to have counterfeit goods impounded.

European Communities (Introduction of Organisms Harmful to Plants or Plant Products) (Prohibition) (Amendment) Regulations 1990 (SI No. 119).

European Communities (Introduction of Organisms Harmful to Plants or Plant Products) (Prohibition) (Amendment) (No. 2) Regulations 1990 (SI No. 346).

European Communities (Introduction of Organisms Harmful to Plants or Plant Products) (Prohibition) (Temporary Provisions) (Amendment) Regulations 1990 (SI No. 282).

European Communities (Life Assurance) (Amendment) Regulations 1990 (SI No. 150).

European Communities (Life Assurance) (Amendment) (No. 2) Regulations 1990 (SI No. 212).

European Communities (Non-Life Insurance) (Amendment) Regulations 1990 (SI No. 211).

European Communities (Prohibition of Certain Active Substances in Plant Protection Products) (Amendment) Regulations 1990 (SI No. 339): amend the 1981 Regulations.

European Communities (Protection of Workers) (Exposure to Noise) Regulations 1990 (SI No. 157): see the Safety and Health chapter, 474-5, below.

European Communities (Protein Feedingstuffs) (Amendment) Regulations 1990 (SI No. 92): amend the 1986 Regulations.

European Communities (Quantitative Analysis of Binary and Ternary Fibre Mixtures) Regulations 1990 (SI No. 275).

European Communities (Radio Interference from Electrical Household Appliances, Portable Tools and Similar Equipment) (Amendment) Regulations 1990 (SI No. 290): amend the 1979 and 1983 Regulations of the same title.

European Communities (Radio Interference from Flourescent Lighting Luminaires) (Amendment) Regulations 1990 (SI No. 291): amend the 1979 and 1983 Regulations of the same title.

European Communities (Restriction of Aeroplane Operations) Regulations 1990 (SI No. 235): requires noise certification to operate in the State.

European Communities (Retirement of Farmers) Regulations 1990 (SI No. 174).

European Communities (Roll Over and Falling Object Protective Structures for Construction Plant) Regulations 1990 (SI No. 202).

European Communities (Safety of Toys) Regulations 1990 (SI No. 32): require that toys marketed in the State must possess an EC safety mark. The

Regulations came into effect on 13 February 1990. The European Communities (Safety of Toys) Regulations 1985 (SI No. 44) apply to toys placed on the market prior to 13 February 1990.

European Communities (Seed of Fodder Plants) (Amendment) Regulations 1990 (SI No. 214): provide a revised scale of fees for the testing of fodder plant seeds.

European Communities (Standards for Heat-treated Milk in Intra-Community Trade) Regulations 1990 (SI No. 124)

European Communities (Surveillance of Certain Textile Products, Footwear and Tableware Imports) Regulations 1990 (SI No. 35).

European Communities (Trade with Iraq and Kuwait) Regulations 1990 (SI No. 215): prohibited trade with Iraq and Kuwait after the invasion by Iraq.

European Communities (Trade with Iraq and Kuwait) (No. 2) Regulations 1990 (SI No. 262): specified penalties for engaging in trade, and provided for trade under licence for medicine and food for humanitarian purposes.

Health (Emulsifiers, Stabilisers, Thickening and Gelling Agents in Food) (Amendment) Regulations 1990 (SI No. 102): update the 1980 Regulations to implement further EC Directives.

Jurisdiction of Courts and Enforcement of Judgments (European Communities) Act 1988 (Section 1(4)) (Declaration) Order 1990 (SI No. 231): specifies the contracting parties to the Brussels Convention.

Restriction of Imports from Iraq and Kuwait Order 1990 (SI No. 217): required a licence for the importation of items connected with the ECSC Treaty.

Road Vehicles (Registration and Licensing) (Amendment) Regulations 1990 (SI No. 287): see the Transport chapter, 586, below.

Winter Time Order 1990 (SI No. 52): gives effect to Directive 89/47/EEC on Summer Time as well as specifying the start of Winter Time.

REFERENCE TO COURT OF JUSTICE

A reference under Article 177 of the Treaty of Rome was refused by the Supreme Court in *Rhatigan v Textiles y Confecciones Europeas SA* [1990] ILRM 825; [1990] 1 IR 126: see the discussion in the 1989 Review, 75.

Family Law

At the introduction to this chapter we enthusiastically welcome the publication of Duncan & Scully's *Marriage Breakdown in Ireland: Law and Practice* (Butterworth (Ireland) Ltd, 1990). The work covers many aspects of family law and involves a very satisfactory intermingling of the academic and practical approaches. It is written with great clarity and contains a wealth of new information. Additional material by Cormac Corrigan, Barrister at Law, in relation to family property and the family home, adds to the value of the book.

ADOPTION

1 Adoption Rules 1990 The Adoption Rules 1990 (SI No. 170 of 1990) prescribe forms to be used for the purposes of the Adoption Acts 1952 to 1988. They replace similar rules made in 1976 and 1984. They relate to such matters as the application for an adoption order, consent to adoption, the adoption order itself and the form (Form 10) which must be furnished by the adoption society to the parent or guardian who proposes to place the child for adoption. Interestingly, the law relating to Form 10 (in its previous incarnation) fell for consideration in a decision in 1990, to which we now turn.

2 Adoption Societies and procedural requirements S. 39 of the Adoption Act 1952 imposes an obligation on registered adoption societies, before accepting children for adoption, to furnish their mother or guardian with a statement in writing in the prescribed form explaining clearly the effect of an adoption order on the rights of the mother or guardian and the provisions of the Act relating to consent to the making of an adoption order; it also obliges the societies to ensure that the mother or guardian understands the statement and signs a document to that effect. These requirements are backed by a criminal sanction with a maximum fine of £100.

In *In re D.G., An Infant: O.G. v An Bord Uchtála and the Protestant Adoption Society* [1991] ILRM 514, Lavan J interpreted s. 39 as requiring that an adoption society, through its servants or duly appointed agents, should actually furnish the mother the statement in writing in the required form and, also through them, should ensure that she understood the statement and signed a document to that effect. Since this had not been done Lavan J held that the adoption order was invalid. (We examine in a moment the other grounds on which he held it invalid).

The Supreme Court reversed (counsel for the mother not seeking to stand over this holding). Finlay CJ (O'Flaherty J concurring) considered that the section was complied with if the society satisfied itself that the statement had been furnished to the mother or guardian and that 'an appropriate person' had 'clearly and responsibly ascertained' that she had understood it and signed a document to this effect. There would, in his view, be no more appropriate person to carry out these tasks on behalf of an adoption society than (as in this case) a professional social worker who had been in constant communication with the mother for a protracted period beforehand.

The Chief Justice expressed the tentative option that, in any event, failure to comply with s. 39 could not vitiate an otherwise valid fully informed and free consent to a placement for an adoption, unless it went so far as to be construed as vitiating the entire adoption procedure in an individual case. McCarthy J, concurring, considered it unfortunate that counsel for the mother had not conceded in the High Court that failure to comply with s. 39 would not invalidate the agreement to place the child for adoption.

The Supreme Court's interpretation of s. 39 must be regarded as an indulgent one. The section imposes an obligation on the adoption society to furnish the relevant document to the mother or guardian. Of course that direct obligation could be discharged through the society's servants or agents; it is, however, an entirely different proposition that a society complies with the section where it does nothing but the mother or guardian happens to receive the documentation from another person not acting under the authority of the society, however responsible that person may be. The society's duty is not simply to ensure that the mother or guardian is furnished with the document: it is to furnish it to her itself.

As to the crucial question of the effect of non-compliance on the validity of the adoption, many will welcome the Supreme Court's holding on pragmatic grounds. The idea that an adoption should be held invalid where the mother freely consented to it, on a fully informed basis, may seem unpalatable. Nevertheless, formal and procedural requirements in legislation sometimes serve the role of ensuring that high standards will be maintained. The requirements of s. 39 represent the essentials of good adoption practice. To treat them as unimportant or optional would seem unwise. The substantive (as opposed to formal) obligations prescribed by s. 39 are, independently, essential to the validity of consent, in that a mother's failure to appreciate the legal effect of adoption or of her requirement for the consent would mean that her consent was not fully informed and thus not legally effective. There is a respectable argument that compliance with s. 39 should be treated as essential to the validity of an adoption so as to encourage adoption societies to ensure that the mother's free consent is obtained. Of course the argument against this approach has many attractions, the most obvious being that it would be wrong to invalidate an adoption (to the detriment of the child, the mother and the adopters), where a full and free consent had in fact been obtained, merely to accomplish the general goal of keeping adoption societies on their toes so far as their compliance with proper procedures is concerned.

The second issue in the case concerned the efficacy of the mother's consent. Lavan J had held that the mother had not given a fully informed and free consent to the placement of the child for adoption; in coming to this conclusion he had been very largely influenced by the view he had reached concerning the manner in which the social workers had counselled and advised the mother. He considered that the social workers had given the mother unsound advice, had acted with a lack of propriety, had been biased towards adoption, as distinct from any other course of conduct for the mother, and had been placed in a situation of a serious conflict of interest in their obligation to the mother and to the adoption society.

The Supreme Court held that there was no foundation in the evidence for these conclusions. The mother's evidence, however, had been to the effect that, having had the matter explained to her by one of the social workers, she believed that she had an unequivocal and unqualified right to the return of her child if she withdrew her consent within six months of having given it. The social worker's evidence had been to the contrary. The course adopted by the Supreme Court, therefore, was to remit the case to the High Court to determine, in the light of the legal principles laid down by the Supreme Court, whether the mother's consent had been effective and if so, whether it should be dispensed with, under s. 3 of the Adoption Act 1974.

McCarthy J noted in this context that, while the case was not an appeal by the social workers, they had a keen interest in its outcome; no less than the parties, they were entitled to feel that they had been treated fairly. A fundamental feature of fairness was that an individual should be given the opportunity of answering any imputation, either personal or professional. No such opportunity had been given here, since counsel for the mother had not made the imputation, put forward by the trial Judge, that the social workers had been involved in a deliberate attempt to blacken the mother's character before the court so as to encourage it to dispense with her consent. McCarthy J considered that '[i]f counsel for the mother did not make such imputations, it was no part of the judge's role to do so'. This criticism was without foundation and should not have formed any part of the reasoning underlying the decision.

This concept of procedural due process to witnesses echoes the approach favoured by the Supreme Court in *M. v M.* [1979] ILRM 160 where the Court, in proceedings for annulment of marriage, held that it was 'not in accordance with the proper administration of justice [for the trial judge to have] cast aside the corroborated and unquestioned evidence of witnesses, still less to impute collusion or perjury to them, when they were not given any opportunity of rebutting such an accusation. To do so in this case was in effect to condemn them unheard, which is contrary to natural justice'. Whereas in *M. v M.* the trial judge's error was apparently to have failed to cross-examine the witness himself (a dangerous course, one might have thought), the trial judge in *In re D.G.* was, in McCarthy J's view, wrong to have reached a conclusion as to certain witnesses' evidence that had not been pressed by counsel for the mother.

There can hardly be a general principle that a judge is debarred from reaching a conclusion of fact or law merely became counsel have not submitted that he should do so. Lavan J's conclusion that the social workers had deliberately attempted to blacken the mother's character, if unsustainable on the evidence, should not have formed part of the reasoning underlying his judgment; but it would have been perfectly proper for it to have done so if it *had* been sustained by the evidence, even if counsel for the mother had not invited him so to conclude.

In relation to s. 3, it is worth noting what the Chief Justice had to say. He thought that it was:

> of obvious importance to state that a mother agreeing to place her child for adoption could not be said to reach a fully informed decision so to agree, unless at the time she made the agreement she was aware that the right which she undoubtedly has to withdraw that consent or to refuse further to consent to adoption, is subject to the possibility that, upon application by the prospective adopting parents, the court could con-clude that it was in the best interests of the child to dispense with the mother's consent, and if following upon such a decision the board decided that it was appropriate to order the adoption of the child, she (the mother) could lose, forever, the custody of the child.

This statement reflects what was said in *G. v An Bord Uchtála* [1980] IR 32, so far as the judgments in that case share a common denominator. What it does not address is the important question as to whether the information regarding the legal effect of s. 3 will suffice if it explains the fact that there is a *possibility* of the court's dispensing with the mother's consent, or whether it should go further and address the *actual likelihood* of this occurring. The reality is that the passage of a relatively short period of time after the mother has placed the child for adoption may well result in the court's holding that the welfare of the child requires that it stay with the would-be adopters. This is clear from the decision of *K. v W. (No. 2)* [1990] ILRM 791, which we discuss later in this Chapter. There is a strong argument that the mother's consent is not a free and fully informed one where there has been a failure to inform her of the potent attraction to courts of the 'trauma' doctrine regarding changes in the custody of young children and the consequent likelihood of her consent's being dispensed with after a few months have elapsed. In fact Form 10 of the Adoption Rules 1990 (SI No. 170 of 1990) is drafted in a legalistic manner which follows closely the language of s3. It gives no indication to the mother of the practical likelihood that if she does not withdraw her consent quickly, she will lose her child.

NULLITY OF MARRIAGE

1 Homosexual orientation In the 1989 Review, pp. 210-15, we analysed in some detail Keane J's judgment in *F. (otherwise H.C.) v C.* [1991] ILRM 65. We noted there that the Supreme Court had reversed Keane J. It will be recalled that the case concerned an application for nullity on the ground that the respondent, at the time he went through a ceremony of marriage with the petitioner, was, on account of his homosexual orientation, unable to form or maintain a normal marital relationship with the petitioner. Keane J disagreed with his High Court colleagues so far as they had recognised and developed the ground of incapacity to form a normal, or a caring and considerate, relationship with the other party.

Crucial to the resolution of the issue was Kenny J's statement in his dissenting judgment in *S. v S.* [1976-7] ILRM 156, at 163, relating to the effect of s. 13 of the Marriage Law (Ireland) Amendment Act 1870. This provided that the newly established Court for Matrimonial Cases and Matters should act and give relief on principles and rules which in its opinion 'shall be as nearly as may be conformable' to those on which the ecclesiastical courts of the Church of Ireland had acted and given relief. Kenny J had observed that s. 13:

> did not have the effect of fossilising the law in its state in that year. That law is, to some extent at least, judge-made, and the courts must recognise that the great advances made in psychological medicine since 1870 make it necessary to frame new rules which reflect these.

Finlay CJ (Griffin, Hederman and O'Flaherty JJ concurring) noted that Keane J had appeared to assume that Kenny J's statement should be interpreted as meaning that the *only* circumstance to which the courts could or should have regard in framing new rules for the application of the jurisdiction of immunity was that of the advances made in psychological medicine. In the Chief Justice's view this interpretation was incorrect and constituted an unsound principle with regard to the jurisdiction of the courts in nullity cases.

The Chief Justice did not expand in express terms on his disagreement with Keane J but the remainder of his judgment suggests that, in denying that advances made in psychological medicine represented the only circumstance to which the court should have regard in framing new rules for the grounds of nullity, the Chief Justice did not commit himself to the broad proposition that the courts are free to create new grounds for any reason that may appeal to them.

Finlay CJ went on to endorse Barrington J's use in *R.S.J. v J.S.J.* [1982] ILRM 263 of the analogy with impotence in recognising as a ground for nullity the incapacity of one party to enter into a caring or considerate relationship with the other. The Chief Justice considered that this analogy was valid not only in cases where the incapacity arose from psychiatric or mental illness so recognised or defined but also in cases where it arose from 'some other inherent quality or characteristic of an individual's nature or personality which could not be said to be voluntary or self-induced.' He also approved of the principles laid down by Costello J in *D. v C.* [1984] ILRM 173.

The Chief Justice could see no reason why the 'apparently fully accepted principle of the development of the law of nullity', by reason of modern advances in psychiatric medicine, should be confined to advances and knowledge which could be placed before the court as strictly coming within the definition of psychiatric medicine and should exclude advances in knowledge and research which had been equally important and widespread in the area of sexual orientation and sexual development of the individual with regard to the origins, causes and consequences of these features of personality:

> Recognition of the existence by psychiatrists of a homosexual nature and inclination, which is not susceptible to being changed, makes it, in my view, a necessary and permissible development of the law of nullity, having regard to the principles which I have already outlined in this judgment, that it should recognise that in certain circumstances the existence in one party to a marriage of an inherent and unalterable homosexual nature may form a proper legal ground for annulling the marriage at the instance of the other party to the marriage in the case, at least, where that party has no knowledge of the existence of the homosexual nature.

The Chief Justice was satisfied that his view of the appropriate extension of development of the law of nullity beyond 'the mere confines of mental or psychiatric illness' found support in Henchy J's judgment in *N. (otherwise*

K.) v K. [1986] ILRM 75; [1985] IR 733, where Henchy J had recognised that, not merely modern psychological and psychiatric advances might properly be applied today in the development of the law of nullity of marriage, but also 'other advances in knowledge and understanding of human affairs'.

Finlay CJ's judgment represents an important milestone in the development of the law of nullity of marriage, in raising the *R.S.J.* ground to Supreme Court status. His point of departure from Keane J is a good deal less radical than might at first appear. Having denied that Kenny J's statement in *S. v S.* had limited the scope of development of grounds for nullity to those where this development is attributable to advances made in psychological medicine, the Chief Justice went on to base the ground of incapacity to form a caring or considerate relationship, in the context of a homosexual orientation, on *advances in psychological understanding in respect of sexual orientation and development*. This seems well capable of falling within even a narrow interpretation of Kenny J's statement. The only basis on which it might be considered to represent an extension is that it resolves the issue which has troubled and divided the courts since *R.S.J.*, namely, whether it is essential that the incapacity should spring from a mental *illness*. The Chief Justice makes it clear that this is not essential: it suffices that it arose from some other inherent quality or characteristic of the party's nature or personality which could not be said to be voluntary or self-induced.

Thus, a party's selfishness and indulgence cannot activate this ground, however damaging such moral weakness may be for the relationship between the parties: but a homosexual orientation over which a party had no control would be capable of coming within the scope of the ground as this would not be 'voluntary or self-induced'. (It is of interest to note that the Chief Justice made no attempt to discuss the question of the difference between an orientation and conduct: this is perhaps less than crucial in the particular context of the *R.S.J.* ground, since, if a party is of exclusively (or virtually exclusively) homosexual orientation, the evidence may be such as to reveal an incapacity to form a caring or considerate relationship with the other party, regardless of whether the homosexual party engages in homosexual conduct).

The effect of Finlay CJ's recognition of the *R.S.J.* ground as extending to cases of incapacity resulting from some inherent quality, other than illness, which is not voluntary or self-induced is that a case of alcoholism might be capable of falling within the scope of this ground without the need for the court to make the increasingly controversial characterisation of alcoholism as an illness. But, for this ground to apply, it would be necessary for the Court to hold that the condition of alcoholism was attributable to causes in the psychological or physical, rather than the moral, order. It would be mistaken to understate the formidable philosophical issues which this question would require the Court to confront.

McCarthy J's concurring judgment is of interest for two reasons. First, he makes no express reference to the distinction between incapacity resulting from mental illness and incapacity resulting from some other inherent quality of an individual's nature which could not be said to be voluntary or self-induced. The tenor of his remarks, however, is clearly in accord with the Chief Justice's thinking on this matter: his reference to the respondent's 'unalterable homosexual proclivity' makes it plain that he did not consider it necessary to characterise that condition as an illness. Secondly, McCarthy J explored the possibility of approaching the matter from the standpoint of the *petitioner*. It was, in his view, unthinkable that a party who was totally ignorant of the other's homosexual proclivity should be held to have entered into a valid contract 'of which one of the implied but most important terms is the commitment to physical consummation and natural satisfaction'. It might be, however, that a contract of marriage could be validly entered into by parties, both of whom were aware of the homosexual proclivity of one of them, where they hoped that their relationship would eliminate or, at least, suppress this homosexual proclivity.

McCarthy J's approach here is not inconsistent with that of the Chief Justice, who recognised that a party's inherent and unalterable homosexual nature might be a ground for nullity at the instance of the other party 'in the case, at least, where that party has no knowledge of the existence of homosexual nature'. Whether knowledge of the condition should *automatically* deprive the non-homosexual party of the right to petition may be debated. The kind of case envisaged by McCarthy J, where the parties hoped (in vain) that the condition would substantially disappear, would seem to be one where the better rule would enable the court to grant a decree, subject to the bar of approbation.

The converse question will surely soon arise. This is where a *homosexual party petitions* on the basis of his own condition. If he was unaware (or not fully aware) of that condition before he went through the ceremony of marriage, then there would not appear to be an objection to a decree's being made, subject to the bar of approbation. Where the petitioner *was* fully aware of his homosexual orientation but kept this fact from the respondent, then normally he should expect to be denied a decree on equitable considerations. We have yet to see which of the following specific approaches will commend itself to the courts. The first would deny a decree in *every* case. This would seem too inflexible a rule, capable of working injustice in some cases. The second would deny a decree in all cases save where the conduct of the respondent prevented her from denying the 'just cause' of the petition. This is based on the analogy with impotence, a ground which, in the courts' view, bears a close analogy with the ground of incapacity to form a normal marriage relationship: cf. *R.S.J., D. v C.* and the instant case. It will be recalled that, in impotence cases, this 'just cause' proviso seemingly applies in all cases where a party petitions on the basis of his or her own impotence. We discuss this whole question in our analysis of Barr J's decision in *E.C. (otherwise M.) v A.M.*, High Court, 5 December 1990, below, pp. 306-8.

The third possible approach would resolve the matter by reference to the bar of approbation. This would seem likely to offer a sensitive and flexible solution. A fourth possible option would seek to distinguish between 'deserving' and 'undeserving' cases even before reaching the issue of approbation (which the court would be free to address in those cases where the petitioner survived the threshold scrutiny).

Another important matter discussed in *F. (otherwise H.C.) v C.* was the question of the standard of proof. In *S. v S.*, Kenny J had noted that one of the principles fundamental in suits of nullity prior to 1870 was that the petitioner had to establish his or her case with a high degree of probability or, as Lord Birkenhead had expressed it in *C. (otherwise H) v C.* [1921] P 399, the petitioner 'must remove all reasonable doubt'. Keane J had referred to Kenny J's remarks, and had noted that the public policy underlying this aspect of the law had been 'emphatically reinforced' by Article 41.2 of the Constitution. Keane J had quoted from Finlay CJ's judgment in *N. (otherwise K) v K.*, [1986] ILRM 75; [1985] IR 733 to the effect that the status of marriage and the related concept of a family receive special provision from the Constitution. He disagreed with McCarthy J's view, expressed in that decision, that the standard of proof in nullity cases was that of the balance of probabilities.

McCarthy J, on appeal, was not enthusiastic about Keane J's analysis. He observed:

> If the observations of Kenny J in *S. v S.* mean, as apparently in the instant case Keane J thought, that there is a greater onus imposed upon a petitioner, then, in my view, this was an incorrect statement of the law applicable to this jurisdiction. There may have been a misunderstanding of the reference to the Constitution contained in *N. v K.*; the guarantee protects the institution of marriage but it does not presuppose the existence of a valid marriage in any given case so as to increase the burden of proof where a petitioner calls in aid s. 13 of the Act of 1870. It begs the question to say that the constitutional guarantee endorses, for instance, the citation from Lord Birkenhead in *C. (otherwise H.) v C.* [*supra*]. The burden of proof point only arises where there is an issue of fact. There was no such issue here. The point is irrelevant to the issue as to what constitutes incapacity.

McCarthy J was surely correct to make it clear that the burden of proof lies in the realm of fact rather than of legal characterisation of proven or admitted facts: there is no 'presumption', one way or the other, as to the merits of any *legal* argument to the effect that, on proven or admitted facts, a marriage is null. It is an entirely different matter, however, to contend that there can be no rules of evidence relating to specific (alleged) marriages, either as regards the burden or the standard of proof. It is well established that the burden of proof rests on those who attack the validity of the marriage and that the standard is a stringent one, more onerous than that of the balance of probabilities. (It is to be hoped that our courts are not tempted to follow the dubious metaphysics of Denning LJ (as he then was) who in *Bater v Bater* [1951] P25, at 37, defined the balance of probabilities as a constant formula having different weightings in different contexts).

Perhaps McCarthy J was thinking on the 'due process' lines which underlay O'Hanlon J's rejection of the (effectively) irrebuttable presumption of paternity in *S. v S.* [1984] ILRM 66; [1983] IR68. There O'Hanlon J emphasised the need for the truth to be told in legal proceedings; evidential rules which frustrated that function were accordingly suspect. It might be argued that the protection of marriage in society does not require, and cannot justify, the imposition of an evidential rule which would have the effect of preventing the court from acting on what seemed more likely to be true than false, applying the balance of probabilities test. If this is so, any more stringent standard would frustrate justice by thus immobilising the court. As against this, a more benign interpretation of the stringent approach in the context of nullity of marriage can be hazarded. Litigation affecting marital status is unlike much of the ordinary run of civil litigation: society has an interest (in marital stability) which in some instances the parties may be tempted to subvert. Collusion is an ever-present danger in cases of this type. It is, of course, notoriously difficult to eradicate; in the absence of a Queen's Proctor or Defender of the Bond, it may be considered reasonable that the judges in nullity proceedings should maintain a cautious stance.

It is worth noting that in *F. (otherwise H.C.) v C.*, Finlay CJ, while agreeing with McCarthy J that, on the facts, the question of the onus of proof did not arise for determination, preferred to reserve his position on what the onus might be, pending a case involving argument on both sides of the question. His recollection of *N. (otherwise K.) v K.* was that the issue of the onus of proof had not been raised as a contentious issue between the parties in it, and he did not think that it could be inferred, as Keane J had done, that the absence of mention of the onus of proof in the other judgments of the court could be taken 'as an affirmation of any previous view concerning it'. This statement might be interpreted simply as a corrective for reading too much into judicial silence: judgments would be particularly burdensome assignments if, from fear of generating unintended inferences from their failure to disagree expressly with their colleagues' remarks, judges they had to engage in an elaborate process of recording their lack of accord. On the other hand, the Chief Justice's characterisation of a well-established principle as a 'previous view' might be considered to evince a certain willingness to examine the issue afresh.

2 Lack of consent In the 1988 Review, 227-9 we discussed Carroll J's judgment, in *D.B. (otherwise O'R.) v N. O'R.*, High Court, 29 July 1988. The facts, briefly, were that the petitioner went through a ceremony of marriage with the respondent in 1966, when the petitioner was sixteen, the respondent nearly ten years her senior. At the time the petitioner was pregnant. From an early age she had lived in an orphanage, though in recent years she had become somewhat closer to her parents, staying with them periodically. When the parents learned of the pregnancy, they brought their daughter back to the convent, blaming the nun in charge for her condition. The nun had then contacted the respondent, who was an Irish soldier in the British army; he had returned and agreed to marry the petitioner. The wedding took place within a month.

The couple had four children. The relationship did not prosper and, after legal proceedings, the petitioner sought an annulment. The essence of her case was that the marriage had been arranged by the nun over her head and that she was scared going into the marriage. Carroll J rejected the petition on the basis that the petitioner's mind had not been overborne by the nun or any other person. Pressure of events 'such as an unwanted pregnancy or fear of being poor of having nowhere to live or of being unable to cope on one's own', might explain the motive for marrying but alone could not constitute duress or 'unreasonable influence'. That had to emanate from a person. In the 1988 Review, 228, we argued that while, of the nature of things, pressure to marry which is of sufficient force to remove free will tends to come from people and other sources of fear rarely have this effect, there can be no *principled* objection to granting a nullity decree where, as a matter of fact, the will has been overborne by such a source.

The Supreme Court, on 13 December 1990, reversed Carroll J. Before we examine Hederman J's judgment (with which Finlay CJ and O'Flaherty J, the other members of the Court, concurred), it should be noted that, during argument before the Court, counsel for the appellant abandoned the grounds of duress and influence 'and relied on the petitioner's incapacity to give a real consent to the marriage'. As we shall see, this was an important change of strategy.

Counsel for the appellant, not surprisingly, relied on Finlay CJ's judgment in the Supreme Court decision of *N. (otherwise K.) v K.* [1986] ILRM 75;

[1985] IR 733, at 739, to the effect that consent to marry 'must, . . . if the
marriage is to be valid, be a fully free exercise of the independent will of the
parties', and that, whilst a court, faced with a challenge to the validity of a
marriage, based on the absence of real consent, should conduct its enquiry
in accordance with these concepts and their legal definition, such defined
legal concepts as duress and undue influence '. . . must remain subservient
to the ultimate objective of ascertaining in accordance with the onus of proof
whether the consent of the petitioning party was real or apparent.'

The respondent was not legally represented. He received a strong com-
mendation for the manner in which he gave his evidence in the High Court
and for the manner and restraint with which he presented his submissions to
the Supreme Court. (It may here be interposed that, from a human standpoint,
the case presents a poignant story; Hederman J's judgment, including parts
of the transcript, fully conveys the moral and emotional dilemmas of the
participants). It is perhaps unfortunate that the respondent did not have the
benefit of legal representation. The petitioner's legal argument emerged
without any forceful counterpoint.

In his judgment Hederman J stated that the fact that the petitioner's will
had not been overborne by the nun or any other person was not sufficient to
determine the issue of consent. He referred to aspects of the evidence: that
the petitioner had never been given any instructions on the nature of the
marriage covenant and its consequences; that no adult had advised her in any
way as to whether or not she should marry or offered her any alternative to
marriage; that she was clearly very shocked on discovering her pregnancy;
that her parents had totally abandoned her and returned her to the convent;
that the marriage had been arranged and that she had complied with this
decision.

The question for the court, said Hederman J was a single one:

> On the facts as proved in evidence and accepted by the learned trial
> Judge, did the petitioner establish that she was not in a position, prior
> to the marriage, freely to exercise her independent will to enter into the
> covenant of marriage[?]

Carroll J had not dealt with this issue. Hederman J considered that
'[c]learly' the evidence could lead to only one conclusion: that the petitioner
was not at the time of the marriage in a position to give a consent to the
marriage and her consent was not a real, but only an apparent, consent.

Hederman J stressed that, in pronouncing a marriage null and void, 'a court
must be extremely cautious and examine all the evidence before it with great
vigilance'. Where there was delay, as here, the court would also have to be
satisfied as to the reason for the delay. He added:

This is not a question of approbation because approbation can never be relevant where there is no true consent but I am concerned with the difficulty of establishing such a case as will discharge the onus of proof in nullity suits.

While there was no doubt that the delay was long in the instant case, nonetheless, the evidence, including that of the respondent, was clear in establishing that there was not a true consent by the petitioner to the marriage.

The case provokes a number of questions. First, it is worth examining the nature of an *apparent* consent for the purposes of the law of nullity of marriage. At the threshold of considering this question, it may be best to clear away the easy cases. It is manifest that a consent may be apparent rather than real where it has been abstracted by duress or undue influence. Equally it is plain that lack of consent may result from mental incapacity of a permanent or even temporary nature, such as intoxication. (The fact that there may be debate about the precise parameters of such incapacity need not here concern us). It is interesting to note that counsel for the petitioner had relied on the petitioner's *incapacity* to give a real consent to the marriage and that Hederman J concluded that at the time of the marriage the petitioner 'was not in a position to give a consent. . . .' It might perhaps be argued that the holding is thus based on what was, in effect, a condition of temporary mental incapacity. We suggest, however, that this would not be a correct reading of the decision. There is nothing in the judgment to suggest that, to invalidate a marriage, the lack of consent in cases not involving duress or undue influence must involve mental incapacity on the part of the party who gives an apparent rather than real consent.If this is so, what other circumstances could result in the vitiation of consent? It seems that they should be limited to cases where there has not been 'a fully free exercise of the independent will of the parties', as Finlay CJ observed in *N. (otherwise K.) v K., supra.* This can occur where the factual circumstances are so oppressive and threatening in their own right they destroy the freedom of the will, without there necessarily being any duress exercised by a human agency. The facts of the instant case involved just such a situation.

It is clear that a party could give an apparent rather than real consent in circumstances where there was *no* oppression: he or she might be lying, in the sense that he or she had no intention to live a married life with the other party. It will be recalled that in the Supreme Court decision of *S. v S.*, [1976-7] ILRM 156, Kenny J was of the view that:

the intention to have sexual intercourse is such a fundamental feature of the marriage contract that if, *at the time of the marriage*, either party has determined that there will not be any during the marriage and none takes place and if the parties have not agreed on this before the marriage or if the ages of the parties make it improbable that they could have intercourse . . ., a spouse who was not aware of the determination of the other is entitled to a declaration that the marriage was null. The intention not to have or permit intercourse has the result that the consent which is necessary to the existence of a valid marriage does not exist.

The question arises as to whether cases of this type of duplicity fall within Finlay CJ's formula in *N. (otherwise K.) v K.* We suggest that they do not, since the duplicitous party is here engaging in 'a fully free exercise' of his or her independent will. The Chief Justice's statement that the court's ultimate objective is to ascertain 'whether the consent of the petitioning party was real or apparent' should be interpreted in its context as relating to the question of the full exercise of an independent will and not embracing other cases of apparent rather than real consent.

The Court's concession that there was no question of approbation 'because approbation can never be relevant where there is no true consent' raises interesting issues, not only from the standpoint of principle but also of policy. The statement is consistent with the premises (i) that the bar of approbation applies only to voidable marriages and (ii) that the category of voidable marriages does not include marriages invalid on the basis of lack of consent. As to the first, this seems beyond argument. When Costello J, in *D. v C.* [1984] ILRM 173, at 189, observed that '. . . the doctrine of approbation . . . applies only to voidable marriages', he was reflecting the orthodox view: see J. Jackson, *The Formation and Annulment of Marriage* (2nd ed., 1969), 331 Lasok, 'Approbation of Marriage in English Law and the Doctrine of Validation' (1963) 26 *Modern L Rev* 249.

As to the second premise, the position is more complicated. The distinction between void and voidable marriages was not originally part of the law of nullity: see Tolstoy, 'Void and Voidable Marriages' (1964) 7 *Modern L Rev* 385 and Goda, 'The Historical Evolution of the Concepts of Void and Voidable Marriages' (1967) 7 *J Family L* 297.

Gradually it came to be accepted without dissent that certain grounds for annulment, such as formal defect, lack of age and prior existing marriage, rendered a marriage void, whereas impotence rendered a marriage voidable. This left a range of grounds in a no-man's land. The common dominator was lack of consent: they included duress, mistake and insanity (save for marriages invalid under the Marriage of Lunatics Act 1811, which were clearly void rather than voidable). To these grounds attached the bar of ratification: see Tolstoy, 'the Validation of Void Marriages' (1968) 31 *Modern L Rev* 656. The concept of ratification looks suspiciously like that of approbation since it has regard to the behaviour of the parties subsequent to the ceremony of marriage and operates on a somewhat similar equitable basis.

It is perhaps unfortunate that the question of charactering the ground of lack of consent which arose in *D.B. (otherwise O'R.) v N. O'R.* should have been approached in formalistic terms, without regard to the underlying principles. Rather than placing the ground in the pigeon-hole of a void marriage, and then, as it were, discovering that approbation could not be a bar since it applies only to voidable marriages, it would have been preferable for the Court to have addressed the larger questions of what the categories of void and voidable marriage are designed to accomplish, and how bars of approbation and ratification should best operate with respect to specific grounds.

3 Impermanent commitment   In *H.H (otherwise H.C.) v J.F.F. D.S.*, High Court, 19 December 1990, Carroll J confronted new issues in Irish nullity law. The petitioner had gone through a ceremony of marriage in 1989 when she was 21 and the respondent was 25. She had been reared in a loving home, the eldest of four children, where she had had a sheltered upbringing. She had worked as a secretary since she left school, and had many friends. In 1988, on a holiday in Portugal, she had met the respondent, and lived with him for the last week of the holiday. He was a foreman with poor English. After she came home, the parties wrote to each other from time to time (in French). The petitioner was seeing other people during this time.

The petitioner obtained a Donnelly Visa in June 1989. She rang the respondent who suggested she go to Portugal. She spent two weeks with him there. She wanted him to come back to Ireland and get a job or to get a job in London. A month later the respondent came to visit her family in Ireland. He was a great success with them, cooking, shopping and helping the petitioner's father to paint the house. Carroll J's judgment records that the parties had no opportunity for sexual intercourse as the petitioner's mother 'was extremely vigilant'.

The parties initially intended to go to London. At that point the petitioner asked the respondent about going to the United States. He said he would go anywhere she was going. She took him to the United States Embassy and told the staff she was married. The judgment records that 'they said there would be no problem claiming him in New York as her husband but he would have to get his papers in order from Portugal'.

In evidence, the petitioner said that she had then asked the respondent to marry her. According to her, the next day he had said they would go through with it as long as they got divorced in the United States. The petitioner telephoned the Registrar of Marriages and discovered that they would have to wait for a week, and that the respondent would have to be three weeks resident in the country. She said nothing to her parents. The petitioner was working full-time for the first two weeks of the respondent's stay and part-time for the last week. On the day arranged for the marriage, she worked for the morning. Two friends acted as witnesses. They had a drink in a pub, went to the pictures and that evening went out to a party until about 2 a.m.

The following weekend the petitioner wanted to stay in Dublin with the respondent while the family went off to the West, but her mother insisted that they come as well. The respondent returned home after that weekend. The marriage was never consummated, although the petitioner said that if her mother had not been so strict it might have been. About ten days later, the petitioner's mother found the marriage certificate. Neither parent could believe it was true. The petitioner saw a solicitor who immediately issued a petition for nullity. The petitioner went off the following day to the United States where she was still working at the time Carroll J delivered her judgment.

On behalf of the petitioner it was argued that the parties had married only to get divorced when the respondent arrived in the United States. Carroll J did not believe the matter could be 'reduced to such simplistic terms'. From several things the petitioner had said in evidence, Carroll J was of opinion that the reality was different. When talking about the ceremony, she had said she wanted the respondent to mean what he was doing, and that he had known what he was doing although he did not understand the words. She had also said that she hoped they would go together for a long time and if all worked out they would be really married, meaning in a Catholic Church. She reckoned if they got married in a Registry Office she could get divorced. She now sees it as a 'rash decision'.

Carroll J was quite prepared to accept that the parties had agreed to marry on the basis that they would divorce if it did not work out; but she did not believe that they had married only on the understanding that they would never have sexual intercourse and that the sole purpose was for the respondent to go to the United States and that when he got there they would divorce. The petitioner was infatuated with the respondent who in turn was prepared to follow her and live with her and to marry her if divorce was an option.

Carroll J analysed the crucial issue as follows:

> [The petitioner] obviously believes that she is not really married in the eyes of God because she was not married in a Church. That is a religious belief which would be shared by all practising Catholics in this State. The marriage before the Registrar was a civil marriage. That civil marriage cannot be considered a nullity because of the petitioner's religious beliefs. If she intended to consent to a civil marriage her religious beliefs do not enter into it.

In Carroll J's view, the petitioner intended to enter into a valid civil marriage which would enable her to claim the respondent in the United States as her husband: 'she wanted him with her and I have no doubt she consented to continue the sexual relationship with him'. The petitioner had made an irresponsible decision. While it had been presented in Court as an impulsive decision, Carroll J noted that the petitioner had had to wait a week to carry it out and therefore had had a week to reflect:

> She was infatuated — but infatuation is not a ground for nullity. An agreement to divorce if things do not work out is not a ground for nullity. Immaturity is not a ground for nullity unless it exists in such a degree as to prevent a person giving a person giving full consent.

Notwithstanding the petitioner's irresponsibility Carroll J considered her capable of contracting a valid marriage; there was no incapacity to form and sustain a normal marriage relationship.

Carroll J addressed and answered three questions. The first was whether the parties had failed to understand the true nature, purpose, requirements and consequences of a normal marriage relationship. Carroll J found no evidence to prove that that either of them had not known what are the elements of a normal marital relationship. The petitioner had grown up in a happy loving home with the example of her parents before her and had the benefit of a normal secondary education. Carroll J had no evidence as to what the respondent's understanding had been about a normal marital relationship. (Although the judgment does not resolve the issue definitively, it seems plain that the respondent did not participat in the proceedings. Unusually, there is no express judicial finding of the absence of collusion.)

The second question was whether the parties had intended 'to sustain or enter into a lasting marital relationship' and whether they lacked the ability to do so. Carroll J answered this by stating:

> They did not intend to sustain a lasting marital relationship if things did not work out between them. There is no evidence that either party lacked the ability to sustain or maintain or enter into a lasting marital relationship. By all accounts they are both young, sexually active, attractive people. Their different backgrounds and nationality are not a bar to a normal marital relationship.

The final question was whether the petitioner had suffered from a level of immaturity which prevented her from giving a true and valid consent to the purported marriage. Carroll J thought not. The petitioner was 21 at the date of her marriage; she had earned her living since leaving school and had performed well at her job; she had been out with many people:

> She decided to have a sexual relationship with the respondent and to renew it a year later. She wanted her own way and she got it. She could not be described as mature but that is not the criterion. Her immaturity was not of such a degree as to interfere with her ability to form a marriage contract.

Accordingly Carroll J refused the application for a decree of nullity.

The case raises several interesting issues. The first concerns Carroll J's approach to the 'sham marriage', or, as it is also known in the international literature, the 'limited purpose marriage'. We have already discussed this subject in the 1989 Review, 214-5, 234-5. We have noted that there is a divergence of viewpoint among courts in common law jurisdictions as to how to treat sham marriages in the context of nullity of marriage. English and Canadian judicial authority is *against* recognising this as a ground for annulment; judicial authority in the United States and Scotland is in *favour* of the ground in at least some narrow circumstances though (as we noted in the 1989 Review, 234), the Scottish Law Commission in its Discussion Paper No. 35, para. 3.18 (1990) prefers the Anglo-Canadian approach.

It seems that Carroll J would not necessarily have been averse to granting a decree for nullity of marriage if the parties had gone through a ceremony of marriage with the sole intention of enabling the respondent to acquire immigrant status in the United States and with no intention of establishing a conjugal relationship. What is less clear is whether she would have been receptive to the argument that a decree of nullity should be available where the shared intention of the parties was for a brief period of cohabitation to be followed by divorce.

Carroll J's apparent willingness to recognise as a ground for nullity the intention to go through the form without the conjugal substance of marriage is in harmony with the approach favoured by Barron J in a number of cases where duress was alleged to have invalidated the marriage. In the 1989 Review, 234, we cautiously hazarded the suggestion that Barron J's approach was not dependent on the dimension of duress and that 'a cool decision to go through a ceremony of marriage, with no intention to commit oneself to a conjugal relationship with the other party but rather to acquire some independent goal (such as an immigrant status) falls within Barron J's analysis . . . .' It seems that Carroll J's approach, evident in the counterpoints of her analysis, is to similar effect.

The second important issue raised by the decision is whether parties who go through a ceremony of marriage on the understanding or express agreement that they will divorce if things do not work out should be entitled to a decree of nullity. Some may argue that, since marriage involves a freely made commitment by the spouses of permanence and exclusivity, a decree of nullity should be the logical corollary (subject, of course, to the bar of approbation or ratification) if it can be established to the court's satisfaction that one (or *a fortiori* both) of the parties did not, as a matter of fact, make this commitment. Others may reply that the act of marrying is *itself a public act of commitment* importing the elements of exclusivity and permanence regardless of what mental reservations the person thus committing himself or herself may have.

Part of the necessary cement of society is the general principle that public commitments should not be subverted by freely chosen private reservations. Whereas it is entirely proper that apparently freely made public commitments should be capable of being revealed as having been vitiated by duress, mistake or insanity, for example, a freely made public commitment, intended to be understood and treated as such by other members of society should arguably be held binding, even in the face of a later revelation that it was modified or contradicted by a private reservation. The basis of this approach is that society must on be able to rely on a presumed consistency between public and private commitment. Indeed that is one of the reasons why marriage is adorned with such ceremonial and unambiguous social markers. In short, parties should not be permitted 'to make their marriage vows as false as dicers' oaths'.

A third line of argument would seek to modify the general principle that a public act of commitment should not be vitiated by a freely chosen private reservation. This would support the view that, where one party's private reservations, unknown to the other at the time of the ceremony, are subversive of true marital commitment, the other party should be entitled to a decree of nullity of marriage. This is the approach which Kenny J favoured in *S. v S.*, *supra*. It raises the question as to the level of subversion at which the marriage is invalidated. Clearly a party who secretly intends to abandon the other party immediately after the ceremony fulfils this criterion, but courts may be reluctant to hold that a secret willingness to contemplate divorce should be similarly characterised.

As these conflicting arguments make clear, the Supreme Court would have had an interesting issue to confront if this case had been appealed. It is also worth considering how the Court should handle the obverse case: where parties go through a *religious* ceremony of marriage, making it clear to all that their commitment is designed to be of a religious rather than legally binding character. Are they nonetheless to be held to have entered a legally binding marriage?

This question is far from academic, since Irish family law is scarred by the religious conflicts of former centuries. The relationship between Church and State in some respects still reflects a nineteenth century compromise: the validity of Catholic marriages is determined in accordance with the finding of the House of Lords in *R. v Millis* (1844), 9 HL Cas 274, 11 ER 735, which treated the pre-Reformation Canon Law, as having been received into English (and Irish) common law, subject to such modifications as the common law might ordain. The holding in *Millis*, relating to the formal requirements of marriage, is believed by most competent scholars to have been without any real historical foundation: Schwelb, 'Marriage and Human Rights' (1963) 12 *Amer J of Comp L* 337, at 355. (See also, Walsh, 'Two Famous Irish Marriage Cases', 21 *Ir Ecclesiastical Record* (4th, series) 449, 579 (1912), 32 *Ir Ecclesiastical Record* 10, 118 (1913)). Whatever the historical merits of *Millis* may be, we now have the situation that the law of the State regards the *formalities* of Catholic marriages as largely a matter for regulation by the Catholic Church (subject to the *Millis* modification) but regards the *substantive* requirements as falling exclusively within the domain of the civil courts.

It is one thing to argue that, where a couple go through a *civil* ceremony before a registrar of marriages, the civil marriage 'cannot be considered a nullity because of the petitioner's religious beliefs. If [he or] she intended to consent to a civil marriage [his or her] religious beliefs do not enter into it'. It is quite another thing to suggest that, where a couple go through a *religious* ceremony, the court may so easily dismiss the effect of the parties' religious beliefs on the commitment that they make.

The question is one with philosophical and political dimensions. Is it possible for a person who makes a commitment of religious dimensions, where that commitment has important social implications, to delimit the terms of that commitment so as to exclude from it any of these social implications? We suggest that the answer must depend on two factors. First, society, through its legal framework, has a legitimate interest in monitoring religious practices with a significant social dimension. Thus, to take an extreme example, society should not be required to permit, on account merely of its religious characterisation, the implementation of a religious belief in the merits of child sacrifice. The sacramental dimension to marriage in no sense contradicts its social dimensions; on the contrary, a sound theological understanding of the sacrament of marriage would accord to it a supreme social significance. The idea that parties could, consistently with marrying as a sacrament, deny to that commitment its social dimension, which is supported by the law of marriage, seems unattractive.

The implication would thus seem to be that parties who marry according to religious norms should not be permitted to prevent the necessary social consequences from attaching to that commitment.

4 Impotence In *E.C. (otherwise M.) v A.M.* High Court, 5 December 1990,

Barr J applied well-established principles in granting a decree of nullity to the petitioner on the ground of her impotence. The petitioner suffered from vaginismus during the five years she spent with the respondent. She made continuing attempts to cure this condition but they proved unsuccessful. The respondent did not provide loving support; he had a drink problem and subjected the petitioner to intermittent physical violence. Some time after the parties separated, and after an ecclesiastical annulment had been granted, the petitioner entered into a relationship with another man which, after some initial difficulty, developed into a normal sexual relationship. The respondent did not oppose the petition before Barr J: correspondence between the parties' solicitors made it clear that he did not wish to uphold the marriage.

In granting the decree, Barr J characterised the case as one of impotence *quoad hunc*. Years of sincere effort on the petitioner's part to cure the condition had established that her psychological impotence towards the respondent was a permanent disability. She had persisted as well as she could and for as long as might reasonably be expected of her. There was nothing to suggest that, if the parties had stayed together, there would ever have been any improvement in the respondent's attitude towards the petitioner.

Barr J proceeded on the basis that an impotent spouse may not be granted a decree of nullity merely on the basis of his or her own impotence unless there has been conduct on the part of the respondent which prevents the respondent from denying the 'just cause' of the petition, as, for example, where the respondent has repudiated the marriage contract and its obligations. Here, the respondent's participation and support of the petition for the ecclesiastical annulment and the correspondence between the solicitors amounted to a 'clear and unequivocal' repudiation by him of the marriage.

The question whether an impotent petitioner should be required to establish conduct on the part of the respondent preventing him or her from denying the 'just cause' of the petition has exercised a number of courts and commentators: see, e.g. *Harthan v Harthan* [1949] P115, Bevan, (1960) 76 *LQ Rev* 267, A. Shatter, *Family Law in the Republic of Ireland*, (3rd ed., 1986), 127-30. On one view, the courts should distinguish between cases on the basis of whether the petitioner, being aware of his or her condition, *deceived* the respondent into going through a ceremony of marriage. Alan Shatter, *op. cit.*, 130, argues that, if such circumstances arise, the decree of nullity should be refused:

> If he knew of his impotence at the time of the ceremony, he entered the marriage with a full realisation of the fact that it would not be con- summated. His own impotence in such circumstances could make no difference to a situation which he had voluntarily accepted. In such a

situation only the potent spouse should be permitted to petition the court. The present law, however, seems to be that if the potent spouse does some act repudiating the marriage, the impotent spouse can succeed on the grounds of his own impotence. It is difficult to understand why a spouse who enters a marriage fully knowing that it cannot be consummated due to his own incapacity, should be permitted to plead such incapacity to obtain an annulment in one situation — i.e. where the other spouse also repudiated the marriage — and be prevented from relying on it in another situation, i.e. where there is an absence of such repudiation. In both situations the impotent spouse enters marriage knowing that it cannot be consummated and the principal cause of action is his own impotence. In such a situation only the other spouse should be permitted to petition.

Perhaps the analysis can be taken a few steps further. Let us begin, not with a deceitful impotent petitioner, but with an unfortunate petitioner who has learnt of his or her condition only after the ceremony of marriage. Should he or she be free to petition without regard to the position of the other party? It is easy to think of cases where this might be unjust. If, for example, the petitioner in the instant case had been treated with loving attention and concern by the respondent, it would seem unjust that she should *automatically* be entitled to a decree of nullity without some judicial regard to the equities of the case. The doctrine of approbation (or, in cases of certain void marriages, ratification) ensures that nullity decrees will not be granted without consideration of these equities. In the context of a petition by an impotent party, the limitation recognised by Barr J, that the conduct of the respondent prevented him or her from denying the 'just cause' of the petition, operates as an equivalent of the bar of approbation: cf. Shatter, *op. cit.*, 137.

If we now consider the case of a deceitful impotent petitioner, who was aware of his or her condition when going through the marriage ceremony, it would seem reasonable that he or she should not be granted a decree of nullity where the conduct of the respondent does not prevent him from denying the 'just cause' of the petition. (Whether there should be such an express rule or instead have the matter determined by applying the general bar of approbation is a matter of discussion). The more debatable question is whether he or she should be entitled to be granted a decree in *all* or *some* other circumstances, or in *no* other circumstances.

Regardless of how this issue is to be resolved, the point worth noting is that it is separate from the desirability or otherwise of the present limitation on the granting of decrees to impotent petitioners.

JUDICIAL SEPARATION

In *O'H. v O'H.* [1991] ILRM 108; [1990] 2 IR 558, the question arose as to whether s. 29 of the Judicial Separation and Family Law Reform Act 1989 is retrospective in its effect. S. 29 enables the court to set aside a 'reviewable disposition' made by a person with the intention of preventing financial relief being granting under the Act to another person or of reducing the amount of that relief. In essence a reviewable disposition is one other than for valuable consideration to a *bona fide* recipient without notice of the disponer's intention to defeat a claim for relief. In cases where the disposition took place less than three years before the application for relief, a presumption can arise, 'unless the contrary is shown', that the disponer had that intention. See the 1988 Review, p. 239. The disposition in the instant case had occurred some months before the Act came into force.

Barron J approached the issue on the basis that it was a matter of *construction* of the particular statute. O'Higgins CJ's judgment in *Hamilton v Hamilton and Dunne* [1982] ILRM 290; [1982] IR 466 (Supreme Court) had been to this effect. There was a presumption against retrospective construction. Barron J also accepted that, in considering whether a statute should be construed retrospectively, a distinction should be drawn between *applying the new law to past events* and *taking past events into account*. To do the latter was not to apply the Act retrospectively.

Applying these principles to the 1989 Act, Barron J held that s. 29 was *not* retrospective in its remit and that thus the court had no jurisdiction to set aside the disposition. He contrasted s. 2 of the Act, which set out six grounds for the granting of a decree of judicial separation. An applicant for a decree was entitled to give evidence as to events that occurred before the Act came into force, for that was 'the purpose of the legislation'. The purpose of s. 29 was different. It did not create a jurisdiction but dealt with powers available to the court in the exercise of that jurisdiction. There was nothing in the language of s. 29 to rebut the presumption against a retrospective construction. If the court set aside a disposition made before the Act came into force, it would be taking away or impairing a vested right acquired under existing laws, or imposing a new duty, or attaching a new disability in respect of transactions or considerations already passed. (This is the language of *Craies on Statute Law* (7th ed.), p. 387, which O'Higgins CJ endorsed in *Hamilton* as being 'based on sound authority'.) Barron J considered that, in the absence of an express intention to this effect, it must be presumed that this was not intended.

The result of the decision is surely in harmony with the mainstream of judicial thinking on retrospection. There is, however, a need for the Supreme Court to deepen its analysis of the principles on which retrospection in legislation is appropriate. We suspect that much of what passes as literal construction has in fact a healthy element of concern for the policies underlying the statute in question.

More fundamentally, the Court must dispense with the artificial props of the presumed intent as to non-retrospection and the presumption of constitutionality and confront the stark question of the extent to which the principle of retrospection is compatible with the Constitution. In his dissenting judgment in *Hamilton*, Costello J showed no sympathy for the approach of 'solving' the retrospection issue by invoking the rule that, if two interpretations of a post-Constitution statutory provision are reasonably open, one of which is constitutional, the other not, the former is to be preferred. It was, he thought, essential that the issue of the constitutionality of the retrospective construction be fully investigated before this rule should be applied against retrospection:

> Of course, the Court must refuse to give effect to an unconstitutional construction of a statute; if the statute can only reasonably be interpreted in that way, it must be declared invalid. Until the Court so rules, it should not ascertain the legislative intent by (a) holding that one of two possible interpretations of the statute *might* be unconstitutional and (b) by then assuming that the other interpretation was what the Oireachtas intended. If the Court reaches no conclusion on the constitutional validity of a disputed interpretation, it can only reject that interpretation for reasons other than its possible constitutional validity.

Hamilton is also interesting in the contrast between O'Higgins CJ and Henchy J's resolution of the constitutional dimension. *Hamilton* raised the issue whether the Family Home Protection Act 1976 was retrospective so as to enable a non-owning spouse to veto (subject to s. 4) the *completion* of a sale of the family home the contract for which had been entered into before the passage of the Act. The Chief Justice considered that the Act could not be construed retrospectively since to do so would constitute an unjust attack upon and a failure by the State to vindicate the property rights of the purchaser and of others similarly situated and would constitute 'a clear infringement' of the provisions of Article 40.3.2°. Henchy J placed the legislation in a broader constitutional framework. He noted that it provided for the protection of the family home, 'presumably as an implementation of the constitutional duty that falls on the State to protect the family and to guard with special care the institution of marriage'. Being of the view that the Act indicated no intention of retrospective effect, he agreed with O'Higgins CJ's conclusion as to its construction but pointedly refrained from expressing a view as to whether the Act would have been unconstitutional if it had been retrospective:

The primary duty of the State in regard to [the protection of] property rights arises under Article 40.3, of the Constitution . . . but such duty would have to be balanced against other constitutional duties, such as the protection of marriage and the family.

It is perhaps worth contrasting the social contexts arising under the Family Home Protection Act 1976 and under s. 29 of the 1989 Act. To have construed the 1976 Act retrospectively would have clearly interfered with the expectations of *bona fide* purchasers for value; in contrast s. 29 can have no application to such persons. To that extent the equities tilt less strongly against retrospection. As against this, it might be argued that s. 29 of the 1989 Act introduces a radically new and wide-ranging jurisdiction to upset transactions relating to *any* property of a spouse rather (than simply the family home), provided the transaction in question is a 'reviewable disposition' with the necessary intent. See further McCormack, 'Contractual Entitlements and the Constitution' (1982), 17 *Ir Jur* 340, at 344.

In this context it is worth noting Professor Casey's observation that the question of balancing constitutional entitlements and duties 'would assume great importance' if legislation were enacted with clear retrospective intent, providing for joint ownership of the matrimonial home: *Constitutional Law in Ireland* (1987), 486. One of the frequently ignored side-effects of judicial developments is, of course, their retrospective effect. In *B.L. v M.L.* [1989] ILRM 528, Barr J's decision had the effect of altering the common understanding of spousal property entitlements in the family home more radically than the Oireachtas would ever dare to contemplate: see the 1988 Review, 213-21, Jackson (1989) 11 DULJ 158. The fact that two of Barr J's colleagues do not agree with the approach he favoured (cf. the 1989 Review, 240-244 and Duncan & Scully, *op. cit.*, paras 10.042-10.049) serves only to complicate the potential for retrospective inequities.

GUARDIANSHIP OF INFANTS

1 Custody dispute between parents In *K. v K.*, High Court, 30 May 1990, Barron J delivered what has since 1981 become a rarity: a written judgment on the custody of a child. The case concerned a boy of nearly twelve; his parents had separated when he was three, the father living in a provincial town, the mother near Dublin. Litigation concerning the boy's custody had gone on since he was four years old. This had involved an accusation, strongly denied and subsequently retracted, that the father had been guilty of sexually abusing his son. The boy had been in his mother's custody since the time of separation. By an agreement reached in 1988, the father was given access at specified periods; the mother undertook to inform and consult the husband on all matters concerning their son's health, schooling, friends, interests and general welfare. It was agreed that the boy would not be removed from his school or doctor without the consent of the father or of the court.

In the present proceedings the father sought custody of the child. He argued that the mother had failed to exercise sufficient discipline and was to blame for the boy's poor progress in his school work. He also contended that his son had reached the stage in his development where he required a father's control.

Barron J rejected the application. He considered that most of the family's problems sprang from the totally different character of the parents. The father was 'obsessed with the desire' to obtain custody of his son and tended to refuse to consider the boy's needs when they conflicted with his own. This was manifested by his refusal to consider a change of school because (among other reasons) this might militate against his chance of obtaining custody. He had, moreover, refused to let the boy join a tennis club because it would interfere with access.

The father pointed to the mother's failure to make the boy persist with piano lessons as an example of her lack of discipline. She had allowed him to take up the guitar and then give that up to return to the piano. The mother said that learning a musical instrument should be a matter of feeling for the instrument and not of compulsion. Barron J found 'nothing wrong' with this approach.

He rejected the father's application. Barron J expressed the view that the boy's welfare required him to stay where he was. If he were to be moved to his father, there would not only be an immediate unhappiness, but 'his quality of life would suffer under the different norms of his father'. His school work was governed by his interest in the subject. If he stayed with his mother, these interests might widen. If he moved to his father, there was a serious danger that he would lose interest rather than gain it in his various school subjects. The boy needed the stability of knowing that his home was in Dublin, where his wider family was living.

Barron J expressed the view that the boy would prosper better under his mother's care:

> she has concern for him and leaves him scope to develop his own personality. With his father, there would be a serious risk that this would be stifled. [The father]'s attitude is, too narrow, too authoritarian and too unyielding.

Finally, Barron J noted that the boy himself wished to stay in Dublin with his mother. All the psychiatrists were agreed on this. He accepted their views that consideration should be given to these wishes.

The case was thus resolved on Barron J's view that the mother's policy on upbringing was a sound one and the father's not. From the presentation of the facts in the judgment, a reader would find it difficult to disagree. Nevertheless, some interesting broader issues are raised by the case. If we accept that certain extremes in childrearing philosophy are clearly unacceptable, the question remains as to whether the court should 'take sides' as between educational philosophies where one parent subscribes to a liberal philosophy and the other adheres to a more conservative approach.

The notion of the child's *welfare*, which is the linchpin of the Guardianship of Infants Act 1964, is more complex than it might first appear. The element of physical welfare, mentioned in s. 2, is a matter primarily referable to empirical evidence, but clearly such elements as the religious and moral welfare of the child inevitably involve a potential conflict of values. Against the background of Articles 41 and 42, which involve the constitutional recognition of the rights of parents to adhere a broad range of approaches towards the rearing of children, it might be argued that the court in custody disputes should be reluctant to commit itself to one educational philosophy rather than another, subject, of course, to a long-stop to deal with positively harmful approaches: (cf *J. O'C. v M. O'C.*, High Court, August 1975, discussed by Shatter, *op. cit.*, 357 and Duncan & Scully, *op. cit.*, para. 14.040. In that case the mother had consistently inflicted severe corporal punishment on her children. Kenny J observed that '[t]he parents who use corporal punishment on young children may think that it is for their good but civilised human beings have long since abandoned this barbaric practice').

In the light of a growing debate as to the merits of some of the educational approaches favoured in the Nineteen Sixties, it may be mistaken for a Court to decide the issue of custody on the basis of its preference for one philosophy rather than another; cf the controversial American decision of *Painter v Bannister*, 258 Iowa 1390, 140 NW 2d 152 (1966).

An issue which the father raised in the case but was not expressly mentioned by Barron J in his resolution of the application was that of sex roles in the upbringing of children. As we noted, the father contended that his son had 'reached the stage in his development where he requires a father's control'. The idea that, at certain ages, a child is better suited for the custody of the mother or the father held a strong appeal for the courts until relatively recently. Thus, in the Supreme Court decision of *MacD v MacD*, (1979) 114 ILTR 60, Kenny J could observe that:

[y]oung children have a much greater emotional need of their mother

than they have of their father who, when they are young, seems to them to be a somewhat remote figure. A mother has an instinctive understanding of child's minds and needs. She provides warmth, visible signs of affection, love, a feeling of security, a last refuge in times of trouble and patience in listening to their petty complaints.

Other judicial contributions on the theme are collected by Binchy, 'The Sex of a Parent as a Factor in Custody Disputes', 77 Incorporated Law Society of Ireland *Gazette* 289 (1983). (For international comparisons, see Mason, 'Motherhood and Equal Treatment', (1990) 29 *J of Family L* 1, at 20 ff, Klaff, 'The Tender Years Doctrine: A Defense', (1982) 70 *Calif L Rev* 335, at 337-42).

It is interesting to note the approach which Barron J adopted towards the claim of an *unmarried* father to custody in *K. v W. (No. 2)* [1990] ILRM 791. While this did not involve a contest between father and mother, the issue did cover the father's suitability as a custodian, and Barron J was satisfied that he passed the test, even in relation to a young child. Of course in that case no question of a mother's intuitive love for her child arose since there the contest was between the natural father and would-be adoptive parents.

Barron J's disposition of the issue of the boy's wishes in *K. v K.* is unusual. Courts have shown themselves willing to heed the wishes of children, especially where the children are reasonably mature and not unduly influenced by one or other of their parents . Barron J appears to treat the issue as one to be mediated by psychiatric evidence. It is of course true that psychiatrists may perform a useful role in articulating for the court the child's attitudes and feelings about those who are competing for his custody (cf. Litwak, Gerber & Fenster, 'The Proper Role of Psychology in Child Custody Disputes', (1980) 18 *J of Family L* 269, at 289); but it is not clear why psychiatrists should determine whether consideration sbould be given to a child's wishes. This is surely an element of the child's welfare on which the court should make its own assessment.

In *J.P.D. v M.G.* [1991] ILRM 217, the Supreme Court addressed the question of the circumstances in which an order might appropriately be made under s. 38 of the Status of Children Act 1987. The issue arose, unusually, in the course of an application by a husband for sole custody of the two children of the marriage, coupled with an application for an injunction against the wife restraining her from removing them from the jurisdiction. The wife sought an order under s. 38 that both children, as well as herself and her husband, should submit to the taking of DNA tests ('genetic finger printing') to ascertain inheritable characteristics. She contended that her husband was not their father. Under the 1987 Act, there was a rebuttable presumption that the husband was the father, based on the fact of his marriage to the mother, buttressed by a further rebuttable presumption based on the registration of the births of the children with his name entered as father.

S. 38(1) provides that, in any civil proceedings before a court in which the parentage of any person is in question the court may, either on its own motion or on an application by any party to the proceedings, give a direction for the use of blood tests. Lavan J made an order under the section.

The husband appealed unsuccessfully to the Supreme Court against the making of this order. McCarthy J (Griffin and Hederman JJ concurring) noted that the wording of the section appeared to be discretionary with the use of the word 'may', but that there was no indication of the criteria to be applied in the exercise of that discretion. It must have been envisaged that there should be some discretion to be exercised judicially, taking into account relevant matters and disregarding what was irrelevant.

The husband has argued that Lavan J had failed to consider the welfare of the children, which was to be given first and paramount consideration under s. 3 of the Guardianship of Infants Act 1964. In particular, the husband said, Lavan J had failed to consider the depth of the relationship existing between the husband and the two children (who were now 12 and 11 years old).

McCarthy J rejected this interpretation of Lavan J's judgment. Whilst this factor had not been mentioned expressly in the considered judgment, that was in no way conclusive. Lavan J had expressed grave doubts as to whether the evidence heard would operate to remove the rebuttable presumption of legitimacy. He had reserved his position as to how positive DNA tests, confirming the wife's claim, could affect the husband's position as guardian and parent with rights in relation to custody and access . For the purposes of his decision in relation to the application, he had accepted the view of the English courts in *S. v Mc (otherwise S.)* [1972] AC 24. Arising from it, he had held that the paramount consideration was the welfare of both children and, secondly, echoing what O'Hanlon J had said in *S. v S.* [1984] ILRM 66; [1983] IR 68, that the truth should prevail over the presumption of legitimacy, subject to the reservations which he had expressed.

McCarthy J was satisfied that there was nothing to show that Lavan J had not considered all relevant matters or had taken into account irrelevant matters. Had McCarthy J been called on to exercise his own discretion in the matter, he would have come to the same conclusion.

As to the benefits of DNA evidence, it is worth recording the words of caution recently expressed in England, in an article in [1991] *Crim L Rev* 264: Young, 'DNA Evidence — Beyond Reasonable Doubt?' On the basis of scientific studies, Mr Young expresses concern regarding the non-use of independent peer review or other external scrutiny, the dearth of publications in the area, the methods by which band-shifting 'corrections' are commonly employed, and the inappropriateness of certain population studies relied on to calculate the odds of a random match. Mr Young considers that the lack of publications seriously reduces the material on which counsel can base an examination of the expert witness. See also Hall (1990), 140 *New L J* 203, McLeod [1991] *Crim L Rev* 583 and Fennell (1991) 1 *ICLJ* 34. See also above, 206-7.

In the present context, Collins & Macleod, 'Denials of Paternity: The Impact of DNA Tests on Court Proceedings', [1991] *J of Social Welfare & Family L* 209, at 213-4, argue that,

> although . . . the claims made for DNA evidence are not as clear cut as originally thought, a distinction needs to be made between forensic and diagnostic tests. When paternity tests are carried out, the procedures governing taking blood samples mean that it is unlikely that the samples will be contaminated. Moreover, the size of the samples allows for re-runs of the tests should ambiguities arise. Similarly the size of the samples avoids the need for sample 'amplification' by the so-called 'PCR' technique. For these reasons many of the difficulties of the forensic laboratory do not apply to paternity testing and the use of the technique for this purpose is relatively uncontroversial.

See further Yaxley, 'Genetic Fingerprinting' (1988) 18 *Family L* 403, Kaye, 'DNA Paternity Provisions' (1990) 24 *Family LQ* 279. One suspects that this controversy may be only beginning.

2 Applications by natural father to be made guardian   In the 1989 Review, pp. 248-57, we discussed in detail the Supreme Court's determination in *K. v W. (No. 1)* [1990] ILRM 121 of questions posed a case stated by Barron J regarding the correct approach to determining an application by a natural father under s. 6A of the Guardianship of Infants Act 1964 (inserted by s. 12 of the Status of Children Act 1987) to be appointed guardian of his child. Barron J had asked if he was correct in interpreting the test as being 'whether the natural father is a fit person to be appointed guardian and, if so, whether there are circumstances involving the welfare of the child which require that notwithstanding he is a fit person he should not be so appointed'. The Supreme Court held that this was not the correct test . The father had merely a right to apply for guardianship with no statutory presumption, however tentative, that his application should be successful. In a key passage, which we analysed at length in the 1989 Review, 252-5, Finlay CJ said that he was satisfied that the submission on behalf of the father that he had a con-stitutional or natural right identified by the Constitution to the guardianship of the child which was acknowledged in s. 6A was:

not correct and that although there may be rights of interest or concern arising from the blood link between the father and the child, no constitutional right to guardianship in the father of the child exists. This conclusion dose not, of course, in any way infringe on such considerations appropriate to the welfare of the child in different circumstances as may make it desirable for the child to enjoy the society, protection and guardianship of its father, even though its father and mother are not married.

The extent and character of the rights which accrue arising from the relationship of a father to a child whose mother he is not married to must vary very greatly indeed, depending on the circumstances of each individual case.

The range of variation would, I am satisfied, extend from the situation of the father of a child concerned as a result of a casual intercourse, where the rights might well be so minimal as practically to be non-existent, to the situation of a child born as a result of a stable and established relationship and nurtured at the commencement of his life by his father and mother in a situation bearing nearly all the characteristics of a constitutionally protected family, when the rights would be very extensive indeed.

In *K. v W.*, the applicant was the unmarried father of a child whom the mother had placed for adoption without the father's knowledge. Only if the father's application were successful would he be able to prevent the adoption, as fathers who are not guardians have no such veto. The Chief Justice said that:

[i]n a case such as the present case where the application for appointment as a guardian is linked to the application for a present order of custody, regard should not be had to the objective of satisfying the wishes and desires of the father to be involved in the guardianship of and to enjoy the society of his child unless the court has first concluded that the quality of welfare which would probably be achieved for the infant by its present custody which is with the prospective adoptive parents, as compared with the quality of welfare which would probably be achieved by custody with the father, is not to an important extent better.

For analysis of this passage, see the 1989 Review, 255-6.

The case went back to Barron J who delivered a judgment on 9 February 1990: *K. v W. (No. 2)* [1990] ILRM 791. Barron J traced the background to the application under s. 6A. The applicant, aged 25, was a machine operator who impressed his employers as being trustworthy, punctual and obedient. He had, however, been sentenced to imprisonment three times for taking or being carried in a car without the owner's consent, and he had convictions for the possession of drugs, as well as receiving the benefit of the Probation Act for petty larceny. The mother was aged 21. When attending a course on child-minding she met the applicant, with whom she started to live some months later. The couple had decided to have a baby. After the mother became pregnant they became engaged but when the mother went home to tell her parents the news, she found she could not do so. Shortly afterwards she broke up with the applicant and went to live at home. The applicant tried to contact her but his efforts were deliberately blocked by her parents. When the child — a daughter — was born, the applicant sought to see the mother but was thwarted. He did, however, see the baby.

Some weeks after he child's birth, the mother placed the child for adoption. Up to then the applicant and his family had been 'fended off [by the mother's family] and . . . led to believe that the child was going to be kept'. A week after the placement the mother told the applicant the news. His immediate reaction was to consult a solicitor.

The child had been placed with a married couple who had no children. The would-be adoptive father had been educated to Leaving Certificate standard and worked for his father. (The judgment does not state the nature of this employment.) The would-be adoptive mother worked as a clerk/typist. The couple had their own home. Their social and financial circumstances were similar to those of the natural mother and her family.

The natural father, in Barron J's view, wished *bona fide* to have custody of the child. His entire family supported his application, and were willing to have the child brought up in their home. There was 'more than adequate' accommodation. The child, if given into the father's custody, would, in Barron J's opinion, be well looked after. If, however, the would-be adoptive parents retained custody, the child would be 'equally well looked after'. She would obtain a higher standard of living and be more likely to remain at school than if she were in the custody of her father.

The crucial factual element in the case concerned the likely short-term and long-term psychological effects which a change in custody might involve for the child. The opinion of a consultant child psychiatrist was that the child (aged about sixteen months) would suffer short-term trauma for at least three weeks. Moreover, in his opinion the child would be more vulnerable to stress in later years and less able to cope with it. She might have difficulty in forming 'trust relationships'. These opinions were based on the theory of attachment. Barron J noted that '[u]nfortunately [the psychiatrist] was unable to instance any case histories in support of his opinion. His evidence was that there was very many variables which can effect what actually occurs'. Barron J went on to observe that the theory of attachment was one which the courts had had propounded to them for at least the past decade with little contrary evidence and had in general been accepted. He accepted the theory, adding that in the absence of any evidence to the contrary he would be wrong not to do so. He took the view, however, that the short-term effects of a change in custody would not be as serious as that suggested by the psychiatrist.

Barron J observed that the differences in the upbringing of the child between the two competing homes:

> spring solely from socio-economic causes and in my view should not be taken into consideration, certainly where one of the parents is a natural parent. To do otherwise would be to favour the affluent as against the less well-off which does not accord with the constitutional obligation to hold all citizens as human persons equal before the law.

In a crucial passage, Barron J said:

> This case is not merely an application for the appointment of a natural father as guardian of his child. This is because if he were so appointed he could effectively bar the adoption process by refusing his consent to it. Accordingly the question to be determined before the applicant can be appointed guardian is should he also be granted custody[?]

Barron J made it clear that, if he had been dealing with an application for guardianship, he would have appointed the father a guardian. He quoted the passage from the Chief Justice's judgment to the effect that the extent and character of the rights of an unmarried father vary greatly depending on whether, at one end of the spectrum, the child was conceived as the result of a casual intercourse or, at the other end, the child was born into a stable and established relationship and nurtured by both parents in a situation bearing nearly all of the characteristics of a constitutionally protected family. Barron J observed that, though the applicant was never in the latter situation, 'nevertheless it was his wish and his intention at the date of the conception of the child that she should be a party to such a stable relationship, though [not] one based upon marriage to the mother'. In Barron J's view, it would have been proper in those circumstances to have acceded to his application if it had been only for guardianship.

Barron J went on to invoke and apply the test laid down by the Chief Justice in relation to the *custody* application by applicant. The key element of this test was that the wishes of the applicant should be disregarded unless the quality of welfare which would probably be achieved for the infant by its existing custody with the adoptive parents as compared with the quality of welfare which would be achieved by custody with the father was not to an important extent better.

The decision gives rise to a couple of observations. First it may be asked why a father applying to be made guardian under s. 6A should apparently be prejudiced by his decision to apply also for custody of his child. The reason the applicant in *K. v W. (No. 2)* failed to be awarded custody was that the trauma doctrine was sufficiently strong to prevent the court from authorising the transfer of the child's custody from the would-be adoptive parents to him. If he had sought merely to be made guardian, this factor would not have been crucial, since he could be guardian without having custody, as many married fathers are when separated from their wives. On principle it seems difficult to justify the defeat of the applicant's claim for guardianship by reason of the contingency of his having also made a separate application for custody.

Lurking beneath the surface is the troublesome question of how to deal with 's. 6A' applications for guardianship where the father is not (or, had he also applied for custody, would not be) entitled to custody of the child. If the father is made guardian, he can prevent the adoption of his child, but the custody will remain with the would-be adopters. They will be in the difficult position of knowing that they can never succeed in adopting the child as long as the father maintains his veto; they will also be reasonably sure in most cases that they will be able to retain custody for the foreseeable future, since the trauma doctrine will have continuing relevance. This solution may substantially frustrate the wishes of all interested parties. If the court takes the view in any case that it would not be in the child's welfare that such a situation should result, no doubt this will affect its determination of the application for guardianship under s. 6A. What is unfortunate is that this determination should be interfered with by the imposition of a different criterion merely because the application for guardianship happens to be accompanied by an application for custody.

The second observation that may be made on Barron J's judgment relates to his view that, in custody proceedings, differences in the upbringing of the child between the two competing homes which spring solely from socio-economic causes 'should not be taken into consideration, certainly where one of the parents is a natural parent'. This view, as we have seen, was based on the premise that to do otherwise would not accord with the constitutional guarantee of equality under Article 40.1. Barron J's approach to this question is novel, and finds scarce reflection in the body of case-law. It raises important and difficult issues.

It is easy to argue that Article 40.1 does not prevent the court from having regard to differences in economic power between two applicants for custody of a child. The award of custody is not 'a prize for good matrimonial behaviour' (*JJW v BMW* (1971), 110 ILTR 45, at 47 (High Court, Kenny J)). The mere fact that an applicant is denied custody does not, without more, constitute a breach of Article 40.1. While parents of children born within marriage have 'a joint right and duty' to provide for their children's education according to their means (*In re Tilson, Infants* [1951] IR 1, at 32), it is clear that a court, in determining a disputed custody case, is not obliged to award joint custody where considerations apart from the child's economic welfare are equal but the consideration of the child's economic welfare points in favour of awarding custody to one of the parents.

Nevertheless it is interesting to recall that in a number of Supreme Court decisions an attempt has been made to ensure that the factor of poverty will not operate against a parent's interest in the assessment of his or her assertion of a constitutionally-guaranteed parental function, such as the exercise of guardianship. Three cases may be mentioned. First, and of most obvious relevance, is the decision in *In re the Adoption (No. 2) Bill 1987* [1989] ILRM 266 (analysed by Paul O'Connor (1988) 6 *ILT* (ns) 271) where the Court held that a failure in parental duty 'due to externally originating circumstances such as poverty' did not constitute a failure such as would in any circumstances warrant the compulsory adoption of a child. Secondly, in *K.C. & A.C. v An Bord Uchtála* [1985] ILRM 302; [1985] IR 375, the Court held that s. 3 of the Guardianship of Infants Act 1964 'must be construed as involving a constitutional presumption that the welfare of the child . . . is to be found within the family [based on marriage] unless the court is satisfied on the evidence that there are compelling reasons why this cannot be achieved or unless the court is satisfied that the evidence establishes an exceptional case where the parents have failed to provide education for the child and continue to fail to provide education for the child for moral or physical reason'. Thirdly, in the context of determining the validity of a mother's consent for her child's adoption, Walsh J expressed the view in *G. v An Bord Uchtála* [1980] IR 32, at 74 that 'a consent motivated by fear, stress or anxiety or consent or conduct dictated by poverty or other deprivations does not constitute a valid Consent'. (In the later High Court decision of *McF. v G. & G., The Sacred Heart Adoption Society, et. al.* [1983] ILRM 228, McWilliam J added the gloss that these factors 'must be considered from a practical point of view . . . [I]f absolute rules as to fear, stress, anxiety or poverty were to be applied, there could hardly be a case found in which one or other of them would not be present so that it could be argued a consent was not valid'.)

Do these cases carry any necessary implications for Article 40.1? The better answer seems to be that they do not. As to the first and second Supreme Court cases, they are concerned with ensuring that the guarantees to families under Articles 41 and 42 are not subverted by principles for judicial intervention which would leave poorer families exposed to the risk of having their children taken from them, by reason of their relative lack of economic resources, and given to persons with greater economic clout. The goals here include effecting social justice and protecting families from unwarranted intrusion by the State. The third case is somewhat different. In contrast to the first two, where the poor parent is regarded as fully autonomous *in spite of his or her state of indigence*, Walsh J approaches poverty as being capable of *defeating* the autonomy of the poor parent. The underlying goal is, however, similar to that in the first two cases. The first two protect poor families from the compulsory taking of their children from them; the third protects a poor mother whose circumstances of dire poverty vitiate her consent of the adoption of her child. The willingness of the Supreme Court to go so far to protect poor parents from social injustice and unwarranted State intervention surely does not commit it to the proposition that, on the basis of Article 40.1, all differences of economic resources must be ignored when determining the custody of a child. Nothing in the caselaw relating to Article 40.1 would appear to support such a radical development.

COSTS IN FAMILY LITIGATION

In *F. v L.* [1990] ILRM 886, Barron J addressed the interesting question of who should bear the costs of matrimonial litigation. The petitioner had sought and obtained a declaration of nullity on the ground of the respondent's incapacity to consummate the marriage. The respondent sought an order for her costs as against the petitioner. The established practice favoured awarding costs to the wife as a general rule, regardless of whether or not she was the successful party: *Courtney v Courtney* [1923] 2 IR 31. Barron J considered that the time had come to change this practice. The old practice had been based on different realities:

> Clearly at a time when married women were legally and factually dependant financially on their husbands it would have been unjust to allow matrimonial proceedings against them to go undefended for lack of funds to employ a solicitor and counsel. Equally, it would have been unjust to prevent them from themselves petitioning for relief. The rule of court which gave them an immediate right to their costs prevented that injustice. . . .

> However, times have changed. In particular since the passing of the Married Women's Status Act of 1957, any fetters which may have existed in relation to a married woman' s right to own property were

removed. In my view the justification for allowing a wife her costs as against her husband in all circumstances is no longer justified. In each individual case, it is the duty of the court to make such order as is just in the circumstances . Save as is recognised by O. 70, r. 75 of the Rules of the Superior Courts 1986, there is no reason why different principles should be applied in the award of costs because the proceedings are matrimonial proceedings. In this case, the petitioner and respondent are both working. Neither would be able without hardship to pay the costs of the other. The proceedings have declared the status of both parties. In my view the proper order as to costs is to require each to bear his or her own costs.

Several issues of principle and policy are raised by this case. First, let us consider the general rule in what we may call 'ordinary' civil litigation that the loser pays the winners costs. In favour of this approach, it has been argued that it would be unfair to require the successful party who has been obliged to resort to litigation either to protect his or her entitlements as a plaintiff or to resist an unwarranted claim to have to pay his or her own legal expenses. They may be very considerable and they have been incurred because of the otber party's conduct. As against this, it has been argued that the fear of paying two sets of costs if the litigation is unsuccessful acts an unwarranted disincentive to litigation for all except the extremely sick or institutional plaintiff or the extremely poor plaintiff who may be able to obtain legal aid. Moreover, in many cases both parties may have good legal arguments to raisei while one of them has to lose this does not necessarily mean that the other was unreasonable in contesting the issue.

There are no easy answers, especially in an unequal society. To require each side to pay its own costs makes the prospect of losing less frightening and thus encourages more litigation, but this may not always be an improvement. It may involve an increase in speculative, divisive, litigation, especially when backed by a contingent fee system, which is engrafted on such a system far more easily than on the present 'winner take all' system (since a lawyer engaging in a contingent free arrangement cannot subsidise an unsuccessful plaintiff in respect of the other party's costs).

When one considers the effects of civil legal aid, the problems are compounded. If a legally aid plaintiff sues a defendant who is not legally aided and the plaintiff loses, who should pay the successful defendant's costs? The plaintiff cannot pay them as he or she has not the resources. If the defendant pays them the effect is arguably discriminatory in that the 'winner take all' principle is displaced, not on account of a better principle, but because of the accidental circumstance of the financial means of the plaintiff. It might be thought that the proper solution would be for the defendant to be entitled to obtain his or her costs from the State; the financial implications of this entirely reasonable proposition have proved so startling that it has been rejected out of hand. In its stead is a narrow discretionary entitlement to award costs to the successful legally unaided defendants only in cases of severe financial hardship.

It is against this background that the problem of costs in matrimonial proceedings must be considered. The truth of the matter is that family litigation is not always the same as, for example, a dispute between neighbours. It would be wrong to treat all of the several instances of matrimonial litigation as involving the same issues of principle and policy, but if we take the case of nullity proceedings, which were in question in *F. v L.*, it may be argued there is a social interest in having such procccdings take place which may have no parallel in relation to at least some other types of civil litigation, such as a nuisance action in tort between neighbours. The settlement of inter-neighbour disputes may be considered generally desirable in the social interest (though even here the issues are far from simple: cf. Fiss, 'Against Settlement' (1984) 93 *Yale LJ* 1073. Where the question of resolving the status of parties to an alleged marriage in concerned, however, the social interest is thwarted rather than advanced by the failure to have the issue resolved through legal proceedings. To the extent that a 'winner takes all' approach to costs discourages nullity proceedings, therefore, it may be acting contrary for the social interest. Parties who want to know their marital status are surely entitled to an answer from the only forum that is lawfully competent to resolve the matter — the court — without having a rule as to costs, which makes sense in relation to other types of proceedings, being applied inflexibly in their context.

A further complicating factor is that, in some instances, the rights of children depend largely or exclusively on the discretion of one of their parents as to whether to institute legal proceedings against the other parent. For example, a child's right to maintenance in a united family normally depends on whether his or her mother is willing to take proceedings against the father under the Family Law (Maintenance of Spouses and Children) Act 1976. (In a small number of cases, the child's entitlement will depend on the father's decision to take proceedings against the mother.) A similar parental discretion exists under the Guardianship of Infants Act 1964 and s. 5 of the Family Home Protection Act 1976. The 'winner takes all' rule for costs would have the effect of discouraging more mothers from taking legal proceedings on behalf of their children lest they be stung for costs. The *cestuis que trustent*, the children, are the losers in such cases.

If the 'winner takes all' rule works unjustly what should replace it? To require the husband to pay in all or most cases would not seem just either. Perhaps the best solution would be for the court to exercise a discretion which would encompass such factors as the strength of the wife's losing case, her *bona fides* and the respective resources of the parties. The argument that, as a general rule, the State should foot the bill for nullity proceedings seems a strong one. In this general context, reference may be made to our critical analysis, above, 144-7, of Gannon J's judgment in *Cosgrove v Legal Aid Board and Ors*, High Court, 17 October 1990.

In *J.P.D. v M.G.* [1991] ILRM 217, which we have already discussed *supra*, pp. 314-6, in relation to the circumstances in which blood tests may be ordered under s. 38 of the Status of Children Act 1987, the trial judge, Lavan J, ordered that the wife should pay her husband's costs in respect of the motion resulting in the order under that section. He came to this conclusion on the basis of an agreement between the parties whereby the husband would not be liable for costs of separation. The Supreme Court set aside this part of the order and reserved the issue for the trial judge when deciding the substantive matter relating to custody. The agreement in guestion was that the husband would not be liable for the costs of divorce proceedings in England. This was 'wholly irrelevant' to the issue of costs in respect of the motion relating to blood tests in custody proceedings.

Fisheries

DETENTION OF VESSELS

Rederij Kennemerland BV v Attorney General [1989] ILRM 821 concerned the 48 hour detention power granted to the District Court or a Peace Commissioner under s.233A of the Fisheries (Consolidation) Act 1959, as inserted by s.12 of the Fisheries (Amendment) Act 1978. The section provides that an application for such an order must be made by a sea fisheries protection officer 'as soon as may be' after a boat has been detained under s.233(1) of the 1959 Act on suspicion of an offence under the Act. In the instant case, the applicants' boats had been detained under s.233(1) on the afternoon of 5 November 1986 and brought before the District Court on the afternoon of the next day to seek a 48 hour detention order from the District Court. Gannon J held that the application had not been made 'as soon as may be' within the meaning of s.233A of the 1959 Act, so that the detention of the boats had been *ultra vires*. This view was upheld by the Supreme Court (Finlay CJ, Walsh, Henchy, Hederman and McCarthy JJ) in an *ex tempore* judgment delivered by the Chief Justice.

The Peace Commissioner who had heard one of the applictions for a 48 hour detention order had also failed to consider in an independent manner the application for the detention order. Gannon J also held, in a phrase approved by the Chief Justice, that the Peaec Commissioner 'did nothing that a judge would do and what he did would not have been done by a judge'. In that sense, the Peace Commissioner had fallen into a trap which had not been apparent up to that time, but which was identified in this case and in cases such as *Byrne v Grey* [1988] IR 31 (1987 Review, 86), which coincidentally was decided by Hamilton P on the same date (9 October 1987) as the decision of Gannon J in the instant case. For further discussion of this see the 1988 Review, 192-4.

Since Gannon J was able to deal with the case on the basis of these findings, he was not required to address the constitutionality of the power of a Peace Commissioner to grant such detention orders. For consideration of some of the issues involved see *O'Mahony v Melia* [1990] ILRM 14; [1989] IR 335 (1989 Review, 92).

ESTREATMENT OF SECURITY FOR FISHING GEAR

In *Attorney General v Sheehy* [1990] 1 IR 704, the Supreme Court held that a sum of money lodged as security for the value of fishing gear by a ship's owner who had been charged under the Fisheries Acts could be estreated against the value of the gear after a successful prosecution.

The circumstances giving rise to the case were as follows. At the conclusion of the trial of a boat owner for failure to keep a log book of a sea fishery vessel as required by Table 1 of the Sea Fisheries (Control of Catches) Order 1985 the respondent Circuit Court judge imposed a fine on the ship's owner, ordered him to pay a sum towards costs and also made a forfeiture order in respect of the owner's catch and gear. Prior to the trial, the owner's boat had been impounded. However, he had obtained its release under s.235 of the Fisheries (Consolidation) Act 1959, as inserted by s.14 of the Fisheries (Amendment) Act 1978, when he deposited a sum by way of security against payment of the maximum fines, the estimated costs and the estimated value of any forfeiture ordered in the event of his conviction. The prosecution requested the respondent to deduct the fines, costs and value of the defendant's catch and gear from the sum deposited as security. The respondent deducted the fine and costs only, but declined to deduct the value of the catch and gear and he then released the security. In the High Court, Murphy J had declined to grant judicial review of the respondent's decision: [1989] ILRM 303; [1988] IR 226 (1988 Review, 257), though he acknowledged that this left awkward administrative problems for the authorities.

The appeal by the Attorney General to the Supreme Court (Finlay CJ, Griffin and McCarthy JJ) obviated the difficulties resulting from the view taken by Murphy J in the High Court. Speaking for the Court, McCarthy J noted that the sum lodged in court prior to the trial was, under s.235 of the 1959 Act, a surety for three different categories of liability: any fine, costs and the value of any forfeitures ordered. Each of the three headings was caught by the power to estreat, McCarthy J noting that there had been no real dispute as to the fine and costs being caught. In such cases, he said, the statutory scheme did not contemplate forfeiture in kind, but the surety stands in the place of the thing to be forfeited. Thus the operation of the forfeiture on the surety, being a statutory consequence of the conviction, should be stated in the order of conviction; and the Court therefore directed the respondent to deduct the value of the catch and gear from the security lodged.

SEA FISHING LICENCE

Cannon v Minister for the Marine [1991] ILRM 261 concerned an application for a sea fishing boat licence.

In 1986, the applicant was granted by the Department of Fisheries a sea-fishing boat licence for a vessel of a particular class and size, under s.222B of the Fisheries (Consolidation) Act 1959, as inserted by the Fisheries (Amendment) Act 1983. The purchase of the boat to which the licence referred fell through. The applicant was concerend about whether an application for a licence for a similar vessel would be granted, and he obtained an assurance in writing in November 1986 that the Minister would grant such an application. Later that month he applied for a licence in respect of another vessel, but this fell through because someone else purchased the vessel before the application could be processed.

In January 1989, the applicant became interested in purchasing a vessel of similar class and size and he applied for a licence for the vessel to the Minister for the Marine who was now responsible for such applications. The applicant was informed that, due to the time elapsed, his previous application was being treated as lapsed; and that in view of the appointment of a Licensing Review Group, the Minister had suspended consideration of all sea-fishing boat licences. The applicant sought judicial review, on the ground that the letter of November 1986 gave rise to a legitimate expectation that his application for a licence would be granted. After liberty to apply had been granted, the Minister informed the applicant that, while the applicant's particular circumstances had been considered, no licence would be issued having regard to current licensing policy. Barr J refused judicial review to the applicant.

He quoted with approval a passage from the judgment of Finlay CJ in *Webb v Ireland* [1988] ILRM 565; [1988] IR 353 (1987 Review, 162-4) on the equitable nature of legitimate expectation. On that basis, he held that the test to be applied was whether in all the circumstances it would be unfair or unjust to allow a party to resile from a position created or adopted by that party which at that time gave rise to a legitimate expectation in the mind of another person that that situation would continue and might be acted on by that other person to their advantage.

In the instant case, he concluded that the State derived no benefit from the concession made in 1986, which was in the nature of gratuitous bureaucratic humanity arising from the temporary difficulty in which the applicant found himself when the purchase of the vessel in question fell through. Nor did he consider that the concession had been intended to be open-ended. Rather he took the view that it was to apply for a reasonable period to enable the applicant to find a suitable alternative vessel. He found it significant that the applicant had made a licence application within one month of the concession.

He concluded that the concession had therefore expired before January 1989 when the applicant re-applied for a licence.

It is unfortunate that the *Webb* case was the only authority relied on by Barr J in his judgment. Consideration of the considerable case law on this issue (see the 1988 Review, 20-30 and the 1989 Review, 9-12) might, of course, have led to the same result. However, it would have been useful to deal with those decisions in order to assess the current status of legitimate expectation.

Garda Síochána

COMPLAINTS BOARD

The Annual Report of the Garda Síochána Complaints Board for 1989 (Pl.7279) was published in May 1990. While considerable backlogs continue, the situation had improved since the publication of its Report for 1988: see the 1989 Review, 275.

DISCIPLINE

1 Dismissal: criminal charges In *McGrath v Garda Commissioner* [1990] ILRM 817 the question at issue was whether criminal charges brought against a member were such as to justify disciplinary proceedings against him.

The applicant member of the Force had been charged with offences under the Larceny Act 1916 in connection with payments made to him in discharge of court orders imposing fines. The applicant admitted that he had not issued official receipts for any of the payments, thus leaving the persons who had paid their fines to him liable to imprisonment. The applicant was returned for trial before the Circuit Criminal Court, but he was acquitted on all counts. Subsequent to his acquittal, he was served with notices under Reg.9 of the Garda Síochána (Discipline) Regulations 1971 (since replaced by the 1989 Regulations of the same title) stating that he might have been in breach of discipline as a result of being charged with criminal offences and of appearing before the District Court and the Circuit Criminal Court. He was then served with detailed forms setting out the alleged breaches of discipline. The first three breaches were of conduct prejudicial to the Force, the particulars being the appearances in the District Court and Circuit Criminal Court. The other three breaches alleged were of corrupt or improper practice, the particulars alleging failure to account for the sums of money received by him in the course of his duty which had been the subject matter of the criminal charges. The applicant applied for judicial review seeking to prohibit the holding of an inquiry into the alleged breaches of discipline. In the High Court, Lynch J acceded to the application in part: [1990] ILRM 90; [1989] IR 241 (1989 Review, 275-6). The Supreme Court (Finlay CJ, Griffin, Hederman, McCarthy and O'Flaherty JJ) upheld this view in dismissing the appeal taken by the Commissioner.

Delivering the leading judgment, Hederman J concluded that, in the particular circumstances of the instant case, it would amount to an unfair procedure for the Commissioner to proceed with a disciplinary hearing alleging corrupt or improper practices after essentially the same issues which would arise at such hearing had been fully heard and determined by a court of competent jurisdiction.

However, two important riders were added to this disposition of the case which are of importance for future cases. First, the Court appeared to be of the view, without expressing a final conclusion, that a charge of improper practice could proceed under the 1971 Regulations. In addition, all five judges indicated that no view would be expressed as to whether the doctrine of *res judicata* applied in the circumstances of the instant case. But in a significant straw in the wind, McCarthy J left as an open question the correctness of the approach taken by O'Hanlon J in *Kelly v Ireland* [1986] ILRM 318 and that of Lardner J in *Breathnach v Ireland* [1989] IR 489. These two cases are discussed in the 1989 Review, 358-61.

2 Dismissal: lewd conduct In *Stroker v Doherty and Ors*, Supreme Court, 26 July 1990, the question at issue was whether certain allegedly lewd conduct of the applicant was sufficiently grave to warrant dismissal from the Force. The Supreme Court declined to quash the applicant's dismissal, holding that the dismissal had not been unreasonable: see 14-6, above, in the Administrative Law chapter. The Court thus reversed the decision of Barron J in the High Court: [1989] ILRM 428; [1989] IR 440 (1989 Review, 276-8).

Health Services

CLINICAL TRIALS

In the 1987 Review, 299-304, we discussed the Control of Clinical Trials Act 1987, which introduced statutory controls into an area formerly governed exclusively by somewhat uncertain constitutional and common law principles. The 1987 Act sets out detailed requirements for the conduct of clinical trials. Only registered medical practitioners or dentists may conduct them, and it is necessary to have obtained the permission of the Minister for Health as well as the approval of an ethics committee.

A difficulty with the 1987 Act arose in relation to s. 10(1), which prohibited a person from conducting a clinical trial unless he established to the satisfaction of the ethics committee that he could provide sufficient security to ensure that adequate funds were available to provide adequate compensation for each participant who might suffer injury or loss as a result of the trial. Ethics committees became concerned lest they should be exposed to civil liability, under common law or for breach of statutory duty, if they failed to exercise due care in the exercise of a function which pertains more to the exercise of a commercial than an ethical judgment.

Most hospital-based ethical committees accordingly either ceased to operate in relation to clinical trials or limited their consideration to trials on products which had licences and were already in current use:, 125 Seanad Debs, col. 1183. As Senator Hederman observed: 'Basically the Clinical Trials Act made research safe by stopping it' (*id.*, col. 1206).

The 1990 Act resolves this difficulty in s. 3 by amending s. 10 of the 1987 Act so as to shift from ethics committees to the Minister the task of ensuring the adequacy of the arrangements for security to compensate injured participants.

S. 5 provoked Dr Upton to comment that '[t]he Minister in this Bill seems to be going around immunising people' (*id.*, col. 1194). Subs. (1) provides as follows:

No action or other proceedings shall lie or be maintainable (except in the case of wilful neglect or default) against

(a) the Minister,
(b) the National Drugs Advisory Board or any person acting as a

member, officer or servant thereof,
(c) an ethics committee or any member thereof,

for the recovery of damages in respect of any injury to persons or property alleged to have been caused or contributed to by reason of or arising from the discharge of any of their functions imposed by or under the Control of Clinical Trials Acts 1987 and 1990.

The Minister of State, Mr Treacy, explained to the Dáil that the Attorney General had recommended this provision, which had parallels in the immunity granted to other State boards, including Eolas and the National Health and Safety Authority.

A key expression here is 'wilful neglect or default'. The tenor of the Ministerial assurances was that the negligent, *non-wilful* default of the Minister, the National Drugs Advisory Board or an ethics committee would *not* be immune from liability:

I trust it is clear that the two categories [of 'wilful neglect' and 'default'] stand alone. If it was intended to cover wilful default the word 'wilful' would be included the second time'. (401 Dáil Debs, col 610).

With respect, this cannot be correct. The expression 'wilful neglect or default' has a long legislative pedigree: it connotes wilful neglect or *wilful* default. If it embraced default, whether wilful or otherwise, the subsection would be futile: it would exempt the named parties from liability only to impale them immediately thereafter on an uncertain basis of liability at least as broad as that of negligence. The notion of default, unencumbered by the qualification of wilfulness, could scarcely be narrower in scope than the notion of 'fault' under the Civil Liability Act 1961.

If we assume that the true interpretation of s. 5(1) is that the named parties are to be liable only for wilful neglect or wilful default, the question arises as to what range of conduct or omission this envisages. Obviously the concept of wilfulness connotes a degree of conscious deliberation. Thus, if an ethics committee were to discharge a statutory function carelessly, in sublime ignorance of their failure to exercise due care, no liability would arise under s. 5(1). But, as will often be the case, if the issue arises during the committee's deliberations as to whether a proposed course of action is legally 'safe', and if the committee, aware of the danger of generating liability, goes ahead and gives the requested permission, then an argument may arise as to whether it was guilty of wilful neglect or default. To be wilful, it would not seem necessary for the committee's neglect or default to have been characterised by the committee as negligent. On the other hand, the mere advertence to, and discussion of, the risk that a proposed course of conduct may be negligent should not, of itself, seem capable of generating liability. Such a rule would penalise conscientious and frank discussion by committees of the question of legal liability. A *via media* would impose liability where (i) the question of the proposed course of action's being negligent was addressed by the committee, (ii) the risk that it was negligent was at least substantial, and (iii) the committee, conscious of that risk, decided nonetheless to go ahead.

S. 5(2) should also be noted in this context. It confers a similar immunity on the National Drugs Advisory Board and a committee established under Article 18 of the National Drugs Advisory Board (Establishment) Order 1966 (SI No. 163 of 1966) in respect of the discharge of any of the Board's functions under Article 4 of that Order. The Minister for State, Mr Treacy, explained that, in order to ensure the continued participation of specialists of the highest standing as members of the board and their specialist committees and thereby maintain their internationally recognised status, this immunity was desirable.

S. 2 of the 1990 Act introduces an important amendment to s. 6(2) of the 1987 Act with regard to the definition of what 'conduct[ing] a clinical trial' means. S6(2)(a)(ii) had exempted from the scope of this definition the conduct of a systematic investigation where the principal purpose of the administration of a substance or preparation on persons 'is the welfare of the patient'. S. 2 substitutes for this formula the test that the principal purpose of that administration should be 'to prevent disease in or to save the life, restore the health, alleviate the condition or relieve the suffering of, the patient'.

During the Oireachtas Debates, the Minister tended to interpret the provision narrowly:

> It refers to a person who would be terminally ill and the possibility that the use of a particular drug might be life-saving. Obviously the drug would be used as a matter of urgency, as distinct from using the drug in the nature of a trial to see what its effect would be. . . . The reason the drug is being used is of central importance. If it is used as one last chance to save a life, that would fall outside the Act; if it is used to see how it will perform, it is very much within the scope of this legislation. 401 Dáil Debs, cols 601-2.

This interpretation is not easy to reconcile with the clear language of the provision. Saving the life of the patient is but one of *five* principal purposes, any of which serves to exclude the activity from the protection of the Act. Thus there need be no situation of urgency; indeed the patient's life need not even remotely be at risk.

What may cause concern about s.2 is that the administration of a drug can fall outside the Act's protection even where it is *not*, on balance, for the patient's welfare. Medical ethics raises well-known issues as to what the precise relationship should be between prolonging a patient's life and easing his or her suffering. The effect of s.2 is to remove from the Act's scrutiny the conduct of a doctor who engages in experimental treatment with drugs which have no likelihood of benefiting the patient in terms of prolonging his or her life or of alleviating his or her condition, and whose only conceivable benefit is in the area of easing suffering. This is the exact antithesis of the rationale in favour of s.2 presented by the Minister. Of course a doctor who engages in this type of treatment has to comply with the criminal law (of murder and manslaughter) and the civil law (of negligence and battery); but the abolition of the requirement that, to avoid the scrutiny of the Act, the principal purpose of the administration should be the welfare of the patient may be regretted.

The suggestion that, if a drug is used to see how it will perform, the administration is 'very much within the scope of the legislation' is worth considering. This is true only if this is the *principal* purpose of the administration. If, however, the principal purpose is one of five mentioned in the provision, then the fact that there are other, even significant, purposes does not bring the administration under the Act's control. Presumably most doctors who engage in clinical trials have the principal purpose of alleviating the condition of their patients or at least of relieving their suffering. Neither the fact that the drug they are using has not an established track record nor the fact that there is another well-tried drug available would necessarily be inconsistent with the existence of that principal purpose. The change brought about by the 1990 Act makes it easier for a doctor to engage in clinical trials without the scrutiny of the Act. Formerly he or she might have had difficulty in convincing a court that in choosing the experimental rather than established treatment he or she had as a principal purpose the welfare of the patient. Now all that has to be shown is one of five principal purposes, none of which need, on balance, be identified with the welfare of the patient.

It is also true that the doctor may be paid for engaging in these trials without coming under the Act's scrutiny. (Senator Brendan Ryan made a valiant, though unavailing, attempt to prevent this: 125 Seanad Debs, cols. 1228-1248).

During the Debates, there was some discussion on s. 6 (2)(b) of the 1987 Act, which appeared in the 1990 legislation in the Table to s. 2, which amended s. 6(2)(a)(ii) of the 1987 Act. S. 6(2)(b) exempts from the definition of the conduct of a clinical trial cases where the substance or preparation concerned:

is to be administered to persons undergoing a course of training leading to a qualification which will entitle such a person to be registered as a registered medical practitioner or as a registered dentist or as a registered pharmaceutical chemist and where it is to be administered as part of such a course of training.

In the Seanad, Dr Upton expressed concern as to why these students should be thus left unprotected. It seemed to him that many of them would:

be in a very difficult position if they say 'no thank you very much' to an over-enthusiastic or, horror of horrors, a nutty or crazy professor who decides to go one over the top in terms of what will or will not be used. 125 Seanad Debs, col. 1196 (20 June 1990).

The Minister of State at the Department of Industry and Commerce's reply was somewhat bland: medical students might 'wish, as part of their training, to experience the effect of medicines so as to understand the effects which these medicines are likely to have on their patients': *id.*, col. 1226. When the matter was raised in the Dáil by Eric Byrne TD, the Minister for Health's response was soothing but perhaps not fully dispositive of the issue. The provision would apply to students:

who might make something themselves in a laboratory and then take it. For example, a pharmaceutical student might make hydrochloric acid or vinegar and then taste it. This gives them a perception of the taste of the substances they are working with and in that way they might be involved in a trial. This subsection allows for that in very controlled circumstances and they would not need to go off and seek authority under the Bill from the Minister for Health. (401 Dáil Debs, col. 605 (July 1990)).

The final change brought about by the 1990 Act is in s.4, amending s. 13 of the 1987 Act which deals with offences and provides for defences in relation to them. s. 13(2)(a) had brought within the net of criminal liability the director, manager, secretary and other officers of bodies *corporate*. S. 13(2)(b) provided a defence for persons who could show that the offence was committed without their knowledge, where they had exercised all due diligence to prevent its commission, having regard to the nature of their position and to all the circumstances. S. 4 now extends the net to the offences of *unincorporated* bodies. The Minister explained that its purpose is to extend the *defences* provided by s. 13(2)(b) to unincorporated bodies of persons, in particular, the ethics committees. 401 Dáil Debs, col. 608.

HEALTH BOARDS

Health board officer: redundancy In *Hickey v Eastern Health Board* [1990] ELR 177, the applicant unsuccessfully sought judicial review of her dismissal as an officer of the respondent health board. The case is discussed in the Labour Law chapter, 356-7, below.

Health board officer: travel In *Osborne v Hickey*, High Court, 2 May 1990, the applicant successfully sought an order of mandamus in respect of the refusal of the respondent chief executive officer to grant him certain travelling allowances: see also 12, above, in the Administrative Law chapter.

HOSPITALS SWEEPS

The Public Hospitals (Amendment) Act 1990 provided for the disposal of unclaimed prize money (totalling £480,000) arising from the operation of the Irish Hospitals Sweepstake. The Act vested the money in the Minister for Health, to be disposed of by the Minister in respect of services by pensioners and certain former employees of Hospitals Trust (1940) Ltd, the company which promoted and operated the hospital sweepstakes. Most of the Act came into operation on 14 December 1990 by virtue of the Public Hospitals (Amendment) Act 1990 (Commencement) Order 1990 (SI No. 299).

MEDICAL PRACTITIONERS

Medical practitioner: registration *Bakht v Medical Council* [1990] ILRM 840; [1990] 1 IR 515 concerned a medical practitioner seeking registration under the Medical Practitioners Act 1978.

The applicant had been given five certificates of temporary registration to practice medicine in the State by the respondent Council pursuant to the terms of s.27 of the 1978 Act. Each certificate of registration was for one year's duration. S.27 of the 1978 Act provides that no more than five such certificates may be granted. The applicant then applied for registration on a permanent basis pursuant to s.27 in accordance with a provision by which the Council may register a person who satisfies it that he has undergone such courses of training and passed such examinations as are specified for the purposes of the section in rules made by the Council. At the time that the applicant applied for registration, the Council had not made any rules under this provision. As a result, the applicant had not been able to practice medicine from January 1988.

In June 1988, the applicant sought, inter alia, an order of mandamus directing the Council to register him, issue rules under s.27 of the 1978 Act and damages for loss of earnings. After the institution of these judicial review proceedings, the Council adopted rules under s.27 specifying examination requirements, and these rules came into effect in October 1989. In the High Court, Gannon J granted an order of mandamus directing the Council to consider the applicant's case and declaring that the Council had been in default in failing to adopt rules under s.27 of the Act. On appeal by the Council the Supreme Court (Finlay CJ, Griffin and Hederman JJ) upheld the main holding by Gannon J.

The Court disagreed with Gannon J on one point only, finding that he had erred in ordering the Council to consider the applicant's case without regard to the rules which the Council, at the time the High Court order was made, proposed to bring in.

However the Supreme Court agreed that the Council had been in default of the requirement to make rules under s.27 of the 1978 Act, since this was a mandatory requirement having regard to the overall purposes of the 1978 Act and the national and European Community obligations of the Council as regards setting standards for registration of medical practitioners.

On the question of damages, the Court decided it could itself assess damages since the cost of referring the matter back to the High Court would be out of all proportion to the amount of damages likely to be awarded in the High Court: see the Court's decision in *Holohan v Donohoe* [1986] ILRM 250; [1986] IR 45. Having regard to the fact that the Council could, having been notified of the applicant's case, had rules in place by late 1988 but had not in fact had them in place until the end of 1989, the Court held the Council was liable for one year's loss of earnings by the applicant, which on the applicant's uncontradicted evidence indicated a total sum of £12,500.

The *Bakht* decision was applied by Costello J in *Philips v Medical Council*, High Court, 11 December 1990 where damages of £41,500 was awarded: see 533, below, in the Torts chapter. The *Philips* case also involved the successful invocation of legitimate expectation: see 10, above, in the Administrative Law chapter.

By way of contrast, in *Banerjee v Medical Council*, High Court, 23 November 1990 Lavan J declined to grant judicial review of a refusal of limited registration by the Medical Council in respect of the applicant, who had not been successful in either an English language test of professional knowledge and who had ceased to practice medicine following her internship. Lavan J cited the decision of the Supreme Court in *The State (Abenglen Properties Ltd) v Dublin Corporation* [1982] ILRM 590; [1984] IR 381 to support his view that, since the 1978 Act comprised a self-contained code, and since judicial review should not be used as an appeal mechanism, he should refuse the relief sought by the applicant.

MENTAL TREATMENT

Murphy v Greene [1991] ILRM 404; [1990] 2 IR 566 involved an unsuccessful application to commence proceedings for damages under s.260 of the Mental Treatment Act 1945: see 147-50, above, in the Constitutional Law chapter.

NURSING

Fitness to practice *K. v An Bord Altranais* [1990] 2 IR 396 dealt with whether an oral hearing was required where an application is made to the High Court to cancel an erasure from the Register of Nurses pursuant to s.39 of the Nurses Act 1985.

Pursuant to an inquiry into allegations of professional misconduct against the applicant and after an opinion had been expressed by the Fitness to Practice Committee under Part V of the 1985 Act, the respondent Board decided that the applicant's name be erased from the Register of Nurses. The applicant had been represented by solicitor and counsel before the Committee and Board. She instituted proceedings under s.39 of the 1985 Act seeking to have the erasure cancelled. Her defence to the allegations were that they were untrue and had flowed from a conspiracy of hostility and malicious invention on the part of witnesses who had appeared before the Fitness to Practice Committee.

Article 7 of the Rules of the Superior Courts (No. 2) 1989, which applied O.95, r.5 of the Rules of the Superior Courts 1986 to an application under s.39 of the 1985 Act, provides that the hearing may be by affidavit. The applicant wished to have the application heard on oral evidence. In the High Court Costello J held that a hearing on affidavit was sufficient but the Supreme Court took a different view.

Costello J was of the view that the High Court's function under s.39 of the 1985 Act was not to re-hear the inquiry into professional misconduct but to review the evidence before the Fitness to Practice Committee and which was considered by the Board; and that a hearing on affidavit only would satisfy this requirement.

Delivering the judgment of the Supreme Court (Finlay CJ, Griffin and McCarthy JJ) the Chief Justice stated that the essence of the application to the High Court under s.39 of the 1985 Act was that the Court must make the vital determinations as to erasure from the Register. He noted that if such determinations were in the hands of the Board the 1985 Act would be in breach of Article 34 of the Constitution, citing *In re the Solicitors Act 1954* [1960] IR 239 and *M v Medical Council* [1984] IR 485 in this context.

He went on to state that where, as in the instant case, the application under s.39 of the 1985 Act depended on the truth or falsity of evidence as to the plaintiff's conduct and not on any question of standards or principles of professional conduct, it was essential that the High Court must reach its own conclusions as to the truth or falsity of the allegations. It was thus necessary to have the issues determined on oral evidence. However, he did note, finally, that a great number of disputes under s.39 of the 1985 Act could be dealt with by way of affidavit where the facts were not in dispute. Here, the facts were clearly in dispute.

Nursing homes   The Health (Nursing Homes) Act 1990 is a framework Act which requires the registration of nursing homes with their local health board. The Act also empowers the Minister for Health to make extensive Regulations concerning the standard of care given to people in such homes. The Act re-enacts, with amendments, the Health (Homes for Incapacitated Persons) Act 1964, and existing Regulations made under the 1964 Act are continued in force by the 1990 Act. For a detailed discussion of the Act see Humphreys' annotation, *Irish Current Law Statutes Annotated.*

Labour Law

ABOLITION OF PERMANENT OFFICE

In *Turley v Laois County Council*, High Court, 29 January 1990, Carroll J held that the plaintiff was entitled to a declaration that he was the holder of the office of rate collector and would continue to do so until lawfully removed by the defendant. The position was a permanent one, which the plaintiff had held since 1975. with the abolition of domestic rates, the work of rate collectors largely fell away. The defendant County Council took active steps to rationalise the position through the twin courses of redundancy and upgrading the office to that of revenue collector, which entailed extra duties. The stumbling block was s. 10 of the Local Government Act 1941, as amended by s. 12 of the Local Government Act 1955. S. 10(5) enables local authorities, with Ministerial consent, to abolish offices, but in the case of an office held by a person in a permanent capacity, the consent of that person is essential.

Here the local authority had not obtained that consent. The plaintiff's attitude had been quietly to stand firm and give his express agreement to none of the proposals put forward by the local authority. The local authority wrongly interpreted the statement of a trade union representative as being to the effect that the plaintiff had given his agreement. When the local authority wrote to him referring to the alleged agreement reached with him and his union representative, and informing him that he had been re-graded as a revenue collector, the plaintiff instructed his solicitor to write back stating that he had never given his consent to the abolition of his office.

The county council argued unsuccessfully that the plaintiff had ratified his appointment as a revenue collector by his silence at meetings and by accepting the salary of a revenue collector. Carroll J considered that no agreement could be implied from his conduct prior to the managerial order purporting to abolish the post; in the absence of consent, the order was made *ultra vires*. The plaintiff's acts after the new post had been created were not solely referable to its acceptance. He had continued collecting rates and working on the electoral register and never worked as a revenue collector. While his conduct could validly be criticised for deliberately keeping quiet after he had made up his mind not to accept re-grading, it was up to the county council to obtain his agreement and this it had not done.

EMPLOYMENT EQUALITY

1 Principle of non-retrospection   In the 1988 Review, 263-6, we analysed Carroll J's judgment in *Aer Lingus v The Labour Court* [1990] ILRN 485; [1990] ELR 113. Aer Lingus's appeal to the Supreme Court was successful.

Walsh J (Griffin and Hederman JJ concurring) agreed with Carroll J that the procedure before the Labour Court was meant to be relatively simple and that the Labour Court was quite entitled to refer a complaint to an equality officer for his or her recommendations without the Labour Court's first having made an initial determination that the complaint was receivable. He also agreed that it would be far preferable that the matter should not be brought to the High Court until after the Labour Court had made its determination as to any matters of law arising. In the instant case, the Labour Court had not yet made any findings on the merits of the case. Normally, therefore, Walsh J would have been quite content to let the case go back to the Labour Court. Since, however, Carroll J had elected to go into the question of whether the acts complained of were capable of constituting unlawful discrimination under ss. 2(b) and 3 of the Employment Equality Act 1977, the Supreme Court could not avoid dealing with this part of her judgment.

As to the complainants' claim, it will be recalled that it raised the troublesome question of whether employment arrangements reflecting rather than transforming the effects previous lawful discrimination are themselves unlawful on the grounds of discrimination. The complainants, air hostesses, had been discriminated against in different ways at different times. First, they had been forced to resign on marriage, prior to August 1970. Secondly, they had been refused permanent employment when other married women who had married later were either taken back by their employers or never forced to resign. Thirdly, when they had been taken back permanently, they had been refused recognition for past service and experience in calculating seniority where other married women who were taken back had been given full recognition.

Carroll J held that this constituted unlawful discrimination as between members of the same sex on the basis of marital status. There was no immutable rule that, because seniority at present affected every aspect of the work, it must continue to do so in the future. Existing work practices based on seniority might not be unchallengeable on account of the legislative time bar, but Aer Lingus could not be allowed to add new examples of discrimination and force the complainants to submit to them. The existing seniority system could not be used as 'a licence to discriminate indefinitely and without limit'.

The Supreme Court rejected this analysis. Walsh J noted that the former compulsory retirement of the complainants was a discriminatory act relating to marital status but was not illegal. The 1977 Act did not have retrospective effect. In his opinion the original discrimination was 'exhausted and spent' when it took effect and was not in any way revived by the subsequent employment of the complainants in a temporary capacity for the relevant subsequent periods. Therefore when the complainants re-entered the service of Aer Lingus in 1980 they were entitled to be protected against any discriminatory acts relating to their sex or marital status *occurring after the date or built into the contract itself.* There was no suggestion of any discrimination because of marital status since 1980; so far as seniority was concerned, the complainants were in exactly the same position as all other women entering the service on a permanent basis at that time.

Walsh J added:

> It has been sought to suggest that there had been indirect discrimination on the grounds that the seniority issue was already predetermined by the events which took place prior to 1970. It is true that the question of seniority was affected by the date of marriage and, that is, by the date of the acquisition of that status. That is different from the status itself. I do not think that the reference to marital status in the 1977 Act can be held to include differences resulting from dates of marriage [or] can amount to discrimination between married women to be classed as a discrimination because of marital status.

In view of the non-retrospective character of the Act, in effect the slate was 'wiped clean' in respect of matters occurring before the Act. The instant claim was an effort to give the Act a retrospective character, asserting that every consequence of the seniority situation must be deemed to be an act of discrimination, when the seniority situation itself could not be established to be an illegal discrimination because it was traceable to a situation which had not been illegal and had been a discrimination which was exhausted many years before the enactment of the 1977 Act:

> Failure to recognise previous service may be thought to be inequitable but that does not amount to illegal discrimination. There was a distinction made between different groups of married women dealing with their respective seniority but that is not a discrimination of marital status nor can it be shown that marital status in the present case, as distinct from date of marriage, was an activating cause in the determination of the seniority. The complainants were not treated less favourably because they were married. All their present complaints refer to the operation of the seniority rule in its ordinary way.

2 Sexual harassment   In *W. (Worker) v A. (Company)* [1990] ELR 187, a female worker who had left her employment in a hotel claimed that she had been constructively dismissed by virtue of having been forced to resign because of sexual harassment and a serious sexual assault by a director of the company. The Labour Court approached the matter on the basis that, to establish constructive dismissal, the worker had to convince the Court, 'through direct corroboration or on the balance of probability' that the employer had acted in a manner that had left her with no reasonable alternative but to resign. This formulation of the test is clearly unfortunate: the issue of the standard of proof cannot be addressed as an *alternative* to that of the requirement of corroboration.

Since there was no corroboration in the case, the issue depended on the credibility of the parties. The Court was satisfied that there was greater credibility on the side of the worker and that the complaint was well founded.

The essence of the worker's case was that there had been repeated and unwarranted sexual harassment during her period of employment. She contended that the director had initially sought to date her but that she had not accepted this arrangement. She said that the director, during the course of business and without prior arrangement, had taken her out for a meal in a hotel, and then booked a bedroom without her agreement. She also claimed that on a number of occasions he had come uninvited to her bedroom in the hotel where she worked. On some of these occasions he undressed and on the final occasion (three days before she resigned) he sexually assaulted her.

The court observed that there was a 'ring of truth' to the worker's account. It considered it important that her doctor had stated in evidence that her medical history was consistent with the account she had given at the hearing. It noted that there had been a complex relationship between the worker and the director. In the business context, he had included her in a small number of employees who had access to sensitive business information, the disclosure of which could be damaging. This, said the court, 'afforded her a position of some small privilege as demonstrated by her unusual freedom in relation to time-keeping and the fact that, though claiming to be critical of her work performance, the director did not at any time attempt to dismiss her. On the contrary, he ignored the threats to resign which she made on a number of occasions'.

The Court stated that, in fact, the worker's position of privilege as perceived by other staff was more 'illusory that real because of her personal and economic need to retain her job and because of her health and emotional condition'.

The director admitted to a sexual interest in the worker. He claimed as a defence that all his actions had been with the consent of the claimant.

In an important passage of its judgment the Court stated that:

> [i]n considering the question of consent, and in view of the worker's denial of consent, the court must have regard to the director's dominant position in the employment relationship with all the power inherent in that position, the fact that he took advantage of the work-related arrangements in the hotel, the fact that he did not have a social relationship with the worker outside the work place, and that he was aware of the personal vulnerability of the worker. In these circumstances the Court does not accept the claim of consent.

With regard to the claimant's specific allegation of sexual assault a few days before she resigned, the Court was convinced that the director's actions 'did not have the consent of the worker even if, as claimed by him, earlier actions had such consent'. It said:

> A sexual relationship between consenting adults does not imply that that consent is unlimited as regards either time-scale or acts which may take place between the parties. Each party has a continuing right to place limitations on what acts may take place and when they may take place, and also a right to withdraw consent totally. These rights acquire the protection of the Employment Equality Act 1977, when the parties concerned are in a relevant employment situation. Consent may be varied at will and, provided the other party is made aware or should be aware of the position, any act committed outside of the immediate consent is in breach of the 1977 Act.

While recognising the compelling need which existed for the worker to retain employment, the Court considered that she had been imprudent to leave herself at risk over an extended period and that she should not have relied to such a degree on her own resourcefulness to protect herself in recurring circumstances of obvious and serious danger, despite the difficulty and unpleasantness which dealing with it would have involved for her. She should have sought counsel and assistance to find a remedy or redress for her situation. The Court took account of this aspect in its determination of compensation, which amounted to £9,000. Since the plaintiff's wages were £145 per week net, this suggests only a relatively small reduction for what in effect if not express characterisation was, in the Court's view, her con-tributory negligence.

Two aspects of the Labour Court's analysis call for brief comment. First, it is surely beyond argument that an employee who embarks on a sexual relationship with an employer, even without any undue pressure by the employer, is perfectly free to call a halt to it at any time. An employer who engages in sexual activity with an employee without the employee's consent, however abruptly that consent may have been withdrawn, is guilty of a serious criminal offence (provided, of course, the necessary *mens rea* is established): see our discussion of the Criminal Law (Rape) (Amendment) Act 1990, in the Criminal Law chapter, above 258-62. There is no question of some twentieth century equivalent of the *droit de seigneur* attaching to employers.

Secondly, there is a certain occlusion about the court's analysis of the circumstances in which an employee's consent to a sexual relationship with an employer is vitiated. Clearly, not every sexual relationship between an employer and an employee is to be characterised as non-consensual on the employee's part: there must surely be some element of abuse of position or dominance by the employer before the consensual element is impugned. To show that an employer had a dominant position in the employment relationship should scarcely automatically suffice. Nor should an employer's taking advantage of the work-related arrangements in the place of employment seem to weigh heavily in favour of an allegation of lack of consent. It *could* do so of course, depending on the nature of the advantage thus taken. The absence of a social relationship with the employee outside the workplace might well be a feature of many affairs between persons of differing social backgrounds; it would not always indicate lack of consent on the part of the person in the less economically powerful position. Again, it would be necessary to know more of a particular case before one could say that a definite indication of lack of consent had been established.

Of the four elements identified by the Court as rendering the employee's consent invalid, only the last, relating to the employer's awareness of the employee's personal vulnerability, carries the clear implication of abuse of position or dominance over the employee. We do not intend to suggest that the other three elements, in conjunction with the fourth, were not relevant in the global assessment of the issue of consent. What is worth noting, however, is that in no sense do they rise above the circumstances of the particular case to represent *principles of general import* by which *other* cases of alleged sexual harassment can easily be assessed. This is not to criticise the Court's analysis or determination, save to the extent that it does not offer a particularly helpful conceptual guide for the development of future jurisprudence on this important subject. For general analysis, see Deirdre Curtin, *Irish Employment Law* (1989), 259-35, Prendeville, 'Equality Legislation — A Success or Failure?' (1991), 1 *Irish Students L Rev* 21, at 28-30.

THE INDUSTRIAL RELATIONS ACT 1990

In contrast to the recent history in Britain, though no doubt reflecting some ideological reverberations from that experience, Ireland has had a relatively tranquil development in its industrial relations legislation in the last few years. The 1990 Act represents a pragmatic compromise on emotive issues, which found support from a surprisingly broad political and social base. For a succinct and incisive analysis of the background to the legislation, see Tony Kerr's Annotation to the Act, *ICLSA*, General Note to the Long Title. Brian Wilkinson offers a provocative critique of the legislation, arguing that it is fundamentally flawed and open to a likely successful constitutional challenge: (1991) 20 *Industrial L J* 21. The Irish Congress of Trade Unions has produced a very readable *Users' Guide* to the legislation, and Michael Forde is on the point of publishing a textbook on the Act.

Part II of the Act has placed the issue of legal liability for strikes and other industrial action on a new footing. It replaces the Trade Disputes Act 1906 (repealed by s. 7) with provisions several of which are largely similar to what went before but which nonetheless contain important differences.

Definition of 'Trade Dispute' A 'trade dispute' is defined by s. 8 as meaning any dispute between employers and workers which is connected with the employment or non-employment, or the terms or conditions of or affecting the employment, of any person. An 'employer' here means a person for whom one or more workers work or have worked or normally work or seek to work having previously worked for that person. The device of separate incorporation so as to break the employer-employee nexus, which succeeded in *Roundabout Ltd v Beirne* [1959] IR 423 has not been expressly killed off by the legislation. The Minister (398 Dáil Debs, col. 329) doubted whether it continued to have vitality today. See further Wilkinson, *op. cit.*, 25, fn. 26. A 'worker' means any person who is or was employed whether or not in the employment of the employer with whom a trade dispute arises, but does not include a member of the Defence Forces or of the Garda Síochána. Disputes between workers (or between trade unions) do not come within the scope of a 'trade dispute'.

Immunities Ss. 10 to 13 confer immunities from liability. That conferred by s. 13 applies only in relation to authorised trade unions which for the time being are holders of negotiation licences under the Trade Union Act 1941 and the immunities conferred by ss.11 and 12 apply only to members and officials of these trade unions: s. 9(1). Moreover, where in relation to the employment or non-employment or the terms or conditions of or affecting the employment of *one* individual worker, there are agreed procedures availed of by custom or in practice in the employment concerned, or provided for in a collective agreement, for the resolution of individual grievances, including dismissals, ss. 10 to 12 apply only where those procedures have been resorted to and exhausted: s. 9(2). Procedures here include resort to a rights commissioner, the Labour Relations Commission (about which more anon), the Labour Court, an equality officer and the Employment Appeals Tribunal, but *not* an appeal to a court: s. 9(4). Procedures are deemed exhausted if at any stage an employer fails or refuses to comply with them: subs. (3).

S. 10 re-enacts the immunity from criminal and civil liability for conspiracy contained respectively, in s. 3 of the Conspiracy and Protection of Property Act 1875 and s. 1 of the 1906 Act. The immunity attaches only to acts 'in contemplation or furtherance of a trade dispute'. As to conspiracy see our discussion, in the Torts Chapter, below, 542-5, of the Supreme Court decision of *Taylor v Smyth*, 5 July 1990. See further McMahon & Binchy, *Irish Law of Torts* (2nd ed, 1990), 582.

S. 12 re-enacts s. 3 of the 1906 Act, with certain extensions of the scope of the immunity which it conferred, by providing that:

> [a]n act done by a person in contemplation or furtherance of a trade dispute shall not be actionable on the ground only that —
> (a) it induces some other person to breach a contract of employment, or
> (b) it consists of a threat by a person to induce some other person to breach a contract of employment or a threat by a person to breach his own contract of employment, or
> (c) it is an interference with the trade, business or employment of some other person, or with the right of some other person to dispose of his capital or his labour as he wills.

S. 12 goes further than s. 3 of the 1906 Act in granting immunity to those who threaten to induce a breach of contract of employment (that is, to *organise a strike*) or who threaten to breach their own contracts of employment (that is, to *go on strike*).

It remains the position that the breach of contract itself may be actionable. Moreover, a business whose commercial contract with an employer is improperly interfered with by one who has immunity under s. 12 may, in appropriate cases, sue for inducement of breach of contract, conspiracy or perhaps the slowly developing generic tort of unlawful interference with economic relationships: see the 1987 Review, 238-9. S. 12 professes to confer immunity only on an inducement to break a 'contract of employment'; it does not extend to an inducement to break other contracts, such as commercial contracts. Thus it would seem that there is continuing vitality in the Supreme Court's holding in *Talbot (Ireland) Ltd v Merrigan* 30 April 1981, extracted in McMahon & Binchy's, *Casebook on the Irish Law of Torts* (1983), 450)52 and discussed by Kerr & White, *op. cit.* 260-1, and by McMahon & Binchy, *op. cit.*, 566-8. It is true that, as Kerr points out (Annotation to the Act, General Note to s.12), the Minister stated (400 Dáil Debs, col. 1978) that the phrase 'shall not be actionable' meant that 'shall not be actionable by any person. . . .' It should be noted, however, that the Minister was seeking to oppose the addition of the words 'by any person', which Deputy Jim Mitchell had proposed to deal with a situation where someone *acting in concert with an employer* might take action. The Minister stated that the legal advice which he had received was to the effect that the subsection as framed already covered the point addressed by Deputy Mitchell. This was no doubt true; it would seem unwise, therefore, to read a broader interpretation into his remarks.

S. 13 gives a limited immunity to trade unions from being sued in tort. It provides as follows:

(1) An action against a trade union, whether of workers or employers, or its trustees or against any members or officials thereof on behalf of themselves and all other members of the trade union in respect of any tortious act committed by or on behalf of the trade union in contemplation or furtherance of a trade dispute, shall not be entertained by any court.

(2) In an action against any trade union or person referred to in subs. (1) in respect of any tortious act alleged or found to have been committed by or on behalf of a trade union it shall be a defence that the act was done in the reasonable belief that it was done in contemplation or furtherance of a trade dispute.

The requirement that the defendant should have done the act *in contemplation or furtherance of a trade dispute (or in the reasonable belief that it is so done)* is new: cf. section 4(1) of the 1906 Act (as amended), McMahon & Binchy, *op cit.*, 583-4.

Limitations inhering in the immunity conferred by s. 4(1) apply also to s. 13 of the 1990 Act. Thus, actions for damages for breach of contract (cf. *O'Neill v Transport & General Workers Union* [1934] IR 633) may be brought against a trade union; similarly actions for quasi-contract (*Universe Tankships Inc of Monrovia v International Transport Workers Federation* [1980] IRLR 363). The development of the doctrine of 'economic duress' carries with it important implications in relation to s. 13: see Atiyah, (1982) 98 *LQ Rev* 197 and (1983) 99 *LQ Rev* 353; Tiplady, (1983) 99 *LQ Rev* 188. This renders unlawful a wide range of economic pressures, extending more broadly than conduct that would constitute the torts of intimidation or inducing a breach of contract, for example. If the doctrine were to be applied without limitation, it 'would rampage at the whim of the judiciary across the face of industrial relations'. Wedderburn, (1982) 45 *Modern L Rev* 556, at 563. See further Wedderburn, 'Labour Law: From Here to Autonomy?' (1987) *Industrial LJ* 1, at 19-20. Finally, it should be noted that in *Hayes v Ireland* [1987] ILRM 65, (High Court, 1986), Carroll J held that s. 4 of the 1906 Act did not confer immunity from action for unlawful interference with a constitutional right. The same rule would appear to apply to s. 13 of the 1990 Act.

As interesting issue arises as to the implications of Henchy J's analysis of the relationship between tort actions and actions for damages for infringement of constitutional rights, in the Supreme Court decision of *Hanrahan v Merck Sharp & Dohme (Ireland) Ltd* [1988] ILRM 629, at 447. He there stated:

> So far as I am aware, the constitutional provisions relied on have never been used in the courts to shape the form of any existing tort or to change the normal onus of proof. The implementation of those constitutional rights is primarily a matter for the State and the courts are entitled to intervene only when there has been a failure to implement or, where the implementation relied on is plainly inadequate to effectuate, the constitutional guarantee in question. In many torts — for example, negligence, defamation, trespass to person or property — a plaintiff may give evidence of what he claims because of what is usually a matter of onus of proof or because of some other legal or technical defence. A person may of course in the absence of a common law or statutory cause of action, sue directly for breach of a constitutional right (see *Meskell v CIE* [1973] IR 121); but when he founds his action or an existing tort he is normally confined to the limitations of that tort. It might be different if it could be shown that the tort in question is basically ineffective to protect his constitutional right.

What should the court say to a plaintiff who claims damages for the infringement of a constitutional right against a trade union where the alleged misconduct falls clearly within the well-established parameters of a particular tort? Is the Court to dismiss the action, or could it hold that this is a case where the tort in question is 'basically ineffective to protect his constitutional right'? A narrow, formalistic answer would be that the tort is perfectly effective and that it is s. 13 which renders it ineffective. As against this, it might be replied that torts are the normal vehicles for effectuation through damages of an individual's constitutional rights. Where these vehicles prove seriously defective for any reason the Court should fall back on its general entitlement to award damages for the particular infringement of constitutional rights. To deny the Court this power would be to create an anomolous and arguably unconstitutional distinction based on an accident of history, since the common law accretion to the corpus of tortious liability over the centuries occurred in sublime ignorance of the relatively recent developments of jurisprudence epitomised in *Byrne* and *Meskell*.

Apart from this difficulty s. 13 must raise constitutional problems in the area of equality. Why should trade unions be *totally* exempt from liability in tort, in the circumstances prescribed by the section, when other persons or bodies have no similar immunity? Two points may be made in reply. The first is that Article 40.1 can have no application since a trade union is not a human person. The precise remit of Article 40.1 is of course a matter of some debate but, even if we assume that it has no reference to inequalities between bodies that are not human persons, on the one hand, and human persons, on the other, there must surely be a principle of fairness underlying the Constitution which protects an abuse of fair play which impinges on the protection of such fundamental rights as those of bodily integrity and of property. The second point in defence of s. 13 is that it deals with a unique situation of regulating trade disputes, to which a distinctive legal response, albeit one impinging on the rights of others, is appropriate, in the interests of giving employees some muscle in the protection of their interests as a group.

Picketing S. 11 modifies the immunity from liability for peaceful picketing. It may be useful to set out the terms of the section in full:

> (1) It shall be lawful for one or more persons, acting on their own behalf or on behalf of a trade union in contemplation or furtherance of a trade dispute, to attend at, or where that is not practicable, at the approaches to, a place where their employer works or carries on business, if they so attend merely for the purpose of peacefully obtaining or communicating information or of peacefully persuading any person to work or abstain from working.
>
> (2) It shall be lawful for one or more persons acting on their own behalf or on behalf of a trade union in contemplation or furtherance of a trade dispute, to attend at, or where that is not practicable, at the approaches to, a place where an employer who is not a party to the trade dispute works or carries on business if, but only if, it is reasonable for those who are so attending to believe at the commencement of their attendance and throughout the continuance of their attendance that that employer has

directly assisted their employer who is a party to the trade dispute for the purpose of frustrating the strike or other industrial action, provided that such attendance is merely for the purpose of peacefully obtaining or communicating information or of peacefully persuading any person to work or abstain from working.

(3) For the avoidance of doubt any action taken by an employer in the health services to maintain life-preserving services during a strike or other industrial action shall not constitute assistance for the purposes of subs. (2).

(4) It shall be lawful for a trade union official to accompany any member of his union whom he represents provided that the member is acting in accordance with the provisions of subs. (1) or (2) and provided that such official is attending merely for the purpose of peacefully obtaining or communicating information or of peacefully persuading any person to work or abstain from working.

(5) For the purposes of this section 'trade union official' means any paid official of a trade union or any officer of a union or branch of a union elected or appointed in accordance with the rules of a union.

As regards subs. (1), which deals with primary picketing, it may be noted that it authorises picketing, not only *at* a place where the employer works or carries on business, but also *at the approaches* to such a place where it is not practicable to picket at the place. Thus, for example, it would be permissible to picket an employer at the entrance to an industrial estate or shopping centre in cases where the picketers were not permitted to enter the estate or centre. See further the ICTU *Users' Guide*, pp. 18-19, Kerr, Annotation to the Act, General Note to s 11. The phenomenon of pickets thus being placed at the entrance to industrial estates or shopping centres (or, indeed, ports or airports) was criticised as less than ideal, from opposing standpoints, during the Oireachtas Debates. Deputy Rabbitte considered that to remove a picketer to such a distance, bearing in mind the vast area involved, meant that 'he might as well be waving his picket at the moon. The picket will have no impact'. 398 Dáil Debs, col 504. Deputy Jim Mitchell, on the other hand, stressed the damage to businesses unconnected with the dispute which might flow from a picket placed at the entrance to an area where many businesses operate: *id.*, cols. 498-9. While commercial common sense may encourage the owner of the area to permit picketing at the place where the employer in the dispute works or carries on business, this will not always be the position.

It may be worth mentioning the (surely faint) hope of trade unionists that a constitutional right of free speech, encapsulated in picketing, might here be held to circumscribe the conditional right of property where the area trespassed upon has a 'public' dimension, as does an airport or shopping centre, for example. In Canada, Laskin CJ, in a dissenting judgment in *Harrison v Carswell* [1976] SCR 200, saw merit in this line of thought. See further Ulmer, 'Picketing in Shopping Centres', (1975) 13 *Osgoode Hall LJ* 879; see also *Rosso v Ontario Jockey Club*, 46 DLR (4th) 359, at 363 (Ontario High Court, Boland J, 1987). In Australia the claim by trespassing trade unionists to immunity by virtue of Articles 19 and 22 of the International Covenant on Civil and Political Rights was given short shrift by Morling J in *Concrete Constructions (NSW) Pty Ltd v Australian Building Construction Employees' and Builders Labourers' Federation*, 83 ALR 385 (Federal Court of Australia, Gen Div, 1988). For brief consideration of the position in the United States see McMahon & Binchy, *op. cit.*, 433, fn. 40.

S. 11(2) introduces a significant restriction on the right to engage in secondary picketing. It makes it necessary for the picketers to believe, on *reasonable grounds* that the picketed employer has *directly assisted their employer for the purpose of frustrating the strike or other industrial action*. Thus, even if the picketed employer's acts have had the *inevitable consequence* of frustrating a strike, this would not suffice: the picketers must have reasonable grounds to believe that the picketed employer actually intends to bring about this consequence.

The requirement of secret ballots S. 14 of the Act (which comes into effect on 18 July 1992) introduces significant new requirements as to holding of secret ballots. These requirements, important in their own right, have equally crucial consequences in relation to the law of tort. Trade unions that do not submit to the Registrar of Friendly Societies a copy of their rules as to statutory ballots will lose their negotiation licence (and thus the protection of ss. 11 to 13): ss. 9(1) and 16. Moreover in proceedings relating to a strike or other industrial action by a trade union or group of workers *in disregard of or contrary to the outcome of a secret ballot relating to the issues involved in the dispute*, the defendants are prohibited from calling ss. 10, 11 or 12 in aid: s. 17(1). Finally, *compliance* with the statutory requirements as to secret ballot gives those engaging in a strike or other industrial action extra entitlements to resist the granting of an *ex parte* injunction on behalf of the employers as well as interlocutory injunctions in many cases (s. 19).

Restriction of right to an injunction S. 19, as we have indicated, provides that, where a secret ballot held in accordance with the requirements of s. 14 favours a strike or other industrial action and the trade union has given the employer at least a week's notice of its intention to engage in the strike or other industrial action, the employer may not apply *ex parte* for an injunction: subs (1). Nor may the court grant an injunction restraining the strike or other industrial action where the respondent establishes a fair case that he was acting in contemplation or furtherance of a trade dispute: subs (2). Neither of these restrictions applies in respect of proceedings arising out of or relating to:

> (a) unlawfully entering into or remaining upon any property belonging to another, or unlawfully causing damage or causing or permitting damage to be caused to the property of another, or
> (b) any action resulting or likely to result in death or personal injury: subs. (3).

Thus malicious damage, violence, threats of violence and even hunger-strikes do not render a respondent immune from an injunction on the basis that he has established a fair case that he was acting in contemplation or furtherance of a trade dispute.

S. 19 gives rise to constitutional difficulties. Subs. (2) is drafted in such a way as to prevent the court from granting an injunction, *even at the suit of a third party*, simply on account of the existence of a fair case that the respondent was acting in contemplation or furtherance of a trade dispute. In many instances, it will be no defence in a tort action for the respondent to establish the fact that he was so acting. S. 19(2) requires the court to stand idly by while an innocent third party's economic or reputational interests, constitutional and legal, are being damaged by a tortfeasor who has no statable defence amd where the balance of convenience is strongly in favour of granting the injunction. Strikes can last a long time. This frustration of the administration of justice may be considered to infringe the victim's constitutional rights; it may also offend against the separation of the powers. It is of course a worthwhile legislative policy to encourage adherence by trade unions to the statutory requirements on ballots; but this is hardly so pressing a *desideratum* as to warrant such overbreadth. The qualifications in subs. (4) go some way, but arguably not sufficiently far, to preserve the constitutional validity of the section as a whole.

Trade union rationalisation With a view to encouraging trade union rationalisation the Act includes a stick and a carrot. S. 21 provides the stick: this is a doubling of the membership requirement for a new union seeking a negotiation licence from 500 to 1000 and a substantial increase in the High Court deposit required by such a union. The idea here is to improve on the attempt made in the Trade Unions Act 1971 'to forestall the establishment of small, poorly financed or breakaway unions in areas already serviced by existing unions': 125 Seanad Debs, col. 2088 (10 July 1990). S. 22 offers the carrot, by extending the scope of the system of grants introduced by the Trade Union Act 1975 in respect of expenses incurred by unions in a merger. Under the 1975 Act the funds were available only when the merger was successfully accomplished. S. 22 enables expenses to be claimed even where an attempt at merger was proved fruitless.

Industrial relations generally Part III effects important changes in the process of industrial dispute resolution. It establishes a new body, the Labour Relations Commission, whose functions include the provision of conciliation and advisory services and the development of codes of practice, with the equality service and the rights Commissioner service acting as independent units of the Commission. The reasoning behind this move was that employers and employees were resorting too quickly to the Labour Court and that it would be preferable to encourage them, as far as practicable, to resolve their disputes themselves. Reflecting one of the tenets of Alternative Dispute Resolution, the Minister argued that '[t]he parties should be more committed to an agreement that they have worked out together through negotiation than to an adjudication handled down by a third party'. 396 Dáil Debs, col. 748.

The statistics afford *some* support for the perception of over-eager reference to the Labour Court but are a good deal less than conclusive. The Court issued about 100 recommendations per annum in the 1960s. By 1983, the number had risen to 1,045. Since then it declined to 708 in 1988 and 646 in 1989. It could be argued that, rather than indicating a significant element of undue reliance on the Labour Court, these statistics primarily reflect changing practices in the broad field of industrial relations over the past decade. The Labour Court resisted the proposed subtraction of an important part of its conciliatory role; it was sceptical as to why the Commission should do a better job in this area than it had done: see Kerr's Annotation to the Act, General Note to s. 24.

The Commission's membership is tripartite, its seven members being appointed by the Minister (s. 24). The Chairman is Mr Dan McAuley, former Director General of the Federated Union of Employers; the other six members come from employer, trade union and other labour-related backgrounds. The Chief Executive (s. 28) is Mr Kieran Mulvey, former General Secretary of the Association of Secondary Teachers, Ireland. The Commission was established on 21 January 1991: Labour Relations Commission (Establishment) Order 1991 (SI No. 7 of 1991).

S. 25 spells out in detail the functions of the Commission. The general remit is one of responsibility for promoting the improvement of industrial relations. Specific functions include the provision of conciliation and industrial relations advisory services, the preparation of codes of practice relevant to industrial relations (cf. ss. 42-43) and assisting joint labour committees (cf. ss. 44-50) and joint industrial councils in the exercise of other functions. Except where there is specific provision for the direct reference of trade disputes to the Labour Court, they are first to be referred to the Commission or its appropriate services: s. 25(3).

The Labour Court is *not* to investigate unless it receives a report from the Commission stating that it is satisfied that no further efforts on its part will advance the resolution of the dispute, and the parties have requested the court to investigate it (s. 26(1). The Court may, however, investigate a dispute, again on the request of the parties, if the Chairman of the Commission (or authorised member or officer) notifies the court that in the circumstances specified in the notice the Commission waives its function of conciliation in the disputer: s. 26(3). Moreover, where the Court, following consultation with the Commission, is of opinion that there are exceptional circumstances which warrant its so doing, it may investigate a dispute which it would otherwise be precluded from investigating: s. 26(5).

INSOLVENCY OF EMPLOYER

The Protection of Employees (Employers' Insolvency) (Variation of Limit) Regulations 1990 (SI No. 17 of 1990) increase the limit of an employee's weekly remuneration from £211.54 to £250 for the purposes of calculating benefits under the Protection of Employees (Employers' Insolvency) Act 1984. The increased ceiling applies to debts arising under the Act where the date of termination of employment or the date of insolvency is on or after 1 February 1990. (In certain circumstances the employee has the option of nominating whichever date is more favourable to him).

NON-RENEWAL OF CONTRACT

In *Hickey v Eastern Health Board* [1990] ELR 177, the applicant was a qualified state registered nurse who had been engaged by the respondent as a part-time temporary staff nurse at a hospital since 1980. This involved successive terms of three months, renewed from time to time. In 1987 her employment was terminated on the basis that this was necessary on account of 'Government Embargo on the non-filling (*sic*) of vacancies and the Board's reduced Budget allocation'. The applicant obtained leave to apply for an order of *certiorari* on the ground that this termination had been made in breach of the rules of constitutional and natural justice in that no hearing was afforded to her before she was dismissed.

Gannon J dismissed the application and the Supreme Court affirmed. In his judgment (with which McCarthy and O'Flaherty JJ concurred), Finlay CJ accepted that the applicant was an officer, as distinct from a servant, of the Board. This followed from Barrington J's judgment in *Western Health Board v Quigley* [1982] ILRM 390. But the Chief Justice was equally satisfied, on the basis of the Supreme Court decision of *Glover v BLN Ltd* [1973] IR 388, that the applicant's rights in regard to dismissal did not depend on any such distinction but rather 'on the question of the grounds for and circumstances of her dismissal'. The Supreme Court decisions of *Garvey v Ireland* [1981] IR75 and *Flynn v An Post* [1987] IR 68 were authorities in support of this proposition.

The Chief Justice was satisfied that, had the applicant been dismissed for *misconduct*, then, irrespective of whether she was an officer or servant, she would have been entitled, as a matter of natural justice, to a fair hearing with knowledge of the charges against her before a decision to dismiss her was taken. *Maunsell v The Minister for Education* [1940] IR 213 did not support the contention that an officer of a statutory or Local Authority Board or of the State had special rights to a hearing, irrespective of the reason for his or her dismissal. *Maunsell* had turned on the individual provisions of the regulations concerning assistant teachers and did not support any general proposition regarding the making of officers redundant.

The reality of the applicant's complaint was that she had been chosen as the person to be made redundant when others whose engagement was not terminated had entered the employment of the Board later than she had done. Finlay CJ admitted that it was possible to understand a sense of grievance arising from that fact but he was satisfied that 'there was not . . . in the facts of this case any legal right to the application of such a principle with regard to the termination of her employment'. The Board in failing to renew her temporary periodic engagement as a part-time staff nurse, had been entitled to so decide and the affidavit filed by it gave valid grounds for that decision. There could be no question, nor had there been any allegation, that the decision had been arbitrary or capricious or induced by a wrong motive. The terms of the letter informing the claimant of the decision were the clearest possible indication of the absence of any suggestion of misconduct.

PENSIONS

The Pensions Act 1990 seeks to protect the pension entitlements of people changing jobs by ensuring that in moving they will not lose rights that have accrued, that the value of these rights will not be wiped out by inflation and that the temptation to cash them in when moving will no longer be capable of being legally given effect. The Act also opens up pension schemes to the gaze of interested parties and improves the range of protection for them in relation to defaulting trustees. It established An Bord Pinsean — The Pension Board, whose functions include supervising the operation of the Act and pensions developments generally; it has wide-ranging investigative powers. The Act also introduces a funding standard, by which pension schemes must have sufficient resources to provide the promised benefits. Finally, the Act implements an EC Directive in relation to equal treatment for men and women in occupational benefit schemes.

Part I: General provisions   In this Part, we need here merely note s. 3, which prescribes that contravention by trustees, actuaries or auditors of schemes of a provision of the Act is an offence, punishable on summary conviction by a maximum penalty of one year's imprisonment and a fine of £1,000 or on indictment by 2 year's imprisonment and a fine of £10,000. The Board may prosecute for summary offences. We consider the effect of s. 3 in the particular context of s. 59, in Part IV, below. Part I came into operation on 21 December 1990: Pensions Act 1990 (Parts I and II) (Commencement) Order 1990 (SI No. 331 of 1990).

Part II: Establishment of Pensions Board   Part II provides for the establishment of An Bord Pinsean — The Pensions Board. Details of its membership and procedures are set out in the First Schedule. Para 8 of the First Schedule provides that the ordinary members are to include a trade union member, an employers' member, two personal representatives of occupational pension schemes, as well as representatives of the actuarial, accounting and legal professions, together with representations of the Ministers for Finance and Social Welfare. As well as these nine members, the Minister for Social Welfare has the right to nominate directly three ordinary members. See further 126 Seanad Debs, col. 580 (17 July 1990). The Board was established on 21 December 1990: Pensions Act 1990 (Part II) (Establishment Day) Order 1990.

S. 10 sets out the functions of the Board. The most important is to monitor and supervise the operation of the Act and pensions developments generally. Other functions include that of advising the Minister for Social Welfare on matters relating to pensions generally and issuing guidance on the representatives of trustees of schemes as well as codes of practice. The Minister of Social Welfare, with the consent of the Minister for Finance, may confer additional functions on the Board: s. 11.

The Board has power to investigate the state and conduct of a scheme, to require employers or trustees to furnish it with information, explanation, books of account and other documents and, through its authorised employees, to enter premises for these purposes: s. 18(1)-(4), Failure to comply with these powers constitutes an offence: s. 18(5). (The Act has wisely avoided the temptation to introduce 'deemed contempt' provisions here). Part II came into operation on 21 December 1990: Pensions Act 1990 (Parts I and II) (Commencement) Order 1990.

Part III: Preservation of benefits Part III deals with the problem, endemic before the legislation was enacted, that so few occupational pension schemes in the private sector made adequate provision to protect the pension entitlements of those who changed jobs, especially in relation to maintaining the real value of these entitlements. This in turn led to the widespread practice of employees seeking a refund of their contributions. The overall result was of course, bad for these mobile employees, but it had wider social implications in that it indirectly placed a greater burden of support on the State when the employees retired.

Part III therefore preserves pension rights with an option to transfer the equivalent value of members' entitlements to another suitable scheme. S. 28 prescribes as a condition of eligibility that the employee must have completed at least 5 years' qualifying service of which at least 2 fall after the commencement of the Act.

We need here only note that ss. 29 and 30 distinguish as between levels of benefit preserved on the basis of whether a 'defined benefit scheme' or a 'defined contribution scheme' is involved. In the case of the former, the scheme must preserve an appropriate part of any benefit for service after the commencement date; in the case of the latter, the amount of preserved benefit is equal to the actuarial value of the contributions accumulated on behalf of the member at the date of payment in respect of that service.

S. 32 provides that a member of a scheme who is entitled to preserved benefit under the scheme is *not* entitled to receive a refund of any contributions paid to it *after the commencement of Part III*. The Minister explained that this prohibition was 'essential, since to do otherwise would not result in any improvement in the existing situation': 126 Seanad Debs, col. 583 (17 July 1990). Refunds will continue to be payable where a member fails to fulfil the qualifying service requirement of 5 years, for preservation of benefit.

In order to deal with the problem of preserved benefits losing their value with the passage of time, s. 33 provides for a *minimum* revaluation at 4% per annum or the increase in the consumer price index, whichever is the lesser. The Minister for Social Welfare, has power to alter the 4% figure. The Minister resisted a proposal from the National Pensions Board that, where the rate of inflation is between 4 and 10%, an additional increase or half the excess over 4% should apply: see 126 Seanad Debs, col. 584.

S. 34 permits a member of a funded scheme who is entitled to a preserved benefit to receive a 'transfer payment' as an alternative to his preserved benefit entitlement. This is equivalent to the actuarial value of the preserved benefit including an appropriate element for revaluation. The member may exercise this right by directing the trustees of the scheme to transfer the payment to another scheme or to purchase an annuity contract from an approved life office. The member has 2 years from leaving on which to exercise this right, or such longer period as the trustees may determine.

S. 37 enables the Minister, by regulations, to exclude from the application of the preservation requirements under Part III schemes already having a comparable system of preservation and revaluation for early leavers. The Minister expressed his intention to exclude public sector schemes operating on these lines: 126 Seanad Debs, col. 586. Part III came into operation on 1 January 1991: Pensions Act 1990 (Part III, IV and V) (Commencement) Order 1990 (SI No. 330 of 1990).

Part IV: Funding standard   Part IV is designed to prevent employers from making pension promises to their employees which are beyond the means of the business to sustain. It introduces a *funding standard*, which will be ratified if, in the opinion of an actuary, the resources of the scheme at the time he gives a certificate would have been sufficient, if the scheme had then been wound up, to provide for its liabilities for pensions in the course of being paid to existing beneficiaries, additional voluntary contributions made, transfer value entitlements and the benefits that have accrued in respect of service from the time of commencement of the Act. Trustees of schemes to which this Part applies (cf. s. 41) must submit to the Board a certificate to this effect; the certificate must be renewed every 3.5 years. After a transition period of 10 years, every such scheme must have reached a funding standard which will enable it to discharge fully the accrued benefit expectations of its members. The certificate at that time will have to address this extra burden.

It seems that accounting bodies, in their Statement of Standard Accounting Practice No. 24, had relatively recently dealt with the question of disclosure of pension costs in the accounts of employees. It already applies in full to quoted Irish registered companies and will apply to non-quoted Irish companies from 1993: see 126 Seanad Debs, col. 589-90. Part IV came into operation on 1 January 1991: Pensions Act 1990 (Parts III, IV and V) (Commencement) Order 1990 (SI No. 330 of 1990).

Part V: Disclosure of information in relation to schemes   Part V deals with the recurrent phenomenon of employees not being given full information about the pension schemes of which they are members. S. 54 prescribes a wide-ranging duty of disclosure on the trustees of the scheme.

They must give the information to members, prospective members, their spouses, those within the application of the scheme and qualifying or prospectively qualifying for its benefits and authorised trade unions representing the members. The information relates to the constitution of the scheme, its administration and finances, the rights and obligations arising under it and such other matters as appear to the Minister relevant to schemes in general or schemes of this particular description.

S. 55 requires trustees to prepare annual reports and s. 56 requires them to obtain actuarial valuations and audited accounts. S. 57 gives the Minister power to reduce the scope of these burdens for schemes where it would be unreasonable having regard to their nature and character and the size of the membership, to require the wider range of duties. The Occupational Pension Schemes (Disclosure of Information) Regulations 1991 (SI No. 215 of 1991) set out detailed provisions as to disclosure. Part V came into operation on 1 January 1991: Pensions Act 1990 (Parts III, IV and V) (Commencement) Order 1990 (SI No. 330 of 1990).

Part VI: Trustees   Part VI is designed to provide extra practical controls on trustees, rather than leave members, as formerly, to the uncertain and expensive course of suing the trustees for breach of trust. First s. 59 spells out the general duties of trustees of schemes as including:

(a) the duty to ensure, so far as is reasonable, that the contributions due to the scheme are received;
(b) the duty to provide for the proper investment of the resources of the scheme in accordance with its rules;
(c) the duty, where appropriate, to make arrangements for the payment of the benefits as provided by the scheme as they fall due; and
(d) the duty to ensure that proper membership and financial records are kept.

The sanctions for breach by trustees of their duties are stark. The High Court, on application of the board, may order the replacement of trustees who have failed to carry out their duties: s. 63. Moreover s. 3 makes it an offence (with maximum penalty on indictment of 2 years' imprisonment and a fine of £10,000) for a trustee to contravene, in his capacity as trustee, a provision of the Act. S. 59 seems to be drafted in such terms as to render a trustee potentially liable under s. 3 for breach of s. 59. If this is so, the question arises as to what *mens rea* requirements, if any, should be read into s. 3 in respect of such a breach. S. 59 prescribes duties which, at a minimum, call for the exercise of reasonable care by the trustees. The idea that an incompetent, good faith exercise of the office of trustee should occasion criminal liability may seem so radical as to give pause for thought. Unfortunately, s. 3 generated little discussion at Committee stage in the Dáil (400 Dáil Debs, cols. 231-38, 19 June 1990), none of it enlightening of the question of *mens rea*, and *no* discussion at Committee stage in the Seanad (126 Seanad Debs, col. 661, 17 July 1990). The Minister's remarks during Second Stage in the Seanad (*id.*, col. 596) support the view that non-compliance with s. 59 may generate liability under s. 3.

The question of the participation by members of schemes in the appointment of trustees had provoked a disagreement within the National Pensions Board. A majority were in favour of it, but a minority considered that it should be encouraged only through voluntary agreement between employers and members. In view of this divergence of views, the majority had recommended that there should be a three year delay before the statutory provision in this regard should come into effect. The solution adopted in the legislation is slightly more cautious. S. 62 empowers the Minister for Social Welfare to provide by regulations for such participation by members. The Minister made it clear that it was his intention to consult with the Board before the end of 1992, and to make regulations in early 1993 which will come into force from January 1994, three years after the Act came into effect: 126 Seanad Debs, col. 577 (17 July 1990).

S. 60 requires trustees of a scheme to ensure that it is registered with the Board within a year after the commencement of the section (on 1 January 1991: Pensions Act 1990 (ss. 60 and 61) (Commencement) Order 1990 (SI No. 329 of 1990) if the scheme was by then already in existence or, if not, within a year after it comes into existence.

Part VI: The equal treatment principle   Part VII of the Act fully implements the requirements of EC Directive 86/378 in relation to equal treatment for men and women in occupational benefit schemes. The main schemes covered are occupational pension and sick pay schemes. In accordance with the Directive, optional benefits, single member schemes and personal schemes are excluded: 126 Seanad Debs, col. 597.

S. 66 lays down the general principle that every occupational benefit scheme is to comply with the principle of equal treatment, which is defined in s. 67(1) as 'that there shall be no discrimination on the basis of sex in respect of any matter relating to an occupational benefit scheme'. This principle applies also to members' dependants: s. 67(2). S. 67(3) spells out an exclusive list of five cases where discrimination on the basis of sex is deemed to occur in this context:

(a) where because of a person's sex, he or she is treated less favourably than a person of the other sex;

(b) where a person is treated by reference to his marital or family status less favourably than a person of the other sex with the same status;

(c) where, because of a person's sex, he or she is unable to comply with a requirement or condition in respect of which the proportion of persons of the other sex able to comply with it is substantially higher than that of his or her sex and which is not justifiable irrespective of the sex of the person to whom it applies;

(d) where a similar inability arises because of a person's marital or family status; and

(e) where a person is penalised for having in good faith exercised his or her entitlements to complain under the relevant provision of Part VII.

S. 72 enables schemes to provide special treatment for women in connection with pregnancy or childbirth. These will not be considered to offend against the principle of equality: s. 69(1)(c).

Disputes relating to pension schemes are to be resolved by the Board: s. 75. Disputes concerning other occupational schemes are to be resolved by equality officers and the Labour Court according to procedures closely similar to the Anti-Discrimination (Pay) Act 1974 and the Employment Equality Act 1977: see ss. 77 to 80 of the 1990 Act.

REDUNDANCY PAYMENTS ACT 1967

In *Winston v The Director, Central Statistics Office* [1990] ELR 222, the claimant had been employed as an enumerator since 1970; he generally worked for two periods of five weeks each year collecting agricultural statistics. From 1983 onwards (save for 1986) he also did the Labour Force Survey each year. His work was subject to PAYE and PRSI deductions; it was paid in a lump sum at the end of each period of work. In 1989, the employer sent a letter to enumerators (including the claimant) explaining that the method of collecting agricultural statistics had changed to a new postal system which would be used in the next survey, so that temporary enumerators would not be required. The letter thanked the enumerators for their interest, commitment and co-operation in the work.

The claimant claimed that he was entitled to redundancy; he claimed that the letter was a dismissal. The Employment Appeals Tribunal found that his service had been continuous; it regarded the periods when he was not working as periods of lay off. S. 8(1)(a) of the Redundancy Payments Act 1967 was crucial. It provides that employees are not to become entitled to redundancy payments by reason of dismissal or lay off until a period equal to the average annual period of lay off over the four year period had elapsed after the date of dismissal or lay off. Here the average annual period of lay off was thirty eight weeks. The claimant's case had been brought before the expiration of this period and thus failed.

RETURN-TO-WORK FORMULA

In *Corcoran v Electricity Supply Board*, High Court, 10 May 1990, Barron J was called on to construe the terms of a clause of a return-to-work formula drawn up by an ESB Industrial Council to end a 'particularly bitter' unofficial strike. This stated:

> In the resolution of disputes of such duration and intensity it is customary as part of a return to work formula to have contained within it a provision that there will not be actions on either side which could be construed as vindictive or retaliation. In that spirit and on (*sic*) the hope that a more peaceful atmosphere will quickly return to the local scene, the Council finally recommends that there should be no victimisation on either side in regard to participation in the industrial action itself. Proven serious cases of endangering life or limb, misappropriation or damage to property or other matters with legal connotations could not of course be covered by a no victimisation clause of the kind the Council has in mind in this recommendation.

The strike ended on the basis of acceptance of this recommendation. The defendant had later sought the dismissal of a number of employees on the basis of their alleged conduct during the strike. The Industrial Council recommended dismissal of the three plaintiffs.

The plaintiffs accepted that, in the light of the formula, they could be dismissed if they had been successfully prosecuted in the courts for offences committed by them during the course of the strike. They conceded, moreover, that the matters alleged against them before the Industrial Council were of a sufficiently serious nature to warrant dismissal if established. They argued however, that the proper construction of the formula was that enforcement of disciplinary procedures was dependent on prior successful criminal proceedings.

Barron J rejected this argument. The formula had been drawn up by both parties, so an ambiguity could not be held against either. He considered that there was nothing in the recommendation to suggest the action by either party was dependent on Court action:

> The recommendation itself seeks to prevent action by the parties

themselves arising out of the strike. It purported to limit that action. If it had intended to impose the condition precedent of Court action on such limitation, it would have been expected that it would have done so. In construing the recommendation, regard should be had to its original 'non legal status'. Thus, it seemed to Barron J that words like 'proven', 'serious' and 'victimisation' had to bear the meanings attributable to them when the recommendation was issued. At that stage, there would have been no thought other than that any action taken would have been within the confines of industrial procedures. 'Proven' would thus have meant 'proved before the Industrial Council'. From this it followed that the proper construction to be placed on the recommendation was that it was intended that disciplinary procedures could be initiated, but whether they came within the terms of its no-victimisation clause and, if not, whether the matters complained of justified any particular action was a matter for the Industrial Council itself.

TERMINATION OF APPOINTMENTS

In *O'Callaghan v Meath Vocational Education Committee, McCormack and the Minister for Education*, High Court, 20 November 1990, Costello J dismissed the claim of a catechetics teacher for unlawful termination of his appointment as a permanent offer of the Vocational Education Committee. The plaintiff had been appointed on a temporary wholetime basis. He could be made permanent if he acquired the requisite qualification in Irish, had an acceptable qualification in another subject of the school programme, had his suitability for the permanent appointment confirmed by the catechetical inspectorate and (by virtue of s. 23 of the Vocational Education Act 1930) his permanent appointment received the approval of the Minister for Education.

The plaintiff's action failed on the simple ground that the requisite Ministerial approval had not been obtained, and that thus he never had acquired permanent status. However, Costello J expressed the view that the failure of the catechetical inspectorate, and the Bishop of Meath, for a year and a half to confirm the plaintiff in a permanent post did not amount to a breach of duty to the plaintiff. The post to be filled was a highly responsible one requiring very special pedagogical skills and it could well happen that a just, fair and conscientious decision on the suitability of an applicant could take this long to reach.

Since the decision, in effect, involved an assessment of the applicant's qualifications to fill a professional academic post, it was entirely different from those decisions taken by administrative bodies in respect of which the law imposed a duty to state reasons. Had proceedings been instituted to quash the Bishop's decision for failure to state reasons, Costello J did not think they would have been successful.

Costello J also dismissed the plaintiff's action for damages for conspiracy: the suggestion that any of the defendants had entered into an agreement to injure him was 'entirely a fanciful one'. Similarly the plaintiff's claim against the Bishop and the Minister for procuring or including the termination of his permanent position was unsuccessful. It had to fail since the applicant had never been appointed to a permanent post; but Costello J was also satisfied that no evidence of any sort supported it.

The plaintiff claimed damages for defamation against all defendants. He contended that the purported termination of his appointment and the summary nature in which it had been done exposed him to ridicule and contempt and portrayed him as incompetent, dishonest, corrupt, unreliable and unqualified.

Costello J rejected this claim for several reasons. The plaintiff had never been of permanent status and his temporary appointment had expired by efflux of time. The termination of an office such as the plaintiff had could not give rise to a claim for damages for defamation:

> If wrongful, the consequence may well result in the disparagement of the office holder in the eyes of reasonable people who learn of the termination. But if this resulted from knowledge they obtained otherwise than by a publication of it to them by the wrongdoer no action lies. The act of wrongful dismissal does not in itself involve the tort of defamation or injurious falsehood.

This is of course true; but it is possible to envisage some wrongful terminations which could indeed be defamatory. If, for example, an employer dismisses an employee summarily, this may constitute a defamation (to which, of course, the defence of qualified privilege may be available in appropriate cases). In this general context, it may be useful to refer to *Corliss and Diggin v Ireland*, High Court, Hamilton J, 23 July 1984: see McMahon & Binchy, *Irish Law of Torts* (2nd ed, 1990), 612.

Costello J also dismissed the plaintiff's claim for damages against the Minister for Education for breach of warranty, misrepresentation and deceit, based on a conversation the plaintiff had had with a civil servant in the Department who had said to him: 'I think you are qualified except for the Ceard Teastais [Gaeilge]'. (Though the plaintiff's version of the conversation was contested, Costello J accepted it for the purposes of the claims). The plaintiff argued that this assurance was at variance with the stance taken later by the Department (and communicated by the same civil servant to the

Vocational Education Committee) that the plaintiff lacked an acceptable qualification in another school subject.

Costello J had no difficulty in dispatching the claim for breach of warranty: there was no contractual relationship at any time existing between the plaintiff and the Minister. (This raises yet again the issue of whether the privity of contract rule needs a critical contemporary examination: see the 1987 Review, 113-4, and the 1989 Review, 121-3) .

As to the claim for misrepresentation, Costello J noted that it had not been pleaded that the civil servant's statement amounted to a tortious negligent misrepresentation. He presumed that this was because, even if a duty of care had existed towards the plaintiff, there was no evidence that the civil servant had arrived at the opinion in a negligent manner or was guilty of any negligence in expressing it or that it was the sort of statement which would found an action for damages for negligent misstatement. The claim for deceit was unsustainable since the statement was one of *opinion* as to the suitability of the plaintiff's qualifications rather than of fact; there had, moreover been no evidence that the civil servant had known the opinion to be wrong or that he had made it recklessly. See further McMahon & Binchy, *op cit.*, (2nd ed, 1990), 664-73. Furthermore the plaintiff had failed to prove that he had suffered any damage by the alleged deceit for which he was entitled to compensation: Costello J did not think that the plaintiff's efforts in acquiring of an extra academic qualification amounted to such a loss. Perhaps some may disagree. Undergoing the study for that qualification may well have caused the plaintiff financial loss as well as the diversion of his energies from other potentially beneficial, economic activities. The fact that an academic qualification represents an achievement which itself may enhance a person's economic standing does not prevent it from ever representing on balance a financial loss for which compensation in the tort of deceit may be forthcoming. Whether it did so in any particular case would seem a matter requiring evidential resolution.

UNFAIR DISMISSAL

1 Appeal procedure S. 10(4) of the Unfair Dismissals Act 1977 provides that a party may appeal to the Circuit Court from any determination of the Employment Appeals Tribunal in relation to a claim for redress under the Act 'within six weeks from the date on which the determination is communicated to the parties'. In *Morris v Power Supermarkets Ltd*, High Court, 9 March 1990, Barron J held that the essence of an appeal under s. 10(4) is neither the issue nor service of a notice of appeal as such but *the invoking of the jurisdiction* of the Circuit Court. This is done by the issue of the originating document, usually a civil bill, but in the present case a notice of application to the Court in the form prescribed by O. 63 of the Circuit Court Rules 1950, In Barron J's view, time ceases to run, as with the Statute of Limitations 1957, when the proceedings are issued and not when they are served.

In the instant case, the notice of application had been issued within the six weeks period but owing to an oversight, and in spite of enquiries made by the applicant's solicitors, not served for some weeks. Barron J held that the application was not statute-barred.

2 Constructive dismissal

(a) 'Cooling off period In *O'Connor v Garvey* [1990] ELR 228, the claimant had been employed as manager of the butcher counter in a branch of the respondent's supermarket. He was transferred to another branch on the basis that he needed more training. This followed a report on a store inspection which had criticised certain aspects of the meat department's operation. When informed of the decision to transfer him, the claimant raised no objection. When the claimant reported for work at the other branch he was assigned to cutting and wrapping cabbage. A person who had come into the shop to service equipment made some unfounded and hurtful remarks about the reason for the claimant's move. This upset the claimant who was, moreover, concerned about the drop in wages which he would sustain since his new work involved less hours. (The precise amount of this drop had not yet been clarified). He went to the manager with a letter of resignation. The manager suggested that he work in another shop; this was not acceptable to the claimant. The manager then proposed that he let the matter rest for a week. The claimant did not return to work. The employer, who assumed he had resigned, did not seek to contact him.

The Tribunal held that the claimant had been constructively dismissed. The claimant should not be held bound by his initial acceptance of the transfer. It was not unreasonable for him, a couple of hours after he had taken up work in the new shop, to have had second thoughts on the matter. The unfounded comments by the service man had the effect of triggering in the claimant's mind that he was being unfairly treated by the respondent company. The Tribunal recognised that the service man was outside the control of the respondent but added (surely by way of *non sequitur*) that 'it was the respondent's decision that caused the claimant to be in the [particular] shop'.

In the Tribunal's opinion, a good employer in a similar situation would not have accepted an employee's resignation but instead would have 'put a hold' on the resignation for a specified period, for the benefit of both sides.

While this had happened, the onus was on the employer, within that period, to consider and investigate the reason for the resignation and to come back to the employee within that period. There had been no evidence of any such effort. Accordingly, the Tribunal was of the view that the claimant had been dismissed one week after he had handed in his letter of resignation.

The Tribunal then considered the question whether the dismissal had been fair. They held that it had not. The respondent company's decision to send the claimant to work in the other branch for an indefinite period, in a lower position and without having informed him of his rate of pay 'amounted to a significant breach in contract of employment'. This holding seems difficult to understand. The precise terms of the claimant's contract of employment were not discussed anywhere in the Tribunal's determination. Moreover, the claimant's case was not expressly based on the breach of this contract. It seems reasonable to hypothesise (in the absence of a reference to any evidence on the point) that a contract of this nature would not be inconsistent with the employers' entitlement to shift an employee to another branch on a temporary basis at a reduced salary (by reason of less hours being worked) if the employee's work record indicated the desirability of such a move. Even if this is not so, and, let us assume, the move was not authorised by the contract of employment, the employers would certainly have been entitled to have sought to secure their employee's agreement to a change in his terms of employment. The evidence suggested that the employee did agree initially to the change (if such it was). When subsequently he evinced unhappiness with the new regime, he did so by professing to resign rather than to contest the entitlement of his employers to act as they had done. Presumably the Tribunal would not commit itself to the radical proposition that any attempt by an employer to secure the agreement by an employee to a variation in the terms of employment is necessarily unfair.

Having found that the claimant had been unfairly dismissed, the Tribunal addressed the question of the appropriate remedy under s. 7. They considered that, since the claimant had contributed to his dismissal, the most appropriate remedy was compensation reduced by 60% to take account of the claimant's contribution.

(b) Undermining manager's authority In *O'Beirne v Carmine Construction and Glaire Enterprises Ltd* [1990] ELR 232, the claimant was manager of a hotel, responsible for the general running of it, the appointment and dismissal of staff and the arrangement of staff rotas. A rift occurred between the managing director (with whom the claimant had a close personal relationship) and the owner of the hotel as to how it should be re-financed. The owner, moreover, was not happy about the personal relationship: in his evidence to the Tribunal he said that he had told the managing director and

the claimant to find accommodation elsewhere.

The gravamen of the claimant's case was that several staff changes were made without her consent, their effect being to completely undermine her position. Employees whom she had engaged and whom she had found satisfactory and competent were dismissed and others whom she had dismissed for valid reasons had been re- employed without consultation. In addition new staff had been taken on without discussion. Quite often she had heard about staff changes from members of the staff or from customers. This embarrassed her and, she said, made her a laughing stock in the eyes of the staff. After having given in her notice on three occasions (according to the evidence of the owner) she resigned.

The tribunal (with one dissentient) decided that she had been constructively dismissed. Her position had been gradually undermined. It appeared that, following the rift with the managing director, the owner's desire was to get rid of the old administration and replace it with his own administration. His interference in relation to the hiring and dismissal of staff which was a function of the manager was 'completely unjustified'. The claimant's belief that she had no option but to leave had been reasonable in the circumstances.

3 Ill-health and incapacity   In *Bolger v Showerings (Ireland) Ltd* [1990] ELR 184 (*ex tempore*), the issue was whether the employee's ill-health rendered him incapable of performing his duties as a forklift driver. The employee had been clearly informed, in correspondence, of the employer's concerns. On three occasions he had been asked to provide his doctor's opinion as to his likely return to work date. In reply, he submitted a letter from a locum of his general practitioner, setting out the general practitioner's view that he would never be able to work and that at some time in the near future he would be admitted to hospital. At no stage was a likely return to work date furnished. The employer dismissed him at this point.

Lardner J approached the issue of the fairness of the dismissal by noting that it was for the employer to show that (1) it was the ill health which was the reason for the dismissal, (2) this was 'substantial reason', (3) the employee received fair notice that the question of his dismissal for incapacity was being considered and (4) the employee was afforded an opportunity of being heard . Lardner J held that, in the circumstances of the case, the employer was not obliged to await the results from the hospital. If this had been the first or one of a very few instances of absence a different view might have been taken but in the light of his case history the employer was entitled to say that the employee himself thought he was unfit to return to work. Different considerations might well have applied if the employer and employee were at odds over his fitness for work: in that case it might well have been appropriate to await the results of the medical tests.

4 Jurisdiction In *Duffy-Finn v Lundbeck Ltd* [1990] ELR 224, the claimant had entered into negotiations with his employer to settle his claim before the Tribunal heard the proceedings. These negotiations were carried on by a trade union representative on his behalf. Settlement was reached five days before then; by its terms, the claimant was deemed to have resigned rather than being dismissed; it also provided that the claimant would withdraw his claim on foot of the employer's affording him a normal reinstatement. The claimant later changed his mind.

The Tribunal held that it had no jurisdiction to hear the case, even though the claimant had never withdrawn the claim. The settlement was binding on the parties. In view of its terms the Tribunal had 'no option but to hold that there was no dismissal, to treat the claimant's claim as withdrawn' and to find that if had no further jurisdiction in the matter. It would perhaps have been better if the tribunal had limited its holdings to its lack of jurisdiction rather than, as well, to make the finding that there was no dismissal. If it had no jurisdiction, it could not, and should not, have purported to make a holding premised on its having that jurisdiction. Moreover, to conclude from the content of the terms of a settlement that any particular factual situation existed would seem quite misconceived.

5 Non-compliance with Management Committee's instructions In *Purcell v The Board of Management, Tallaght Community School* [1990] ELR 218, the claimant was employed as a manager at the respondent's sports complex. Certain irregularities with regard to the running of the complex came to light. An investigation was initiated. A meeting of the Management Committee took place at which the claimant was present. He was instructed to close a particular account (the Water Babies Account), which was used for the payment of wages to certain employees from whom tax and PRSI were not being deducted. He was also instructed to deduct tax and PRSI from all employees. At a joint meeting of the Board of Management and Management Committee a year and a half later, the claimant informed those present that all employees were subject to these deductions; he also told the meeting that all books and accounts were available to the auditors. It later transpired that neither the Water Babies Account nor another account had been submitted to the auditors.

Two months later, the school Principal learned about the continuing vitality of the Tallaght Water Babies Account. He also was told by a part-time employee that a separate account had been opened to pay part-time instructors in cash and avoid tax and PRSI deductions.

It transpired that, a few months before the joint meeting of the Board of Management and Management Committee, the claimant had called a meeting of part-time instructors and suggested to them that, in order to avoid the payment of tax and PRSI, the instructors could form themselves into an independent club. He expressed his willingness to be president of the club but said that he would withdraw from the club when it was in operation. The claimant was the sole operator of the account, of whose existence the auditors of the management committee were unaware.

On learning these facts the board of management suspended the claimant with pay. It sent him a questionnaire relative to the matters under investigation. He replied to this two months later. A meeting took place between the parties after a further two months. A series of questions to be put to the claimant at the meeting had been sent to him in advance of the meeting. He attended the meeting, with his union representative. The board's decision was that the claimant could not be re-instated because his credibility was in question. The claimant refused to resign. A fortnight later the board decided to dismiss the claimant. It informed him of this intention, inviting him to make any submission he wished over the coming weeks to show why he should not be dismissed. The claimant obtained an extension of this period but, as matters transpired, made no submission. He was then dismissed.

The Employment Appeals Tribunal held that the dismissal was not unfair. The principal reason for it had been the board's lack of confidence in him as a result of his setting up the club and his handling of the club account. The Tribunal, therefore, did not take into consideration any of the other matters referred to by the board. The Tribunal made no finding as to whether the club accounts had been properly managed.

The Tribunal found that the claimant had opened the club account for the purpose of avoiding the deduction of tax and PRSI from the part-time instructors. He had done this without informing the management committee and contrary to an instruction which he had received from them to make these deductions. He had, too, misled the management committee and board of management when he told them that tax and PRSI were being deducted from the wages of all employees. These actions amounted to misconduct warranting dismissal.

6 *Pregnancy*   In *Maxwell v English Language Institute* [1990] ELR 226, the claimant had been employed as a secretary by the respondent. There was a conflict of evidence as to whether the employment was on a permanent basis (as the claimant alleged) or on a temporary basis which might be changed to permanent if she worked well (as the respondent alleged). Within a week of her having given the respondent's director a letter of her intention to take maternity leave, she was dismissed. The claimant said in evidence that she had never been reprimanded about her work and had been late for

work on only one occasion. The respondent's director said that the claimant had been unsatisfactory in her work, but that no warning had been issued (save on the occasion when she was late) because, since the claimant was temporary, there was no point in taking disciplinary action against her. The termination of her employment, the director insisted, had not been related to her pregnancy. The managing director gave similar evidence as to the claimant's temporary status and the reason for termination of her employment.

The tribunal, with one dissentient, was satisfied on the balance of probabilities that the claimant had been dismissed by reason of pregnancy, and that the dismissal was thus unfair by virtue of s. 6(2) of the 1977 Act.

7 Third party concerns In *Sheehan v Keating's Bakery Ltd* [1990] ELR 155, the claimant was employed by the respondent as a merchandiser of its products to a supermarket chain. At one of the supermarkets, an incident occurred. The claimant picked up a carton of orange and was looking at it; what happened when the assistant manager came in was the subject of later disagreement. The assistant manager said that the claimant threw the carton on the bottom shelf; the assistant manager characterised this as theft. The claimant, however, said that the assistant manager asked him what he was doing and told him to put the carton back and get back to work.

The claimant was subsequently barred from all the supermarkets in this chain. Since he could no longer do the work for which he had been employed, his employer dismissed him, even though it did not believe the allegation of larceny.

The Tribunal held that the claimant had been unfairly dismissed. An unascertainable allegation had been made against him with unfortunate consequences flowing from it. The respondent had attempted to undo the wrong but had failed to do so comprehensively in its dealings with the supermarket chain, in spite of its *bona fides*. The obligations owed by an employer to an employee in such circumstances were very high. A grave allegation having been made, steps such as requesting a meeting at the highest level with the supermarket chain should have been taken so as to have had the matter dealt with. An endeavour should have been made to have the details of the allegation clarified. The Tribunal accepted that the employer was under 'enormous pressure' in its dealings with the supermarket chain, but was of the view that the dismissal had nonetheless been unfair.

The approach of the Tribunal was thus to concentrate on the employer's obligation to negotiate with the third party rather than to confront the issue of principle. The strong response of the third party to the incident gives little reason for believing that further communications would have led to a change in its stance. The issue of general principle is whether an employee whose ability to do the job is frustrated in effect by a decision made by a third party can insist on his employer finding some other employment for him. Does the answer depend on whether the third party's attitude is (i) *correct* in that it is based on accurate factual premises, bearing a proportionate relationship to the facts or (ii) *reasonable* in that it bears a proportionate relationship to factual premises which are reasonable to adopt though not necessarily factually correct? Or is an employer free to fire an employee on the basis of the decision of the third party however unreasonable or malicious?

Perhaps the answer is that an employer is not, as it were, vicariously answerable for the prejudices of a third party but that the employer has to seek, so far as is practicable, to mitigate the effects of arbitrary, malicious or simply mistaken action taken to the detriment of an employee. This principle may be considered to underlie the verdict of the tribunal.

8 Unauthorised computer access In *Mullins v Digital Equipment International BV* [1990] ELR 139, the Employment Appeals Tribunal held that there had been substantial grounds justifying a dismissal where the employee had tried to gain access on the employer's control computer systems to the master directory account, the accounts of three of his supervisors and the account of one of his fellow employees. The Tribunal found that the employee had been aware at all times of what he was doing, thus rejecting his explanation to his employers that he had been 'looking for games'.

9 Adequacy of warning In *Carroll v The Foxrock Inn Ltd* [1990] ELR 236, the claimant had been employed by the respondent originally as a lounge boy but for the five months before his dismissal had been working behind the counter. A specific procedure was in place for 'off-sales' after closing time, when the tills were not operational. This involved writing down details as to what had been sold and the price, and ringing it up properly in the register afterwards. All the staff, including the claimant, were aware of this procedure. One evening, after closing time, the manager observed the plaintiff taking money from a customer for a purchase and putting it into the lounge till. (The manager told the Tribunal that this represented an 'off-sales' transaction: the Tribunal's determination makes no further reference to this element in the case). In the bar, the manager found a glass with £16 in it but no record of the off-sales transaction. The claimant explained to him that it was for off-sales. The manager dismissed the claimant the following morning, as he had lost trust and confidence in him.

The claimant told the Tribunal that he had not put a record of the off-sales in the glass as he was the only one behind the bar and he would remember the sales. Although the manager had spoken to the staff three weeks previously regarding the need to follow correct procedures, the claimant had never been pulled up on the procedure before.

The Tribunal determined that the dismissal had been unfair. The procedures prescribed by the manager were reasonable, but a reasonable employer would make it clear in the form of a written warning that the procedures had to be carried out, otherwise jobs would be at stake. The claimant had been 'left with an uncertain situation'.

The Tribunal found that the claimant's contribution towards his dismissal was 10%.

WORKER PARTICIPATION

The Worker Participation (State Enterprises) Act 1988 (Irish Fertilizer Industries Ltd) Order 1990 (SI No. 70 of 1990) enables employees of IFI to participate in the election of employee representatives to the Board of Nitrigín Éireann Teoranta.

Land Law

CONVEYANCING

1 Duty of Care   In *Hanafin v Gaynor*, High Court, 29 May 1990, Egan J addressed the question of how a solicitor discharges the duty of care in relation to conveyancing, and held that the defendant solicitor had not been guilty of professional negligence. We discuss the case in the Torts Chapter, below, 522-3.

2 Undertakings   In *Shangan Construction Ltd v T.P. Robinson & Co.*, High Court, 10 July 1990, Barron J had to consider the legal position where the defendant, a solicitor, was dilatory in fulfilling an undertaking on behalf of the vendor of land, to obtain a release from a mortgagee with respect to a mortgage where the moneys borrowed had been repaid. The plaintiff company, the purchaser, was, to the solicitor's knowledge, intent on building houses on the land with a view to their sale. The plaintiff company's solicitor had for some considerable time pressed the solicitor to honour the undertaking. The plaintiff company suffered financial loss as a result of the delay since it could not proceed with sales of houses it had built until the matter of the undertaking was satisfactorily resolved.

Barron J held that, once the defendant had given his undertaking, 'he had an immediate obligation to take the necessary steps to obtain the release and to go on doing whatever was necessary until it was furnished to him. Not to have done so was not only a breach of contract but professional misconduct'. Barron J rejected the defendant's argument that the plaintiff should have issued contracts to intending purchasers. In the light of evidence from several solicitors given on behalf of both parties as to the relevant conveyancing law and practice, Barron J came to the following conclusions:

> The release was an essential document. A solicitor for a vendor would not have been prepared to bind his client to a completion date unless he knew that the document would be available on completion. For this reason, the solicitor would have inserted a special condition in the contract to protect his client. The nature of such a condition could have varied between permitting a purchaser to rescind without remedy to compelling him to close on an undertaking. If such a condition had been included, it was unlikely to have been accepted since it was imposing

possible liabilities on the purchaser. He might have been unable to obtain finance or he might run into problems similar to those of the vendor on a resale, or have found himself without a house at a time when prices were rising.

The longer an undertaking remained unperformed, the less likely it was that a special condition would be accepted. In this case, the lender whose release was missing was a bank, the solicitor who had given the undertaking was a reputable solicitor and the presence of the mortgage with the deeds indicated that the loan had been paid off. Nevertheless in January 1983 the undertakings were over a year old, the bank was out of the jurisdiction and the vendor solicitor was unable to say when the release would be forthcoming. Any prudent solicitor acting for a purchaser would have been wary.

Apart from the purchaser' s solicitor it would have been necessary to satisfy the solicitor for the lending institution. While solicitors for local authorities do close on an undertaking, solicitors for building societies do, but not often. . . . However, the circumstances here were such as to lead them to expect trouble if they did so. I do not think a building society solicitor in the present case, certainly in 1983, would have closed on an undertaking. An additional factor would have been that the performance of the undertaking was outside the control of the vendor solicitor.

Having regard to this view and to the financial problems with which the plaintiff would certainly have been faced if he had bound his clients unconditionally, Barron J was satisfied that the plaintiff's solicitor was justified in his belief that contracts should not be executed until the release was available. Similarly, the defendant should have anticipated this difficulty since he was aware that the land was being bought for building, that it was likely that all the purchasers would require financing to complete their purchases and that it would therefore be necessary to satisfy not only their solicitors but also solicitors for the lending institutions.

In this context, Barron J observed that, having heard the evidence, he accepted that 'practical conveyancing does not depend upon strict rules of procedure, or of law, but rather upon the actual approach which might be anticipated from a solicitor acting for the other party'.

Barron J, while imposing liability on the defendant, went on to find that the plaintiff's solicitor (who was a party to the litigation, as second named plaintiff) had been guilty of 25% contributory negligence in failing to have minimised the damage, by not having sought 'to throw all prospective losses onto the defendant'. Barron J considered that he:

> should have written to the defendant to explain to him that he could wait
> no longer for the release; that he intended to issue contracts on the basis
> that the release was available to him; and that if he could not complete
> by reason of the absence of the release he would hold the defendant
> liable for any loss sustained as a result. It would have been prudent for
> him to ask the defendant to assent to such a course and to undertake to
> indemnify the plaintiff against any such loss, indicating that, if he did
> not, he would not issue contracts but would hold the defendant
> responsible for losses sustained by reason of his inability to issue
> contracts. If the defendant had refused to co-operate in this way then
> [the plaintiff's solicitor] would have been justified in the course he
> adopted, knowing that he had done all he could and that probably the
> defendant would have to carry the burden of any losses which might be
> sustained.

This finding seems difficult to support. The plaintiff's solicitor had made
it plain to the defendant the nature of the financial losses which the company
would continue to sustain as long as the delay in furnishing the release
continued. To have adopted the course envisaged by Barron J would perhaps
have been a justifiable one (though in the eyes of another judge it might
possibly be regarded as exacerbating rather than mitigating damages). The
failure to have adopted this course, however, should scarcely be regarded as
contributory negligence.

REGISTRATION OF TITLE

In *Crumlish v Registrar of Deeds and Titles and Gillen* [1991] ILRM 37,
Lynch J gave a useful clarification of the scope of the powers of the Registrar.
A particular piece of land had apparently been transferred on two separate
occasions; the first, in 1978, to two persons as joint tenants in fee simple, for
valuable consideration; the second, in 1980, to one person, again for valuable
consideration. Both transfers were dealt with in the Land Registry on the
same day in 1980. An error occurred in the Registry, whereby the different
parties were registered as full owners of the same plot. The Registrar sought
to rectify the error. Acting under the powers purportedly conferred on him
by the Registration of Title Act 1964 and the Land Registration Rules 1972,
the Registrar made an order in 1988 on the basis that the second transfer had
been null and void. The person to whom this transfer was made specifically
refused to consent to the making of any such order. Having failed to prevent

it, he applied for judicial review in the form of *certiorari* to quash the Registrar's order.

Lynch J considered the several possible statutory bases on which the Register's entitlement to make the order might conceivably have been based. S. 19 of the 1964 Act provides that a person aggrieved by any order or decision of the Registrar may appeal to the court, which may annul or confirm the Registrar's order or decision. This, in Lynch J's view, did not itself *confer* on the Registrar any power to make any orders. It merely made *ancillary provision* for cases where the Registrar had power to make orders under other sections of the Act or under the 1972 Rules.

S. 30(1) provides that, subject to the provisions of the Act regarding registered dispositions for valuable consideration, any disposition or charge which if unregistered would be fraudulent or void 'shall, notwithstanding registration, be fraudulent and void in like manner'. Lynch J interpreted the section as declaratory only, conferring no powers on the Registrar. S. 31, which expressly gives the court power to respond to fraud or mistake by directing the register to be rectified, does not empower the Registrar so to act, said Lynch J. And s. 32 clearly required the consent of all interested parties if the Registrar was to make an order rectifying an error originating in the Land Registry.

Having clarified the position and established that the Registrar had no statutory authority to make the order he had done, Lynch J made an order for *certiorari* quashing the Registrar's order. He made it clear that, although the High Court (and Circuit Court in cases within its jurisdiction) might make orders consequential on s. 30 and pursuant to s. 31, it would be quite inappropriate for him to do so in proceedings for judicial review only on affidavit. Proceedings by way of plenary hearing between the contending parties was essential. His order in no way affected the jurisdiction of the Circuit Court, before which proceedings were pending, to determine the issues and make any order that might appear just and equitable.

RESTRICTIVE COVENANTS

In *Whelan v Cork Corporation* [1991] ILRM 19, critically analysed by Lyall, 'Freehold Covenants and What To Do With Them', (1991) 9 *ILT* (ns) 157, Murphy J gave some useful guidance to practitioners on practical aspects of restrictive covenants, while leaving effectively unresolved an important constitutional issue relating to the ground rents legislation of 1978. The Supreme Court upheld Murphy J's judgment in an *ex tempore* judgment.

The complicated facts may be briefly summarised as follows. The lessee of a lease created in 1908 subdemised certain lands to an underlessee in 1937 and extended the underlessee's interest in 1958. The underlessee's interest vested in the plaintiffs, by assignment, in 1989 subject to the covenants on the part of the underlessor contained in it. In 1948 the lessee subdemised adjacent lands to a second underlessee, and extended his interest in 1964. The second underlessee assigned his interest to the defendants in 1984, subject to the covenants on the part of the lessee contained in it. The lessee's interest in the 1948 and 1964 leases was assigned to the defendants in 1989 and a week later the freehold of these lands was conveyed to the defendants subject to and with the benefit of the 1908 lease and the 1948 lease in reversion; the intent was that the leases should merge with and be extinguished in the freehold reversion.

The 1937 underlease contained a covenant that the lessors should not permit building on the adjacent land above a certain height. The 1948 sub-demise of these adjacent lands contained a covenant against building on the lands above this height. The covenant was repeated in the 1964 lease in reversion. The defendants began roadworks which involved building higher than the stipulated height. The plaintiffs sought an injunction to restrain them from breaching the restrictive covenants in their lease. The parties agreed to treat the application as the trial of the action.

The cardinal principle was, of course, laid down in *Tulk v Moxhay*, 2 Ph 774 (1848). As Pringle J said in *Williams & Co. Ltd v LSD and Quinnsworth*, High Court, 19 June 1970, this principle is to the effect that:

> a negative bargain, as for instance a covenant against a particular use of land retained on a sale or lease of part of an estate, may be enforced by any person entitled in equity to the benefit of that bargain against any person bound in equity by notice of it, either express or to be imputed by the acquisition of his title.

See generally Preston & Newsom's *Restrictive Covenants Affecting Freehold Land* (8th ed., by G.L. Newsom, 1991), chapters 1, 3.

The defendants claimed, first, that they had purchased the lands without knowledge or notice of the restrictive covenant. It was agreed that they did not have actual knowledge in 1984, but the plaintiffs contended that such knowledge should be imputed to the defendants on the basis of enquiries and inspections which they ought reasonably to have made. No evidence as to the practice of conveyancers was tendered by either side, and Murphy J was left to resolve the issue as a matter of law, assisted, however, by, albeit conflicting, submissions of 'two experienced conveyancers' (Mary Laffoy SC for the plaintiffs, Thomas McCann SC for the defendants).

It seemed to Murphy J that a purchaser acquiring by way of lease property which was by its terms subject to a particular covenant for the benefit of the lessor was unlikely in ordinary circumstances to enquire as to whether any other parties were entitled by virtue of any other transaction to enforce as against the lessee a covenant to the same effect, in view of the purchaser's obligation to perform the covenant in any event. The issue would be more likely to arise when the purchaser contemplated relieving himself of the covenant by acquiring the interest of his immediate lessor. It would be prudent at that stage to ensure that no other persons were entitled to enforce the covenants contained in the lease. In the circumstances of the case, the defendants had been put on actual notice of the plaintiffs' entitlement to the benefit of the restrictive covenant in 1989.

The defendants argued secondly that the terms in which the covenant was expressed were not sufficiently wide to capture them. Murphy J, while accepting that restrictive covenants as to the letting or user of property should be strictly construed, held on authority *(Holloway Brothers Ltd v Hill* [1902] 2 Ch 612, *Ricketts v Churchwardens of the Parish of Enfield* [1909] 1 Ch 544) that a restrictive covenant by a lessor, his heirs, executors, administrators and assigns will in fact bind a lessee of the lessor. Cf. Preston & Newsom, op. cit., para. 2-84.

Murphy J expressed the view that it would generally be more helpful to express impersonally the obligations imposed by a restrictive covenant than to identify the covenant with a particular group of persons.

The defendants' third argument was that the restrictive covenant was not 'a contract concerning the lands' and accordingly could not be enforced by a tenant against an assignee of his landlord, having regard to the provisions of s. 13 of the Landlord and Tenant Law Amendment (Ireland) Act 1860 (Deasy's Act). Murphy J had no hesitation in rejecting it: the extent to which a lessor or lessee (or their respective assigns) might sue each other by virtue of the relationship of lanalord and tenant was entirely distinct from the doctrine in *Tulk v Moxhay*. Liability in equity on foot of a restrictive covenant arose merely by virtue of the actual or imputed knowledge of the restriction at the time of the acquisition by the purchaser. There was no reason why a person acquiring leasehold property should be in any better or worse position in relation to his liability in equity to comply with that restriction than one acquiring a freehold interest though clearly there might be practical differences as between them regarding the enquiries or inspection that should be made.

The defendants' fourth and final argument was that, when a lessee enlarges his interest under s. 8 of the Landlord and Tenant (Ground Rents) (No. 2) Act 1978, the effect, by virtue of s. 28 of that Act, is that all covenants subject to which the lessee held the land, including those in favour of third parties, cease to have effect. The plaintiffs contended in reply that s. 28 should be given a restricted meaning: it should be limited to covenants between lessor and lessee and should not extend to covenants in favour of third parties. They argued against a literal interpretation of 'all covenants subject to which [the lessee] held the land', in favour of one that would not infringe constitutional rights which the benefit of the restrictive covenant involved.

Murphy J considered that the Oireachtas in s. 28 had shown a 'clear and unambiguous intention' to eliminate a wide range of covenants, including those for the benefit of third parties, where the fee simple is acquired under the provisions of the 1978 Act. This did not necessarily render the section unconstitutional; indeed it would be impossible to reach that conclusion without the benefit of hearing argument from the Attorney General to the contrary.

Murphy J speculated on possible approaches which would save the constitutional validity of s. 28. It might be the case that the plaintiffs or other covenantees in the same position could claim under s. 17 of the Landlord and Tenant (Ground Rents) Act 1967 or otherwise to have paid to them some apportioned part of the purchase price payable by the lessee acquiring the fee simple interest. (Such a crumb of comfort, we suggest, could scarcely suffice). Alternatively, it might be suggested that the statutory termination without the payment of compensation of covenants affecting lands comprised in a building or proprietary lease did not constitute an unjust attack on the property rights of the covenantees:

> Perhaps . . . the Attorney General would argue that the rights such as those enjoyed by the plaintiffs over the lands of others are now more effectively and more justly protected and vindicated under the Local Government (Planning and Development) Acts 1963 to 1982 and by the evolution and general acceptance of environmental planning which regulates property rights of this nature in accordance with the principles of social justice.

It was impossible to anticipate all the arguments that the Attorney General might raise on a constitutional issue, still less to adjudicate on them in advance of a plenary hearing. It was sufficient for the purposes of the case that Murphy J was not convinced that a literal interpretation of s. 28 would necessarily render it unconstitutional. In any event, he considered that the words used were so clear and unambiguous that they did not admit of the interpretation which the plaintiffs sought to place on them. Murphy J accordingly dismissed the plaintiff's claim.

The constitutional question the plaintiffs raised would seem to have passed the *Campus Oil* test, had the injunction they sought been of an interlocutory nature. To have this constitutional issue disposed of without the participation of the Attorney General, in the necessarily tentative manner to which Murphy

J was obliged to have recourse, is less than fully satisfactory, from the standpoint of the legal system as a whole. Lawyers advising clients on the issue can make only enlightened guesses as to its ultimate judicial resolutions. Of course, it would be wrong to criticise parties for adopting whatever litigation strategies they considered most desirable, and for having failed to pay any disinterested and altruistic regard to the wider legal canvass.

Conveyancing experts will no doubt be interested in Dr Lyall's observations (*op. cit.*, at 158-60) on possible strategies, on the one hand of using *Whelan* creatively to discharge unwelcome convenants (by first granting a lease to a purchaser which qualifies as a ground rent and then enlarging it to a fee simple): or, on the other hand to use the Renewable Leaseholds Conversion Act 1849, Deasy's Act 1860 or s. 65 of the Conveyancing Act 1881 to make the burden of either positive or negative covenants run effectively under *Tulk v Moxhay*.

WILLS

The Supreme Court decision of *In re Glynn deceased' Glynn v Glynn* [1990] 2 IR 326 involved an interesting discussion of principles relating to the testamentary capacity and the execution of wills, but ultimately reduced itself to a narrow issue of fact.

The deceased, an elderly farmer, who lived with his sister, gave instructions to a priest in the presence of a friend to draw up a will for him leaving the bulk of his substantial estate to his second cousin, with his sister benefitting only by a legacy of £20,000. After the priest had done this but before it was executed, the deceased suffered a massive stroke. Fifteen days later the priest and the friend visited him in hospital. Neither of them consulted his medical attendants. He was at the time totally incapable of writing or of speech. The two had the will with them. Hamilton P's judgment, in a crucial passage, records that:

> [t]hey spoke to him for about 10-15 minutes and were satisfied that he understood them as he nodded from time to time and smiled. Then [the friend] said to [the deceased] that he was there to do what he had promised to do and asked [the priest] to produce the will. Both [the priest] and [the friend] were satisfied that the deceased understood. [The priest] asked him if he was happy with the will that [the priest] had drawn up [earlier] and he nodded. He then read the will slowly and distinctly. He stopped at each sentence and the deceased nodded. [The priest] stated that the deceased was 'with him all the time' [The friend]

was satisfied that the deceased knew what was being said and 'looked eager to take the pen' and 'looked determined to sign the will'. He, with difficulty, made an X at the end of the document.

He did so in the presence of [the priest] and [the friend] . . . and it was witnessed by them in the presence of the testator and each other. [The friend] asked him was he satisfied and he nodded with a smile.

The evidence of one of the doctors in charge at the time was that the deceased had been given the last dose of a drug designed to improve his level of consciousness on the morning of the day the will was read to him and presented to him for his execution. While he was more alert that day than he had been he was still disorientated and unable to follow commands. The doctor was of the opinion that the deceased was not fit to make a will because he would not have been able to communicate his ideas or intentions in regard to it, ideas would have to be suggested to him and a code of communication would have to be worked out, which in his opinion would be extremely difficult to do. He also testified that it is extremely difficult to assess the intellectual function of a person who is unable to speak. Another doctor gave evidence to the same effect.

Hamilton P held that the deceased had been of sound disposing mind and that the will had been properly executed. The Supreme Court by a majority (McCarthy J, Hederman J concurring; Walsh J dissenting) affirmed Hamilton P's judgment.

McCarthy J approached the matter on the basis that a certain degree of compression is permissible where what is involved is confirmation of earlier instructions. He accepted as a guiding principle what Lord MacNaghten had said in the Privy Council case of *Perera v Perera* [1901] AC 354:

If a person has given instructions to a solicitor to make a will, and the solicitor prepares it in accordance with those instructions, all that is necessary to make it a good will, if executed by the testator, is that he would be able to think this far:

'I gave my solicitor instructions to prepare a will making a certain disposition of my property; I have no doubt that he has given effect to my intention, and I accept the document which is put before me as carrying it out'.

McCarthy J considered that if on the date he was visited in hospital, the deceased had been required to give instructions for the making of any sort of testamentary document, even as simple as the one in question, it might be that the validity of its execution could be challenged. That was not what he was doing: he was confirming instructions already given. He was told that the document represented, as it did, what he had expressed to be his testamentary wishes. There had been 'ample evidence' before Hamilton P that the testator had fully appreciated what was going on and that the terms of the document on which he placed his mark fully represented what he wanted done with regard to his property. The opinion or conclusion of the priest and the friend as to the understanding of the deceased was 'immaterial'.

Walsh J dissenting, stressed the lack of medical evidence of capacity. No code of communication, which the doctors had considered an essential prerequisite, had in fact been established. It could not therefore be said that the testator was of sound disposing mind at the time of execution. Walsh J quoted from the unanimous judgment of the Court in *In bonis Corboy; Leahy v Corboy* [1969] IR 148, at 167 to the effect that 'nothing less than prior medical evidence by a doctor in a position to assess the testator's mental capacity could suffice to discharge the onus of proving him to have been a capable testator. No doctor was brought to see him. . . . Such evidence as was adduced does nothing to aid matters. The testator said nothing and one does not have any material on which a judgment can be found as to his mental capacity. . . .' In the instant case the entire basis of the finding that the deceased had the necessary understanding was based on the interpretation put on his smiles and nods.

The issue in the case was the correctness of the assessment by two non-medical witnesses of what was essentially a medical problem. In the light of the medical evidence Walsh J was of opinion that it could not be proved that at the time of execution of the will the deceased was of sound disposing mind. Hamilton P's decision had been based only on the opinion of these witnesses 'who, having no medical expertise whatever, based their opinion on their previous acquaintance with the deceased, though they had never seen him in that condition before, as against the expert medical testimony of the medical practitioners attending the deceased'. Walsh J noted that the two witnesses did not appear even to have known how serious was the condition of the deceased or that he had suffered a stroke.

The decision provokes a number of comments. The first is one of general impression. Based on the discussion of the evidence in the judgments of Hamilton P, McCarthy J and Walsh J, it is difficult not to agree with Walsh J's conclusion.

Secondly, one might not necessarily concur with McCarthy J's interpretation of the medical evidence as being, '[i]n sum', that the first doctor (with whom the second agreed) 'appeared to think that if a code of communication could have been established then [the deceased] had testamentary capacity'. What this doctor had testified was that the deceased on the fateful day was 'still disorientated', that it was practically impossible to communicate with him and that 'it may very well be the case . . . that he didn't understand what was being said to him'. What the doctor had to say about the possibility of devising a code of communication seems more easily interpreted as containing a description of what would be necessary to test the deceased's capacity rather than as an unqualified endorsement of the existence of this capacity.

A third issue concerns the position of a testator who, when of full capacity, has given instructions for a will but who at the time of execution has lost the capacity to give such instructions. For the will to be valid in these circumstances, is it sufficient that the testator has retained sufficient mental capacity to *confirm* instructions already given? The majority in *Glynn* seemed receptive to the view that it was. Walsh J was more circumspect. There is perhaps good reason for caution before accepting too quickly a 'two-tier' approach, which could result in upholding wills executed by persons of insufficient mental capacity. It is, of course, true that, in cases where a testator gives instructions for a will of *particular* complexity, the mere fact that at the time of execution his mind was no longer sufficiently subtle to repeat this achievement should not be a reason for failing to uphold his execution of it. But rather than endorsing the second tier standard of what Walsh J described as 'nod[ding] through' a will, would there not be merit in requiring proof of sufficient capacity not merely to nod through but also to give basic instructions for a will? A possible drawback to such a test is that it requires the medical witnesses to address the question of capacity in respect of hypothetical facts.

Law Reform

The Law Reform Commission published three Reports in 1990: a Report on Child Sexual Abuse (LRC 32-1990), which we consider in the Criminal Law Chapter, above, 246-53; a Report on Sexual Offences Against the Mentally Handicapped (LRC 33-1990), which we also consider in the Criminal Law Chapter, above, 253-8; and a Report on Oaths and Affirmations (LRC 34-1990), which we consider in the Practice and Procedure Chapter, below, 442-7.

Other bodies were also active in the area of law reform. We examine the Report of the Committee to Enquire into Certain Aspects of Criminal Procedure, chaired by Judge Martin, in the Criminal Law Chapter, above, 240-2. We discuss the Report of the Committee, on Public Safety and Crowd Control, chaired by Hamilton P, in the Safety and Health Chapter, below, 476. The Fair Trade Commission Report into Restrictive Practices in the Legal Profession is discussed briefly in the Chapter on Practice and Procedure, below, 437-8.

Licensing

INTOXICATING LIQUOR

Extinguishment of licence   In *O'Rourke and Flanagan v Grittar* [1990] ILRM 877, the applicants objected to the grant of two new off-licences to the respondent, an unlimited company. The company had submitted to the Circuit Court two on-licences for extinguishment, in substitution for which the new off-licences were sought. The applicant objectors argued on case stated from the Circuit Court that the company's application should not be granted under s.13 of the Intoxicating Liquor Act 1960 since it required that the licences to be extinguished must be of the same character' as those to be granted in substitution. Gannon J upheld the objections.

He referred to the judicial interpretation of pre-1960 Act intoxicating liquor legislation requiring the extinguishment of a licence of the same character as that for which a new licence was being sought. In particular, he referred to the decisions in *R. (Collins) v Donegal Justices* [1903] 2 IR 533 and *R. (Henderson) v Louth Justices* [1911] 2 IR 312 in concluding that it was irrelevant to argue in the instant case that the existing on-licences were in some senses 'greater' or 'more extensive' than the off-licences which were sought to be created. In his extensive references to and quotations from the *Collins* and *Henderson* decisions, Gannon J cast doubt on certain *dicta* of Walsh J in *Power Supermarkets Ltd v O'Shea* [1988] IR 206, which had appeared to support the view put forward by the respondent in the instant case.

Limitation of Actions

THE DISCOVERABILITY TEST

Barron J's decision in *Hegarty v O'Loughran* [1987] ILRM 603, which we discussed in the 1987 Review, 246-50, was unsuccessfully appealed to the Supreme Court: [1990] ILRM 403; [1990] 1 IR 148. It will be recalled that the case involved a claim for damages for injuries to the plaintiff's nose alleged to have resulted from medical treatment. The defendants contended that the action was statute-barred under s. 11(2)(b) of the Statute of Limitations 1957. The resolution of the defendants' argument depended on the time at which the cause of action should be considered to arise. The plaintiff did not claim that s. 11(2)(b) was constitutionally invalid.

During argument before the Supreme Court, three possible constructions of s. 11(2)(b) were canvassed. According to the first, the cause of action should be deemed to have accrued when the wrongful act was committed. According to the second, it accrued only when personal injury manifested itself. On the third, which the plaintiff championed, the cause of action accrued only when the injured party could, by the exercise of reasonable diligence, have discovered that the injury had been caused by the wrongful act complained of.

In his judgment (with which Griffin J concurred) Finlay CJ favoured the *second* of these constructions. He disagreed with Carroll J's approach in *Morgan v Park Developments Ltd* [1983] ILRM 156, which had proceeded on the basis that, if two or more possible constructions for s. 11(2)(a) were open, the one in harmony with the Constitution should be preferred. In the view of the Chief Justice, whilst this general approach to construction was a sound one, it had no relevance to the construction of s. 11(2)(a) or (b), since these provisions did not lend themselves to more than one construction.

The inclusion within the legislation of s. 71(1), which prevented time from running in the event of fraudulent concealment, would have been entirely redundant if s. 11(2)(a) or (b) were to be construed as preventing the cause of action from accruing until the time the plaintiff discovered or ought to have discovered that he or she had a cause of action. Similar considerations appeared to apply to s. 48, dealing with disability, at least in so far as that disability consisted of unsoundness of mind.

The extent and nature of the provisions of England's Limitation Act 1963, which introduced the discovery test into English law, and the recommendations of the Irish Law Reform Commission with a like objective, strongly supported the conclusion that 'to interpret this subsection as being based on discoverability, though possibly very desirable, would be to legislate'.

Noting that no challenge to the constitutional validity of the subsection had been made in the proceedings, Finlay CJ went on to say that he did not accept that to construe it as meaning that 'the time limit commenced when provable personal injury, capable of attracting monetary compensation occurred' was necessarily to construe it as a constitutionally flawed provision.

In a crucial passage, the Chief Justice said:

> In legislation creating a time limit for the commencement of actions, the time provided for any particular type of action; the absolute or qualified nature of the limit; whether the court is vested with a discretion in certain cases in the interests of justice; and the special instances, if any, in which exceptions from the general time limit are provided are with others all matters in the formulation of which the legislature must seek to balance between, on the one hand, the desirability of enabling persons with causes of action to litigate them, and on the other hand, the desirability of finality and certainty in the potential liability which citizens may incur into the future.

> It is quite clear that what is sometimes classified as the harshness and injustice of a person failing to bring a cause of action to trial by reason of exceeding a time limit not due to his or her own particular fault, may well be counterbalanced by the harshness and injustice of a defendant called upon to defend himself at a time when by the passage of years his recollection, the availability of his witnesses and even documentary evidence relevant to a claim in tort or contract have disappeared.

> If and when a challenge is made to the constitutional validity of this subsection by a person adversely affected by it, and the matter is fully argued on the facts established in a particular case, it will be necessary for the courts to make a decision upon it. Until that time, however, I would reserve my view on the question of its constitutional validity other than to presume it constitutional, as I must do.

Finlay CJ therefore concluded that the proper construction of the subsection was that contended for on behalf of the defendant and that time began to run 'when a provable personal injury, capable of attracting compensation, occurred to the plaintiff which was the completion of the tort alleged to be committed against her'. Applying this test to the facts of the case, the Chief

Justice held that the time limit had well expired when the proceedings were commenced. The plaintiff, on Barron J's finding, 'was dissatisfied with the operation by . . . 1976'. This referred to the plaintiff's dissatisfaction with the results of the second operation, which had been performed in 1974. Since proceedings were not begun until 1982, it appeared that this was 'upwards of five to six years' after the time limit has expired.

In his concurring judgment, Griffin J clearly adhered to the Chief Justice's construction. He did not address the merits of the third construction that had been posited during argument.

McCarthy J, who also held in favour of the defendants, did so on a more radical basis. Time begins to run from the date at which the wrongful act 'has caused personal injury beyond what can be regarded as negligence, even when that injury is unknown to and cannot be discovered by the sufferer'. This is the test stated by Lord Reid in *Cartledge v E. Jopling & Sons Ltd* [1963] AC 758, at 771. McCarthy J found Lord Reid's reasoning 'wholly convincing'. In his opinion, the words of s. 11(2)(b) were 'so clear as not to admit of any interpretation save that expressed in *Cartledge*'.

Later in his judgment, McCarthy J said:

> [T]he more one peruses the outpourings, both judicial and academic, on the topic, the clearer it is that one must revert to first principles. The fundamental principle is that words in a statute must be given their ordinary meaning and, for myself, I am unable to conclude that a cause of action accrues on the date of discovery of its existence rather than on the date on which, if it had been discovered, proceedings could lawfully have been instituted. I recognise the unfairness, the harshness, the obscurantism that underlies this rule, but it is there and will remain there unless qualified by the legislature or invalidated root and branch by this Court. It may be that special provision ought to be made to deal with medical malpractice cases . . ., but that is for the legislature, which might consider it appropriate to provide a saving clause based upon whether or not the court considers in all the circumstances that it is reasonable to extend the time. If the discovery principle is to be applied, I see no logical reason why it should not extend to discovery of actionable cause. I reject either construction as being inconsistent with the wording of the statute.

McCarthy J went on to note that, in medical negligence cases, the patient, as potential plaintiff, is at a disadvantage, since he or she is likely to continue as a patient of the doctor against whom the action may lie. This factor makes it most unlikely that the plaintiff will appreciate the relationship, if any, between the treatment and the now discovered condition, and, if he or she does make that connection, the doctor 'will, quite *bona fide*, seek to allay any such suspicion'. Experience did not encourage McCarthy J to believe that other medical practitioners in Ireland would be prepared to point the finger of blame.

In an important passage at the conclusion of his judgment McCarthy J said:

> In its *Report on Statute of Limitations: Claims in Respect of Latent PersonalInjuries* (LRC 21-1987), the Law Reform Commission recommended that the discoverability test should be incorporated explicitly in legislative provisions and further that time should begin to run only where the plaintiff becomes or ought to become aware that the injury is attributable, in at least some degree, to the conduct of another. I share these views but I recognise that such legislative provision would increase the spread of a different harm to society. The increase in the number of medical malpractice suits has, it is said, led to the practice of defensive medicine, which has patient/practitioner, social and economic effects. The case for a no-fault system of compensation for those who suffer injury as a result of medical treatment seems so strong as to be virtually unanswerable. That also is a matter for the legislature.

Hegarty v O'Loughran provokes several questions. The first is of real practical significance since the Oireachtas has since enacted the Statute of Limitations (Amendment) Act 1991, s. 2(1) of which incorporates a discoverability test in respect of personal injuries, under which time begins to run only where the plaintiff first has knowledge of the injury, the fact that it is significant, the fact that it is attributable to tortious conduct and the identity of the defendant.

Will this legislation withstand constitutional scrutiny? We suggest that it will, for two principal reasons. First, with the exception of *O'Brien v Keogh* [1972] IR 144, the Supreme Court has not shown itself overanxious to strike down legislation dealing with limitation of actions. (As we shall see presently, there is a good reason why the court can afford to take this approach.) The passage from Finlay CJ's judgment relating to the function of the Oireachtas in seeking to strike a balance between the conflicting goals of facilitating litigation for those with causes of action and 'the desirability of finality and certainty in the potential liability which citizens may incur into the future' suggests some degree of sympathy for, and deference to, the Oireachtas in the exercise of this task. This reflects the approach of Henchy J in *Hynes-O'Sullivan v O'Driscoll* [1988] IR 436 in relation to legislation on defamation (cf. the 1988 Review, 442-3), and of the Chief Justice himself, in *Webb v Ireland* [1988] IR 353, in relation to legislation on the protection of historical cultural treasure.

Secondly, the Supreme Court has made it easier to uphold the constitutionality of legislation such as the 1991 Act by its (controversial) develop-development and extension of the right to dismiss proceedings on broadly equitable grounds where, having regard *inter alia* to the length of time that has elapsed, it would be unjust to the defendant to let the proceedings continue. Armed with this power, courts need not worry about legislation prescribing even the most generous of discoverability tests: the longer the period the legislation gives the plaintiff to initiate proceedings, the more assured the courts will be in the exercise of their discretionary power of dismissal.

Against this confidence in the constitutional validity of the Act may be marshalled a number of instances where judges have evinced an apparent preference for legislation providing for a *discretionary* judicial power to extend the limitation period in deserving cases. (Interestingly, this is a mirror image of the discretionary power of *dismissal* which the courts have already developed). In *Cahill v Sutton* [1980] IR 269, at 288, Henchy J referred to English legislation of 1963 which contained a judicial discretionary power of extension of the limitation period and went so far as to observe that:

> the justice and fairness of attaching . . . [such] a saver . . . are so obvious that the enactment by our Parliament of a similar provision would merit urgent consideration.

This approach was echoed by Costello J in *Brady v Donegal County Council*, High Court, 6 November 1987 (reversed by Supreme Court, [1989] ILRM 282 (see the 1987 Review, 264 and the 1988 Review, 125-6)). As we have seen, in *Hegarty v O'Loughran* Finlay CJ referred to the possibility of the courts' being vested with a discretion in certain cases in the interests of justice; and McCarthy J observed that the legislature 'might consider it appropriate to provide a saving clause based upon whether or not the court considers in all the circumstances and it is reasonable to extend the time'. It would be wrong, however, to attach too much significance to these remarks: McCarthy J, after all, said that he shared the views of the Law Reform Commission as to the appropriate discoverability test. The Commission was no enthusiast for a discretionary judicial power of extension: cf LRC 21-1987, p. 42 and the 1987 Review, 246.

In the light of *Hegarty v O'Loughran*, the question arises as to what is the position in cases not involving personal injury. The principles on which the decision is based seem to be that the second construction should apply in this context. Thus, for example, if a purchaser of premises became aware of damage to the property, time would begin to run against him even though he could not have been aware that the damage sprang from a tortious act or omission. Cases of physical damage to property present a clear analogy to cases of personal injury, but what of *pure economic loss*? If, for example, a solicitor acts negligently in circumstances which lead to a will being condemned, so that an intended beneficiary, who had no expectation of receiving a bequest, is deprived of it, the beneficiary being unaware of the circumstances, will naturally never experience the sense of any damage or loss: he will, without knowing it, have failed to obtain a benefit. In such circumstances, at what moment should time start running? *Hegarty v O'Loughran*, with its trigger of perceived damage, presents no clear solution. For excellent comparative analysis of the subject, see Mullany (1991) 54 *Modern L Rev* 216 and 349.

DISCRETIONARY POWER OF DISMISSAL

In the 1987 Review, 250-3, we discussed in some detail the Supreme Court's judgment in *Toal v Duignan (No. 1)* [1991] ILRM 135 (1987), suggesting that it was 'a watershed decision, with profoundly disturbing implications for the victims of "sleeping" torts'. It will be recalled that the case involved allegations of medical negligence against several defendants. The plaintiff, who was born in 1961, claimed that he learned in the summer of 1983 that he suffered from a condition of sterility as a result of an undescended testicle at the time of his birth. His proceedings against the defendants concerned with events in 1961 were dismissed but the plaintiff had other strings to his bow. These related to his medical treatement when he was ten years old.

In June 1971 the plaintiff has been diagnosed as suffering from mumps. The plaintiff alleged that, following his discharge from hospital, the eighth defendant examined him and failed to discover the condition that had continued since birth. He claimed that as a result his condition was let deteriorate, his testis becoming atrophic.

The eighth defendant had been employed primarily as a locum from 1967 to 1978, when she retired. She did not keep records of the visits she made to patients in the course of this work, though she kept notes in notebooks. At the time of the litigation, she had only one of the notebooks, which contained no references to attendances on the plaintiff.

The sixth, seventh and eighth defendants sought orders dismissing the plaintiff's proceedings against them on the basis that it would be unjust for them to be called on to defend themselves after such a length of time on which elapsed. (This was the ground on which the defendants in *Toal v Duignan (No. 1)* had succeeded in obtaining a dismissal against them). Lynch J refused the relief they sought: Irish Times Law Reports, 27 March 1989. The Supreme Court dismissed the appeals of the sixth and seventh defendants but allowed the appeal of the eighth defendant: *Toal v Duignan (No. 2)* [1991] ILRM 140 (1990).

The sixth defendant was the Chairman of the Board of Governors and Directors of Harcourt Street Children's Hospital, and the seventh defendant was the Board and Governors and Directors of that hospital. The Supreme Court was satisfied that the position of both defendants was different from that of the Coombe Hospital, which had been sued in respect of alleged defaults of the gynaecologist and paediatrician who had attended the plaintiff's birth in 1961 and that of the junior medical and nursing staff. By the time the litigation had progressed, both the gynaecologist and paediatrician were dead. Their records were 'wholly incomplete and wholly inadequate': *id.*, at 145 (*per* Griffin J). In contrast, so far as the sixth and seventh defendants were concerned, the doctor involved was alive and apparently had personal records as well as some personal recollection. There was no real evidence of a concrete kind with regard to the records which were available nor any attempt by the hospital to ascertain the whereabouts or availability of other persons who were involved with the treatment of the plaintiff at the relevant time. The Supreme Court accordingly affirmed Lynch J's order with respect to the sixth and seventh defendants.

The eighth defendant had been permitted in the interests of justice to file an affidavit by way of supplement to the affidavit she had supplied in the High Court. The Supreme Court (McCarthy J dissenting) held that proceedings against her should be dismissed since there was no form of written record which was of any assistance to her concerning the crucial period.

What is of considerable interest in the case is the fundamental cleavage of approach between the majority (Finlay CJ and Griffin J) and McCarthy J, who dissented. The Chief Justice reconsidered the principles laid down in his judgment in *Toal v Duignan (No. 1)* as to the jurisdiction of the court in the interests of justice to dismiss a claim where the length of time that has elapsed between the events out of which it arises and the time when it comes for hearing is in all circumstances so great that it would be unjust to call on a particular defendant to defend himself or herself against the claim made. He adhered to the view that the court had such an inherent jurisdiction; to conclude otherwise would 'give to the Oireachtas a supremacy over the courts which is inconsistent with the Constitution'. He considered that:

> [i]f the courts were to be deprived of the right to secure to a party in litigation before them justice by dismissing against him or her a claim which by reason of the delay in bringing it, whether culpable or not, would probably lead to an unjust trial and unjust result merely by reason of the fact that the Oireachtas has provided a time limit which in the particular case has not been breached would be to accept a legislative

intervention in what is one of the most fundamental rights and obligations of a court to do ultimate justice between the parties before it.

The Chief Justice stressed that the power of dismissal on this ground was a jurisdiction 'which could be frequently or lightly assumed'. As against this, he repeated what he had said in *Toal v Duignan (No. 1)* that the evidence of culpable negligence on the part of the plaintiff was of considerable relevance but was not an essential ingredient for the court's exercise of this jurisdiction.

Griffin J expressed complete agreement with Finlay CJ's analysis of this issue. McCarthy J dissented. He did not accept that, without the culpable delay which existed in *Ó Domhnaill v Merrick*, the court should dismiss the claim of a non-culpable plaintiff. He was not satisfied that this issue had been argued. In any event he found it:

> impossible to accept that justice requires of the courts that an injured plaintiff, innocent of any responsibility for delay, and unaware of the existence of his cause of action at least in part because of the very failure in communication of which he complains in the substantive action itself, should lose his case without a trial on the merits because the doctor whom he sues is less adequately equipped to defend the case because she has lost or destroyed comtemporaneous records which may or may not be relevant to the case itself. In short, the very negligence alleged is, itself, a direct cause of the delay because of which, it is said, the plaintiff is to lose his case. It is a variation of Joseph Heller's *Catch 22*.

In the 1987 Review, 252, we expressed our lack of enthusiasm for the approach favoured by the majority in *Toal v Duignan (No. 2)*. The implications of that approach are worth examining. The majority appears to support the view that there is a constitutional imperative, by virtue of the separation of powers which the Constitution prescribes, for the courts to retain a discretionary power of dismissal in the interests of justice even where the plaintiff's conduct is unimpeachable in any way. Now it is no doubt true that the courts have a special function to protect the administration of justice (cf the controversial decision of *The State (DPP) v Walsh* [1981] IR 412), but justice is a very large concept and it is scarcely the case that, on account merely of the fact that an issue of justice arises in the context of the maintenance of judicial proceedings, it thereby becomes a matter on which the courts should have the last word. The laws of evidence relate to the administration of justice and the maintenance and conduct of judicial proceedings, but that surely does not mean that a statute specifying a list of cases where privilege arises, would, by reason only of the fact that the Oireachtas has ventured into this area, fall under the shadow of constitutional invalidity.

Of course legislation must ensure that the courts can protect adequately the demands of justice in the conduct of legal proceedings but the question whether the relationship between doctor and patient should be subject to legal privilege — to take one controversial instance — is a matter on which the Oireachtas may have a legitimate interest.

Similarly, the subject of limitation of actions is surely one raising complex issues of justice and social policy. If, for example, a long discoverability period is permitted, this may have important practical implications for some professions and enterprises (such as the pharmaceutical industry). The question may arise as to the likely consequences for insurance and the downstream effects in terms of the provision of the service or product in question. The idea that these complex issues can be reduced to a simple value judgment as to fairness, which only the courts, and not the Oireachtas, can determine, may seem to be mistaken.

Even if one approaches the question of justice as between the parties in relation to the issue of limitation of actions without regard to the social and economic policy dimensions, and treats the matter as one of simple principle, it does not lend itself to easy resolution. Finlay CJ himself emphasised the dilemma in *Hegarty v O'Loughran*, as we have seen. It is not easy to know where to draw the line when to draw it in any particular place will have clearly identifiable unpalatable effects for one party to the other. If a long period is allowed to elapse this can work hardship for the defendant — as *Toal v Duignan* makes plain. Equally, where a court dismisses the action on the basis of that hardship, this creates resulting hardship to an entirely innocent plaintiff who may be the victim of the defendant's wrong. It would be a brave court which would assert that *its* value position on this troublesome question was inevitably preferable to that of the Oireachtas. In truth it seem to be quintessentially a matter on which a broad margin of appreciation should be conceded to the Oireachtas.

Perhaps this lies at the base of the Chief Justice's assurance that the court's jurisdiction to dismiss proceedings on the ground of delay is one that should not be 'frequently or lightly assumed' but it may be debated whether such restraint converts the jurisdiction into a 'long-step' guarantee against a manifestly unjust legislative regime. The point of intervention favoured by the majority in *Toal v Duignan (No. 2)* scarcely fits easily within such a characterisation.

We have already noted the broad judicial hints over the years in favour of a statutory framework (such as was adopted in England in 1963) which lays down reasonably short limitation periods but which confers on the court a power to extend the period on a broad discretionary basis in individual cases. Such a structure is no doubt appealing to the judiciary because it reserves to the courts the dominant role in relation to a matter which they consider has been placed under their care by the Constitution. There is, however, a significant price to be paid for this solution. It results in uncertainty and in variation from judge to judge. If one purpose of limitation periods is to give potential defendants a degree of security in planning their affairs, a regime of discretionary extension significantly interferes with this security.

REGISTERED CHARGES ON LAND

In *First Southern Bank Ltd v Maher* [1990] 2 IR 477, Barron J addressed the interrelationship between contractual liability and registered charges on land, so far as limitation of actions is concerned. A landowner in 1980 had executed a promissory note in favour of the plaintiff bank. This was repayable over the next three years by several instalments over three years. The note provided that, in the event of default in payment for one month from its due date of any of the instalments, the whole of the outstanding amount should immediately become due. The landowner also executed a deed of charge over the lands in the plaintiff's favour as security for the amount owing. This included a provision for 'payment on demand'.

No monies were paid on foot of the promissory note. The landowner died in 1983. The following year the plaintiff demanded payment from the deceased's representatives. In 1989 the plaintiff issued proceedings against the executrix on foot of the charge, seeking possession of the lands under s. 62(7) of the Registration of Title Act 1964.

Barron J dismissed the proceedings. The contractual remedy, based on the promissory note, had expired two years after the landowner's death (Civil Liability Act 1961, s. 9(2)(b)). This did not mean that the claim under the registered charge should necessarily suffer the same fate. The crucial question was whether the provision relating to a demand for payment was a pre-condition of the commencement of the cause of action. Barron J thought not. Repayment of the principal money secured by the instrument of charge had become due when there had been a month's default in payment of the first instalment. There was nothing in the deed to suggest that the security could not be enforced until the demand was made: the document could have so provided but had not done so.

SUSPENSION OF RUNNING OF TIME

In *Rohan v Bord na Móna* [1991] ILRM 123, the plaintiff received serious head and facial injuries in an explosion while he was at work in the defendant's employment in February 1985. Proceedings were issued in September 1988. The defendant pleaded that the cause of action was barred by lapse of time. The plaintiff countered this defence by invoking s. 49(1)(a) of the Statute of Limitations 1957, which provides that:

> [i]f, on the date when any right of action accrued for which a period of limitation is fixed by the Act, the person to whom it accrued was under a disability, the action may . . . be brought at any time before the expiration of six years from the date when the person ceased to be under a disability or died, whichever event first occurred, notwithstanding that the period of limitation has expired.

Two questions thus arose: first as to whether the plaintiff was under a disability at the relevant date, and secondly, if he was, whether s. 49(1)(a) required that he be in that condition at that date *before* the time of the accident.

As to the first question, the plaintiff contended that he was of unsound mind. This expression is not defined in the legislation, though s. 48(2) makes it clear that, without prejudice to the generality of the provision, a person is conclusively presumed to be of unsound mind while detained in pursuance of any enactment authorising the detention of persons of unsound mind, or criminal lunatics.

From the conflicting medical evidence in the case given by a consultant neuroradiologist, a consultant neurosurgeon, a consultant psychiatrist, a consultant neurologist and a clinical psychologist (as well as the plaintiff's solicitor and brother in law), Barron J concluded that the plaintiff had sustained a severe injury and that he suffered from intellectual impairment which placed him in the mildly mentally handicapped class. He was unable to manage his own affairs and had been in law a person of unsound mind from the instant he had sustained his injuries.

Barron J did not expressly refer to the basis of the connection between inability to manage one's own affairs and unsoundness of mind. It has the support of the decision of the English Court of Appeal in *Kirby v Leather* [1965] 2 QB 367, which, as we shall see, Barron J followed in relation to the second question raised in the case. In *Kirby v Leather*, Lord Denning MR had pointed out that the phrase 'of unsound mind' in a statute must be construed in relation to the subject-matter with which the statute is dealing rather than having one inflexible meaning throughout the law. Incapacity to manage one's affairs was an appropriate meaning in the present context, since it was similar to the test relevant to the appointment of a guardian *ad litem* or next friend. Danckwerts LJ agreed: bringing an action for compensation, he thought, 'is obviously a business matter'. Winn LJ, while in general agreement, counselled that:

> Care must be taken not to confuse the decision which has been announced in these judgments with any such proposition as . . . that there can be a suspension of the running of the statutory limitation period during such time as an injured person is unconscious or ill or in a state of delirium without more being shown . . . Had [the plaintiff] merely been unconscious . . . unable to recognise any member of his family, ... but had there been lacking cogent and convincing medical evidence that throughout that period of unconsciousness and amnesia his mental powers had been so affected as to make him in the relevant sense of unsound mind, I would not have thought that there would have been any suspension of the running of the statutory period of limitation.

Winn LJ was surely right to emphasise that under the legislation (in Britain as also here) time is suspended on the basis of unsoundness of mind rather than by virtue of some general inability, from whatever cause, to manage one's affairs. But if it is true that not every case of such inability falls within the definition of unsoundness of mind, and if such inability is thus a necessary but not sufficient ingredient, the question still must be resolved as to what are the parameters of what one might call the mental component in this formula. For Winn LJ mere unconsciousness is not enough, though this state is undoubtedly a mental one. One suspects that what he envisages is a degree of mental illness involving interference with cognitive capacity or other brain damage over and above the single fact of unconsciousness.

Turning to the second issue arising in *Rohan*, Barron J noted that counsel for the defence had submitted that s. 49(1)(a) so was intended to apply only to persons *who were of unsound mind already at the time of the incident giving rise to the cause of action*. Barron J did not agree, considering it to be 'an unlikely intention' on the part of the Oireachtas. He said:

> The purpose of the provision is to save a cause of action for someone to whom it has accrued but because of a disability may be unable to pursue it. If so, it is immaterial whether the plaintiff was at the date of the accident or immediately as a result thereof became of unsound mind. He requires the same protection in either case. Whether or not this is what the Oireachtas intended is not in any event to be decided by a presumption. The intention must be determined by the words used. Taking the words 'on the date' in their normal meaning, this means at any time on such date. I see no reason for seeking any other construction.

The plaintiff's proceedings were accordingly not defeated by the statute.

Barron J's interpretation is in harmony with that of the English Court of Appeal in *Kirby v Leather, supra*. There, Lord Denning MR had adopted a similarly literal approach:

> 'On the date' means, I think, at any time before the end of the day, because the law takes no account of fractions of a day.

That Lord Denning should here have ridden the literalist horse when he was such a champion of the teleological approach is reason for close scrutiny of his remarks. The truth of the matter is that the conclusion at which he (and Barron J in *Rohan*) arrived is one that may be supported from a teleological standpoint even though a strong — possibly stronger — teleological interpretation to the opposite effect is also worth serious consideration. It is of interest that, while professing fidelity to the literal approach, Barron J also went outside its narrow straitjacket, venturing the conclusion that the construction advocated by counsel for the defendant 'seems an unlikely intention on the part of the Oireachtas', and addressing the purpose of the provision and the need for protection of a plaintiff of unsound mind even where that condition has resulted immediately from the incident giving rise to the cause of action.

Which side of the teleological interpretation is more impressive? In favour of the approach favoured by *Rohan* and *Kirby v Leather* it may be argued that a plaintiff who is rendered mentally incompetent immediately on the accrual of his right to action is just as vulnerable as one who was in that condition immediately beforehand. As Barron J observed, '[h]e requires the same protection in either case'. From the start, he is not in a position properly to look after his interests so far as vindicating his right of action is concerned.

As against this, Brady & Kerr, *The Limitation of Actions in the Republic of Ireland* (1984) 20, argue that this approach . . . 'can be objected to on principle because the [question] of whether time runs depends on an artificial distinction drawn between disability supervening in the course of the same calendar day as that on which the accident occurred and disability supervening at the end of that day'.

The truth of the matter is that anomalies are the inevitable consequence of *either* interpretation, not because of deficiencies in the interpretation but because of the inherent arbitrariness and ineffectiveness of suspending the running of the period of limitation on account of unsoundness of mind at the date of accrual on the cause of action. Of course unsoundness of mind at this point may often make it difficult for the plaintiff to protect his interests through litigation but, if the underlying premise is that *those who are unable through no fault of their own to protect their interests should be entitled to a suspension of the statute*, s. 49(1)(a) gives effect to that goal in a most unsatisfactory manner.

First it is *underinclusive* in that it gives no protection to a plaintiff who becomes of unsound mind very shortly after the cause of action accrues. As we have seen, Brady & Kerr criticise the interpretation favoured in *Kirby v Leather* because of its anomalous implications in this context; they note (*op. cit.*, 20) that it 'prevents time running against a person who is knocked down by a car and is immediately rendered mentally ill, but allows time to run against him if the accident merely causes twenty four hours' unconsciousness followed by mental illness'.

The suspension based on the plaintiff's unsoundness of mind is *over-inclusive*, so far as its underlying policy is concerned, since it can result in an extension of time, not just to vulnerable plaintiffs whose hapless condition led to the delay, but also to plaintiffs, albeit of unsound mind, whose dilatoriness springs, not from haplessness but from independent causes, entirely unrelated to their condition. In *Rohan*, the plaintiff's solicitors had launched a preliminary letter on his behalf *less than seven weeks' after the explosion had occurred*. Now it may be true that a person of unsound mind can be at a disadvantage in pursuing a claim even where he (or someone who cares about his welfare) had sufficient perspicacity to consult solicitors; but the effect of s. 49(1)(a) is that the clock does not start ticking against a plaintiff of unsound mind even where, on the facts, no difficulty in the prosecution of his claim is attributable to his mental condition.

Is there not a strong argument that the court should consider invoking its discretionary jurisdiction (under *Ó Domhnaill v Merrick/Toal v Duignan* principles) to dismiss an action where a plaintiff seeks to rely on the suspension of a limitation period in circumstances where the facts show that the policy basis in favour of the suspension will not be effectuated in any way?

It is interesting to consider how the *Rohan* principle intersects with the law as stated in *Hegarty v O'Loughran, supra*. If a cause of action accrues only where 'provable personal injury, capable of attracting compensation' has occurred, then the fact that the plaintiff was of unsound mind at the time the tort was committed will not suspend the operation of the statute if the plaintiff is no longer of unsound mind at the time this damage occurs.

This can lead to curious results. Let us imagine the case of a person suffering from a serious mental illness. During the period of his disability he is the victim of a wrong (such as a negligent medical diagnosis, or a negligently caused injury when a passenger in a car) in circumstances where the damage is insidious and incapable of being appreciated by anyone, sane or insane. If that person a year later regains his sanity and some time thereafter notices that he is suffering from a slowly developing injury, there is a far greater likelihood than in the case of a person who was at all times sane that he will be unable to trace the injury to its tortious source. How could he be expected to have a clear memory and understanding of what happened to him when he was mentally ill? The discovery principle as stated in *Hegarty v*

O'Loughran would in these cases work with particular harshness. It may be contrasted with the approach adopted in the 1991 Act which has the effect of at least preventing the clock from starting to tick against the plaintiff until he ought reasonably be aware both of the fact that the injury was the result of a tort and of the identity of the wrongdoer.

One should keep a sense of reality here, however. If the formerly mentally ill person is unable to identify the source of the injury because it occurred during the period of his disability, in most cases the fact that the clock has not started ticking will be of no substantial benefit to him because he will *never* be able to make the necessary connection between injury, tort and tortfeasor. There will nonetheless be a small number of actual cases where the *Hegarty v O'Loughran* approach would exclude formerly mentally ill plaintiffs whose access to the courts is guaranteed by the 1991 Act.

TRANSPORT

S. 3 of the International Carriage of Goods by Road Act 1990 provides that, notwithstanding s. 7 of the Statute of Limitations 1957, Part III of the 1957 Act is to apply in relation to action in respect of or arising out of carriage to which the Convention on the Contract for the International Carriage of Goods by road (CMR) applies. We examine this legislation in detail in the Conflict of Laws Chapter, above, 129-39. Briefly, the effect of s. 3 is to apply to these actions the 1957 Act's provisions regarding extension of limitation periods in cases of fraud, mistake and disability, as Article 32(3) of CMR requires.

Local Government

BUILDING CONTROL

The Building Control Act 1990 is the long-awaited legislative framework for the establishment of statutory Building Regulations in this State. The Local Government (Planning and Development) Act 1963, in ss.86 to 88, had provided a similar framework but these sections were never brought into force: see Cooney, Annotation, *Irish Current Law Statutes Annotated*. The current legal position, pending the implementation of the 1990 Act, is that certain local authorities had approved bye-laws in respect of buildings but that there were wide discrepancies between those that had. Clearly there was a greater difficulty in those local authority areas which had approved no bye-laws of any description. Draft Building Regulations under the 1963 Act had been circulated to local authorities by the Department of the Environment. These were given semi-legal status in the wake of the Stardust Fire in Dublin in 1981 when the Department issued a Circular requesting each local authority to have regard to the Draft Building Regulations in determining applications for planning permission and for bye-law approval. Updated Proposed Building Regulations were published by the Department in October 1988. That these are likely to form the basis for the Regulations to be made under the 1990 Act may be gauged form the fact that they run to over 250 pages of printed text.

S. 2 of the 1990 Act provides that local authorities and any council which is also a fire authority under the Fire Services Act 1981 will also now be designated Building Control Authorities. Such Authorities will be responsible for enforcing the Regulations made under the Act. As under the 1981 Act, Authorities may enter into 'sharing' agreements for the purposes of the 1990 Act.

S. 3 of the Act is a comprehensive framework for the making of Building Regulations under the Act, and in many respects it goes much further than the terms of ss.86 to 88 of the 1963 Act (which will be repealed when the 1990 Act comes into effect). Such Regulations will concern the actual design, structure, alteration and fitting out of buildings. The Regulations to be made under the Act will only apply to buildings being constructed after the Regulations come into operation (including buildings in the control of the State, with the exception of new prisons and places of detention). Material alterations to old buildings will, however, also be subject to the Regulations.

Ss.4 and 5 of the Act allow for dispensations and relaxation of the Regulations.

S. 6 of the Act provides for the making of Building Control Regulations: these Regulations, by way of contrast with those to be made under s.3, will detail the mechanisms by which the s.3 Regulations will be enforced. The essence of the system is one of self-certification by the construction industry itself, and this approach led to criticism from the opposition in the course of the Act's passage: see Cooney, Annotation, above. Fire safety certificates are, on the other hand, subject to positive approval by the relevant Building Control Authority, a provision which follows the recommendations of the *Report of the Tribunal of Inquiry into the Stardust Fire* (1982, Pl.853).

Although the Act will, in general, be based on self-certification, it also provides, in ss.8 and 9, for enforcement mechanisms to be used by Building Control Authorities to ensure compliance with Building Regulations, and of inspection powers for authorised officers (s.11). Such officers can be appointed by the Authorities, by the Minister for the Environment or by An Bord Pleanála.

It is of interest to note that s.21 of the 1990 Act provides that no civil proceedings may be instituted by reason of a contravention of any provision of the Act, or of any Regulation made under it. S.21 may be contrasted with s.60 of the Safety, Health and Welfare at Work Act 1989, which provides that nothing in ss.6 to 11 of the 1989 Act may found a civil claim. However, s.60(2) of the 1989 Act also expressly provides that Regulations made under the 1989 Act may be actionable, unless otherwise expressly provided. And the 1989 Act allows for the making of Regulations by the Minister for Labour in connection with the design and construction of buildings so as to ensure the safety and health of persons employed in such buildings (see Fourth Schedule of 1989 Act).

Despite the difference in approach between s.21 of the 1990 Act and s.60 of the 1989 Act, the actual effect is, in fact, less than a first glance might indicate. As Cooney notes in his Annotation, s.21 will not affect the current position by which building cases will be determined by reference to tort and contract. Nor will it necessarily render 'off limits' the Building Regulations when they are eventually promulgated under the Act. Assuming that the present Draft Building Regulations are based on the standards applicable in the construction context, they will continue to be relevant even though, as s.21 provides, they may not in themselves found an action. Thus, the Regulations, when signed, will continue to be relevant in that sense in future litigation.

S. 23 of the 1990 Act provides that, when the Act is brought into force, s.4 of the Local Government (Multi-Storey Buildings) Act 1988 will cease to apply. This will have the effect that multi-storey buildings completed before the 1988 Act came into force will then become subject to the 1990 Act. On the 1988 Act see the 1988 Review, 306-7.

Finally, it should be noted that no Commencement Order has been made under the 1990 Act at the time of writing.

CHARGES

1 Trade effluent In *Ballybay Meat Exports Ltd v Monaghan County Council* [1990] ILRM 864 Gannon J held that the respondent Council was not entitled to impose a charge for connecting the applicant's drains into the public sewer system. The case arose in the following way.

As part of an expansion of its meat processing plant, the applicant company applied in 1987 for a licence under s.16 of the Local Government (Water Pollution) Act 1977 to discharge trade effluent from the plant into the respondent's sewer. In August 1987 the respondent Council granted such a licence under the 1977 Act subject to a number of conditions, including an annual fee of £400 for effluent monitoring costs. In the same month, the applicant received from the Council outline planning permission for the expansion at its meat processing plant. The conditions attaching to the permission required the applicant to apply to the respondent, as sanitary authority, for formal sewer and watermain connections as required. The applicant applied for the sewer connection in March 1988. By letter of May 1988, the respondent agreed to provide a connection, subject to certain conditions. These conditions included a requirement that the applicant pay either (i) a capital (once-off) contribution of £42,014 plus an annual running charge of £3,600 or (ii) an annual charge of £12,394 (the latter subject to annual review). The applicant then sought relief by way of judicial review, on the ground that the respondent was not authorised, as sanitary authority, to impose the charges referred to in the letter of May 1988. The applicant further argued that the licence under the 1977 Act was a valid and subsisting licence. Gannon J granted the relief sought.

Applying, in effect, the old *ultra vires* rule (see now s.6 of the Local Government Act 1991) Gannon J noted towards the end of his judgment that the Council:

> is a body whose authority and functions are prescribed by legislation, and consequently it may be required to establish that its actions accord not only as to purpose but also as to form prescribed by the legislature.

In the instant case, he held that it was clear that the legislature had made distinctions as respects the Council's different capacities as sanitary authority under the Local Government (Financial Provisions) Act 1983 and as local authority under the 1977 Act, but that the Council had failed to recognise these distinctions. That the Council might be forgiven for failing to do so was, perhaps, implicitly recognised by Gannon J himself, because he pointed out that the precise distinction in the relevant legislation between a sanitary authority and a local authority had not been opened in argument.

As to the detailed provisions in issue, he held that s.23 of the Public Health (Ireland) Act 1878 conferred a public right on an owner or occupier to cause his drains to empty into the sewer of a sanitary authority without charge. Significantly, this was not an individual service provided by the sanitary authority to an individual, nor was the sanitary authority entitled to impose any charge by way of condition attaching to permission to connect. Turning to s.2 of the 1983 Act, which allows for the imposition of charges, Gannon J noted that this related to the functions performed by the respondent as local authority, and thus had no bearing on the provisions of s.16 of the 1977 Act, under which the respondent had granted a licence as sanitary authority.

Applying these views to the case before him, he concluded that the purported conditions attaching to the letter of May 1988 were *ultra vires* the range of authority conferred on the respondent by s.23 of the 1878 Act, and amounted to an invalid attempt to review the licence which had been granted under s.16 of the 1977 Act. As to any such review, he noted that there was a particular mechanism for review contained in s.17 of the 1977 Act. Finally, Gannon J confirmed that the licence granted under the 1977 Act remained a valid and subsisting licence.

2 Water supply In *O'Donnell v Dun Laoghaire Corporation* [1991] ILRM 301, Costello J delivered two judgments concerning the validity of charges for domestic water supply raised by the defendant Corporation. The first judgment held that the charges levied for certain years were *ultra vires*, and the second judgment dealt with the consequential declaratory relief to which the plaintiffs were entitled.

The plaintiffs resided in the administrative area of the defendant Corporation. The Corporation, through its Manager, purported to raise water charges for the years 1983, 1984 and 1985. These were levied in purported compliance with s.65A of the Public Health (Ireland) Act 1878, as inserted and amended by s.7 of the Local Government (Sanitary Services) Act 1962 and s.8 of the Local Government (Sanitary Services) Act 1983. The amendments effected by the 1983 Act to s.65A of the 1878 Act came into force in July 1983. S.65A provided that the charges when levied were payable by two equal instalments and that, in the absence of any contrary indication from a particular Order raising a water charge, were to be payable on 1 April and 1 October of the year in question. The defendant's managerial Order raising the 1983 water charge was made in September 1983; the 1984 Order was made in July 1984 and that for 1985 in June of that year. As we will see below, Costello J found that the water charges for these three years were *ultra vires*.

Although not mentioned in Costello J's judgment, the levying of charges was a controversial political issue and it was significant that no charges were levied in the immediate aftermath of the 1985 local government elections. By virtue of the County Management (Reserved Functions) Order 1985, the function of raising water charges was transferred to the elected members of the Council. It was not until December 1987 that the elected members of the defendant Corporation passed a resolution providing for water charges for the year 1988, and also provided that the instalments were payable on 15 March and 15 July 1988. As we will see, Costello J held that this levy was valid.

The plaintiffs challenged the validity of the water charges for each of the four years in question. As already indicated, Costello J held that the charges levied for 1983, 1984 and 1985 were *ultra vires* s.65A of the 1878 Act, as inserted and amended by the 1983 Act. This was, briefly, because the managerial Orders were each made after 1 April in the years in question, and since no alternative dates were specified for payment, it was thus impossible for the instalments to have been paid by the time specified in s.65A of the 1878 Act.

As to the Order made by the elected members of the Corporation for 1988, Costello J concluded that this was valid since it expressly provided for payments by instalments. He did not consider it was necessary that the period between the dates for payment be as great as the six month gap indicated in s.65A of the 1878 Act.

On the basis of his findings in his first judgment, Costello J then heard further submissions as to the relief (if any) to which the plaintiffs were entitled. The relevant circumstances were these. The Corporation had disconnected the plaintiffs' water supply in late 1988 after a notice of disconnection had been served on them. This notice referred to the failure to pay the water charges for 1983, 1984, 1985 and 1988. Apparently, the plaintiffs' supply was re-connected on more than one occasion without the Corporation's permission, but the Corporation ultimately disconnected the supply effectively. The plaintiffs claimed declarations that the disconnections were *ultra vires* and sought damages for the inconvenience which resulted. The Corporation argued that declaratory relief should not be granted and that damages were not available. Costello J granted declaratory relief only.

He held that the disconnections had been *ultra vires* because although the water charges for 1988 were overdue for in excess of 2 months (a matter required by s.65A of the 1878 Act, as inserted by s.7 of the 1962 Act), the notices for disconnection had also referred to the *ultra vires* water charges for 1983, 1984 and 1985. This reference to sums which were not lawfully due invalidated the disconnections, he concluded.

This did not end the matter, because the Corporation pointed out that the power to grant declaratory relief in the instant case had been conferred by s.155 of the Chancery (Ireland) Act 1867, and Costello J agreed that the power was was therefore discretionery in nature. But he held that the plaintiffs were not barred from claiming declaratory relief merely because they had not established an inability to claim judicial review. He made reference to the development of declaratory relief as a public law remedy and noted that the Supreme Court in *Transport Salaried Staffs' Association v CIE* [1965] IR 180 had effectively removed the requirement to prove inability to obtain certiorari prior to seeking a declaration. To that extent, Costello J stated that the decision of Gavan Duffy J in *O'Doherty v Attorney General* [1941] IR 659 no longer represented good law.

Nor did he consider it to be an abuse of the process of the court for the plaintiffs to obtain declaratory relief in a plenary action merely because declaratory relief was also now available under O.84 of the Rules of the Superior Courts 1986. Costello J pointedly declined to follow the controversial decision of the House of Lords in *O'Reilly v Mackman* [1983] 2 AC 237 in this context, this being the second occasion in recent years in which he has shown a certain disdain for mainstream English precedents in this area: see *Tromso Sparebank v Beirne and Ors (No. 2)* [1989] ILRM 257 (1988 Review, 331-4). Costello J held that O.84 of the 1986 Rules could not be regarded as an exclusive public law remedy and that there were sufficient protections against vexatious proceedings for public bodies in O.20 and O.21 of the 1986 Rules which could be exercised by analogy with O.84.

Applying this analogy approach he stated that, in line with the provision in O.84 of the 1986 Rules, the Court could refuse relief to the plaintiffs for unreasonable delay in challenging the Corporation's charges. However, he concluded that in the instant case there were good reasons for the plaintiffs' delay. Following the majority Supreme Court decision in *The State (Furey) v Minister for Defence* [1988] ILRM 89, he noted that since the plaintiffs had been involved with a residents association in objecting to the charges and had also later concluded that any legal issues concerning them would be dealt with in enforcement proceedings brought by the Corporation, and since no third party rights were affected, the plaintiffs were entitled to the declaratory reliefs sought.

Finally, on the declaratory relief issue, he did not consider that there was any basis on which the Court could refuse declaratory relief merely on the ground that to do so would be detrimental to the good administration of the

Corporation's administrative area. In this respect he also declined to accept
the reasoning of the House of Lords in *R. v Dairy Produce Quota Tribunal,
ex p Caswell* [1990] 2 AC 738, primarily on the basis that the 'good
administration' ground existed as an express statutory basis for refusing relief
in Britain, whereas no such ground existed under the 1986 Rules. Costello J
was happy to confine the Irish High Court's discretion to those established
in decisions such as *Furey*, above, and *The State (Cussen) v Brennan* [1981]
IR 181.

On the question of damages, the plaintiffs were not successful. Costello J
followed the decision of the Supreme Court in *Pine Valley Developments Ltd
v Minister for the Environment* [1987] ILRM 747; [1987] IR 23, holding that
since the Corporation had not committed any tort in disconnecting the
plaintiffs' water supply, and since it had acted bona fide in the ultra vires
exercise of its statutory powers, the plaintiffs were not entitled to damages
arising from the inconvenience which they had suffered. See the discussion
of this point in the Torts chapter, 549-51, below.

DERELICT SITES

The Derelict Sites Act 1990, which repealed the Derelict Sites Act 1961, is
the most recent legislative attempt to prevent land becoming derelict, particularly in urban areas. For a full analysis see Delany's Annotation, *Irish
Current Law Statutes Annotated*.

S.3 of the Act defines the term 'derelict site' as meaning a site which
detracts from the amenity, character or appearance of neighbouring land
because of: (a) the existence of structures which are in a ruinous, derelict or
dangerous condition; or (b) the neglected, unsightly or objectionable condition of the site; or (c) the presence of any litter, rubbish, debris or waste on
the site (unless the presence of such litter etc. results from the exercise of a
legal right). This definition is substantially wider than that under the 1961
Act.

S.8 of the Act places a statutory duty on local authorities to compile a
Register of Derelict Sites in their functional areas. Ss.9 and 10 of the Act
impose a duty on owners of land and local authorities, respectively, to 'take
all reasonable steps' to prevent land from becoming or continuing to be a
derelict site. Land in the occupation of a Minister of State or of the Office of
Public Works are exempt by virtue of s.2 of the Act.

The 1990 Act also provides for improved enforcement mechanisms. S.11
empowers a local auhtority to serve a notice requiring specified improve-
ments be carried out by the owner of the site in question. The Act also

authorises the compulsory acquisition of a derelict site, subject to compensation (this re-enacts provisions from the 1961 Act).

Of particular importance is s.23 the Act, which provides for the imposition of an annual levy on urban derelict sites, with a view to encouraging development of such sites. The amount of the levy is a matter for determination by the Minister for the Environment. Such a levy would appear to be similar to the industrial training levy which withstood constitutional challenge in *Cityview Press Ltd v An Chomhairle Oiliúna* [1980] IR 381; but see the comments on s.23 by Delany, Annotation, above, for an alternative view.

See also the Derelict Sites Regulations 1990 (SI No. 192).

ELECTIONS

1 Double registration The decision of the Supreme Court in *Quinn and Ors v Waterford Corporation* [1991] ILRM 433; [1990] 2 IR 507 established what may turn out to be a short-lived right to be registered in two different electoral constituencies: see 175, above in the Constitutional Law chapter.

2 Postponement of elections The Local Elections (Specification of Local Election Year) Order 1990 (SI No. 104), made under s.2 of the Local Elections Act 1973, had the effect of postponing the local government elections until 1991. At the time, the postponement caused considerable political controversy.

ENVIRONMENTAL CONTROL

Air Pollution *Cork County Council v Angus Fine Chemicals Ltd* [1991] ILRM 173; [1990] 2 IR 365 concerned a prosecution for failure to comply with the terms of the Air Pollution Act 1987: see 469, below, in the Safety and Health chapter.

Environmental impact assessment The Regulations made in 1990 are referred to 418, below.

HOUSING

Fitness for habitation The decision of the Supreme Court in *Burke v Dublin Corporation*, Supreme Court, 26 July 1990 concerning the duty of care of a housing authority under s.66 of the Housing Act 1966 was discussed in the 1989 Review, 117-25.

House grants   The Housing Act 1988 (Commencement) Order 1990 (SI No. 33) brought into effect from 16 February 1990 the following sections of the 1988 Act: s.3 (house-buying subsidy), s.25 (first-time buyer subsidy for separated couples) and s.26 (housing grants for elderly and other categories of persons). The Housing (New House Grants etc.) Regulations 1990 (SI No. 34), as amended by the Housing (New House Grants etc.) (Amendment) Regulations 1990 (SI No. 301), give detailed effect to the implementation of these sections.

MALICIOUS INJURIES

In *Duggan v Dublin Corporation* [1991] ILRM 330 the Supreme Court held that, in most circumstances, a claim under the Malicious Injuries Act 1981 cannot be made in respect of property stolen during a robbery.

The applicant was the owner of a jewellery shop. The shop was entered by a three man gang, who committed extensive property damage inside the shop, struck the applicant on the arm with a baseball bat (breaking his arm in three places) and stole a number of trays of rings and other items of jewellery. The gang escaped in a car driven by a fourth member. The jewellery stolen was valued at £10,650, while the damage done to the display cases in the shop was in the sum of £750. The applicant claimed damages against the Corporation under s.6 of the 1981 Act, which provides that a malicious injuries claim for stolen property can be made arising from a situation in which 'three or more persons . . . are tumultuously and riotously assembled together . . . .' The applicant's claim was dismissed in the Circuit Court, and on a case stated to the Supreme Court (Finlay CJ, McCarthy and O'Flaherty JJ) that view was affirmed.

Delivering the Court's leading judgment, Finlay CJ concentrated on the correct interpretation of thr words 'tumultuously and riotously assembled' in s.6 of the 1981 Act. He rejected the applicant's argument that 'and' should be construed in a disjunctive sense, because to do so would be to amend the section. Such an interpretation was impermissible, he stated, having regard in particular to s.5 of the Act, which dealt with claims for damage to property as opposed to stolen property. S.5 had used the phrase 'unlawfully, riotously or tumultuously', and this difference lent force to the conclusion that 'and' in s.6 should be construed in the conjunctive sense. For another 'conjunctive or disjunctive' problem see *Capemel Ltd v Lister* [1989] IR 319 (1989 Review, 125-6).

A connected problem arose, however, because of the reference to 'three or more persons' in s.6 of the 1981 Act. Quoting the judgment of Lyell J in *Dwyer Ltd v Metropolitan Police District Receiver* [1967] 2 QB 970, Finlay

CJ concluded that the reference to three persons might have been included in s.6 to reflect the common law definition of 'riot'. The Chief Justice accepted that while the idea of three persons engaged in an activity might not be readily consistent with the concept of a 'tumultuous' as well as a 'riotous' assembly, it did not render s.6 inoperable. He also accepted the description of 'tumultuosly' given by the late Gibson LJ in *Fosters of Castlereagh Ltd v Secretary of State* [1976] NI 25. Having reviewed these authorities, Finlay CJ provided this guidance as to the future application of s.6:

> In short and in layman's language, I take the view that the proper meaning of this section is that it was intended in respect of property which has been stolen, as distinct from damaged, to confine the right to compensation to cases where looting had taken place as part of a riot. So construed as to its intention, the necessity to prove a tumultuous assembly separately from and in addition to a riotous assembly becomes plain and meaningful.

The result, as McCarthy J noted in a separate concurring judgment, would appear to be that s.6 of the 1981 Act should be interpreted as providing redress for loss sustained through looting, and in that respect the apparent disharmony between ss.5 and 6 of the 1981 Act can be resolved.

MULTI-STOREY BUILDINGS

Building control On the effect of the Building Control Act 1990, see 405-6, above.

Certification The Local Government (Multi-Storey Buildings) (Amendment) Regulations 1990 (SI No. 95) amend the 1988 Regulations by providing for a new form of certification and for the time within which they must be submitted.

OFFICE HOLDER

Turley v Laois County Council, High Court, 29 January 1990 is an important decision on the circumstances in which a local authority office may be abolished pursuant to s.10 of the Local Government Act 1941. The case is discussed in the Labour Law chapter, 341, above.

PLANNING

Advice of inspectors   The validity of the planning permission given to the 'Radio Tara' transmission mast was considered in *O'Keeffe v An Bord Pleanála and Anor*, High Court, 31 July 1990; Supreme Court, 15 February 1991. The case is discussed in the Administrative Law chapter, 16, above.

In essence, the Supreme Court held (reversing the High Court) that in the instant case, the applicant had not discharged the onus placed on him to establish that the respondent Board had acted unreasonably in granting the planning permission for the mast. In particular, even though the Board had before it reports from its own experts which indicated the hazards of granting the permission the Supreme Court held that the Board had been entitled to reach the conclusion it did on a perusal of the entire of the Reports before it, notwithstanding the strength and clarity of the actual recommendations against granting permission made in them.

Bord Pleanála: minutes   In the *O'Keeffe* case, above, the Supreme Court also rejected a point on the Board's procedure for keeping minutes. It held that there was no obligation on the Board to keep contemporaneous minutes of its proceedings; and that, in any event, having regard to the failure of the applicant to seek a minute of its proceedings its procedure was not infirm for judicial review purposes. This would appear to limit to some extent the range of the decision of the Supreme Court itself in *P. & F. Sharpe Ltd v Dublin City and County Manager* [1989] ILRM 565; [1989] IR 701 (1988 Review, 296-301).

Compensation for refusal   The Local Government (Planning and Development) Act 1990 amended substantially the provisions of the 1963 Act concernning compensation for a refusal of planning permission. The 1990 Act results from a number of years of public disquiet and Oireachtas pressure on successive governments concerning well-publicised awards of compensation. For some years, the suggestion had been made that the 1963 Act was required as a mechanism for ensuring that property rights under Articles 40.3 and 43 of the Constitution were not infringed. But in *XJS Investments Ltd v Dun Laoghaire Corporation* [1987] ILRM 659, McCarthy J had doubted whether the somewhat extravagent effects of the compensation regime was constitutionally proper (1987 Review, 101). Further public disquiet emerged in the wake of the long-running *Grange Developments* litigation: see the 1988 Review, 312-4. It also emerged that, in order to avoid payment of compensation, planning authorities had in some instances given undertakings to developers which were not, perhaps, in the best interests of overall planning policy. The 1990 Act emerged from this general background.

In essence, the Act places greater limits on the circumstances in which compensation for refusal may be sought. The Second Schedule to the 1990 Act sets out the list of developments in respect of which a refusal of planning permission will not attract compensation. The Third Schedule sets out an extensive list of reasons for refusal of planning permission which, when used by a planning authority, exclude compensation. And the Fourth Schedule to the Act is a list of conditions which may be imposed by a planning authority on the granting of planning permission, again without attracting compensation.

The Local Government (Planning and Development) (Compensation) Regulations 1990 (SI No. 144) set out the detailed procedures to be followed under the 1990 Act.

Development plan   The effect of breaching a Development Plan arose in two cases in 1990.

In *Wilkinson v Dublin County Council* [1991] ILRM 605, the issue arose again in the context of providing halting sites for members of the travelling community. The respondent Council, through an order made by the County Manager, proposed the development of land as a halting site for over 60 families of the travelling community. It was intended to develop the site with hard core surfaces, water points, communal toilet facilities and refuse skips. The applicant sought judicial review of the Manager's order on the ground, *inter alia*, that it constituted a material contravention of the Council's Development Plan and was therefore not authorised under s.39 of the Local Government (Planning and Development) Act 1963. Costello J quashed the Manager's order.

He noted that the Council's development plan permitted the use of caravans designed for year-round human habitation of the type used by the travelling community, and that the Council had effected certain amendments to the Plan in light of the decision of O'Hanlon J in *O'Leary v Dublin County Council* [1988] IR 150, also a case concerning halting sites: see the 1988 Review, 308-9.

However, Costello J also pointed out that the Council was required by the terms of the 1963 Act to consider the proper planning and development of the area in question. Having regard to that general obligation, he concluded that the nature and size of the proposed halting site was one which no reasonable planning authority could consider was consistent with the proper planning and development of the area; and having regard to the evidence presented he could not accept that the site could be regarded as a short-term emergency measure. He concluded:

> In my opinion, such a development, whether it is called a halting site or a residential caravan park, is a material contravention of the plan because no reasonable planning authority could regard this development as being consistent with the proper planning and development of the area. For this reason the Manager's Order was *ultra vires* his powers and should be quashed. This does not mean that the site cannot be developed as a halting site; it means that it cannot be developed as a halting site on the scale now proposed.

The last sentence in this quotation is of interest, because the County Manager later adopted a more modest plan for development of the site. This was held by MacKenzie J to constitute a material contravention of the Development Plan and was also one which required a decision of the elected councillors. The Council obtained an expedited appeal to the Supreme Court. On appeal, the Court held, in *ex tempore* judgments, that the new plan was valid: *Irish Times*, 8 November 1990. Speaking for the Court, Finlay CJ was reported as saying that the plan did not contravene any zoning provisions; that since the matter was not explicitly a reserved function under the County Management Acts the courts should not make it so; and (implicitly disagreeing with the view taken by Costello J in the *Wilkinson* case) that the courts should not go behind the evidence of the Manager that the site would be a temporary arrangement. While this would, in the ordinary course, have been an end to the matter, a number of residents of the area were not prepared to allow the revised plan to proceed. Successful applications were made by the Council to have three men jailed for contempt of court, and they spent a week in prison. A further application to commit 10 other residents was also brought by the Council. This application was ultimately adjourned, with undertakings given by the residents to obey all relevant court orders, when a further revised plan for a yet more limited development formed the basis for agreement between the Council and the residents and the members of the travelling community affected by the plan: see *Irish Times*, 13 and 15 December 1990.

For completeness, we should mention that in the *Wilkinson* case Costello J dealt with other points which the parties had raised in the case but which in the end did not affect the outcome. He held that s.13 of the Housing Act 1988 empowered the Council to provide halting sites for the travelling community, and since this was not expressed to be a reserved function, it could be carried out by the County Manager on behalf of the Council, and thus the Manager had acted *intra vires* in that respect. Nor did Costello J consider that the applicant had established that his constitutional rights of property were infringed by the failure of the Council to consult him prior to the proposed development. Finally, since the land in question was owned by the Council he held that it was free to use it as it thought fit provided it was not in breach of the development plan or did not involve the commission of a tort.

The second case in 1990 in which a breach of a Development Plan arose was *Griffin v Galway City and County Manager*, High Court, 31 October 1990. The applicant was the owner of a six acre holding of land, divided into two fields. The frontage of the holding was on a national primary route. In 1987, the applicant sought planning permission for the erection of a dwelling house on one of the fields. This was refused on the ground that it would breach the Galway County Development Plan, which provided that frontage development outside the 30 mph speed limit was to be restricted in order to preserve the effectiveness of the roads in regard to safe speed and capacity. In 1988, the applicant was granted permission to retain a splayed access gate to the land, subject to the condition that it be used for agricultural purposes only. In 1989 the applicant sought planning permission for the erection of a dwelling house on the other field which comprised the holding. Permission was refused on the same grounds as given in the 1987 application.

A further application was also made in 1989, with the difference that access was sought through the gateway for which agricultural use had been granted in 1988. It was indicated to an elected councillor that this application would also be refused. This councillor, along with two other councillors, then put down a motion under s.4 of the City and County Management (Amendment) Act 1955 requiring the respondent Manager to grant the planning permission requested. At the Council meeting that considered the s.4 motion, an engineer's report was presented which referred to the applicant's agricultural business, and councillors who spoke also referred to the needs of the applicant to have a dwelling on the holding in order to conduct his business. The respondent Manager informed the meeting that permission would be in breach of its Development Plan. Nonetheless, the s.4 motion was passed. The Manager, after consultation with the Council's Law Agent, declined to implement the resolution. The applicant then applied for judicial review to implement the s.4 resolution. Blayney J refused the relief sought.

Central to his conclusions were the Supreme Court decision in *P & F Sharpe Ltd v Dublin City and County Manager* [1989] ILRM 565; [1989] IR 701 (1988 Review, 296-301) and Blayney J's own decision in *Flanagan v Galway City and County Manager* [1990] 2 IR 66 (1989 Review, 330-1). In *Griffin*, he held that the Council had acted *ultra vires* in granting the permission, since it was clear from the minutes of the meeting that the councillors did not have regard to the proper planning and development of the area as required by s.26 of the Local Government (Planning and Development) Act 1963. In particular, the provisions of the Development Plan had not been taken into account, and the councillors had also taken into account the irrelevant considerations of the personal business circumstances of the applicant. In those circumstances, he concluded that the respondent Manager had correctly declined to implement the s.4 resolution.

Discretion to refuse relief   This was discussed in *Molloy v Dublin County Council* [1990] ILRM 633; [1990] 1 IR 90: see, 420-1, below.

Duty of care   In *Sunderland v Louth County Council* [1990] ILRM 658, the Supreme Court held that the defendant Council did not owe a duty of care under the Local Government (Planning and Development) Act 1963 to the plaintiffs as purchasers of a house for which permission had been granted by the Council as planning authority: see the discussion in the Torts chapter, 545-9, below.

Environmental impact assessment   A number of Regulations concerning environmental impact assessment (EIA) were made in 1990. The Local Government (Planning and Development) Regulations 1990 (SI No. 25) further incorporated the EIA requirements into the planning code, including the procedure to be followed on appeal to An Bord Pleanála. The Regulations also deal with developments carried out by local authorities. The Fisheries (Environmental Impact Assessment) Regulations 1990 (SI No. 40) apply the EIA requirements to applications for the culture of salmon at sea and require that the EIA be sent to various specified bodies, including An Taisce. The Fisheries (Environmental Impact Assessment) (No. 2) Regulations 1990 (SI No. 41) apply the EIA requirement to an application for an aquaculture licence under s.54 of the Fisheries Act 1980. The Gas Act 1976 (Sections 4 and 40A) Regulations 1990 (SI No. 51) specify the period within which EIAs must be sent to specified bodies where required for developments under the 1976 Act. The Air Navigation and Transport (Environmental Impact Assessment) Regulations 1990 (SI No. 116) specify those bodies to whom EIAs concerning air transport developments are to be sent. The Petroleum and Other Minerals Development Act 1960 (Section 13A) Regulations 1990 (SI No. 141) set out the prescribed bodies to whom EIAs are to be sent for comment and the prescribed period within which they must be considered in respect of developments under the 1960 Act. The Foreshore (Environmental Impact Assessment) Regulations 1990 (SI No. 220) prescribe the time limits within which EIAs must be considered and the prescribed bodies to which they must be sent in respect of developments on the foreshore. The Arterial Drainage Acts 1945 and 1955 (Environmental Impact Assessment) Regulations 1990 (SI No. 323) require EIAs under the Acts to be sent to each Department of State, a somewhat more limited list than under the other 1990 Regulations.

Exempted development: garage In *Murray v Buckley*, High Court, 5 December 1990 Barron J held that a 1,500 square foot garage came within the terms of Class 3 of Part 1 of the Third Schedule to the Local Government (Planning and Development) Regulations 1977 as an exempted garage development. It should be noted that, in this case, the house with which the garage was connected was a particularly large structure, that the garden attached to the house was large and that, in the case of the respondent owner Barron J stated that '[i]t is not unreasonable that the owner should require to keep three cars under cover.'

Exempted development: water pollution notice *Clarke v Brady*, High Court, 30 October 1990 involved the question of the interaction between the planning code and the water pollution legislation. The respondent, a farmer, had been served with a notice from Meath County Council under s.12 of the Local Government (Water Pollution) Act 1977. This required him, in order to reduce the danger of polluting matter from entering waters, to carry out certain measures, including the provision of sealed holding tanks for all contaminated farm effluence, the details of which were to be supplied to the Council prior to commencement of construction. The respondent supplied the Council with an engineer's report which indicated the works he intended to carry out pursuant to the s.12 notice. The Council approved the works but indicated that they might require planning permission. The respondent proceeded to carry out the works. The applicant sought an order under s.27 of the Local Government (Planning and Development) Act 1976 restraining the respondent from continuing the construction of certain walls and roofs of a slurry tank and silage area until planning permission had been obtained for them. The respondent argued that the works were an exempted development under Art.4 of the Local Government (Planning and Development) Regulations 1984 (which amended the principal 1977 Regulations) since they were being carried out pursuant to the s.12 notice. Hamilton P accepted this argument in part but also restrained some works until planning permission was obtained.

The central issue in the case was whether the works in question were necessary to comply with the s.12 notice. The President of the High Court concluded that the proportion of the work being carried out by the respondent concerning the construction of a new shed and its roofing and walls as well as additional cattle cubicles was not necessary to comply with the s.12 notice and so was not exempted development under the 1984 Regulations. However, he also held that the construction of a new silage slab and of a slatted area over the holding tank was necessary to ensure compliance with the notice. That portion of the works was, therefore, exempted under the 1984 Regulations.

Non-compliance with regulations *Molloy and Anor v Dublin County Council* [1990] ILRM 633; [1990] 1 IR 90 concerned a number of different points.

The plaintiffs were the occupiers of adjoining cottages. The second plaintiff was entitled to the beneficial ownership of the cottage under a will, though he had not been formally registered as owner. The plaintiffs applied to the defendant Council for planning permission to erect a petrol filling station on the site of the cottages. The address for notification of the Council's decision was given as the first plaintiff's. The Council sought clarification of the second plaintiff's entitlement to ownership of the cottage he occupied, and this was furnished by letter from the second plaintiff's sister. The Council refused the application for permission, but this was notified by letter to the second plaintiff's sister, and no notification was sent to the plaintiffs.

The plaintiffs sought a declaration that, since the two month time limit had expired under the Planning Acts, they must be deemed to have obtained the permission. The Council argued that: notification to the second plaintiff's sister was sufficient since she was deemed to be an agent of the plaintiffs'; the plaintiffs should have applied for permission to demolish the cottages prior to seeking planning permission; the court should exercise its discretion to refuse the relief sought on the basis that the plaintiffs had not exhausted the appeal mechanisms in the Planning Acts; and that the application did not comply with the Local Government (Planning and Development) Regulations 1977. Blayney J rejected all the Council's arguments and granted the plaintiffs the declaration they sought.

As to the adequacy of the notification, he rejected the argument that the second plaintiff's sister had held herself out, in her letter replying to the Council's request for information, as the plaintiffs' agent in the planning application. He thus concluded that no valid notification had been sent to the plaintiffs.

As to the failure to seek permission to demolish the cottages, Blayney J considered that the Council could not rely on this point now since it had originally dealt with the application without any reference to this course of action. While he described this as a 'mistake' on the Council's part, he appeared to be indicating that the Council was estopped from raising this point at this stage of the proceedings.

Then he dealt with the discretion point raised by the Council, which he also rejected. He distinguished the instant case from that in *Creedon v Dublin Corporation* [1983] ILRM 339; [1984] IR 428. In *Creedon*, a refusal had been notified within the statutory time limit, and the plaintiff sought a declaration that the refusal was invalid. The Supreme Court declined the application on the basis that the statutory appeal mechanism had not been exhausted. Blayney J pointed out that in the instant case no valid notification had taken place so that no appeal could have been taken. This approach appears to conflict with that taken by Costello J in the later decision *O'Keeffe v An Bord Pleanála*, High Court, 31 July 1990 (17, above, in the Administrative Law chapter), where an *ultra vires* decision was held to be appealable. It also seems to ignore what might be described as the 'motives' test adopted by the Supreme Court in *The State (Abenglen Properties Ltd) v Dublin Corporation* [1982] ILRM 590; [1984] IR 381.

Finally, Blayney J dealt with what he described as the main submission in the case, namely whether the plaintiffs had complied with the requirements of the Local Government (Planning and Development) Regulations 1977. He quoted with approval the judgment of Henchy J in *Monaghan UDC v Alf-A-Bet Promotions Ltd* [1980] ILRM 64, where a 'substantial compliance' test was adopted and where Henchy J accepted that certain non-compliance could be ignored under the *de minimis* rule. Blayney J considered that the instant case fell within the *de minimis* rule. He accepted that some of the documentation was inadequate but that, looked at in the overall, all necessary information was available to the Council to enable it to make its decision.

Blayney J added a rider to his judgment. He stated that he had reached his decision 'with considerable regret', acknowledging that it had the effect of granting a permission which the Council had not intended to grant. He accepted that the two month notification rule in s.26(4) of the Local Government (Planning and Development) Act 1963 was intended to ensure decisions were made within a reasonable time, but he felt that the consequence of non-compliance was disproportionate. He felt it would be relatively simple to devise some alternative sanction, and he hoped that the Oireachtas might give serious consideration to this suggestion.

Notification This point was dealt with in the *Molloy* case, above.

Practice: judicial review The Supreme Court in *O'Keeffe v An Bord Pleanála and Anor*, High Court, 31 July 1990; Supreme Court, 15 February 1991 (16, above, in the Administrative Law Chapter) issued what amounted to a Practice Direction on aspects of appeals in planning cases. Delivering the Court's leading judgment, the Chief Justice made two important points at the end of that judgment. First, an applicant for judicial review must seek to join, and the court should normally join, any party who is likely to be affected by the avoidance of the decision impugned. Second where judicial review is by way of a plenary summons, the action should be presented by way of oral evidence, unless the court by express order directs a hearing on affidavit or accepts from the parties an expressly agreed statement of facts.

SANITARY SERVICES

Bradley and Anor v Meath County Council [1991] ILRM 179 concerned the extent of the respondent Council's obligation as sanitary authority to deal with domestic refuse. Costello J held that there was no mandatory duty on it to provide such a service.

The applicants sought judicial review of the decision of the respondent Council to discontinue its domestic refuse collection service and to contract it out to a private company. The first applicant was an elected councillor. The second applicant was a householder in the Council's administrative area. The private refuse collector declined to collect the second applicant's refuse and the nearest approved dump was 25 miles from her home. The applicants claimed that the respondent Council was in breach of statutory duty in failing to provide for a domestic refuse collection service. Costello J held against the applicants on all grounds put forward.

The main argument centred on s.52 of the Public Health (Ireland) Act 1878. In *Louth County Council v Matthews*, High Court, 14 April 1989 (1989 Review, 336-7) the parties had accepted for the purposes of that case that s.52 laid down a mandatory duty on a Council to provide a domestic refuse collection service. No such concession was made in the *Bradley* case. Costello J concluded that s.52 did not impose a statutory duty on a sanitary authority to provide a refuse collection service, but merely empowered the authority to do so in non-mandatory terms. Similarly, he held that a sanitary authority was not obliged to make byelaws under s.54 of the 1878 Act as to a domestic refuse collection service, since that section was also couched in non-mandatory terms. Thus, the Council was not obliged to lay down conditions for a private refuse collector if it chose not to do so.

Two further arguments were also rejected by Costello J. The applicants pointed to the duty imposed on a local authority under s.7 of the Housing of the Working Classes Act 1885 as to the condition of housing provided under that Act. He held that the duty in s.7 must be read in the context of that Act as a whole; and since the 1885 Act was intended to deal with the general physical condition of dwellings it would not be apt to construe it as imposing a duty to provide a domestic refuse collection service. Finally, Costello J held that while the respondent Council had in the instant case exercised the power conferred on it by Reg.5 of the European Communities (Waste) Regulations 1979 to issue a licence for the collection of domestic refuse, the Regulations could not be construed as imposing a statutory duty on sanitary authorities themselves to undertake the collection of household refuse. Nor did he think that the 1979 Regulations could be taken to extend the duty under the 1878 Act or to lead to a construction of the 1878 Act other than from the Act's own provisions.

ULTRA VIRES RULE

The problems associated with the old *ultra vires* rule for local authorities were illustrated by the decision of Gannon J in *Ballybay Meat Exports Ltd v Monaghan County Council* [1990] ILRM 864: see 406-7, above. With the maze of legislation involved, it is not surprising that judges took differing views of the extent of the powers given to authorities: contrast *Louth County Council v Matthews*, High Court, 14 April 1989 (1989 Review, 336) with *Bradley v Meath County Council* [1991] ILRM 179 (422, above). The general change to the *ultra vires* rule effected by s.6 of the Local Government Act 1991 (to be discussed in the 1991 Review) may make such cases less frequent.

VALUATION (RATING)

Annual letting value The relevant factors to be taken into account in determining the annual letting value of premises for rating purposes were considered in the important judgment of Barron J in *Irish Management Institute v Commissioner of Valuation* [1990] 2 IR 409.

The IMI premises in Dundrum, County Dublin comprise a large administrative and teaching complex on 13 acres with substantial car-parking facilities. A rateable valuation of £2,400 had been placed on the premises by the respondent Commissioner, but this was reduced to £1,900 by the Valuation Tribunal. The Tribunal had reduced the valuation on the basis of a comparison with the annual letting value of certain other premises. S.11 of the Valuation (Ireland) Act 1852 requires a valuation be based on the rent which a hypothetical tenant would pay for the hereditament taking one year with another. The 'comparison' basis was established to take account of the effects of inflation. This long-established practice was given statutory backing in s.5(1) of the Valuation Act 1986. S.5(2) of the 1986 Act provides that in making such comparisons 'regard shall be had, in so far as is reasonably practicable, to the valuations of tenements and rateable hereditaments which are comparable and of similar function and whose valuations have been made or revised within a recent period.' The Valuation Tribunal held that additions to Trinity College Dublin made in 1969 and 1979 constituted the closest comparison with the IMI complex but it also took into account that those attending IMI courses would be more affluent than Trinity College students and that the valuation should reflect this. The Tribunal also rejected a comparison with FÁS training centres on the ground that valuations of those premises were tied directly to commercial values.

Barron J held that the fundamental basis on which valuations are made under s.11 of the 1852 Act had not been altered by s. 5(1) of the 1986 Act; it was simply that the relevance of inflation was recognised in statutory form. He continued:

> The sub-section [s. 5(1)] is seeking to establish an overall ratio between annual letting values and valuation. This overall ratio will alter with inflation since annual letting values will alter with inflation while valuations remain the same. It was the gap caused by failure to provide the satisfactory mechanism for these circumstances in earlier legislation which s. 5 of the Act of 1986 was intended to fill. Notwithstanding this general intention, [s. 5] sub section (2) recognizes that the overall ratio may differ as between rateable hereditaments of different function for example as between offices on the one hand and, say, shops on the other.

Barron J therefore pointed out that s. 5(1) and (2) should be considered together, as two parts of one overall test, rather than separately, and he considered that the Tribunal had split the two subsections in the instant case. Second, he held that three factors must be taken into account in the application of s. 5(2): (a) valuations which are comparable; (b) valuations which relate to tenements and hereditaments of similar function; and (c) valuations which have been made or revised within a recent period.

On the specifics of the comparison premises referred to by the Tribunal, Barron J held that it had been right to disregard evidence as to commercial use. However, he held that the rent of FÁS training centres should have been taken into account if such premises were as a matter of fact of similar function. Similarly, once the Tribunal had found that the Trinity College buildings were comparable to the IMI premises, it was making a finding that they had the same net annual value. The relative affluence of the students then became immaterial, he held, because that factor must have been an element taken into account by the hypothetical tenant under the s.11 formula and so had already been taken into account in finding equality on net annual value.

Tanks: containment or process of change   *Caribmolasses Co Ltd v Commissioner of Valuation* [1991] ILRM 1 was another case on the issue as to whether certain industrial structures were rateable. In this instance, the issue arose in the context of the recent amendments to the rating code in the Valuation Act 1986.

The company owned and operated two large tanks at Dublin Docks. Crude molasses was pumped into the tanks from ships, and hot water was later added to the molasses externally to achieve a standardised consistency for the company's customers. The Commissioner of Valuation determined that the tanks were rateable hereditaments under the valuation code. The company appealed to the Valuation Tribunal which held that the tanks were non-rateable in accordance with s. 8 of the 1986 Act. S. 8, inserting a new Schedule into s. 15 of the Annual Revision of Rateable Property (Ireland) Amendment Act 1860, provides that 'constructions which are designed or used primarily for storage or containment (whether or not the purpose of such containment is to allow a natural or a chemical process to take place)' are rateable. The section also exempts from rating any such constructions 'designed or used primarily to induce a process of change in the substance contained or transmitted'. Gannon J, upholding the decision of the Tribunal, agreed that, under the 1986 Act, the tanks in question were exempt.

Gannon J attempted to provide a summary of the effect of s. 8 of the 1986 Act, acknowledging that the application of the valuation code had 'now become as difficult for the Commissioner of Valuation as for the layman setting up in business.' He distinguished between two types of containment of a substance under s. 8:

> The one is primarily designed or used for storage or containment. If it is so used it is a rateable hereditament even though during the period of storage some natural or chemical process takes place. (No reference is made here to a change of substance.) The other is primarily designed or used 'to induce a process of change in the substance contained'. If it is so used it is not a rateable hereditament even though the process requires containment for a determined or indeterminate period. The use of the qualifying word 'primarily' indicates some degree of latitude in relation to factual circumstances of purpose. It also conveys to my mind that it is not intended that the mere containment should be the only means of inducing change of substance. It seems to me that if the containment assists in or is an integral part of the process of change, even though merely as ancillary to some other catalytic agency, it comes within the ambit of being used to induce a process of change. In such circumstances the construction is not a rateable category of plant. That is, I think, a necessary corollary to the circumstances prescribed in which by contrast it would be a rateable hereditament notwithstanding that the process of change might take place.

On this basis, he concluded that the company's tanks were non-rateable under s. 8 of the 1986 Act since they were used primarily to induce a process of change in the substance contained in them, even though the containment was merely ancillary to some other catalytic agency.

Gannon J noted earlier in his judgment that similar cases in the past had concentrated on the question whether such tanks constituted 'machinery' for the purposes of the valuation code: see *Beamish & Crawford Ltd v Commissioner of Valuation* [1980] ILRM 149 and *Pfizer Chemical Corp v Commissioner of Valuation*, High Court, 9 May 1989 (1989 Review, 337). Gannon J did not find these decisions particularly helpful. While Costello J in the *Pfizer* case had expressed the hope (quoted by Gannon J in the instant case) that the 1986 Act had dispelled the difficulties which the older cases had given rise to, it may be that the level of resulting clarity may be similar to that of the substance held in the tanks in the instant case.

Tanks: grain silo   *D. Coakley & Co Ltd v Commissioner of Valuation*, High Court, 29 May 1990 concerned structures quite similar to those in the *Caribmolasses* case, above, though the focus of attention was on a different provision in the valuation code.

The applicant company operated a grain silo. The silo consisted of a number of grain bins, each of which was fed by a number of conveyers and elevators and other machinery. The respondent Commissioner accepted that the conveyors and elevators were not rateable as they constituted manufacturing plant for the purposes of s. 7 of the Annual Revision of Rateable Property (Ireland) Amendment Act 1860. This section of the 1860 Act has been amended by s. 7 of the Valuation Act 1986, though the relevant provisions for the instant case remain unchanged (but the judgment in *Coakley* does not indicate whether the valuation raised in the case predated the 1986 Act).

In the Circuit Court, Judge Fawsitt found that the silo itself also constituted a manufactory for the purposes of s. 7 of the 1860 Act. The Commissioner requested a case stated. Judge Fawsitt had retired at the time the High Court heard the case stated, which created a slight procedural difficulty to which we will return presently.

On the substantive point, Barron J held that, on the authorities cited to him (which he does not specify) the silos constituted machinery within s. 7 of the 1860 Act, but he found the question as to whether the silos constituted a 'manufactory' within s. 7 much more difficult. On this, he referred exclusively to a number of revenue authorities which dealt with the vexed question of 'manufacture'. Citing *dicta* of Murphy J in *Cronin v Strand Dairy Ltd*, High Court, 18 December 1985, as approved by the Supreme Court in *C. McCann Ltd v Ó Culacháin* [1986] IR 196, Barron J pointed out that while various functions were performed on the grain to make it suitable for sale to the company's customers these did not purport to produce a different product. Since the essential purpose of a silo was to handle grain, he concluded that it could not constitute a 'manufactory' within s. 7 of the 1860 Act.

Since there was no evidence in the case stated to justify the findings of the Circuit Court that the silos constituted a manufactory within s.7 of the 1860 Act, the normal course might have been to return the matter to the Circuit Court. However, since Judge Fawsitt had retired, Barron J considered that the correct approach was, simply, to make an order that the silos were not exempt from rating. He noted that, in the somewhat similar circumstances which had arisen in *North Western Health Board v Martyn* [1988] ILRM 519; [1987] IR 565, neither party had requested a remittal for further findings of fact and the Supreme Court had held that in those circumstances the findings must be taken to have been justified. He distinguished that case by reference to the retirement of Judge Fawsitt.

Finally, Barron J rejected two estoppel-type points raised by the applicant company. He held that, although the Commissioner's concession that the machinery in the silos were not rateable must have been based, in part, on a view that the entire plant was a manufactory, he was not estopped from raising an issue of fact in the instant case. Nor did he consider that he could decide in the company's favour even though Judge Fawsitt had, it appeared, found that similar plant in the premises next door to the applicant was exempt from rating and that this decision had not been appealed. This approach would appear to be in line with the general principle in cases such as *McMahon v Leahy* [1985] ILRM 423; [1984] IR 525. Barron J commented, however, that: 'It seems wrong to me that like premises should be treated differently, if that be so.'

WATER POLLUTION

The Local Government (Water Pollution) (Amendment) Act 1990 is discussed in the Safety and Health chapter, 470-3, below.

Practice and Procedure

APPELLATE COURT FUNCTION

1 Assessment of damages In *Bakht v Medical Council* [1990] ILRM 840, the Supreme Court assessed damages on the basis that the cost of remitting the matter to the High Court for assessment would be out of all proportion to the level of damages likely to be awarded there: see 338, above.

2 Grounds of appeal In *The State (Gallagher Shatter & Co.) v de Valera (No. 2)*, Supreme Court, 8 February 1990 (dealt with below, 430), the Chief Justice indicated that parties should discontinue what appeared to him to be an expanding practice of submitting grounds of appeal to the Supreme Court which contain no more than a mere statement of grievance with an order of the High Court. No doubt this requirement for more specific grounds would be of assistance in assessing the length of an appeal and thus help in a small way towards alleviating the Court's backlog of appeals.

3 Review of trial court's findings The well-established limitations on an appeal court's functions of review in an appeal on a point of law were applied by the Supreme Court in *The People v Egan (L.)* [1990] ILRM 780 (see 193, above).

CASE STATED

Form of case stated In *D.P.P.(Crowley) v Connors*, High Court, 10 May 1990, Lavan J bemoaned the mechanism of posing a general question of law for the High Court on case stated. See the advice of Blayney J in the 1989 Review, 345.

Judge retired The correct approach to the situation that arises where a Circuit Court judge who has stated a case retires before the case reaches the High Court was discussed in *D. Coakley Ltd v Commissioner of Valuation*, High Court, 29 May 1990 (see 427, above, in the Local Government chapter).

CHAMPERTY

In *McElroy v Flynn* [1991] ILRM 294, the plaintiff, trading under the name Irish Genealogical Services, specialised in tracing next-of-kin where people died intestate. He located the defendants, who were cousins of such a deceased person. The plaintiff told the defendants that he believed they were entitled to a share in an estate. He also told them that he did not know the name of the person involved, though he did in fact know the name of the deceased at that time. The defendants signed deeds of assignment which appointed the plaintiff to represent them and that in consideration of the plaintiff informing them of their entitlement they would assign him 25% of their respective shares in the estate. The defendant lodged the defendants' claim, but the defendants later repudiated the deeds of assignment. The plaintiff instituted the proceedings claiming the 25% share, but Blayney J held that the deeds of assignment were void for champerty. The case is discussed above, 270-1, in the Equitable Remedies chapter.

CONSOLIDATION

In *O'Neill v Ryan, Ryanair Ltd and Ors (No. 2)*, High Court, 21 May 1990 the Court was faced with an application for consolidation, or alternatively, simultaneous hearing of two sets of proceedings. The plaintiff's first set of proceedings against the defendants was for relief under s. 205 of the Companies Act 1963, and the other was for damages for, *inter alia*, misrepresentation, breach of contract and conspiracy. The first defendant applied to have the proceedings consolidated under O.49, r.6 of the Rules of the Superior Courts 1986 or to have them heard simultaneously. Blayney J declined to order consolidation but agreed that a simultaneous hearing was appropriate.

He noted that the relief sought under s. 205 of the Companies Act 1963 was quite different in nature from the common law relief in damages sought in the second set of proceedings, so that it would not be proper to order consolidation. Nor was it, he considered, appropriate therefore to allow the first defendant to make one lodgment under O.22, r.1(5) of the 1986 Rules in respect of the two proceedings.

A simultaneous hearing was ordered, however. Blayney J agreed that the court had an inherent jurisdiction to order that the proceedings be heard together, the dominant factors being whether there was the possibility of substantial saving of expense or inconvenience, citing *Malone v Great Northern Railway Co.* [1931] IR 1 in support. He concluded that, on the evidence to date, it was clear that there would be substantial saving of expense and that the plaintiff would not be unduly prejudiced by the joint trial, on balance there were good grounds for ordering a simultaneous hearing of the two actions. This presumption in favour of a single set of proceedings is, of course, entirely consistent with recent decisions of the Supreme Court: see the 1989 Review, 353-4.

COSTS

1 Follow the event In *Society for the Protection of Unborn Children (Irl) Ltd v Coogan and Ors (No. 2)* [1990] 1 IR 273, the Supreme Court applied the normal rule that the losing party must bear its own costs and that of the successful party: see the 1989 Review, 106-7. It may be noted that in many constitutional cases this usual approach is waived: see for example the approach of Hamilton P in a previous case involving the same plaintiff, *Society for the Protection of Unborn Children (Irl) Ltd v Open Door Counselling Ltd* [1987] ILRM 477, at 502-3 (no order as to costs made). See further Collins and O'Reilly, *Civil Proceedings and the State in Ireland*, 165-6.

2 Matrimonial proceedings In *F. v L.* [1990] ILRM 886, Barron J indicated that costs in matrimonial cases should, in general, be based on general principles: see the discussion in the Family Law chapter, 322, above.

3 Solicitor instructing self In *Bourke v W.G. Bradley & Sons (No. 2)*, Irish Times LR, 28 May 1990 Blayney J held, in an *ex tempore* judgment, that a firm of solicitors which instructs itself in proceedings in which it is defendant is entitled to recover costs awarded against the other party to the proceedings. In the substantive proceedings, *Bourke v W.G. Bradley & Sons* [1990] 1 IR 379 (1988 Review, 369-70), the High Court had awarded costs against the applicant inspector of taxes. The respondent firm of solicitors had instructed itself in the case and Blayney J held that it was entitled to recover costs in the usual way. While the substantive proceedings had indicated that the respondent firm were providing services for clients of an insurance company, Blayney J held that this did not detract from his conclusion. He noted that in many personal injuries actions either side might be indemnified by an insurance company in respect of their legal costs, yet this did not prevent the successful party from seeking costs from the unsuccessful party.

4 Taxation In *The State (Gallagher Shatter & Co.) v de Valera (No. 2)*, Supreme Court, 8 February 1990 the well-established principles on taxation of costs were applied by the Supreme Court, upholding the High Court decision of Barrington J in the case: [1987] ILRM 555; [1987] IR 55 (1987 Review, 279-80).

The prosecutors, a firm of solicitors, had originally brought *certiorari* proceedings challenging the jurisdiction of the respondent Taxing Master to tax a bill of costs more than 12 months after its delivery and where it had already been paid. The prosecutors were successful in the Supreme Court ([1986] ILRM 3) and they were awarded their costs. The respondent Taxing Master then requested taxation. On reference to taxation, another Taxing Master deducted a percentage from the brief and refresher fees which had been agreed between the prosecutors and their counsel; the basis given for this deduction was that the fees 'erred on the side of excess'. The prosecutors appealed to the High Court against the taxation, and Barrington J reinstated the fees holding that the Taxing Master had erred in reducing the fees. The respondent unsuccessfully appealed that decision to the Supreme Court (Finlay CJ, Walsh and McCarthy JJ).

Delivering the principal judgment, the Chief Justice quoted with approval a passage from the leading decision of Gannon J in *Dunne v O'Neill* [1974] IR 180, and also expressly approved the nine principles enumerated by Hamilton J (as he then was) in *Kelly v Breen* [1978] ILRM 63. From these, Finlay CJ held that, at a general level, the Taxing Master had erred in failing to consider whether a solicitor acting reasonably carefully and reasonably prudently could have made the disbursements by way of counsel's fees which were made in the instant case. He concluded that the reduction made by the Taxing Master here indicated that the Taxing Master had substituted his own view for that of the solicitor in the instant case.

Finlay CJ then dealt with a specific point adverted to by the Taxing Master, namely that there was a great disparity between what counsel for the prosecutors had marked on their brief and what the State had agreed as a fee with its counsel. The Chief Justice pointed out (and it had been accepted by the respondent) that there was, historically, a great difference between the fees charged by counsel for the State and those for the other side, and so this was not in itself a reason for overturning Barrington J's conclusion. On this disparity, the Court might have referred to the decision of Barr J in *Crotty v An Taoiseach (No. 2)* [1990] ILRM 617 in support (see the 1989 Review, 346-7).

Nor did Finlay CJ consider relevant the circumstance that there had been an indemnity against costs granted by the State to the respondent in the instant case, an arrangement which he described as 'very unusual indeed.' One might question whether such an arrangement is, in fact, unusual: see for example the comments of the Minister for Labour in the course of the Oireachtas debates on s. 40 of the Safety, Health and Welfare at Work Act 1989, referred to in Byrne, Annotation, *Irish Current Law Statutes Annotated*. This is, however, probably a moot point in the context of the particular issue before the Court in the *Gallagher Shatter* case.

DELAY

Prejudicial delay   The Supreme Court dealt again with the issue of striking out proceedings for prejudicial delay in *Toal v Duignan (No. 2)* [1991] ILRM 140: see 394-8, above.

Promptness   In *Director of Public Prosecutions v McDonnell (Dumbrell, Notice Party)*, High Court, 1 October 1990, Gannon J declined to hear a judicial review application even though it had been made within the three month time limit specified in the Rules of the Superior Courts 1986. The application was, admittedly, made on the last day provided for under the Rules and Gannon J held that there was an obligation on an applicant to seek relief with promptness: see 11, above, in the Administrative Law chapter.

DISCOVERY

Affidavit of discovery: claiming privilege   Two decisions of the Supreme Court in 1990 restated long-standing requirements that claims for privilege must be made in specific terms in an affidavit of discovery, thus halting what appeared to be a trend towards blanket claims.

In February, the Court signalled this approach in an *ex tempore* judgment in the long-running case *Bula Ltd v Tara Mines Ltd*, Irish Times Law Reports, 20 August 1990. This was confirmed in *Bula Ltd and Ors v Crowley and Ors* [1990] ILRM 756.

The plaintiffs had instituted proceedings against the defendants which involved, *inter alia*, claims of negligence and breach of duty in connection with lending transactions made between the defendants and the plaintiffs. The proceedings were instituted in 1986 and they related to transactions dating back to the early 1970s and continuing thereafter. In the course of the proceedings, an affidavit of discovery filed on behalf of one of the defendants claimed legal professional privilege in respect of certain documents without identifying the precise documents in question. Another defendant also resisted discovery in respect of communications generated after the institution of the proceedings. Finally, discovery was also resisted in respect of certain documents relating to loan transactions made prior to 1974. Another defendant had acknowledged, in a previous affidavit of discovery, the relevance of pre-1974 documents to the proceedings. The Supreme Court (Finlay CJ, Griffin and O'Flaherty JJ) ordered discovery.

The Chief Justice stated that, whatever the practice may have been in the past, privilege could not be claimed in a blanket manner in an affidavit of discovery. Relying in particular on the judgment of Walsh J in the February *Bula* case, he held that the appropriate form for such an affidavit under O.31, rr.12 and 13 of the Rules of the Superior Courts 1986 was to identify each document in question and the particular basis on which privilege was claimed. He also noted that this was consistent with the decision of the Court in *Smurfit Paribas Bank Ltd v AAB Export Finance Ltd* [1990] ILRM 588 (discussed below, 435-6). The defendants in question were therefore ordered to file a further and more detailed affidavit of discovery in connection with the claim for legal professional privilege.

Affidavit of discovery: scandalous material The long-running Bula litigation provided another point of interest in preliminary applications with the judgment of Murphy J in *Bula Ltd and Ors v Tara Mines Ltd and Ors*, High Court, 17 September 1990.

The substantive proceedings between the parties involved allegations that the defendants trespassed on the plaintiffs' ore body and that the defendants caused economic loss to the plaintiff by various means with a view to taking over the plaintiffs' ore body. In the course of motions seeking further and better discovery of documents, the plaintiffs filed a supplemental affidavit of 88 paragraphs which included a large amount of hearsay evidence concerning various meetings alleged to have been attended by the defendants since 1984 which were said to concern the circumstances giving rise to the proceedings as well as indicating that certain material remained to be discovered by the defendants. The defendants applied to have the affidavit struck out either under O.40, r.12 of the Rules of the Superior Courts 1986 as containing scandalous material or as an abuse of the process of the court. Murphy J declined to strike out the affidavit.

Applying the decision in *Savings & Investment Bank Ltd v Gasco Investments BV* [1984] 1 WLR 271, he held that since this was an interlocutory application, the plaintiffs were entitled to refer to hearsay material in the affidavit. That well-established rule is also supported by the Supreme Court's approach in *Society for the Protection of Unborn Children (Irl) Ltd v Coogan and Ors* [1990] ILRM 70; [1989] IR 734 (see 1989 Review, 150).

Murphy J went on to accept that the Court might have jurisdiction under O.40, r.12 of the 1986 Rules to strike out irrelevant material from an affidavit, and that it certainly had an inherent jurisdiction to do so. As to the instant case, he stated that while it was understandable that the defendants did not wish to respond to each of the hearsay allegations in the plaintiffs' supplemental affidavit, it would not be safe to strike out the affidavit in its entirety as being irrelevant to the issues between the parties. And while he acknowledged that responding to the affidavit would impose a considerable burden on the defendants, this was catered for in the substantial adjournment he granted to enable them to respond. He also added that it might not be necessary to respond to each of the allegations.

Privilege: documents generated after proceedings begun In *Bula Ltd and Ors v Crowley and Ors* [1990] ILRM 756, above, 432, the Supreme Court also dealt with discovery of documents generated after the institution of the proceedings. The Court was alive to the requirement that it should be satisfied as a matter of probability of the relevance of documents to the proceedings and in particular should not allow a party to indulge in an exploratory or fishing expedition in seeking further discovery. Nonetheless, because of the interrrconnected nature of the claims in the case, the Court concluded that there was sufficient indication from the statement of claim that documents generated after the institution of the proceedings could be relevant; and since the relevance of documents concerning loans given by the defendants to the plaintiffs prior to 1974 had been acknowledged already by another defendant, and having regard to the wide-ranging nature of the claim in the proceedings, such documents were discoverable.

Privilege: law enforcement function In *Director of Consumer Affairs v Sugar Distributors Ltd* [1991] ILRM 395 Costello J held that privilege attached to certain material communicated to the Director of Consumer Affairs and Fair Trade as part of his enforcement of consumer protection legislation.

The Director had instituted proceedings against the defendant company alleging that it was in breach of the Restrictive Practices (Groceries) Order 1987. A complaint had been made to the Director by a company, ASI International Foods Ltd, to the effect that the defendant had entered into contracts with a view to eliminating or restricting competition in the sugar market in Ireland. ASI was a company involved in the importation and distribution of sugar, and the defendant company was a subsidiary of the Irish Sugar Co. Ltd (now Greencore plc). The defendant applied for discovery, and the Director claimed privilege in respect of certain documents in his possession, being from ASI to a company to whom it distributed sugar. Costello J upheld the claim to privilege.

Citing with approval the decision of the House of Lords in *D. v NSPCC* [1978] AC 171, Costello J noted that the law of evidence had long recognised that the public interest may require that relevant documents should be excluded from inspection or even disclosure in both civil and criminal proceedings where such documents relate to affairs of state and also to the prevention and detection of crime. However, he also pointed out that such decisions ultimately rested not with the parties but with the courts. In accordance with the decision of the Supreme Court in *Murphy v Dublin Corporation* [1972] IR 215, any such claims to privilege must be subject to judicial decision as to whether inspection or refusal of inspection would do least harm to the public interest.

Turning to the position of the Director, he noted that the Director had been conferred with extensive powers under the Restrictive Practices (Amendment) Act 1987: to investigate the operation of orders made under restrictive practices legislation (s. 6); to enter and search premises (s. 17); to institute criminal proceedings (s. 22); and to seek injunctive relief to enforce compliance with orders (s. 55). In order to protect the proper functioning of such powers, Costello J concluded that the courts must give protection to all documents forwarded to the Director by a complainant, so that the Director can assure such complainants that information given will be treated in confidence. He added that a court should not order inspection of any documents forwarded to the Director unless, on examination by the court, they might tend to show that the defendant had not committed the wrongful acts alleged against him. Having perused the documents in the instant case, he concluded that none of them tended in any way to show that the defendant was not guilty of the offences alleged, and so inspection was refused.

The approach taken by Costello J on the question of privilege would appear to lean more towards the approach taken by the House of Lords than by the Supreme Court. In *Murphy*, the Supreme Court had expressly left for future consideration the question as to the privilege attaching to informers. In the *NSPCC* case, the House of Lords in effect decided that privilege should attach in order to further the interests of law enforcement. It is also unfortunate that Costello J did not appear to have his attention drawn to the decision of Keane J in *DPP (Hanley) v Holly* [1984] ILRM 149, in which Keane J had taken the line that no category of information could claim special status, and that each document must be examined by a court. While Costello J did actually examine the documents in question in the *Sugar Distributors* case, the reasoning he used would not appear to be as strong, in terms of the assertion of the judicial function, as that indicated in the *Murphy* case.

Privilege: legal professional In 1990, the Supreme Court confirmed the recent judicial trend against extending privilege.

In *Smurfit Paribas Bank Ltd v AAB Export Finance Ltd* [1990] ILRM 588, the defendant claimed privilege in respect of certain correspondence between it and the solicitor who at that time had acted for it in connection with a proposed floating charge which was the subject matter of the instant proceedings. The documents in question did not contain any legal advice about the proposed floating charge but they did refer to the defendant's instructions to its solicitors to enable the necessary documentation to be drafted. In the High Court, Costello J held that the correspondence was not privileged. The defendant's appeal to the Supreme Court (Finlay CJ, Walsh and McCarthy JJ) was dismissed.

At a general level, the Chief Justice (with whom Walsh J concurred) quoted with approval the comment in *Murphy v Dublin Corporation* [1972] IR 215 that it was a matter exclusively for the judicial power, exercised under Article 34.1 of the Constitution, to determine whether a party to litigation is to be compelled to produce particular evidence. As McCarthy J pointed out in his concurring judgment there was no question here of one side consenting to production: the final arbiter would be the Court.

Applying that general principle, the Court held that communications between solicitor and client attracted privilege only insofar as they arise in circumstances which can be identified as securing an objective which, in the public interest in the administration of justice, can be said to outweigh the disadvantage arising from the restriction of the disclosure of all the facts. The Court accepted that privilege attached to communications seeking advice connected to actual or potential litigation; the question posed was whether this should be extended to those cases in which the client merely seeks legal assistance. The suggestion in *Minter v Priest* [1929] 1 KB 655; [1930] AC 558 that such an extension might be recognised was expressly rejected by the Court. It concluded that the privilege was thus confined to circumstances where legal advice was sought, since in such circumstances there was the possibility of a challenge as to the correctness of such advice, and it could therefore be connected with potential litigation. In the instant case, the Court held that the communications were for legal assistance without a connection to potential litigation, and they were thus not privileged.

Finally, it may be regretted that the Court did not advert to the decision of Costello J in *Tromso Sparebank v Beirne and Ors (No. 2)* [1989] ILRM 257, where a similar restrictive approach to legal professional privilege was taken: see the 1988 Review, 331-4. The result is that the courts have shown a clear reluctance to extend the traditional boundaries of privilege; the constitutional influence has been particularly significant in this context.

Privilege: public interest   In *Ahern v Minister for Industry and Commerce (No. 2)*, High Court, 19 February 1990 (the judgment being reported on other aspects at [1990] 1 IR 55: see 10-11, above), Blayney J applied accepted principles in ordering discovery of certain documents in respect of which public interest privilege was claimed. In respect of one batch of documents, the details of which are not revealed in the judgment (but which almost certainly involved communications within the Department of Industry and

Commerce), Blayney J ordered discovery on the basis that it would not be adverse to the public interest to the public interest to permit their inspection. He expressly approved comments of Walsh J in *Murphy v Dublin Corporation* [1972] IR 215 in this context (see also above in the *Smurfit Paribas Bank* case).

In respect of a letter from the Controller of Patents, Designs and Trade Marks to the Secretary of the Department, marked 'Confidential' and a letter from the Controller to the Personnel Officer in the Department, also marked 'Confidential', Blayney J also ordered discovery. This was on the basis that it would be contrary to the interest of the administration of justice that the applicant be precluded from having access to a document which concerned himself. Thus, Blayney J distinguished such confidential documents from those found not to be discoverable in *Geraghty v Minister for Local Government* [1975] IR 300.

For an earlier discovery application in these proceedings see *Ahern v Minister for Industry and Commerce*, High Court, 11 March 1988 (discussed in the 1988 Review, 334-5) and for the final outcome, see 6-7, above.

DISTRICT COURT

Fit person order   The nature of the investigations to be conducted by the District Court when being asked to make a 'fit person' order under the Children Act 1908 was considered by the Supreme Court in *The State (F.) v Superintendent of B. Garda Station* [1990] ILRM 243 (HC); [1990] ILRM 767 (SC): see the 1989 Review, 267-9.

ENFORCEMENT OF JUDGMENTS: EUROPEAN COMMUNITIES

In *Rhatigan v Textiles y Confecciones Europeas SA* [1990] ILRM 825; [1990] IR 126, the Supreme Court dealt with important formalities to be dealt with in order to obtain judgment under the Jurisdiction of Courts and Enforcement of Judgments (European Communities) Act 1988: see the 1989 Review, 73-6.

FAIR TRADE COMMISSION REPORT

The Fair Trade Commission *Report Into Restrictive Practices in the Legal Profession* was published in June 1990, having been submitted to the Minister for Industry and Commerce in March 1990. Running to over 300 pages, it contained a large number of proposals for reform of the legal profession and of other aspects of practice. Essentially, the Commission was limited to considering whether certain activities amounted to restrictive practices for the purpose of the Restrictive Practices Acts 1972 and 1987. A number of recommendations were made.

1. The Solicitors Act 1954 should be amended to abolish what is commonly known as the solicitor's conveyancing monopoly. Consideration might be given to licensing conveyancers.

2. The drawing up of legal documents should not be confined to solicitors.

3. There should be a right of representation in the courts for what are known in Britain as McKenzie friends.

4. The Commission did not recommend that there be a fused legal profession, but that nothing should be done to frustrate such a development.

5. On access to the legal profession, the Commission saw the possibility of abuses arising from the current regulatory system, and recommended, *inter alia*, the consideration of a common vocational course for solicitors and barristers. This could require the establishment of an Institute of Legal Education. In addition the Commission recommended the establishment of an Advisory Committee on Legal Education and Training.

6. The Commission recommended that the Irish language requirement be abandoned.

7. Mandatory membership of the Law Library for barristers should also be abolished, the Commission recommended.

8. The Commission also recommended altering the distinction betweeen senior and junior counsel.

9. The Commission recommended the Law Society should encourage solicitors to take greater advantage of the right of audience granted by the Courts Act 1971.

10. The Commission recommended changes in the requirement that a barrister may only be briefed through a solicitor.

11. The rule that a junior counsel be briefed with a senior counsel should also be removed, the Commission stated.

12. The Commission also recommended considerable changes in the prohibition on barristers forming partnerships with other barristers. Differences emerged on whether professional indemnity insurance should be mandatory from the date of entry into the legal profession.

13. The Commission recommended that greater freedom from scale fees be allowed for solicitors and barristers.

14. The Commission accepted that the 'no foal, no fee' approach to personal injuries litigation had advantages to impecunious litigants, and recommended that the legislation on maintenance should be repealed to

clarify the legailty of such arrangements. Differences emerged on the question of contingency/percentage fees.

15. The Commission recommended that fee advertising be allowed.

16. The Commission recommended greater freedom be allowed for employed members of the legal profession to engage in legal work.

17. The Commission welcomed the emergence of legal executives.

18. The Commission recommended lay representation on the disciplinary bodies for the Bar and the Law Society, and the establishment of a Legal Ombudsman.

19. The Commission also dealt with other miscellaneous matters concerning the courts including: consideration of the appointment of solicitors as judges of the higher courts; alterations to the length of the working days and of the vacations of the higher courts; raising the jurisdiction of the lower courts; consideration by the Bar of the continued wearing of wigs in court; and consideration of the establishment of a Tribunal to hear personal injuries claims.

It is clear form this brief summary of the Commission's recommendations that any changes resulting would have a profound effect on the provision of legal services in the State. Many of the Commission's recommendations were criticised by the Law Society and the Bar Council when they were published. Legislation is required to effect changes in areas concerning solicitors but the Bar is freer to effect change in the absence of statutory regulation. Some changes have in fact been made by the Bar in response to the Commission's Report. These include an extension of direct access to barristers, the abandonment of mandatory scale fees in some instances and changes in the disciplinary procedure. At the time of writing, the Bar has postponed consideration of the abandonment of wigs, an issue which has received a striking amount of media attention. It is also unclear to what extent the Department of Industry and Commerce (to which the Commission reported) or the Department of Justice (which has responsibility for the operation of the courts) will be prepared to bring forward legislative proposals to implement any of the Commission's recommendations. The publication of the Solicitors (Amendment) Bill 1991, in October 1991, indicated some movement in this area. We will discuss the Bill in the 1991 Review.

FATAL INJURIES

The decision of Lavan J in *Mahon v Burke* [1991] ILRM 59 is discussed in the Torts chapter, 563-5, below.

HEARSAY

In the absence of legislation implementing the Law Reform Commission's Report on the Rule Against Hearsay in Civil Cases (LRC 25 – 1988) (see the 1988 Review, 340-3), the courts continue to operate a somewhat outdated set of principles. In *Hughes v Staunton*, High Court, 16 February 1990 Lynch J accepted that had it not been for the agreement of the parties in the case certain valuable medical records might have been ruled out under the hearsay rule in accordance with the decision in *Myers v Director of Public Prosecutions* [1965] AC 1001. Although the Law Reform Commission has noted that some doubts have been raised here as to the correctness of *Myers* (Report, p.11) the hearsay rule continues to exercise considerable influence, as the *Hughes* case illustrates. It may be, of course, that if the Oireachtas fails to act in this area, the courts may examine whether the hearsay rule might in some respects be inconsistent with, for example, Article 34.1 or Article 40.3 of the Constitution, as has happened in recent years with other common law rules of evidence: see the cases cited in the 1988 Review, 151.

IN CAMERA HEARINGS

Recent judicial uneasiness about *in camera* hearings where such are not necessary in the interests of justice (see the 1989 Review, 351-3) found an echo in the judgment of Keane J in *The People v Neilan* [1991] ILRM 184; [1990] 2 IR 267. The judge discouraged the practice which had operated for some years by which applications for release by a person found guilty but insane were heard in chambers: see further, 162, above.

IRISH LANGUAGE

Two important issues as to the status of the Irish language were dealt with by O'Hanlon J in *Delap v Minister for Justice and Ors*, High Court, 13 June 1990, in which judgment was delivered in the Irish language sub nom. *Delap v An tAire Dlí agus Cirt, Éire agus an tÁrd Aigne.*

The applicant sought, *inter alia, mandamus* directing the respondents to publish an Irish language version of the Rules of the Superior Courts 1986. The respondents argued that they were not required to provide such a version pursuant to Article 8 of the Constitution and that it was sufficient that an English language version be published. It was indicated, however, that without prejudice to this argument an Irish language text of the 1986 Rules was in the course of preparation and would be available shortly after the case was being heard. O'Hanlon J gave a decision which gave some comfort to both parties.

First, he concluded that it was not required by Article 8 of the Constitution that, for the 1986 Rules to have legal effect, an Irish language version be published. In this respect he was prepared to follow dicta of Kingsmill Moore J in *Attorney General v Coyne* (1967) 101 ILTR 17, in which it was accepted that publication in either of the official languages was sufficient. This conclusion removes, for the present at least, the spectre of mass invalidity of legislation.

O'Hanlon J did, however, find in favour of the applicant on the alternative submssion put forward, namely that having regard to the right of the applicant to conduct his case before the courts in the Irish language, the respondents were required to facilitate this by making available an Irish language version of the 1986 Rules. In this respect, he followed dicta of his own in *The State (MacFhearraigh) v MacGamhnia*, High Court, 1 June 1983 concerning the right to conduct proceedings in either of the official languages and in *Ó Murchú v Registrar of Companies*, High Court, 21 September 1988 on the text of official forms (see the 1988 Review, 323). O'Hanlon J therefore granted the applicant a declaration to that effect, but since the respondents had stated that an Irish language version of the 1986 Rules was in preparation, he did not consider it appropriate to issue an order of *mandamus*, but the applicant was granted his costs.

JUDGE AND JURY

Direction for disagreement In *McIntyre v Lewis*, Supreme Court, 17 December 1990 (see 554 and 576, below, in the Torts chapter) the Supreme Court rejected the notion that a trial judge was required to inform the jury that they could disagree on a verdict if less than nine of them were unable to agree on an issue (nine votes being required under the Courts of Justice Act 1924). The Court noted that no authority had been cited to support the proposition being put forward.

JUDICIAL INFLUENCE

On 22 March 1990, Mr Justice Brian Walsh retired as a judge of the Supreme Court. His influence on the development of Irish law over the 30 years he held judicial office is reflected in the editorial note in (1990) 12 DULJ

106-14. That note, of course, reflects just some of the areas of Irish law on which Walsh J has had a major impact. See also Morgan, *Irish Times*, 27 March 1990. The concern of Walsh J with access to the courts was also reflected in his remarks on retirement from the Supreme Court. He referred to the 17th Interim Report of the Committee on Court Practice and Procedure (1972), of which he was Chairman, which recommended that court fees be abolished. Walsh J was reported as having doubted the constitutional validity of such fees. A full report of the speeches made on the occasion of Walsh J's retirement is contained in (1990) 8 *ILT* 100.

LEGAL AID

Cosgrove v Legal Aid Board and Ors, High Court, 17 October 1990 was the first major legal challenge to the operation of the non-statutory Scheme of Civil Legal Aid and Advice (Prl. 8543, 1979). The case is discussed in the Constitutional Law chapter, 144-7, above.

OATHS

In its *Report on Oaths and Affirmations* (LRC 34-1990), the Law Reform Commission makes the radical and controversial proposal to abolish the oath for witnesses, jurors and deponents submitting affidavits in all proceedings, civil and criminal, and to replace it by a solemn statutory affirmation.

Under present law any person who objects to taking an oath on the basis that he has no religious belief or that the taking of an oath is contrary to his religious belief may affirm; this affirmation is treated for all purposes as of the same force and effect as an oath: Oaths Act 1888, s. 1, Juries Act 1976, s. 18(2). The three principal options considered by the Commission were (1) to leave the present law unchanged; (2) to permit a person choose to take the oath or affirm on the basis of his conscience, without judicial scrutiny for his reasons for doing so; (3) to abolish the oath completely, replacing it by an affirmation.

Option 1: *To leave the present law unchanged*   The Commission does not in fact expressly examine this as an option. Instead it simply describes what it perceives as the unsatisfactory features of the present law.

The first difficulty identified by the Commission is that 'many forms of oath are at best embarrassing and at worst offensive to the religious beliefs of the persons to whom they are meant to apply'.

Some may wonder whether any significant case for change is here presented. The offensiveness and embarrassment which the Commission identifies may be traced to an article written in an Australian journal fifteen years ago (Weinberg, 'The Law of Testimonial Oaths and Affirmations' (1976) 3 *Monash UL Rev* 268) which reported problems for Buddhists, Moslems, Sikhs and Chinese witnesses in accommodating their religious principles with a system of oaths allegedly conforming to the beliefs of these religions but not in fact doing so. Before one could decide whether this represents a problem in Ireland it would have been useful to learn in the Report of any criticism of the existing law that has been made by any members of these groups; the Report makes no reference to any such criticism. It expresses gratitude to a Catholic theologian (Rev Enda McDonagh of Maynooth) and the Dean of Christ Church (The Very Rev John Paterson) for the assistance they offered in their personal capacity but gives no indication as to the comments it may have received from members of other religions.

Other unsatisfactory features with the present law identified by the Commission include the suggestion (by an American author, (1977) 75 *Mich L Rev* 1681, at 1681) that the oath has become a technical adjunct to perjury, 'more a genuflection performed out of habit than a ceremony sacred or significant to the law'; the suggestion (by the Ontario Law Reform Commission and Scottish Law Commission) that the process of ascertaining people's religious beliefs or lack of them is impractical in the daily administration of justice; the particular incongruity of requiring resort to an oath for minor cases such as those relating to traffic offences (this criticism coming from England's Criminal Law Revision Committee); and the invasion of religious privacy involved in requiring a person who wishes to affirm to make a public declaration of his or her religious beliefs or their absence (a criticism made by the Scottish Law Commission and the Law Reform Commission of Canada).

Option 2: *A choice between oath and affirmation* This option would dispense with the requirement that, to affirm, a witness must state that taking an oath is contrary to his religious belief or that he has no religious belief . Instead the witness should be free to choose between them without any public declaration as to his religious beliefs.

The Commission freely acknowledges the widespread appeal which this option has had for legislators and law reform agencies throughout the common law world. In the United States, it is incorporated in Rules 603 and 610 of the Federal Rules of Evidence. It has received the support of the Australian Law Reform Commission, the New South Wales Law Reform Commission and the Canadian Task Force on Uniform Rules of Evidence. Moreover in England, Scotland, Ontario and Canada at the federal level, where abolition of the oath was first recommended, the preferred solution has ultimately been to introduce legislation providing for choice as between an oath and an affirmation.

Option 3: *To abolish the oath and replace it by a solemn statutory option*
The Commission addresses this option by examining whether and to what extent:

(a) the oath would be more successful than the affirmation in encouraging witnesses to speak the truth and to take care in giving evidence;

(b) the triers of fact may consciously or unconsciously and unjustifiably prefer the evidence of the witness who took the oath as compared to the witness who affirmed; and

(c) the abolition of the judicial oath would be contrary to the provisions of the Constitution, in particular Article 44.

(a) The oath as security for truth   The central question here is whether the oath is more successful than the affirmation in encouraging truthful, careful evidence. The Canadian Law Reform Commissioner, now Chief Justice, La Forrest thinks it does:

> To those who take the oath seriously (and this covers a great many people) the certain demands of conscience are more likely to elicit the exact truth than the highly uncertain threat of a prosecution for perjury.

In accord is Family Solidarity:

> To deny people the opportunity to call on God to witness the truth of what they say in court would limit their human freedom, as well as denying the judge and jury . . . the opportunity to hear evidence supported by as solemn a guarantee of truthfulness as it is possible to have. . . . [T]he calling of God to witness the truth of what one has said is so much part of human experience (and by no means only Irish culture) that its extirpation would need a coherent justification [though this is not] to suggest that every witness who takes the oath tells the truth or that a solemn non-religious affirmation would not be treated in a moral and responsible way by most witnesses.

The Commission's reply is that '[t]he confidence of these conclusions is, however, not shared by most legal commentators and is, moreover, unsupported by scientific evidence'. The Commission goes on to state that '[s]uch psychological studies as have been available to [it] in this area are of little assistance and appear to be out of date'. It adds that it is not aware of any convincing body of expert opinion which would support the view that an oath would have 'greater psychological consequences' for the speaker than an affirmation. It would perhaps have been helpful for the Commission to make it clear to the reader that there is equally no convincing body of expert opinion refuting the view that the oath would have greater psychological consequences for the speaker than an affirmation. The truth is that there appear to be *no* recent psychological studies on the issue, *one way or the other*, recorded by law reform agencies which have analysed the subject. The studies to which the Commission refers appear to be those discussed by the Australian Law Reform Commission in a research paper. It is quite true that they are 'of little assistance' but, although they are old, it is untrue that they 'appear to be out of date', since they have not been refuted by subsequent research and the nature of their subject-matter and findings seems incapable of being rendered obsolete by the mere passage of time. What is noteworthy about these studies is that, far from refuting the proposition that oath-taking enhances reliability, they are supportive of that proposition, to the very limited and qualified extent to which they are helpful at all.

The legal commentators called in aid by the Commission make a somewhat motley and less than convincing group. Writing in 1843, Bentham argued that religious belief is essentially a private matter for the conscience of the individual, so that the external ceremony can have no effect on the incidence of perjury: *Rationale of Judicial Evidence* p. 308. Bentham no doubt had many virtues but the logic of this argument is clearly suspect. It rejects on *a priori* grounds the possibility that the conscience of an individual may be called to account more effectively by requiring him, before giving evidence, to commit himself solemnly and publicly to the most profound standard of truthfulness in his universe. The notion of a person's conscience being a static equilibrium rather than capable of stimulation and neglect is at variance with human experience in all societies, whether religious or otherwise. It is an invariable phenomenon of legal systems that, on matters of particular importance, there is provision for the making of declarations in circumstances of solemnity.

The English Law Reform Commission echoed Bentham in also resorting to a process of logical analysis of doubtful strength:

> For a person who has a firm religious belief, it is unlikely that taking the oath will act as any additional incentive to tell the truth. For a person without any religious belief, by hypothesis, the oath can make no difference. There is value in having a witness 'solemnly and sincerely' promise that he will tell the truth, and from this point of view the words of the affirmation are to many at least more impressive than the customary oath. The oath has not prevented an enormous amount of

perjury in the courts. A witness who wishes to lie and who feels that the oath may be an impediment can easily say that taking an oath is contrary to his religious beliefs. (Eleventh Report, on Evidence, p. 165).

This argument suffers from the same weakness as Bentham's, in denying, *a priori*, the potential effect on a person's veracity of publicly and solemnly calling on God to witness the truth of what he says. Of course those of firm religious belief appreciate the necessity of truthfulness on all occasions but the idea that these people are simply *incapable* of benefiting from the assistance of social structures, such as the possibility of taking an oath, suggests a certain naivete as to the effects of religious belief on ordinary mortals. *Logically* those who believe should be saints, but the very religions which seek to inspire such sanctity reveal a realistic insight into the nature of humanity. Props are necessary to encourage fidelity to moral norms. The oath is just such a prop. Consideration of its efficacy can scarcely be dismissed on the basis that those of firm religious belief need no additional incentive to tell the truth.

The Commission goes on to quote, without dissent, the argument of an American commentator to the effect that:

> [O]aths are essentially archaic self-curses. Our modern judicial oath may include remnants of pagan, prereligious and, indeed, preanimistic beliefs in the omnipotence of man and in his power to create by the magic of language a self-operative entity, the curse, which will haunt him, if he fails to keep his promise. . . . (Silving, *Essays on Criminal Procedure* (1964), p. 239).

One wonders what the theologians whom the Commission consulted had to say on this characterisation of the oath. Certainly those of religious conviction are treated somewhat inconsistently by the Commission. Having been lavished with exaggerated praise, to the effect that their religion is so dear to them that the oath cannot act as an additional incentive to them to tell the truth, they are then accused of harbouring in their souls the remnants of pagan, prereligious and preanimistic beliefs!

(b) Potential prejudice resulting from choice of affirmation The Commission argues that, although taking an oath offers no greater security for the veracity of a witness's evidence, there is a danger that some jurors and judges will, quite unjustly, regard the quality of evidence given on affirmation as impaired because it has not been given on oath. The Commission accepts that 'this might appear to be a veiled imputation of bigotry to all triers of fact in Irish courts', but replies that 'the danger that such a consideration will be

unconsciously taken into account in evaluating the evidence is a real one, and is recognised as such by the Cadian Task Force and by others who favour retention of the oath'. The Commission goes on to argue that '[i]t is precisely becase religion plays a more important part in Irish life than in other societies where secular values predominate that the risk of evidence . . . given on affirmation being treated as a form of second-rate evidence is significantly greater'.

Who are these triers of fact? Juries, of course, in serious criminal cases and in a handful of civil cases. But, in the overwhelming majority of judicial proceedings in Irish courts, the triers of facts are *judges*, the large majority being District Judges. This accusation of bias against the Irish Bench, if made by a body less august than the Commission, could well constitute contempt by scandalising! (See the Commission's own *Consultation Paper on Contempt of Court*, pp. 50-7 (1991).) It may be, of course, that the Commission's accusation of bias was intended to be directed exclusively at juries. If so, the scaffolding of the argument for abolition of the oath (as opposed to giving the witness the cboIce of affirming) capsizes, so far as almost all civil proceedings and all summary criminal proceedings are concerned.

(c) Constitutional considerations The Commission goes on to consider whether there is any constitutional bar to the abolition of the oath. It concludes that there is no problem. To abolish the oath would not hold God's name in any less reverence nor demonstrate any lack of respect or honour for the free practice and profession of religion. Freedom of conscience cannot 'take precedence over the public interest in the administration of justice'. Any person making an affirmation 'may continue privately to call on God to witness the truth of his statements if he so desires'.

It must be said that this latter part of the Commission's analysis is a good deal more convincing than what precedes it. The core of the argument in favour of abolition of the oath rests on two unproven hunches, neither of which is even presumptively true.

PLEADING

1 Creating estoppel In *Taylor v Smyth and Ors*, Supreme Court, 5 July 1990 (542-5, below), the Court held that the manner in which a case is pleaded may preclude a party from asserting to the contrary in the course of the proceedings. It is therefore clear that, in certain circumstances, the form of pleadings remains quite important in a substantive sense.

2 Res ipsa loquitur In *Mullen v Quinnsworth Ltd* [1990] 1 IR 59 (see 516-7, below) the Supreme Court gave contradictory signals as to whether the doctrine of *res ipsa loquitor* must be expressly pleaded. Griffin J clearly stated that it need not be expressly pleaded, since it was a matter arising from the circumstances of a particular case. He cited *Bennett v Chemical Construction Ltd* [1971] 1 WLR 1572 in support of this. McCarthy J, on the other hand, merely stated that the Court should apply a reasonableness test, regardless of whether *res ipsa loquitor* should be expressly pleaded. The third member of the Court, the Chief Justice, concurred with both judgments. Although Griffin and McCarthy JJ were in agreement as to the disposal of the appeal in the case, it is unfortunate that Finlay CJ did not advert to this important pleading point in expressing concurrence with both judgments. In *O'Reilly v Lavelle*, High Court, 2 April 1990 (see 551, below in the Torts chapter) Johnson J followed the approach taken by Griffin J in *Mullen*, though without adverting to the slight confusion in the Supreme Court decision. The balance of opinion, therefore, appears to be that the doctrine need not be specifically pleaded.

PLENARY HEARING

In *K. v An Bord Altranais* [1990] 2 IR 396 it was held that a plenary hearing was required, in an appeal under the Nurses Act 1985, where the truth or falsity of certain events were in issue: see further 339, above, in the Health Services chapter.

PRECEDENT

1 Analogy   In *U.F. v J.C.* [1991] ILRM 66 (292, above, in the Family Law chapter) the Court acknowledged that analogy plays an important part in the development of the doctrine of precedent.

2 High Court   In *Lynch v Burke* [1990] 1 IR 1, O'Hanlon J felt bound by a decision of the Supreme Court of the Irish Free State, *Owens v Greene* [1932] IR 225. He indicated that he was particularly unhappy with the *Owens* decision, going to some lengths to quote from a number of authorities which had doubted the conclusions in that case. He also expressed a hope that his decision might be appealed to the Supreme Court where *Owens* might be reconsidered. Whether the present High Court is bound by the decision of the courts established prior to 1961 is an issue which, in itself, has not been resolved: see Byrne and McCutcheon, *The Irish Legal System*, 2nd ed, p.122. The Supreme Court might also take the opportunity to clarify this point.

3 Supreme Court In *Finucane v McMahon* [1990] ILRM 505; [1990] 1 IR 165 the Supreme Court declined to follow its own decision in *Russell v Fanning* [1988] ILRM 333; [1988] IR 505: see 212-6, above, in the Criminal Law chapter.

4 Supreme Court declining to address point In *McDaid v Sheehy* [1991] ILRM 250 (see 464-5, below, in the Revenue Law chapter) the Supreme Court declined to address the constitutional point dealt with by Blayney J in the High Court [1989] ILRM 342: see the 1989 Review, 111-4. As was suggested in the 1989 Review, the views expressed by Blayney J on the constitutional invalidity of the Imposition of Duties Act 1957 could be regarded as *obiter*. This was the view taken by the Supreme Court. Thus, the comments of Blayney J would have little value in terms of precedent, though no doubt the issue may arise again if the Oireachtas does not seek to clarify the difficult issues arising from the continued use of the 1957 Act.

RES JUDICATA

The judgments of Lardner J in *Breathnach v Ireland* [1989] IR 489 and of Blayney J in *Breathnach v Ireland (No. 2)*, High Court, 14 March 1990 were discussed in the 1989 Review, 358-61. The issue of *res judicata* arose again, peripherally, in *McGrath v Garda Commissioner* [1990] ILRM 5 (HC); [1990] ILRM 817 (SC), where McCarthy J noted the connection between estoppel and *res judicata*: see the discussion at 330-1, above.

The point was also discussed in *Reamsbottom v Raftery*, High Court, 30 May 1990. Johnson J held that *res judicata* should not apply in respect of a previous action in which the defendant had successfully sued the owner of the car which the plaintiff was driving when she suffered the injuries that were the subject matter of the present case. The plaintiff had not been a party to the previous case, and Johnson J applied the 'privity' rule discussed by O'Donnell LJ in *Shaw v Sloan* [1982] NI 410. In this respect, he also distinguished the instant case from that in *Donohue v Browne* [1986] IR 90. Johnson J's decision could also be supported by reference to the decisions in *McCarthy Construction Ltd v Waterford County Council*, High Court, 6 July 1987 (1987 Review, 263) and *Gilroy v McLoughlin* [1989] ILRM 133 [1988] IR 44 (1989 Review, 343-4), neither of which he would appear to have been referred to.

RULES OF COURT

The following rules of court were made in 1990.

Civil Bill   The Circuit Court Rules (No. 2) 1990 (SI No. 155), *inter alia*, amend O.10 of the 1950 Rules as to the stamping and issuing of a Civil Bill.

Case stated: Circuit Court   The Circuit Court Rules (No. 2) 1990 (SI No. 155), *inter alia*, amend the proecdure for cases stated under O.77 of the 1950 Rules.

Commissioners for Oaths   The Rules of the Superior Courts (No. 4) 1990 (SI No. 281) prescribes the fees payable to a Commissioner for Oaths with effect from 30 November 1990.

Costs: District Court   The District Court (Costs) Rules 1990 (SI No. 67) prescribe solicitors' costs and revoke the 1982 Rules. The District Court (Costs) (Amendment) Rules 1990 (SI No. 194) provide for the recoupment by successful parties of VAT payable to them in respect of costs awarded to them in appropriate cases.

Courts-Martial: legal aid   The Courts-Martial (Legal Aid) Regulations 1990 (SI No. 68) amend the 1986 Regulations (as previously amended by the 1989 Regulations).

Enforcement of judgments   The Circuit Court Rules (No. 2) 1990 (SI No. 155), *inter alia*, adapt the 1950 Rules to the Jurisdiction of Courts and Enforcment of Judgments (European Communities) Act 1988 (1988 Review, 90-104). The Jurisdiction of Courts and Enforcement of Judgments (European Communities) Act 1988 (Section 1(4)) (Declaration) Order 1990 (SI No. 231) sets out the contracting States for the purposes of the 1988 Act.

Family law   The Rules of the Superior Courts (No. 1) 1990 (SI No. 97) prescribe the procedure to be followed in family law applications, with effect from 1 May 1990. The Circuit Court Rules (No. 1) 1990 (SI No. 152) deal with applications by a father to be made guardian under the Status of Children Act 1987; applications for declaration of parentage under the 1987 Act; and with blood tests in connection with civil proceedings.

Furnishing costs: Circuit Court   The Circuit Court Rules (No. 2) 1990 (SI No. 143), *inter alia*, amend O.58 of the 1950 Rules concerning furnishing of costs and tendering discharge.

Landlord and tenant   The Circuit Court Rules (No. 2) 1990 (SI No. 143), *inter alia*, deal with the time for service under the Landlord and Tenant (Ground Rents) Act 1967.

Lodgments: Circuit Court   The Circuit Court Rules (No. 2) 1990 (SI No.

143), *inter alia*, amend O.12 of the 1950 Rules as to additional lodgments and payment out.

Lodgments: High Court   The Rules of the Superior Courts (No. 3) 1990 (SI No. 229) amend the Rules concerning payments into court to take account of the Courts Act 1988 (1988 Review, 454-6).

Maritime Conventions   The Rules of the Superior Courts (No. 2) 1990 (SI No. 143) give effect to the changes required by the Jurisdiction of Courts (Maritime Conventions) Act 1989 (1989 Review, 69-73).

Motion for judgment: Circuit Court   The Circuit Court Rules (No. 2) 1990 (SI No. 155), *inter alia*, amend O.24 of the 1950 Rules as to motions for judgment.

Vacation sittings   The Circuit Court Rules (No. 2) 1990 (SI No. 155), *inter alia*, deal with vacation sittings of the Circuit Court.

STRIKING OUT

Action seeking set aside   In *Din and Arborfield Ltd v Banco Ambrosiano SPA and Ors*, High Court, 30 November 1990 the plaintiffs instituted proceedings seeking to set aside the judgment and order of the Supreme Court in *Banco Ambrosiano SPA v Ansbacher & Co. Ltd* [1987] ILRM 669. The plaintiffs claimed that the decision in those proceedings had been obtained in breach of the rules of natural justice by virtue, *inter alia*, of the failure of Banco Ambrosiano SPA to disclose documents which had been available to the Bank prior to the decision of the Supreme Court but which only became available to the plaintiffs in 1988. The failure to disclose the documents was claimed to arise either from mistake or a deliberate concealment. The plaintiffs claimed that if these documents had been available to them at the time of the previous proceedings, they would have led them to engage in a course of enquiry which might have had a material effect on the outcome of those proceedings. The defendants sought to have the plaintiffs' action struck out as an abuse of the process of the courts. Murphy J acceded to the defendants' argument and struck out the plaintiffs' claim.

The first issues dealt with was the extent to which the plaintiffs would be entitled to set aside a final judgment. Murphy J held that such a judgment would not be set aside merely on the discovery of new evidence, except where this is done in the course of an appeal on a point of law (see the cases discussed in the 1989 Review, 341-3). However, approving the decision of Barrington J in *Waite v House of Spring Gardens Ltd*, High Court, 26 June 1985 and of the House of Lords in the *Ampthill Peerage Case* [1977] AC 547, Murphy J conceded that the finality of the decisions of the Supreme

Court pursuant to Article 34.4.6 of the Constitution was limited in the sense that a decision of the Court could be set aside for fraud since such a decision would in fact be a nullity. He went on to hold that in order to set aside a judgment on grounds of fraud, the fraud must be pleaded with particularity, and ultimately established on the balance of probabilities.

As to the instant case, Murphy J noted that the only duty to disclose documents in proceedings arises from failure to discover documents under O.31, r.12 of the Rules of the Superior Courts 1986. He pointed out that at least one document referred to by the plaintiffs as the basis for setting aside the *Ansbacher* decision had been in their possession at all material times. He had also examined other documents referred to by the plaintiffs, and concluded that they would not have materially advanced the plaintiffs' claim. He was prepared to accept that they might have led to some train of enquiry which might have resulted in some further evidence, but that this was not sufficient to establish fraud with any particularity, as required.

The plaintiffs had also referred to a 1988 decision of an Italian court which had differed from the Supreme Court decision in the *Ansbacher* case as to the effect of certain documents in Italian law, but Murphy J held that it was not sufficient to set aside a final decision of the Supreme Court merely because it might have been based on a misunderstanding of foreign law.

Finally, he did not consider that the judgment of the Italian court should be recognised over the Supreme Court decision under the Jurisdiction of Courts and Enforcement of Judgments (European Communities) Act 1988, since the Italian decision had been given in a matrimonial claim and Article 27 of the Brussels Convention expressly provided that such judgments fell outside the recognition rules of the Convention.

SUMMARY SUMMONS

In *Calor Teo v Colgan*, Supreme Court, 22 June 1990 the Court, in an important *ex tempore* judgment held that where leave to defend summary proceedings was granted by the High Court under O.37, r.3 of the Rules of the Superior Courts 1986, no lodgment conditions should be attached to such leave. In the instant case, the defendant was relying on the *non est factum* defence. Having been satisfied that a *prima facie* defence had been made out, requiring a plenary hearing, Lynch J had held that the defendant should lodge £12,500 in court. This was regarded as an unacceptable fetter on the defendant's right of access to court. The note of the Court's judgment is quoted in the very informative article by Doyle, 'Summary Procedure: Leave to Defend and Lodgments' (1990) 8 *ILT* 255. The article discusses the case law on O.37, r.3 as well as the constitutional dimension raised by the decision.

SUPREME COURT

1 Appellate court   Many issues as to the appellate nature of the Supreme Court's jurisdiction are dealt with under the Appellate Court Function heading, above, 428.

2 Fresh evidence: interlocutory hearing   In *Toal v Duignan (No. 2)* [1991] ILRM 140 (see 394, above) Finlay CJ (with Griffin J concurring) was of the view that in an interlocutory hearing the Supreme Court was free to hear additional evidence under O.58, r.8 of the Rules of the Superior Courts 1986. McCarthy J doubted the Court's jurisdiction on this point.

3 Malicious injuries appeals   In *W.J. Prendergast & Son Ltd v Carlow County Council* [1990] ILRM 749 the Supreme Court dealt with the extent to which it could be involved in malicious injuries appeals. The applicant brought proceedings in the Circuit Court under the Malicious Injuries Act 1981 seeking compensation from the respondent Council. It may be noted that this application arose prior to the severe limits on such claims that were introduced in the Malicious Injuries (Amendment) Act 1986. The applicant was successful on the issue of liability in the Circuit Court, but on appeal to the High Court, O'Hanlon J held (3 June 1988) that compensation was not payable under the 1981 Act.

The applicant then purported to lodge an appeal to the Supreme Court against the decision of the High Court. The applicant also applied to O'Hanlon J for a case stated to the Supreme Court. O'Hanlon J held that no case stated could lie having regard to the terms of ss. 38 and 39 of the Courts of Justice Act 1936, s. 38 providing for a rehearing in the High Court of Circuit Court civil proceedings and s. 39 providing that the High Court decision on such appeal shall be 'final and conclusive and not appealable.' In essence, the Supreme Court (Finlay CJ, Griffin, Hederman, McCarthy and O'Flaherty JJ) upheld O'Hanlon J's view by deciding that no appeal could be brought in the instant case. However, the Court indicated there was a possible form of appeal available in such future cases as might be litigated under the terms of the post-1986 malicious injuries code.

Delivering the only judgment, McCarthy J held that neither an appeal on a point of law or appeal by way of case stated could lie from the High Court in the circumstances of the instant case. He drew this conclusion from a close reading of the statutory scheme of the 1981 Act which, 'although somewhat awkwardly devised, is clear' and which indicated, he considered, that it was subject to the provisions of ss. 38 and 39 of the Courts of Justice Act 1936. This conclusion, he said, affirmed the finality of a High Court decision in a Circuit appeal.

However, he also noted that s. 18 of the 1981 Act provided, by way of consultative case stated, for a malicious injuries claim to be referred to the Supreme Court either from the District Court or from the Circuit Court. He noted that such form of case stated left the ultimate resolution of the case in the hands of the Court which sought the case stated.

4 Stay of execution pending appeal   In *Corish v Hogan*, Irish Times LR, 21 May 1990, the Supreme Court (Finlay CJ, Walsh and Hederman JJ) held, in an *ex tempore* judgment delivered by the Chief Justice, that in general a party was not entitled to an unconditional stay on a High Court order where an appeal is lodged. Only where there was a reasonable prospect of the verdict being overturned could such even be considered. However, the Court approved the usual stays where there is an undertaking to pay a certain sum to the successful party.

TIME

The Winter Time Order 1990 (SI No. 52), made under s. 1 of the Standard Time Act 1971, as well as specifying when Winter Time begins, also gives effect to the Directive on Summer Time 89/47/EEC.

Prisons

CONDITIONS

The riot in Strangeways Prison in Manchester was the impetus for the establishment of the Woolf Inquiry into English Prisons. The year also saw unusual controversy in Ireland arising from the leaked publication of the 1988 Report of the Mountjoy Prison Visiting Committee: *Irish Times*, 1 May 1990. The Visiting Committee criticised conditions in the prison and also alleged ill-treatment of prisoners by prison officers. These led to the unusual step of the Minister for Justice publishing a rejection of the points made by the Committee when the Annual Report on Prisons 1988 was ultimately published later in the year. The Oireachtas Joint Committee on Women's Rights later recommended the closure of the Women's Unit in Mountjoy Prison in the wake of the suicide of a 19 year old woman: *Irish Times*, 13 July 1990. The 1989 Report of the Mountjoy Visiting Committee again criticised conditions in Mountjoy: *Irish Times*, 12 December 1990. In addition to these factors, the absence of secure accommodation for young offenders also gave rise to controversy: see the discussion in the Criminal Law chapter, 264, above.

At the end of the year, the Minister for Justice announced a substantial reform package which included, *inter alia*, phased implementation of 'in-cell sanitation' in existing prison accommodation, which would eventually remove the need for 'slopping out': see *Irish Times*, 11 December 1990. The Minister also stated that recommendations from a Working Party on Prison Suicides would be followed through by the training of medical orderlies. Earlier in the year, the Minister had appointed a new Director of Medical Services for the Prison Service: *Irish Times*, 27 July 1990. These changes and proposals reflect some of the key recommendations in the 1985 Report of the Whitaker Committee of Inquiry into the Penal System (Pl.3391).

DISMISSAL

Whelan v Minister for Justice, High Court, 29 June 1990 concerning the purported dismissal of a probationer prison officer under the Civil Service Regulation Act 1956 is discussed in the Administrative Law chapter, 3-4, above.

RULES

The Detention of Offenders (Wheatfield) Regulations 1990 (SI No. 218) amend the 1989 Regulations to allow for the detention of 15 year old persons at Wheatfield.

TEMPORARY RELEASE (PAROLE)

Sherlock v Governor of Mountjoy Prison, High Court, 21 December 1990 represents a significant change in the judicial approach to the withdrawal of temporary release under the Criminal Justice Act 1960. It will be recalled that in *Ryan v Governor of Mountjoy Prison* [1988] IR 198, Murphy J had described temporary release as a privilege or concession and thus subject to an almost unfettered discretion. We had suggested in the 1988 Review, 350-2, that this approach did not reflect the correct approach to the grant or withdrawal of temporary release. The *Sherlock* decision would appear to support our view though, regrettably, the *Ryan* decision was not alluded to.

In *Sherlock*, the applicant had been convicted of murder in 1970 and sentenced to penal servitude for life. In November 1978, he was released for a period of time on temporary release granted under s.2 of the 1960 Act. From that time until November 1990, he was at liberty under the 1960 Act pursuant to approximately 15 renewals of his temporary release, such renewals being granted on his surrender at the expiry of each temporary release order. In November 1990, the applicant reported on the expiry of his temporary release to the Training Unit of Mountjoy Prison. He was informed that his temporary release was not being renewed. He was taken into custody and issued with prison clothing. He sought an inquiry under Article 40.4 of the Constitution into the legality of his detention. The applicant argued that the reasons for the non-renewal of his temporary release should be provided and that the non-renewal in the instant case was in breach of the rules of natural justice. Johnson J ordered the Governor to provide the reasons for the non-renewal.

While Johnson J accepted that the applicant had no right as such to temporary release under the 1960 Act, he also noted that the process was hedged around with the procedural requirements laid down in *The State (Murphy) v Kielt* [1982] ILRM 475; [1985] ILRM 141; [1984] IR 458. Thus, he commented that:

> a situation has developed whereby over some 12 years and at least 15 temporary releases, they were granted without question and it would appear to me that the applicant had developed a legitimate expectation that, either, he would get a renewal of his temporary release or, if that

was not done that he would be given an explanation as to why it was not being done and be given an opportunity to be heard in that regard, and to answer any allegations which might be made against him.

The allusion to a legitimate expectation indicates that, in this instance Johnson J applied it in its procedural fairness mode rather than its equitable estoppel form. It is unfortunate that his judgment does not contain any further references to the decisions which have followed in the wake of *Webb v Ireland* [1988] ILRM 565; [1988] IR 353 (see the 1988 Review, 20-30 and the 1989 Review, 9-12). The passage also reflects the recent case law requiring reasons be given for decisions: see the 1988 Review, 17-18 and 16-20, above in the Administrative Law chapter.

This approach is, as already indicated, quite at variance with the 'concession' view taken by Murphy J in the *Ryan* case. Although not referred to by Johnson J in his judgment in *Sherlock*, the *Ryan* case must now be a dubious authority. This appears to have been conceded to some extent by the approach of the authorities on appeal to the Supreme Court. When the case came before the Court on 5 June 1991, the Minister for Justice was added as a party to the proceedings, the appeal was withdrawn, the order of the High Court affirmed and the Minister undertook to give reasons to the applicant for his continued detention within three weeks: *Irish Times*, 6 June 1991. Although this was obviously a consent order and lacks the authority of a decided case, it indicates that the authorities accepted that the view taken by Johnson J in the High Court reflects current orthodoxy.

TRANSFER FROM ST PATRICK'S INSTITUTION TO PRISON

The Prisons Act 1970 (Section 7) Order 1990 (SI No. 165) continued s.7 of the 1970 Act in operation until 27 July 1991. As to s.7, see the 1988 Review, 353.

Revenue

As with previous Reviews, this chapter focuses on case law during 1990. For a detailed analysis of the Finance Act 1990, see Kennedy's Annotation, *Irish Current Law Statutes Annotated*. As well as giving effect to the tax changes announced in the 1990 Budget, some of the substantive changes effected by the 1990 Act were as follows:

Personal injuries actions S. 5 of the Act exempts from income tax the income on the proceeds from a personal injuries action, but only where the recipient is permanently and totally incapacitated by reason of mental or physical infirmity from maintaining himself or herself. This provision was inserted at Committee Stage after public disquiet was expressed concerning the taxation of income from the settlement entered into in *Dunne v National Maternity Hospital* [1989] ILRM 735; [1989] IR 91 (see the 1989 Review, 424-5).

HIV Trust Fund S. 7 of the Act exempts from taxation any payments made by the Haemophilia HIV Trust to beneficiaries of the Trust.

Self-assessment The 1990 Act provides that, under the self-assessment procedure, all income will be taxed on a current year basis. Changes are also effected in the returns system and there is a more stringent surcharge for late submission of returns.

Revenue appeals S. 28 of the Act extends the right to be heard before the Appeal Commissioners to members of the Institute of Taxation in Ireland. This had previously been limited to accountants. Note this does not involve a right to plead, still confined to solicitors and barristers.

Plant S. 70 of the 1990 Act reverses the effect of the decision of the Circuit Court in *G. v O'C.*, Circuit Court, 24 October 1989 (1989) 4 *Irish Tax Review* 481 (1989 Review, 368). S. 241 of the Income Tax Act 1967 has been amended to provide that plant and machinery must be 'wholly and exclusively' used as plant in order to qualify for a capital allowance. However, apportionment will still be possible for, say, a car which is used partly for business and partly for personal use.

ACCOUNTING METHODS

The value of expert evidence from an accountant in Revenue matters was underlined again in *Murnaghan Bros Ltd v Ó Maoldomhnaigh*, High Court, 2 October 1990. The company was involved in building operations, and thus qualified as a company engaged in trade within s.17 of the Finance Act 1970. It bought 103 acres of agricultural land for £300,000 and intended to use the land for building purposes at some time in the future. It sought stock relief under s. 62 of the Income Tax Act 1967, as applied by s. 31 of the Finance Act 1975 in respect of the land.

The question at issue was whether the land could be regarded as 'trading stock' within s.17 of the 1970 Act. The case revolved, to some extent, around the question whether the company had taken possession of the land for the accounting period in respect of which relief was being claimed. The company had not actually obtained possession at the relevant time and, pursuant to the decision in *Tempany v Hynes* [1976] IR 101, this indicated that beneficial title only had passed. However, Murphy J did not consider that this posed an insuperable barrier to the company's case. The company's accounts for the year in question had included the purchase price of £300,000 and the accountant giving evidence for the company had stated in the Circuit Court that this was consistent with good accountancy practice. Ultimately, Murphy J was satisfied that this disposed of the case in the company's favour. He referred with approval to the decision of Carroll J in *Carroll Industries plc v Ó Culacháin* [1989] ILRM 552; [1988] IR 705, where although an accounting practice had been disapproved (1988 Review, 354-5) the general principle that accounting methods were of great importance had been accepted.

ASSESSMENT IN DEFAULT

In *Deighan v Hearne* [1990] 1 IR 499, the Supreme Court upheld the constitutionality of an inspector's power to issue an assessment in default of a tax return. The plaintiff was assessed for income tax under Schedule D of the Income Tax Act 1967 on default of making returns of income. The assessment was made under s.184 of the 1967 Act which requires an Inspector of Taxes to make an assessment in accordance with his best judgment of what was due by the taxpayer. The plaintiff failed to respond to the assessments made and, pursuant to s. 416 of the 1967 Act, the assessments became final and conclusive. S. 485 of the 1967 Act empowers the Collector General to issue a Certificate of tax due in default upon receipt of which a sheriff is entitled to levy execution of the sum on the taxpayer's property. The plaintiff challenged the constitutional validity of the powers in the 1967

Act on the ground that they amounted to an administration of justice, contrary to Article 34 of the Constitution, or that they were harsh and unnecessarily stringent, contrary to his property rights in Article 40.3. He also challenged certain aspects of the particular assessment raised, including whether the Revenue Commissioners were able to establish that proper notifications had been issued pursuant to their automated system. In the High Court, Murphy J dismissed the plaintiff's claim ([1986] IR 603) and this view was upheld by the Supreme Court (Finlay CJ, Walsh, Griffin, Hederman and McCarthy JJ).

The judgment of the Court on the constitutional issue, delivered by the Chief Justice, relied strongly on the Court's own decision in *Kennedy v Hearne* [1988] ILRM 531; [1988] IR 481 (1988 Review, 355-6), where similar assessment powers had been upheld. In *Deighan*, the Court concluded that the powers exercised by an Inspector of Taxes pursuant to ss. 184 and 485 of the 1967 Act did not amount to the administration of justice because an assessment in default did not impose a binding liability on any person unless and until it became final and conclusive by reason of failure to appeal, and it did not therefore create any justiciable controversy between the taxpayer and the Revenue Commissioners.

Nor did the Court consider that the provisions of s. 416 of the 1967 Act were unjustly wide or harsh, bearing in mind that the taxpayer had an opportunity to appeal within 21 days, subject to an extension in cases of sickness or other reasonable cause. The Court pointed out that the exercise of the Inspector's powers were also subject to judicial review if, for instance, the inspector acted capriciously or unreasonably.

On the particular circumstances of the case, Finlay CJ delivered a separarte judgment with which the other members of the Court agreed. He held that the plaintiff was not entitled to seek to challenge in the High Court the factual issue as to whether he was a furniture wholesaler at the time of the assessments, since he had not pursued the appropriate appeal mechanisms provided for this purpose under the income tax code. Nor, he held, was the plaintiff entitled to expect proof of individual mailings to him of assessments from the Revenue, who posted thousands of such assessments. He therefore agreed with Murphy J that the court should act on the evidence of the operation of a system which established, as a matter of probability, that the various documents had been posted to the plaintiff.

AVOIDANCE

The fact that avoidance schemes continue to play an important role in Irish revenue law after the decision in *McGrath v McDermott* [1988] ILRM 647; [1988] IR 258 (1988 Review, 356-8) was confirmed in *O'Grady v Laragan*

Quarries Ltd, High Court, 27 June 1990.

A number of road hauliers entered into agreements with the respondent company, Laragan, by which they agreed to sell quarry materials to Laragan and also agreed to transport the material to the destinations specified by Laragan. The rate per ton of material was to be paid by Laragan together with the supply of all necessary fuel. All materials were to be purchased from another company, Hanley Bros Ltd, with which Laragan was associated. The hauliers entered into a simultaneous agreement with Hanley Bros Ltd by which all sums owed to Hanley Bros Ltd for the purchase of quarry materials be deducted from the amount owed to the hauliers by Laragan for the supply of quarry materials. The hauliers regularly collected quarry material from Hanley Bros Ltd, were debited with the cost and then delivered the material to Laragan's customers. At the end of each month, Laragan prepared an account in which the cost price of the material due to Hanleys was debited against the sale price payable by Laragan and a cheque for the balance was paid to the hauliers. Laragan conceded that this cheque represented the total of the transport charges involved.

The inspector argued that the payments were made in respect of 'haulage for hire of materials for use in construction operations' and that, pursuant to s.17 of the Finance Act 1970 (as inserted by s. 21 of the Finance Act 1976), a deduction of 35% should have been made at source and forwarded to the Revenue. In the Circuit Court, it was held that the payments did not come within s. 17, and on a case stated Murphy J upheld this approach.

The case came down, essentially, to a question of the proper interpretation of the contracual commitments which had been entered into. Murphy J relied on the views expressed by the Supreme Court in *Gatien Motor Co. Ltd v Continental Oil Ltd* [1979] IR 406, using it to explain the Court's later decision in *Irish Shell BP Ltd v J. Costello Ltd* [1981] ILRM 66.

Relying on the judgment of Griffin J in the *Gatien* case, Murphy J stated that while the Court should attempt to ascertain the substance of a contract, it should not ignore the actual bargain between the parties by attempting to substitute an agreement more in harmony with the commercial realities of the situation. While he accepted that, in general, the parties own labels will not determine the outcome, the transaction itself must be examined. For further discussion of this point see the Contract Law chapter, 183-6, above.

Applying these general rules to the instant case he held that there was no reason why the agreements should not take effect in accordance with the clear terms entered into between the hauliers and Laragan. In this light, he expressly pointed out that the parties had deliberately arranged their affairs so that the relationship between them would not in law constitute a hiring. Thus, s. 17 of the 1970 Act (as inserted by s.21 of the 1976 Act) did not apply in the circumstances.

DESIGNATED AREA ALLOWANCE

McNally v Ó Maoldomhnaigh [1990] 2 IR 513 concerned the question whether exclusive use of plant and machinery in a designated area was required to attract the investment allowance provided under the tax code.

The taxpayer carried on business as a plant hire contractor in County Monaghan, a designated area for the purposes of claiming investment allowances for machinery and plant pursuant to s. 22 of the Finance Act 1971. The 1971 Act referred expressly to the scheme of designated areas contained in the Industrial Development Act 1969, which was intended to encourage industrial activity in certain areas by the provision, *inter alia*, of grants for investment in those areas designated by the Minister for Industry and Commerce. The taxpayer had purchased a crane, with a value of over £100,000, which he then let out on hire, and it was agreed that for 94% of the time it was used in a designated area. The inspector of taxes took the view, however, that exclusive use in a designated area was required to qualify for relief under s.22. This view was upheld by the Circuit Court and High Court (1988 Review, 363) but on further appeal the Supreme Court (Finlay CJ, Hederman and O'Flaherty JJ) reversed this and held that the taxpayer was entitled to the allowance.

Delivering the leading judgment the Chief Justice indicated that the statutory provisions required interpretation from first principles. This is apparent from the cases cited by counsel for the taxpayer. Finlay CJ stated that in providing that the investment allowance was to be for plant and equipment 'provided for use' in a designated area, s. 22 of the 1971 Act did not unambiguously indicate that it applied only where plant was used exclusively in a designated area, as had been argued by the Revenue. The Court was thus required to examine the overall purpose of the section.

It was noted that by the use of a direct reference to the designated areas provisions in the 1969 Act, the 1971 Act had clearly and unequivocally identified its objective as intended to further and support the objectives of s. 33 of the 1969 Act. Having regard to the evidence that the plant was used in a designated area for 94% of the time and that the taxpayer exclusively employed persons from designated areas in connection with the use of the plant, the Court held that the taxpayer was entitled to the allowance in question.

Finally, the Chief Justice doubted whether Murphy J had been correct in expressing the view that plant hired out by the taxpayer could fall within s. 22, even if used exclusively in a designated area.

EMPLOYMENT DISABILITY PAYMENTS

Cahill v Harding and Ors, High Court, 3 May 1990 concerned payments made to the respondents, each of whom had been employed by Henry Ford & Son Ltd in Cork and each of whom also had a degree of disability to one extent or another. The issue raised was whether the payments attracted an exemption from tax under s. 115 of the Income Tax Act 1967.

In 1984, the company announced the closure of its production plant in Cork. Prior to 1984, the company had developed a scheme by which it encouraged disabled employees to take disability retirement thus avoiding compulsory disability retirement. In July 1984, protective dismissal notices were issued to the entire workforce, and in August the company forwarded to the Revenue a list of employees (including the respondents) whose employment was being terminated for disability. The Inspector replied that tax should be deducted from all lump sum payments to employees, and the company did so. On receipt of the payment, each employee signed a statement stating that the payment was in full and final settlement of any rights, claims and demands arising from the closure. Subsequently, the company received 60% of the statutory element of the sums paid to each employee whose employment was terminated. The respondents claimed that no deduction should have been made as the payments were made on account of disability and were thus exempt under s. 115 of the 1967 Act. Two of the respondents were production workers whose jobs were to go in the closedown, while the other three respondents' jobs were to continue. In the Circuit Court the judge held that each of the payments were exempt under s. 115. On appeal Carroll J held that some only were entitled to claim that exemption.

First of all, she dealt with a preliminary point. She held that the respondents were not estopped from making their present claim by reason of the documentation used in accepting the payment or by the fact that the company recouped 60% of the statutory element of the sums paid to the employees.

On the substantive point arising, she held that the three respondents whose jobs were to continue were entitled to the exemption from tax under s. 115 of the 1967 Act since the payments were made on account of their disabilities. However, the two production workers were not entitled to the exemption since, although the payment was made to someone suffering from a disability, it had not been made on account of the disability because their jobs were not continuing after protective notice had been served. Citing *Mara v Hummingbird Ltd* [1982] ILRM 421, Carroll J held that since this was a mixed question of fact and law, the Court was entitled to overturn the decision of the Circuit Court judge on this point.

EXCISE DUTIES

McDaid v Sheehy [1989] ILRM 342 (HC); [1991] ILRM 250 (SC), which raised a storm when the High Court declared invalid the Imposition of Duties Act 1957, turned out to be a more mundane affair when it reached the Supreme Court.

The applicant had been convicted in the District Court of the offence of keeping in his vehicle certain hydrocarbon oil chargeable with an excise duty on which a rebate of duty had been allowed under the Imposition of Duties (No. 221) (Excise Duties) Order 1975, contrary to s. 21 of the Finance Act 1935, as amended, inter alia, by the 1975 Order. The conviction had been upheld by the respondent Circuit Court judge. The 1975 Order was made pursuant to s.1 of the Imposition of Duties Act 1957, by which the government are empowered to impose customs duties, by statutory order, with or without limitations 'of such amount as they think proper on any particular description of goods imported into the State'. S. 2 of the 1957 Act provides that any such excise Order shall have effect only until the end of the calendar year in which it is made, unless it is confirmed by Act of the Oireachtas. The 1975 Order had been confirmed by s. 46 of the Finance Act 1976, and the applicant had been convicted in respect of an offence alleged to have been committed in 1984. The applicant sought judicial review of his conviction.

In the High Court ([1989] ILRM 342) Blayney J held that the 1975 Order was unconstitutional as an impermissible delegation of the law-making power of the Oireachtas under Article 15.2.1 of the Constitution, but he declined to quash the applicant's conviction on the basis that the confirmation of the Order by the 1976 Act could be interpreted as an intention to validate the order without intending to breach Article 15.2.1 (see the 1989 Review, 111-4). On appeal, the Supreme Court (Finlay CJ, Griffin, Hederman, McCarthy and O'Flaherty JJ) unanimously agreed that the 1976 Act validated the 1975 Order so that the applicant's conviction was valid. Significantly, the Court (with McCarthy J a lone dissentient) declined to address the constitutional issue which had resulted in Blayney J ordering that the 1957 Act was invalid.

Delivering the leading judgment, Finlay CJ dealt quickly with the substantive issue, agreeing that Blayney J had been correct in concluding that s.46 of the 1976 Act constituted a valid confirmation of the 1975 Order and that the applicant's conviction should therefore stand. No particular authority was cited for this conclusion, though the Chief Justice might have referred to the Court's own decision in *Doyle v An Taoiseach* [1986] ILRM 693, which dealt with similar issues and on which Blayney J had relied.

He went on to explain why the Court would not address, and the High

Court should not have addressed, the constitutional issue. In view of the Court's decision on the effect of the 1976 Act, he noted that the applicant could have no conceivable interest in pursuing the constitutional issue. He then referred to, and quoted from, what he termed an almost unbroken line of decisions of the Supreme Court by which it avoided dealing with a constitutional issue where a case could be determined on some other ground, including *Cooke v Walsh* [1984] ILRM 208; [1984] IR 710 and *Murphy v Roche* [1987] IR 106. Only *McDonald v Bord na gCon* [1964] IR 350 stood out as an exception. Finlay CJ stated that a number of factors supported this abstension from making a moot decision, among them being that in a full constitutional action the Court would be required to take into consideration a variety of matters pertaining to the precise effect of a statutory provision on the interests of the citizen impugning it; and in the particular issue arising in this case, he noted that the constitutional validity of the 1975 Order might be considered without necessarily affecting the 1957 Act itself, citing *Harvey v Minister for Social Welfare* [1990] ILRM 185; [1990] 2 IR 232 as an example (see the 1989 Review, 394-5). To the extent that the *McDonald* case was out of line with this approach the Court decided that it should not be followed.

Arising from this analysis, the Chief Justice concluded that the portion of Blayney J's decision dealing with the constitutional issue should be deemed to be obiter dictum, and the portion of his order declaring s.1 of the 1957 Act to be constitutonally invalid was therefore set aside. The remainder of the High Court order, which upheld the applicant's conviction, was affirmed.

McCarthy J alone delivered a dissenting judgment on the constitutional issue (agreeing with the other members of the Court on the other point raised). He felt that, in view of the overriding importance to the executive branch of a definitive determination of the constitutional issue in question, the Court should determine that issue. This approach, like that in relation to locus standi in constitutional matters, did not find favour. In this respect, there has been in recent years a clear break from the more open approach to such issues in the 1960s and early 1970s, exemplified by the *McDonald* case, and others such as *East Donegal Co-Op Ltd v Attorney General* [1970] IR 317 and *O'Brien v Keogh* [1972] IR 144, the latter two effectively overruled by *Cahill v Sutton* [1980] IR 269. For comments which might be closer to McCarthy J than of the majority, see the 1987 Review, 83-5.

PENAL WARRANTS

In *Murphy v Wallace and Ors*, High Court, 17 July 1990 Barron J held unconstitutional the penal warrant provisions of s.90 of the Excise Management

Act 1827, as amended by s. 76 of the Courts of Justice Act 1936.

The plaintiff had been convicted of offences under the Betting Acts and fined a total of £5,200. Having failed to pay the fines, distress warrants were issued in the District Court. When the Gardaí found that the plaintiff's assets were insufficient to meet the fines, the respondent Justice issued penal warrants to the Revenue Commissioners pursuant to s. 90 of the 1827 Act as amended by s. 76 of the 1936 Act. S. 90, as so amended, provided that where a penal warrant in a Revenue matter is issued, the person in question shall be committed to a prison and that the Revenue Commissioners are required to release the person at the expiration of six months whether the penalty for the Revenue offence has or has not been paid. The plaintiff sought a declaration that s. 90, as amended, was inconsistent with the Constitution, and Barron J granted the declaration.

Relying on the decision of the Supreme Court in *Deaton v Revenue Commissioners* [1963] IR 170, he held that s. 90 of the 1827 Act, as amended by s. 76 of the 1936 Act, was inconsistent with the Constitution since it vested a discretion in the Revenue Commissioners as to the length of time which a defaulter may be kept in prison. This, he held, was fatal to the validity of the power, since a person against whom a penal order is made is entitled to know exactly the length of time which he will be required to spend in prison.

Applying the severability test to s. 90 (see *Maher v Attorney General* [1973] IR 141), Barron J ordered that the whole of s. 90 of the 1826 Act and of s. 76 of the 1936 Act were invalid, because to delete only the part which conferred the discretion on the Revenue would be leave a power which had not been intended by the legislature.

He concluded that it would not be appropriate to remit the matter to the District Court under O.84, r.26(4) of the Rules of the Superior Courts 1986 because there was no basis on which the respondent Justice could reconsider the matter of the penal warrants. However, as the convictions against the plaintiff stood the Director of Public Prosecutions might be entitled to make an application in accordance with law.

As Barron J himself noted, one effect of the decision was to make clear that the whole question of the enforcement of penalties imposed in summary Revenue matters required legislative consideration.

PLANT

The perennial problem of what constitutes 'plant' for the purposes of the Income Tax code arose in *Ó Culachain v McMullen Bros Ltd*, High Court, 31 July 1990. Lardner J held that forecourt canopies at petrol stations did constitute plant.

The respondent company carried on the business of selling petrol and oil products to various 'Maxol' retail filling stations in respect of which they had granted franchises to individuals. The company had erected forecourt canopies at a number of such filling stations and claimed that the canopies constituted 'plant' within s. 241 of the Income Tax Act 1967 as amended by s. 26 of the Finance Act 1971 and extended to corporation tax by s. 21 of the Corporation Tax Act 1976. The company therefore claimed to be entitled to make a deduction against corporation tax of the capital expenditure involved in the erection of the canopies. The appellant tax inspector declined to allow the deduction claimed.

In the Circuit Court, the evidence indicated that the company had decided in the early 1980s to provide a new and sophisticated image for its petrol products, that most of its outlets were self-service, that motorists expected a service station to include a large canopy, that the type of canopies involved covered the entire area where the petrol pumps were situated, that market research by the Texaco petrol company had indicated that the presence of a large canopy communicated the particular image of a given brand of petrol and also advertised the station and the product. It was accepted that the canopy played no direct part in the actual process of dispensing petrol. The Circuit Court (Judge Martin) found that the canopies constituted plant, and as already indicated, on case stated Lardner J upheld this view.

Lardner J first referred to the Supreme Court decision in *Mara v Humming-bird Ltd* [1982] ILRM 421 in support of the view that, on a case stated, the High Court was limited to accepting the findings of primary facts made in the Circuit Court where there was evidence to support those findings.

Approaching the instant case, he felt that there was ample evidence to support the conclusions that the canopies fulfilled functions over and above that of shelter, namely the provision of an attractive setting for the sale of the company's products, the creation of an overall impression of efficiency and the attraction of customers. Lardner J also approved the functional test used by Judge Martin in the Circuit Court, and Lardner J also cited in support the decision of the Court of Appeal in *Benson v Yard Arm Club Ltd* [1979] 2 All ER 336 and of Murphy J in *Ó Srianan v Lakeview Ltd* (1984) ITC Leaflet No. 125. Since, he held, the canopies were more than merely the place at which the business in question was carried on, but performed a function in the actual carrying out of the trade and were thus part of the means by which the trade was carried on in the appropriately prepared setting, he agreed that Judge Martin's conclusion had been justified by the evidence presented.

It is unfortunate that, in citing certain English authority on the question of plant, Lardner J did not refer to the decision in *Dixon v Fitch's Garage Ltd* [1975] 3 All ER 455 that forecourt canopies did *not* constitute plant. It is of interest to note that the *Dixon* case was approved in the Court of Appeal in *Benson*.

STAMP DUTY

In *Irish Nationwide Building Society v Revenue Commissioners*, High Court, 2 October 1990 Murphy J held that a deed of transfer under which the Society acquired premises for use as a place of business was not exempt from stamp duty under the First Schedule of the Stamp Act 1891 (as amended). This was so even having regard to the provisions of s. 91 of the Building Societies Act 1976, which exempts from stamp duty certain instruments executed by a building society. Murphy J held that this section must be interpreted as limited to instruments concerning the internal workings of the building society. He did not consider that it could have been intended to effect a wide ranging exemption from stamp duty by oblique means.

URBAN RENEWAL

The Finance Act 1987 (Designation of Urban Renewal Areas) Order 1990 (SI No. 206) and the Finance Act 1987 (Designation of Urban Renewal Areas) (No. 2) Order 1990 (SI No. 315) extended the areas for which tax relief may be claimed.

Safety and Health

ENVIRONMENT

Air pollution: offence *Cork County Council v Angus Fine Chemicals Ltd* [1991] ILRM 173; [1990] 2 IR 365 concerned a narrow but important point concerning failure to notify an air pollution emission from industrial plant. The defendant had been prosecuted by the Cork County Council under s. 29 of the Air Pollution Act 1987 for failing to notify the Council of an accidental emission of material which was likely to cause air pollution. The defendant accepted that the emission occurred but argued that it was exempt from the notification requirement under s. 30(3) of the 1987 Act.

S. 30 provides that regulations may require existing industrial plant to apply for an air emission licence; and s. 30(3) provides that in the period before a licence is granted or refused, the operation of the industrial plant 'shall . . . be deemed not to have contravened the provisions of this Act. ...' The Air Pollution Act 1987 (Licensing of Industrial Plant) Regulations 1988 were made pursuant to s. 30 of the 1987 Act, and they provided that existing industrial plant shall not be in operation after 1 March 1989 unless there was a licence in force for the plant in question. The defendant had applied for, and obtained, a licence under the 1988 Regulations. The emission complained of occurred in the period after the defendant had applied for an emission licence but before it had been granted. On a case stated from the District Court, Blayney J held that an offence under s. 29 of the 1987 Act had been committed.

He stated that the requirement in s. 29 of the 1987 Act to notify the Council of an emission likely to cause air pollution was operative once the 1987 Act was brought into force by Commencement Order in September 1987. This, he held, was not affected by the coming into force of the 1988 Regulations, which did not immediately affect the right of the defendant to carry on its business, so that the requirement to notify continued up to 1 March 1989. He considered that the exemption contained in s. 30(3) of the 1987 Act did not extend to the notification requirement under s. 29 of the 1987 Act, and was concerned only with the actual operation of the industrial plant to which the Act applied; and since s. 29 was stated in clear terms the question whether he was required to interpret it in a strict manner did not arise. In any event, it may be noted that, although the 1987 Act creates criminal offences, the courts will not always apply the strict construction rule since the legislation is also intended to protect health and safety, and this acts to some extent as a countervailing factor: see, for example, *Harrison v National Coal Board* [1951] AC 639, at 650.

Asbestos The Air Pollution Act 1987 (Emission Limit Value for Use of Asbestos) Regulations 1990 (SI No. 28) establish the maximum permissible asbestos emission levels from industrial plant under the 1987 Act. The European Communities (Asbestos Waste) Regulations 1990 (SI No. 30) concern the procedures to be adopted for the transport and disposal of asbestos waste. The European Communities (Control of Water Pollution by Asbestos) Regulations 1990 (SI No. 31) concern offences connected with pollution of watercourses by asbestos.

Coal The Air Pollution Act 1987 (Marketing, Sale and Distribution of Fuels) Regulations 1990 (SI No. 123) constituted a key part of the Department of the Environment's strategy on combatting smog in Dublin. Revoking the Air Pollution Act 1987 (Retail Sale of Fuels) Regulations 1989 (1989 Review, 373), the 1990 Regulations prohibited the sale of bituminous coal in the Dublin area from 1 September 1990.

Control areas The Special Control Area (Ballyfermot Area D) Order 1989 (Confirmation) Order 1990 (SI No. 26) confirmed with modification the designation under the Air Pollution Act 1987 which had been made by Dublin Corporation.

Emission limits The Air Pollution Act 1987 (Commencement) Order 1990 (SI No. 29) brought s. 51 of the 1987 Act into effect from 1 March 1990. S.51 allows the setting of maximum permissible emission levels under Regulations to be made by the Minister for the Environment. Emission levels for asbestos were the first such set of Regulations: see above.

Environmental impact assessment A number of Regulations concerning environmental impact assessment (EIA) were made in 1990. These are referred to in the Local Government chapter, 418-9, above.

Water pollution The Local Government (Water Pollution) (Amendment) Act 1990 strengthens the legal controls on water pollution, contained in earlier legislation, notably the Local Government (Water Pollution) Act 1977.

S. 3 amends the scope of the defence to a charge under s. 3 of the 1977 Act. Henceforth the accused will avoid liability if he proves that he took all reasonable care to prevent the entry to waters to which the charge relates by providing, maintaining, using, operating and supervising facilities, or by employing practices or methods of operation, that were suitable for the purpose of that prevention.

S. 3 also replaces s. 3(5)(a) of the 1977 Act by a provision clarifying the effluents to which the general prohibition does not apply; these, briefly, are discharges of trade effluents or sewage effluents under licence; sewage effluents complying with the standard prescribed under s. 26 of the 1977 Act and trade or sewage effluents to which regulations under s. 4(10) of the 1977 Act apply. The Minister is given power to restrict or repeal by Regulations the exemption set out in s. 3(5) and (6) of the 1977 Act.

Ss. 5 and 13 extend the grounds on which reviews of effluent discharge licences and licences for discharges to sewers may be made and introduce a power of revocation in addition to the power of amendment prescribed by the 1977 Act. A local authority may conduct a review at any time if it has reasonable grounds for believing that the discharge authorised by the licence is or is likely to be injurious to public health or renders or is is likely to render the waters concerned unfit for use for domestic, commercial, industrial, fishery (including fish-farming), agricultural or recreational uses.

S. 7, substituting a new section for s. 10 of the 1977 Act, extends to any person, whether or not with an interest in the waters concerned, the power to apply for a court order requiring one who is causing or permitting water pollution to mitigate any effects of the pollution and to pay the costs of the applicant, or of any other person as may be specified in the order, which were incurred in investigating, mitigating or remedying the effects of the pollution. S. 8 amends s. 11 of the 1977 Act by extending the circumstances in which a person may obtain a High Court order. These are where the Court is satisfied:

> (a) that unauthorised polluting matter is being, has been or is likely to be caused or permitted to enter waters;
> (b) that a similar position exists in relation to unauthorised trade effluent or sewage effluent; and
> (c) that polluting matter has escaped, is escaping or is likely to escape accidentally from premises to waters.

The High Court is given wide-ranging express and discretionary powers as to the range of orders it may make.

The local authorities' power to serve notices regulating practices which, in their opinion, could result in water pollution is clarified (s. 9); the powers of sanitary authorities and local authorities to intervene directly to prevent, mitigate or remedy pollution widened (s. 10); a power to make a water quality management plan jointly is conferred on two or more local authorities (s. 11); and a more flexible system for calculating charges for monitoring, treating and disposing of trade effluent discharges to sewers is introduced (s. 12). As regards licensing and appeals to An Bord Pleanála, regulations may require the payment of fees: s.14. The appeals function was transferred from the Minister for the Environment to An Bord Pleanála in 1978 by the Local Government (Water Pollution) Act 1977 (Transfer of Appeals) Order 1978. S. 16 of the 1990 Act now expressly provides for this, with the Minister retaining the power to regulate procedural matters.

The powers of local and sanitary authorities to require specified particulars of abstractions from, or discharges to, waters or sewers are extended by s. 17 to enable them to seek relevant information from persons who have custody or control of any polluting matter in their functional area or who are engaged in activities or practices which, in their opinion, may cause or permit polluting matter to enter the waters.

S. 20 is a provision of considerable importance. It prescribes *civil* liability for pollution, save in cases covered by s. 3(5) or 4 of the 1977 Act or s. 171 of the Fisheries (Consolidation) Act 1959. S. 20(1) provides as follows:

> Where trade effluent, sewage effluent or other polluting matter enters waters and causes injury, loss or damage to a person or to the property of a person, the person may, without prejudice to any other cause of action that he may have in respect of the injury, loss or damage, recover damages in any court of competent jurisdiction in respect of such injury, loss or damage — (a) from the occupier of the premises from which the effluent or matter originated unless the entry to the waters was caused by an act of God or an act or omission of a third party over whose conduct such occupier had no control, being an act or omission that such occupier could not reasonably have foreseen and guarded against, or (b) if the entry to the waters was occasioned by an act or omission of any person that, in the opinion of the court, constitutes a contravention by the person of a provision of the Principal Act or this Act, from that person.

Thus two heads of civil liability arise. The first, in respect of the occupier of the premises from which the effluent or matter entered the waters, covers much the same ground as the case in *Rylands v Fletcher*, and is subject to broadly similar defences. In an important respect it is wider, in that the plaintiff will not have to show that the use of the effluent or other polluting matter was 'non-natural': cf. McMahon & Binchy, *op. cit.*, 483-6, Kadirgamar, 'The Escape of Water from Domestic Premises', 37 *Conv* (ns) 179 (1973). It seems narrower, however, in that the occupier will escape liability if responsibility lies with a third party over whose conduct the occupier had 'no control', where the act was one which the occupier could not reasonably have foreseen and guarded against. The rule in *Rylands v Fletcher* extends liability to the acts of an independent contractor, over whom the occupier will not necessarily exert control.

An aspect of this first head worth noting is that liability is based, not on any breach of pollution legislation but (subject to the specific defences) the mere entry into the waters of the effluent or matter from the defendant's premises.

An occupier who has a defence to a charge under s. 3(3) of the 1977 Act (as amended by the 1990 Act) is not on that account relieved of civil liability under s. 20(1)(a).

The scope of the second heading is also worth noting. Most obviously it attaches liability to an occupier or other person who discharges effluent or other matter in contravention of the law. Here no question of the defences specified in paragraph (a) arises. Instead the defendant may invoke only such defences as are available in *criminal* law. In this context s. 3 of the 1977 Act (as amended) is important in giving the defendant what amounts, in effect, to the affirmative defence of due care.

Other provisions in the Act which are worthy of particular note are the new powers for local authorities to make bye-laws regulating or prohibiting specified agricultural activities in their functional areas, where they consider this necessary to prevent or eliminate the entry of polluting material to waters (s. 21); the increase in penalties under the 1977 and 1959 Acts (ss. 24 and 25) and the repeal of the provision of the 1977 Act which provided for the establishment of the Water Pollution Advisory Council (s. 30). This was never brought into operation and the regional fisheries boards continued to take prosecutions under s. 171 and 172 of the 1959 Act: see the *Explanatory and Financial Memorandum to the Bill as Initiated*, p. 7 (An Roinn Comhshaoil, Eanair 1989).

INDUSTRIAL STANDARDS

The Industrial Research and Standards (Section 44) (Perambulators and Pushchairs) Order 1990 (SI No. 240) prohibits the marketing of prams and pushchairs unless the are in accordance with Eolas or EC standards.

MERCHANT SHIPPING

Collision Regulations The Collision Regulations (Ships and Water Craft on the Water) (Amendment) Order 1990 (SI No. 36) amends the 1984 Order of the same title to give effect to further requirements of the International Maritime Organisation (IMO).

Fire The Merchant Shipping (Fire Protection) (Amendment) Rules 1990 (SI No. 86) amend the 1985 Rules of the same title.

Navigational equipment The Merchant Shipping (Navigational Equipment) (Amendment) Rules 1990 (SI No. 84) amend the 1985 Rules of the same title by requiring that certain ships carry echo sounder installations.

Training The Merchant Shipping (Musters and Training) Rules 1990 (SI No. 86) revoke the 1983 Rules of the same title and establish new rules for musters and training.

OCCUPATIONAL SAFETY (GENERAL)

Dangerous Substances The Dangerous Substances (Storage of Liquefied Petroleum Gas) Regulations 1990 (SI No. 201) set out obligations on occupiers of commercial premises as to the storage of LPG. The Regulations are couched in general terms such as 'adequacy' and 'reasonably practicable' but significantly they state that such terms should be interpreted by reference to any Code of Practice approved by the National Authority for Occupational Safety and Health, established by the Safety, Health and Welfare at Work Act 1989 (1989 Review, 379-93). NSAI Standards on the storage of LPG were, in fact, approved as Codes of Practice pursuant to s. 30 of the 1989 Act by the Authority almost simultaneously with the promulgation of the Regulations: *Iris Oifigiúil*, 7 August 1990.

Inquests The Safety Health and Welfare at Work Act 1989 (Repeals) Order 1990 (SI No. 103) repealed s. 28 of the Dangerous Substances Act 1972 concerning inquests. S. 56 of the 1989 Act deals with inquests arising from fatalities at all places of work, so that s. 28 of the 1972 Act had become redundant.

Protection against noise The European Communities (Protection of Workers) (Exposure to Noise) Regulations 1990 (SI No. 157) include important new statutory duties placed on virtually all employers in the State in respect of preventive measures to be taken to protect workers from noise induced hearing loss (formerly better known, perhaps, as industrial deafness). The 1990 Regulations, which came into effect on 1 July 1990, revoke the Factories (Noise) Regulations 1975, but it is important to bear in mind that while the 1990 Regulations apply to industrial activity they also apply to places of work outside the factory context. Thus, local authorities, forestries and discos are covered by the 1990 Regulations. In implementing the EC Noise Directive (86/118/EEC) the 1990 Regulations apply to all employees, except those on board sea transport or air transport. Thus, for example, employees working on the ground for Aer Lingus or Aer Rianta would appear to be covered by the 1990 Regulations. The principal elements of the 1990 Regulations are as follows.

Noise levels must be assessed and measured to identify employees exposed to 85 dB(A) (decibels measured at the ear), based on an eight hour day exposure, or in respect of employees who may be exposed to high levels of instantaneous sound pressure (e.g. employees working with pneumatic drills). Results of these measurements must be kept for 3 years. Where noise levels exceed 90dB(A), the employer must draw up and implement a Noise Programme, including measures to reduce exposure to noise 'so far as is reasonably practicable', thus allowing the employer to take account of cost factors (see the 1989 Review, 385).

Whether commercial realities will be relevant in this context, for example, in the application of the Regulations to discos, remains to be seen. It is of interest to note that, while the 1990 Regulations are limited in their apparent scope to the protection of 'workers' the proprietor of a disco would be well advised not to ignore the potential damage to clients on the premises. Common law occupier's liability rules will, of course, be relevant in this context. In addition, s. 7 of the Safety, Health and Welfare at Work Act 1989 imposes a general duty on an employer to ensure 'so far as is reasonably practicable' the safety and health of non-employees arising from the place of work. This duty would appear highly relevant in the context of noise.

Where noise levels exceed 90 dB(A), the 1990 Regulations provide that hearing protection for employees is mandatory and areas with such levels must be marked off, access restricted and warning signs must be posted. Training and information must also be provided to employees as to the risks involved in exposure to high levels of noise.

In addition, the employer must 'make available' hearing checks for employees exposed to 85 dB(A), indicating that such checks are not actually mandatory. It is a matter for the employee to decide to avail of such checks. However, once an initial test is availed of, mandatory follow up checks are required, at intervals specified in the Regulations and in Guidelines issued in August 1990 by the National Authority for Occupational Safety and Health (the Health and Safety Authority).

OFFSHORE INSTALLATIONS

The Safety, Health and Welfare (Offshore Installations) Act 1987 (Commencement) Order 1990 (SI No. 274) brought the 1987 Act into effect from

30 November 1990. The implementation of the Act had been delayed pending discussion between 1987 and 1990 with interested parties on four sets of Regulations. The results of these discussions were published as draft Regulations in December 1990 and were signed into law in January 1991. Most of the Regulations (SIs Nos. 13 to 16 of 1991) came into effect in May 1991. They will be discussed in the 1991 Review.

PUBLIC SAFETY

The Report of the *Committee on Public Safety and Crowd Control* (Pl.7107) was published in February 1990. Chaired by Hamilton P, the Committee had been established in the wake of the Hillsborough stadium disaster. The Committee's Report made extensive recommendations on the procedures to be followed to protect public safety particularly at outdoor sporting occasions and concerts. The Report recommended that a statutory National Authority for Safety at Sports Grounds be established to oversee and enforce codes of practice concerning crowd control. Such codes are currently operated on a voluntary basis, and the Committee considered that while these had operated satisfactorily there was a justification for putting them on a sounder legal footing. The Committee also made a substantial number of recommendations on crowd capacities at major sports venues, the appointment of safety officers and the need to liaise with the Garda authorities.

TOBACCO

The Tobacco (Health Promotion and Protection) Regulations 1990 (SI No. 39), which came into effect on 1 May 1990, introduced major restrictions on tobacco smoking in, for example, public offices, schools and colleges, cinemas and theatres, health premises, food preparation areas and canteens. The Regulations were made under the Tobacco (Health Promotion and Protection) Act 1988 (1988 Review, 377-8).

Social Welfare

For a detailed analysis of the Social Welfare Act 1990, see Clark, Annotation, *Irish Current Law Statutes Annotated*. As well as giving effect to the changes in benefits announced in the 1990 Budget, the 1990 Act introduced a number of important substantive changes. Among these changes were the following.

Lone parent's allowance S.12 provides for a gender-free lone parent's allowance to replace the previous social assistance schemes for single mothers. The Social Welfare Act 1990 (Part III) (Commencement) Order 1990 (SI No. 270) and the Social Welfare Act 1990 (Section 15) (Commencement) Order 1990 (SI No. 271) brought this into effect from 29 November 1990. The Social Welfare (Lone Parent's Allowance and Other Analogous Payments) Regulations 1990 (SI No. 272) set out the details. The Social Welfare Act 1989 (Part III) (Commencement) Order 1990 (SI No. 273) brought connected provisions of the 1989 Act into effect from 29 November 1990.

Carer's allowance S.17 introduced a carer's allowance, operative from 1 November 1990: Social Welfare Act 1990 (Part IV) (Commencement) Order 1990 (SI No. 241). The details of the carer's allowance are set out in the Social Welfare (Carer's Allowance) Regulations 1990 (SI No. 242).

Appeals system Part V of the Act implement changes in the appeals system, the main effect of which is to develop some element of independence for the Chief Appeals Officer by establishing a separate executive office. Part V came into effect on 1 February 1991: Social Welfare Act 1990 (Commencement) (Part V) Order 1990 (SI No. 345). The necessary changes to the appeal procedure are effected by the Social Welfare (Appeals) Regulations 1990 (SI No. 344), which also came into effect on 1 February 1991. For criticisms of the pre-1990 Act situation see Whyte and Cousins, (1989) 7 *ILT* 198.

Social Insurance Fund Ss.23 to 31 provide for amalgamation of the Occupational Injuries Benefit Fund and the Redundancy and Employers Insolvency Fund into the newly established Social Insurance Fund. This is intended to achieve smoother administration and effect some savings. The

Protection of Employees (Employers' Insolvency) (Occupational Pension Scheme) (Forms and Procedure) Regulations 1990 (SI No. 121) revoke the 1985 Regulations of the same title and take account of the amalgamation of Funds effected by the 1990 Act. The Redundancy (Rebates) Regulations 1990 (SI No. 122) similarly take account of the 1990 Act changes.

Occupational injuries disablement S.39 of the 1990 Act, in force from 1 May 1990, provides that any payment in respect of an occupational injuries disablement of less than 10% shall be by way of gratuity only: Social Welfare Act 1990 (Section 39) (Commencement) Order 1990 (SI No. 113).

DISABILITY BENEFIT

In *McHugh v AB (Deciding Officer) and Ors*, High Court, 23 November 1990 Lavan J held invalid certain provisions of the Social Welfare (Overlapping Benefits) (Amendment) Regulations 1987. The applicant had been in receipt of unemployment benefit. In September 1988, she applied for and received unmarried mother's allowance in respect of her child. Following the award of this allowance, the applicant's unemployment benefit was reduced by one half pursuant to Article 4 of the 1987 Regulations.

The applicant suffered from epilepsy and from September 1989 she suffered an increase in attacks to such an extent that she was advised not to go out. She therefore ceased signing on for unemployment benefit as she was no longer available for work. She applied for disability benefit, but was refused under Article 5 of the 1987 Regulations. By virtue of the changes effected in the Regulations in April 1990, the applicant became entitled to both the disability benefit and the unmarried mother's allowance. However, the question remained as to whether the applicant had been entitled to both prior to this. Lavan J held she was.

Quoting s.8 (disability benefit), s.130 (making of Regulations) and s.197 of the Social Welfare (Consolidation) Act 1981, Lavan J agreed that the applicant had been entitled under the Act to both the benefit and the allowance. He referred by way of analogy to the Supreme Court decision in *Harvey v Minister for Social Welfare* [1990] ILRM 185; [1990] 2 IR 232 (1989 Review, 394-5) in support of his conclusion that Article 4 of the 1987 Regulations were *ultra vires* the Minister's powers, and he granted relief to the applicant accordingly.

PRE-RETIREMENT ALLOWANCE

The Social Welfare Act 1988 (Section 28) (Commencement) Order 1990 (SI

No. 75) brought the pre-retirement allowance scheme established by s.28 of the 1988 Act into effect from 27 March 1990. The Social Welfare (Pre-Retirement Allowance) Regulations 1990 (SI No. 76) set out the details of the scheme.

REGULATIONS

In addition to the Regulations referred to above, the following Regulations were made in 1990 in relation to social welfare.

Social Welfare (Adult Dependent) (Amendment) Regulations 1990 (SI No. 137).

Social Welfare (Amendment of Miscellaneous Social Insurance Provisions) Regulations 1990 (SI No. 188).

Social Welfare (Assistance) Regulations 1990 (SI No. 279).

Social Welfare (Claims and Payments) (Amendment) Regulations 1990 (SI No. 247).

Social Welfare (Contributions) (Amendment) Regulations 1990 (SI No. 88).

Social Welfare (Contributions) (Amendment)(No. 2) Regulations 1990 (SI No. 264).

Social Welfare (Family Income Supplement) (Amendment) Regulations 1990 (SI No. 189).

Social Welfare (Family Income Supplement) (Amendment) (No. 2) Regulations 1990 (SI No. 263)

Social Welfare (Miscellaneous Provisions) Regulations 1990 (SI No. 114).

Social Welfare (Modification of Insurance) (Amendment) Regulations 1990 (SI No. 89)

Social Welfare (Normal Residence) (Amendment) Regulations 1990 (SI No. 280).

Social Welfare (Overlapping Benefits) Regulations 1990 (SI No. 342).

Social Welfare (Overlapping Benefits) (Amendment) Regulations 1990 (SI No. 90).

Social Welfare (Overlapping Benefits) (Amendment) (No. 2) Regulations 1990 (SI No. 261).

Social Welfare (Payments to Appointed Persons) Regulations 1990 (SI No. 248).

Social Welfare (Preservation of Rights) (Amendment) Regulations 1990 (SI No. 178).

Social Welfare (Rent Allowance) (Amendment) Regulations 1990 (SI No. 187).

Social Welfare (Rent Allowance) (Amendment) (No. 2) Regulations 1990 (SI No. 302).

Social Welfare (Temporary Provisions) Regulations 1990 (SI No. 278).

Solicitors

FAIR TRADE COMMISSION

The recommendation of the Fair Trade Commission Report on the Legal Profession are discussed above, 437, in the Practice and Procedure chapter.

NEGLIGENCE

The unsuccessful claim in negligence, *Hanafin v Gaynor*, High Court, 29 May 1990, is discussed below, 522-3, in the Torts chapter.

PRACTICING CERTIFICATES

The Solicitors Acts 1954 and 1960 (Fees) Regulations 1990 (SI No. 324) specify revised fees for obtaining practicing certificates.

SOLICITOR AND CLIENT PRIVILEGE

The limits to discovery of material passing between solicitor and client was discussed by the Supreme Court in *Smurfit Paribas Bank Ltd v AAB Export Finance Ltd* [1990] ILRM 588: see 435, above, in the Practice and Procedure chapter.

UNDERTAKINGS

The decision in *Shangan Construction Ltd v TP Robinson & Co.*, High Court 10 July 1990 is discussed in the Land Law chapter, 376, above.

Statutory Interpretation

Breach of statutory duty   In *Sunderland v Louth County Council* [1990] ILRM 658, the Supreme Court held that obligations imposed on the Council by the Local Government (Planning and Development) Act 1963 did not give rise to a duty of care to the plaintiffs: 545-9, below, in the Torts chapter. By way of contrast, the Court in *Burke v Dublin Corporation*, Supreme Court, 26 July 1990 held that obligations imposed by the Housing Act 1966 did give rise to a duty to the plaintiffs: see the 1989 Review, 117-25.

Mandatory   In *Bakht v Medical Council* [1990] ILRM 840; [1990] 1 IR 515, the Supreme Court described as mandatory certain provisions of the Medical Practitioners Act 1978: 337, above, in the Health Services chapter.

Overall purpose   In *Director of Consumer Affairs v Irish Permanent Building Society* [1990] ILRM 743 Murphy J referred to the overall purpose of a statutory provision in order to construe it: see 29-30, above, in the Commercial Law chapter.

Plain meaning   In *Mahon v Burke* [1991] ILRM 59, Lavan J applied the plain meaning rule to a provision in the Civil Liability Act 1961: 563, below, in the Torts chapter.

Prospective effect   In *Aer Lingus Teo v Labour Court* [1990] ILRM 485; [1990] ELR 113 (342, above, in the Labour Law chapter), *O'H. v O'H.* [1991] ILRM 108; [1990] 2 IR 558 (309, above, in the Family Law chapter) and *McDaid v Sheehy* [1991] ILRM 250 (464, above in the Revenue chapter) the presumption that legislation operates prospectively only was applied.

Punctuation   In *Hegarty v Fitzpatrick* [1990] 2 IR 377, Murphy J referred to a problem of punctuation in s.14 of the Courts Act 1971: see 199-200, above, in the Criminal Law chapter.

Singular and plural   In *Ellis v O'Dea (No. 2)* [1991] ILRM 346, the Supreme Court referred to the provision in s.11 of the Interpretation Act 1937 concerning the presumption that the use of the singular does not exclude reference to the plural: 218, above, in the Criminal Law chapter.

Strict interpretation This issue was adverted to in *Cork County Council v Angus Fine Chemicals Ltd* [1991] ILRM 173; [1990] 2 IR 365 (469, above, in the Safety and Health chapter).

Teleological approach The limits to the teleological approach of interpretation were discussed by Murphy J in *Dowling v Ireland*, High Court, 18 January 1990: see 282-3, above, in the European Communities chapter.

Telecommunications

BROADCASTING

General   The Broadcasting Act 1990 follows on legislation enacted in 1988 (analysed in the 1988 Review, 399ff) which established for private sector radio broadcasting and the establishment of a national television programme service under contract with the Independent Radio and Television Commission, which was created by the 1988 legislation. The 1990 Act introduces a miscellany of provisions, the most politically controversial of which related to the regulation of economic incentives and controls applying to RTE relative to its competitors. The Bill as initiated proposed that a grant, equivalent to a proportion of the licence fee, would be payable to the Independent Radio and Television Commission for disbursement to the sound broadcasting and television services established under the 1988 Act. This approach met with such opposition that what emerged in the Act was a watered down version, still contentious but far less than the original proposal. For a very helpful analysis of the Act and its background, see David Barniville's Annotation of the Act, *ICLSA*.

Advertising broadcasts by RTE   S. 3 introduces a statutory time limit on advertising on RTE's services of 7.5% of total daily programme transmission time, as against 10% formerly. It also introduces a maximum of five minutes of advertising in any one hour, as against the former maximum of 7.5 minutes.

The section goes on to place a limit on the revenue RTE may derive annually from advertising, sponsorship or other forms of commercial promotion in broadcasts equal to the amount of the grant paid to it in respect of licence fees in the preceding financial year, that amount having been adjusted by the increase in the consumer price index compiled by the Central Statistics Office for the preceding financial year.

The Minister expected that these measures would lead to the diversion of around £12 million in advertising revenue in a full year.

Codes of practice relating to advertising and other commercial promotions   S. 4 is designed to ensure a uniformity of standards across all broadcasting services. It applies to RTE services and to services established under the 1988 Act. It enables the Minister to draw up enforceable codes governing standards of practice and prohibitions in advertising, sponsorship or other forms of commercial promotion in broadcasting services. These codes may prescribe the extent to which RTE or a sound broadcasting contractor or television programme service contractor may provide for the extent to which its promotion of its own commercial activities within its own broadcasting services is to be treated as advertising for the purposes of complying with the limits set out in s. 3. Thus, promotions for the *RTE Guide* or video-cassette compilations will count as advertising.

Television programme service contract S. 6 permits the Independent Radio and Television Commission to enter into a contract with the television programme service contractor, in addition to the basic one envisaged under s. 4(2)(b) of the 1988 Act, under which the television programme service contractor will have the right and duty to establish, maintain and operate television broadcasting transmitters. Translated into everyday language, the TV3 operator, in addition to cable and MMDS modes of transmission, will have the opportunity of a separate conventional VHF transmission system. This will mean that it will be able to reach those households which do not have cable and MMDS: see the Minister's observations, 126 Seanad Debs, cols. 289-90.

Accounts and audits S. 7 gives RTE the function of appointing its own auditors. Formerly the Comptroller and Auditor General had this responsibility. Because of pressure on that office, there had been delays which had led, unfairly, to criticism of RTE. The change had therefore been actively sought by RTE for some years: see 399 Dáil Debs, cols. 1578-9. An Post and Telecom Éireann have a similar entitlement.

One provision worth noting in s. 7 is subs. (2)(c), which requires RTE, after the audit, to send to the Minister a statement certified by the auditors in respect of the total revenue derived by RTE from advertising, sponsorship or other forms of commercial promotion in its broadcasts. This requirement is 'basically a cross-check' on compliance with the advertising renewal cap imposed by s. 3: see 399 Dáil Debs, col. 1579.

Complaints to Broadcasting Complaints Commission S. 8 amends the Broadcasting Authority (Amendment) Act 1976 by extending the ambit of the Broadcasting Complaints Commission to cover complaints by persons that an assertion was made, in a broadcast, of inaccurate facts or information in relation to them which constituted an attack on their honour or reputation. It also requires RTE (unless the Commission considers it inappropriate) to broadcast the Commission's decision in favour of the complainant, including any correction of inaccurate facts or information, at a time and in a manner corresponding to that in which the offending broadcast took place.

This 'right of reply' model echoes the approach in several European legal systems: see The Law Reform Commission's *Consultation Paper on the Civil Law of Defamation* (1990), paras. 470-1. It is necessitated by the EC Directive on Broadcasting Activities, adopted by the Council of Ministers on 3 October 1989, and will facilitate Ireland's ratification of the Council of Europe's Convention on Transfrontier Television, which was opened for signature in May 1989. Formerly the Commission's findings were only published in the *RTE Guide*, save in those rare cases which were sufficiently newsworthy to attract the attention of other media.

The EC Directive and the Council of Europe's Convention relate only to television services. The mechanism already existing under s. 11 of the Broadcasting and Wireless Telegraphy Act 1988 to extend the ambit of the Broadcasting Complaints Commission to all the services operating under that Act and the Minister explained that it was his intention to do so: 399 Dáil Debs, cols. 1581-2.

Unauthorised interception of cable services and MMDS services Ss. 9 to 15 of the Act deal with the growing problem of unauthorised interception of cable services and MMDS services. In the case of the Cablelink system in Dublin it was estimated that there were about 12,000 unauthorised connections, resulting in a loss of over £600,000 in rental revenue *per annum*: 399 Dáil Debs, col 1582. The practice also interfered with the quality of reception, which in turn led to consumer dissatisfaction and further indirect financial losses.

Larceny laws and criminal damage provisions, in the hands of 'creative' courts, can be bent sufficiently to catch some of these interceptions, but the easier solution is obviously to create specific offences, and this is what is done in s. 9, prohibiting interception of such services, and s. 10, prohibiting owners or those in the control or management of persons knowingly to premit breaches of s. 9 to occur on the premises. The maximum penalty for either offence, on conviction on indictment, is a term of imprisonment and a fine of £20,000: s. 11(1). Moreover the court may order the forfeiture of any equipment used in the commission of the offence: s. 12.

S. 15 creates *civil* remedies, prospective and retrospective. Where a licensee or service provider alleges that any activity or conduct prohibited by s. 9 is being, has been or is about to be carried on and that, as a result, he has suffered, is suffering or may suffer damage he is entitled to seek the following remedies against the person responsible:

(a) an injunction;
(b) damages or, at his option, an account of profits.

The section does not address the questions of the onus and standard of proof. On one view, it would be necessary to prove the case beyond reasonable doubt since this would be necessary to establish criminal liability under s. 9. On another view, which seems more likely to commend itself to the courts, the normal civil standard of the balance of probabilities applies: the defendant found liable under s. 15 is not being convicted of an offence and the fact that, in a criminal trial, proof beyond reasonable doubt is necessary is not relevant to his civil liability. Since s. 15 envisages judicial intervention even where *no* activity in breach of s. 9 has occurred, it would be odd that the *likelihood* of such breach in the future should have to be adjudicated by the criminal standard of proof. The idea that the section envisages differing standards of proof, depending on whether the activity has occurred or is apprehended, seems most unconvincing. As to the burden of proof, it might seem reasonable to assume that, in proceedings under s. 15, the plaintiff should be permitted to avail himself of the advantage given the prosecution by s. 13, which relieves it of the necessity, to negative by evidence the existence of an agreement with a licensee or service provider, in proceedings for an offence under s. 9 or 19. Since, however, the proceedings are civil rather than criminal, and involve different parties, the point is uncertain.

S. 16 empowers the Minister to extend the provisions of ss. 9 to 15 to services transmitted by wireless telegraphy where the operator of the service charges a fee. The most obvious example is an encrypted satellite television programme service. It is expected that international institutions such as the Council of Europe, will afford similar protection in due course: 399 Dáil Debs, col. 1584.

Technical amendments S. 17(1) makes it clear that the Minister's licensing powers under s. 5 of the Wireless Telegraphy Act 1926 include the power to limit the number of licences in the interests of the efficient and orderly use of apparatus for wireless telegraphy. This has proved important in relation to MMDS service and the mobile business radio area: 399 Dáil Debs, col. 1584. S. 17(2) gives the Minister power to recognise licences for various types of radio systems in other countries, thus avoiding the red tape of temporary licences for visitors here.

S. 18 corrects an oversight in the Broadcasting and Wireless Telegraphy Act 1988 by extending the period for prosecution from six months to two years for the basic offences under s. 3 of the Wireless Telegraphy Act 1926 (as amended by s. 12 of the 1988 Act). S. 6(4) of the 1988 Act had introduced a similar extension for the various offences relating to illegal broadcasting which that Act created. S. 3 of the 1926 Act involves offences relating to the possession, maintenance or installation of unlicensed wireless telegraphy apparatus.

Restrictions on broadcasting   Under the Broadcasting Authority Act 1960 (Section 31) Order 1990 (SI No. 11), effective until 19 January 1991, spokespersons for certain named and proscribed organisations are prohibited from broadcasting any material on Radio Telefís Éireann, including party political broadcasts. For discussion, see *The State (Lynch) v Cooney* [1983] ILRM 89; [1982] IR 337.

DATA PROTECTION

The Data Protection (Fees) Regulations 1990 (SI No. 80) amended the registration fees applicable under the Data Protection Act 1988 (1988 Review, 390-9). For a data controller with more than 25 employees, the fee was increased to £200 (from £100), while for other data controllers the fee was decreased to £50 (also from £100).

POSTAL SCHEMES

The Inland Post Amendment (No. 46) Scheme 1990 (SI No. 320) allows An Post to carry on a 24 hour parcel service within the State.

TELECOM SCHEMES

General   The Telecommunications Scheme 1990 (SI No. 91) consolidated with amendents the detail concerning all Telecom Éireann services (other than telemessage and foreign telegram services). See also the Telecommunications (Amendment) (No. 2) Scheme 1990 (SI No. 245).

Telephone   The Telecommunications (Amendment) Scheme 1990 (SI No. 179) provided for the standardisation of business, residential and auxiliary telephone rentals and for the liberalisation of the telephone set market.

Torts

STANDARD OF CARE AND REMOTENESS OF DAMAGE

In *Fitzsimons v Bord Telecom Éireann and the Electrical Supply Board*
[1991] ILRM 276 (High Court, 1990), Barron J had to resolve issues of the
standard of care and remoteness of damage in relation to an unusual, tragic,
factual situation. On a Saturday in winter, a telephone line in a rural area
broke in a severe storm. The first defendant was aware of this by 10 p.m. The
following evening, at 6.30 p.m. the line became live by coming into contact
with an electricity power line above it. The manner in which this occurred
was not certain; the most likely hypothesis was that a passing car had caught
the telephone line which whiplashed over the power line and draped back
onto the ground. At all events, the line was sizzling and started a fire on the
grass margin. When the deceased went to investigate, he tried to pull the wire
away with a stick, but was electrocuted and died instantly.

In fatal injuries proceedings brought by the deceased's family, the
evidence showed that the telephone and electricity authorities had established
a pattern whereby, if their lines crossed, the party who came second (and thus
caused the crossing) took the bulk of safety precautions. This approach did
not appeal to Barron J, who considered that, if safety precautions were
desirable in one case they should be followed in both. He was also critical
of the relative lack of liaison. If there had been a joint safety committee or
some similar cooperation, standardised features would almost certainly have
been adopted in all cases, and appropriate precautions would have been
taken, such as lessening the span of a telephone line or putting it underground.

Barron J was of the view that the case fell within the principles articulated
in the Supreme Court decision of *Kelly v St Laurence's Hospital* [1989]
ILRM 437, which we analysed in the 1988 Review, 410-18. That decision
related to the standard of care appropriate for the monitoring of a patient who
had been admitted to hospital for observation where his normal medication
was being withheld. The patient had been injured when he fell from a window
in a toilet attached to his ward, which he had been able to visit without
supervision from the staff. The trial judge had sought to define the test of
negligence in terms of probability of injury. The Supreme Court held that
this was not the proper approach: reasonable care was the test, not some
specific inflexible point on the gradation of probability. Walsh J said:

In this case the reasonable person concerned and the standard involved was the reasonable hospital administration and nursing service. In my view, it would not be correct to tell the jury that they must be satisfied that what has to be foreseen is a probability of injury. To maintain that position would amount to saying to the jury that, even if they were satisfied that the nursing staff foresaw not merely that there was a possibility which was more than a vague or a very remote possibility, but even a substantial possibility . . . because it did not reach the height of being a probability, . . . they could safely take no precautions. In my view, once there is a foreseeable possibility then the persons involved are on notice. Undoubtedly the standard of care which might reasonably be expected may be sufficient if it is commensurate with the degree of possibility, but that is different from saying that no standard of care is expected until the possibility reaches such a high degree as to be classified as a probability.

Barron J quoted this passage with approval. He was of opinion that 'there should also be added that the standard of care should take into account the *nature of the danger*' (emphasis added). Walsh J's remarks in *McNamara v ESB* [1975] IR 1, at 14 were authority for this.

Barron J considered that, once the telephone wire was known to have fallen, it could not be ignored. In *Kelly*, the patient's abnormal behaviour might not have been foreseen, but behaviour of *that type* was to have been foreseen. In the instant case, it was foreseen that a telephone wire might break, that a broken telephone wire might whiplash and that, if it did, it would behave in an unpredictable fashion. Once An Bord Telecom was aware that the telephone wire was down, it had an obligation to ensure that it was made safe:

It was aware that it was a danger and that it could behave in an unpredictable manner. And it was liable for its failure to render it safe even though what happened was a freak accident which occurred in a manner which itself was not foreseeable. . . .

Once it creates a source of danger which in itself is unpredictable, it must be taken to be responsible for whatever that very quality of unpredictability causes. In my view, that is the situation here. This was a freak accident only in the sense that the actual manner in which the telephone wire caught on the power line could not have been foreseen.

Barron J considered that it was not necessary for the plaintiff to 'go beyond' *Kelly's* case to rely on *Hughes v Lord Advocate* [1963] AC 837 (HL

(Sc)), where the House of Lords made it plain that the test of reasonable foreseeability which displaced that of directness in *The Wagon Mound (No. 1)* [1961] AC 388 (PC), as appropriate to determining remoteness of damage, should not be interpreted so narrowly as to exclude compensation for injury of a kind that was reasonably foreseeable even if the precise manner in which the accident unfolded could not reasonably have been foreseen.

Barron J appears to have treated *Kelly* and *Hughes* as addressing different, albeit closely related, issues. From a doctrinal standpoint, the question may be asked as to how the court should approach the test of reasonable fore-seeability, which (according to Irish no less than British law) governs *both* the issue of the *standard of care* ('Did the defendant act so unreasonably that his conduct should, in the circumstances be characterised as negligent?') and the issue of *remoteness of damage* ('Assuming that the defendant acted negligently, was the injury of which the plaintiff complains reasonably foreseeable?'). Is it possible that the same verbal test could yield different outcomes, depending on which issue is in focus?

The Privy Council appeared to think that this was *not* possible. In *Wagon Mound (No. 1)*, Viscount Simonds, speaking for the Judicial Committee, said:

> It is, no doubt, proper when considering tortious liability for negligence to analyse its elements and to say that the plaintiff must prove a duty owed to him by the defendant, a breach of that duty by the defendant, and consequent damage. But there can be no liability until the damage has been done. It is not the act but the consequences on which tortious liability is founded. Just as (as it has been said) there is no such thing as negligence in the air, so there is no such thing as liability in the air. Suppose an action brought by A for damage caused by the carelessness (a neutral word) of B, for example a fire caused by the careless spillage of oil. It may, of course, become relevant to know what duty B owed to A, but the only liability that is in question is the liability for damage by fire. It is vain to isolate the liability from its context and to say that B is or is not liable, and then to ask for what damage he is liable. For his liability is in respect of that damage and no other. If, as admittedly it is, B's liability (culpability) depends on the reasonable foreseeability of the consequent damage, how is that to be determined except by the foreseeability of the damage which in fact happened — the damage in suit? And, if that damage is unforeseeable so as to displace liability at large, how can the liability be restored so as to make compensation payable?

One suspects, however, that courts do not in fact proceed on the basis that the issue of reasonable foreseeability should be treated as one question. Barron J's remarks seem to confirm this suspicion. While of course it is necessary, in determining the issue of a defendant's alleged negligence, to have regard not merely to what he did but also to the effects of his action, there is a natural tendency to take these aspects in sequence. The first question (of characterising the act as negligent) examines the reasonableness of the conduct primarily in the light of the probability of accident, the gravity of threatened harm, the social utility of the defendant's act and the cost of prevention. While of course adverting to the injury which resulted, it concentrates on the normative quality of the defendant's conduct in the light of the circumstances prevailing at the time the defendant acted. The second question (of remoteness of damage) is addressed only where the first has been resolved against the defendant. Now the court concentrates its attention on the injury which the plaintiff has sustained and enquires whether it is within the bounds of reasonable foreseeability. In determining that question, the court again must have regard to the four factors of *probability, gravity, social utility* and *cost of prevention* (see *The Wagon Mound (No. 2)* [1967] 1 AC 617), but in *most* instances its attention will be concentrated on the first (and to a lesser extent the second) of these factors.

It is on this basis that *Hughes v Lord Advocate* can best be understood. The notion of a *type* of accident that is foreseeable clearly relates to the first and second of these factors exclusively. A plaintiff who complains of an injury which the defendant seeks to characterise as unforeseeable will invoke *Hughes* to show that the injury was of a type that was foreseeable. If he succeeds in convincing the court that this was so he will win his case, but he will have interested the court in this question only where the court is willing, in the light of all *four* factors of probability, gravity, social utility and cost of prevention, to characterise as negligent the conduct in which the defendant engaged.

It would be wrong to interpret *Fitzsimons* as holding that, in *all* cases where there is a foreseeable risk of an unpredictable reaction or behaviour the person who created that risk is inevitably liable for injury caused by that reaction or behaviour. It is only in those cases where, in the light of the four factors, the court adjudicates that generating that risk was negligent that liability will attach.

At all events, having found An Bord Telecom liable, Barron J proceeded to address the issue of the ESB's liability. He accepted the submission of counsel for the ESB that the inadequacy of the safety features where the lines crossed was not *a causa causans* of the accident (on the basis of *Conole v Redbank Oyster Co.* [1976] IR 1), since An Bord Telecom had failed to make the fallen wire safe. Nevertheless he held that the ESB could not be relieved of liability in the light of its failure to have responded adequately to the danger. Two systems of response were available: the earth neutral system (in which only the affected line would be cut out when a fault was detected) and the isolated neutral system (in which all lines serviced by the sub-station had to be cut out whenever a fault was detected on any of the lines). Each system had its advantages and drawbacks; Barron J, in the light of the somewhat incomplete evidence on this issue, could not say that the ESB had been wrong to use the latter system. But it *had* been negligent in letting a live power line remain in that condition for two hours. If it had had an operator present in the sub-station at all times, he or she could have identified the dangerous line within ten minutes, isolated it, and restored power to the other lines. Barron J accepted that the ESB was entitled to balance the risk inherent in a faulty line with its desire to maintain continuity of supply; discontinuation could itself cause danger when supply was cut off to such outlets as hospitals, factories and traffic lights. But this did not justify leaving the live power line for that period.

A slight difficulty with this analysis is that the deceased had come into contact with the power line *half-an-hour* after it had become live. The fact that the ESB took two hours to respond effectively may well have constituted negligence in respect of a contact occurring *after the elapse of that two hours*; the real question was whether that negligence *caused* the accident occurring after the relatively shorter period. The crucial question related thus to the minimum amount of time which the ESB had in which to respond before its failure could be stigmatised as negligent. If the period was greater than half an hour, then the ESB, in spite of its negligence, should have been relieved of liability. Cf. *Barnett v Chelsea and Kensington Hospital Management Committee* [1969] 1 QB 428.

THE RESCUE DOCTRINE

In *Phillips v Durgan* [1991] ILRM 321, the Supreme Court for the first time addressed the position in tort law of a rescuer. The defendant owned and lived in a house in which his late mother had also lived prior to her death in 1975. The house was not in a good state of upkeep: the kitchen was in a condition of extreme dirt and filth, most of which consisted of many years' accumulation of grease from constant frying on a gas cooker. The linoleum which covered the floor was broken in one particular place, in front of the cooker. From this hole newspapers protruded; they had originally been put under the linoleum as a lining between it and tiles. There was also an accumulation on the floor of many greasy paper bags which had originally contained fish and chips. The cooker was deeply embedded with grease on all parts of it, and the wall immediately adjoining it was also heavily coated with grease.

In 1981 the defendant entered into a contract with the first plaintiff, who was his sister, for her to paint and decorate the house for a price of £100. Neither the first plaintiff nor the second, her husband, had been in the kitchen since some time before the death of the first plaintiff's mother. The defendant gave neither of them any warning about the condition of the kitchen. The first plaintiff was driven by her husband to the house to start the work. Since she did not drive and the house was some distance from their home, the Supreme Court was satisfied that it must have been within the contemplation of the defendant that the second plaintiff 'would at least be involved in coming with his wife to the house to drive her there and probably would also take part in carrying out the work': *id.*, at 323 (*per* Finlay CJ). When they arrived they went into the kitchen where the first defendant tried to provide herself with hot water to use with detergents and wire wool which she had brought. The geyser did not work and, after trying all four jets on the cooker, she succeeded in getting one to light in a defective, 'stuttering' fashion. She placed a kettle of water to boil on that jet, and then started to scrape away grease from the cooker and the wall. She stumbled, due probably to the greasy condition of the floor. The cloth in her hand came in contact with the flame under the kettle. The cloth immediately took light because of the grease which had already accumulated on it. She dropped it on the floor and tried to extinguish the flame by stamping on it but, in what both plaintiffs described as an extraordinarily short time, the whole area around the cooker, as well as the cooker itself, appeared to be on fire. The first plaintiff was extensively burned as a result of the fire on the floor catching onto her slippers and then her clothes. Her husband dragged her out. He was also injured in the process of doing so as well as in his attempts to put out the fire.

At trial, Egan J had imposed liability on the defendant in respect of both plaintiffs' claims, not because of a failure to *warn* the plaintiffs of the dirty condition of the floor (since they could see the condition themselves) but because the dirty condition 'in some way contributed to this fire occurring'. The Supreme Court, affirming Egan J, based liability on the failure to warn and the foreseeability of the husband's rescue attempt.

Finlay CJ (Griffin and Hederman JJ concurring) said that he was:

> satisfied that what is described as the principle of rescue, and what is dealt with in the case of *Ogwo v Taylor* [1987] 3 All ER 961, truly consists only of a situation in which the court will rule as a foreseeable consequence of the negligent commencement of a fire that persons seeking to put out that fire, either by reason of their duty as officers of a fire brigade or by reason of their desire to prevent damage, whether to persons or property, may be injured by the existence of the fire. It is

essentially, therefore, a doctrine of foreseeability and cannot . . . come into operation without an initial negligence causing the fire.

The Chief Justice disagreed with Egan J's basis for imposing liability, which did not appear to require negligence on the part of the defendant in causing the fire, but he also disagreed with Egan J's acquitting the defendant of negligence contributing to the fire by reason of the fact that the plaintiffs could see the condition of the premises. Having regard to the earlier Supreme Court decisions of *O'Donoghue v Greene* [1967] IR 40 and *Morley v Eye, Ear and Throat Hospital Inc* [1967] IR 143, as well as Griffin J's judgment in *Foley v Musgrave Cash and Carry Ltd*, Supreme Court 20 December 1985, he was satisfied that the defendant was obliged 'to warn the plaintiffs of the particular risks and hazards which could reasonably be foreseen in the type of work which he was asking them to carry out [under contract], and to provide them either with a means of carrying out that work which was safe, or to issue to them a warning, prior to their arrival for the commencement of the work, of the sort of preparations which might be necessary and the sort of equipment which it might be necessary to being in order to carry out the work with safety'.

Since the primary facts were not in dispute, and having regard to the fact that nearly a decade had passed since the occurrence of the accident, Finlay CJ had no doubt that the interests of justice were that the Supreme Court should decide the issues between the parties. He held the defendant negligent: the particular task which the defendant had asked the plaintiffs to carry out in the kitchen was 'a most unusual task of cleaning which no ordinary person could be expected to anticipate'. He owed the plaintiffs a duty to give some consideration to how it might be done with safety. This he had not done, since he had neither arranged any method of providing hot water, which was essential for the job, without permitting the lighting of a jet on the cooker, nor had he given the plaintiffs any specific warning as to the condition of the cooker or the geyser. The duty of care could have been discharged in a number of ways, the most obvious being to have the geyser repaired. A warning to the first plaintiff as to the fact that there was no way of making hot water otherwise than by the flame in an excessively greasy area would also have been sufficient, in view of her experience as a housekeeper.

The fact that the plaintiffs could see the condition of the kitchen was relevant to contributory negligence. The second plaintiff could not be found guilty of negligence contributing to the accident: what he had done after the fire had started 'was the natural and obvious thing to do, and could not be an act of contributory negligence, namely, an attempt to put out the fire to save his wife'.

The first plaintiff was in a different position, however. She was aware of the 'stuttering' nature of the flame under the kettle, as well as the extremely greasy nature of the cooker and the condition of the floor. A standard of reasonable care for her own safety would have required her to take some special precautions about where she was working until such time as the kettle had been boiled and the flame had been turned off. Accordingly her damages were reduced by 15%.

In his concurring judgment, Griffin J noted that it had been accepted by counsel that the rescue principle had been neither raised nor argued in the High Court. He endorsed the statement of Lord Denning MR in *Videan v British Transport Commission* [1963] 3 WLR 374, at 385, that:

> . . . if a person by his fault creates a situation of peril, he must answer for it to any person who attempts to rescue the person who is in danger. He owes a duty to such a person above all others. The rescuer may act instinctively out of humanity or deliberately out of courage. But, whichever it is, so long as it is not wanton interference, if the rescuer is killed or injured in the attempt, he can recover damages from the one whose fault has been the cause of it.

Griffin J also accepted the principles of liability set out in *Ogwo v Taylor, supra*. It was 'clear therefore that in both rescue and fire-fighting cases there can be no liability unless there was negligence on the part of the person creating the situation of peril in the former case and on the part of the person starting the fire in the latter case'.

The decision raises a number of interesting issues in relation to the rescue principle. Judicial attitudes towards the rescuer have changed radically over the past half century. As Fleming has observed: 'Once the Cinderella of the law he has since become its darling' *(The Law of Torts*, 155 (7th ed, 1987)). Formerly the courts would congratulate the rescuer for his heroism and hold that his action amounted to voluntary assumption of risk: cf *Cutler v United Dairies (London) Ltd* [1933] 2 KB 297. Today there is the danger of their going too far in the opposite extreme, in compensating professional rescuers, such as firemen, whose motivation in choosing their career may well be admirable but who are paid to engage in rescue activity as part of the terms of their employment.

The conceptual elements of the rescue principle have been widely debated. Among the leading analysis are Tiley, 'The Rescue Principle', (1967) 34 *Modern L Rev* 25, Linden, 'Rescuers and Good Samaritans' (1971) 34 *Modern L Rev* 241 (1971) and Rose, 'Restitution for the Rescuer' (1989) 9 *Oxford J of Legal Studies* 176. What might be called the orthodox position, which most easily harmonises with the general principles of the law of negligence, is that a defendant should be liable if, *and only if,* his conduct or omission negligently induces a reasonably foreseeable rescue attempt by the plaintiff. Thus the rescuer's claim is an independent one, not deriving from any necessary breach of duty by the defendant to another. Of course in most cases *(as in Phillips v Durgan)* there will be a primary victim in danger in respect of whom the defendant will be guilty of negligence; but the rescuer's claim does not evaporate if the danger was apparent rather than real. The rescuer's claim stands or falls on whether the defendant is guilty of negligence *to the rescuer* in inducing the rescue attempt on the basis of apparent danger to another.

A more controversial aspect of the orthodox position is that the plaintiff's rescue attempt must have been *reasonably foreseeable.* In the famous Canadian case of *Horsley v MacLaren (The Ogopogo),* [1972] SCR 446, liability was denied on this basis to a rescuer who, heroically, but rashly, dived into the icy waters of Lake Ontario in the Spring to rescue his friend who had fallen overboard. For consideration of the decision see Binchy, 'The Good Samaritan at the Crossroads: A Canadian Signpost?' (1974) 25 *N. Ireland LQ* 147. Some courts and commentators are uncomfortable with this limitation and would prefer to handle the element to unforeseeability exclusively by the mechanism of contributory negligence, rejecting a rescuer's claim completely only where it is 'wanton', to use Cardozo J's expression in *Wagner v International Railroad Co.,* 232 NYS 176, 133 NE 437 (1921). As we have seen Lord Denning MR, availed himself of this word in *Videan v British Transport Commission, supra.*

The question arises as to whether Griffin J's endorsement of Lord Denning MR's remarks places Griffin J in the heterodox camp of this issue. The answers seems that it does not, since *Ogwo v Taylor,* which he also endorsed, clearly requires foreseeability as an ingredient. It is nonetheless true that, on a narrow parsing of his judgment, it could be argued that it is at least consistent with the proposition (difficult to justify from the standpoint of principle or policy) that, whereas it is essential that the injuries suffered by the plaintiff in fighting a fire should be foreseeable, no such requirement applies to rescuers responding to other situations of peril.

On this matter, Finlay CJ's judgment (with which, as we have noted, Griffin J concurred) seems on first reading to include an unequivocal requirement that the rescue be foreseeable: '[i]t is essentially . . . a doctrine of foreseeability . . .'. Nevertheless another interpretation can (hesitatingly) be proferred of the Chief Justice's remarks — that they are to the effect that the court should bring rescuers as a class within the pale of foreseeability, without investigating that issue on an individuated basis having regard to the facts of the particular case. The 'principle of rescue', he says, 'truly consists only of a situation in which the court will rule as a foreseeable consequence of the negligent commencement of a fire that persons seeking to put out that fire, either by reason of their duty as officers of a fire brigade or by reason of their desire to prevent damage, whether to persons or property, may be injured by the existence of the fire. It is essentially, therefore, a doctrine of foreseeability and cannot, in my view, come into operation without an initial negligence causing the fire'.

In this passage, the Chief Justice does not suggest that that negligence should foreseeably risk injury to the particular rescuer in the particular circumstances of the case. Of course the reason for this is that the nature of a fire is to induce rescue attempts, but it would be mistaken to suggest that *all* rescue attempts are foreseeable. The Chief Justice mentions the case of a person intervening 'to prevent damage'. So far as property damage (as opposed to personal injury) is concerned, it is possible to envisage rescue attempts which would be quite unforeseeable, where the value of the endangered property bears no proportion to the risk of injury.

The Supreme Court's finding of negligence against the defendant seems to have been on the generous side. The accident happened at a time when the first plaintiff had become fully apprised of the condition of the kitchen floor, the geyser the cooker and its 'stuttering' jet. In other words, all that the defendant had negligently failed to tell her had by now become apparent to her. Finlay CJ was satisfied that the defendant would not have been liable if he had brought the facts to the first plaintiff's attention. It is, however, true that Griffin J, while concurring with the Chief Justice, appeared to be of opinion that, in view of the condition of the floor and the cooker, the first plaintiff could not efficiently carry out the work she was doing for the defendant without exposing herself to the risk of injury, even having been apprised of this condition.

Some other questions arise. Should not the first plaintiff, in view of her carelessness, also have been held liable in negligence to the second plaintiff, with her liability and that of the defendant's being subject to the provisions relating to concurrent wrongdoers? It is well established that a person guilty of a careless lack of concern for his or her own safety may be liable to one injured in carrying out a foreseeable rescue attempt to remove the careless person from a position of danger: *Dupuis v New Regina Trading Co.*, [1943] 4 DLR 275, *Harrison v British Railways Board,* [1981] 3 All ER 679. It seems that in *Phillips v Durgan* there was no claim for contribution against the first plaintiff on these lines; the explanation may possibly be that, in view of the likelihood of a small percentage being ascribed to the plaintiff, to have argued the case on this somewhat defeatist line might well have been considered counter-productive.

In *Ogwo v Taylor*, which received the support of the Supreme Court in *Phillips v Durgan*, the House of Lords rejected the 'fireman's rule', which still commands very widespread support in the United States. Lord Bridge had 'no doubt whatever' that the doctrine had no place in English law. It is perhaps worth examining its rationale since, in view of the fact that the second plaintiff was *not* a fireman, the Supreme Court's endorsement of the holding in *Ogwo v Taylor* scarcely commits it to necessary agreement in relation to an issue not before the Court.

In *Krauth v Geller,* 31 NJ 270, 157 A 2d 126 (1960), Weintraub CJ provided the following rationale for the fireman's rule:

> Stated affirmatively, what is meant is that it is the fireman's business to deal with that very hazard and hence, perhaps by analogy to the contractor engaged as an expert to remedy dangerous situations, he cannot complain of negligence in the creation of the very occasion for his [engagement]. In terms of duty, it may be said there is none owed the fireman to exercise care so as not to require the special services for which he is trained and paid. Probably most fires are attributable to negligence, and in the final analysis the policy decision is that it would be too burdensome to charge all who carelessly cause or fail to prevent fires with the injuries suffered by the expert retained with public funds to deal with these inevitable, although negligently created, occurrences. Hence, for that risk, the fireman should receive appropriate compensation from the public he serves, both in pay which reflects the hazard and in workmen's compensation benefits for the consequences of the inherent risks of the calling.

Firefighters in the United States are not totally bereft of protection: even where the fireman's rule applies, they may sue for injuries caused by hidden dangers about which the occupier failed to warn them — the same test as applies in Irish law to licensees. Lest we dismiss the American approach as obviously wanting, we should remember that, on this side of the Atlantic, courts have experienced much the same difficulty in categorising persons entering property by legal right (such as firefighters and police): see Fleming, *The Law of Torts* (7th ed., 1987), 428-9.

The central policy issue can perhaps be encapsulated in the following example. A householder negligently causes a fire in his chimney. He calls the firebrigade, and a fireman is injured when he comes to fight the fire. On the basis of *Ogwo v Taylor,* the householder must compensate the fireman for his injuries. If, however, the firebrigade was on strike and the householder had to rely on the expensive services of a private contractor, would he have to compensate the contractor if he was similarly injured? To impose such an obligation in the latter case would seem debatable. The high price for the contracted service reflects the element of risk inherent in this type of work (as it does for roofrepairers, for example). The contractor offers his services, with sublime indifference as to whether the need for them originated in an act of negligence. Is it too unkind to suggest of the professional fireman that he has chosen a mode of employment with inherent risks of injury? The fact that he looks to the local authority rather than the householder for payment should arguably not distinguish his case from that of the contractor who is paid directly by the householder. Moreover the fireman can expect the courts to be solicitous in protecting his physical safety in their implementation of the principles of employers' liability, to judge by *Heeney v Dublin Corporation*, High Court, 16 May 1991.

Having raised these questions, we should mention that the practical likelihood of the Supreme Court's endorsing the fireman's rule without qualification seems small, in view of the stance it took in relation to the duty of care owed to soldiers in *Ryan v Ireland* [1989] IR 177, which we analysed in the 1989 Review, 410-18.

EMPLOYERS' LIABILITY

1 Interrelationship with action for breach of statutory duty Barron J's judgment in *Dunne v Honeywell Control Systems Ltd and Virginia Milk Products Ltd* [1991] ILRM 595 raises interesting and difficult questions in relation to the underlying policies served by employers' liability and actions for breach of statutory duty.

The plaintiff was an electrical technician employed by Honeywell. Honeywell had supplied a control system to Virginia Milk Products Ltd and maintained this equipment under a service contract. The plaintiff went to Virginia's premises to free a control valve which operated the flow of steam to a processor. The machine on which he was required to work was housed on the roof of the control room, access to which was by a vertical ladder fixed to a wall. He brought with him the necessary equipment and tools, contained in a case which had been provided by Honeywell. In previous employments, he had used a satchel which he could carry over his shoulder, leaving both hands free when using a ladder; Honeywell, however, thought that a case gave his work a better image.

When the plaintiff was descending the ladder he lost his balance and sustained severe injuries. He sued Honeywell and Virginia for negligence and breach of statutory duty.

Barron J found that the design of the ladder included several features which created a potential danger to those using it. It has been added to the factory premises and thus needed to be built within the constraints of the existing structure. There was insufficient space for the person using it at a certain point. The space available at the roof was less than the recommended width in the relevant British standard for ladders issued in 1985. One of its rails could be dangerous because it was close to a pipe which at times was hot. The steps were both too narrow and too deep, again in breach of the British standard. There were no protective hoops around the ladder, which 'would almost certainly have prevented the plaintiff from falling'.

The case which the plaintiff carried caused problems when negotiating the ladder. It weighed twenty five pounds and was an awkward shape. To bring the case down with him as he descended the ladder required the plaintiff to engage in what Barron J described as 'a particularly awkward manoeuvre', which involved moving his body away from the ladder to accommodate the case, thereby shifting his centre of gravity away from the ladder. Barron J found that the plaintiff sustained his injuries from a combination of the deficiencies presented by the case.

Barron J first addressed the question of breach of statutory duty. He was satisfied that the plaintiff could invoke s. 37(1) of the Factories Act 1955, as amended by s. 12(1) of the Safety in Industry Act 1980, which requires that:

> [e]very place at which any person has at any time to work shall be made and kept in a safe condition and in addition to the foregoing there shall so far as is reasonably practicable be provided and maintained safe means of access to and egress from every such place.

Barron J considered that, in the light of the words used in Part III of the Act, there was no reason why the section should be given a construction linking its protection to servants of the factory owner:

> The plaintiff was required to work on the factory premises for the purposes of the factory and was accordingly entitled to the benefit of the section.

Barron J then turned to the plaintiff's claim in negligence. His analysis here was coloured by the question of who is the employer *for the purposes of vicarious liability*. The courts, in deciding the issue of vicarious liability, have rightly or wrongly proceeded on the basis that where an employee of a permanent employer is engaged to work for a temporary employer, only one of the two employers can be vicariously liable for the purposes of vicarious liability: see *Lynch v Palgrave Murphy Ltd* [1964] IR 150, *Treacy v Robinson,* Supreme Court, 29 July 1936, *McMahon v CIE,* [1961] IR 30 (Supreme Court 1958). Cf. McMahon & Binchy, *Irish Law of Torts* (2nd ed., 1991), 751 fn. 11: 'It might be wondered why both the permanent and temporary employer should not be considered masters for the purposes if vicarious liability. Has the biblical injunction that one cannot serve two masters affected judicial attitudes here?'

Barron J, having referred to *Lynch v Palgrave Murphy*, said:

> The present case differs in the sense that the question is not, which employer should be vicariously liable for the acts of the plaintiff, but which employer owed him the duty of care owed by a master to his servant. But the test is the same, was the control exercisable by the person for whom he was working such as to make that person in reality the master? When it is, then it is that person who will be liable.

It may be suggested that Barron J reached the right conclusion after embarking on a route that could have led to quite inappropriate diversions. The truth is that the principles underlying employers' liability have no necessary identity with those underlying vicarious liability. In imposing liability on employers in negligence, courts seek to identify wrongful behaviour on the part of employers relative to their employees. Vicarious liability involves no such an inquiry: an employer is liable not because of any wrong on his part but because of what may be called the intensity of relationship between him and the employee. Employers are vicariously liable for the torts of their employees committed in the course of their employment because (rightly or wrongly) it is considered appropriate that they should foot the bill. One may debate the merits of vicarious liability: *why* should the mere fact of employing someone generate responsibility for the wrongs he or she commits in the course of his or her employment? Is the basis one of enterprise liability or is it based on some crude utilitarian calculus that employers tend to be better marks than employees? Could the fact that employers tend to be insured be the explanation and, if so, how should the court deal with a case where the defendant has not, in fact, obtained insurance cover?

Whatever may be the merits of the philosophy underlying the imposition of vicarious liability, it bears no necessary connection with that underlying employers' liability in negligence. Barron J interpreted *control* as the key element. We suggest that, while this concept may be useful in many cases, it should not be treated as crucial. Though it forms the essential test in vicarious liability, it would not yield a totally satisfactory solution to employers' liability cases since there should be no objection to imposing liability on *both* permanent and temporary employer in appropriate cases.

Barron J went on to say:

> Here the plaintiff was performing a maintenance contract on behalf of Honeywell. Employees of Honeywell were regularly at the factory for that purpose. How the plaintiff carried out the maintenance of the

processor and dealt with the control valve which required to be freed was a matter for him. It was because of his particular skill that he was required to do the work rather than an electrician employed by Virginia. To this extent Virginia had no control over him as he went about his actual work. Nevertheless he was doing that work for the benefit of Virginia. If his work impinged on other work being carried out, Virginia was entitled to order the work to suit itself. Virginia had a control over the plaintiff to that extent. This control did not make Virginia the plaintiff's master. Nevertheless, it seems to me that the employer for the benefit of whose business the employee is working owes a duty of care to that employee commensurate with the extent of the control he is entitled to exercise over him. If the employee does or does not do something which it would be within the employer's control to prevent or require, as the case may be, he is in breach of duty.

It seems that Barron J considered that Virginia's duty to the plaintiff derived from the *degree of control that Virginia exercised over the plaintiff*. A more conventional approach might have been to characterise the relationship as one of occupier and entrant and to examine *Virginia's degree of control of the premises*. This element was highlighted in the English decision of *Wheat v E. Lacon & Co. Ltd* [1966] AC 552.

On the facts of *Dunne v Honeywell Control Systems Ltd and Virginia Milk Products Ltd*, there was, of course, no doubt that Virginia exercised the requisite control. The more relevant questions related to the precise status of the plaintiff and the nature of the duty owed to him. Assuming that the law still distinguishes between contractual entrants, invitees and licensees (cf. below, 508-21), the plaintiff would appear at least to have the status of invitee, since his visit was designed to confer an economic benefit on Virginia. Possibly he could be considered a contractual entrant, in view of the service contract between his employer and Virginia. The problem of privity might perhaps be overcome by an ascription of agency to Honeywell in making this contract, so far as concerned its employees whose presence on the premises was being assured by the terms of the contract.

We suggest that in the next case in which an employee is injured on premises to which he is assigned by his employer on foot of a contract between the employer and the occupier of those premises, the easiest approach, from the plaintiff's standpoint, is that of occupier's liability. (One may surely at this point assume that a plaintiff who would win under a straightforward negligence test would not now find his case rejected because he could not establish an 'unusual danger' as required by *Indermaur v Dames* (1866) LR ICP 274, at 287.)

Having said this, it remains true that in some instances the relationship between the plaintiff and the occupier may be one capable of being characterised as one of employment. In such cases the straightforward negligence test would usually yield the same result, regardless of whether the case proceeded on the basis of occupiers' liability or employers' liability. There are, however, some instances where employers' liability will range more widely, by virtue of the principle that an employer's duty of care to his employee is *non-delegable*: see *McDermid v Nash Dredging & Reclamation Co. Ltd* [1987] 2 All ER 878.

Barron J went on to hold that Virginia was in breach of its duty, as employer, to the plaintiff. The plaintiff would normally have had the assistance of one of Virginia's electricians. If Virginia had a duty, as he had, to tell its own electrician not to carry cases or other materials as he ascended or descended the ladder, it had an equal duty to the plaintiff to give him a similar instruction.

Honeywell was similarly in breach of its duty of care to the plaintiff. Its employees had gone regularly to Virginia's premises and it was reasonable for Honeywell to have inspected them in advance to ascertain the nature of the access to the workplace which would be provided for its employees. The plaintiff should have been warned not to carry his whole case of tools onto the roof. Virginia was entitled to expect that Honeywell would have performed its duty of care to the plaintiff to this extent. Once Virginia saw how the work was in fact being done, it should have prevented it and provided an alternative method for getting the tools to where they were required.

Barron J considered that the plaintiff was guilty of contributory negligence to the extent of 10%. He 'ought to have realised the danger'. This applied to the plaintiff's action in common law. But his action for breach of statutory duty involved a different rule. Here (following Ó Dálaigh CJ's judgment in *Kennedy v East Cork Foods* [1973] IR 244, at 249), Barron J held that, to amount to contributory negligence, something more than mere inattentiveness was required. As the Chief Justice had said, the plaintiff must enter into the realm of 'downright carelessness' because the Factories Act had been passed 'for the express purpose of saving factory workers from their own carelessness, and their own inattention'. The plaintiff in the instant case had taken insufficient care for his own safety, not through any positive act on his part, but because the danger had not occurred to him. He therefore should not be found guilty of contributory negligence in his claim based on breach of statutory duty and was entitled to recover in full against Virginia.

The distinction in approach as between actions for common law negligence against employers and actions for breach of statutory duty is well established: see McMahon & Binchy, *op. cit.*, 392-5. It arose at a time when the implications of a finding of contributory negligence were stark: the plaintiff simply lost his case. The mitigating effects of the doctrine of the 'last clear chance' did not usually apply since in most industrial accidents (as opposed to road accidents) the defendant did not have the last clear chance. (If one of his co-workers had such a chance and handled the situation carelessly the defence of common employment would defeat the plaintiff's case). Today, when contributory negligence reduces a plaintiff's damages rather than defeating his case completely and common employment has been laid to rest, one may enquire whether the distinction between common law negligence and breach of statutory duty is not too crude. It may well be right to interpret the duties laid down by the Factories Acts as involving such a strongly protective policy as to limit, if not completely defeat, the defence of contributory negligence: cf. *Bexiga v Havir Manufacturing Corporation*, 60 NJ 402, 290 A 2d 281 (1972), discussed in the 1987 Review, 336. But it may also be the case that *common law negligence* in the employment context should involve a similar constriction of the defence, at least in cases where the employer's negligence consists of exposing the employee to risk of injury from the employee's own foreseeable carelessness in performing his work tasks.

2 *'Non-delegable' duties*   In *Connolly v Dundalk Urban District Council and Mahon & McPhillips* [1990] 2 IR 1, the plaintiff, an assistant caretaker at the Council's waterworks, was severely injured when he inhaled a dense cloud of chlorine gas which had escaped when a plastic pipe carrying chlorine mixed with water became disconnected from a rigid plastic pipe. The point of connection, O'Hanlon J held, had been inadequately secured. The type of joint used was 'quite unsuitable for its purpose and was likely to fail at some stage, and the failure of the joint, which should have been foreseeable to the plaintiff's employers, was the primary cause of the accident. . . .' Accordingly, O'Hanlon J held that the Council had failed in its duty as employer to the plaintiff to take all reasonable steps to ensure that his place of employment was safe and free from danger of a type which should have been foreseen by it.

The second defendant had erected the waterworks for the first defendant in 1968. Having completed the design and construction of the waterworks, the contractors at a later stage agreed to service the installation by providing three service visits *per annum*.

Expert evidence adduced in the case was to the effect that, while alarm systems and ventilation systems were not at the time part and parcel of the conventional installation where chlorine gas was used for water treatment, these additional protective features had since become commonplace, being widely used for many years prior to 1986, when the plaintiff met with his accident. The Council was at the time of the accident in the process of arranging for their introduction. O'Hanlon J stated that, while the Council had obviously been activated at all times by the desire to keep the waterworks up to the best standards of safety, he was forced to conclude that it again must be held liable, for failing to acquaint itself in time with the development of safety procedures which had come to be regarded as standard for some significant time before the accident and to give effect to them in the plaintiff's place of employment.

The Council had sought to avoid liability on the basis that the responsibility for any failure of the pipework or any failure to implement safety measures should be laid at the door of the second defendant who was responsible for the original design and installation and for all aspects of service and maintenance of the system. O'Hanlon J considered it:

> well-established . . . that an employer owes a duty to his employee to provide a safe place of work, and cannot escape liability for breach of such duty by employing an independent contractor — no matter how expert — to perform the duty for him.

He invoked two English authorities in support, one judicial, the other academic. In *Paine v Colne Valley Electricity Co.* [1938] 4 All ER 803, at 807, Goddard LJ said: 'This is a duty which cannot be avoided by delegation. It is no answer to say . . . "We employed competent contractors to provide a safe place or plant."' And *Charlesworth on Negligence* (4th ed., para 845) states:

> The employer is liable if the failure to execerise reasonable care and skill is that of an independent contractor, and is only excused from liability if the danger is due to a latent defect not discoverable by reasonable care and skill on the part of anyone.

The notion of a 'non-delegable duty' is worth considering briefly. Conceived with the purpose of mitigating the former doctrine of common employment, it operates as a tacit principle of vicarious liability. Characterised, in effect, by Lord Wright in *Wilsons and Clyde Coal Co. v English* [1938] AC 57 as a warranty that reasonable care will be taken, subsequent courts have preferred to treat the duty as one lying in tort: see, eg. *McDermid v Nash Dredging and Reclamation Co. Ltd* [1987] All ER 878 noted by Hepple, *All ER Review* 1987, at 298-9. While courts in England (*Davie v New Merton Board Mills Ltd* [1959] AC 604) and Ireland (*Keenan v Bergin* [1971] IR 192) have held that this duty does not extend to insuring the safety of equipment supplied by a reputable supplier, they are nonetheless willing to impose liability in respect of the default of an independent contractor engaged in work on the premises or otherwise impinging on the duty owed by the employer to the employees. The dividing line is not entirely clear, but, in view of the existence of the service contract in *Connolly v Dundalk Urban District Council*, it is not surprising that the Council was held liable in respect of the second defendant's negligence.

Turning to the question of the liability of the second defendant, O'Hanlon J concluded on the evidence that in all probability the joint had been inadequate for a considerable time before the accident and that this inadequacy should have been noted and acted upon when the periodical servicing was taking place. Moreover, having designed and erected the waterworks, and having thereafter undertaken for reward the periodical servicing and maintenance of the equipment installed, the second defendant owed an obligation to the Council to keep it informed as to changes which modern standards might require in the system from time to time. It should have reacted sooner to the developments in its field and should have been aware of serious accidents which had occurred elsewhere and which could be guarded against by technology which had evolved since the waterworks had been constructed.

O'Hanlon J imposed liability on both defendants on an equal basis.

An interesting issue of principle and policy arises as to the second basis of liability of the second defendant. Let us imagine a case where an employer has taken all reasonable care with respect to the safety of his premises and where the negligence of a servicer consists exclusively of its failure to inform the employer of the need to improve safety standards on the premises as a result of changes in technology. Is an employee injured by that negligence to be able successfully to sue the employer on the basis of a non-delegable duty of care? The answer we suggest is in the affirmative only to the extent that the employee is a foreseeable victim of the servicer's breach of duty of care to the employee. In the instant case the plaintiff clearly was such a foreseeable victim and indeed in the overwhelming majority of cases this will also be the situation; but the point worth noting is that a servicer's liability to the employer for failure to advise about changing safety standards is not necessarily identical in scope with the service's duty of care to a plaintiff employee.

A second point worth considering in relation to the case is whether the issue of *novus actus interveniens* was relevant. O'Hanlon J found, after all, that the Urban District Council was negligent in failing to have taken due care with regard to the premises and in failing to acquaint themselves with the development of safety procedures. Could it not be argued that these two elements of negligence insulated the second defendant from liability? Perhaps the answer depends on whether the Urban District Council knowingly confronted the dangerous connection to the piping and negligently omitted too repair it. See our discussion of *Crowley v Allied Irish Banks* [1988] ILRM 225; [1987] IR 282 (Supreme Court), in the 1987 Review, 326-9.

508

OCCUPIERS' LIABILITY

1 Duty, proximity and foreseeability   In *Smith v Coras Iompair Éireann*,
Supreme Court, 29 November 1990 the plaintiff was severely injured one
summer's evening when struck by a train at Inchicore, not very far from
Heuston Station. At the time he and a companion were chasing one of two
youths who had been riding a mare owned by the plaintiff which was in an
adjoining field. The plaintiff had already tripped and fallen but had picked
himself up and continued to chase. While running along the uneven ground
between two sets of tracks he saw a train, with lights, coming towards him.
He again tripped and fell, having come in contact with a length of railway
track which had been placed between the regular tracks roughly parallel to
them. He was then struck by the train. In evidence he explained that his
objective in trying to catch the youth was 'to beat him up'. He was running
'flat out'. His entire concentration was on the youth.

The plaintiff's action for negligence concentrated on the fact that the
defendant had allowed a wall to become partially broken down with the result
that local residents had carved out a short cut through it, down a precipitous
embankment of about fifteen feet and across the railway tracks, to give them
quicker access to a public house and some shops. This was the route availed
of by the plaintiff, his companion and the youths they were chasing.

At trial, the plaintiff had argued that the defendant should have been aware
that he was likely to be proximate to them, that the danger of his running at
speed should have been reasonably foreseeable and that the defendant
consequently owed him a duty of care. At the close of the plaintiff's case,
counsel for the defendant had sought a non-suit, not on the basis that any
lower duty was owed to him by virtue of his status as a trespasser, but solely
on the criteria of foreseeability and proximity. The trial judge, Egan J, had
granted the non-suit, applying the test stated by McCarthy J in *Foley v
Musgrave Cash and Carry Ltd*, Supreme Court, 20 December 1985.

The Supreme Court dismissed the plaintiff's appeal. Griffin J, delivering
the judgment of the Court, said that, since counsel for the defendant had again
relied on the issues of foreseeability and proximity, it was:

> not necessary for this Court to consider whether, and if so to what extent,
> the conventional law in relation to the classification of invitees, licen-
> sees and trespassers and the duties owed to each of them, is still
> applicable. That question should accordingly be reserved for an
> occasion on which it is fully argued and may be necessary for decision.

Griffin J went on to enlarge upon Walsh J's pioneering statement in *Purtill
v Athlone UDC* [1968] IR 205, at 212 that:

[w]hen the danger is reasonably foreseeable, the duty to take care to avoid injury to those who are proximate, when their proximity is known, is not abrogated because the other party is a trespasser. The duty to those in proximity is not based on any implied term of an invitation or a licence, or upon any warranty for safety which might be thought to be inherent in any such invitation or licence. Rather is it based upon the duty that one man has to those in proximity to him to take reasonable care that they are not injured by his acts. What amounts to sufficient care must vary necessarily with the circumstances, the nature of the danger, and the age and knowledge of the person likely to be injured.

Griffin J did not think that Walsh J there intended or purported to enumerate all the circumstances which were to be considered; those mentioned were the appropriate ones in that case. To them should be added those of time and place (including the nature of the surface of which use was being made), the persons who might be expected to be exposed to danger, and the presence and conduct of the person coming onto the premises.

Griffin J considered that *Foley* did not assist the plaintiff. In that case a customer in a supermarket had been injured when she fell over a trolley. Her 'proximity was known', said Griffin J. The Court had held that, as a customer, she could not reasonably be expected to look down at her feet while walking along an aisle looking at the shelves displaying the goods on sale.

In the instant case, the circumstances were entirely different. There was no evidence that the defendant was aware that persons used the railway as a short cut. Even if the defendant had tolerated the crossing of the line for use as a short cut, the question arose as to whether it was reasonably foreseeable to the defendant that any adult would go onto the railway line, not for the purpose of taking a short cut, but to act and conduct himself in the manner which the plaintiff had done. To answer this question, all the prevailing circumstances had to be taken into account. These would include the time at which, and the state of light when, the events took place, the nature of the surface on which the plaintiff was running, the speed at which he ran, the fact that having fallen once he got up and started again, and that, although he saw a train approaching in close proximity to him, he continued to run as fast as he could when all he need have done to avoid any danger was to pull up or step to his left.

In Griffin J's opinion it would be perverse to hold that the defendant could or should reasonably have foreseen that any adult would have conducted himself as the plaintiff had done. In the circumstances, the defendant 'owed no duty to the plaintiff'.

The judgment gives rise to a number of observations. The first is to remark yet again on the curious reluctance of the Supreme Court to carry through the logic of the *Purtill* decision and sweep away the 'categorical' approach to occupiers' liability. To take this step would not mean that all entrants could insist on the same level of care: the court would be required to attach such significance as appeared appropriate to the purpose of the entrant in going on the defendant's property. Even under a simple negligence formula the court should distinguish radically between injuries sustained on a defective stair by a guest who has outstayed his welcome and injuries suffered by a burglar on the same stair during a nocturnal visit. That distinction is not reducible simply to the relative foreseeability of their presence on the property. I owe no greater duty to a man who announces his intention of breaking into my home and killing me than to one who comes suddenly through the window with the same purpose. What abolition of the categorical approach will accomplish is the removal of *undue* and inflexible attribution of significance to the question of the entrant's status, as well as the *arbitrary limitations attaching to the duty* owed to invitees and licensees, respectively. Why should the duty to invitees be limited to *unusual* danger? And why should the duty of licensees be limited to *warning* of *patent* dangers? The Supreme Court itself evinced discomfort with such a strait-jacket in *Rooney v Connolly* [1986] IR 572, while professing to apply the traditional duty owed to licensees. The sweeping away of all these unnecessary technicalities would be desirable, leading as it would to an unencumbered determination of the negligence issue in the light of all the circumstances of the case.

The second feature of *Smith v Coras Iompair Éireann* which is worth noting is the judicial treatment of the concepts of duty, *proximity* and *reasonable foreseeability*. These are at the core of the negligence lexicon. According to the orthodox doctrine, the notion of a duty of care is an essential ingredient in liability, over and above carelessness on the part of the defendant resulting in reasonably foreseeable injury to the plaintiff.

When does a defendant owe a duty of care? The orthodox answer goes back to the attempt by Lord Esher and A.L. Smith LJ in *Le Lievre v Gould* (1893) 1 QB 491 (developing on what Lord Esher (then Brett MR) had said in *Heaven v Pender* (1883) 11 QBD 503) to define the basis in terms of proximity. In *Donoghue v Stevenson* [1932] AC 562, at 580, Lord Atkin raised the robust formula to the metaphysical order: proximity should 'not [be] confused to mere physical proximity, but [should] be used, as I think it was intended, to extend to such close and direct relations that the act complained of directly affects a person whom the person alleged to be bound to take care would be directly affected by his careless act'. The Irish courts have been happy to endorse this approach: see McMahon & Binchy, *op. cit.*, 95-6.

The concept of reasonable foreseeability, on the other hand, serves a different function. This is to define the scope of liability in negligence. A defendant is not liable to persons who are not reasonably foreseeable victims; even if they pass this barrier, the defendant will not as a general rule be liable for unforeseeable injuries which they sustain (subject to the 'egg shell skull' proviso).

As we have already noted, the notion of reasonable foreseeability is in fact ambiguous. The decision of the Privy Council in *Overseas Tankship (UK) Ltd v Morts Dock and Engineering Co. Ltd (The Wagon Mound (No. 1))* [1961] AC 388 has forced courts to consider as a single question what really involves two separate issues: first, whether the defendant acted unreasonably in the circumstances, and, second, whether some or all of the injuries the plaintiff sustained ought reasonably to have been within the defendant's contemplation. The first issue raises questions that are not reducible exclusively to what might be called an assessment of the *predictability* of the accident. That is of course a factor, but other matters must also be weighed, such as the *gravity* of the threatened injury (however unlikely its occurrence may be), the social utility of the defendant's conduct and the cost of preventing an accident.

The relationship between the concepts of reasonable foreseeability and duty should be noted. As we have seen, there are cases where a defendant, even if guilty of careless conduct resulting in reasonably foreseeable injury to the plaintiff, will not be liable because he owed him no duty of care. A drunken advocate can shelter behind the immunity afforded by *Rondel v Worsley* [1969] 1 AC 191. Of course it is always possible to say that a defendant who has not risked or caused reasonably foreseeable injury to the plaintiff owed him no duty of care in that, for a duty to arise in the first place, the plaintiff must have been within the radius of the risk of reasonably foreseeable injury; but this is a tautological conclusion which does not contribute to the clarity of analysis.

Against the background of this summary of orthodox doctrine it is useful to examine Griffin J's handling of these three concepts. It would appear to involve some degree of elision between them. In essence the case can best, and most easily, be understood as raising the issue of reasonable foreseeability. The conclusion that that a non-suit was warranted on the basis of the absence of such *reasonable foreseeability* seems eminently justified on the facts. Why, therefore, should there have been a discussion of the issue of proximity and why should Griffin J have concluded that the defendant 'owed no duty' to the plaintiff? We suggest that the answer lies in history. In former times injured adult trespassers received short shrift and little sympathy from the courts. The occupier owed them no duty of care; he would be liable only for injuries inflicted intentionally upon trespassers or in reckless disregard of their presence. *Purtill* represented a flank attack on this general immunity. Walsh J did not seek to challenge the general rule that occupiers owed no duty of care to trespassers, but he held that a duty of care could nonetheless be generated, on the basis of proximity or relationship between the parties, in a context which did not *depend* on the occupier-trespasser relationship. It will be recalled that the essence of the plaintiff's case in *Purtill* was that of negligent custodianship of chattels tempting and dangerous to children. At the time of his injury, his trespass had ceased. It was not difficult to displace the tough immunity towards trespassers by a special finding of proximity.

By the time the Supreme Court decided *McNamara v ESB* [1975] IR 1, the notion of a proximity-based duty of care to a trespasser had been transformed. Emboldened by *Purtill*, the Court (with varying degrees of emphasis in the different judgments) *displaced* the general immunity by a general duty of care. Only Henchy J baulked at doing so. He considered that, '[a]s a general rule' trespassers do not come within Lord Atkin's definition of 'neighbour' in *Donoghue v Stevenson*. By the time the Supreme Court addressed the issue in *Keane v ESB* [1981] IR 44, Henchy J no longer sought to exclude the general run of trespassers from the scope of the duty of care, and instead concentrated on the question of the foreseeability of their presence on the property.

It is interesting to note that, in England, twelve years after the House of Lords, in *British Railways Board v Herrington* [1972] AC 877, had displaced the *Addie v Dumbreck* formula by one of common humanity, the Occupiers Liability Act 1984 still falls short of embracing trespassers, as a class, within the scope of the duty of care. S. 1 leaves it to the court in each case to determine whether the risk of injury to the trespasser resulting from a danger due to the state of the premises was one against which in all the circumstances the occupier might reasonably be expected to offer him some protection.

This background may explain why the issues of proximity and duty featured so strongly in Griffin J's judgment. The truth is that the courts, since the changes brought about in *Purtill*, have not yet been faced with the claims of what might be called an unattractive adult trespasser whose presence was even arguably foreseeable, and that thus they have not had to consider whether the writ of proximity runs so widely as to embrace *all* trespassers. It can hardly be the case that such a nexus should *inevitably* arise, requiring the issue to be resolved in terms of the test of reasonable foreseeability. An intending murderer entering a premises is *not* in a relationship with the occupier which generates any duty of care and the courts should say so without embarrassment.

In *Smith v CIE*, Griffin J rightly perceived that a genuine issue of proximity arose. Apart altogether from the question or reasonable foreseeability, a railway company (albeit one that may have tolerated the development of a short cut across their tracks) surely does not inevitably owe a duty of care to a person who goes onto that area, not for the purposes of a short cut, but to assault another person.

One can therefore understand why Griffin J might wish to hold that the defendant *owed no duty* to the plaintiff; it is also understandable, on the evidence, that the plaintiff's claim should have been dismissed on the basis of lack of reasonable foreseeability. What should not be acceptable from an orthodox doctrinal standpoint in tort law is that the issues of duty, proximity and reasonable foreseeability should be blurred as though they were but one issue.

Having said this it may be useful to record the anti-metaphysical stance of members of the House of Lords in *Caparo Industries plc v Dickman* [1990] 2 AC 605. Lord Oliver observed that:

> 'proximity' is, no doubt, a convenient expression so long as it is realised that it is no more than a label which embraces not a definable concept but merely a description of circumstances from which, pragmatically, the courts conclude that a duty of care exists.

And Lord Roskill considered that:

> It is now to be accepted that there is no simple formula or touchstone to which recourse can be had in order to provide in every case a ready answer to the questions whether, given certain facts, the law will or will not impose liability for negligence or, in cases where such liability can be shown to exist, determine the extent of that liability. Phrases such as 'foreseeability', 'proximity', neighbourhood', 'just and reasonable', 'fairness', 'voluntary acceptance of risk' or 'voluntary assumption of responsibility' will be found used from time to time in the different cases. But . . . such phrases are not precise definitions. At best they are but labels or phrases descriptive of the very different factual situations which can exist in particular cases and which must be carefully examined in each case before it can be pragmatically determined whether a duty of care exists and, if so, what is the scope and extent of that duty.

Irish courts have so far shown no enthusiasm for de-constructing the conceptual elements of negligence in this manner. This does not mean, of course, that they are blind to policy considerations, as is plain from the Supreme Court decision in *Sunderland v Louth County Council* [1990] ILRM 658, which we consider below, 545-9.

2 *Duty to keep bathing place safe*   In *Nolan v Kilkenny County Council* 8 *ILT* (ns) 210 (Circuit Court, 1990), the plaintiff was injured when he stood on a piece of jagged glass when bathing in a river, at a point which was a traditional bathing place for the city of Kilkenny. The defendant Council maintained a ramp and rudimentary diving board there; it also provided a series of steps and a lifebelt, as well as employing a lifeguard. The lifeguard's contractual duties included inspecting his patrol area and, where possible, removing any dangerous items; if he was unable to deal with the matter, he was required immediately to report to his supervisor. The accident took place on an August afternoon.

The first question concerned the status of the defendant. Judge Sheridan considered that since the Council clearly did not own the river, it therefore was not occupier of the area of the accident. The notion of *proximity*, however, as articulated by Walsh J in *Purtill v Athlone Urban District Council* [1968] IR 205, at 210, was relevant to the instant case. The defendant was 'certainly in proximity to the plaintiff', in view of the manner in which it had acted in relation to the bathing place.

Perhaps a case can be made out that precisely these actions, of maintaining steps, equipment and the services of a lifeguard, constituted a sufficient degree of *control* on the part of the council to warrant its characterisation as occupier.

At all events, nothing appears to have hinged on the issue of occupation, since Judge Sheridan did 'not think it would have made a great deal of difference' even if he had found that the defendant was occupier.

Having held that there was sufficient proximity between the parties to warrant the imposition of a duty of care, Judge Sheridan went on to consider whether the plaintiff had passed the test of *reasonable foresight*. He held that he had not. The river was near a public road and therefore it would not be surprising if it received debris from members of the public apart altogether from that which might be carried downstream when the river was in flood.

The question essentially was whether it was reasonably foreseeable that every piece of debris within the radius of 1700 square yards, or even the smaller area nearer the driving platform, would, with reasonable care, be discovered. To sweep the area in question might have the effect of uncovering hidden dangers which themselves might become new dangers. In Judge Sheridan's opinion, 'it would be asking too much of the defendants to trawl the area and particularly having regard to the time of the year and the proximity to the public road this would have to be done daily in case there was something secreted on the bed of the river which was a danger completely unknown to the defendants'.

The case involves a classic application of the four elements of the negligence formula: the *likelihood* of injury; the *gravity* of the threatened injury;

the *social utility* of the defendant's conduct; and the *cost of prevention*. See McMahon & Binchy, *op. cit.*, 110-19. Judge Sheridan was clearly satisfied with the high social utility of the defendant's conduct in supplying the facilities at the traditional bathing place: this had been done 'for the best possible motives'. To have reduced the risk of injury to bathers further than the Council had done would unquestionably have been possible (even taking account of the consequential risk of uncovering new dangers); but the cost in engaging in such reduction on a daily basis would no doubt have been such as to encourage the council to think twice about maintaining its facilities on the river.

3 Liability of supermarkets for falls on premises   Accidents in supermarkets have provoked a significant volume of litigation in recent years. The relevant legal principles are well established: a supermarket proprietor is not the insurer of his patrons' safety. The plaintiff has to show, not only that he or she was injured by encountering something in the wrong place — a packet of yoghurt that has spilled on the ground, for example; it is necessary also to establish that the supermarket failed to take proper care to protect the injured patron from injury. Clearly it is possible for slips and falls to occur without any negligence on the part of the proprietor or his employees: the offending item may have been knocked from the shelf by another customer only a moment previously, and no scheme of monitoring the aisles can guarantee total safety. So the question usually reduces itself to one of the supermarkets's *modus operandi* in terms of the frequency of 'sweepers' going through the store as well as the standing orders for staff as regards reporting spillages.

The fact that the issue essentially reduces itself to one of whether the supermarket exercised due care in this specific context has encouraged the courts to define the duty owed by the supermarket in terms of negligence rather than occupiers' liability to invitees. This is because none of the distinctive aspects of the duty owed to invitees under the *Indermaur v Dames* formula need divert the court's attention from a consideration of the issue in straightforward terms of negligence. It is scarcely arguable that a yoghurt spilled on the aisle is an 'unusual danger'. It would be wrong therefore, to conclude automatically from the repeated judicial incantation of the negligence formula in these cases that the *Purtill — McNamara* restatement of occupiers' liability to trespassers in terms of negligence has necessarily filtered up to the duty owed to invitees.

In *Mullen v Quinnsworth Ltd t/a Crazy Prices* [1990] 1 IR 59, the plaintiff, aged seventy four, slipped and fell when shopping in the defendant's super-market. The cause of her fall was cooking oil, which covered 'a reasonably wide area of the floor' and which persons, even keeping a proper look-out, would not be able to see. At the end of one of the shelves nearby was an 'end display' of cooking oil.

In the plaintiff's action for negligence, breach of statutory duty and nuisance Barrington J withdrew the case from the jury. The Supreme Court reversed and directed a re-trial.

The supermarket in question was just under 25,000 square feet in area, with eighteen main aisles. It stocked 7,500 individual lines, of which 60% were breakable. Four employees were engaged as 'sweepers', three working in high risk areas such as the check out area and the vegetable area, the fourth (a 'floater') continuously sweeping the main floor and wiping up spillages encountered. The floater's journey around the store was estimated as taking between ten and fifteen minutes. The evidence disclosed that, when cooking oil was knocked from the shelves, nine times out of ten the plastic broke.

In holding that a reasonable jury might have found the defendant liable, Griffin and McCarthy JJ referred in particular two facts: the colourless quality of the cooking oil and the length of time that would elapse at a point of particular danger between one patrol of the 'floater' and the next.

Barrington J, in withdrawing the case from the jury, had been persuaded that the system 'would appear to be a very sensible down-to-earth system, and that there is no expert evidence to suggest other supermarkets do things differently or do things better or that there is anything defective in the way the defendant's operate this system'. McCarthy J considered that:

> such a conclusion overlooks the essential issue which it appears to me to be one that, at the time of the trial, was for a jury to determine — the adequacy of the system, with particular reference to the time scale.

McCarthy J was surely correct in rejecting any suggestion that a universal or widespread practice of supermarkets could immunise them from liability in negligence. The value-judgment involved in determining whether a supermarket system of protecting customers from injury is adequate is well within the competence of a judge or jury; running a supermarket bears no parallel to engaging in a professional activity, to which, rightly or wrongly, the courts afford some degree of deference to accepted practice: cf *Dunne v National Maternity Hospital* [1989] ILRM 735; [1989] IR 91, which we discussed in the 1989 Review, 421-5.

Two other issues were also considered by the Supreme Court. The first related to *res ipsa loquitur*. This had not been pleaded at trial. McCarthy J showed little enthusiasm for the argument that it could be raised on appeal, though he expressed no final view on the matter. In contrast Griffin J embraced the doctrine warmly. He was of the opinion that:

if there is such a slippery substance on the floor, as in the present case, and a customer steps on it and falls, the maxim *res ipsa loquitur* applies — the circumstances of the accident raise a sufficient presumption of negligence on the part of the occupier of the premises. . . .

In the instant case, the floor was under the management of the defendants or their servants and the accident was such as, in the ordinary course of things, would not happen if the floors are kept free from spillages of this nature. The onus is therefore on the defendants to show that the accident was not due to any want of care on their part.

The plaintiff's failure to plead the doctrine was not fatal. *Bennett v Chemical Construction Ltd* [1971] 1 WLR 1571 supported the proposition that, if the facts pleaded and proved showed that the doctrine was applicable to the case, this sufficed.

Griffin J's analysis of the issue is interesting and may provoke debate. It may be argued that the *res ipsa loquitur* doctrine does not apply merely because the accident was 'such as, in the ordinary course of things, would not happen if the floors are kept free from spillages of this nature'. The essence of the *res ipsa loquitur* doctrine is that the accident was such, as in the ordinary course of things, would not happen 'if those who have the management use proper care . . .': *Scott v London & St Katherine Docks Co.*, 3 H & C 596, at 601, 159 ER 665, at 667 (*per* Erle CJ, 1865). The requirement that the close association between *negligence* and accidents be so clear that accidents of the type in question do not usually occur without negligence is different from the requirement of merely a close association between the *presence of spillages on floors* and the occurrence of accidents. The latter involves merely a relationship between two facts, while the former involves a relationship between a fact and a legal phenomenon. Perhaps the best way of raising the doctrine of *res ipsa loquitur* is to enquire whether customers in supermarkets, in the ordinary course of things, do not fall on spilled items if those in charge of the supermarket use proper care.

Of course, the *res ipsa loquitur* doctrine may be criticised for its uncertainty in two respects. The first is the conceptual problem of the statistical scope of 'the ordinary course of things': is it 30%, 50% or 90% of cases? Is this percentage a constant or a variable figure? Why should the courts shy away from specifity? The second is an empirical problem: how is the factfinder in legal proceedings to know whether the accident is such as in the ordinary course of things does not happen if those who have the management use proper care? In *Mahon v Osborne* [1939] 2 KB 14, the English Court of Appeal was divided on whether expert evidence was admissible on this matter. It would seem frankly impossible without expert evidence for a factfinder to make any reasonable assessment as to whether accidents involving customers in supermarkets do not in the ordinary course of things occur without negligence on the part of the supermarkets. To answer this question, it would be necessary to engage in an empirical study involving in a scrutiny of the 'sweeper' system in each supermarket in which an accident occurred. To compound the difficulty of this problem, some accepted criterion or criteria of due care would have to be applied before any conclusion would be warranted.

The other issue raised in *Mullen v Quinnsworth* arose more or less by accident. At trial, counsel for the defendant had submitted to the judge that, if the case were allowed to go to the jury, 'there would be absolute liability'. The premise of this submission was undoubtedly that the case should properly be determined by the standard of due care rather than of strict (or *a factiori*, absolute) liability. Yet on appeal to the Supreme Court McCarthy J wheeled the scrum: he seemed attracted to the idea that supermarkets might indeed be subjected to absolute liability, though, in view of the fact that the case had not been argued on this ground, he acknowledged that his observations should be construed as tentative.

McCarthy J developed his analysis as follows:

> The supermarket is a modern phenomenon derived from a combination of events such as cash and cash only purchasing, efficient and attractive packaging, competition itself, convenience of customers, the increase in the number of gainfully employed housewives, the growth of family shopping, the availability of 'fast foods', the purchasing power of store chains or other groups of traders, the efficiency and speed of transport, both traders and private customers, and, no doubt, a variety of other circumstances. The supermarket has supplanted the family grocer in whose shop the risk of an accident such as befell the plaintiff was virtually non-existent. If a customer on taking a package from the grocer were to let it fall she would know it; it would not arise that another customer would come so near as to be endangered. The customer in the supermarket has sacrificed the personal touch of the family grocer for the sake of lower prices and possibly other advantages but she has taken on a very much greater risk of personal injury.

Having referred to the rule in *Rylands v Fletcher*, LR1 Ex 285 (1866), aff'd LR 3 HL 330 (1868), and noted the insistence in *Read v Lyons* [1947] AC 156, at 168, on the requirement of *escape* from the place of the defendant's occupation or control, McCarthy J went on to quote the following passage from McMahon & Binchy's *Irish Law of Torts*, 505 (1st ed., 1981):

Whether an Irish court would look with sympathy on the American refinement of the rule, so as to impose strict liability for ultra-hazardous activities irrespective of any question of escape is difficult to predict. It would have the advantage of rationalising the policy basis of the rule, but would possibly involve too radical a departure from established principles to encourage the court here to take this step. In the light of recent experience with the not unrelated subject of occupier's liability, however, it would be unwise to exclude this possibility.

In a crucial comment, McCarthy J observed that:

[i]t remains for another day to consider whether or not, by way of application of the rule in *Rylands v Fletcher* or otherwise, balancing the rights of people and the rights of property, a principle of absolute liability may be appropriate to claims arising out of certain forms of accidents occurring in large supermarkets.

While these observations were *obiter*, it is worth noting that McCarthy J appeared to consider them worthy of being regarded not as *en passant* comments but rather as an amber light, warning of possible future developments. This interpretation is supported by his statement that the matter was 'of such importance to the public at large and to the owners and occupiers of supermarkets' that it was 'but fair' that he should express a tentative view on the subject of absolute liability. It would seem premature, however, for supermarket proprietors, or their insurers, to panic: Griffin J's reservation on the issue gave no hint of enthusiasm for, or opposition to, such a change. (But then that is precisely what a proper reservation on any issue should do!)

It is worth considering briefly the nature and source of the absolute liability postulated by McCarthy J. Although the rule in *Rylands v Fletcher* was quoted and discussed, it may not at first seem to afford a particularly helpful model for developing new principles of liability. The rule involves *strict* rather than *absolute* liability: among the defences are acts of a stranger, act of God and (if intentional release comes within its scope) necessity: *Rigby v Chief Constable of Northamptonshire* [1985] 2 All ER 985. Moreover, as *Read v Lyons* indicates, proof of an *escape* from the defendant's premises is necessary. McCarthy J certainly seemed to be telegraphing a preference for the American doctrine of 'ultrahazardous activities', which is not premised on escape but rather on the peculiarly dangerous nature of those activities; but can it credibly be suggested that a visit to a supermarket that is properly managed bears any great similarity to working in a munitions factory? Supermarkets are no doubt less safe places than grocers' shops and falls occur from time to time; but to characterise them as inherently unsafe enterprises may be different to sustain, especially when, if run properly, they may be very safe for customers. In short, the negligence formula contains the key for the courts to regulate the level of safety which they consider appropriate in supermarkets. With the abolition of juries in these cases, the trial judges and the Supreme Court have a good deal more control over this process.

It is true that the notion of 'non-natural' user under the rule in *Rylands v Fletcher* contains more than a germ of ultrahazardousness. It will be recalled that in *Rickards v Lothian* [1913] AC 263, Lord Moulton, for the Judicial Committee of the Privy Council, defined this as 'some special use *bringing with it an increased danger to others,* and . . . not merely . . . the ordinary use of land or such a use as is proper for the general benefit of the community' (emphasis added). This forces us to enquire whether running a supermarket should be categorised as a non-natural user for the purposes of the rule in *Rylands v Fletcher*? The answer must be that, according to the sum of decisions in common law jurisdictions other than the United States over the past fifty years, it should not. In *Read v Lyons* [1947] AC, at 169-70 and 173-4, respectively, Viscount Simon and Lord Macmillan doubted whether running a munitions factory on land in wartime constituted a non-natural use. Mines would normally be considered more dangerous places than super-markets; yet in *Rouse v Gravelworks Ltd* [1940] 1 KB 489, the English Court of Appeal held they fell outside the rule.

The truth of the matter is that the definition of non-natural user in *Rickards v Lothian* contains a ragbag of criteria borrowed from those applicable to the determination of whether any particular conduct constitutes *negligence.* In a negligence action the court must have regard to the *probability* of an accident, the *gravity* of the threatened injury, the *social utility* of the defendant's conduct and the *cost* of eliminating the risk. How much weight should be afforded to each of these factors involves a value-judgment by the court, but the entitlement of each factor to be weighed is not questioned in a negligence action. In cases where the rule in *Rylands v Fletcher* is an issue, however, the position is different. The court must make a single characterisation: did the defendant's use of his property constitute a non-natural user? If it *did,* then the rule applies and strict liability attaches to any escape; if it did not, then the plaintiff loses under *Rylands v Fletcher* though of course he or she may nonetheless succeed in many instances on some other ground such as negligence. If the essence of non-natural user were the ultrahazardousness of the process, that might indeed be an excellent reason for imposing strict liability; no-one needs to engage in ultrahazardous activities, any more than he needs to own an elephant for example, but, if he does and injury results, then, according to a rough-and-ready sense of justice, it is not unfair that he should pay up. The problem with the definition of non-natural user in that it lacks any such clarity. It contains the element of 'increased danger to others' but also two other notions: some 'special' rather than 'ordinary' use of land and a use that is other than 'proper for the general benefit of the community'. There are many activities which contain a relatively high degree of risk, are scarcely 'ordinary', and are certainly not philanthropic, but that is not necessarily a sufficiently coherent reason for demanding of those who engage in them that they pay up when things go wrong without any fault on their part. The negligence test seems a far more sensitively calibrated test to determine liability than the all-or-nothing characterisation which the rule in *Rylands v Fletcher* requires.

Finally it is worth considering whether the true reason for McCarthy J's serious consideration of imposing absolute liability on 'certain forms of accidents occurring in large supermarkets' is not traceable to the ultra-hazardous quality of shopping in the vicinity of 4500 breakable items but instead rooted in a value judgment related to contemporary socio-economic realities. What is striking about the judgments of both McCarthy and Griffin JJ sn their nostalgic and sympathetic perception of the grocer's shop of former times. Griffin J recalled that, in traditional grocer shops, 'a great many of which have now fallen by the wayside', customers rarely handled the goods, which were wrapped by assistants:

> Where the order was substantial, and therefore difficult to carry, the goods were delivered either to the house of the customer or to the vehicle to which the customer came if that was near-by.

Supermarkets appeared 'to be growing bigger and bigger'. As we have seen, McCarthy J observed that '[t]he customer in the supermarket has sacrificed the personal touch of the family grocer for the sake of lower prices and possibly other advantages . . .'.

Could it be argued that the idea of imposing absolute liability of large supermarkets for certain injuries suffered by customers is based in some part on a conservative disdain for these new cathedrals of commerce? The business is a notoriously tough one; the profits, on very narrow margins, can be large. Perhaps McCarthy J felt that a duty to compensate all customers who fall on spilled products is a small price for these enterprises to pay. It may not be insignificant that he referred to *large* supermarkets when canvassing the question of absolute liability. The risk of spillages is not dependent on the size of the supermarket, but the sentiment that it is fair to impose what would be a species of enterprise liability might well rest more comfortably if limited to the giants in the industry.

PROFESSIONAL NEGLIGENCE

In *Hanafin v Gaynor,* High Court, 29 May 1990, the plaintiff unsuccessfully sued the defendant solicitor for professional negligence. The plaintiff had purchased premises on an industrial estate for over half a million pounds. As a result of planning defects, he had to sell it at a very substantial loss. The plaintiff claimed that the defendant had negligently recommended to the plaintiff that he should buy the premises, which could be worth over a million pounds. Egan J rejected this on the evidence, as he did the plaintiff's claim that the defendant had warranted, represented or advised that the property had full planning permission and bye-law approval for light industrial and office use.

At contract stage, certain documents had been furnished to the defendant, including a planning permission in 1970 for a proposed industrial building on the site of the premises. Proper requisitions of title by the defendant ensued; Egan J was satisfied that 'one would certainly assume from reading the replies that this 1970 permission was the only permission in existence which affected the property'. Nothing was disclosed about a permission in 1972. Searches handed over revealed that there had been a permission in 1973. The defendant had made a query about this and was told in reply that it did not affect the site being sold. In Egan J's opinion, the defendant had had no reason to query the accuracy of this reply, nor to believe that a 1972 permission was in existence.

Applying the test for professional negligence spelt out by the Supreme Court in *Roche v Peilow* [1985] IR 232 and *Dunne v National Maternity Hospital, supra,* Egan J held that the defendant was not guilty of professional negligence. He had been perfectly entitled to accept the reply to his query regarding the 1973 permission. The existence of the 1972 permission had never been disclosed even though professional law searchers had carried out searches, 'so how was the defendant to know about it?'. Egan J rejected the plaintiff's argument that the defendant should have carried out a further search *before closing*: the plaintiff or his tenants 'were actually in possession during this period and [the defendant] would have known, therefore, that nothing could have occurred affecting planning permission during this period'. (Whether lawyers should thus be able to transfer the burden onto non-lawyers may be debated.)

Egan J stressed that the title had been accepted by the solicitor of the plaintiff's financiers as by the *vendor's* solicitor, who was actually buying the property for his own clients while at the same time selling it to the plaintiff.

Egan J concluded that it could not be said that the defendant was guilty of such failure as no other solicitor of equal status and skill would be guilty of it acting with ordinary care. He did not address in express terms the question whether the evidence had revealed any professional practice which had inherent defects which ought to have been obvious to any person giving the matter due consideration. Presumably he considered this proviso irrelevant to the evidence in the case.

In *O'Connor v First National Buiding Society et. al.* [1991] ILRM 208 Lynch J addressed the question whether it is negligent for a solicitor to fail to inform his or her client who is intending to purchase a house of the need to have an independent valuation rather than rely on the building society's valuation. We discuss the case later in the chapter, below, 529-32.

PSYCHIATRIC NEGLIGENCE

In *Armstrong v Eastern Health Board and St. Patrick's Hospital*, High Court, 5 October 1990, Egan J had to deal with an allegation of negligence by psychiatrists — a subject raising difficult issues of law and policy.

The plaintiff was a married woman aged 39. Her troubles were manifold: she had had two children before marriage, whom her relations were rearing; she and her husband were unemployed, living in accommodation which they found intolerable; she had a long psychiatric history, going back nearly twenty years. Between 1979 and 1982 she had been admitted about fourteen times to St. Loman's Hospital. Many of these admissions were for what were called 'social' reasons, that is, reasons which a lay person would consider to constitute ordinary depression as distinct from clinical depression. She suffered from simple schizophrenia and was diagnosed as having a socio-pathic and low IQ; apart from medication, she had also received ECT to help her depression.

In the three month period before the incident which resulted in the injuries of which she complained, she had attended St. Patrick's Hospital on eight occasions. Since she had formed the habit of largely ignoring out-patient appointments, preferring to attend on an emergency basis, a policy decision was taken by the team of psychiatrists whose patient she was that she should thenceforth be seen only in the out-patients section. This was to bring about some regularity and system in her treatment.

The plaintiff at the time was seriously concerned about her living conditions: her Corporation flat was in a poor state and had no proper cooker. She and her husband had lost a better flat when they went briefly to live in England. Both were very angry about their housing situation and she demanded of the psychiatrist who was treating her that she should give them a letter there and then to take to the Corporation for a transfer. The psychiatrist told the plaintiff of the policy decisions regarding her treatment. A month later the plaintiff came again to the hospital, as an emergency patient. She was in a most angry mood when the psychiatrist saw her. She demanded that the psychiatrist should provide her with a furnished flat by the afternoon. Her husband tried to explain to her that the psychiatrist could do little about their housing situation.

Nine days later, the psychiatrist received a message that the plaintiff's husband was in the out-patients section demanding to see her. The psychiatrist, who was attending her own in-patients, sent him a message that, if the plaintiff was unwell, she should go to a general practitioner for a referral letter. This the plaintiff did and came to the hospital shortly afterwards with the referral letter, in which the general practitioner stated that the plaintiff was very restless and agitated and had suicidal ideas; it went on to say that there was inappropriate affect and that the plaintiff felt she required hospitalisation.

The psychiatrist who had been treating the plaintiff up to then did not go to see her. Instead she gave another psychiatrist, who had never met the plaintiff, the diagnosis that the plaintiff had simple schizophrenia, personality disorder and low IQ. She also told her that at no stage of her contact with the plaintiff had she found her to be seriously depressed or psychotic. She expressed the view that the plaintiff's main problems related to housing and to her marital situation. She made no mention of suicidal tendencies.

The other psychiatrist, without consulting the plaintiff's chart or log-book, and (Egan J concluded with some hesitation) without having read the general practitioner's letter of referral, conducted her assessment of the plaintiff, as a result of which she formed the conclusion that she was not clinically depressed or suicidal and that there was no medical necessity to admit her. When the plaintiff and her husband were told that there was no bed available for her at St. Patrick's or another hospital, they became very angry and left, threatening that they would bring legal proceedings. Shortly afterwards the plaintiff threw herself over a balcony at the block of flats where she lived; she received serious injuries.

Egan J imposed liability. He accepted without question the principle that a doctor is not negligent merely because his or her assessment is wrong. The reason why there was negligence in this case was that the assessment was based on insufficient information. Had the psychiatrist consulted the chart and log- book, she would have discovered two recent entries, one of which was to the effect that the plaintiff had attempted to throw herself over the balcony because of exacerbation of her auditory hallucinations, the other (twelve days before the incident) in which the plaintiff had made a similar threat. The psychiatrist who had been treating the plaintiff until the day of her fall knew the details of the second of these entries but knew nothing about the first entry. She did not mention the second when orally briefing the psychiatrist who assessed the plaintiff that day. Egan J noted that medical evidence had been given in the proceedings that many threats of suicide are not genuine but that they must be taken more seriously when an actual method of committing suicide is mentioned.

While the psychiatrist who examined the plaintiff on the fateful day stated in evidence that, even if she had read the relevant documentation, her assessment would have been the same, Egan J concluded that as a matter of probability she would have hospitalised the plaintiff that day had she been in possession of the information it contained.

In an important passage, Egan J said:

> I do not hold that clinical notes or entries in log-books must always be read in all circumstances. There must be many occasions when there is simply not sufficient time and an emergency decision is required. Notes, however, are made for a purpose and should be read in the ordinary course. I imagine it was not unusual for one doctor to rely on a verbal summary given by another doctor who was well acquainted with the patient but this cannot always be excused.

Egan J went on to acquit the plaintiff of any contributory negligence as 'she was not really in control of her thoughts when she jumped from the balcony'.

Armstrong raises a number of interesting issues in relation to psychiatric negligence. A requirement that clinical notes should be read 'in the ordinary course' may be considered by some psychiatrists working in busy hospitals to impose a burden that is inappropriate to the circumstances of their practice. It is one thing to penalise as negligence a diagnosis based on an oral communication between psychiatrists, made in the knowledge that the recipient will probably not read the clinical notes; it is another thing to require the recipient of oral information from a reliable professional source to read the notes under pain of being held negligent. Of course the failure to read clinical notes can in some circumstance generate civil liability (cf. *Meyer v Gordon*, 17 CCLT 1 (BC Supreme Court, Legg J, 1981): but a suggestion that there should be a general obligation to do so save in exceptional cases may seem to some psychiatrists to lead to counter-productive results, most notably delay in dealing with urgent cases. Having said this, it must be re-emphasised that the information available to the doctor from clinical notes is undoubtedly a factor of considerable potential relevance in determining whether his or her diagnosis was made with due care: see Jackson & Lovell's *Professional Negligence* (2nd ed, 1987), para 6.68, Touquet & Harris, 'Accident and Emergency', in Powers & Harris eds., *Medical Negligence* (1990), paras 21.10-21.15.

A more general question arises as to the duty and standard of care in the psychiatric context. Too broad a definition of the range of duty and too onerous an imposition of the standard of care may not be in the interests of psychiatric patients as a group. Faced with the possibility of being sued if he or she fails to commit a patient and the patient thereafter commits suicide or kills or injures another person, the doctor can secure his or her own position by simply committing the patient. The result may be that too many patients will be incarcerated, simply to make life easier for their psychiatrists. Cf. Stone, 'The *Tarasoff* Decisions: Suing Psychotherapists to Safeguard Society', (1976), 90 *Harv L Rev* 358, Anon, Note (1990) 103 *Harv L Rev* 1192.

NEGLIGENCE ON THE ROADS

In *Moore v Fullerton* [1991] ILRM 29, the plaintiff a nine year old boy, received very serious severe injuries in a traffic accident in the village of Burnfoot in Co Donegal, when he was crossing the street on an October afternoon. The road was about twenty four feet wide. On the day in question, a mart was being held in the village in the immediate vicinity. There was, as was usual on such days, a considerable amount of traffic, and trucks, motor cars and trailers were parked on both sides of the road for some distance.

The trial judge, Costello J, hearing the case without a jury, found that the accident had occurred when the plaintiff ran across the road and in the path of the defendant's large, laden lorry, which had come into the village at about 23 to 24 miles per hour but, on seeing another lorry crossing the road, had slowed down to a speed of 12 to 14 miles per hour. Just as the other lorry had straightened out, the defendant had seen the plaintiff running into his path.

Costello J had refused an application for a direction at the conclusion of the plaintiff's case but, after hearing the evidence of both sides, had held in favour of the defendant on the basis that there was 'no evidence of negligent driving' on his part. The Supreme Court (Finlay CJ, Hederman J concurring, O'Flaherty J dissenting) affirmed.

In his judgment, Finlay CJ accepted that the Supreme Court was bound by Costello J's findings of primary fact and his acceptance of the defendant's version of the accident. The Chief Justice was, however, satisfied that the question whether that version constituted evidence of negligence on the part of the defendant was a matter of law which the Supreme Court had to investigate. He was satisfied on the facts that there was no such evidence. To hold the driver liable would be to impose on him an artificially high and unreasonable standard of care.

O'Flaherty J, dissenting, considered that, while the emergence of the other lorry contained no problem for the defendant in the sense that he could get by on his side of the road, the defendant must have known that it cut off completely his view of anything that might be happening on the other side of the road and also cut off the view of anyone on the other side of the road to traffic approaching from his direction. Moreover, the defendant was fully aware that there was a large popular gathering taking place in the village. He had travelled through the village earlier that day and, in any event, had often travelled through it on mart-days. While, in the ordinary way, what the defendant had done would not have been negligent, regard must be had to the time and place of the accident:

> The fact that it was on this day a place of popular concourse and commerce called for a special vigilance and the driver should have appreciated that the [other] lorry — while it created no problem for him on his side of the road — was a source of danger in that it hid what was happening on the other side. In a word, his speed, while slow, should have been slower still. He was required to pick his way with the greatest care.

In O'Flaherty's view, therefore, the defendant should not have been completely acquitted of negligence and the issues of the plaintiff's contributory negligence and of damages should be determined on a re-trial.

The case is interesting in the light of the abolition in 1988 of juries in personal injuries litigation in the High Court: see the 1988 Review, 454-6. The issue in *Moore v Fullerton* was not the same as that which had usually presented itself to the Supreme Court, namely, whether the trial judge should (or should not) have withdrawn the case from the jury. Here, as we have mentioned, Costello J decided the case on its merits after both sides had given evidence. It is of course possible for an appellate court to substitute its own judgment as to secondary findings of fact: of *Northern Bank Finance Corporation Ltd v Charlton* [1979] IR 149, *Banco Ambrosiano Spa v Ansbacher & Co. Ltd* [1987] ILRM 669, *In re M, an Infant; IM v An Bord Uchtála* [1988] ILRM 203 and the 1987 Review, 208-9, 274-5. Whether the finding of negligence or no negligence should be regarded as exclusively a finding of fact is most doubtful. The issue whether in the circumstances the defendant ought to have acted as he did is unquestionably one of *value*, based on factual evidence rather than of fact alone.

In these circumstances, the Irish courts need to be aware of the dangers of resurrecting in a new context and with some new clothes the old and largely discredited doctrine of negligence as a matter of law. It is interesting that traffic accidents in the past encouraged courts into favouring this approach.

In *O'Beirne v Hannigan* [1937] IR 237 (Supreme Court), the plaintiff, dazzled by the defendant's lights, continued driving at a speed of 15 to 20 miles per hour. Fitzgibbon J held that this was 'a negligent act, *per se*'. This characterisation later gave way to a contextualised test, depending on all the circumstances of the case: see, eg, *O'Reilly v Evans* [1956] IR 269, at 273-274; cf. McMahon & Binchy *op. cit.*, 285-286.

O'Flaherty J's judgment lies somewhere between these two extremes. Nevertheless it would amount to a judicial 'rule of the road', with some considerable degree of specificity. As to its merits, one may perhaps debate whether liability should be imposed for travelling at such a low speed as the defendant's, even if he should have realised the other lorry would represent a visual occlusion for others. Surely those others could be expected to heed the danger rather than insist that the defendant should drive on the assumption that they would not. In this context it should be noted that O'Flaherty did not base his judgment on the presence of *children*, such as was the case in *O'Donnell v CIE* (1955) 89 ILTR 181.

ONUS OF PROOF

In *Sheehy v Faughnan*, High Court, 14 December 1990 (Circuit Appeal), the plaintiff sent his mare to the defendants' stud for servicing. It was expected that she would be there for about three weeks. The mare died four days after arriving at the stud, but the defendant did not inform the plaintiff for nearly a fortnight. The mare had not suffered external injuries and the cause of her death was never established.

The plaintiff's action for negligence was successful. Barron J considered it 'immaterial whether cases of this nature are brought in detinue or in negligence. In either case, the onus of proof lies on the defendant to show that the loss did not occur through lack of reasonable care on his part'. Barron J was satisfied that the defendant had not *deliberately* failed to contact the plaintiff immediately after the mare's death but this failure was nonetheless unreasonable in the circumstances. Had the plaintiff then been contacted he would have arranged for a *post mortem* which would probably have determined the cause of death. The defendant had thus failed to discharge the burden of proof resting on him since his fault in failing to notify the plaintiff had left the matter a mystery.

The case is interesting in a number of respects. Clearly the facts could not justify a claim for detinue, since there was no question of the plaintiff's having made a demand for the return of the mare with which the plaintiff declined to comply. Cf. McMahon & Binchy, *op. cit.*, 528-31, *Treasure Island Ltd v Zebedee Enterprises Ltd*, High Court, Carroll J, 29 May 1987 (noted in the

1987 Review, 340). Rather than characterise the matter as detinue, it might have been desirable to treat it in terms of the duty of care of a bailee under a contract of bailment.

Barron J did not expressly address the principles of *res ipsa loquitur* in this context. (Cf. *M'Lachin v London & NW Ry & Co.* (1907) 41 ILTR 139, mentioned by McMahon & Binchy, *op. cit.*, 138).

On the broader front, it is worth considering whether a similar duty should rest on a defendant in a *res ipsa loquitur* situation, *outside the context of bailment*. If this were so, then a prospective defendant against whom the *res ipsa loquitur* doctrine might be invoked would be under a duty to provide the plaintiff with an immediate opportunity of discovering the cause of his injury under the legal sanction that, if he did not do so, he could not argue that the cause was unknowable if such an immediate investigation would probably have unearthed it. It might be thought that this does not represent a significant development in the law. In fact it does, since the traditional application of the *res ipsa loquitur* doctrine permits a defendant to escape liability where, without establishing the actual cause of the injury, and certainly without providing the plaintiff immediate facilities for doing so, he convinces the court that he was not negligent or even (on some renditions of the doctrine) cogently posits an explanation equally consistent with the absence of his negligence.

The requirement to facilitate an immediate inspection harmonises with the Supreme Court's general approach in *Hanrahan v Merck, Sharp & Dohme (Ireland) Ltd* [1988] ILRM 629, where Henchy J (for the Court) observed that the rationale behind the shifting of the onus of proof in *res ipsa loquitur* cases 'would be palpably unfair to require a plaintiff to prove something which is beyond his reach and which is peculiarly within the range of the defendant's capacity of proof'. Whether this rationale in fact truly represents the traditional basis of the *res ipsa loquitur* doctrine may, however, be debated: see our comments in the 1988 Review, 448-9. Morris J was attracted to it in *Lindsay v Mid-Western Health Board*, High Court, 30 May 1991, which we will analyse in the 1991 Review.

NEGLIGENCE TOWARDS HOUSEBUYERS

Until quite recently the old principle of *caveat emptor* continued to apply to purchases of real property. The 'neighbour' principle of *Donoghue v Stevenson* [1932] AC 562, at 580 was not considered to extend its protection that far. In the past decade, the position has been reversed. The old immunity from the duty of care has been swept away and courts have in some cases extended the scope of paternalistic protection very widely. This has been particularly evident where the purchaser is of limited means and is buying from, or with the assistance of, a local authority, but even in cases lacking this dimension courts have on occasion gone very far to protect purchasers, even to the extent of overriding or sidestepping orthodox principles of contract law. The law of contract proceeds on the basis that agreements should as a general principle be binding unless vitiated by a defect such as mistake or duress. The law of negligence, especially by resort to the *Hedley Byrne* principle, has enabled some purchasers to neutralise the doctrines of contract law. Where this fails, the statutory policy underlying legislation controlling unfair terms has been called in aid: see *Smith v Bush; Harris v Wyre Forest District Council* [1989] 2 All ER 514, Kaye 'Surveying the Scene: A Valuer's Duty of Care', (1989) 52 *Modern L Rev* 841.

In *O'Connor v First National Building Society* [1991] ILRM 208, a bus driver who had retired permanently on the ground of ill-health and was living on a social welfare pension was, with his wife, anxious to buy a somewhat larger house that the one in which they were at present living, which had been bought with a mortgage from the defendant building society. After consulting with the building society, he was informed of its approval of a loan of £15,000 provided the house to be purchased would be adequate security for that amount.

The plaintiffs found a house that interested them. They looked over it and noted that it was in a very bad state of decorative repair though it seemed otherwise to be sound. They agreed to buy it for £21,500 and paid the auctioneer a booking fee of £1,000. They then obtained a loan application from the building society, which they returned having filled in most of it. They completed the form on the society's premises with the assistance of a representative of the society. During their discussion with the representative, they enquired whether or not they should obtain an independent inspection of the house. The representative indicated that such an inspection might cost £100 or £200 or even as much as £700 but that a vendor would never allow an inspection of such detail as to cost £700; he also pointed out that the society would be having its own valuation or survey or inspection of the premises and, if it showed up anything structurally serious or any rot of a serious nature, the society could not advance a loan on the security of that house. The plaintiffs paid the society £29.80 in respect of the cost to be incurred by the society in having the premises valued or surveyed or inspected. The loan application form which they completed specifically provided in clause 8 that '[n]o responsibility can be accepted by the society for the condition of the property'. This paragraph occurred immediately above the plaintiffs' signatures. Lynch J was satisfied that the plaintiffs were aware 'in a general way' of this clause.

A few days later, the plaintiffs went to see a member of the staff of their solicitors. They brought him up to date as to how matters had progressed. While the solicitor was obtaining particulars from Mr O'Connor, Mrs O'Connor, by way of interjection, sought to enquire whether they should arrange for their own survey of the premises; the solicitor brushed this enquiry aside as he was concentrating on what Mr O'Connor had to say. The solicitor advised Mr O'Connor to jump on certain floors and to test walls to see if the plaster was sound. The solicitor was under the impression that Mr O'Connor was in the building trade; because of this, because Mr O'Connor had said the premises were in very poor condition and because the purchase price seemed relatively cheap, the solicitor did not think it necessary to advise that the plaintiffs should have any independent inspection or survey by a suitably qualified person. Equally he did not seek to dissuade them from doing so. Had he known of Mr O'Connor's actual qualifications he would have advised that an independent survey be obtained.

The plaintiffs, having purchased the house, found that it contained a number of defects in the chimney and flues. They sued their building society and solicitors in negligence.

Lynch J dismissed their claim against the building society. They had to be fixed with notice of the provisions and meaning of clause 8. The society's representative had told them nothing but the truth as regards the cost of independent inspections and of the implications of the society's inspection revealing serious structural faults. His remarks about the cost of independent inspections was 'undoubtedly offputting' so far as the plaintiffs' thoughts about obtaining an independent inspection were concerned, but it was nevertheless true, and many purchasers economised and took a chance in not obtaining an independent investigation. Insofar as the representative might have referred to the valuation which the society might obtain as a 'survey', Lynch J did not consider that the plaintiffs would have been in any way misled as to the nature of what was being obtained, having regard to the contrast between the price they had to pay for this valuation and the figures for an independent inspection mentioned by the representative:

> It must have been clear to the plaintiffs that whatever valuation or survey might be obtained by the [society] for the £29.80 fee could hardly be anything other than a walk around and visual inspection.

(It will be recalled that in *Ward v McMaster* [1989] ILRM 400; [1988] IR 337 the plaintiffs' reasonable inferences from the payment of a small fee for what they believed was a valuation were construed somewhat differently; but the facts of that decision were in many respects different from those in *O'Connor*.)

Lynch J imposed liability on the firm of solicitors. He accepted that there

could be no absolute rule of law that a solicitor must always advise a
purchaser that he ought to have an independent inspection of the property by
a suitably qualified person, but, having regard to the evidence of Mr John
Buckley from the Law Society Conveyancing Committee about established
practice, he thought that:

> such a duty *prima facie* arises and it is for a solicitor who contends that
> no such duty arose in any particular case to show circumstances such
> as [where the purchaser is an architect who has himself carefully
> examined the property] if he is to negative the existence of the duty.

Since Mr O'Connor was no more than a do-it-yourself enthusiast, rather
than the person with experience in the building trade who the solicitor
believed him to be, a duty arose to advise an independent inspection. Had it
been carried out, it would have revealed the defects and the plaintiffs would
have withdrawn from the purchase. One suspects that solicitors around the
country are quaking in recollection of many transactions in which they failed
to adhere to this very onerous test.

CONTRIBUTORY NEGLIGENCE

1 Conveyancing   In the Chapter on Land Law, 376-8, we discuss Barron
J's decision in *Shangan Construction Ltd v TP Robinson & Co.*, High Court,
10 July 1990.

2 Mitigation of damages   In *Philips v The Medical Council*, High Court,
11 December 1990, which we consider below in the present chapter, 533, as
well as in the Equity Chapter, 277, Costello J held that the plaintiff had not
been guilty of failure to mitigate his damage in not claiming a social welfare
benefit of £30 per week. The plaintiff's claim was for loss of earnings (at
approximately £20,000 per annum) for a period of after three years while the
Medical Council unreasonably delayed in determining his application for full
registration of the General Register of Medical Practitioners. The plaintiff
had not considered it worth his while applying for this benefit. Costello J
regarded this attitude as 'a reasonable one'.

3 Rescue attempts   In *Phillips v Durgan* [1991] ILRM 321, the Supreme
Court was not called on to address some interesting but complicated issues
that arise where one plaintiff's contributory negligence, combined with the
negligence of the defendant, induces a rescue attempt by another plaintiff in
which that other plaintiff is injured. We discuss the case and these issues,
earlier in the chapter, above, 493-500.

4 Mental disability In *Armstrong v Eastern Health Board and St Patrick's Hospital*, High Court, 5 October 1990, Egan J held that a patient who had attempted to commit suicide was not guilty of contributory negligence because she was 'not really in control of her thoughts' at the time. We discuss the case, earlier in the chapter, above, 523-6.

5 Interrelationship between employers' liability and statutory duty In *Dunne v Honeywell Control Systems Ltd and Virginia Milk Products Ltd* [1991] ILRM 595. Barron J analysed the interrelationship between employers' liability and proceedings for breach of statutory duty, so far as the plaintiff's contributory negligence is in issue. We discuss the case earlier in the chapter, above, 500-05.

BREACH OF STATUTORY DUTY

1 Registration of Medical Practitioner In *Philips v The Medical Council*, High Court, 11 December 1990, Costello J awarded the plaintiff over £40,000 for breach by the Medical Council of its statutory duty under the Medical Practitioners Act 1978 to determine his application for full registration on the General Register of Medical Practitioners within a reasonable time. The evidence in the case revealed an unhappy state of affairs as regards the formulation, publication, rescission and revision of rules to govern applications of this type: see the Equity Chapter, above, 277. Costello J considered that three months would have been a reasonable time within which the Council could have considered the plaintiff's application; yet it had not done so three years later.

The evidence established that, on the balance of probabilities, the plaintiff's action would have been successful. The case was thus one in which damages were appropriate.

An interesting element in the judgment is that, as well as ordering the defendant to pay damages for its failure to have considered his application within a reasonable time Costello J declared that the Medical Council should consider and determine this application. Thus the Council had to determine an issue on which Costello J had held that the plaintiff would have succeeded had the Council made that determination earlier.

Costello J did not refer to the questions whether the 1978 Act had been enacted for the benefit of the public or a specific category of persons (cf. McMahon & Binchy, *op. cit.*, 377- 80) or, if so, whether the plaintiff fell within that favoured category. He did, however, note that the Medical Council 'is not a body established to manage the affairs of the medical profession or to protect its interests; it is a statutory body entrusted with important statutory functions to be performed in the public interest. In particular the register of medical practitioners which it is required to maintain has been established to ensure that those who practice medicine in the State are properly qualified to do so'. While this passage emphasises the public policy grounding of the legislation it in no sense excludes the possibility of interpreting the legislation as also being designed to protect the legitimate interests of medical practitioners, including applicants for full registration in the General Register. The interests of the public may perhaps be regarded as dominant, but the legitimate interests of medical practitioners were no less the concern of the legislation.

Eight months before Costello J delivered his judgment in *Philips,* the Supreme Court, in *Bakht v The Medical Council* [1990] ILRM 840 had awarded damages against the same defendant arising from its delay in making the rules. The discussion of the legal dimensions of this claim was rudimentary. (We consider *Bakht* more fully in the Health Services Chapter above, 337-8.)

2 *Duty to employee*   We discuss Barron J's judgment in *Dunne v Honeywell Control Systems Ltd and Virginia Milk Products Ltd* [1991] ILRM 595, above, 500-5.

DEFAMATION

1 *Prior restraint*   In [X] v RTE, Supreme Court, 27 March 1990, aff'g High Court, Costello J 27 March 1990, Irish Times, 28 March 1990, the plaintiff sought an injunction restraining RTE from naming him as a person who had been involved in the Birmingham bombings of 1974, in a television programme due to be published that evening. His affidavit stated that he had been informed and believed it to be true that his name was to be thus mentioned in the programme. He stated that such assertion was completely untrue and added:

> Such publication would not only defame me but also expose me to the risk of personal violence by persons excited by animosity against me. I do not believe that damages would be a sufficient remedy if the programme were broadcast.

The plaintiff's solicitor, in an affidavit, stated that she had received instructions from the plaintiff the previous evening, that she had telephoned RTE and that there was nobody there who could deal with the particular matter. At 9.50 on the morning of the hearing she had sent a letter by fax to RTE in which she indicated her belief that her client was going to be named as one of the bombers in the forthcoming programme. She had asked for an undertaking that the programme broadcast would not include any such reference and said that in the absence of an undertaking she must assume that RTE intended to show the programme with defamatory matter and that she would be forced to act accordingly. She also asked for permission to look at the programme.

Permission was not granted. She received a letter, before 11 a.m., in which RTE stated that it found it 'impossible to give the undertaking in her letter'.

Costello J refused the plaintiff's application on two grounds. First, he was not satisfied, having regard to the plaintiff's failure to name the person who had informed him that his name was going to be used as suggested in the programme, that there was sufficient proof of an apprehension of defamation; secondly, that the plaintiff's delay in moving with regard to an *ex parte* application disentitled him to relief.

The Supreme Court affirmed. Finlay CJ stated that he understood the general principle applicable to injunction applications in regard to the publication of defamatory matter to be that, if a defendant indicated an intention in the proceedings to justify the matter complained of and provided some substantial grounds to satisfy the Court that he had a reasonable chance of doing so, then, ordinarily, the publication would not be restrained. That general principle seemed to him to make it absolutely essential that if, in regard to a publication, the precise time and date of which had been publicly notified more than a week in advance, a plaintiff seeking *ex parte* an injunction against publication should have compelling reasons indicated to the Court why he had not moved earlier than on a time scale which made it impossible for the defendant to be heard.

In this concurring judgment, McCarthy J expressed the opinion that the constitutional guarantee of the vindication of the good name of every citizen had to be read in the context of the constitutional guarantee of freedom of expression. That good name might be vindicated in damages but a restraint on freedom of expression could not be similarly remedied.

The Court's approach and holding in this decision are controversial. Of course there should be stringent judicial controls on 'gagging writs', and a close scrutiny of the plaintiff's case before an injunction is granted. But there are surely some limits to this approach. If a plaintiff can credibly assert that the publication of the allegedly defamatory material is likely to expose him to the risk of being murdered, this must be a factor of such significance as to be afforded great weight. The idea that it should be swept aside by his delay in taking the proceedings seems bizarre. Being penalised in costs is one thing; being subjected to the risk of death another. Of course it may be that in some cases, the circumstances of the delay will be so striking as to warrant the inference that the asserted risk of being killed is fanciful: if a plaintiff was slow in seeking the court's protection it may suggest that he did not himself believe that the publication would be likely to provoke violence against him. If this was the basis of the Court's holding, it would perhaps have been desirable for the Court to have said so clearly.

A more difficult aspect of the problem relates to the question of the defamatory character of a statement made about a plaintiff who produces credible evidence that its publication will expose him to the serious risk of being killed. How is a court to weigh the competing interests of the parties? If the plaintiff passes the *Campus Oil* threshold on the issues of the defamatory quality of the statement and the risk of his being killed, how substantial a counterweight is the right of free speech? Does the answer in any way depend on the strength of the plaintiff's case as to the defamatory quality of the statement, or is that aspect to be treated as a constant rather than variable factor once it is shown that there is a serious question to be tried on that issue? These are troublesome questions to which courts may be reluctant to provide frank answers in their judgments. Here it is often a case of having to *infer* these principles from the orders actually made in the case, with the judgments offering only limited assistance in this task.

The question of the constitutional protection of free speech in the context of interlocutory orders in defamation proceedings would need detailed judicial consideration which, of the nature of things, is almost impossible to provide in cases of urgency where an *ex tempore* judgment is called for. It is a radical proposition that Article 40.6.1 confers a general right to defame another, leaving the victim to a subsequent claim for damages, provided the defendant can produce some substantial grounds for showing that he has a *reasonable chance* of succeeding with the defence of justification. This proviso might be acceptable (subject to the exception we mention in a moment) if the likelihood of the defence of justification succeeding was considerably greater than that of it failing.

Whatever about a general rule in this area, the courts should surely be sensitive to the *differences* between cases. It is one thing to permit a defendant cause the plaintiff financial injury, since that can (in principle at least) be remedied by an award of damages. It is quite another thing to permit a defendant by indirect means to occasion the destruction of a person's life, or of his or her family relationships (as might be the case with the publication of a false allegation of child sexual abuse, for example). From the constitutional standpoint, apart from the right to one's good name (under Article 40.3.2), other rights also need to be considered, such as the rights to life, health and bodily integrity.

Even in cases where the plaintiff's apprehended injury is entirely financial, difficult issues arise in the constitutional dimension. Is the court to hold that the Constitution protects free speech in cases where the plaintiff is likely to be left with an entirely theoretical entitlement to damages because the defendant has no money, or is the right of free speech to be restricted to those who can pay for their defamatory statements? The former approach would seem to deny a plaintiff effective protection; the latter raises questions of equality and social justice.

The question of the constitutional dimensions of free speech has excited much academic discussion in the last few years. See, e.g. M. McDonald, *Irish Law of Defamation* (1989), K. Boyle & M. McGonagle, *A Report on Press Freedom and Libel* (National Newspapers of Ireland, December 1988), O'Dell, 'Does Defamation Value Free Expression?', (1990) 12 *DULJ* (ns) 50, O'Dell, 'Reflections on a Revolution in Libel', (1991) 9 *ILT* (ns) 181. We do not intend here to enter into an extended consideration of the subject, since we will be addressing it in detail in the 1991 Review when analysing the Law Reform Commission's proposals on defamation. All we need here record is that, from the historical standpoint, there is an attractive argument to be made that Article 40.6.1 does not seek to address the constitutional dimensions of civil defamation law but is concerned rather with giving a guarantee, *as between State and citizen*, not to *punish* citizens for the free expression of their opinions and convictions nor to censor or otherwise repress their publication outside the contexts of subversion, public order and morality. In other words the guarantee is *against State totalitariarism* rather than an attempt to regulate the relationship between speech and good name *as between citizens*. This seems clearly to have been de Valera's understanding of the provision. Whether an argument on these lines would easily be harmonised with all judicial utterances is another matter, but the instant case perhaps offers a warning against treating too seriously the casual invocation of Article 40.6.1.

Of course, defamation law inevitably has a constitutional dimension: the guarantee of protection for the citizen's good name under Article 40.3.2 ensures this, and it would not be surprising if the courts were to develop principles involving an interrelationship between Article 40.6.1 and the personal rights of the citizens under Article 40.3. But it is surely unwise of the courts to invoke Article 40.6.1 for rhetorical rather than substantive purposes. It should not be forgotten that in the Supreme Court decision of *Hynes-O'Sullivan v O'Driscoll* [1989] ILRM 349; [1988] IR 436, where Henchy and McCarthy JJ gave extended consideration of the constitutional dimensions to the law of defamation, this analysis offered scant support for the view that Article 40.6.1 has rewritten the common law principles of defamation law. It will be recalled that Henchy J considered that:

[t]he public policy which a new formulation of the law would represent should more properly be found by the Law Reform Commission or by those others who are in a position to take a broad perspective as distinct from what is discernible in the tunnelled vision imposed by the facts of a single case. That is particularly so in a case such as this, where the law as to qualified privilege must reflect a due balancing of the constitutional right of freedom of expression and the constitutional protection of every citizen's good name. The articulation of public policy on a matter such as this would seem to be primarily a matter for the Legislature.

See further our discussion of *Hynes-O'Sullivan* in the 1988 Review, 439-45 and McDonald (1989) 11 *DULJ* 94.

The relationship between the torts of defamation and negligence is worth noting briefly in this context. Whilst it has recently been observed that '[a]ny attempt to merge defamation and negligence should be resisted' (*Balfour v Attorney General* [1991] 1 NZLR 520, at 529), the fact remains that negligence is the quintessential tort for dealing with personal injury (especially of indirect causation, which does not fit into the historical tort of trespass). Negligent communications leading foreseeably to another's death generate liability in negligence with no great ado. If a drugs company produced a product with potentially lethal directions on the bottle, their asserted constitutional right of free speech would be given short shrift in injunction proceedings for removal of the label. Courts should be watchful against being hypnotised by evocative legal labels.

2 Defamation by conduct In *O'Callaghan v Meath Vocational Education Committee, McCormack and the Minister for Education,* High Court, 20 November 1990, Costello J dismissed a claim for defamation resulting from an alleged termination of employment. We analyse the case in the Labour Law Chapter, above, 365-7.

DECEIT

In *O'Callaghan v Meath Vocational Education Committee, McCormack and the Minister for Education, supra,* Costello J dismissed the plaintiff's action for deceit in the context of his job prospects. We analyse the case in the Labour Law Chapter, above, 365-7.

TREES ADJOINING THE HIGHWAY

The liability of occupiers of property adjoining the highway for injury or damage to persons using the highway has generated much controversial litigation. At the heart of the judicial analysis is the debate as to whether ordinary principles of negligence should be applied or whether a stricter test should be adopted in the interests of the public. An uneasy and unconvincing compromise was reached in the English Court of Appeal decision of *Wringe v Cohen* [1940] 1KB 229, whereby strict liability was limited to cases involving injury by artificial structures. Fleming, *The Law of Torts* (7th ed., 1987, 399, criticises this distinction on the basis that 'a tree planted by human hand is as much an artificial structure as a gable or a lamp fixed to a wall'.

In *Lynch v Hetherton* [1990] ILRM 857 (Circuit Court Appeal), O'Hanlon J was faced with a narrower issue. The plaintiff, who had been driving his car along a country road in County Westmeath, ran into a falling ash tree which came from the defendant's property. The car was damaged. The plaintiff's claim was framed in negligence and nuisance. The Circuit Court judge found in favour of the plaintiff (subject to a reduction for contributory negligence). O'Hanlon J reversed, holding that the defendant was not liable.

The parties were agreed on the general principle that a landowner having on his lands a tree or trees adjoining a highway or his neighbour's land is bound to take such care as a reasonable and prudent landowner would take to guard against the danger of damage being done by a falling tree. Thus there was no argument as to whether concern for public safety might require the imposition of a stricter test. The difficulty in the case concerned the definition of *the degree of care* to be expected of the reasonable and prudent landowner.

The House of Lords had addressed this question in *Caminer v Northern & London Investment Trust Ltd* [1951] AC 88. Some nuances of difference among the speeches are worth noting.

Lord Normand said:

> The test of the conduct to be expected from a reasonable and prudent landlord sounds more simple than it really is. For it postulates some degree of knowledge on the part of landlords which must necessarily fall short of the knowledge possessed by scientific arboriculturists but which must surely be greater than the knowledge possessed by the ordinary urban observer of trees or even of the countryman not practically concerned with their care. . . . If a landlord is aware of his ignorance about elms he should obtain the advice of someone better instructed, not a scientific expert in the ordinary case, but another landlord with greater experience or a practical forester, for example.

Lord Oaksey obtained that landowners 'are not all experts in the management of trees and those who are not perform their duty if they take reasonable steps to employ persons who are experts'.

Lords Radcliffe and Reid emphasised the relevance of the *location* of the occupier's premises in the determination of the appropriate steps for the occupier to take. In *Caminer*, the accident happened in a busy street in London, and Lord Reid expressed no opinion about the extent of the duty of one with trees near an unfrequented highway. Lord Reid addressed the question of adequate inspection as follows:

> Plainly it would be no use to send a person who knew nothing about trees. The alternatives put forward were that he should be an expert or that he should have at least such knowledge and experience of trees as a landowner with trees on his land would generally have. As the question depends upon on what a reasonable man would do I think that it may be put in this way. Would a reasonable and careful owner, without expert knowledge but accustomed to dealing with his trees and having a countryman's general knowledge about them, think it necessary to call in an expert to advise him or would he think it sufficient to act at least in the first instance on his own knowledge and judgment.

Thus, while for Lord Normand the degree of knowledge 'must surely be greater' than that of the countryman not practically concerned with the care of the tree. Lord Reid was willing to tolerate 'a countryman's general knowledge' without subdividing countrymen into those with, or without, a practical concern with the care of the tree in question.

In *Gillen v Fair* 90 ILTR 119 (1955), Lavery J applied the principles expressed in *Caminer,* without any fine parsing of the language in the several speeches. He is reported as saying that he 'did not think that every farmer in the country should employ an expert to examine every tree growing on their lands beside a highway'. Echoing the emphasis placed on location by Lords Radcliffe and Reid, he expressed the view that the standard of care required of a farmer in Co. Mayo having trees growing on his land adjoining a highway might not be as high as that required of an owner of a tree growing beside a highway in a thickly-populated, built-up area.

An English decision subsequent to *Caminer* throws some light on the subject. In *Quinn v Scott* [1965] 2 All ER 588 (QB Div), Glyn-Jones J considered that, by way of qualification of what Lord Normand had to say, there might be circumstances in which it is incumbent on a landowner to call in somebody skilled in forestry to advise him; in the instant case, Glyn-Jones J thought that such a duty arose, since the defendant (the National Trust) owned a belt of hardwood trees bordering a busy main country road which had three traffic lanes. Glyn-Jones J expressed sympathy for the National Trust, which had to be concerned about the amenity value of growing trees; he stressed, however, that the safety of the public had to take precedence over the preservation of the amenities and he could 'not hold that the Trust's duty of care for the countryside diminishes in any degree the duty not to subject users of this highway to unnecessary danger'. Perhaps it may be suggested that the fact that the defendant was a public institution rather than a farmer of limited resources made it easier to impose the duty to secure the advice of one skilled in forestry. The location of the trees was scarcely one of pronounced public danger.

In *Lynch v Hetherton* the plaintiff gave evidence that the tree which fell on his car was rotten inside. Evidence tendered on his behalf fell somewhat short, however, of establishing that this rotten state had been perceptible externally before the accident. The defendant gave evidence that the tree was located on an out-farm, which he passed five days a week. He had tightened a row of wire on a ditch, which was connected to the tree, with staples ten days before the accident at a point two feet above ground level and at that point it was very sound and firm. He had inspected all his trees, though he did not employ an expert to look at them, and had cut down several before the accident.

O'Hanlon J held in favour of the defendant. Having regard to the principles enunciated in *Caminer*, *Gillen v Fair* and *Quinn v Scott*, he considered that the defendant had exercised the degree of care that would have been exercised by a reasonable and prudent landowner in satisfying himself that the tree which fell should not be regarded as a danger to persons using the highway. Even if a higher degree of care were demanded of him, such as arose in the particular circumstances of *Quinn v Scott*, involving the employment of an expert to advise about the condition of the tree, the evidence failed to satisfy O'Hanlon J as a matter of probability that the intended decay would have been detected as a result of that expert examination.

Where does this case leave landowners as regards the discharge of their duty of care in relation to trees adjoining the public highway? The fact that the defendant was held not to have been liable on the facts should not encourage any false sense of security. In the light of *Caminer* and *Quinn v Scott* a landowner whose premises adjoin a highway with any significant traffic flow, even in a rural area, would be well advised to engage on a periodical basis the services of a professional person of experience, such as a practical forester. The test is one of due care, but, in the light of the manifest danger to the public from falling trees, the standard is not to be interpreted in a manner indulgent to the landowner.

Finally it is worth noting that O'Hanlon J sought to carve no distinction between the torts of negligence and nuisance so far as the scope of liability was concerned. (It appears that neither of the parties had suggested that he should). The precise role of negligence is the determination of actions for private nuisance is a matter of ongoing discussion (see Gearty, 'The Place of Private Nuisance in the Modern Law of Torts', 48 *Camb LJ* 214 (1989)). Many will sympathise with Markesinis's observation that 'it would be ridiculous to say that a case will succeed if pleaded in nuisance but fail if it is argued on negligence principles': 'Negligence, Nuisance and Affirmative Duties of Action', 105 *LQ Rev* 104, at 118 (1989). Nevertheless it would as yet be premature to write off private nuisance as a tort separate from negligence in its balancing of competing interests: good neighbourliness is not *quite* the same as discharging one's duty to his Atkinian 'neighbour', wheresoever encountered. Moreover, the tort of *public* nuisance is manifestly not easily reducible to an identity with that of negligence, though again there is a considerable overlap: cf. Spencer, 'Public Nuisance — A Critical Examination', 48 *Camb LJ* 55, at 75-76 (1989).

NEGLIGENT MISSTATEMENT

In *O'Callaghan v Meath Vocational Education Committee, McCormack and the Minister for Education*, High Court, 20 November 1990, Costello J explained why, on the facts of the case, liability for negligent misstatement could not be successfully asserted. We analyse the case in the Labour Law Chapter, above, 365-7.

POLLUTION

In the Chapter on Safety and Health, above, 470-3, we discuss the Local Government (Water Pollution) Amendment Act 1990, s. 20 of which prescribes civil liability for water pollution.

INDUCING A BREACH OF CONTRACT

In *O'Callaghan v Meath Vocational Education Committee, McCormack and the Minister for Education*, *supra*, the plaintiff unsuccessfully sought damages against two of the defendants for inducing a breach of an employment contract. We analyse the case in the Labour Law Chapter, above, 365-7.

CONSPIRACY

In *Taylor v Smith, Kape Investments Ltd, et. al.*, Supreme Court, 5 July 1990, analysed by Kerr, (1990) 12 *DULJ* 166, two important issues relating to the tort of conspiracy arose. The first concerned the question whether there is any legal reason why a company and a person who controls that company should not be capable of being held liable in tort for having conspired with each other to the plaintiff's detriment. We discuss that issue in the Chapter on Company Law, above, 119.

The second issue, which we here consider, concerns the *intent* of the conspirators. This matter has caused some controversy in England in recent years. In *Lonrho Ltd v Shell Petroleum Co. Ltd* [1982] AC 173 the House of Lords radically narrowed the scope of the tort of conspiracy from what had formerly been the common understanding of its remit. It was of the view that conspiracy to injure should still be tolerated as a basis of liability but that conspiracy by unlawful means where there is no intention of injuring the plaintiff's interests should not be actionable. Lord Diplock (for the Court) noted that it had:

> an unfettered choice whether to confine the civil action of conspiracy to the narrow field to which alone it has an established claim or whether to extend this already anomalous tort beyond those narrow limits that are all that common sense and the application of the legal logic of the decided cases require.

> I am against extending the scope of the civil tort of conspiracy beyond acts done in execution of an agreement entered into by two or more persons for the purpose not of protecting their own interests but of injuring the interests of the plaintiff.

Commenting on this passage, McMahon & Binchy, *op. cit.*, 579 observed:

> It remains to be seen whether our courts will take the same view. . . . [A] vital aspect of Irish law, which of course has no counterpart in Britain, is the notion, recognised in *Meskell v CIE* [1973] IR 121, of conspiracy in respect of the infringement of constitutional rights. Our courts will have to determine the precise role of and necessity for, intention to injure in this context rather than embrace uncritically the *Lonrho* restatement of the tort.

In *Taylor*, McCarthy J (Finlay CJ and Hederman J concurring) rejected the *Lonrho* modification in holding that, 'if there be a combination to use unlawful means to achieve a particular aim, that is actionable conspiracy, whether or not such means amount to an infringement of constitutional rights'. He emphasised that it was the very combination itself that strengthened the hands of the wrongdoers. It was 'entirely logical' that what was actionable when done by unlawful means, such as procuring a breach of contract, was actionable against an individual, even though his purpose might be solely one of self interest; it should not cease to be actionable when done in combination by a group with a like purpose.

McCarthy J endorsed the Supreme Court's analysis in *McGowan v Murphy*, 10 April 1967 (extracted in McMahon & Binchy's, *Casebook of the Irish Law of Torts* (1983), 461-5). He went on to observe that,

> [i]f conspiracy be inchoate it is difficult to see how it can have caused damage, a necessary ingredient of every tort. If it be executed, then the cause of action derives from the execution whether it be because of the unlawful nature of the act done or the unlawful means used. Neither of these circumstances, however, would warrant condemning the existence of the tort itself if for no other reason than because of its evidential features.

This latter consideration featured in a critique by John Eekelaar ((1990) 106 *LQ Rev* 223) of Lord Diplock's speech in *Lonrho*. Eekelaar had argued that it 'would be a strange reversal of the common perception that combination strengthens the hands of wrongdoers'; he had gone on to identify the evidential advantage as the major one in framing the action in conspiracy when unlawful means are used.

The Supreme Court's decision in *Taylor* provokes a number of observations. First, it is interesting to contrast its rationale with that which it had adopted in *Dillon v Dunne's Stores (George's Street) Ltd*, 20 December 1968 (extracted in McMahon & Binchy's *Casebook on the Irish Law of Torts* (1983) 460-1). There Ó Dalaigh CJ had quoted, with apparent approval, Denning LJ's objection, in *Ward v Lewis* [1955] 1 WLR 9, at 11, to permitting a plaintiff sue for conspiracy to commit a tort where the defendants are guilty of the substantive tort:

> It is sometimes sought, by charging conspiracy, to get an added advantage, for instance in proceedings for discovery, or by getting in evidence which would not be admissible in a straight action in tort or to overcome substantive rules of law, such as . . . the rules about republication of slander.

What seemed to be a vice in 1968 is regarded as a virtue in 1990.

In this context it is worth recalling that the failure to characterise as tortious conspiracy a consummated conspiracy to commit a tort, breach of contract or breach of trust causing injury to the plaintiff does not prevent the plaintiff from suing the defendants as *concurrent wrongdoers*: cf. the Civil Liability Act 1961, s. 11(2).

An interesting provision, which has tended to be overlooked, is s. 11(6) of the 1961 Act, which provides that, '[f]or the purpose of any enactment referring to a specific tort, an action for a conspiracy to commit that tort shall be deemed to be an action for that tort'. The meaning of this subsection is clear enough in at least certain respects. Thus, for example, provisions in the Statute of Limitations 1957 prescribing specific periods of limitation for specific torts must be construed as including a reference to actions for conspiracy to commit these torts. This is something different, however, from snuffing out actions for conspiracy to commit these torts, save where the tort *is itself a statutory creation*. S. 11(6), far from accomplishing the consummation devoutly wished by Denning LJ, seems more consistent with its antithesis since, if there were a general rule preventing an action for conspiracy with respect to a completed tort, s. 11(6) would be otiose.

We should note here that, in *O'Callaghan v Meath Vocational Education Committee, McCormack and the Minister for Education*, High Court, 20 November 1990, Costello J dismissed a claim for damages for conspiracy. We analyse the case in the Labour Law Chapter, above, 365-7.

PUBLIC AUTHORITIES

1 Planning permission The question of the duty of care in negligence cases has raised difficult issues in relations to the liability of public authorities. The range of functions which these authorities have to discharge is awesome. The manner in which they go about doing so has a large element of what might be called political discretion, involving, as it necessarily must, tough decisions as to the allocation of scarce resources.

In *Sunderland v Louth County Council* [1990] ILRM 658, the defendant county council, pursuant to its power under the Local Government (Planning and Development) Act 1963, granted one McGreavey permission to build a house at a particular location. McGreavey, who had no previous building experience, went ahead without checking on the suitability of the site. He later discovered that planning permission did not apply to the site on which he had built the house and, pursuant to s. 28 of the Act, obtained a permission for its retention. The plaintiffs bought the house from McGreavey, following an inspection but without carrying out a survey. The county council confirmed to the plaintiffs' solicitors 'that in general the conditions of the planning permission granted have been complied with'.

The plaintiffs, in buying the house, 'also bought disaster' (*per* McCarthy J, at 659). Because of the unsuitability of the site and the way the septic tank had been built, the house and garden were constantly in a state of dampness, with periodic flooding. The house was thus uninhabitable.

The plaintiffs obtained judgment against McGreavey who was no mark. Their action against the county council failed before Lardner J ([1987] IR 372) and on appeal to the Supreme Court. The essence of the plaintiffs' case against the county council was that the council breached a duty of care to them, as foreseeable and proximate persons liable to be detrimentally affected by the council's failure properly to exercise in functions in the granting of planning permission. To grant planning permission, the plaintiffs argued, implied that the development would at least not be at variance with the county development plan nor be an environmental or health hazard. The council ought to have refused planning permission on the ground that there was no effective drainage.

On the evidence the council might well have been held in breach of its duty of care to the plaintiffs if such a duty existed. They had carried out no inspection of the constructed house before granting planning permission; there had been no investigation of the site; all that had occurred was an inspection carried out by a planning assistant, who was a geographer or economist. It was conceded by the plaintiffs that the council owed no duty of care to McGreavey. The essence of their case was that the council owed a duty to them *as occupiers*, over and above such duty as it owed to the public as a whole, pursuant to the statutory obligations imposed by the Planning Act.

In rejecting the plaintiffs' argument that the council owed them a duty of care, McCarthy J, delivering the judgment of the Court, developed his analysis as follows:

> In *Siney v Dublin Corporation* [1980] IR 400 a legal relationship of landlord and tenant existed between the parties; in *Ward v McMaster* [1989] ILRM 400; [1988] IR 337], a mortgagor-mortgagee relationship existed. True it is that the damage that was caused to the plaintiffs could be foreseen; but it would require that the council could reasonably foresee that a prospective occupier would not carry out an investigation to learn whether or not the site was suitable for drainage by means of a septic tank; that, equally, future purchasers would not carry out such an inspection. Both *Siney* and *Ward* were cases where the statutory duty of the local authority arose under the Housing Act 1966, an Act which is demonstrably and unequivocally designed towards the protection and improvement of the housing conditions of persons who are not able by their own resources to provide it for themselves. So also a number of the English cases cited ... were cases under the Public Health Act 1937, an Act directed towards the protection of the public health and welfare

or, in *[Governors of] Peabody [Donation Fund v Sir Lindsay Parkinson & Co. Ltd* [1985] AC 210], under the London Government Act 1963 which prohibited the erection of buildings unless drains were constructed to the satisfaction of the council.

McCarthy J went on to state:

The fundamental difference between what may be called planning legislation and housing legislation is that the first is regulatory or licensing according to the requirements of the proper planning and development of the area but the second is a provision in a social context for those who are unable to provide for themselves; if they are unable to provide for themselves then the duty on the provider reaches the role that would be taken by professional advisers engaged on behalf of the beneficiary. This is in marked contrast to the watchdog role that is created under the Planning Act, a watchdog role that is for the benefit of the public at large. This is emphasised by the existence of the appeals procedure, formerly to the relevant minister of the government, assigned by him to a junior minister, and since 1976 carried out by the planning appeals board (An Bord Pleanála). This latter body has a national jurisdiction but must still deal with any planning appeal by the test of local standards — the proper planning and development of the area. It would follow from the plaintiffs' argument that there would be imposed upon the planning appeals board, in the case of an application for retention of a dwelling house constructed without permission, a duty to carry out an examination of the drainage system including the suitability of the soil, presumably irrespective of whether or not the applicant for such permission had done so. Such a duty would lie upon the board as much in the case of a large scale housing development, and, presumably, separately in respect of each house, as it would for a single development such as here. The liability, whether it be of the planning authority or of the planning appeals board, would remain indefinitely towards any occupier.

I point to these consequences, not *in terrorem* but, rather, to seek to identify on a reasonable approach the intention of the legislature in enacting the relevant parts of the Planning Act. That Act was to make provision, in the interest of the common good, for the proper planning and development of cities, towns and other areas, whether urban or rural; the Act permits the making of building regulations, which, if they had existed, might well enure to the benefit of the plaintiffs. There are no such regulations relevant to County Louth.

On the basis of this analysis, McCarthy J concluded that, in conferring statutory powers on planning authorities, the Oireachtas 'did not include a purpose of protecting persons who occupy buildings erected in the functional area of planning authorities from the sort of damage which the plaintiffs . . . suffered'. This being so, the council, in the exercise of those powers, owed no duty of care at common law to the plaintiffs.

The holding is likely to be greeted with approval by most commentators. To have engrafted onto the 1963 Act such as onerous duty of care as the plaintiffs asserted would surely have laid too heavy a burden on local authorities and An Bord Pleanála.

Having said this some points remain for analysis. The first relates to the relationship between statutory interpretation and the duty of care. On the one hand, the courts have the function of interpreting legislation in order to determine whether the Oireachtas has intended to impose a statutory duty enforceable by court action at the suit of a person injured by *breach* of that duty: see McMahon & Binchy, *op. cit.*, 373-95. (In some circumstances, the courts may find that the Oireachtas intended to confer a *statutory right* on a person, enforceable by an action for damages (cf. *Cosgrave v Ireland* [1982] ILRM 48) or, it seems, injunction.) On the other hand, the courts must develop the law of negligence, examining new cases in which a duty of care is asserted by a plaintiff. In determining whether to recognise such a duty of care, the court will often have to pay close attention to statutory provisions which prescribe functions (usually powers) to public bodies such as county councils. It usually is precisely because of the existence of these statutory functions that it has occurred to the plaintiff to assert that a duty of care should be imposed. But the point to note in this context is that the plaintiff seeks the imposition of a duty of care, *not because the Oireachtas intended to impose such a duty*, but because, in the context of the existence of these statutory functions, *the courts should apply the common law tort of negligence* to compensate victims of the careless discharge of these functions. In other words, the courts in negligence actions are not called on merely to engage in an exercise of statutory interpretation as to the intentions of the Oireachtas. Of course, the courts would do well to examine the purpose of the legislation and the intentions of the Oireachtas, but at the end of the day the fact that the Oireachtas did not intend to impose a statutory liability to compensate victims of the negligent exercise of the powers which it prescribed is not of itself a conclusive barrier to the court's imposing a duty of care in negligence in relation to these powers.

Secondly, it is interesting to consider whether the Supreme Court's holding in *Sunderland* gives any ground for believing that the Court is disposed to resile from the position it favoured in *Ward v McMaster, supra*. Such a temptation might seem possible in view of the recent retreat of the

House of Lords from a number of propositions to which it adhered in earlier decisions. In *Murphy v Brentwood DC* [1990] 3 WLR 414 the House of Lords departed from its earlier decision in *Anns v Merton London Borough* [1978] AC 728 and held that a local authority is not liable in negligence for the negligent breach of its statutory duty to ensure that foundation plans are in compliance with its bye-laws, where this results in the plaintiff being faced with the situation that property he has acquired is at risk of causing physical injury or damage and, to prevent this, he will sustain economic loss. This holding applied to local authorities the principle which the House of Lords had accepted in respect of private defendants in *D & F Estates v Church Commissioners for England* [1989] AC 187: see Binchy, 'Defective Building Work: Who Should Pay?', (1989) 83 Incorp L Soc of Ireland *Gazette* 41 (1989), McMahon & Binchy, *op. cit.*, 185-6, 250-54. Lords MacKay, Keith and Jauncey reserved on the more radical question of whether the authority might be under no liability to third persons for consummated, as well as threatened, dangers, and Lord Bridge assumed that liability might attach to the former category only for the purposes of argument. Lord Keith's remarks indicated only tentative support for the imposition of liability in that context. See Duncan Wallace, '*Anns* Beyond Repair', (199) 107 *LQ Rev* 228, at 233.

We suggest that the Supreme Court will hesitate before sounding such a radical retreat. The arguments of principle and policy in favour of imposing liability for negligently bringing about a situation threatening injury unless the plaintiff takes remedial action are very strong. So far as this element of *D. & F.* and *Murphy* is concerned, it would be most unfortunate if the Supreme Court were to take the same course.

As to the proposition that local authorities should not be liable in negligence arising from the careless exercise of their statutory functions, we think it most unlikely that the Supreme Court will give it its benediction. Of course it is wrong to impose too wide-ranging a liability of this type: to do so assists the careless private party who is the primary villain. But so long as the Court is sensitive to the danger of spreading the net of liability too widely, it is surely preferable that there be no *a priori* restriction on the development of the law in this area. Thus far, all the cases involving local authorities which have reached the Supreme Court, save for *Sunderland*, have involved situations where social paternalism suggested imposing liability. It is surely significant that in *Sunderland*, where this dimension was lacking, the Court was willing to exempt the local authority from a duty of care.

2 Ultra vires action In *O'Donnell v Dun Laoghaire Corporation* [1991] ILRM 300, the plaintiffs, a married couple, claimed (*inter alia*) damages in relation to the defendant corporation's *ultra vires* action in disconnecting their water supply. Costello J rejected their claim. While there was no doubt that the plaintiffs had suffered hardship arising from the defendant's actions, there was, in his view, no legal basis for their claim for compensation.

The plaintiffs' claim was not one for damages for breach of satutory duty or breach of a common law duty of care. Following the Supreme Court in *Pine Valley Development Ltd v Minister for the Environment* [1987] ILRM 747 [1987] IR 23, Costello J approved of the summary in Wade's *Administrative Law* (5th ed., 1982) 673 of the circumstances where an *ultra vires* administrative action which is not actionable merely as a breach of duty will found an action for damages:

(1) If it involves the commission of a recognised tort, such as trespass, false imprisonment or negligence.

(2) If it in actuated by malice, eg personal spite or a desire to injure for improper motives.

(3) If the authority making the administrative act knows that is does not possess the power which it purports to excerise.

In the instant case, Dun Laoghaire Corporation had committed no tort when it cut off the plaintiff's water supply; it had not been activated by malice but rather was 'carrying out its difficult responsibility in an impartial and unbiased manner, satisfied that it possened the statutory power to cut off defaulting householders, like the plaintiff[s] who failed to pay the charges which it believed had been validly imposed'.

This approach is in line, not merely with *Pine Valley*, but also the decision of O'Hanlon J in *CW Shipping Co. Ltd v Limerick Harbour Commissioners* [1989] ILRM 416, which we discussed in the 1988 Review, 426-8.

Although the Corporation was, in the circumstances, not guilty of a tort, it may be useful to speculate on the general question of the tortious implications of the cutting off of the supply of utilities to domestic premises. The tort of intentional infliction of emotional suffering (cf. McMahon & Binchy, *op. cit.*, 407-9) may seem somewhat melodramatic, though some American courts have granted a remedy for this type of physical interference.

A more promising candidate is *negligence* in the exercise of statutory functions. It may be that the broad deference given by the courts in this context to policy determination, as opposed to operational default, would result in the non-imposition of liability. Indeed the plaintiffs would find it hard to comply with Lord Wilberforce's statement in *Anns v Merton London Borough Council* [1978] AC 728, at 755 that the burden on those complaining of negligence is to prove that action taken 'was not within the limits of a discretion *bona fide* received before [they] can begin to rely on a common law duty of case'.

It is interesting to note in this context that the English Court of Appeal, in *McCall v Abelesz* [1976] QB 585, held that a landlord whose failure to pay the gas, electricity and water bills for premises in which its tenant resided resulting in the suspension of the supply of these utilities, could not be sued for the putative tort of harassment and that the tenant's remedies lay in trespass, breach of contract and breach of covenant. The requirement in the tort of trespass that there be some element of incursion (cf. McMahon & Binchy, *op. cit.*, 428-36) might render this action ineffective, depending on *where* the supply is cut off.

LIABILITY FOR ANIMALS

In *O'Reilly v Lavelle*, High Court, 1 April 1990, Johnson J was called on to interpret the meaning of s. 2 of the Animals Act 1985, which, it will be recalled, abolished the rule in *Searle v Wallbank* [1947] AC 341, whereby an owner of an animal that strayed onto the highway and caused damage there was not liable for the damage. This old immunity, increasingly anachronistic in times of rapid and widespread motor traffic, had frequently been criticised and narrowly interpreted. Indeed, in *Gillick v O'Reilly* [1984] ILRM 402 at 405 McWilliam J had cast strong doubt on the justice of the rule in modern times:

> It seems to me that, in each age, circumstances arise, different from those of previous ages, which entail that acting or failing to act in the way in which a reasonable man might be expected to act constitutes a breach of duty to others. In determining negligence the circumstances must be considered in each case so that there cannot be any hard and fast rules governing all cases. I am of opinion that this applies equally to consideration of the liability for negligence with regard to animals wandering the public road. An unfenced road running through rough mountain pasture gives rise to different considerations from those arising on a modern main motor road running though fenced farm land and I cannot see any logical reason for a principle which ignores the entirely different circumstances of each when considering the duty owed to users of the road.

The Law Reform Commission, in their *Report on Civil Liability for Animals* (LRC 2-1982), had recommended that this immunity be swept away, and s. 2 of the 1985 Act does this as follows:

> (1) So much of the rules of the common law relating to liability for negligence as excludes or restricts the duty which a person might owe to others to take such care as is reasonable to see that damage is not caused by animals straying on to a public road is hereby abolished.

(2) (a) Where damage is caused by an animal straying from unfenced land on to a public road, a person who placed the animal on the land shall not be regarded as having committed a breach of the duty to take care by reason only of placing it there if—

(i) the land is situated in an area where fencing is not customary, and
(ii) he had a right to place the animal on that land.

(b) In this subsection 'fencing' includes the construction of any obstacle designed to prevent animals from straying, and 'unfenced' shall be construed accordingly.

In *O'Reilly v Lavelle*, the plaintiff, driving his motor vehicle after dark at 50 mph, with full headlights on, at about 10pm a couple of days after midsummer's night in County Monaghan, collided with a friesian calf. The calf died and the plaintiff's vehicle was severely damaged. The plaintiff gave evidence that the calf had been one of eight to ten cattle that suddenly darted across the highway into his path. After the accident, the other animals had disappeared up a laneway dividing the defendant's lands. The defendant's son, who arrived on the scene twenty minutes later, identified the calf as theirs. When the Garda arrived, the defendant, who had by now also come to the scene, showed one of them his field on one side of the highway which contained his cattle. Examination of the gate and fencing facing the highway showed that they were not defective in any way. The Garda did not, however, examine the fencing on the laneway.

A motorist who had travelled the road an hour before the accident testified that he had observed animals grazing on the side of the highway at the spot where the accident later occurred.

At the end of the plaintiff's case, counsel for the defendant sought a direction on the ground that no negligence had been established against the defendant. There was, he said, no evidence that the defendant had failed to take reasonable care; the evidence on behalf of the plaintiff had been that the defendant's gate and fencing facing the roadway were sound. *Res ipsa loquitur* did not apply as it was possible that some stranger could have left the gate on the defendant's field open. Johnson J, impressed by a decision on this issue by District Justice Brennan, *McCaffrey v Lundy* (1988) 6 *ILT* 245, agreed with the holding of the District Justice that s. 2 created a *res ipsa loquitur* presumption. Johnson J said:

Cattle properly managed should not wander on the road and therefore the burden of proof in this case shifts to the defendant to show that he took reasonable care of his animals. I believe that there is no matter more appropriate for the application of the doctrine of *res ipsa loquitur* than cattle wandering on the highway.

The defendant then gave evidence that he had passed the accident spot just before the accident and there were no cattle on the roadway and that all his cattle were then in his field. He had examined his gates and fences and they were in sound condition. He could give no explanation as to how his animals escaped from and returned to his field and he believed that it was only the calf who met with the accident that had escaped. The defendant's son 'corroborated his father's evidence'. A neighbour testified that his lands adjoined the defendant's and that in ten years the defendant's cattle had never broken into his land; nor had he ever known of their being on the road in that period.

Johnson J accepted the accuracy of the plaintiff's evidence. He held that the defendant had failed to discharge the onus of proof that the fencing in his field was not defective in that his cattle had escaped from and returned to it on the occasion in question. It was highly impossible that some stranger had opened the gate of the field, remained there until the animals at their leisure returned, and then closed it. Accordingly he awarded damages to the plaintiff.

The case is of course of general interest, not only to the legal profession but also to the farming community. The holding seems eminently reasonable on the facts. Nevertheless some issues of general principle need to be addressed.

First, it may be asked, as a *matter of statutory interpretation* whether s. 2 introduced a statutory shift of the onus of proof onto the defendant. Certainly it did not do so expressly. What the section does is to remove an immunity from the duty of care in respect of damage caused by animals straying on to a public road. It lays down no specific content for the duty of care: that is a function of the courts. It clearly has nothing to say on the questions of either the mode or onus of proof. But in letting the courts address the issue of liability, the Oireachtas has thereby enabled them to handle the related matter of *res ipsa loquitur* in such a manner as they wish. In other words s. 2 neither requires nor prevents the court from applying the *res ipsa loquitur* doctrine in respect of some or all of the cases covered by s. 2. It may well be that a court, confronting for the first time the damage caused by straying animals, may consider this type of case to be enimently suitable for the application of the *res ipsa loquitur* doctrine: thus Johnson J was perfectly entitled to take the view that 'there is no matter more appropriate for the application of the doctrine . . . than cattle wandering on the highway'. The point to note is that this approach is facilitated rather than required by s. 2, and that the matter is one to be determined in accordance with common law rather than statutory principles.

The next question worth considering is whether it would be appropriate to shift the onus onto the defendant in every case where a plaintiff sues for negligence in respect of damage caused by straying cattle. The answer depends on the degree of contextual reference afforded to the element of the *res ipsa loquitur* doctrine which requires that 'the accident [be] such as in the ordinary circumstances does not happen if those who have the management use proper care'. If the court takes what might be called a specific or contextualised approach, the application or non-application of the doctrine would not be an all-or-nothing issue; in some cases the doctrine might be applied, in others not.

What kind of distinction could a court make on the basis of a contextualised approach? Perhaps the easiest would be to treat differently cases where animals stray near urban areas with a high motor traffic density, on the one hand, and cases where they stray at the top of a mountain miles away from any centre of population, with little traffic flow, on the other. S. 2, after all, merely removes the owner's immunity from the duty to exercise due care. He does not thereby fall under any duty to fence his lands, as opposed to taking such care as is reasonable to see that damage is not caused by animal straying on to a public road. A man living in a remote area who lets his cattle stray is not necessarily guilty of negligence in doing so. All will depend on how the court, *in the particular circumstances* of the case, weighs the elements of the likelihood (or unlikelihood) of damage, the extent of possible damage if it occurs, the social utility of the defendant's act and the cost of prevention. It should be noted in this context that a court is perfectly free to hold that a defendant whose cattle strayed exercised due care even in a case which does not fall within the terms of s. 2(2)(a). If context is vital and thus an owner is not necessarily guilty of lack of due care by virtue of the fact that he permitted his cattle to stray, then it would seem quite wrong that the owner up the mountain, for example, should find himself subjected to the weight of a *res ipsa loquitur* burden to prove that he was not negligent. A contextual rather than universalist approach to *res ipsa loquitur* seems far preferable in negligence actions arising from damage caused by straying cattle.

MALICIOUS PROSECUTION

In *McIntyre v Lewis, Dolan, Ireland and the Attorney-General*, Supreme Court, 17 December 1990, the plaintiff had been awarded £5,000 by a High Court jury for assault and false imprisonment and over £60,000 for malicious prosecution. He had been attacked by members of the Garda Síochána and charged with assaulting his attackers. He had been sent forward to the Circuit

Court for trial where a jury had acquitted him. On appeal a number of the defendants had contended that, in an action for malicious prosecution, the plaintiff must establish an absence of reasonable and probable cause for bringing the prosecution.

The Supreme Court did not demur from this proposition but nonetheless held that the disposition of the malicious prosecution issue at trial had been satisfactory. The trial judge's direction to the jury had been correct in stating that the onus rested on the plaintiff to show that the prosecution had been brought against him without reasonable cause. Once the jury had accepted that the plaintiff had been the victim rather than the offender in respect of the assault, it could not, on the evidence, have brought in a verdict for the defendants on either the issue of malicious prosecution or false imprisonment; to have done so would have rendered its verdicts inconsistent. Hedermen J observed that:

> [w]hile there may be cases where the trial judge should decide the issue of 'reasonable and probable cause', this in not one of them. There may be cases where, as the authors of McMahon and Binchy, *Irish Law of Torts* (2nd edition), p. 678 point out, '. . . the plaintiff has the somewhat daunting task of proving a negative'. No such problem arises in this case. There was a single, solitary, stark fact to be determined: who had committed the assault. Those with the obligation to determine the facts in this case were the jury and once they had made a finding that the assault had been committed by the Gardai and not the reverse then everything else inevitably followed.

McCarthy J's concurrence was based on the 'overwhelming case of the absence of reasonable and probable cause', once the jury accepted that the defendants had been the aggressors in the assault. He made no reference to the role of the judge in the determination of this issue.

The Supreme Court's gloss on the rule that the judge rather than the jury is to determine whether there was reasonable and probable cause may be compared with the approach favoured in *Cruise v Burke* [1919] 2 IR 182, where Kenny J observed (at 188) that '[i]t is for the Judge at trial, and not for the jury, to decide as to the existence of reasonable and probable cause, after he has taken the opinion of the jury on such controversial matters of fact as he deems necessary'. In England, if the plaintiff gives evidence of facts permitting the inference that the defendants *did not in fact* believe in the plaintiff's guilt, that issue must be left to the jury. *Street on Torts* (8th ed, by M. Brazier, 1988) 436-7, explains that:

> [t]his question to the jury must be formulated precisely and should not

refer to reasonable cause. It should be either: 'Did the defendant honestly believe in the plaintiff's guilty', or 'Did he honestly believe in the charges he was preferring?' It must not be: 'Did he honestly believe that there were reasonable grounds for the prosecution?' For that would cause the jury to pass on the whole issue of reasonable and probable cause [citing *Tempert v Snowden* [1952] 1 KB 130].

In *McIntyre*, the trial judge's direction to the jury had stated that the onus lay on the plaintiff to show that the Gardai had abused their position and 'brought a prosecution against [the plaintiff] for a completely wrongful motive and in the circumstances *in which there was no reasonable cause to bring it at all'*. (Emphasis added).

In England, *after Glinski v McIver* [1962] AC 726, if the plaintiff does not give evidence permitting the inference that the defendant did not believe in the plaintiff's guilt, sufficient to be left to the jury, he must show that a person 'of ordinary prudence and caution would not conclude, in the light of the facts in which he honestly believed, that the plaintiff was probably guilty': *Street*, 437. *Street* goes on to record (*id.*) that:

[i]t is for the judge and not the jury to determine whether a man of ordinary prudence would have so concluded. It is for the judge alone to determine whether there was reasonable and probable cause. The trouble experienced in splitting the functions of judge and jury in consequence of this rule accounts for most of the complexities of this tort. There is the ever-present danger that the questions addressed to the jury will be so general that the ultimate question left to the judge of reasonable cause is instead improperly decided by the jury. In conducting the trial the judge had two alternatives: he may direct the jury that, if they find certain facts, or arrive at certain answers to specific questions which he puts to them, there is reasonable and probable cause, leaving it to the jury to find a general verdict on this hypothetical direction; his alternative — and this is the better course — is to direct the jury to settle the facts in dispute, whereupon he decides, upon the whole case, whether there is reasonable and probable cause'. (Citations omitted.)

What the Supreme Court in *McIntyre* appears to have endorsed, in effect, is the bifurcated approach favoured in *Glinski v McIver*.

VICARIOUS LIABILITY

1 Cowardly employees In *Reilly v Ryan* [1991] ILRM 449 (Circuit Appeal, 1990), Blayney J was faced with a troublesome issue relating to vicarious liability. The plaintiff, who had gone into the defendant's city-centre public house to talk to the manager, was standing close to the bar, in the company of around thirty to thirty five people, when a man wearing a balaclava came in with a knife in his hand and shouted to the manager: 'Give me £40 out of the till'. The manager grabbed the plaintiff by the shoulders and pulled him over in front of him, using him as a shield. The plaintiff tried to get out of his grip. While in this position the plaintiff was stabbed in the right arm by the intruder. The manager then got a snooker cue as a weapon; when he saw this, the intruder ran out of the bar, dropping his knife as he went. The plaintiff sued the defendant; the precise basis of the claim is not mentioned in the judgment save for the element of vicarious liability, but it may be presumed to have sounded in negligence and battery (at a minimum).

The defendant in evidence said that the manager, who had held the position for the previous fourteen years, had instructions to look after the customers' needs and safety. He had not authorised the manager to do what he had done on the occasion in question.

The central issue in the case was whether, in behaving as he had done, the manager was acting in the course of his employment. In approaching that issue, Blayney J stated that his conclusion on the evidence was that the manager had been 'thinking more of his own safety than of his master's property' when he grabbed the plaintiff and used him as a shield. 'He was protecting himself from the intruder's knife rather than protecting the cash in the till. He may also have had this in mind but it seems probably that his own safety was upper-most'.

Blayney J accepted as correct the statements of law in *Winfield on Tort*, 568, 570, 574 (13th ed.) and *Salmond on Torts*, 89 (10th ed) (and p. 437 of the 18th ed by Professor Heuston & Mr Chambers); in *Poland v John Parr & Sons* [1927] 1 KB 240, the English Court of Appeal had endorsed the following passage from p. 89 of the 10th edition of *Salmond*:

> A master is not responsible for a wrongful act done by his servant unless it is done in the course of his employment. It is deemed to be so done if it is either (a) a wrongful act authorised by the master; or (b) a wrongful and unauthorised mode of doing some act authorised by the master.

In that case a carter in the employment of the defendants had struck a boy whom he thought, reasonably and honestly, to be stealing sugar from a bag on the wagon. The carter's employers were held vicariously liable for the boy's injury as the carter had had implied authority to make reasonable efforts to protect and preserve his employers' property. Atkin LJ had posed the question as being 'whether the act is one of the class of acts which the servant is authorised to do in an emergency'. The carter's mode of doing what he was authorised was not such as to take it out of this class.

In the light of these statements of law, Blayney J considered that a crucial issue was whether the manager had exceeded what was required by the emergency and if so whether that excuse was such as to take his action outside the class of acts impliedly authorised. Blayney J was willing to accept that the manager's conduct had been impliedly authorised, whether it was directed to protecting his employer's property or defending himself:

> *Poland v John Parr* is clear authority to protect his master's property and I consider that, where an employee, who is in charge of his master's premises in the course of his employment, is attacked by an intruder intent upon stealing his master's property, it would be unreasonable to hold that he did not also have implied authority to defend himself. To hold otherwise would involve deciding that he was acting in two separate capacities in warding off the attack — acting as the defendant's servant in protecting the latter's property but acting in his personal capacity in defending himself, and to make such a distinction would in my opinion be unreal.

Blayney J concluded, however, that what the manager did exceeded what was required by the emergency:

> There were two options open to him, to accede to the intruder's demand and give him the £40 or to resist. He chose the latter. But the means he employed went well beyond what was reasonable. One could have imagined him picking up some makeshift implement in order to resist the intruder (such as the snooker cue with which he did arm himself after the plaintiff had been stabbed) and if in the course of using it he had, by accident, injured one of the customers, the latter would have a good cause of action against the defendant. What [the manager] did was very different. He choose to interpose a human barrier between himself and the intruder. His involved a physical assault on the plaintiff and putting him in a position of great danger. It was a wholly unreasonable and excessive means of dealing with the emergency.

> Was it so excessive as to take it out of the class of acts which are impliedly authorised? In my opinion it was. What he did has to be looked

at in the context of his duties as the defendant's manager. His principal duty was to serve the defendant's customers. But, instead of looking after the plaintiff's safety, as was his duty, [the manager] was the cause of his being injured. His reaction was accordingly excessive in the sense that what he did went wholly outside what he was employed to do being in fact the precise opposite of what his duty was at the time. Instead of trying to protect the plaintiff, he assaulted him and was the cause of his being injured. In my opinion it could not be said that such behaviour was impliedly authorised by the defendant.

Accordingly, Blayney J held that the plaintiff's action against the owner of the public house should fail.

The result seems intuitively wrong. It may be useful to try to examine the relevant legal principles and policies in order to find why this should be so. By way of introduction it may be asked why a cowardly (probably instinctive) response of an employee to an emergency arising during his employment should be considered to fall outside the scope of his employment. Blayney J perceived the manager's motivation to protect his own skin as placing his acts outside the course of his employment; but that would have the effect of denying to the victims of employees whose negligence consists of cowardice the benefits of the vicarious liability doctrine.

The situation arising in this case straddles the barrier between negligent and intentional acts. In the New Zealand case of *Auckland Workingmen's Club and Mechanics Institute v Rennie* [1976] 1 NZLR 278, at 282, Mahon J quoted the passage from *Salmond* which found favour with Blayney and went on to observe that:

[W]here an employer is alleged to be vicariously liable for an act of negligence it is sufficient to apply the broader test as to whether the servant was acting in the course of his employment. But where an employer is claimed to be vicariously liable for an intentional tort committed by his servant the plaintiff faces a more difficult task. I suppose it might be said, broadly speaking, that there is a logical difficulty in comprehending a unified liability shared by a blameless employer and a servant who has done an intentional wrong. For this reason the cases in respect of intentional torts seem to have required proof, where vicarious liability is sought to be established, not merely that the servant was acting within the course of his employment but also that he had real or ostensible authority from his employer to commit the deliberate act which constitutes the gist of the plaintiff's cause of action. In other words, the scope of vicarious liability on the part of the employer seems to have been narrowed in those reported cases where an intentional tort has been committed by placing greater emphasis on the first division of the concept of course of employment which I have quoted from *Salmond.*

There have been several cases (many concerned with acts of aggression by bar employees) where the courts have had to determine whether the violent act generated vicarious liability: see, e.g., *Pettersson v Royal Oak Hotel Ltd* [1948] NZLR 136, *Deatons Pty Ltd v Flew*, 79 Comm LR 370 (1949), *Rutherford v Hawke's Bay Hospital Board* [1949] NZLR 400, *Griggs v Southside Hotel Ltd* [1947] 4 DLR 49, *Bigcharles v Merkel* (1972) 32 DLR (3d) 511, *Lakatosh v Ross* (1974) 48 DLR (3d) 694, *Keppel Bus Co. Ltd v Ahmad* [1974] 2 All ER 700, *Q v Minto Management Ltd* (1985) 15 DLR (4th) 581, affirmed (1986) 34 DLR (4th) 767, and *Auckland Workingmen's Club v Rennie, supra* (critically analysed by Rose (1976) 39 *Modern L Rev* 720). For general discussion see Rose, 'Liability for an Employee's Assaults' (1977) 40 *Modern L Rev* 420.

In *Reilly v Ryan*, the employee's instinctive action, if capable of being characterised as intentional (cf. *Larin v Goshen* (1974) 56 DLR (3d) 719), surely bore no relation to cases where the employee, for reasons of anger, retribution or the desire to dominate, engaged in violent conduct. The situation was surely akin to that of the 'agony of the moment' in negligence (cf McMahon & Binchy, *op. cit.*, 355-7).

There are echoes in Blayney J's analysis of an approach which formerly held sway, to the effect the notion of implied authority should not extend to the commission of an illegal act: cf *Barry v Dublin United Tramways Co.*, (1890) 26 LR Ir 150, *Kinsella v Hamilton* (1890) 26 LR Ir 671, *M'Namara v Brown* [1918] 2 IR 215. This approach no longer commands general support: see *Bigcharles v Merkel, supra.*

Let us take the analysis a stage further and enquire whether an act of self-defence by an employee in a raid on his employer's premises falls within the scope of his employment. In *Kinsella v Hamilton*, 26 LR Ir at 689, Palles CB appeared to think not, but it is interesting to note that in *M'Namara v Brown*, [1918] 2 IR, at 224, Campbell CJ confessed that he was 'not altogether convinced by this reasoning'. We suggest that the Chief Justice's doubts were well-based and that an excessive non-retributive act of self-defence against an assailant or one who threatens an attack should fall within the scope of vicarious liability. If this is so, it is not difficult to accept that a cowardly act of self defence, involving an innocent victim, should also be capable of falling within the net.

2 *Partners   Allied Pharmaceutical Distributors Ltd and All-Phar Services Ltd v Walsh et. al.*, High Court, 14 December 1990 is of interest in that it involved the imposition of liability on partners for the breach of duty of care of one of them towards the plaintiff company where the conduct in which the partner engaged was not such as would necessarily have bound the partnership on general *Hedley Byrne* principles. The complicated and un-usual fact situation may be summarised briefly. The defendant accountancy partnership did work (including auditing) for the plaintiff company. One of the partners acted as a personal executive for the plaintiff company, taking crucial decisions as to its financial investments. Over the years, he invested some of the plaintiff company's money in his family company which eventually became insolvent, resulting in loss to the plaintiff company.

The relationship between this family company and the partnership was described by Barron J as 'a somewhat unusual one'. The partnership provided a secretary for the company; all its books were kept in the financial executive's office in the partnership offices. Other partners had for a time been the company's Secretary and a director and at that time several members of the partnership had borrowed small loans from it. Its accounts were audited for a period by employees of the partnership and its tax affairs were dealt with by the tax division of the partnership.

The partners unsuccessfully argued that, since their ordinary business did not include giving investment advice, they should thus not be liable for the financial executive's advice and actions in that regard. Barron J considered that this was not the true issue; that was whether in doing what he had done the financial executive was carrying out the ordinary business of the part-nership. It was 'clearly' the ordinary business of the partnership to allow one of its number to be a director and even chairman of a board of directors of a client company. It was its ordinary business to allow a partner in that position to take deposits from client companies for his own private company. It was moreover its ordinary business that, in those positions, the partner should make decisions in regard to how client companies should apply their monies. In these circumstances what the financial executive had done *was* within the ordinary business of the partnership.

It was, however, essential that there should have been a representation by the partnership to the plaintiff that such conduct had its approval. This could be done by conduct, which was the normal way in which an ostensible authority was established. Since the partnership had acted as auditor of the plaintiff and thus was aware of the transactions with the investment company, its failure to suggest that there was anything unusual or improper in making the deposits amounted to a sufficient representation by conduct that the financial executive had their authority to direct the making of these deposits. Barron J considered that:

the position is stronger [than a case of principal and agent] when the alleged agency arises between partners. The basis of partnership is mutual trust between the partners. When one partner is put into a position of trust with a client in my view that alone is a representation that the partnership trusts that partner and will stand over whatever he does.

Barron J rejected the defendants' claim that the plaintiff had been guilty of contributory negligence. There was no evidence to suggest that it knew or ought to have known of the financial state of the investment company.

The effect of the decision was that the partnership was liable, in the unusual circumstances of the case, when it would not normally have been liable under ordinary *Hedley Byrne* principles: cf. McMahon & Binchy, *op. cit.*, 157-58.

3 Agency In *Irish Permanent Building Society v O'Sullivan* [1990] ILRM 598 (Circuit Appeal, Blayney J, 1989, *ex tempore*), the manager of the plaintiff building society in a country town also carried on an auctioneering business from the same office, with the knowledge of the building society. The defendants, who 'did not know much about the situation regarding buying houses', explained to the manager that they wanted to buy a house and that they needed a loan. He advised them to open a savings account with the plaintiff society. Some time later, when they had saved some money with the society, the manager told the defendants that they qualified for a loan. He told them that he was selling a house on behalf of a named client. The defendants, who 'saw him only as the manager of the building society', looked at the house, which was at least 100 years old. The manager informed them that the house was in good condition and needed only wallpapering and painting. Relying on this statement, the defendants bought the house for £18,100, with a loan of £17,100.

When the plaintiffs started to decorate the house, the mortar came away with the old paper. It transpired that the house, though structurally ground, needed some repair. The plaintiffs later fell behind with their mortgage payments. The plaintiff sought recovery of possession and the defendants counterclaimed for damages for (*inter alia*) negligence. Judge O'Higgins granted the plaintiff possession but awarded the defendants £10,973. On appeal to the High Court, Blayney J disallowed the plaintiff's appeal and varied the award to a decree of £12,991 for the defendants with liberty to execute for £8,473 (the reduced sum taking into account the amount of the arrears on the loan).

Blayney J considered that because the plaintiff building society had allowed their manager to operate in a dual role, they ought to have anticipated that members of the public might conclude that [he] was their agent in selling houses and might suffer loss through acting on that belief. They were under a duty therefore to ensure that it was made clear to members of the public that, in selling houses, [he] was not acting as a principal. The plaintiff building society failed to discharge this duty and the defendant suffered damage as a result. It was because of their belief that [the manager] was the agent of the plaintiff building society that they relied on his representations about the house. The plaintiff building society is accordingly liable in damages to the defendants'.

This analysis is interesting. It establishes liability in negligence in the part of the building society by a very direct route rather than relying on the more traditional concepts of ostensible authority (cf. *Allied Irish Banks v Murnane*, High Court, 21 December 1988, noted in the 1988 Review, 425-6) and vicarious liability. If the defendants, believing the manager was speaking in his capacity as manager, would in fact have relied on his representations about the house regardless of whether they had been made in the capacity of auctioneer or of manager, should not the building society also be held liable for what he said, not necessarily because of a breach by the building society of a duty of care to the defendants but on the basis of the manager's ostensible authority?

One may also wonder whether in *all* cases the prior clarification by the building society that their manager was acting, not as their agent, but as a principal in an auctioneering business of his own, would immunise the society from liability in negligence. The confusion of roles might in some instances be regarded as so intertwined as to leave a purchaser with the impression that, while in the particular transaction the manager was acting under a different hat, the society blessed the practice of changing hats and thus impliedly endorsed the accuracy and reliability of what the manager might have to say when wearing his auctioneer's hat.

FATAL INJURIES

1 Relationship with survival of actions In *Mahon v Burke and Mid-Western Health Board* [1991] ILRM 59 the deceased had been a patient of both defendants who had sued them for negligence in diagnosis and treatment. The action had been settled by a compromise in 1985 for £123,000 and costs. Shortly afterwards the deceased had died. In the instant case, the plaintiff, the deceased's widow, brought fatal injuries proceedings under s. 48 of the Civil Liability Act 1961 on behalf of the dependants as well as proceedings on behalf of the deceased's estate under s. 7 of that Act.

In the Circuit Court Judge Gleeson held that the plaintiff could recover funeral expenses under s. 49(2). On appeal by the parties Lavan J held that the defendants should succeed.

Counsel for the plaintiff argued that, to succeed under s48, the plaintiff did not have to prove that there was vested in the deceased a cause of action before his death. He sought to defend Judge Gleeson's view that s. 49(2) enabled the plaintiff to maintain an action for funeral expenses in spite of the compromise.

Lavan J noted that at common law an action in tort did not survive the death of tortfeasor or victim. The effect of Part II of the 1961 Act was that a cause of action for personal injuries, *vested in the deceased before his death*, survived his death for the benefit of his estate. Where the deceased's death was occasioned by a tort, there was vested in him before his death, and, where the death was instantaneous, immediately before his death, a cause of action against the tortfeasor which likewise survived for the benefit of the deceased's estate.

English judicial authorities were to the effect that the settlement or suing to judgment by the victim of a personal injuries action precluded the victim's dependants from bringing a fatal injuries claim on his death. Lavan J agreed with this approach.

Nor could Lavan J interpret s. 49(2) in the manner that Judge Gleeson had done. The language of s. 49(1) was clear in providing the machinery for determining the heads of damages to which dependants, properly entitled to sue by reason of s. 48, were to be compensated. S. 49(2) should be similarly interpreted. To hold otherwise would subject a defendant to two actions arising from one cause of action.

The decision raises interesting issues of principle and policy, which have troubled courts in other jurisdictions. In the United States, the majority approach is in harmony with that favoured by Lavan J and the English courts. The fear of permitting double recovery has encouraged this view. See *Prosser & Keeton on Torts* (5th ed, 1984) 955-957. The minority approach is conscious of the danger of double recovery and seeks to deal with it either by deducting from the award to the dependants the amount paid to the decedent for the permanent destruction of his earning capacity or by taking the possibility of the survivors claim into account when assessing the decedents damages. There is, of course, a strong element of speculation and uncertainty in the latter approach but some may think it preferable to an inflexible exclusion, especially in cases where the deceased made a compromise based on false hopes as to the chances of his survival or did so in callous disregard of the interests of his family. It is interesting in this context to note that Dr John White favours the minority approach: see *Irish Law of Damages for Personal Injuries and Death* (1989), vol 1, para 8.3.06.

2 *Effect of remarriage on quantum of compensation* Later in this chapter (below, 268-74), under the heading of Damages, we discuss two decisions which dealt with the question of the effect of actual or possible remarriage of a surviving spouse on the quantum of compensation. The decisions are *Fitzsimons v Bord Telecom Éireann and ESB* [1991] ILRM 276 and *Cooper v Egan*, High Court, 20 December 1990.

DAMAGES

1 General damages In *Connolly v Dundalk UDC* [1990] 2 IR 1 the plaintiff, a married man aged 6, suffered devasting psychiatric injuries resulting from inhaling a dense cloud of chlorine gas at the defendant's waterworks, where he was employed. O'Hanlon J was satisfied that the plaintiff's personality and life-style had been profoundly depressed, aggressive and unpleasant to live with; he was quite unfit to undertake any type of painful employment, even in a sheltered workshop, or to enjoy any form of recreation; his marital relations had ceased. In short, he was 'condemned to a miserable, stagnant existence, where he mopes round the home, in a state of total dependence on his wife for all his needs'.

Having awarded the plaintiff over £100,000 for loss of earnings, O'Hanlon J went on to consider general damages. He observed the disastrous effect the accident would in all probability have on the plaintiffs for the rest of his life. He also had regard to two factors:

> one, the award of a very large sum for loss of earnings, totalling £104,127.77, and the other, my belief based on the evidence I have heard, and from seeing and listening to the plaintiff, that no award of damages, however large, is likely to enhance his enjoyment of life or bring him much in the way of comfort or consolation.

O'Hanlon J awarded in all the sum of £175,000 for general damages.

This approach, so far as the first factor is concerned, echoes that favoured by Costello J in *Burke v Blanch*, High Court, 28 July 1989. In the 1989 Review, 435-6, we expressed doubts as to its merits from the standpoint of principle. It appears to distinguish between victims of identical devastating injuries, on the basis of their respective economic positions. The compensation which a victim receives for loss of earnings may be large or small, depending on his particular loss. If his loss is large, the victim should be no happier in having that loss alleviated than would a victim with a small loss of earnings on being compensated for that loss. The fact that a large sum is awarded may give the illusion that the victim should in some sense be more satisfied but this ignores the relationship between compensation and loss.

As to the second factor, the plaintiff seems to have received less than he would have if the award would have enhanced his enjoyment or brought him much comfort or consolation. This approach raises a somewhat different and important issue of principle: what is the basis for the award of general damages? On one approach, the function of general damages is objective — to compensate the plaintiff for losses to his *human capacities*. Thus, in the Supreme Court decision of *Arnott v O'Keeffe* [1977] IR 1, at 15, Walsh J could observe that:

> [s]o far as the subject of general damages . . . is concerned, it should be viewed as a form of capital compensation for injury to a capital asset, namely, the bodily integrity of the plaintiff which has been permanently damaged and which, too that extent, represents a capital loss of the assets which he brought to his life.

On this approach, an award of damages is to reflect the damage that has been done to the plaintiff's capacities, regardless of whether the award will be successful in making him happy. The objective damage is the measure of the loss, not simply the plaintiff's putative reaction to a particular amount of compensation.

Under another approach, the award of general damages should seek to reflect the *loss of happiness* which the plaintiff has suffered, by comparing the degree of happiness he would have enjoyed if the accident had not occurred with the degree of unhappiness he has experienced and is likely to experience as a result of the injury. Whether there is any way of converting this felicific calculus into a real, rather than metaphorical, measure may be debated.

Under the third approach, the concentration is on *solace*. As Dickson J explained in *Andrew v Grand & Troy Alberta Ltd*, 83 LRD (3d) 452, at 476 (Supreme Court, Canada, 1979):

> rather than attempting to set a value on lost happiness, [the functional approach] attempts to assess the compensation required to provide the person 'with reasonable solace for his misfortune'. 'Solace' in this sense is taken to mean physical arrangements which can make his life more endurable than 'solace' in the sense of sympathy.

In the High Court of Australia case of *Skelton v Collins*, 115 CLR 94, at 131 (1965), Windeyer J made this philosophy clear:

> I do not for a moment doubt that a man who has deprived of the

opportunity to live his life as he would have wished, and for as long as he might have expected, may, if he retains sufficient intellectual capacity to know his misfortune, feel distressed and frustrated. He is, I do not doubt, entitled to compensation for what he suffers. Money may be a compensation for him if having it can give him pleasure or satisfaction. If his expected years of life have been made less, money may enable him to cram more into the time that remains. If he has been deprived of the ability to do some things that he had enjoyed doing or had hoped to do, then money may enable him to enjoy other things instead. But the money is not then a recompense for a loss of something having a money value. It is given as some consolation or solace for the distress that is the consequence of a loss on which no monetary value can be put.

While the solace-oriented approach has met with the support of the Supreme Court of Canada it had not yet proved victorious in either Australia (Windeyer J who in a minority of one in *Skelton v Collins)* or in England: see *Lim Poh Choo v Camden and Islington Area Health Authority* [1980] AC 174, the English Law Commission in their *Report on Personal Injury Litigation: Assessment of Damages* para 31 (Eng. Law Com No. 56, 1973) reiterated the view they had expressed in their Working Paper No. 41 (1971) on the subject, to the effect that the solace-orientated approach should be rejected. In para 91 of that Working Paper they had observed that:

> *Prima facie* it might seem unworkable to make an award turn on whether the plaintiff can use it. It would be necessary to distinguish between money which *will not* be used by the plaintiff (e.g. money awarded to a very rich man) and money which *cannot* be used for the plaintiff's benefit; there are also considerable difficulties in defining what is meant by 'use'. Is money used if it is bequeathed by will? Some might feel amply compensated by being able to leave money to their children or give it directly during their lifetime. It is possible to draw a line between disposing of money by one's will or allowing it to pass under an intestacy; and does it make any difference if the plaintiff is in no condition to appreciate that his money is passing to relatives, or to the Treasury? . . .

The Pearson Commission did not agree. It considered that non-pecuniary damages should be awarded 'only where they can serve some useful purpose, e.g., by providing the plaintiff with an alternative source of satisfaction to replace one that he has lost': *Royal Commission on Civil Liability and Compensation for Personal Injury*, vol 1, para 398 (1978).

Irish courts have yet to confront these competing philosophies directly. It is fair to say, however, that the effect of a number of decisions over the past decade is to forward the goal of solace. Thus in *Sinnott v Quinnsworth Ltd* [1984] ILRM 523, O'Higgins CJ referred to 'the things on which the plaintiff might reasonably be expected to spend money' as a factor to be taken into account in determining compensation. Moreover, in *Cooke v Walsh (No. 2)* [1984] ILRM 208 at 218, Griffin J, for the majority, held that 'compensation should be moderate' where the plaintiff was badly injured that he had only a mild awareness of his condition on account of brain damage. McCarthy J prepared to reserve on this question, since the matter had not been fully debated on the hearing of the appeal. There is much to be said for his caution. The issue goes to the heart of the philosophy of compensation in tort law and should be resolved only after deep and considered analysis.

2 Effect of remarriage on quantum of compensation   Two decisions in 1990 dealt with the troublesome question of the effect of remarriage on compensation under the fatal injuries code. One was concerned with the remarriage of a widow, the other of a widower. Interesting issues arise as to the extent to which the same principles should apply to both cases.

In *Fitzsimons v Bord Telecom Éireann and ESB* [1991] ILRM 276, the deceased, whose death in 1979 was caused by the defendants' negligence, left a widow aged 34 and five children whose ages ranged from two to eleven. The widow remarried in 1985 and had another child. No evidence was adduced in the case in relation to damages: the parties sought judicial guidance on the question whether the benefits arising from the widow's remarriage should be taken into account in assessing damages and, if so, on what basis.

The nearest Irish authority to the issue is the Supreme Court case of *Byrne v Houlihan* [1966] IR 274. There, the deceased's substantial estate passed to her husband on her death intestate. Their children claimed compensation for the loss of the reasonable expectation of sharing in the income of her estate during her lifetime and of succeeding to it on her death testate in the course of time. The defendant accepted this claim, but contended that there should be off-set against this reasonable expectation the reasonable expectation that they would benefit to a similar, if not greater, extent from their *father* out of the same funds. At the date of the trial, the father had remarried. Kingsmill Moore J accepted that there was a reasonable expectation, at the date of the mother's death, that the father would provide for the children out of the income and eventually bequeath them a considerable proportion and perhaps all of the capital. Noting that the husband had remarried and might have further children, he added:

This would go to reducing the expectation of the children of the first marriage and may be taken into account by the jury in their estimation of damages. But that a reasonable expectation still exists I cannot doubt.

In *Fitzsimons,* Barron J interpreted this passage as supporting the proposition that 'for a benefit to be taken into account there must be a reasonable expectation of it at the date of death, but the actual amount to be taken into account will depend upon the circumstances existing at the date of assessment'. Kingsmill Moore J's remarks may perhaps be best interpreted as requiring that there be a reasonable expectation of benefit at the date of death and at the time of trial. He evinced caution as to whether *Peacock v Amusement Equipment Co. Ltd* [1954] 2 QB 347 (CA) had been 'in all respects correctly decided'; it conflicted with the later decision of the English Court of Appeal in *Mead v Clarke Chapman & Co. Ltd* [1956] 1 All ER 44. *Peacock* had concentrated on the question of reasonable expectation at the time of death; *Mead* had referred to the time of trial, without requiring that a similar expectation should have existed at the time of death.

At all events, Barron J in *Fitzsimons* saw:

no reason why there should not be a recognised principle under which benefits received should or should not be taken into account. The basis of the assessment of damages for fatal injuries is the balancing of losses and benefits. Like any other balance sheet, it seems appropriate to determine first what items can appear on the balance sheet and then secondly the amount of such items. There can be little doubt but that the amount of the items must be determined as of the date of assessment. Perhaps also whether the item can appear should be determined as of the same date. But it seems more logical that if you are establishing a balance sheet required by reason of a death that the items to appear on it should be determined as of that date. There is nothing unusual in this two tier approach. There are many cases in our law where a judge must decide as a matter of law whether or not there is sufficient evidence to support a particular allegation and then it must be decided as a matter of fact whether that allegation has been established. A decision whether or not there was a reasonable expectation of a particular benefit accruing is no different from a decision whether or not a head of damages is too remote. The latter is determined as of the date the cause of action accrues. In my view, the former should also be determined as of that date, i.e. the date of death.

Barron J considered that there was no reason in principle why remarriage of a widow should be treated any differently from any other circumstance giving rise to a benefit to be off-set against losses sustained. It had been suggested that the reason for taking the possibility, or fact, of remarriage into account was that otherwise the widow would be receiving support from two husbands at the same time; but the same could be said of children taken in by relatives, whose damages were not reduced, or of any other case where a benefit was disregarded other than by reason of a statutory provision.

So far as the children were concerned, he thought it reasonable to assume that, if their mother remarried, they would go to live with her and their stepfather. If the benefits to them from a stepfather fell to be assessed, they could not be disregarded on the basis that they were voluntary:

> Voluntary benefits are disregarded not because they are voluntary, but because at the date of the death there was no reasonable expectation that they would occur. This is so equally in respect of losses. Many of the items in respect of which damages are awarded relate to voluntary payments or voluntary services made or provided by the deceased to one or more of the dependants. Such items are allowed when there is a reasonable expectation that the payments or services would have continued but for the death.

In the light of his analysis, Barron J concluded that the proper approach to adopt in relation to the assessment of damages in the case was that the evidence relating to remarriage should be directed in the first instance to establish whether or not there was a reasonable expectation at the date of the death that this would occur. On the basis that this was established, the evidence should then be directed to determining the then value of the benefits accruing to each of the dependants by reason of that remarriage. The onus of proof in each case lay on the defendants. The standard of proof of reasonable expectation was that of reasonable probability.

Barron J's approach has much to recommend it since it offers a useful accommodation between the time of death and the time of the hearing. It is, however, capable of yielding results that are not entirely satisfactory. Whereas most people will accept that a child's *good* fortune should not tell against it if the surviving parent unforeseeably remarries and the stepparent lavishes care and financial assistance on the child, it is not so clear that the court should similarly ignore a child's *bad* fortune which has come to pass before the hearing through an unforeseeable remarriage resulting in diversion of expected benefit (such a share in the surviving spouse's estate) away from the child.

A question of characterisation arises here. If the court were to treat in an identical fashion unforeseeably good and bad outcomes which have occurred by the time of the hearing, it would have to award the child in the case of a bad outcome a low sum of money by reason of the fact that the remarriage to a spouse who is now likely to scoop the pool could not have been reasonably expected at the date of the death. This event not having been reasonably probable, it must (on Barron J's formula) be put out of consideration. But if on the same facts the court were to characterise as the central question *the foreseeability of the surviving spouse's benefitting the child on the surviving spouse's death*, rather than the *foreseeability of remarriage*, then the court would seem entitled to apply the two stage process envisaged by Barron J to yield a quite different result. The court would first hold that it was foreseeable that the child would thus benefit on the death of the surviving spouse; this element in the computation of damage now having passed the first stage, the court would go on to examine it in the light of present realities and would discover that by virtue of the remarriage and of the surviving spouse's (and child's) relationship with the new spouse, it is unlikely that the child will benefit under the surviving spouse's estate. The amount of compensation would accordingly be increased. Whether such a devise of recharacterising the issue is harmonious with the *ipsissima verba* of Barron J's judgment is, however, doubtful.

Barron J's rationale for disregarding voluntary benefits in general, on the basis of their lack of foreseeability, raises interesting policy issues. It could perhaps be argued that this rationale underlies s. 50 of the Civil Liability Act 1961, which requires the court when assessing fatal injuries damages not to take account of sums payable on the death of the deceased under any contract of insurance or by way of pension. If a statutory exclusion is required, does not this suggest that otherwise the court would have subtracted these benefits (subject to a foreseeability test)? It can, however, be replied that the statutory exclusion encapsulates a social policy that certain benefits, regardless of the question of their foreseeability, should not be deducted, because to do so would penalise the prudent forward-planners for their virtue, as well as generally discouraging the taking of such socially beneficial steps, and giving an unjustified windfall to wrongdoers. (Similar social policy issues affect the issue of the deductibility of social welfare payments to victims of personal injury: see *O'Loughlin v Teeling* [1988] ILRM 617, analysed in the 1988 Review, 457-9). In the light of these policy factors, it may be wise to modify Barron J's general principle by the qualification that, while foreseeability of benefit is a precondition of subtraction from the total amount of compensation, it may not be a sufficient justification to make that subtraction if there are good policy reasons for not doing so.

In *Cooper v Egan*, High Court, 20 December 1990, Barr J had to deal with the troublesome question of compensating a man for the death of his wife. The plaintiff was aged 27 at the time of the accident caused by the defendants' negligence. His wife was aged 20. At the time of her death, the wife was looking after the couple's baby, then aged four months old, and 'also performed a normal wifely role in caring for her husband and in assisting her mother-in-law with household chores'. As a result of the accident, the plaintiff and his mother suffered serious personal injuries, so the baby was immediately taken care of by the deceased wife's parents who were still doing so at the time of accident. The child, now five, regarded his grandparents as his actual parents, though he had regular contact with his father.

The plaintiff wished to provide a home for his son, who he felt was tending to grow apart from him as time went by. Barr J did not think it his function to consider the wisdom or otherwise of this plan: as a parent he was entitled to provide a home for his child. Accordingly the plaintiff and his son were entitled to compensation for the loss of the deceased wife's services as a housewife and a mother.

Barr J accepted the plaintiff's evidence that he had no intention of marrying in the foreseeable future. In these circumstances the plaintiff was entitled to compensation for the loss of his wife's services for life, with a modest deduction in the capital value of that loss to take account of his possible re-marriage at some future date as well as the contingency that, had she lived, his wife might not have provided these services for the life of the plaintiff.

Barr J considered that what the plaintiff needed was a local woman who would work in his home five days a week from about 1 p.m. to 2 p.m., her function being to collect the boy from school or the school bus; to make lunch for him and the plaintiff; to perform housework in the afternoon; and to prepare the evening meal for the family. On the basis that this would cost £100, including PRSI, and taking into account the contingencies to which he had referred, Barr J assessed the capital value of this loss at £90,000. To this he added £1,000 for 'occasional weekend babysitting' over the following eight years.

That a husband whose deceased wife rendered services within the home as a fulltime housewife should be permitted to recover damages for the loss of these services has long been recognised: see *Barry v Humm & Co.* [1915] 1 KB 627, cited with apparent approval by Kingsmill Moore J in *Byrne v Houlihan, supra*, at p. 283. What is more controversial is whether a discount should be made in this context in respect of the actual or likely remarriage by the widower. Barr J's judgment proceeds on the basis that such a discount should indeed be made in appropriate cases. This was also the view favoured by the English courts with respect to the remarriage prospects of widowers and widows prior to statutory intervention in relation to widows in 1971: *Mead v Clarke Chapman & Co. Ltd* [1956] 1 All ER 44, *Goodburn v Thomas Cotton Ltd* [1968] 1 QB 845. The same approach has been favoured in Australia: *Jones v Schiffman* 124 CLR 303 (1971), *Hermann v Johnston*

[1972] WAR 121. In *The State (Hayes) v The Criminal Injuries Compensation Tribunal* [1982] ILRM 210, at 214, Finlay P noted that '[t]here is no statutory provision in this country inhibiting a court from making a deduction from compensation in a fatal injury case in respect of the possibility of re-marriage by a widow dependant'.

Dr John White has put forward the challenging thesis that it is not possible to distinguish the benefits obtained by a surviving spouse and children, upon the remarriage of the surviving spouse, from other voluntary benefits, and that accordingly, since the benefits deriving from remarriage do not accrue 'in consequence of the death', the occurrence or prospect of remarriage should be regarded as irrelevant in the damages calculation: *Irish Law of Damages for Personal Injuries and Death*, vol. 1, para 9.4.21 (1989). He relies on the English decision of *Hay v Hughes* [1975] 1 QB 790, where the Court of Appeal held that the services given by a grandmother to her orphaned grandchildren should not be taken into account by way of reduction since it was more realistic to say that they 'resulted from a decision made by her on her own initiative after the accident than that they resulted from the . . . deaths [of the children's parents] in the accident. . . . [G]enerosity does not result from death'.

Whether *Hay v Hughes* compels this conclusion may be debated. Certainly the English courts have not appeared to think so (cf. *Regan v Williamson* [1976] 2 All ER 241), though it is only fair to record that they have not had to confront the issue directly. Dr White is surely right in sounding a warning note to courts that it would be wrong to assume automatically that a widower's remarriage automatically will involve the assumption of domestic responsibilities by a stay-at-home second wife. Although the second wife will be marrying in the knowledge that her prospective husband has children who need care, there should be no unthinking assumption that she will necessarily opt for work within rather than outside the home.

At the heart of this issue is the question whether a court should adopt any normative position on whether a second wife should work within the home. It will not be forgotten that, in *L. v L.* [1989] ILRM 528, Barr J considered it 'evident that the Constitution envisages that, ideally, a mother should devote all her time and attention to her duties in the home and that it is desirable that she ought not to engage in gainful occupation elsewhere unless compelled to do so by economic necessity'. Of course, he was speaking in the context of the State's obligation to women rather than the responsibilities of married women relative to their family. Nevertheless, the defendant in a fatal accidents case, with a view to reducing damages, may assert that a second wife who marries the plaintiff widower, knowing of his children's need for care, is not to be treated in the same way as the grandmother in *Hay v Hughes.* If she decides to work in the home, the defendant may say, she should not be regarded as generous but rather merely as doing what might be expected of her.

We suspect that the courts will be very hesitant to commit themselves to a normative position on this issue. They may well prefer to achieve substantially the same result by addressing the issue in terms of the objective *likelihood* of a second wife's engaging in activities within the home. In cases where the husband has *already* remarried, however, this way out will not be available. If the second wife prefers to work outside the home, the court may again take no normative position and hold that the care costs must continue to be attributable to the defendant's default. It is noted that Barr J in *Cooper v Egan* did not think it his function to consider the wisdom or otherwise of the plaintiff's plan to provide a home for his son rather than leave him in the care of his grandparents. This is perhaps an indication the court would prefer to stand back from taking a particular position on the question of the choice of spousal roles in relation to a situation after a widower remarries.

In England, concern for the sensibilities of widows in having their remarriage prospects assessed by the courts led to the abolition in 1971 of the entitlement of the court to take this factor into account. The Pearson Commission on Civil Liability and Compensation for Personal Injury, which reported in 1978 (Cmnd. 7054), recommended (vol. I, para 411) that a remarriage that had *already* occurred at the date of trial should be taken into account but were divided on the question whether a *reasonable prospect* of remarriage should affect the quantum of damages. Two members of the Commission proposed that the issue should be resolved by reference (para 416) to the national statistics for remarriage. It is doubtful whether a rule which distinguished between surviving spouses on the basis of sex would be valid under the Irish Constitution: the humane motivation underlying a statutory change would appear equally applicable to cases involving the remarriage of widowers as well as widows.

3 Compensation for distress and uncertainty In *O'Brien v McInerney (Civil Engineering) Ltd and Coleman Tunnelling (Ireland) Ltd*, High Court, 1 October 1990, Barr J awarded compensation to two plaintiffs for 'distress and uncertainty'. The defendants, while building a tunnel for a sewage scheme under the foundations of the plaintiffs' premises in a country town, had an accident involving an explosion, which shook and damaged both premises. The senior representative of the contractors on the site met the plaintiffs on the day of the accident and gave them a written undertaking to put right the damage. Some initial work was done but each premises was left in a state with extensive cracking and other defects.

Barr J was clearly unimpressed with the breach of this undertaking. He awarded the first plaintiff, who carried on business as a publican in his premises but did not live there, £5,000 for the distress and uncertanty. The second plaintiff, aged 81, resided in the premises that were damaged. In addition to the inconvenience of having to live with the obvious signs of damage around him for over five years, the medical evidence established that since the accident the plaintiff had developed stress problems which had affected in his health, involving a susbtantial loss of weight. Barr J awarded him £10,000 under this head.

Historically courts have been reluctant to award compensation for mental distress falling short of psychiatric disturbance. Even with respect to psychiatric disturbance, there is continuing debate as to whether entitlement to compensation should be controlled by rigid policy limitations: see *Mulally v CIE*, High Court, Denham J, June 1991, *Jones v Wright* [1991] 3 All ER 88.

On the facts of *O'Brien*, it seems that the second plaintiff would come within the scope of psychiatric disturbance such as would entitle him to recover under the head of 'nervous shock'. The fact that his injury was not traceable to fear or concern for human safety, whether of himself or another, is not a crucial objection (cf. *Attia v British Gas plc* [1987] 3 All ER 455) though the question whether to compensate a plaintiff for a psychiatric disturbance resulting from a failure by the defendant to repair damage caused by his completed wrong may give rise to possible policy objections. In *Mullin v Hynes*, Supreme Court, 13 November 1972 (extracted in McMahon & Binchy's *Casebook on the Law of Torts*, 1st ed, 1983, p. 524, the continuing noise from the defendant's ballroom in a country village had the effect of rendering an elderly semi-invalid hypersensitive to the point of being unable to tolerate even the reduced degree of noise that later emanated from the hall. The court took the view that in obeying an injunction against undue noise the defendants had to take account of this plaintiff's present state. Henchy J observed that, since the defendant had unlawfully brought it about, it did not lie with him to say, in effect that 'she must either put up with that noise, to the probable further detriment of her health, or else go to live elsewhere'.

There are of course clear differences between *O'Brien* and *Mullin*: *O'Brien* involved a claim for damages, *Mullin* an injunction, followed by contempt proceedings. Moreover in *Mullin* the defendant had persisted in a continuing wrong, whereas in *O'Brien* the explosion was a once-off occurrence. There is, however, in Barr J's judgment such a strong deprecation of the breach of promise by the senior representative of the contractors that it may be fair to characterise the wrong as of a continuing nature, akin to a continuing trespass. Every day that the premises were left unrepaired added to the distress and disturbance of the second plaintiff.

4 *Exemplary (or punitive damages)*   In *McIntyre v Lewis, Dolan, Ireland and the Attorney General*, Supreme Court, 17 December 1990, the facts of which we have already mentioned above, 554-5, the Supreme Court resolved a question that has been troubling academic commentators and the courts in recent years: Is there a conceptual difference between *punitive* and *exemplary* damages?

In *Kennedy and Arnold v Ireland* [1988] ILRM 472; [1987] IR 587, Hamilton P thought that there was. He noted that, in s. 7(2) of the Civil Liability Act 1961, there was a reference to 'punitive damages' in the context of survival of actions and in s. 14(2), there was a reference to 'exemplary damages' in the context of concurrent wrongdoers. On this basis he thought it 'quite clear' that Irish law recognised a distribution between these two concepts.

In the 1987 Review, 344, we took the view, which is later asserted in McMahon & Binchy's *Irish Law of Torts* (2nd ed, 1990), 776-7, that there is in fact no difference between punitive and exemplary damages. The concepts are used interchangeably throughout the common law world. It is, of course, curious that the 1961 Act should have used separate expressions if it envisaged a single category of damages, but the true explanation lies in the statutory sources of inspiration for the 1961 Act. S. 7(2) traces its origins to s. 1(2) of England's *Law Reform (Miscellaneous Provisions) Act 1934*, while s. 14(4) derives from s. 4(4) of Glanville Williams's model legislation, in his *Joint Torts and Contributory Negligence*, 501 (1951). Thus, as was argued in the 1987 Review, 344 and in McMahon & Binchy, p. 777, 'the inconsistency in terminology of the 1961 Act may . . . be traced, not to nuances of meaning between the concepts of "punitive" and "exemplary" damages, but to the promiscuity of our borrowings from British legislation'.

In *McIntyre v Lewis, Dolan, Ireland and the Attorney General*, the Supreme Court endorsed this view. McCarthy J quoted the passage from McMahon & Binchy's text. He saw 'no real difference of meaning between the two terms'. Hederman and O'Flaherty JJ came to the same conclusion on this issue.

The Court did not seek to resolve the more fundamental question as to the circumstances in which it is proper to award punitive damages. Over a quarter of a century has passed since the House of Lords, in *Rookes v Barnard* [1964] AC 1129, narrowed the conditions of eligibility replacing a broad discretion to award punitive damages in cases involving circumstances of particular outrages, by an entitlement limited to (1) cases of unconstitutional action by servants of the Crown, (2) cases where the defendant invested in the tort, hoping to make a profit from it after discounting damages, and (3) cases where statute permitted the award of punitive damages.

In *McIntyre v Lewis, Dolan, Ireland and the Attorney General*, the Court was divided as to the desirability of the *Rookes v Barnard* limitations. Of course the factual circumstances demonstrably fell within the first of *Rookes v Barnard's* three categories; this made it unnecessary for the Court to address the position arising in a case falling outside any of the categories. Nevertheless, what the judges had to say is of considerable interest.

Hederman J observed merely that:

> [i]n cases, like this, where there is an abuse of power by employees of the State, the jury are entitled to award exemplary damages. One of the ways in which the rights of the citizen are vindicated, when subjected to oppressive conduct by the employees of the State, is by an award of exemplary damages.

For two reasons, it would seem wrong to interpret this passage as endorsing *Rookes v Barnard*. First, Hederman J made no express statement that he was taking *any* position on the issue; nor did he have to, since the outcome of the case in no way depended on whether the eligibility for punitive damages was broadly or narrowly drawn. Secondly, Hederman J's expressed criterion for eligibility, of 'oppressive conduct by the employees of the State' is less than fully faithful to the first criterion of *Rookes v Barnard* which speaks of *unconstitutional* rather than *oppressive* conduct. The range of unconstitutional conduct is clearly far wider than that of oppressive conduct. Even if our courts favoured a wider interpretation of oppression than did the English Court of Appeal in *R. v Fulling* [1987] QB 426 (a case dealing with the law of evidence which should not, perhaps, be considered to have any real bearing in the present context), it seems obvious that many unconstitutional acts, even if inflicted on citizens by employees of the State lack the element of oppression. (Conversely, it seems reasonable to accept that the mere fact that oppressive conduct relative to a citizen, engaged in by a State employee, even if it is tortious or otherwise contrary to the law, is not *necessarily* unconstitutional).

O'Flaherty J reserved his position on the question whether exemplary damages may be awarded only along the lines of *Rookes v Barnard's* three categories; this was 'obviously not the case to decide', this issue (presumably because it fell within the first of these categories). He did, however, adopt the three consideration which Lord Devlin said should always be borne in mind when awards of exemplary damages are being considered. These are (1) that the plaintiff may not recover exemplary damages unless *he is the victim of the punishable behaviour*; (2) that there is a need for *restraint* in awarding exemplary damages, and (3) that the *means of both plaintiff and defendant are material* in the assessment of exemplary damages.

McCarthy J, in contrast had no hesitation in exorcising the spectre of the *Rookes v Barnard* categories from Irish law. That decision, he noted, had been the subject of significant adverse comment in other common law jurisdictions. In his view, it was inconsistent with the dynamism that characterises the common law to delimit in any restrictive way the nature of its development. Many will welcome McCarthy J's conclusion that the power to award punitive damages should not be restricted in the somewhat arbitrary way that *Rookes v Barnard* prescribed. One might, however, hesitate before interpreting McCarthy J's remarks as involving the far broader thesis that no principles of limitation (as opposed to expansion) of tortious liability are permissible because they inhibit the growth of the common law. A system of civil liability without parameters would be an alarming prospect. Courts at different times may define those boundaries broadly or narrowly, but it would be wrong to oppose the phenomenon of making any particular boundary at any partcular point on the ground that this inhibits a later relocation of the boundaries. The expansion and contraction of the principles of negligence in Britain over the past two decades is proof of the fact that the dynamism of the common law need not be a one-way process.

In *McIntyre*, it will be recalled, the jury had awarded the plaintiff £5,000 for assault and false imprisonment and over £60,000 for malicious prosecution by members of the Garda Síochána. It was accepted in the Supreme Court that the award of damages for malicious prosecution must have included an element of exemplary damages.

On an appeal against the quantum of this award (but not that of £5,000) the Supreme Court, by a majority (Hederman and O'Flaherty JJ), held that was too high. Finding a clear *ratio* is, however, not easy. Hederman J proceeded on the basis of the principle that the amount awarded for exemplary damages should bear some relation to the amount that would be proper for general damages. He was of the view that the maximum that could be given for malicious prosecution in the circumstances of the case was in the region of £5,000. He considered that the award of punitive damages should be reduced to £20,000. The ratio thus acceptable to him was that of four to one. Hederman J also expressed support for the quite different principle that the damages awarded for the assault and for the malicious prosecution had 'to bear some relation to each other'.

O'Flaherty J, who concurred with Hederman J's judgment, stated:

> The award of exemplary damages in anomalous and where such damages are awarded — which should be very rarely in my judgment — the judge or jury must keep them on a tight rein. If the compensatory amount awarded includes aggravated damages then I believe if any award is made by way of exemplary damages it should properly be a

fraction rather than a multiple of the amount awarded by way of compensatory damages (including aggravated damages).

O'Flaherty J did not expressly endorse Hederman J's view that £5,000 was the maximum amount that could have been awarded by way of compensatory damages for malicious prosecution. Nor did O'Flaherty J give any indication as to the quantum of *aggravated* damages which he considered would be appropriate with respect to the malicious prosecution award.

Interestingly, O'Flaherty J appeared to endorse Hederman J's separate basis for reducing the damages. He observed that, when he looked at the amounts awarded in the case, there was no dispute that the award of £5,000 for assault and false imprisonment was appropriate. He went on to say:

> I would accept that that award cannot have any exemplary component in it. It represented rather modest damages. Accepting that the award of £60,000 damages for malicious prosecution has an exemplary component, nevertheless, in my judgment, a reasonable proportion must be kept between the two awards. In fact one exceeds the other by a multiple of twelve. This is too great a disparity'.

McCarthy J dissented. He referred to the fact (expanded upon in Hederman J's judgment) that the initial verdict of the jury had recorded £30,000 for special damages and £30,000 for general damages in respect of the malicious prosecution. The trial judge had pointed out that the agreed special damages were only £1,787.50, and the jury after a very short retiral returned to court, with the appropriate sum entered for special damages and the sum for general damages increased to £60,000. McCarthy J considered (surely correctly) that the jury's initial verdict suggested that they were contemplating a separate award for exemplary damages. The award, in his view, 'did contain a significant element in respect of exemplary damages because of the abuse of power in the breach of the plaintiff's rights of the first and second defendants'.

McCarthy J went on to point out that the plaintiff, from the time of the original incident until his criminal trial, had had to undergo a period of some fifteen months of significant anxiety and concern, not knowing what its outcome might be and knowing that the Gardai were conspiring against him:

> How was he to know that he would be acquitted? He might well have believed that he had little chance of acquittal and would inevitably have to serve a sentence of imprisonment. If one assumes that approximately half of the damages were compensatory in nature, in my view they are in no way excessive. Compared to the anguish caused by defamatory

material published of any citizen, the plight of the plaintiff in this case seems to me to have been considerably worse. Yet awards of damages for defamation well in excess of £30,000 have become a feature of our courts. As exemplary damages for the shocking use of police power by the first and second defendants, I consider a further sum of £30,000 as a perfectly acceptable level of award'.

The majority holding in *McIntyre* gives rise to two crucial questions, which we consider in turn.

(i) Proportionality as between awards of damages for different torts   Both Hederman J and O'Flaherty J were agreed that the damages awarded for the assault and those awarded for the malicious prosecution had to bear some relation to each other, and that this relationship had been exceeded by awards which bore a multiple of twelve. Neither judge explained the basis of their holdings on this crucial issue. We can only speculate, therefore, as to what it may have been.

It surely could *not* have been that there is some general principle that awards of damages for different torts must not exceed some particular mathematical relationship. Clearly, the fact that a plaintiff has been the victim of two torts rather than one at the hands of a defendant should not prevent him from being properly compensated for both merely because the damages is one were small and in the other very large. The multiple is a matter of utter contingency, which should not affect the quantum of either award in any way.

In *McIntyre*, there was much discussion in the majority's judgments as to the subject of exemplary damages, but, when it came to articulating the principle of proportionality as between awards for different torts, neither Judge expressly identified the exemplary element in the award for malicious prosecution as being crucial to the principle.

One possible basis of a principle of proportionality as between awards for different torts would have some attraction, but only in relation to a relatively narrow range of cases. This is where a plaintiff claims damages for several torts arising from one incident, and these torts nearly overlap. If it takes some mental effort to distinguish conceptually between the torts, then there may be some merit in either merging them when it comes to assessing damages (as was done in *McIntyre* in respect of the torts of assault and false imprisonment) or, if not, in ensuring that the plaintiff is not doubly compensated for his injury.

In a case where a plaintiff was grabbed by a Garda, placed in a police van and beaten up there, an appellate court could legitimately form some global assessment of the appropriate damages for the *incident as a whole*. If it concluded that the sum of £20,000 was about right, then it surely would be correct in striking down, as excessive, two separate awards (for battery and false imprisonment, respectively) of £20,000 each.

But equally it would surely be *incorrect* to strike down, on some principle of proportionality, an award of £18,000 for battery where the jury awarded £2,000 for false imprisonment. The global amount of £20,000 would be appropriate, and, since the two torts were closely related so far as the incident as a whole was concerned, it is arguably a matter of indifference as to how the global amount in apportioned.

Where an incident of the type we have just been considering warrants an award of *exemplary* damages, the principle of proportionality has even less a claim for application. A plaintiff who has been beaten up and placed in a police van deserves punitive damages in respect of the incident as a whole. The defendant is to be punished for the incident. It can be quite artificial to attribute specific proportions of this punitive element in the damages to the two torts. The truth of the matter is that the plaintiff will receive compensatory damages for the torts *plus an extra amount for the punitive element*. Some juries may divide this equally as between the two torts; others may add it on to one of the awards. If in either case the *global* amount awarded is appropriate, then surely the way in which the jury chooses to allocate this amount should be a matter of indifference.

If this is so, and if the facts in *McIntyre* involved what was essentially a single incident where the separate torts more or less merged into each other, then the question which the Supreme Court should have considered was whether the global sum of £66,787.50 (ie. £5,000 plus £61,787.50) was excessive. In this context it is significant that the defendants (prudently) did not appeal against the award of £5,000 for assault and false imprisonment. Hederman J was of the view that the jury had been 'entitled to award exemplary damages' in respect of either assault and false imprisonment or of malicious prosecution or of assault, false imprisonment *and* malicious prosecution. He noted that counsel for the plaintiff had 'argued that while, as he contended, it was on the low side it was not such as would call for the intervention of this Court'. O'Flaherty J observed that there had been no dispute that the £5,000 award for assault and false imprisonment was appropriate. He added that he 'would accept that that award cannot have any exemplary component in it. It represented rather modest damages'. (O'Flaherty J's use of the word 'cannot' here appears to refer to what the jury *must have intended* to award rather than what they were *obliged* to award).

Thus, the picture that emerges from the majority's analysis of the award of £5,000 is that it was on the low side, judged by the compensatory criterion, and that it contained no element of exemplary damages, *though it would have been permissible for the jury to have included an amount in respect of exemplary damages.* What would the majority have decided if the jury, instead of awarding £61,787.50 punitive damages for malicious prosecution, had added £30,000 to the £5,000 award for assault and false imprisonment and reduced the amount awarded malicious prosecution to £31,787.50? The principle of proportionality would be satisfied, so no objection could be raised on that account. If the result of applying the principle of proportionality is to strike down a jury award where the global amount awarded for punitive damages is appropriate but it is spread unevenly as between awards for separate torts, we suggest that this is a principle that should be abandoned. A jury which chooses to add the punitive element to one award rather than spread it evenly between awards for separate torts in acting quite rationally and with complete propriety. Nothing whatever is achieved, and no useful principle is effectuated, by spreading the punitive element of the global award in some mathematically proportionate manner between the awards for separate torts.

(ii) Proportionality as between the awards for compensatory and exemplary damages As we have seen, Hederman J considered the amount that awarded for exemplary damages 'should bear some relation to the amount that would be proper for general damages'. O'Flaherty J, in his concurring judgment, stated:

> The award of exemplary damages is anomolous and where such damages are awarded — which should be very rarely in my judgment — the judge or jury must keep them on a tight rein. If the compensatory amount awarded includes aggravated damages then I believe if any award is made by way of exemplary damages it should properly be a fraction rather than a multiple of the amount awarded by way of compensatory damages (including aggravated damages).

These observations give pause for thought. Of course juries should not be too quick to award exemplary damages nor too unrestrained in those cases where exemplary damages are appropriate; but the idea of some necessary relationship of proportionality seems unattractive. It is the essence of exemplary damages that their quantum is not determined by reference to a compensatory function. It is a matter of contingency whether the quantum appropriate to fulfil the compensatory function will be high or low; it is just as much a matter of contingency as to whether in any particular case the defendant's conduct warrants high or low exemplary damages. Whether the respective amounts bear a close relationship or are hugely different cannot be preordained by a rule requiring that the exemplary damages not exceed a specific ratio relative to what is awarded by way of compensatory damages. It is, of course, true that the seriousness of the injury inflicted by the defendant may be reflected in the quantum of the award of punitive damages, but the extent to which it does so depends on other factors, such as the outrageousness of the defendant's conduct.

As to O'Flaherty J's suggestion that aggravated damages should, in effect, carry most of the load, to the extent that exemplary damages should be merely a fraction rather than a multiple of the amount awarded by way of compensation, two comments seem appropriate.

First, there is perhaps a danger of overloading the process of compensation with too many closely related concepts. Exemplary and aggravated damages, while quite distinct conceptually, are nonetheless very closely related. The truth of the matter is that the category of aggravated damages is a judicial device, conceived with the purpose of facilitating the award of what are, to all intents and purposes, exemplary damages. If this reality is accepted, then there would seem little attraction to the idea that, in a case where the defendant has behaved outrageously, the judge or jury (as the case may be) if disposed to award aggravated damages, should make sure to divide the global award so that the quantum of aggravated damages is *more than* that of exemplary damages. Nothing would be gained by this elaboration and the practical difficulties in directing a jury on these lines can easily be appreciated. If, on the other hand, the court proceeds on the basis that the conceptual difference between aggravated and exemplary damages should be taken at face value, then there is a separate difficulty with the proposition that the quantum of aggravated damages, if these are awarded, should exceed that of exemplary damages. It is possible to conceive of cases where the appropriate amount of exemplary damages is well in excess of that which should be awarded by way of aggravated damages. Take the following example. A policeman, anxious to ingratiate himself with his superiors, arrests two men on a charge of attempted burglary. The men are completely innocent, the policeman's purpose being to have an impressively high rate of detections to his credit. This may well be regarded as a case calling for exemplary damages. If the two men spend the night in a cell before the truth emerges, both could sue for false imprisonment and malicious prosecution. The experience would no doubt be such as to warrant an award of aggravated damages, if the court were so disposed. Now it could be that the two men's circumstances were quite different: the first may have been a highly intelligent person, fully conscious of the enormity of the torts that were being committed; the second may have been mentally handicapped, intrigued by the experience but completely unaware of its ramifications. If (let us assume), an award of aggravated damages were justified in both cases, is there any defensible reason why the quantum of punitive damages in relation to the second plaintiff should have to be less than the sum awarded him for aggravated damages? Unquestionably the first plaintiff suffered more but is that a reason for distinguishing radically as between the amounts of punitive damages that may be awarded to the two men?

Transport

AIR NAVIGATION

Eurocontrol fees The Air Navigation (Eurocontrol) (Route Charges) (Amendment) Regulations 1990 (SI No. 312) extend the area of application of Irish airspace and further amend the 1989 Regulations.

Fees The Air Navigation (Fees) Order 1990 (SI No. 321) revokes and re-enacts with amendments the 1985 Order.

Interception of aircraft The Air Navigation (Interception of Aircraft) Order 1990 (SI No. 12) gives detailed effect to the terms of the Air Navigation and Transport Act 1988 (see the 1988 Review, 467-9).

INTERNATIONAL CARRIAGE OF GOODS BY ROAD

General The International Carriage of Goods by Road Act 1990 is discussed in the Conflict of Laws chapter, 129-39, above.

Licences The Road Transport Act 1978 (Section 5) Order 1990 (SI No. 180) exempts from the licensing requirements of the Road Transport Act 1935 certain UK vehicle drivers engaged in this State in the international carriage of goods by road, provided they have documentation indicating that they have been licensed in the UK.

RIVERS

The Shannon Navigation Act 1990 grants comprehensive powers to the Commissioners of Public Works to ensure the maintenance of navigation on the Shannon and to restore certain parts of the Shannon navigation which had not previously been under the Commissioners' control. The vesting day for the purposes of the Act, on which the Commissioners were given care and control over the areas specified in the Act, was 20 August 1990: Shannon Navigation Act 1990 (Vesting Day) Order 1990 (SI No. 209). The

Commissioners are given various powers of entry on land and of compulsory acquisition to carry out their functions. The Shannon Navigation Act 1990 (Forms) Regulations 1990 (SI No. 296) set out the forms in respect of the CPO procedure under the Act.

ROAD TRAFFIC

Agricultural trailers   The Road Traffic (Licensing of Trailers and Semi-Trailers) (Amendment) Regulations 1990 (SI No. 286) amend the 1982 and 1983 Regulations by excluding agricultural trailers from their licensing requirements.

Licence plates   The Road Vehicles (Registration and Licensing) (Amendment) Regulations 1990 (SI No. 287) require that new licence plates must include: the name of the county or city of registration in Irish over the number; the EC flag; and the international signification IRL. Post-1987 number plates may also be converted to the new form.

Removal of vehicles   The Road Traffic (Removal, Storage and Disposal) Regulations 1990 (SI No. 24) increased the charges payable under the 1983 Regulations.

Index